GENOCIDE

Genocide: A Comprehensive Introduction is the most wide-ranging textbook on genocide yet published. The book is designed as a text for upper-undergraduate and graduate students, as well as a primer for non-specialists and general readers interested in learning about one of humanity's enduring blights.

Fully updated to reflect the latest thinking in this rapidly developing field, this new edition:

- Provides an introduction to genocide as both a historical phenomenon and an analytical-legal concept, including an extended discussion of the concept of genocidal intent, and the dynamism and contingency of genocidal processes.
- Discusses the role of state-building, imperialism, war, and social revolution in fueling genocide.
- Supplies a wide range of full-length case studies of genocides worldwide, each with an accompanying box-text.
- Explores perspectives on genocide from the social sciences, including psychology, sociology, anthropology, political science/international relations, and gender studies.
- Considers "The Future of Genocide," with attention to historical memory and genocide denial; initiatives for truth, justice, and redress; and strategies of intervention and prevention.

Written in clear and lively prose, liberally sprinkled with over 170 illustrations and maps, and including personal testimonies from genocide survivors, *Genocide: A Comprehensive Introduction* has established itself as the core textbook of the new generation of genocide scholarship. An accompanying website (www.genocidetext. net) features a broad selection of supplementary materials, teaching aids, and Internet resources.x

Adam Jones, Ph.D., is Associate Professor of Political Science at the University of British Columbia Okanagan in Kelowna, Canada. His recent books include *Gender Inclusive: Essays on Violence, Men, and Feminist International Relations* (Routledge, 2009) and *Crimes Against Humanity: A Beginner's Guide* (Oneworld, 2008). He is co-founder and executive director of Gendercide Watch (www.gendercide.org).

PRAISE FOR THE FIRST EDITION

With its interdisciplinary approach and bevy of case studies, *Genocide: A Comprehensive Introduction* will surely become the seminal text for students of genocide. Written in an engaging and conversational style, the book not only explores existing frameworks, but expands the boundaries of genocide studies with attention to issues such as gender and the future of genocide. Perhaps best of all, Jones educates and inspires the reader to become an active and responsible global citizen.

Nicholas A. Robins, Duke University, USA

This is the best introductory text available to students of genocide studies. Written in clear, elegant prose and supported by a wealth of authoritative sources, *Genocide: A Comprehensive Introduction* is likely to become the gold standard by which all subsequent introductions to this enormously important subject will be measured.

Kenneth J. Campbell, Professor of Political Science,
University of Delaware, USA

This wide-ranging inquest into the dynamics of genocidal violence stands as a major contribution to the dismal science of 'massacrology.' More than a collection of case studies, it offers a depth of critical insight and a richness of data seldom matched in comparative studies of genocide. Informed by a formidable erudition, and a deep personal sensitivity to the horrors that he describes, Adam Jones's splendid book is a milestone in the literature on mass crimes and genocide.

René Lemarchand, Department of Political Science,
University of Florida, USA

The subtitle says it all: unique in the literature, this book provides a thorough, comprehensive introduction to the subject of genocide. Jones delivers a very readable, intellectually stimulating text. The overall perspective is interdisciplinary. Relevant research and insights from psychology, sociology, and anthropology are included; maps and illustrations complement many of the examples and case studies. The historical coverage ranges from discussions of genocide in the Hebrew Bible to contemporary abominations in Sudan's Darfur region. Commendably, there are thoughtful chapters on the significance of gender, memory and denial, and postgenocide tribunals. The book concludes with strategies to anticipate future genocides and intervene when necessary. Readers are encouraged as responsible citizens to consider their reactions to genocide. Summing Up: Essential. All readership levels.

P. G. Conway, SUNY College at Oneonta,
writing in Choice - Reviews Online

PRAISE FOR THE SECOND EDITION

Already the most wide-ranging, accessible and clear-sighted introduction to the subject, the significantly expanded second edition unflinchingly extends the range of its discussion to include contentious issues such as 'cultural' genocide, whether post 9/11 terrorism falls under the rubric, and the wider scope of Ottoman violence against Christian 'minorities' in 1915. Compassionate, searching, up-to-the minute and sometimes even electrifying in its prose, this is *the* book I will be particularly recommending to my university students of genocide.

Mark Levene, University of Southampton, UK

Based on immense scholarship, *Genocide: A Comprehensive Introduction* is much more than an indispensable text for students of this seemingly intractable phenomenon. With its global and interdisciplinary perspectives, it consistently advances our understanding of genocidal events on many fronts. Provocative yet balanced, Adam Jones's second edition at once summarizes and defines this burgeoning field.

A. Dirk Moses, University of Sydney and the European University Institute, Florence

GENOCIDE

A Comprehensive Introduction

2nd Edition

Adam Jones

Routledge
Taylor & Francis Group

LONDON AND NEW YORK

First published 2006
by Routledge

Second Edition published 2011
by Routledge
2 Park Square, Milton Park, Abingdon, Oxon, OX14 4RN

Simultaneously published in the USA and Canada
by Routledge
711 Third Avenue, New York, NY 10017

Routledge is an imprint of the Taylor & Francis Group, an informa business

© 2006, 2011 Adam Jones

Typeset in Garamond by
Keystroke, Tettenhall, Wolverhampton
Printed and bound by Edwards Brothers Malloy, Lillington, NC

All efforts have been made to contact copyright holders. The publishers
would be grateful to hear from any copyright holder who is not acknowledged
and will undertake to rectify any errors or omissions in future editions.

British Library Cataloguing in Publication Data
A catalogue record for this book is available from the British Library

Library of Congress Cataloging in Publication Data
Jones, Adam, 1963–
Genocide : a comprehensive introduction / Adam Jones. — 2nd ed.
p. cm.
Genocide. 2. Genocide—Case studies. I. Title.
HV6322.7.J64 2010
304.6'63—dc22
2010003010

ISBN: 978–0–415–48618–7 (hbk)
ISBN: 978–0–415–48619–4 (pbk)
ISBN: 978–0–203–84696–4 (ebk)

For Jo and David Jones, givers of life,
and for Dr. Griselda Ramírez Reyes, saver of lives.

One gains power over the nightmare by calling it
by its real name.
Martin Buber, *I and Thou*

CONTENTS

ILLUSTRATIONS

FIGURES

MAPS

BOXES

ABOUT THE AUTHOR

 Adam Jones, Ph.D., was born in Singapore in 1963, and grew up in England and Canada. He is currently Associate Professor of Political Science at the University of British Columbia Okanagan in Kelowna, Canada. From 2005–07, he was Associate Research Fellow in the Genocide Studies Program at Yale University. Jones was selected as one of *Fifty Key Thinkers on the Holocaust and Genocide* for the book of that title, edited by Paul Bartrop and Steven Jacobs (Routledge, 2010). He has published various sole-authored and edited works on genocide and related themes, including *Evoking Genocide: Scholars and Activists Describe the Works That Shaped Their Lives* (The Key Publishing House, 2009); *Crimes Against Humanity: A Beginner's Guide* (Oneworld, 2008); *Gender Inclusive: Essays on Violence, Men, and Feminist International Relations* (Routledge, 2008); *Gendercide and Genocide* (Vanderbilt University Press, 2004); and *Genocide, War Crimes and the West: History and Complicity* (Zed Books, 2004). He has also published books on the mass media and political transition. Jones serves as book review editor of the *Journal of Genocide Research*, and is co-founder and executive director of Gendercide Watch (www.gendercide.org). His journalism and photojournalism, along with a selection of scholarly writings, are available at http://adamjones.freeservers.com. Email: adam@genocidetext.net. (Photo by Griselda Ramírez – Kazan, Russia, 2008)

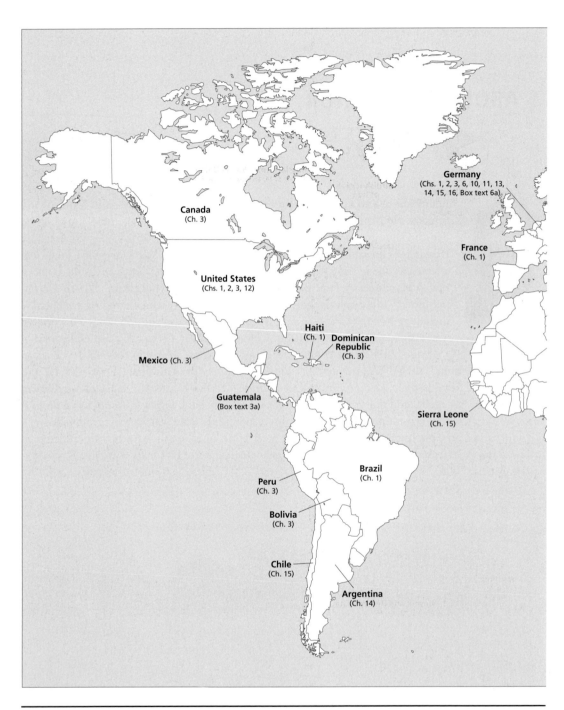

World Map Cases of genocide and mass conflict referenced in this book

Source: Chartwell Illustrators

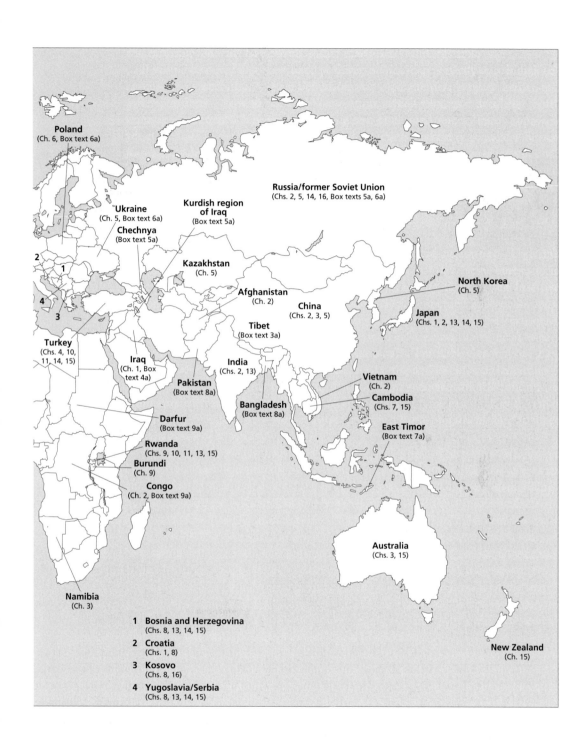

Poland
(Ch. 6, Box text 6a)

Russia/former Soviet Union
(Chs. 2, 5, 14, 16, Box texts 5a, 6a)

Ukraine
(Ch. 5, Box text 6a)

Kurdish region
of Iraq
(Box text 5a)

Chechnya
(Box text 5a)

Kazakhstan
(Ch. 5)

North Korea
(Ch. 5)

Afghanistan
(Ch. 2)

China
(Chs. 2, 3, 5)

Japan
(Chs. 1, 2, 13, 14, 15)

Tibet
(Box text 3a)

2

1

4

3

Turkey
(Chs. 4, 10,
11, 14, 15)

Iraq
(Ch. 1, Box
text 4a)

India
(Chs. 2, 13)

Vietnam
(Ch. 2)

Pakistan
(Box text 8a)

Cambodia
(Chs. 7, 15)

Bangladesh
(Box text 8a)

East Timor
(Box text 7a)

Darfur
(Box text 9a)

Rwanda
(Chs. 9, 10, 11, 13, 15)

Burundi
(Ch. 9)

Congo
(Ch. 2, Box text 9a)

Australia
(Chs. 3, 15)

Namibia
(Ch. 3)

1 Bosnia and Herzegovina
   (Chs. 8, 13, 14, 15)

2 Croatia
   (Chs. 1, 8)

3 Kosovo
   (Chs. 8, 16)

4 Yugoslavia/Serbia
   (Chs. 8, 13, 14, 15)

New Zealand
(Ch. 15)

Preface

WHY STUDY GENOCIDE?

"Why would you want to study *that*?"

If you spend time seriously investigating genocide, or even if you only leave this book lying in plain view, you will probably have to deal with this question. Underlying it is a tone of distaste and skepticism, perhaps tinged with suspicion. There may be a hint that you are guided by a morbid fixation on the worst of human horrors. How will you respond? Why, indeed, study genocide?

First and foremost, if you are concerned about peace, human rights, and justice, there is a sense that with genocide you are confronting the "Big One," what Joseph Conrad called the "heart of darkness." That can be deeply intimidating and disturbing. It can even make you feel trivial and powerless. But genocide is the *opposite* of trivial. Whatever energy and commitment you invest in understanding genocide will be directed towards comprehending and confronting one of humanity's greatest scourges.

Second, to study genocide is to study our historical inheritance. It is unfortunately the case that all stages of recorded human existence, and nearly all parts of the world, have known genocide at one time or another, often repeatedly. Furthermore, genocide may be as prevalent in the contemporary era as at any time in history. Inevitably, there is something depressing about the prevalence and repetition of genocide in world history: Will humanity ever change? But there is also interest and personal enlightenment to be gained by delving into the historical record, for which genocide serves as a point of entry. I well remember the period, a decade ago, that I devoted to voracious reading of the genocide studies literature, and exploring the diverse themes this opened up to me. The accounts were grim – sometimes relentlessly so. Yet they were also spellbinding, and they gave me a better grounding not only in world history, but also in sociology, psychology, anthropology, and a handful of other disciplines.

This points to a third reason to study genocide: it brings you into contact with some of the most interesting and exciting debates in the social sciences and humanities. To what extent should genocide be understood as reflecting epic social transformations such as modernity, the rise of the state, and globalization? How has warfare been transformed in recent times, and how are the wars of the present age linked to genocide? How does gender shape genocidal experiences and genocidal strategies? How is history "produced," and what role do memories or denial of genocide play in that production? These are only a few of the themes to be examined in this book. I hope they will lead readers, as they have led me, towards an engagement with debates that have a wider, though not necessarily deeper, significance.

In writing this book, I stand on the shoulders of giants: the scholars without whose trail-blazing efforts my own work would be inconceivable. You may find their approach and humanity inspiring, as I do. One of my principal concerns is to provide an overview of the core genocide studies literature; thus each chapter and box-text is accompanied by recommendations for further study.

Modern academic writing, particularly in the social sciences and humanities, is often riddled with jargon and pomposity. It would be pleasant to report that genocide studies is free of such baggage. It isn't; but it is less burdened by it than most other fields. It seems this has to do with the experience of looking into the abyss, and finding that the abyss looks back. One is forced to ponder one's own human frailty and vulnerability; one is even pressed to confront one's own capacity for hating others, for marginalizing them, for supporting their oppression and annihilation. These real-izations aren't pretty, but they are arguably necessary. And they can lead to humility – a rare quality in academia. I once described to a friend why the Danish philosopher Søren Kierkegaard (1813–55) moved me so deeply: "It's like he's grabbing you by the arm and saying, 'Look. We don't have much time. There are important things we need to talk about.'" You sense the same in the genocide-studies literature: that the issues are too vital, and time too limited, to beat around the bush. George Orwell famously described political speech – he could have been referring to some academic writing – as "a mass of words [that] falls upon the facts like soft snow, blurring the outlines and covering up all the details."[1] By contrast, the majority of genocide scholars inhabit the literary equivalent of the tropics. I hope to take up residence there too.

Finally, some good news for the reader interested in understanding and con-fronting genocide: your studies and actions may make a difference. To study genocide is to study processes by which *hundreds of millions* of people met brutal ends. Yet there are many, many people throughout history who have bravely resisted the blind rush to hatred. They are the courageous and decent souls who gave refuge to hunted Jews or desperate Tutsis. They are the religious believers of many faiths who struggled against the tide of evil, and spread instead a message of love, tolerance, and common-ality. They are the non-governmental organizations that warned against incipient genocides and carefully documented those they were unable to prevent. They are the leaders and common soldiers – American, British, Soviet, Vietnamese, Indian, Tanzanian, Rwandan, and others – who vanquished genocidal regimes in modern times.[2] And yes, they are the scholars and intellectuals who have honed our understanding of genocide, while at the same time working outside the ivory tower to alleviate it. You will meet some of these individuals in this book. I hope their stories and actions will inspire you to believe that a future free of genocide and other crimes against humanity is possible.

But . . .

Studying genocide, and trying to prevent it, is not to be entered into lightly: as the French political scientist Jacques Sémelin asks, "Who is ever really prepared for the shock of tales of cruelty in all their naked horror?"[3] The psychological and emotional impact that genocide studies can have on the investigator has yet to be systematically studied. How many genocide students, scholars, and activists suffer, as do their counterparts in the human rights and social work fields?[4] How many experience depression, insomnia, and nightmares as a result of having immersed themselves in the most atrocious human conduct?

The trauma is especially intense for those who have actually witnessed genocide, or its direct consequences. During the Turkish genocide against Armenians (Chapter 4), the US Ambassador to Constantinople, Henry Morgenthau, received a stream of American missionaries who had managed to escape the killing zone. "For hours they would sit in my office with tears streaming down their faces," Morgenthau recalled; many had been "broken in health" by what they had witnessed.[5] In 1948, the Jewish jurist Raphael Lemkin, who learned when World War II ended that dozens of his family members had perished in the Holocaust (Chapter 6), wrote: "Genocide has taken the lives of my dear ones; the fight against genocide takes my health."[6] My friend Christian Scherrer, who works at the Hiroshima Peace Institute, arrived in Rwanda in November 1994 as part of a United Nations investigation team, only a few months after the slaughter of perhaps a million people had ended (see Chapter 9). Rotting bodies were still strewn across the landscape. "For weeks," Scherrer writes,

> following directions given by witnesses, I carefully made my way, step by step, over farmland and grassland. Under my feet, often only half covered with earth, lay the remains of hundreds, indeed thousands . . . Many of those who came from outside shared the experience of hundreds of thousands of Rwandans of continuing, for months on end, or even longer, to grieve, to weep internally, and, night after night, to be unable to sleep longer than an hour or two.

Scherrer described the experience as "one of the most painful processes I have ever been through," and the writing of his book, *Genocide and Crisis*, as "part of a personal process of grieving." "Investigation into genocide," he added, "is something that remains with one for life."[7]

I encourage you – especially if you are just beginning your exploration of genocide – to be attentive to signs of personal stress. Talk about it with fellow students, colleagues, family, or friends. Dwell on the positive examples of bravery, rescue, and love for others that the study of genocide regularly provides (see, e.g., pp. 402–12, Box 10.3). If necessary, seek counseling through the resources available on your campus or in your community.

It is also worth recalling that genocide scholars are far from alone as members of a profession that must confront suffering and mortality. Indeed, we are often privileged to maintain an arm's-length distance from those realities, unlike many other (often underappreciated and poorly recompensed) workers. The point was made to me by Meaghen Gallagher, an undergraduate student in Edmonton, Canada, who in October 2009 encountered the field of comparative genocide studies for the first time. She wrote,

> Really, you chose a very interesting field of study, in my opinion. It might be dark, but it is something that people are so afraid to talk about, when it really needs to be brought into light . . . I guess it is just like anything. Nurses, police, emergency technicians, philanthropists, they all have to deal with some pretty tough things, but someone has to do it, right?[8]

WHAT THIS BOOK TRIES TO DO, AND WHY

I see genocide as among history's defining features, overlapping a range of central historical processes: war, imperialism, state-building, and class struggle, from antiquity to the present. It is intimately linked to key institutions, in which state or broadly political authorities are often but not always principal actors, such as forced labor, military conscription, incarceration, and female infanticide.

I adopt a comparative approach that does not elevate particular genocides over others, except to the extent that scale and intensity warrant special attention. I argue that virtually all definable human groups – the ethnic, national, racial, and religious ones that anchor the legal definition of genocide, and others besides – have been victims of genocide, and are vulnerable in specific contexts today. Equally, most human collectivities – even vulnerable and oppressed ones – have proven capable of inflicting genocide. This can be painful for genocide scholars to acknowledge. But it will be confronted head-on in this volume. Taboos and tender sensibilities take a back seat to *getting to grips with genocide* – to reduce the chances that mystification and wishful thinking will cloud recognition, and thereby blunt effective opposition.

The first part of *Genocide: A Comprehensive Introduction* seeks to ground readers in the basic historical and conceptual contexts of genocide. It explores the process by which Raphael Lemkin first named and defined the phenomenon, then mobilized a nascent United Nations to outlaw it. His story constitutes a vivid and inspiring portrait of an individual who had a significant, largely unsung impact on modern history. Examination of legal and scholarly definitions and debates may help readers to clarify their own thinking, and situate themselves in the discussion.

The case study section of the book (Part 2) is divided between longer case studies of genocide and capsule studies that complement the detailed treatments. I hope this structure will catalyze discussion and comparative analysis.

The first three chapters of Part 3 explore social-scientific contributions to the study of genocide – from psychology, sociology, anthropology, and political science/international relations. Let me indicate the scope and limitations of this analysis. I am a political scientist by training. As well as devoting a chapter to perspectives from this discipline, I incorporate its insights elsewhere in the text (notably in Chapter 2 on "State and Empire; War and Revolution," and Chapter 16 on "Strategies of Intervention and Prevention"). Likewise, Chapter 14 on "Memory, Forgetting, and Denial" touches on a significant discussion among professional historians, while the analysis of "Justice, Truth, and Redress" (Chapter 15), as well as parts of Chapter 1 on "The Origins of Genocide," explore relevant developments and debates in international law.

However, even if a synoptic examination of all these disciplines' insights were possible, given space limitations, I would be unable to provide it. The proliferation of academic production, of schools and subschools, has effectively obliterated the "Renaissance" man or woman, who once moved with facility among varied fields of knowledge. Accordingly, throughout these chapters, my ambition is modest. I seek only to introduce readers to some useful scholarly framings, together with insights that I have found especially relevant and simulating.

This book at least engages with a field – genocide studies – that has been inter-disciplinary from the start. The development of strict disciplinary boundaries is a modern invention, reflecting the growing scale and bureaucratization of academia. The barriers it establishes among disciplines are artificial. Political scientists draw on insights from history, sociology, and psychology, and their own work finds readers in those disciplines. Sociology and anthropology are closely related: the former developed as a study of the societies of the industrial West, while in the latter, Westerners studied "primitive" or preindustrial societies. Other linkages and points of interpenetration could be cited. The point is that consideration of a given theme under the rubric of a particular discipline may be arbitrary. To take just one example, "ethnicity" can be approached from sociological, anthropological, psychological, and political science perspectives. I discuss it principally in its sociological context, but would not wish to see it fixed there.

Part 4, "The Future of Genocide," seeks to familiarize readers with contemporary debates over historical memory and genocide denial, as well as mechanisms of justice and redress. The final chapter, "Strategies of Intervention and Prevention," allows readers to evaluate options for suppressing the scourge.

"How does one handle this subject?" wrote Terrence Des Pres in the Preface to *The Survivor*, his study of life in the Nazi concentration camps. His answer: "One doesn't; not well, not finally. No degree of scope or care can equal the enormity of such events or suffice for the sorrow they encompass. Not to betray it is as much as I can hope for."[9] His words resonate. In my heart, I know this book is an audacious enterprise, but I have tried to expand the limits of my empathy and, through wide reading, my interdisciplinary understanding. I have also benefited from the insights and corrections of other scholars and general readers, whose names appear in the acknowledgments.

While I must depict particular genocides (and the contributions of entire academic disciplines) in very broad strokes, I have tried throughout to find room for individuals, whether as victims, perpetrators, or rescuers. I hope this serves to counter some of the abstraction and depersonalization that is inevitable in a general survey. A list of relevant internet sources, along with links, teaching resources, and an extensive "Filmography of Genocide and Crimes against Humanity," can be found on the Web page for this book at http://www.genocidetext.net.[10]

NOTE TO THE SECOND EDITION

The core structure of *Genocide: A Comprehensive Introduction* remains unaltered from the first edition, and many sections are reproduced virtually intact. However, data, analysis, and references have all been updated, and content revised throughout. In the introductory chapter, I have added discussions of the concept of "destruction," especially as it pertains to "cultural genocide" and the question of whether physical killing defines genocide. I still lean toward the killing-focused definition advanced in the first edition, but I want to do justice to this debate, particularly for readers who find my framing too limiting. I have included a box text on the "other -cides" of genocide, and another providing a lexicon of key modern genocides. I have added discussions of multiple and overlapping identities in genocide, as well as dynamism and contingency, and have reworked the section on genocidal intent.

Chapter 2, retitled "State and Empire; War and Revolution," focuses more closely on genocide and nation-state formation and expansion, a central theme in some recent investigations (notably historian Mark Levene's two-volume *Genocide in the Age of the Nation-State*). The first case-study chapter, on "Genocides of Indigenous Peoples" (Chapter 3), has had the Guatemala micro-study extracted, considerably expanded, and redeployed as a supplementary case-study (Box 3a). The original box text, on the Chinese despoliation of Tibet, has been incorporated in somewhat condensed form into a revised Chapter 5, which has shifted from a study of "Stalin's Terror" to a wider consideration of the two great communist tyrants of the twentieth century, Joseph Stalin and Mao Zedong (including Mao's targeting of Tibetans). It was at the urging of Israel Charny, former president of the International Association of Genocide Scholars (IAGS), that I first considered this dual approach. I thank Israel for the suggestion, and for the many lively discussions I have had with him over the years.

Chapter 4 has been reconfigured as "The Ottoman Destruction of Christian Minorities." In its original form, it offered a straightforward study of the Armenian genocide, with some peripheral comments on the destruction of Assyrian, Greek, and Chaldean populations. Since that edition appeared, a successful campaign has been mounted – in which I have played a role – to expand our framing of the genocide of the 1910s and early 1920s to appreciate the diverse *genocides* (plural) inflicted upon the Christian minorities of Anatolia. My chapter thus includes more material on the Greek and Assyrian catastrophes, while still addressing in detail the Armenian genocide, which together with the Holocaust was so central to the emergence of the field of comparative genocide studies.

Elsewhere, the box-text (4a) on the Anfal Campaign against Iraqi Kurds in 1988 has been replaced by a study of more recent genocidal events in Iraq, following the

US-British invasion of 2003. The original Anfal treatment is still available on the book's website (www.genocidetext.net). I have also replaced two of the personal "stories" in the case-study chapters (Chapters 4 and 7) with fresh voices. Chapter 13, on gender, and Chapter 14, on "Memory, Forgetting, and Denial," have been significantly revised and expanded. Finally, in Chapter 16, I have included a long box-text on cases that might be considered "success stories" of coexistence and genocide prevention.

Other changes are more minor and incremental. The intention throughout has been to provide a comprehensive updating, revision, and sometimes rethinking. Readers' comments and feedback on the first edition were most helpful in preparing its successor. I especially thank the educators around the world who have adopted *Genocide: A Comprehensive Introduction* as a core text for their undergraduate and graduate courses, and who shared with me their evaluations of how it works as a teaching tool. I welcome comments, criticisms, and suggestions for future editions: please write to me at adam@genocidetext.net.

NOTES

1 George Orwell, "Politics and the English Language" (1946), in *Inside the Whale and Other Essays* (Harmondsworth: Penguin, 1974). Available on the Web at http://www.resort. com/~prime8/Orwell/patee.html.

2 The Second World War Allies against the Nazis and Japanese; Tanzanians against Idi Amin's Uganda; Vietnamese in Cambodia in 1979; Indians in Bangladesh in 1971; soldiers of the Rwandan Patriotic Front in 1994. See also Chapter 16.

3 Jacques Sémelin, *Purify and Destroy: The Political Uses of Massacre and Genocide* (New York: Columbia University Press, 2007), p. 6.

4 Writing the first in-depth study of the Soviet "terror-famine" in Ukraine in 1932–33 (see Chapter 5), Robert Conquest confronted only indirectly the "inhuman, unimaginable misery" of the famine; but he still found the task "so distressing that [I] sometimes hardly felt able to proceed." Conquest, *The Harvest of Sorrow: Soviet Collectivization and the Terror-Famine* (New York: Oxford University Press, 1986), p. 10. Donald Miller and Lorna Touryan Miller, who interviewed a hundred survivors of the Armenian genocide, wrote: "During this project our emotions have ranged from melancholy to anger, from feeling guilty about our own privileged status to being overwhelmed by the continuing suffering in our world." They described experiencing "a permanent loss of innocence about the human capacity for evil," as well as "a recognition of the need to combat such evil." Miller and Miller, *Survivors: An Oral History of the Armenian Genocide* (Berkeley, CA: University of California Press, 1999), p. 4. After an immersion in the archive of S-21 (Tuol Sleng), the Khmer Rouge killing center in Cambodia, David Chandler found that "the terror lurking inside it has pushed me around, blunted my skills, and eroded my self-assurance. The experience at times has been akin to drowning." Chandler, *Voices from S-21: Terror and History in Pol Pot's Secret Prison* (Berkeley, CA: University of California Press, 1999), p. 145. Brandon Hamber notes that "many of the staff" working with the Truth and Reconciliation Commission in South Africa have experienced "nightmares, paranoia, emotional bluntness, physical problems (e.g. headaches, ulcers, exhaustion, etc.), high levels of anxiety, irritability and aggression, relationship difficulties and substance abuse related problems." Hamber, "The Burdens of Truth," in David E. Lorey and William H. Beezley, eds, *Genocide, Collective Violence, and Popular Memory: The Politics of Remembrance in the Twentieth Century* (Wilmington, DL: Scholarly Resources, Inc., 2002), p. 96.

5 Peter Balakian, *The Burning Tigris: The Armenian Genocide and America's Response* (New York: HarperCollins, 2003), p. 278.

6 Lemkin, quoted in John Cooper, *Raphael Lemkin and the Struggle for the Genocide Convention* (London: Palgrave Macmillan, 2008), p. 169.

7 Christian P. Scherrer, *Genocide and Crisis in Central Africa: Conflict Roots, Mass Violence, and Regional War* (Westport, CT: Praeger, 2002), pp. 1, 7.

8 Meaghen Gallagher, personal communication, October 11, 2009.

9 Terrence Des Pres, *The Survivor: An Anatomy of Life in the Death Camps* (Oxford: Oxford University Press, 1976), pp. v–vi.

10 Readers who are interested in the background to my engagement with genocide studies can consult the short essay, "Genocide: A Personal Journey," at http://www.genocidetext.net/personal_journey.htm.

Acknowledgments

Genocide: A Comprehensive Introduction was born over a 2003 dinner in Durban, South Africa, at which I chanced to sit beside Taylor & Francis commissioning editor Craig Fowlie. I am truly grateful for Craig's early and enduring support. He also provided encouragement and guidance in the crafting of this second edition. Thanks to Nadia Seemungul, Steve Thompson, Nicola Parkin, and Emily Senior on the administrative side at Routledge; and to Ann King and Susan Dunsmore for their sterling copy-editing.

The bulk of the first edition of *Genocide: A Comprehensive Introduction* was written while working as a researcher at the CIDE institute in Mexico City. My research assistant, Pamela Huerta, compiled comprehensive briefs for the Cambodia case study and the Tibet and Congo/Darfur materials. Her skill and enthusiasm were greatly appreciated.

Much of the first edition was written in 2004 during travels through Argentina's Córdoba province, and holed up in an apartment in vibrant Buenos Aires. My thanks to the Argentine friends who welcomed me, especially Julieta and Juan Pablo Ayala; to the hoteliers, and apartment agents who put me up along the way; and to the restaurant staff who kept me fueled with that awesome steak and *vino tinto*.

The manuscript was completed in the Mexico City home of Jessica and Esperanza Rodríguez; my warm thanks to both. In Puebla, Fabiola Martínez asked challenging questions, engaged in probing discussions, and supplied tender care besides. *Gracias, mi Fabi-losa*.

What one could call "post-production" on the first edition took place at Yale University, where I was fortunate to obtain a two-year postdoctoral fellowship in the Genocide Studies Program for 2005–07. I was honored by the opportunity to conduct research at one of the world's leading universities, and am deeply grateful to Ben Kiernan, director of Yale's Genocide Studies Program (GSP), for his interest in my work and support of it over the past few years. I also acknowledge with gratitude the financial assistance of Frederick J. Iseman, Esq., whose donation to the GSP substantially funded the post-doctoral fellowship that brought me to the program, and allowed me to finish work on *Genocide: A Comprehensive Introduction* with access to the rich human and material resources at Yale. The Whitney and Betty MacMillan Center for International and Area Studies at Yale co-sponsored the fellowship, and provided me with a memorable teaching opportunity. Many thanks to its director Ian Shapiro, associate director Richard Kane, and the many wonderful academics, administrators, students, and guest speakers whom I encountered during my time in residence.

My colleagues in the Political Science program at the University of British Columbia Okanagan (UBCO), which I joined in 2007, have been most welcoming and supportive. Students in my "Genocide: An Interdisciplinary Perspective" and "Crimes against Humanity" courses have consistently challenged and enlightened me. I also wish to acknowledge the sterling research assistance, for this and closely related projects, provided at UBCO by Sasha Johnston and Jill Mitchell. Sasha was indispensable in helping me to organize and collate by subject the years' worth of "Media Files" on genocide and crimes against humanity that I have disseminated through my blog (http://jonestream.blogspot.com). Jill had the thankless task of checking all the Web links in this book, which she did efficiently and with panache.

Kenneth J. Campbell, Jo and David Jones, René Lemarchand, Benjamin Madley, and Nicholas Robins generously read the entire manuscript of the first edition. I benefited enormously from their feedback. Jo and David's meticulous proofreading might have landed them in the dedication to this volume even if they weren't my parents. As for Ben Madley, our weekly or biweekly lunches at Yale, when we went through his insightful comments on the manuscript, were simply the most stimulating and thought-provoking discussions I have ever had about genocide. As with Jo and David, there are few pages of this book that do not bear Ben's stamp.

All three of these parties read much or all of the second edition as well, saving me – and sparing you – more soggy verbiage and outright errors than I care to recall. Bless them. Other scholars, professionals, and general readers who read and commented on various chapters of the first and second editions include: Jennifer Archer, Peter Balakian, Donald Bloxham, Peter Burns, David Gaunt, Thea Halo, Alex Hinton, Kal Holsti, Craig Jones, Ben Kiernan, Mark Levene, Evelin Lindner, Linda Melvern, Kathleen Morrow, A. Dirk Moses, Margaret Power, John Quigley, Victoria Sanford, Christian Scherrer, and Hannibal Travis. Although I have not always heeded these individuals' suggestions, their perspectives have been crucial, and have rescued me from numerous mistakes and misinterpretations. I accept full responsibility for those that doubtless remain.

This second edition is much richer in images than the first, and I am grateful to the individuals who both contributed visual materials (as credited in the text) and helped me to arrange reprint rights when necessary. For the latter, thanks to Magnus Bergmar at the World's Children's Prize Foundation; Elisa Marquez at AP Photo;

Michael Shulman at Magnum Photos; Victoria Enaut and Catina Tanner at the International Criminal Tribunal for the Former Yugoslavia (ICTY); Melanie Modlin at the National Library of Medicine in Bethesda, Maryland; Raymond Pettit of the Equipo Argentino de Antropología Forense (EAAF); Martha Smalley at the Yale Divinity School Library; Betty Smith of International Publishers; Tanya Elder and Tammy Kiter, archivists at the American Jewish Historical Society; Pierre Sauvage of the Chambon Foundation; and Ying-Ying Chang, mother of the late Iris Chang.

Friends and family have always buttressed me, and stoked my passion for studying history and humanity. This book could not have been written without the nurture and guidance provided by my parents and my brother, Craig. Warmest thanks also to Atenea Acevedo, Carla Bergman, David Buchanan, Charli Carpenter, Mike Charko, Ferrel Christensen, Katelyn Craig, Terry and Meghan Evenson, Jay Forster, Andrea and Steve Gunner, Alison and Gen Houweling, Henry Huttenbach, María Johnson, David Liebe, John Margesson, the late Eric Markusen, Peter Prontzos, Hamish Telford, and Miriam Tratt.

Dr. Griselda Ramírez Reyes shares the dedication of this work. Griselda is a pediatric neurosurgeon at the Siglo XXI medical center in Mexico City. I have stood literally at her elbow as she opened the head of a three-week-old girl, and extracted a cancerous tumor seemingly half the size of the infant's brain. (I hope to open a few minds myself with this work, but I would not pretend the task compares.) Since this book was first published, Griselda has accompanied me on journeys to a number of the sites that resonated with me as I prepared this new edition – among them Tuol Sleng, My Lai, the Plain of Jars, Ground Zero in New York City, Lidice, Auschwitz-Birkenau, and (on a more optimistic note) the cosmopolitan city of Kazan in Tatarstan, Russia. It is a huge salve and pleasure to have her company while I try to absorb this material and make some sense of it.

Adam Jones
Kelowna, BC, April 2010
adam@genocidetext.net

PART 1 OVERVIEW

CHAPTER 1

The Origins of Genocide

This chapter analyzes the origins of genocide as a global-historical phenomenon, providing a sense of genocide's frequency through history. It then examines the origin and evolution of the concept, unravels some central theoretical debates, and explores "contested cases" that test the boundaries of the genocide framework. No other chapter in the book tries to cover so much ground, and the discussion may at points seem complicated and confusing, so please fasten your seatbelts.

GENOCIDE IN PREHISTORY, ANTIQUITY, AND EARLY MODERNITY

"The word is new, the concept is ancient," wrote sociologist Leo Kuper in his seminal 1981 text of genocide studies.[1]* The roots of genocide are lost in distant millennia, and will remain so unless an "archaeology of genocide" can be developed.[2] The difficulty, as Frank Chalk and Kurt Jonassohn pointed out in their study *The History and Sociology of Genocide*, is that such historical records as exist are ambiguous and

---

* Throughout this book, to reduce footnoting, I gather sequential quotations and citations from the same source into an omnibus note at the end of the passage. Epigraphs for chapters and sections are not footnoted. All Web links cited in the notes were "live" as of early 2010. If you find one broken, search the title of the source in quotation marks; often it will be archived elsewhere. I have included link addresses for media and other reports when they are in a reasonably concise format. Where I consider them too lengthy and ungainly to print, a Web search by author and title will generally bring them up.

undependable. While history today is generally written with some fealty to "objective" facts, many past accounts aimed to praise the writer's patron (normally a powerful leader) and to emphasize the superiority of one's own religious beliefs. They may also have been intended as good stories – so that when Homer quotes King Agamemnon's quintessential pronouncement of root-and-branch genocide, one cannot know what basis it might have in fact:

> We are not going to leave a single one of them alive, down to the babies in their mothers' wombs – not even they must live. The whole people must be wiped out of existence, and none be left to think of them and shed a tear.[3]

Factually reliable or not, Agamemnon's command encapsulates a fantasy of kings and commoners alike. Humanity has always nurtured conceptions of social difference that generate a sense of in-group versus out-group, as well as hierarchies of good and evil, superior and inferior, desirable and undesirable. As Chalk and Jonassohn observed:

> Historically and anthropologically peoples have always had a name for themselves. In a great many cases, that name meant "the people" to set the owners of that name off against all other people who were considered of lesser quality in some way. If the differences between the people and some other society were particularly large in terms of religion, language, manners, customs, and so on, then such others were seen as less than fully human: pagans, savages, or even animals.[4]

The fewer the shared values and standards, the more likely members of the out-group were (and are) to find themselves beyond the "universe of obligation," in sociologist Helen Fein's evocative phrase. Hence the advent of "religious traditions of contempt and collective defamation, stereotypes, and derogatory metaphor indicating the victim is inferior, sub-human (animals, insects, germs, viruses) or super-human (Satanic, omnipotent)." If certain classes of people are "pre-defined as alien . . . subhuman or dehumanized, or the enemy," it follows that they must "be eliminated in order that we may live (Them or Us)."[5]

An example of this mindset is the text that underpins the Christian, Jewish, and Muslim cultural traditions: the Old Testament (particularly its first five books, the Pentateuch). In general, these texts depict God as "a despotic and capricious sadist,"[6] and his followers as eager *génocidaires* (genocidal killers). The trend begins in the Book of Genesis (6:17–19), where God decides "to destroy all flesh in which is the breath of life from under heaven," with the exception of Noah and a nucleus of human and animal life.[7] In "the most unequivocally extirpatory of [the] Old Testament texts,"[8] 1 Samuel 15: 2–3, "the Lord of hosts" declares: "I will punish the Amalekites for what they did in opposing the Israelites when they came up out of Egypt. Now go and attack Amalek, and utterly destroy all that they have; do not spare them, but kill both man and woman, child and infant, ox and sheep, camel and donkey."[9]

The Midianites in Numbers 31: 7–18 fare little better, but even the minimal selectivity at the outset vexes Moses:

They warred against Midian, as the Lord commanded Moses, and slew every male.
. . . And the people of Israel took captive the women of Midian and their little
ones; and they took as booty all their cattle, their flocks, and all their goods. All
their cities . . . they burned with fire. . . . And Moses was angry with the officers
of the army. . . . [He] said to them, "Have you let all the women live? Behold, these
caused the people of Israel, by the counsel of Balaam, to act treacherously against
the Lord . . . and so the plague came to the congregations of the Lord. Now,
therefore, kill every male among the little ones, and kill every woman who has
known man by lying with him [sexually]. But all the young girls who have not
known man by lying with him, keep alive for yourselves.[10]

As this passage suggests, genocides in prehistory and antiquity were often designed
not just to eradicate enemy ethnicities, but to incorporate and exploit *some* of their
members. Generally, it was children (particularly girls) and women (particularly
virgins, or those in the associated age group) who were spared murder. They were
simultaneously seen as the group least able to offer resistance, and as sources of
offspring for the dominant group, descent in patrilineal society being traced through
the male bloodline. By contrast, "every male" was often killed, "even the little ones."
We see here the roots of *gendercide* against men and boys, including male infants,
discussed further in Chapter 13.

A combination of gender-selective mass killing and root-and-branch genocide
pervades accounts of ancient wars. Chalk and Jonassohn provide a wide-ranging selection of historical events such as the Assyrian Empire's root-and-branch depredations
in the first half of the first millennium BCE,* and the destruction of Melos by Athens
during the Peloponnesian War (fifth century BCE), a gendercidal rampage described
by Thucydides in his "Melian Dialogue."

The Roman siege and eventual razing of Carthage at the close of the Third
Punic War (149–46 BCE) has been labeled "The First Genocide" by historian Ben
Kiernan. The "first" designation is debatable; the label of genocide, less so. Fueled
by the documented ideological zealotry of the senator Cato, Rome sought to suppress
the supposed threat posed by (disarmed, mercantile) Carthage. "Of a population
of 2–400,000, at least 150,000 Carthaginians perished," writes Kiernan. The
"Carthaginian solution" found many echoes in the warfare of subsequent centuries.[11]

Among Rome's other victims during its imperial ascendancy were the followers
of Jesus Christ. After his death at Roman hands in 33 CE, Christ's followers were
subjected to persecutions and mass murder. The scenes of torture and public spectacle
were duplicated by Christians themselves during Europe's medieval era (approximately the ninth to fourteenth centuries CE). This period produced onslaughts such
as the Crusades: religiously sanctified campaigns against "unbelievers," whether in
France (the Albigensian crusade against Cathar heretics), Germany (against Jews),
or the Holy Land of the Middle East.[12]

---

* "BCE" means "Before the Common Era," and replaces the more familiar but ethnocentric "BC"
(Before Christ). "CE" replaces "AD" (*Anno Domini*, Latin for "year of the Lord"). For discussion, see
ReligiousTolerance.org, "The Use of 'CE' and 'BCE' to Identify Dates," http://www.religioustolerance.
org/ce.htm.

Further *génocidaires* arose on the other side of the world. In the thirteenth century, a million or so Mongol horsemen under their leader, Genghis Khan, surged out of the grasslands of East Asia to lay waste to vast territories, extending to the gates of Western Europe; "entire nations were exterminated, leaving behind nothing but rubble, fallow fields, and bones."[13]

In addition to religious and cultural beliefs, a hunger for wealth, power, and "death-defying" glory seems to have motivated these acts of mass violence (see Chapter 10). These factors combined to fuel the genocides of the early modern era, dating from approximately 1492, the year of Caribbean Indians' fateful encounter with Christopher Columbus. The consequences of contact between expansionist Europeans and indigenous peoples are detailed in Chapter 3. The next section focuses briefly on two cases from the early modern era: one from Europe, presaging the genocidal civil wars of the twentieth century; and one from Africa, reminding us that genocide knows no geographical or cultural boundaries.

The Vendée uprising

In 1789, French rebels, inspired by the American revolutionaries, overthrew King Louis XVI and established a new order based on the "Rights of Man." The French revolution provoked immediate opposition at home and abroad. European armies massed on French borders, and in March 1793 – following the execution of King Louis and the imposition of mass military conscription – revolt erupted in the Vendée. The population of this isolated and conservative region of western France declared itself opposed to conscription, and to the replacement of their priests by pro-revolutionary designates. Well trained and led by royalist officers, Vendeans rose up against the rapidly radicalizing central government: the "Terror" of the Jacobin faction was instituted in the same month as the rebellion in St.-Florent-le-Vieil. The result was a civil war that, according to French author Reynald Secher, constituted a genocide against the Vendeans – and for historian Mark Levene, a turning point in the evolution of genocide.[14]

Early Vendean victories were achieved through the involvement of all demographic sectors of the Vendée, and humiliated the Republican government. Fueled by the ideological fervor of the Terror, and by foreign and domestic counter-revolution, the Republicans in Paris implemented a campaign of root-and-branch genocide. Under Generals Jean-Baptiste Carrier and Louis Marie Turreau, the Republicans launched a scorched-earth drive by the *colonnes infernales* ("hellish columns"). On December 11, 1793, Carrier wrote to the Committee of Public Safety in Paris, pledging to purge the Vendean peasantry "absolutely and totally."[15] Similar edicts by General Turreau in early 1794 were approved by the Committee, which declared that the "race of brigands" in the Vendée was to be "exterminated to the last." Targeted victims included even children, who were "just as dangerous [as adults], because they were or were in the process of becoming brigands." Extermination was "both sound and pure," the Committee wrote, and should "show great results."[16]

The slaughter targeted all Vendeans, including Republicans (these victims were seen as "collateral damage"). Specifically, none of the traditional gender-selective exemptions was granted to adult females, who stood accused of fomenting the rebellion through their defense of conservative religion, and their "goad[ing] . . . into martyrdom" of Vendean men.[17] In the account of a Vendean abbé, perhaps self-interested but buttressed by other testimony:

> There were poor girls, completely naked, hanging from tree branches, hands tied behind their backs, after having been raped. It was fortunate that, with the Blues [Republicans] gone, some charitable passersby delivered them from this shameful torment. Elsewhere . . . pregnant women were stretched out and crushed beneath wine presses. . . . Bloody limbs and nursing infants were carried in triumph on the points of bayonets.[18]

Perhaps 150,000 Vendeans died in the carnage, though not all were civilians. The character of the killings was conveyed by post-genocide census figures, which evidenced not the usual war-related disparity of male versus female victims, but a rough – and unusual – parity. Only after this "ferocious . . . expression of ideologically charged avenging terror,"[19] and with the collapse of the Committee of Public Safety in Paris, did the genocide wane, though scattered clashes with rebels continued through 1796.

In a comparative context, the Vendée uprising stands as an example of a mass-killing campaign that has only recently been conceptualized as "genocide." This designation is not universally shared, but it seems apt in light of the large-scale murder of a designated group (the Vendean civilian population).

Zulu genocide

Between 1810 and 1828, the Zulu kingdom under its dictatorial leader, Shaka Zulu, waged an ambitious campaign of expansion and annihilation. Huge swathes of present-day South Africa and Zimbabwe were laid waste by Zulu armies. The European invasion of these regions, which began shortly after, was greatly assisted by the upheaval and depopulation caused by the Zulu assault.

Oral histories help document the scale of the destruction:[20] "To this day, peoples in Zimbabwe, Malawi, Zambia, Tanzania, Kenya, and Uganda can trace their descent back to the refugees who fled from Shaka's warriors."[21] At times, Shaka apparently implemented a gender-selective extermination strategy that may be unique in the historical record. In conquering the Butelezi clan, Shaka "conceived the then [and still] quite novel idea of utterly demolishing them as a separate tribal entity by incorporating all their manhood into his own clan or following," thereby bolstering his own military; but he "usually destroyed women, infants, and old people," who were deemed useless for his expansionist purposes.[22]

However, root-and-branch strategies reminiscent of the French rampage in the Vendée seem also to have been common. According to historian Michael Mahoney, Zulu armies often aimed not only at defeating enemies but at "their total destruction. Those exterminated included not only whole armies, but also prisoners of war, women, children, and even dogs."[23] In exterminating the followers of Beje, a minor

Kumalo chief, Shaka determined "not to leave alive even a child, but [to] exterminate the whole tribe," according to a foreign witness. When the foreigners protested against the slaughter of women and children, claiming they "could do no injury," Shaka responded in language that would have been familiar to the French revolutionaries: "Yes they could," he declared. "They can propagate and bring [bear] children, who may become my enemies . . . therefore I command you to kill all."[24]

Mahoney has characterized these policies as genocidal. "If genocide is defined as a state-mandated effort to annihilate whole peoples, then Shaka's actions in this regard must certainly qualify." He points out that the term adopted by the Zulus to denote their campaign of expansion and conquest, *izwekufa*, derives "from Zulu *izwe* (nation, people, polity), and *ukufa* (death, dying, to die). The term is thus identical to 'genocide' in both meaning and etymology."[25]

NAMING GENOCIDE: RAPHAEL LEMKIN

Genocide is an absolute word – a howl of a word . . .

Lance Morrow

Until the Second World War, genocide was a "crime without a name," in the words of British Prime Minister Winston Churchill.[26] The man who named the crime, placed it in a global-historical context, and demanded intervention and remedial action was a Polish-Jewish jurist, a refugee from Nazi-occupied Europe, named Raphael Lemkin (1900–59). His story is one of the most remarkable of the twentieth century.

Lemkin is an exceptional example of a "norm entrepreneur" (see Chapter 12). In the space of four years, he coined a term – genocide – that concisely defined an age-old phenomenon. He supported it with a wealth of documentation. He published a lengthy book (*Axis Rule in Occupied Europe*) that applied the concept to campaigns of genocide underway in Lemkin's native Poland and elsewhere in the Nazi-occupied territories. He then waged a successful campaign to persuade the new United Nations to draft a convention against genocide; another successful campaign to obtain the required number of signatures; and yet another to secure the necessary national ratifications. Yet Lemkin lived in penury – in surely his wittiest recorded comment, he described himself as "pleading a holy cause at the UN while wearing holey clothes,"[27] and he died in obscurity in 1959; his funeral drew just seven people. Only in recent years has the promise of his concept, and the UN convention that incorporated it, begun to be realized.

Growing up in a Jewish family in Wolkowysk, a town in eastern Poland, Lemkin developed a talent for languages (he would end up mastering a dozen or more), and a passionate curiosity about the cultures that produced them. He was struck by accounts of the suffering of Christians at Roman hands, and its parallel in the pogroms then afflicting the Jews of eastern Poland. More generally, as John Cooper notes, "growing up in a contested borderland over which different armies clashed . . . made Lemkin acutely sensitive to the concerns of the diverse nationalities living there and their anxieties about self-preservation."[28]

Thus began Lemkin's lifelong study of mass killing in history and the contemporary world. He "raced through an unusually grim reading list"[29] that familiarized him with cases from antiquity and the medieval era (including Carthage, discussed above, and the fate of the Aztec and Inca empires, described in Chapter 3). "I was appalled by the frequency of the evil," he recalled later, "and, above all, by the impunity coldly relied upon by the guilty."[30] *Why?* was the question that began to consume Lemkin. A key moment came in 1921, while he was studying at the University of Lvov. Soghomon Tehlirian, an Armenian avenger of the Ottoman destruction of Christian minorities (Chapter 4), was arrested for murder after he gunned down one of the genocide's architects, Talat Pasha, in a Berlin street. In the same year, leading planners and perpetrators of the genocide were freed by the British from custody in Malta, as part of the Allies' postwar courting of a resurgent Turkey. Lemkin wrote that he was "shocked" by the juxtaposition: "A nation was killed and the guilty persons were set free. Why is a man punished when he kills another man? Why is the killing of a million a lesser crime than the killing of a single individual?"[31]

Lemkin determined to stage an intellectual and activist intervention in what he at first called "barbarity" and "vandalism." The former referred to "the premeditated destruction of national, racial, religious and social collectivities," while the latter he described as the "destruction of works of art and culture, being the expression of the particular genius of these collectivities."[32] At a conference of European legal scholars in Madrid in 1933, Lemkin's framing was first presented (though not by its author; the Polish government denied him a travel visa). Despite the post-First World War prosecutions of Turks for "crimes against humanity" (Chapters 4, 15), governments and public opinion leaders were still wedded to the notion that state sovereignty trumped atrocities against a state's own citizens. It was this legal impunity that rankled and galvanized Lemkin more than anything else. Yet the Madrid delegates did not share his concern. They refused to adopt a resolution against the crimes Lemkin set before them; the matter was tabled.

Undeterred, Lemkin continued his campaign. He presented his arguments in legal forums throughout Europe in the 1930s, and as far afield as Cairo, Egypt. The outbreak of the Second World War found him at the heart of the inferno – in Poland, with Nazi forces invading from the West, and Soviets from the East. As Polish resistance crumbled, Lemkin took flight. He traveled first to eastern Poland, and then to Vilnius, Lithuania. From that Baltic city he succeeded in securing refuge in Sweden.

After teaching in Stockholm, the United States beckoned. Lemkin believed the US would be both receptive to his framework, and in a position to actualize it in a way that Europe under the Nazi yoke could not. An epic 14,000-mile journey took him across the Soviet Union by train to Vladivostok, by boat to Japan, and across the Pacific. In the US, he moonlighted at Yale University's Law School before moving to Durham, North Carolina, where he became a professor at Duke University.

In his new American surroundings, Lemkin struggled with his concepts and vocabulary. "Vandalism" and "barbarity" had not struck a chord with his legal audiences. Inspired by, of all things, the Kodak camera,[33] Lemkin trawled through his impressive linguistic resources for a term that was concise and memorable. He settled

Figure 1.1 Raphael Lemkin (1900–59), founder of genocide studies.

Source: American Jewish Historical Society.

on a neologism with both Greek and Latin roots: the Greek "genos," meaning race or tribe, and the Latin "cide," or killing. "Genocide" was the intentional destruction of national groups on the basis of their collective identity. Physical killing was an important part of the picture, but it was only a part:

> By "genocide" we mean the destruction of a nation or an ethnic group. . . .
> Generally speaking, genocide does not necessarily mean the immediate destruction of a nation, except when accomplished by mass killings of all members of a nation. It is intended rather to signify a coordinated plan of different actions aiming at the destruction of essential foundations of the life of national groups, with the aim of annihilating the groups themselves. The objectives of such a plan would be disintegration of the political and social institutions of culture, language, national feelings, religion, and the economic existence of national groups, and the destruction of the personal security, liberty, health, dignity, and even the lives of the individuals belonging to such groups. Genocide is directed against the national group as an entity, and the actions involved are directed against individuals, not in their individual capacity, but as members of the national group. . . . Genocide has two phases: one, destruction of the national pattern of the oppressed group; the other the imposition of the national pattern of the oppressor. This imposition, in turn, may be made upon the oppressed population which is

allowed to remain, or upon the territory alone, after removal of the population and the colonization of the area by the oppressor's own nationals.[34]

The critical question, for Lemkin, was whether the multifaceted campaign proceeded under the rubric of policy. To the extent that it did, it could be considered genocidal, even if it did not result in the physical destruction of all (or any) members of the group.[35] The issue of whether mass killing is definitional to genocide has been debated ever since, by myriad scholars and commentators. Equally vexing for subsequent generations was the emphasis on ethnic and national groups. These predominated as victims in the decades in which Lemkin developed his framework (and in the historical examples he studied). Yet by the end of the 1940s, it was clear that political groups were often targeted for annihilation. Moreover, the appellations applied to "communists," or by communists to "kulaks" or "class enemies" – when imposed by a totalitarian state – seemed every bit as difficult to shake as ethnic identifications, if the Nazi and Stalinist onslaughts were anything to go by. This does not even take into account the important but ambiguous areas of cross-over among ethnic, political, and social categories (see "Multiple and Overlapping Identities," below).

Lemkin, though, would hear little of this. Although he did not exclude political groups as genocide victims, he had a single-minded focus on nationality and ethnicity, for their culture-carrying capacity as he perceived it. His attachment to these core

Figure 1.2 Samantha Power's book *"A Problem from Hell": America and the Age of Genocide* (2002) won both the Pulitzer Prize and the National Book Critics Circle Award, and contributed to the resurgence of public interest in genocide. Power's work offered also the most detailed and vivid account to that date of Raphael Lemkin's life and his struggle for the UN Genocide Convention. As of 2010, Power was on leave from the Harvard Kennedy School, serving as a special advisor on foreign policy to the Barack Obama administration. She is shown here speaking at Columbia University, New York, in March 2008.

Source: Courtesy Angela Radulescu/www. angelaradulescu.com.

concerns was almost atavistic, and legal scholar Stephen Holmes, for one, has faulted him for it:

> Lemkin himself seems to have believed that killing a hundred thousand people of a single ethnicity was very different from killing a hundred thousand people of mixed ethnicities. Like Oswald Spengler, he thought that each cultural group had its own "genius" that should be preserved. To destroy, or attempt to destroy, a culture is a special kind of crime because culture is the unit of collective memory, whereby the legacies of the dead can be kept alive. To kill a culture is to cast its individual members into individual oblivion, their memories buried with their mortal remains. The idea that killing a culture is "irreversible" in a way that killing an individual is not reveals the strangeness of Lemkin's conception from a liberal-individualist point of view.

This archaic-sounding conception has other illiberal implications as well. For one thing, it means that the murder of a poet is morally worse than the murder of a janitor, because the poet is the "brain" without which the "body" cannot function. This revival of medieval organic imagery is central to Lemkin's idea of genocide as a special crime.[36]

It is probably true that Lemkin's formulation had its archaic elements. It is certainly the case that subsequent scholarly interpretations of "Lemkin's word" have tended to be more capacious in their framing. What *can* be defended is Lemkin's emphasis on the collective as a target. One can philosophize about the relative weight ascribed to collectives over the individual, as Holmes does; but the reality of modern times is that the vast majority of those murdered *were killed on the basis of a collective identity – even if only one imputed by the killers*. The link between collective and mass, then between mass and large-scale extermination, was the defining dynamic of the twentieth century's unprecedented violence. In his historical studies, Lemkin appears to have read this correctly. Many or most of the examples he cites would be uncontroversial among a majority of genocide scholars today.[37] He saw the Nazis' assaults on Jews, Poles, and Polish Jews for what they were, and labeled the broader genre for the ages.

Still, for Lemkin's word to resonate today, and into the future, two further developments were required. The UN Convention on the Prevention and Punishment of the Crime of Genocide (1948), adopted in remarkably short order after Lemkin's indefatigable lobbying, entrenched genocide in international and domestic law. And beginning in the 1970s, a coterie of "comparative genocide scholars," drawing upon a generation's work on the Jewish Holocaust,* began to discuss, debate, and refine Lemkin's concept – a trend that shows no sign of abating.

---

* I use the word "holocaust" generically in this book to refer to especially destructive genocides, such as those against indigenous peoples in the Americas and elsewhere, Christian minorities in the Ottoman empire during the First World War, Jews and Roma (Gypsies) under the Nazis, and Tutsis in Rwanda in 1994. Most scholars and commentators capitalize the "h" when referring to the Nazi genocide against the Jews, and I follow this usage when citing "the Jewish Holocaust" (see also Chapter 6, n. 1).

DEFINING GENOCIDE: THE UN CONVENTION

Lemkin's extraordinary "norm entrepreneurship" around genocide is described in Chapter 12. Suffice it to say for now that "rarely has a neologism had such rapid success" (legal scholar William Schabas). Barely a year after Lemkin coined the term, it was included in the Nuremberg indictments of Nazi war criminals (Chapter 15). To Lemkin's chagrin, genocide did not figure in the Nuremberg judgments. However, "by the time the General Assembly completed its standard sitting, with the 1948 adoption of the Convention on the Prevention and Punishment of the Crime of Genocide, 'genocide' had a detailed and quite technical definition as a crime against the law of nations."[38]

The "detailed and quite technical definition" is as follows:

Article I. The Contracting Parties confirm that genocide, whether committed in time of peace or in time of war, is a crime under international law which they undertake to prevent and to punish.

Article II. In the present Convention, genocide means any of the following acts committed with intent to destroy, in whole or in part, a national, ethnical, racial or religious group, as such:

(a) Killing members of the group;
(b) Causing serious bodily or mental harm to members of the group;
(c) Deliberately inflicting on the group conditions of life calculated to bring about its physical destruction in whole or in part;
(d) Imposing measures intended to prevent births within the group;
(e) Forcibly transferring children of the group to another group.

Article III. The following acts shall be punishable:

(a) Genocide;
(b) Conspiracy to commit genocide;
(c) Direct and public incitement to commit genocide;
(d) Attempt to commit genocide;
(e) Complicity in genocide.[39]

Thematically, Lemkin's conviction that genocide needed to be confronted, whatever the context, was resoundingly endorsed with the Convention's declaration that genocide is a crime "whether committed in time of peace or in time of war." This removed the road-block thrown up by the Nuremberg trials, which had only considered Nazi crimes committed after the invasion of Poland on September 1, 1939.

The basic thrust of Lemkin's emphasis on ethnic and national groups (at the expense of political groups and social classes) also survived the lobbying and drafting process. In the diverse genocidal strategies cited, we see reflected Lemkin's conception of genocide as a "coordinated plan of different actions aiming at the destruction of essential foundations of the life of national groups, with the aim of annihilating the groups themselves." However, at no point did the Convention's drafters actually define "national, ethnical, racial or religious" groups, and these terms have been subject to considerable subsequent interpretation. The position of the International Criminal Tribunal for Rwanda (ICTR), that "any stable and permanent group" is in fact to be accorded protection under the Convention, is likely to become the norm in future judgments.

With regard to genocidal strategies, the Convention places "stronger emphasis than Lemkin on *physical and biological destruction,* and less on broader *social destruction,*" as sociologist Martin Shaw points out.[40] But note how diverse are the actions considered genocidal in Article II – in marked contrast to the normal understanding of "genocide." One does not need to exterminate or seek to exterminate every last member of a designated group. In fact, *one does not need to kill anyone at all to commit genocide!* Inflicting "serious bodily or mental harm" qualifies, as does preventing births or transferring children between groups. It is fair to say, however, that from a legal perspective, genocide unaccompanied by mass killing is rarely prosecuted.[41] (I return below to the question of killing.)

Controversial and ambiguous phrases in the document include the reference to "serious bodily or mental harm" constituting a form of genocide. In practice, this has been interpreted along the lines of the Israeli trial court decision against Adolf Eichmann in 1961, convicting him of the "enslavement, starvation, deportation and persecution of . . . Jews . . . their detention in ghettos, transit camps and concentration camps in conditions which were designed to cause their degradation, deprivation of their rights as human beings, and to . . . cause them inhumane suffering and torture." The ICTR adds an interpretation that this includes "bodily or mental torture, inhuman treatment, and persecution," as well as "acts of rape and mutilation." In addition, "several sources correctly take the view that mass deportations under inhumane conditions may constitute genocide if accompanied by the requisite intent."[42] "Measures to prevent births" may be held to include forced sterilization and separation of the sexes. Sexual trauma and impregnation through gang rape have received increasing attention. The destruction of groups "as such" brought complex questions of motive into play. Some drafters saw it as a means of paying lip-service to the element of motive, while others perceived it as a way to sidestep the issue altogether.

Historically, it is intriguing to note how many issues of genocide definition and interpretation have their roots in contingent and improvised aspects of the drafting process. The initial draft by the UN Secretariat defined genocide's targets as "a group of human beings," adoption of which could have rendered redundant the subsequent debate over *which* groups qualified.

Responsibility for the exclusion of political groups was long laid at the door of the Soviet Union and its allies, supposedly nervous about application of the Convention to Soviet crimes (see Chapter 5). Schabas quashes this notion, pointing out that "rigorous examination of the *travaux* [working papers] fails to confirm a popular impression in the literature that the opposition . . . was some Soviet machination." Political collectivities "were actually included within the enumeration [of designated groups] until an eleventh-hour compromise eliminated the reference."[43]

In the estimation of many genocide scholars, this is the Convention's greatest oversight.[44] As for the provision against transferring children between groups, it "was added to the Convention almost as an afterthought, with little substantive debate or consideration."[45]

In its opening sentence, the Convention declares that the Contracting Parties "undertake to prevent and to punish" the crime of genocide. A subsequent article (VIII) states that "any Contracting Party may call upon the competent organs of the United Nations to take such action under the Charter of the United Nations as they consider appropriate for the prevention and suppression of acts of genocide or any of the other acts enumerated in Article III." Yet this leaves actual policy obligations vague.

BOUNDING GENOCIDE: COMPARATIVE GENOCIDE STUDIES

Between the 1950s and the 1980s, the term "genocide" languished almost unused by scholars. A handful of legal commentaries appeared for a specialized audience.[46] In 1975, Vahakn Dadrian's article "A Typology of Genocide" sparked renewed interest in a comparative framing. It was bolstered by Irving Louis Horowitz's *Genocide: State Power and Mass Murder* (1976), and foundationally by Leo Kuper's *Genocide: Its Political Use in the Twentieth Century* (1981). Kuper's work, including a subsequent volume on *The Prevention of Genocide* (1985), was the most significant on genocide since Lemkin's in the 1940s. It was followed by edited volumes and solo publications from Helen Fein, R.J. Rummel, Frank Chalk and Kurt Jonassohn, and Robert Melson, among others.

This early literature drew upon more than a decade of intensive research on the Holocaust, and most of the scholars were Jewish. "Holocaust Studies" remains central to the field. Still, rereading these pioneering works, one is struck by how inclusive and comparative their framing is. It tends to be global in scope, and interdisciplinary at many points. The classic volumes by Chalk and Jonassohn (*The History and Sociology of Genocide*) and Totten *et al.* (*Century of Genocide*) appeared in the early 1990s, and seemed to sum up this drive for catholicity. So too, despite its heavy focus on the Holocaust, did Israel Charny's *Encyclopedia of Genocide* (1999). A rich body of case-study literature also developed, with genocides such as those against the Armenians, Cambodians, and East Timorese – as well as indigenous peoples worldwide – receiving serious and sustained attention.

The explosion of public interest in genocide in the 1990s, and the concomitant growth of genocide studies as an academic field, has spawned a profusion of humanistic and social-scientific studies, joined by memoirs and oral histories. (The wider culture has also produced a steady stream of films on genocide and its reverberations, including *The Killing Fields, Schindler's List*, and *Hotel Rwanda*.)[47]

To capture the richness and diversity of the genocide-studies literature in this short section is impossible. What I hope to do is, first, to use that literature constructively throughout this book; and, second, to provide suggestions for further reading, encouraging readers to explore the bounty for themselves.

With this caveat in place, let me make a few generalizations, touching on debates that will reappear regularly in this book. Genocide scholars are concerned with two basic tasks. First, they attempt to *define* genocide and *bound* it conceptually. Second, they seek to *prevent* genocide. This implies understanding its comparative dynamics, and generating prophylactic strategies that may be applied in emergencies.

Scholarly definitions of genocide reflect the ambiguities of the Genocide Convention and its constituent debates. They can be confusing in their numerous and often opposed variants. However, surveying most of the definitions on offer, and combining them with the Lemkin and UN framings already cited, we can group them into two broad categories, and isolate some key features and variables.

BOX 1.1 GENOCIDE: SCHOLARLY DEFINITIONS (in chronological order)

Peter Drost (1959)

"Genocide is the deliberate destruction of physical life of individual human beings by reason of their membership of any human collectivity as such."

Vahakn Dadrian (1975)

"Genocide is the successful attempt by a dominant group, vested with formal authority and/or with preponderant access to the overall resources of power, to reduce by coercion or lethal violence the number of a minority group whose ultimate extermination is held desirable and useful and whose respective vulnerability is a major factor contributing to the decision for genocide."

Irving Louis Horowitz (1976)

"[Genocide is] a structural and systematic destruction of innocent people by a state bureaucratic apparatus . . . Genocide represents a systematic effort over time to liquidate a national population, usually a minority . . . [and] functions as a fundamental political policy to assure conformity and participation of the citizenry."

Leo Kuper (1981)

"I shall follow the definition of genocide given in the [UN] Convention. This is not to say that I agree with the definition. On the contrary, I believe a major omission to be in the exclusion of political groups from the list of groups protected. In the contemporary world, political differences are at the very least as significant a basis for massacre and annihilation as racial, national, ethnic or religious differences.

Then too, the genocides against racial, national, ethnic or religious groups are generally a consequence of, or intimately related to, political conflict. However, I do not think it helpful to create new definitions of genocide, when there is an internationally recognized definition and a Genocide Convention which might become the basis for some effective action, however limited the underlying conception. But since it would vitiate the analysis to exclude political groups, I shall refer freely . . . to liquidating or exterminatory actions against them."

Jack Nusan Porter (1982)

"Genocide is the deliberate destruction, in whole or in part, by a government or its agents, of a racial, sexual, religious, tribal or political minority. It can involve not only mass murder, but also starvation, forced deportation, and political, economic and biological subjugation. Genocide involves three major components: ideology, technology, and bureaucracy/organization."

Yehuda Bauer (1984)

n.b. Bauer distinguishes between "genocide" and "holocaust":

"[Genocide is] the planned destruction, since the mid-nineteenth century, of a racial, national, or ethnic group as such, by the following means: (a) selective mass murder of elites or parts of the population; (b) elimination of national (racial, ethnic) culture and religious life with the intent of 'denationalization'; (c) enslavement, with the same intent; (d) destruction of national (racial, ethnic) economic life, with the same intent; (e) biological decimation through the kidnapping of children, or the prevention of normal family life, with the same intent . . . [Holocaust is] the planned physical annihilation, for ideological or pseudo-religious reasons, of all the members of a national, ethnic, or racial group."

John L. Thompson and Gail A. Quets (1987)

"Genocide is the extent of destruction of a social collectivity by whatever agents, with whatever intentions, by purposive actions which fall outside the recognized conventions of legitimate warfare."

Isidor Wallimann and Michael N. Dobkowski (1987)

"Genocide is the deliberate, organized destruction, in whole or in large part, of racial or ethnic groups by a government or its agents. It can involve not only mass murder, but also forced deportation (ethnic cleansing), systematic rape, and economic and biological subjugation."

Henry Huttenbach (1988)

"Genocide is any act that puts the very existence of a group in jeopardy."

Helen Fein (1988)

"Genocide is a series of purposeful actions by a perpetrator(s) to destroy a collectivity through mass or selective murders of group members and suppressing the biological and social reproduction of the collectivity. This can be accomplished through the imposed proscription or restriction of reproduction of group members, increasing infant mortality, and breaking the linkage between reproduction and socialization of children in the family or group of origin. The perpetrator may represent the state of the victim, another state, or another collectivity."

Frank Chalk and Kurt Jonassohn (1990)

"Genocide is a form of one-sided mass killing in which a state or other authority intends to destroy a group, as that group and membership in it are defined by the perpetrator."

Helen Fein (1993)

"Genocide is sustained purposeful action by a perpetrator to physically destroy a collectivity directly or indirectly, through interdiction of the biological and social reproduction of group members, sustained regardless of the surrender or lack of threat offered by the victim."

Steven T. Katz (1994)

"[Genocide is] the actualization of the intent, however successfully carried out, to murder in its totality any national, ethnic, racial, religious, political, social, gender or economic group, as these groups are defined by the perpetrator, by whatever means." (n.b. Modified by Adam Jones in 2010 to read, "murder in whole or in part. . . .")

Israel Charny (1994)

"Genocide in the generic sense means the mass killing of substantial numbers of human beings, when not in the course of military action against the military forces of an avowed enemy, under conditions of the essential defencelessness of the victim."

Irving Louis Horowitz (1996)

"Genocide is herein defined as a *structural and systematic destruction of innocent people by a state bureaucratic apparatus* [emphasis in original]. . . . Genocide means the physical dismemberment and liquidation of people on large scales, an attempt by those who rule to achieve the total elimination of a subject people." (*n.b.* Horowitz supports "carefully distinguishing the [Jewish] Holocaust from genocide"; he also refers to "the phenomenon of mass murder, for which genocide is a synonym".)

Barbara Harff (2003)

"Genocides and politicides are the promotion, execution, and/or implied consent of sustained policies by governing elites or their agents – or, in the case of civil war, either of the contending authorities – that are intended to destroy, in whole or part, a communal, political, or politicized ethnic group."

Manus I. Midlarsky (2005)

"Genocide is understood to be the state-sponsored systematic mass murder of innocent and helpless men, women, and children denoted by a particular eth-noreligious identity, having the purpose of eradicating this group from a particular territory."

Mark Levene (2005)

"Genocide occurs when a state, perceiving the integrity of its agenda to be threatened by an aggregate population – defined by the state as an organic collectivity, or series of collectivities – seeks to remedy the situation by the systematic, *en masse* physical elimination of that aggregate, *in toto*, or until it is no longer perceived to represent a threat."

Jacques Sémelin (2005)

"I will define genocide as that particular process of civilian destruction that is directed at the total eradication of a group, the criteria by which it is identified being determined by the perpetrator."

Daniel Chirot and Clark McCauley (2006)

"A genocidal mass murder is politically motivated violence that directly or indirectly kills a substantial proportion of a targeted population, combatants and noncombatants alike, regardless of their age or gender."

Martin Shaw (2007)

"[Genocide is] a form of violent social conflict, or war, between armed power organizations that aim to destroy civilian social groups and those groups and other actors who resist this destruction."

Donald Bloxham (2009)

"[Genocide is] the physical destruction of a large portion of a group in a limited or unlimited territory with the intention of destroying that group's collective existence."

Discussion

The elements of definition may be divided into "harder" and "softer" positions, paralleling the international–legal distinction between hard and soft law. According to Christopher Rudolph,

> those who favor hard law in international legal regimes argue that it enhances deterrence and enforcement by signaling credible commitments, constraining self-serving auto-interpretation of rules, and maximizing 'compliance pull' through increased legitimacy. Those who favor soft law argue that it facilitates compromise, reduces contracting costs, and allows for learning and change in the process of institutional development.[48]

In genocide scholarship, harder positions are guided by concerns that "genocide" will be rendered banal or meaningless by careless use. Some argue that such slack usage will divert attention from the proclaimed uniqueness of the Holocaust. Softer positions reflect concerns that excessively rigid framings (for example, a focus on the total physical extermination of a group) rule out too many actions that, logically and morally, demand to be included. Their proponents may also wish to see a dynamic and evolving genocide framework, rather than a static and inflexible one.

It should be noted that these basic positions do not map perfectly onto individual authors and authorities. A given definition may even alternate between harder and softer positions – as with the UN Convention, which features a decidedly "soft" framing of genocidal strategies (including non-fatal ones), but a "hard" approach when it comes to the victim groups whose destruction qualifies as genocidal. Steven Katz's 1994 definition, by contrast, features a highly inclusive framing of victimhood, but a tightly restrictive view of genocidal outcomes: these are limited to the total physical destruction of a group. The alteration of just a few words turns it into a softer definition that happens to be my preferred one (see below).

Exploring further, the definitions address genocide's *agents, victims, goals, scale, strategies*, and *intent*.

Among *agents*, there is a clear focus on state and official authorities – Dadrian's "dominant group, vested with formal authority"; Horowitz's "state bureaucratic apparatus"; Porter's "government or its agents" – to cite three of the first five definitions proposed (note also Levene's exclusively state-focused 2005 definition). However, some scholars abjure the state-centric approach (e.g., Chalk and Jonassohn's "state or other authority"; Fein's [1993] "perpetrator"; Thompson and Quets's "whatever agents"; Shaw's "armed power organizations"). The UN Convention, too, cites "constitutionally responsible rulers, public officials or private individuals" among possible agents (Article IV). In practice, most genocide scholars continue to emphasize the role of the state, while accepting that in some cases – as with settler colonialism (Chapter 3) – non-state actors may play a prominent and at times dominant role.[49]

Victims are routinely identified as social minorities. There is a widespread assumption that victims must be civilians or non-combatants: Charny references their "essential defencelessness," while others emphasize "one-sided mass killing" and the destruction of "innocent and helpless" victims (Midlarsky; see also Dadrian, Horowitz, Chalk and Jonassohn, and Fein [1993]). Interestingly, however, only Sémelin's 2005 definition, and Shaw's 2007 one, actually use the word "civilian." The groups may be internally constituted and self-identified (that is, more closely approximating groups "as such," as required by the Genocide Convention). From other perspectives, however, target groups may and must be defined by the perpetrators (e.g., Chalk and Jonassohn, Katz).[50] The debate over political target groups is reflected in Leo Kuper's comments. Kuper grudgingly accepts the UN Convention definition, but strongly regrets the exclusion of political groups.

The *goals* of genocide are held to be the destruction/eradication of the victim group, whether this is defined in physical terms or to include "cultural genocide" (see below). But beyond this, the element of motive is little stressed. Lemkin squarely designated genocidal "objectives" as the "disintegration of the political and social institutions of culture, language, national feelings, religion, and the economic existence of national groups." Bauer likewise emphasizes "denationalization"; Martin Shaw, the desire to destroy a collective's (generally a minority's) social power. Dadrian and Horowitz specify that genocide targets groups "whose ultimate extermination is held to be desirable and useful," while Horowitz stresses the state's desire "to assure [*sic*] conformity and participation of the citizenry."

As for *scale*, this ranges from Steven Katz's targeting of a victim group "in its totality" and Sémelin's "total eradication," to phrasing such as "in whole or part" (Harff, the UN Convention, my modification of Katz's definition) and "in whole or in large part" (Wallimann and Dobkowski). Irving Louis Horowitz emphasizes the absolute dimension of "mass" murder "for which genocide is a synonym."[51] Some scholars maintain a respectful silence on the issue, though the element of mass or "substantial" casualties seems implicit in the cases they select and the analyses they develop.

BOX 1.2 A LEXICON OF GENOCIDES AND RELATED MASS CRIMES

Groups targeted for genocide and related crimes sometimes develop terms in their local languages to denote and memorialize their experiences. The following is a sample of this nomenclature.

Churban – the "Great Catastrophe" – the Yiddish term for the Holocaust/Shoah (see below) of Jews at Nazi hands.

Holocaust – Derived from the Greek word meaning a sacrificial offering completely consumed by fire. In modern usage, "holocaust" denotes great human destruction, especially by fire. It was deployed in contemporary media coverage of the Ottoman genocides of Christian minorities from 1915–22 (see Chapter 4). Today, "the Holocaust" (note: capital "H") is used for the Nazis' attempted destruction of Jews during World War II (Chapter 6; but see also Shoah, below). The phrase "Nazi H/holocaust" is also sometimes used to encompass both Jewish and non-Jewish victims of the Nazis (Box 6a). Use may be made of "holocaust" (with a lower-case "h") to describe "especially severe or destructive genocides" throughout history, as in my own framing (see note, p. 12).

Holodomor – the Ukrainian "famine-extermination" of 1932–33 at the hands of Stalin's Soviet regime (Chapter 5); "a compound word combining the root *holod* 'hunger' with the verbal root *mor* 'extinguish, exterminate'" (Lubomyr Hajda, Harvard University).

Itsembabwoko – used by Rwandans to describe the genocide of 1994 (see Chapter 9) – Kinyarwanda, "from the verb 'gutsemba' – to exterminate, to massacre, and 'ubwoko' (ethnic group, clan)" (PreventGenocide.org; see their very useful resource page, "The Word 'Genocide' Translated or Defined in 80 Languages," http://www. preventgenocide.org/genocide/languages-printerfriendly.htm). Rwandans also use **jenosid**, an adaption of the English/French "genocide/génocide."

Lokeli – the "Overwhelming" – term used in the Longo language to describe the ravages of the Congo "rubber terror" at the turn of the twentieth century (Chapter 2).

Mec Ejer'n – the "Great Calamity" in Armenian – the Armenian genocide of 1915–17 (Chapter 4).

Naqba – in Arabic, the "Catastrophe" of the Palestinian people uprooted and dispossessed in 1947–48 by the forces of the nascent Israeli state (see Chapter 6).

Porrajmos – the "Devouring" – Romani term for the holocaust of the Roma/Sinti ("Gypsy") population of Europe under Nazi rule from 1941 to 1945 (see Box 6a).

Sayfo – "Year of the Sword" – term used by Assyrian populations to refer to the Ottoman genocide of Christian minorities during World War I (Chapter 4).

Shoah – from the Hebrew for "Catastrophe" – an alternative term for the Jewish Holocaust (Chapter 6), preferred by those who reject the religious-sacrificial connotations of "holocaust."

Sokümü – the "Unweaving" – Turkish term for the atrocity-laden expulsions of Muslims from lands liberated from the Ottoman Empire, from the 1870s to the end of the Balkan wars in 1913 (see Chapter 4).

(With thanks to Mark Levene for his suggestions; readers are invited to submit other terms for inclusion in the next edition of this book.)

Many people feel that lumping together a limited killing campaign, such as in Kosovo in 1999, with an overwhelmingly exterminatory one, such as the Nazis' attempted destruction of European Jews, cheapens the concept of "genocide." However, it is worth noting how another core concept of social science and public discourse is deployed: *war*. We readily use "war" to designate conflicts that kill "only" a few hundred or a few thousand people (e.g., the Soccer War of 1969 between El Salvador and Honduras; the Falklands/Malvinas War of 1982), as well as epochal descents into barbarity that kill millions or tens of millions. The gulf between minimum and maximum toll here is comparable to that between Kosovo and the Jewish Holocaust, but the use of "war" is uncontroversial. There seems to be no reason why we should not distinguish between larger and smaller, more or less exterminatory genocides in the same way.

Diverse genocidal *strategies* are depicted in the definitions. Lemkin referred to a "coordinated plan of different actions," and the UN Convention listed a range of such acts. For the scholars cited in our set, genocidal strategies may be direct or indirect (Fein [1993]), including "economic and biological subjugation" (Wallimann and Dobkowski). They may include killing of elites (i.e., "eliticide"); "elimination of

national (racial, ethnic) culture and religious life with the intent of 'denationalization'"; and "prevention of normal family life, with the same intent" (Bauer). Helen
Fein's earlier definition emphasizes "breaking the linkage between reproduction and
socialization of children in the family or group of origin," which carries a step further
the Convention's injunction against "preventing births within the group."

Regardless of the strategy chosen, a consensus exists that genocide is "committed
with intent to destroy" (UN Convention), is "structural and systematic" (Horowitz),
"deliberate [and] organized" (Wallimann and Dobkowski), "sustained" (Harff),
and "a series of purposeful actions" (Fein; see also Thompson and Quets). Porter and
Horowitz stress the additional role of the state bureaucracy.

There is something of a consensus that group "destruction" must involve physical
liquidation, generally in the form of mass killing (see, e.g., Fein [1993], Charny,
Horowitz, Katz/Jones, Bloxham). In Peter Drost's 1959 view, genocide was "collective
homicide and not official vandalism or violation of civil liberties. . . . It is directed
against the life of man and not against his material or mental goods."[52] This is central
to my own framing of genocide.

My definition of genocide, cited above, alters only slightly that of Steven Katz as
published in his 1994 volume, *The Holocaust in Historical Context, Vol. 1.*[53] Katz
stresses physical (and mass) killing as the core element of genocide, as do I. Like him,
I prefer to incorporate a much wider range of targeted *groups* under the genocide
rubric, as well as an acceptance of diverse genocidal *agents* and *strategies*. Unlike Katz,
I adopt a broader rather than narrower construction of genocidal *intent* (see further
below). I also question Katz's requirement of the actual or attempted *total* extermination of a group, substituting a phrasing of "in whole or in part," following in this
respect the UN Convention's definition.

In my original (2000) reworking of Katz's definition, reproduced in this book's first
edition, my alteration read "in whole or in *substantial* part." This was an attempt to
emphasize that large numbers (either in absolute numbers or as a proportion of the
targeted group) needed to be attacked in order for the powerful term "genocide" to
take precedence over, for example, "homicide" or "mass killing." However, on recon-
sideration, this was to view genocide from the perspective of its elite planners and
directors. What of those who kill at the grassroots, and perhaps murder "only" one
or several individuals? From this perspective, there is something to commend former
UN Secretary-General Kofi Annan's evocative declaration, in his Nobel Peace Prize
acceptance speech in 2001, that "a genocide begins with the killing of one man –
not for what he has done, but because of who he is. . . . What begins with the failure
to uphold the dignity of one life, all too often ends with a calamity for entire
nations."[54] Moreover, legal scholars including William Schabas and Chile Eboe-Osuji
have cautioned against unnecessarily restricting the application of a genocide
framework to "substantial" killing. In Eboe-Osuji's eloquent analysis of the UN
definition:

> the theory of *reading in* the word "substantial" to the phrase "in part" is clearly
> hazardous to the preventive purpose of the Genocide Convention, while arguably
> not enhancing its punitive purpose. It does not enhance the punitive purpose
> since it will be harder to convict any single accused of the crime of genocide.

Not only will it be more difficult to show that the accused intended to destroy a substantial part of the group, but it arguably needs to be shown that the accused was in a position to destroy the substantial part of a protected group. . . . The "substantial" part theory is, worse still, hazardous to the preventive purpose. For in the throes of an unfolding apparent genocide, it will, in most cases, be difficult to ascertain the state of mind of the perpetrators and planners in order to establish whether or not they harbour joint or several intent to destroy a "substantial" part of the group. The longer the delay in establishing whether or not the perpetrators and planners harboured that intent, the longer it will take for the international community to react and intervene with the level of urgency and action required.[55]

Eboe-Osuji's framing allows us to bring into the ambit of "genocide" such cases as exterminations of indigenous people which, in their dimension of direct killing, are often composed of a large number of relatively small massacres, not necessarily centrally directed, and generally separated from each other spatially and temporally. A final example of its utility is the case of the lynching of African Americans, discussed in Chapter 13. If there is a case to be made that such murders were and are genocidal, then we must reckon with a campaign in which usually "only" one or two people were killed at a time.

In the cases of both colonial exterminations and lynching, however, what *does* appear to lift the phenomena into the realm of genocide, apart from genocidal intent (see below), is the fact that the local-level killing occurred as part of a "widespread or systematic" campaign against the groups in question – to borrow an important phrase from the legal language of crimes against humanity (see pp. 538–41). What united the killers was a racial-cultural animus and sense of superiority, in which individual actors were almost certainly and always aware that their actions were taken to bolster and "defend" the wider perpetrator group. Demonstrating such a consciousness is not a requirement for a legal finding of genocide, as it appears to be for the findings of crimes against humanity. Nonetheless, in practice, it seems that acts of murder are unlikely to be defined as genocidal – whether in law or in the wider scholarship on the subject – unless they are empirically part of a "widespread or systematic" campaign. The reader should be aware that this requirement, unspoken hereafter, guides the analysis of genocide offered in this book, and the range of cases presented to illustrate it.

The reader should keep in mind throughout, however, that there is just one international-legal definition of genocide. When I touch on legal aspects of genocide, I highlight the UN Convention definition; but I deploy it and other legal framings instrumentally, not dogmatically. I seek to convey an understanding of genocide in which international law is a vital but not a dominant consideration. In part, this is because at the level of international law, genocide is perhaps being displaced by the framing of "crimes against humanity," which is easier to prosecute and imposes much the same punishments as for genocide convictions. The result may be that "genocide," in the coming years and decades, will prove more significant as *an intellectual and scholarly framework* (a heuristic device, for the jargon-inclined), and as *a tool of advocacy and mobilization*. I return to this argument in Chapter 16.

BOX 1.3 THE OTHER "-CIDES" OF GENOCIDE

The literature on genocide and mass violence has given rise to a host of terms derived from Raphael Lemkin's original "genocide." A sampling follows.

Classicide. Term coined by Michael Mann to refer to "the intended mass killing of entire social classes." *Examples:* The destruction of the "kulaks" in Stalin's USSR (Chapter 5); Cambodia under the Khmer Rouge (Chapter 7). *Source:* Michael Mann, *The Dark Side of Democracy* (Cambridge University Press, 2004).

Democide. Term invented by R.J. Rummel to encompass "the murder of any person or people by a government, including genocide, politicide, and mass murder." *Examples:* Rummel particularly emphasizes the "megamurders" of twentieth-century totalitarian regimes. *Source:* R.J. Rummel, *Death by Government* (Transaction Publishers, 1997).

Ecocide. The wilful destruction of the natural environment and ecosystems, through (a) pollution and other forms of environmental degradation and (b) military efforts to undermine a population's sustainability and means of subsistence. *Examples:* Deforestation in the Amazon and elsewhere; US use of Agent Orange and other defoliants in the Vietnam War (see p. 76); Saddam Hussein's campaign against the Marsh Arabs in Iraq (see Figure 1.3).[56] *Source:* Jared Diamond, *Collapse: How Societies Choose to Fail or Succeed* (Viking, 2004).

Eliticide. The destruction of members of the socioeconomic elite of a targeted group – political leaders, military officers, businesspeople, religious leaders, and cultural/intellectual figures. (*n.b.* Sometimes spelled "elitocide.") *Examples:* Poland under Nazi rule (1939–45); Burundi (1972); Bosnia-Herzegovina in the 1990s. *Source:* "Eliticide," in Samuel Totten, Paul R. Bartrop, and Steven L. Jacobs, *Dictionary of Genocide*, Vol. 1 (Greenwood Press, 2007), pp. 129–30.

Ethnocide. Term originally coined by Raphael Lemkin as a *synonym* for genocide; subsequently employed (notably by the French ethnologist Robert Jaulin) to describe patterns of cultural genocide, i.e., the destruction of a group's cultural, linguistic, and existential underpinnings, without necessarily killing members of the group. *Examples:* The term has been used mostly with reference to indigenous peoples (Chapter 3, Box 5a.1), to emphasize that their "destruction" as a group involves more than simply the murder of group members. *Source:* Robert Jaulin, *La paix blanche: Introduction à l'ethnocide* ("White Peace: Introduction to Ethnocide") (Seuil, 1970).

The UN Declaration on the Rights of Indigenous Peoples (2007) declares (Article 8): "Indigenous peoples and individuals have the right not to be subjected to forced

Figure 1.3 Two members of the Madan community in southern Iraq, known as the "Marsh Arabs," pole along a waterway in a traditional *mashoof* boat. The marshes and their population were viewed as subversive redoubts by the Saddam Hussein dictatorship, which waged a campaign of "ecocide" against the Madans in the 1990s, draining the marshes and turning much of the delicate ecosystem into a desert. The recovery of the wetlands has been one of the few bright spots of the post-2003 period in Iraq, but only about 20,000 Madans remain of an original population of some half a million.

Source: Hassan Janali/US Army Corps of Engineers/Wikimedia Commons.

assimilation or destruction of their culture," and instructs states to "provide effective mechanisms for prevention of, and redress for . . . any action which has the aim or effect of depriving them of their integrity as distinct peoples, or of their cultural values or ethnic identities . . . "[57]

Femicide/Feminicide. The systematic murder of females for being female. *Examples:* Female infanticide; killings in Ciudad Juárez, Mexico, in the 1990s and 2000s; the École Polytechnique massacre in Montreal (1989). (See also Gendercide.) *Source:* Diana E.H. Russell and Roberta A. Harmes, eds, *Femicide in Global Perspective* (Teachers College Press, 2001).

Fratricide. Term coined by Michael Mann to describe the killing of factional enemies within political (notably communist) movements. *Examples:* Stalin's USSR (Chapter 5); Mao's China (Chapter 5); the Khmer Rouge (Chapter 7). *Source:* Michael Mann, *The Dark Side of Democracy* (Cambridge University Press, 2004).

Gendercide. The selective destruction of the male or female component of a group, or of dissident sexual minorities (e.g., homosexuals, transvestites). Term originally coined by Mary Anne Warren in 1985. *Examples:* Female infanticide; gender-selective massacres of males (e.g., Srebrenica, Bosnia in 1995) (see Chapter 13). *Source:* Adam Jones, ed., *Gendercide and Genocide* (Vanderbilt University Press, 2004).

Judeocide. The Nazi extermination of European Jews. Term coined by Arno Mayer to avoid the sacrificial connotations of "Holocaust" (see also Shoah). *Example:* The Jewish Holocaust (1941–45). *Source:* Arno J. Mayer, "Memory and History: On the Poverty of Remembering and Forgetting the Judeocide," *Radical History Review*, 56 (1993).

Linguicide. The destruction and displacement of languages. *Examples:* The forcible supplanting of indigenous tongues as part of a wider ethnocidal campaign (see "Ethnocide," above); Turkish bans on the Kurdish language in education and the media (repealed in 2009).[58] *Source:* Steven L. Jacobs, "Language Death and Revival after Cultural Destruction: Reflections on a Little Discussed Aspect of Genocide," *Journal of Genocide Research*, 7: 3 (2005).

Memoricide. The destruction "not only . . . of those deemed undesirable on the territory to be 'purified,' but . . . [of] any trace that might recall their erstwhile presence (schools, religious buildings and so on)" (Jacques Sémelin). Term coined by Croatian doctor and scholar Mirko D. Grmek during the siege of Sarajevo. *Examples:* Israel in Palestine;[59] Bosnia-Herzegovina in the 1990s. *Source:* Edgardo Civallero, "'When Memory Turns into Ashes' . . . Memoricide During the XX Century," *Information for Social Change*, 25 (Summer 2007).

Omnicide. "The death of all": the blanket destruction of humanity and other life forms by weapons of mass destruction, especially nuclear weapons. Term coined by John Somerville. *Examples:* None as yet, fortunately. *Source:* John Somerville, "Nuclear 'War' is Omnicide," *Peace Research*, April 1982.

Politicide. Barbara Harff and Ted Gurr's term for mass killing according to political affiliation, whether actual or imputed. *Examples:* Harff and Gurr consider "revolutionary one-party states" to be the most common perpetrators of genocide. The term may also be applied to the mass killings of alleged "communists" and "subversives" in, e.g., Latin America during the 1970s and 1980s. *Source:* Barbara Harff, "No Lessons Learned from the Holocaust? Assessing Risks of Genocide and Political Mass Murder since 1955," *American Political Science Review*, 97: 1 (2003).

Poorcide. Coined by S.P. Udayakumar in 1995 to describe "the genocide of the poor" through structural poverty. *Example:* North–South economic relations. *Source:* S.P. Udayakumar, "The Futures of the Poor," *Futures*, 27: 3 (1995).

Urbicide. The obliteration of urban living-space as a means of destroying the viability of an urban environment, undermining the sustainability of its population and eroding the cosmopolitan values they espouse. The term was apparently coined by Marshall Berman in 1987 in reference to the blighted Bronx borough in New York; it was popularized by former Belgrade mayor Bogdan Bogdanovic and a circle of Bosnian architects to describe the Serb siege of Sarajevo (1992–95). *Examples:* Carthage (146 BCE); Stalingrad (1942); Sarajevo (1992–95); Gaza (2008–09). *Source:* Martin Coward, *Urbicide: The Politics of Urban Destruction* (Routledge, 2008).

WHAT IS DESTROYED IN GENOCIDE?

Many framers of genocide have emphasized physical killing as primary in the equation – perhaps essential. For others, however – including Raphael Lemkin, and to an extent the drafters of the UN Genocide Convention – physical and mass killing is just one of a range of genocidal strategies. These observers stress the destruction of the group *as a sociocultural unit*, not necessarily or primarily the physical annihilation of its members. This question – what, precisely, is destroyed in genocide? – has sparked one of genocide studies' most fertile lines of inquiry. It is closely connected to sociologist Martin Shaw, who in his 2007 *What Is Genocide?* called for a greater emphasis on the social destruction of groups. For Shaw,

> *Because groups are social constructions, they can be neither constituted nor destroyed simply through the bodies of their individual members.* Destroying groups must involve a lot more than simply killing, although killing and other physical harm are rightly considered important to it. The discussion of group "destruction" is obliged, then, to take seriously Lemkin's "large view of this concept," discarded in genocide's reduction to body counts, which centred on social destruction. . . . The aim of "destroying" social groups is not reduced to killing their individual members, but is understood as destroying groups' social power in economic, political and cultural senses. . . . [Genocide] *involves mass killing but . . . is much more than mass killing.*[60]

Daniel Feierstein, and the emerging Argentine "school" of genocide studies, have likewise stressed the destruction of social power and existential *identity* as the essence of genocide. For Feierstein, the "connecting thread" among cases of genocide is "a technology of power based on the 'denial of others,' their physical disappearance (their bodies) and their symbolic disappearance (the memory of their existence)." The partial (physical) elimination of the victim group "is intended to have a profound effect on the survivors: *it aims to suppress their identity by destroying the network of social relations* that makes identity possible at all . . . The main objective of genocidal destruction is the transformation of the victims into 'nothing' and the survivors into 'nobodies,'" that is, their social death (see further discussion of this theme on pp. 119–20).[61]

The question of whether forms of destruction short of, or other than, physical killing can *in themselves* constitute genocide touches directly on one of the oldest debates in genocide studies and law: over *cultural genocide*. We have noted that Lemkin placed great emphasis on human groups as culture carriers, and on the destruction of cultural symbols as genocidal in and of itself: "*the destruction of cultural symbols is genocide*, because it implies the destruction of their function and thus menaces the existence of the social group which exists by virtue of its common culture."[62] However, Lemkin felt that cultural genocide had to involve "acts of violence which are qualified as criminal by most of the criminal codes":[63] he was always concerned that patterns of gradual cultural assimilation, for example, should not be depicted as genocidal, or even necessarily malign.

Debates over cultural genocide were some of the most vigorous in the drafting stages of the Genocide Convention, and it was Lemkin's most personally wounding experience in that process to see his concept jettisoned. The UN Secretariat draft of 1947, prepared with Lemkin's direct input as well as that of legal experts Vespasian Pella and Henri Donnedieu de Vabres, "divided genocide into three categories, physical, biological and cultural genocide."[64] But the Sixth Committee of 1948 eliminated cultural genocide, and the Convention as subsequently passed privileged physical killing first and foremost (even more so in its actual application).

Nonetheless, the Sixth Committee did grant that one aspect of the cultural genocide framework be reinserted in the Convention. It is enshrined as Article 2(e), which outlaws "forcibly transferring children of the group to another group," and the consequent elimination of those children as culture-bearers for the victimized group. Article 2(e) has not, by itself, sustained a conviction for genocide in international law. But it *has* figured in an important quasi-legal process, the Australian governmental commission that issued a report on the forcible transfer of aboriginal children to white families and institutions, *Bringing Them Home* (1997). We will see in Chapter 3 that this report controversially used the language of "genocide" on the basis of Article 2(e).

Unsurprisingly, it is aboriginal and indigenous peoples, and their supporters in activist circles and academia, who have placed the greatest emphasis on cultural genocide in issuing appeals for recognition and restitution. Indigenous peoples who experienced settler colonialism, as sociologist Robert van Krieken has argued, have in common "a heartfelt and persistent sense of inflicted violence, pain and suffering at the heart of the settler-colonial project." As a result, they have evinced a "particularly strong . . . support for an understanding [of genocide] which goes beyond outright killing"[65] – a phenomenon explored in Buffy Sainte-Marie's masterful song, "My Country 'Tis of Thy People You're Dying" (see pp. 112–14).[66]

Also unsurprisingly, it was the settler-colonial regimes who were most "anxious to exclude cultural genocide" from the Genocide Convention, as Raphael Lemkin's biographer John Cooper points out. South Africa, settler-conquered and racially-ruled, of course voted to delete the clause. So too did "many members of the Commonwealth with indigenous populations," including Canada and New Zealand.[67]

Nonetheless, despite this early and enduring sidelining of cultural genocide from legal understandings of genocide, the concept has resurged in this setting in the 1990s – *not as genocidal in itself, but as powerfully indicative of genocide*. Specifically, as John

Quigley notes, "the destruction of cultural objects may provide evidence that such acts were done with intent to destroy the group."[68] This was most prominent in the proceedings of the International Criminal Tribunal for the Former Yugoslavia (ICTY), established in 1993 as war and genocide in the Balkans were still raging. Serbian obliteration of Bosnian Muslim cultural symbols, especially mosques (see Figure 1.4) and the main library complex in Sarajevo, was entered into evidence to demonstrate Serbian intent to destroy Bosnian Muslims as a group, though individual convictions for genocide were based on the perpetrators' physical killing of group members, or the infliction of "serious bodily . . . harm" upon them.

Since the first edition of this book appeared, explorations of genocide as including the destruction of "social power" and group culture have been among the most fertile lines of investigation in genocide studies. Martin Shaw's framing of genocidal destruction resonates in the mind long after one has read it, and seems to me one of the most searching conceptualizations of the subject. Notions of cultural destruction as suggestive (or legally indicative) of genocidal intent strike me as persuasive and highly meaningful. The full-scale and semi-official destruction of cultural symbols

Figure 1.4 UN peacekeepers walk past a destroyed mosque in Ahmiçi, Bosnia-Herzegovina, in April 1993. *Génocidaires* often attempt to obliterate a group's cultural, religious, and intellectual symbols as part of their broader campaign of destruction. For Raphael Lemkin, these constituted cultural forms of genocide, and were essential to his understanding of the phenomenon. International law, and most scholarship, has generally made mass killing definitional to the crime of genocide; but such attacks on a group's cultural integrity *are* considered indicative of a wider genocidal strategy, for legal purposes. Thus, the image shown here was tagged for submission as evidence to the International Criminal Tribunal for the Former Yugoslavia (ICTY) in The Hague, Netherlands (see Chapter 15).

Source: Courtesy International Criminal Tribunal for the Former Yugoslavia (ICTY), www.icty.org.

seems entirely relevant to the study of genocide (notably with regard to indigenous peoples), and to legal prosecutions of genocide in the contemporary period. Lower-level acts of vandalism, defacing, hate speech and graffiti, and book-burning are also significant in developing strategies of prevention and intervention (Chapter 16). They occupy a position on the "genocidal continuum" described by the anthropologist Nancy Scheper-Hughes (Chapter 11). As such, they not only point to everyday patterns of anathematization and exclusion that may otherwise be overlooked, but *may* serve as harbingers of serious acts of violence against targeted groups – up to and including genocidal outbreaks. As such, they should prompt serious concern in the national communities in question, and the international community as well.

The question remains, however, whether strategies of social and cultural "destruction" should be considered genocidal *in the absence of systematic killing, or at least widespread physical attack.* I believe they should not be. I will cite two examples, situated at different points on the "genocidal continuum," to make my point.

One of the principal cultural divides in Canada is between descendants of Anglo-Saxon and Gallic civilizations in Western Europe. Quebec's "Quiet Revolution" in the 1960s radically destabilized the longstanding hegemony of the Anglos in the province. Francophone nationalism spilled over, at the end of the 1960s, into small-scale acts of terrorism and political assassination, but also gave rise to a mass political movement that brought the separatist Parti Québécois (PQ) to power in 1976. In ensuing years, the PQ pursued a broad nationalist campaign that included seeking political separation through referenda, institutionalizing French-language requirements in all schools and public signage (Bill 101), and requiring bilingualism in workplaces with over 50 employees. Graffiti began to appear around Montreal reading "101 ou 401" – accept the nationalist legislation of Bill 101, or take Highway 401 from Montreal to the Anglo bastion of Toronto in next-door Ontario.

The Anglo community in Montreal and elsewhere in Quebec organized to resist these measures, and a regular feature of their discourse was the language of mass atrocity to describe the Anglophone plight in Quebec. PQ cabinet minister Camille Laurin, depicted as "the father of Bill 101," was accused of inflicting "linguistic genocide" on the English minority.[69] "Words like 'cultural re-engineering' and 'akin to ethnic cleansing' were printed" at the time,[70] and they remain popular to the present day.[71]

I think most readers will agree that such rhetoric was and is overheated. Yet the result of more than four decades of francophone ascendancy in Quebec has indeed been the real displacement of the Anglo community. Hundreds of thousands of Anglos chose Highway 401 over Bill 101. The native English-speaking population of Quebec declined precipitously, from 13.8 percent in 1951 to 8.2 percent in 2006.[72] French is now a requirement of most middle- and upper-level positions in society, politics, and the economy. Proposed measures to ban even the apostrophe in the name of the department store "Eaton's" were overturned in court battles; in 1993, the UN's Human Rights Committee, ruling on a case brought by representatives of Quebec's English minority, found the province's sign laws in contravention of international rights treaties. "A State may choose one or more official languages," declared the UNHCR, "but it may not exclude outside the spheres of public life, the freedom to express oneself in a certain language."[73] Even in the wake of those decisions, French text must be at least twice as large as English on all commercial signage, and street signs are French-only outside spheres of federal jurisdiction.[74]

So has Anglo power been "destroyed" in Quebec, in whole or in substantial part? Arguably, yes. But as with similar affirmative-action measures in countries like Malaysia and (for a while) Lebanon, Bill 101 seems to have achieved a reconfiguration of power relations that is largely acceptable to the Anglos that remain.[75] Again, the genocide framing seems unhelpful and outsized, because whatever measures of positive discrimination/affirmative action have been instituted to benefit the francophone majority, and redress longstanding disadvantages vis-à-vis the Anglos, they have not spilled over into systematic violence, severe persecution, and murderous rampages against the targeted minority.

Consider a second case. In August 1972, the Ugandan dictator Idi Amin – an incarnation of evil in the 1970s – issued a stunning order. All Ugandan citizens of Asian (overwhelmingly Indian) descent were to be stripped of their property and forced either to leave the country within 90 days, or to accept "banishment to remote and arid areas, where they could occupy themselves as farmers" – a familiar motif in mass atrocity campaigns, forcing a commercially-identified subgroup to engage in "productive" agricultural labour. Despite international protest, noted Leo Kuper in his seminal 1981 volume, "the expulsions took their uninhibited course. The victims were brutally treated, a few were killed, and they were systematically stripped of their possessions, which were distributed to, or seized as booty by, soldiers and other supporters of the regime."[76]

Here we have an instance of persecution, dispossession, forcible uprooting, and expulsion. The result was the *total* destruction of the Indian-descended community of Uganda as a social entity, and the internal displacement or forced exile of the vast majority of its members (about 75,000 people). This would surely meet Shaw's requirement that the essence of the genocidal enterprise be sought in its attempted destruction of a group's social power. Yet Shaw does not mention Uganda's Indians in his book. As for Kuper's early analysis, it is not clear to me that he considers the targeting of the Indians to be genocidal as such – he certainly places more emphasis on "the slaughter . . . [of] almost every conceivable category of victim" in Amin's wider political and ethnic liquidations, nearly all of which occurred *after* the Indian expulsions.[77] Since Kuper's book appeared, I have not seen the Ugandan Indians explored as a case of genocide in the comparative literature – nor do I feel the need to correct a perceived oversight in this regard. The reason for the widespread silence seems to be that Ugandan Indians were largely preserved from the large-scale slaughter that Amin meted out to other political and ethnic opponents. The substantial undermining or even outright destruction of a group's social, economic, political, and cultural power and presence does not seem, by itself, to warrant the "genocide" label, if it is not accompanied by mass killing. To reiterate, though, where such systematic forms of cultural targeting and persecution can be isolated, their significance is considerable for the interpretation, prosecution, and prevention of genocide.

◼ MULTIPLE AND OVERLAPPING IDENTITIES

Huge controversy has attended the Genocide Convention's exclusion of all but four human categories – national, ethnic, racial, and religious groups – from the convention's list of protected groups. We are also, as noted, increasingly conscious that the alleged stability and integrity of these groups is very much open to question – not least because group identity is often imposed (even imagined) by perpetrators rather than claimed by targets.

Less recognized is the fact that these identities, along with the "big three" missing from the Genocide Convention (political, social, and gender groups), *never* exist in isolation. Genocidal targeting is *always* the result of a blurring and blending of identities. As psychologist David Moshman has written, "All genocides involve multiple motives, complex interactions of causal factors, *and groups that can be divided and defined in multiple ways.* . . . A purist definition of genocide requiring unmixed motives, singular causes, and discrete groups would render the concept irrelevant to the actual social worlds of human beings."[78]

This is why victims may be simultaneously viewed as (for example) representatives of a dangerous ethnicity, an insurgent or rapacious social class, a threatening political entity, and a malevolent gender group – in fact, with that particular recipe, we have just sketched the outline of a great many modern genocides. It is also why the "other -cides" of genocide studies, rather than being frivolous, are vital to identifying the interwoven threads of identity, whether claimed or imputed. Hence, "a given campaign of mass killing can easily be labeled as genocidal, democidal, politicidal, eliticidal, and gendercidal all at once – with each of these designations representing an analytical cut that exposes one aspect of the campaign and serves to buttress comparative studies of a particular 'cide.'"[79]

The "hard" test for these assertions is the genocide that many still see as having been impelled by perhaps the fiercest racial-ethnic-biological animus imaginable: the Jewish Holocaust (Chapter 6). In his detailed exploration of Nazi anti-semitic propaganda, *The Jewish Enemy*, historian Jeffrey Herf delivered a surprising verdict: "that the radical anti-Semitic ideology that justified and accompanied the mass murder of European Jewry was first and foremost *a paranoid political, rather than biological, conviction and narrative.*" What was vital was not "the way Jews were said to look" but what "Hitler and his associates . . . believed 'international Jewry *did* . . .'"[80] This was the foundation of the *mixed* political-ethnic construction of "the threatening Jewish-Bolshevik danger," in the language of a 1943 press report.[81] "Judeo-Bolshevism" was the international communist conspiracy allegedly headed by Jews in order to advance their project of political/economic/ethnic-racial/religious/sexual conquest and domination.[82] A Nazi propaganda pamphlet from 1941 described "Bolshevism" – "this system of chaos, extermination and terror" – as "conceived and led by Jews":

> Through subversion and propaganda, world Jewry attempts to gather the uprooted and racially inferior elements of all peoples together in order to lead an extermination battle [*Vernichtungskampf*] against everything positive, against native customs and the nation, against religion and culture, against order and morals. The goal is the introduction of chaos through world revolution and the establishment of a Jewish state under Jewish leadership.[83]

Figure 1.5 "Nazi antisemitic propaganda frequently linked Jews to the fears of their German and foreign audiences. This [1943] poster, displayed in the German-occupied Soviet Union to foment both anti-Soviet and antisemitic fervor, uses the stereotype of the bloodthirsty 'Jewish Bolshevik commissar' to associate 'the Jew' with the murder of more than 9,000 Soviet citizens in Vinnytsia, Ukraine, an atrocity committed by Stalin's secret police in 1937–38. German forces uncovered the massacre in May 1943." The identities that *génocidaires* impute to their victims – here, a mix of racial/ethnic, political, and gender ones – overlap and interpenetrate in complex ways (the Cyrillic caption reads "Vinnytsia." See also Figure 13.10, p. 488).

Source: Library of Congress, Prints and Photographs Division, Washington, DC.

In a single sentence ("Through subversion . . ."), the Judeo-Bolshevik is depicted as a "racial," "nation[al]," "religi[ous]" and "cultur[al]" enemy, seeking to erode German "customs," social "order," and "morals" for good measure. Add the identification of the Jew as a *military* enemy – as the Nazi wartime adage had it, "Wherever there is [a] partisan, there is a Jew, and wherever there is a Jew, there is a partisan"[84] – and one has the essential ingredients of the ideological pastiche and *mortal terror* that fuelled the architects and perpetrators of the Holocaust.[85] According to Martin Shaw,

> SS *Einsatzgruppen* reports in the wake of the invasion of the Soviet Union identified no fewer than forty-four overlapping "target groups" . . . When an *Einsatzgruppen* killer pulled his trigger, could victims always tell – or care – whether they were killed as Slavs, as communists or as Jews, even if the perpetrators later produced grisly reports claiming to itemize the numbers of victims in different categories? Can we, historians and sociologists many decades later, make these distinctions with certainty?[86]

DYNAMISM AND CONTINGENCY

In Chapter 6, we will explore how the historiography of the Holocaust evolved from an "intentionalist" position – depicting the attempted extermination of European Jews as a policy intended from the very outset of the Nazi movement – to a more "functionalist" perspective, emphasizing contingency and situational context, and finally to a synthesis of the two perspectives. Broadly speaking, the Nazi agenda underwent a *cumulative radicalization*. An exterminatory agenda evolved, shaped (though in no way mechanistically determined) by forces beyond the control of the principal perpetrators. Discriminatory legislation gave way to outright persecution, forced migration, ghettoization, enslavement, massacre, and finally industrialized mass killing. In the phrase coined by Karl A. Schleunes, it was a "twisted road to Auschwitz" – and Schleunes can take credit for first supplying an "interpretation of the Final Solution as a product of unplanned evolution rather than premeditated 'grand design,'" in historian Christopher Browning's words.[87]

At each stage, objective factors – notably the bureaucratic challenges of realizing and administering the master-race fantasy – influenced outcomes chosen by at least *somewhat* rational perpetrators. Nonetheless, hateful ideologies and persecutory programs were evident from the outset, and throughout, so that a clear line of connection *can* be drawn from the earliest Nazi activity after World War One, and the exterminatory outburst against Jews and others that we know as the Holocaust.

Genocide studies has displayed a similar intellectual trajectory. In tandem with an increased recognition of multiple and overlapping identities, monocausal models of carefully-planned and long-nurtured mass slaughters have given way to a recognition that genocide, in Mark Levene's words, "is not necessarily preordained but will come out of a concatenation or matrix of ingredients and contingencies . . . *only* crystallising in specific and usually quite extraordinary circumstances of acute state and societal crisis." In the colonial collision with indigenous peoples worldwide, for example, Levene sees "the same scenario . . . played out time and time again":

> Whether on coastal shore, distant prairie or desert interior, both North America and Australia witnessed essentially the same native-settler dynamic: first contact in which there were tentative and strained efforts at co-existence; mounting native resistance to increasing and insupportable settler depredations; a redoubled settler determination to seize absolute territorial control; an ensuing crisis leading to a genocidal explosion; finally an aftermath in which any surviving . . . natives either retreat elsewhere or are allowed to exist as subjugated dependants on the margins of the now established and victorious white society.[88]

Historian Benjamin Madley has emphasized that indigenous resistance to conquest and exploitation often led to colonial genocides against native peoples.[89] Levene has likewise noted that native resistance can create "a dynamic in which perpetrator-state violence leads to tenacious *people* resistance, provoking in turn a ratcheting up of the perpetrator's response" and a genocidal consequence.[90] Dirk Moses, another leading scholar of colonial and imperial genocides, agrees: "Resistance leads to reprisals and counterinsurgency that can be genocidal when they are designed to ensure that never again would such resistance occur."[91] Nor is the pattern limited to colonial cases. Examining the Rwandan genocide in his 2006 book *The Order of Genocide*, political scientist Scott Straus argued that far from a "meticulously planned" extermination,

> a dynamic of escalation was critical to the hardliners' choice of genocide. The more the hardliners felt that they were losing power and the more they felt that their armed enemy was not playing by the rules, the more the hardliners radicalized. After the president [Juvénal Habyarimana] was assassinated [on April 6, 1994] and the [RPF] rebels began advancing, the hardliners let loose. They chose genocide as an extreme, vengeful, and desperate strategy to win a war that they were losing. Events and contingency mattered.[92]

THE QUESTION OF GENOCIDAL INTENT

Most scholars and legal theorists agree that intent defines genocide.[93] A "special intent" must be shown to target members of a particular group "as such." Leaving aside the question of what "as such" can mean when genocide always targets its victims on the basis of multiple identities (see above), what defines special intent for legal purposes?

We can begin by distinguishing *intent* from *motive*. According to Gellately and Kiernan, in criminal law, including international criminal law, the specific motive is irrelevant. Prosecutors need only to prove that the criminal act was intentional, not accidental.[94] As legal scholar John Quigley notes,

> In prosecutions for genocide, tribunals have not required proof of a motive . . . . The personal motive of the perpetrator of the crime of genocide may be, for

example, to obtain personal economic benefits, or political advantage or some form of power. The existence of a personal motive does not preclude the perpetrator from also having the specific intent to commit genocide.[95]

A holistic understanding of "special intent" to commit genocide combines *specific* intent, on the one hand, with *general* intent, on the other. Specific intent implies a direct and manifest connection between act and outcome: for example, executing in cold blood a member of a designated group. For some scholars, a charge of genocide should not be considered if a specific intent cannot be demonstrated; many would consider it probative of a kind of "first-degree" genocide.[96]

With *general* intent, the act and its genocidal consequences may be relatively widely separated in geographical and temporal terms. This "includes cases in which the perpetrators did not intend to harm others but should have realized or known that the behavior made the harm likely." For example, "forcibly removing other members to reservations and then withholding food and medicine, and kidnapping many of their children to raise as slaves outside of the group's culture clearly results in the destruction of that group of people, even if that result is neither intended nor desired."[97]

Note again that motive is not central in the equation. When colonists removed indigenous populations from their historic territories to barren reservations, their primary motive was to gain possession of land and resources, not to exterminate natives for the simple satisfaction of destroying an "execrable race." Nevertheless, if the coveting of native lands led to the removal of indigenous populations to territories incapable of sustaining life; if this unsustainability was "reasonably foreseeable," and confirmed when the deported population started to die *en masse*;[98] and if the policies were not promptly reversed or ameliorated, then genocidal intent may still be said to have existed – albeit in a general form.[99]

Recent legislation and case-law have incorporated this understanding of general as well as specific intent. The Rome Statute of the International Criminal Court (1998), for instance, declares that "a person has intent where . . . in relation to conduct, that person means to cause that consequence *or is aware that it will occur in the ordinary course of events.*"[100] Likewise, the International Criminal Tribunal for Rwanda stated in its historic *Akayesu* judgment (1998) that "the offender is culpable because he knew *or should have known* that the act committed would destroy, in whole or in part, a group."[101] As John Quigley points out, the trial chamber in this case decided "that the intent required for liability, even as a principal, can be satisfied by less than purpose"[102] – that is, by a general intent, rather than a specific one.

Establishing the *mens rea* (mental element) of genocidal intent poses significant challenges. How can one know what is in the perpetrator's mind? In the absence of a formal confession, intent must be *inferred*. In the *Akayesu* case of the International Criminal Tribunal for Rwanda, for example,

the Trial Chamber submitted that genocidal intent could be inferred from a number of indicators, such as a general range of criminal acts systematically targeting the same group, committed by the same perpetrator or others, the scale and nature of these acts, and the fact that victims were systematically and deliberately singled out because of their membership of a group, in contrast to non-group members.[103]

CONTESTED CASES OF GENOCIDE

With the varied academic definitions of genocide, and the ambiguities surrounding both the Genocide Convention and historical interpretation, it is not surprising that nearly every posited case of genocide will be discounted by someone else. Even the "classic" genocides of the twentieth century have found their systematic minimizers and deniers (see Chapter 14). With this in mind, let us consider a few controversial events and human institutions. What can the debate over the applicability of a genocide framework in these cases tell us about definitions of genocide, the ideas and interests that underlie those definitions, and the evolution in thinking about genocide? I will offer my own views in each case. Readers are also encouraged to consult the discussion of "famine crimes" in Chapters 2 and 5, and of genocide against political groups in Chapter 5 on Stalin's USSR.

Atlantic slavery – and after

Slavery is pervasive in human societies throughout history. Arguably in no context, however, did it result in such massive mortality as with Atlantic slavery between the sixteenth and nineteenth centuries.[104]

A reasonable estimate of the deaths caused by this institution is fifteen to twenty million people – by any standard, a major human cataclysm.[105] However, Atlantic slavery is rarely included in analyses or anthologies of genocide. A notable exception – Seymour Drescher's chapter in *Is the Holocaust Unique?* – avoids the "genocide" label, and stresses the differences between slavery and the Holocaust.[106] (Admittedly, these are not few.) More recently, the human rights scholar Michael Ignatieff has cited slavery-as-genocide arguments as a leading example of the tendency to "banalize" the genocide framework:

> Thus slavery is called genocide, when – whatever else it was – it was a system to exploit the living rather than to exterminate them. . . . Genocide has no meaning unless the crime can be connected to a clear intention to exterminate a human group in whole or in part. Something more than rhetorical exaggeration for effect is at stake here. Calling every abuse or crime a genocide makes it steadily more difficult to rouse people to action when a genuine genocide is taking place.[107]

Ignatieff's argument – that it was in slaveowners' interest to keep slaves alive, not exterminate them – is probably the most common argument against slavery-as-genocide. Others point to the ubiquity of slavery through time; the large-scale collaboration of African chiefs and entrepreneurs in corraling Africans for slavery; and the supposedly cheery results of slavery for slaves' descendants, at least in North

Figure 1.6 The deaths of millions of enslaved Africans – before, during, and after the dreaded "Middle Passage" to the Americas and Caribbean – were accompanied on the plantations by a culture of terror and violence, aimed at keeping slaves quiescent and in a state of "social death." Peter, a whipped slave in Baton Rouge, Louisiana, displayed his scars in April 1863. "Overseer Artayou Carrier whipped me," Peter told the photographer. "I was two months in bed sore from the whipping."

Source: US National Archives and Records Administration/Wikimedia Commons.

America. Even some African-American commentators have celebrated their "deliverance" from strife-torn Africa to lands of opportunity in America.[108]

My own view is that these arguments are mostly sophistry, serving to deflect responsibility for one of history's greatest crimes. To call Atlantic slavery genocide is not to claim that "every abuse or crime" is genocide, as Ignatieff asserts; nor is it even to designate all slavery as genocidal. Rather, it seems to me an appropriate response to *particular* slavery institutions that inflicted "incalculable demographic and social losses" on West African societies,[109] as well as meeting every other requirement of the UN Genocide Convention's definition.[110] Moreover, the killing and destruction were intentional, whatever the incentives to preserve survivors of the Atlantic passage for labor exploitation. To revisit the issue of intent already touched on: If an institution is deliberately maintained and expanded by discernible agents, though all are aware of the hecatombs of casualties it is inflicting on a definable human group, then why should this not qualify as genocide?

The aftermath of Atlantic slavery – reverberating through African-American societies to the present – also produced one of the very first petitions ever presented to the United Nations on the subject of genocide. In December 1951, "only 11 months after the Genocide Convention went into effect," a petition titled *We Charge Genocide* was submitted by African-American activists, headed by the lawyer and communist activist William L. Patterson, and the great actor, scholar, and singer Paul Robeson. Nearly sixty years later, the document must be regarded as one of the central, and earliest, documents of the US civil rights era. It is also nuanced in its reading of the Genocide Convention, claiming to have "scrupulously kept within the purview" of the new law. It specifies Article II(c) ("deliberately inflicting on the group conditions of life . . ."), that is indirect/structural genocide, as a foundational aspect of the claim. It also "pray[s] for the most careful reading of this material by those who have always regarded genocide as a term to be used only where the acts of terror evinced an intent to destroy a whole nation," arguing instead for a recognition that the Convention prohibits the selective/partial destruction of a group, as well as its wholesale extermination.[111]

BOX 1.4 WE CHARGE GENOCIDE

To the General Assembly of the United Nations:

The responsibility of being the first in history to charge the government of the United States of America with the crime of genocide is not one your petitioners take lightly. . . . But if the responsibility of your petitioners is great, it is dwarfed by the responsibility of those guilty of the crime we charge. Seldom in human annals has so iniquitous a conspiracy been so gilded with the trappings of respectability. Seldom has mass murder on the score of "race" been so sanctified by law, so justified by those who demand free elections abroad even as they kill their fellow citizens who demand free elections at home. Never have so many individuals been so ruthlessly destroyed amid so many tributes to the sacredness of the individual. The distinctive trait of this genocide is a cant that mouths aphorisms of Anglo-Saxon jurisprudence even as it kills. . . .

Our evidence concerns the thousands of Negroes who over the years have been beaten to death on chain

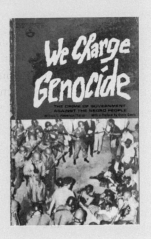

Figure 1.7 *We Charge Genocide*, the text of one of the first genocide declarations ever issued – in 1951, against the US government for its policies toward "the Negro people." This is the cover of the 1970 International Publishers edition.

Source: International Publishers/www.intpubnyc.com.

gangs and in the back rooms of sheriff's offices, in the cells of county jails, in precinct police stations and on city streets, who have been framed and murdered by sham legal forms and by a legal bureaucracy. It concerns those Negroes who have been killed, allegedly for failure to say "sir" or tip their hats or move aside quickly enough, or, more often, on trumped up charges of "rape," but in reality for trying to vote or otherwise demanding the legal and inalienable rights and privileges of United States citizenship formally guaranteed them by the Constitution of the United States, rights denied them on the basis of "race," in violation of the Constitution of the United States, the United Nations Charter and the Genocide Convention.

We shall offer proof of economic genocide, or in the words of the Convention, proof of "deliberately inflicting on the group conditions of life calculated to bring about its destruction in whole or in part." We shall prove that such conditions so swell the infant and maternal death rate and the death rate from disease, that the American Negro is deprived, when compared with the remainder of the population of the United States, of eight years of life on the average. . . .

We have proved "killing members of the group" [Article II(a) of the UN Genocide Convention] – but the case after case after case cited does nothing to assuage the helplessness of the innocent Negro trapped at this instant by police in a cell which will be the scene of his death. We have shown "mental and bodily harm" in violation of Article II[(b)] of the Genocide Convention but this proof can barely indicate the life-long terror of thousands on thousands of Negroes forced to live under the menace of official violence, mob law and the Ku Klux Klan.[112] We have tried to reveal something of the deliberate infliction "on the group of conditions which bring about its physical destruction in whole or in part" [Article II(c)] – but this cannot convey the hopeless despair of those forced by law to live in conditions of disease and poverty because of race, of birth, of color. We have shown incitements to commit genocide, shown that a conspiracy exists to commit it, and now we can only add that an entire people, not only unprotected by their government but the object of government-inspired violence, reach forth their hands to the General Assembly in appeal. Three hundred years is a long time to wait. And now we ask that world opinion, that the conscience of mankind as symbolized by the General Assembly of the United Nations, turn not a deaf ear to our entreaty.

From *We Charge Genocide: The Historic Petition to the United Nations for Relief from a Crime of the United States Government against the Negro People* (New York: International Publishers, 1970 [originally issued in December 1951]), pp. 4–5, 195–96.

Among the atrocities, abuses, and discrimination detailed in *We Charge Genocide* (see Box 1.4) was the murder of "10,000 Negroes . . . on the basis of 'race,'"[113] many of them the widespread "vigilante" lynchings of the post-slavery period. These atrocities were inflicted with the tacit and often enthusiastic approval of local communities and authorities, as I explore in further detail in Chapter 13 (pp. 482–87). Nevertheless, the United Nations General Assembly, still dominated by the US at that early stage of the UN's evolution, refused to accept the petition.[114]

Area bombing and nuclear warfare

Controversy has swirled around the morality both of the area bombing of German and Japanese cities by British and US air forces, and the atomic bombing of Hiroshima and Nagasaki in August 1945. The key issue in both cases is at what point legitimate military action becomes genocide. The line is difficult to draw, in part due to the intimate relationship between war and genocide, discussed in detail in Chapter 2. In the case of "area" bombing (in which cities were blanketed with high explosives), the debate centers on the military utility and morality of the policy. "The effects [themselves] are clear and undisputed," according to Markusen and Kopf: "By the end of the war in 1945, every large and medium-sized German city, as well as many smaller ones had been destroyed or badly damaged by the Allied strategic-bombing offensive. . . . Estimates of deaths range from about 300,000 to 600,000 . . . . Most of the civilian victims were women, infants, and elderly people."[115]

Similar destruction was inflicted on Japan, where some 900,000 civilians died in all. A single night's fire-bombing of Tokyo (March 9–10, 1945) killed 90,000 to

Figure 1.8 The almost unimaginable devastation inflicted on German and Japanese cities in the Allied area bombing campaigns of 1943–45 led some observers to allege that a "just war" spilled over into genocide. This photo shows the heart of the historic German city of Dresden, destroyed by a firestorm generated by US and British incendiary bombing on February 13–15, 1945. An estimated 25,000–35,000 civilians were killed.

Source: Deutsche Fotothek/Wikimedia Commons.

Figure 1.9 A destroyed temple amidst the ruins of Nagasaki, Japan, following the atomic bombing of August 9, 1945, three days after Hiroshima. An estimated 70,000 people were killed at Nagasaki, either in the explosion or from burns and radiation sickness afterward. The "conventional" Allied bombing of Tokyo on March 9–10, 1945 killed even more.

Source: Lynn P. Walker, Jr./Wikimedia Commons.

100,000 people, more than in the atomic bombing of Nagasaki.[116] Was this militarily necessary, or at least defensible? Did it shorten the war, and thereby save the lives of large numbers of Allied soldiers? Should daylight bombing have been pursued, even though it was of dubious efficacy and led to the deaths of more Allied pilots? Or was the bombing *in*defensible, killing more civilians than military requirements could justify?

From a genocide-studies perspective, at issue is whether civilian populations were targeted (1) outside the boundaries of "legitimate" warfare, and (2) on the basis of their ethnic or national identity. Answers have differed, with Leo Kuper arguing that area and atomic bombing *were* genocidal.[117] After a nuanced consideration of the matter, Eric Markusen and David Kopf agreed.[118] Others rejected the genocide framework. The Nuremberg prosecutor Telford Taylor argued that the area bombings "were certainly not 'genocides' within the meaning of the Convention . . . Berlin, London and Tokyo were not bombed because their inhabitants were German, English or Japanese, but because they were *enemy* strongholds. Accordingly, the killing ceased when the war ended and there was no longer any enemy."[119]

The genocide framing is perhaps more persuasively applied in the Japanese case, given the racist propaganda that pervaded the Pacific War, including a common depiction of Japanese as apes and vermin (see Chapter 2). As well, the bombing reached a crescendo when Japan was arguably prostrate before Allied air power – though this would also apply to the destruction of Dresden in Germany, when total Allied victory was already assured. At times in both the German and Japanese cases, but particularly in the latter, the destruction caused by the "thousand-bomber" raids and similar assaults appears to have been inflicted as much to test what was technically and logistically possible as to pursue a coherent military objective.

Fewer ambiguities attach to the atomic bombings of Japan at war's end. Both of the Supreme Allied Commanders, General Dwight D. Eisenhower and General Douglas MacArthur, considered them to be "completely unnecessary."[120] Other options were also available to the US planners – including a softening of the demand for unconditional surrender, and demonstration bombings away from major population centers. The destruction of Nagasaki, in particular, seemed highly gratuitous, since the power of atomic weaponry was already evident, and the Japanese government was in crisis talks on surrender.[121]

UN sanctions against Iraq

Following Saddam Hussein's invasion and occupation of Kuwait in August 1990, the United Nations, spearheaded by the US and Great Britain, imposed sweeping economic sanctions on Iraq. These lasted beyond the 1991 Gulf War and, with modifications, were maintained through to the invasion and occupation of Iraq in 2003.

It soon became evident that the sanctions were exacting an enormous human toll on Iraqis, particularly children. According to a "criminal complaint" filed by former US Attorney General Ramsey Clark before a people's tribunal in Madrid, the policies were nothing short of genocidal:

The United States and its officials[,] aided and abetted by others[,] engaged in a continuing pattern of conduct . . . to impose, maintain and enforce extreme economic sanctions and a strict military blockade on the people of Iraq for the purpose of injuring the entire population, killing its weakest members, infants, children, the elderly and the chronically ill, by depriving them of medicines, drinking water, food, and other essentials.[122]

The resulting debate has sparked controversy and some rancor among genocide scholars. A majority rejects the idea that genocide can be inflicted by "indirect" means such as sanctions, or assigns the bulk of responsibility for Iraqi suffering to the corrupt and dictatorial regime of Saddam Hussein. Such arguments also emphasize the modifications to the sanctions regime in the 1990s, notably the introduction of an "Oil-for-Food" arrangement by which limited food and humanitarian purchases could be made with Iraqi oil revenues under UN oversight.[123]

Those, including myself, who hold that the Iraq sanctions did constitute genocide acknowledge the despotic nature of the Iraqi regime (see, e.g., Box 4a). However, they point to the human damage linked by many impartial observers to the sanctions, and the awareness of that damage among key leadership figures. In legal scholar John Quigley's estimation, "the deaths being caused by the sanctions were widely known, even as the UN Security Council repeatedly voted to extend sanctions."[124] Critics also cite the notorious comments of then-US Secretary of State Madeleine Albright in May 1996. Asked about statistics indicating 500,000 child deaths from sanctions, Albright said: "I think this is a very hard choice. But the price – we think the price is worth it."[125] Is this "infanticide masquerading as policy," as US Congressman David Bonior alleged?[126]

The reticence about the effects of sanctions may reflect the difficulty that many Western observers have in acknowledging Western-inflicted genocides. In 1998 the UN Humanitarian Coordinator for Iraq, Denis Halliday – who witnessed the impact of sanctions at first hand – resigned in protest over their allegedly genocidal character. "I was made to feel by some that I had crossed an invisible line of impropriety," he stated in the following year. "Since then I have observed that the term 'genocide' offends many in our Western media and establishment circles when it is used to describe the killing of others for which we are responsible, such as in Iraq."[127]

9/11: Terrorism as genocide?

The attacks launched on New York and Washington on the morning of September 11, 2001 constituted the worst terrorist attack in history.[128] Perhaps never outside wartime and natural disasters have so many people been killed virtually at once. But were the attacks, apparently carried out by agents of Osama bin Laden's al-Qaeda movement, more than terroristic? Did they in fact constitute genocidal massacres, by Leo Kuper's definition?[129]

In the aftermath of September 11, this question was debated on the H-Genocide academic list. Citing the UN Convention, Peter Ronayne wrote: "[It] seems at least on the surface that the argument could be made that Osama bin Laden and his ilk

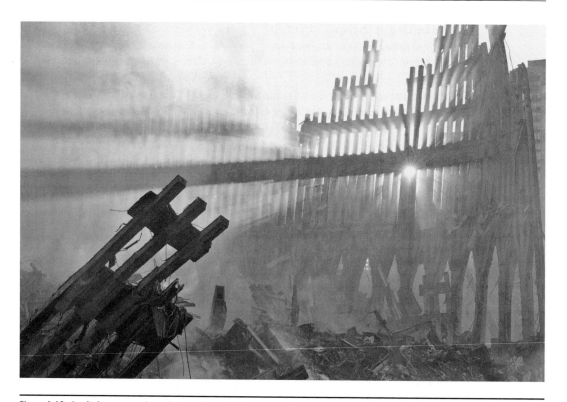

Figure 1.10 Sunlight streams through the still-smoldering ruins of the World Trade Center in lower Manhattan on September 15, 2001, four days after al-Qaeda terrorist attacks on New York and Washington in which nearly three thousand people were killed, overwhelmingly civilians. Was it an act of genocide?

Source: Andrea Booher/FEMA Photo Library/Wikimedia Commons.

are intent on destroying, in whole or in part, a national group, and they're more than willing to kill members of the group." Robert Cribb, an Indonesia specialist, differed. "Surely the attacks were terrorist, rather than genocidal. At least 20% of the victims were not American, and it seems pretty likely that the destruction of human life was not for its own sake . . . but to cause terror and anguish amongst a much broader population, which it has done very effectively."[130]

Expanding on Ronayne's reasoning, if we limit ourselves to the UN Convention framing, the 9/11 attacks resulted in "killing members of the group," intentionally and (in most cases) "as such." Also, the "destruction[,] . . . terror and anguish" they inflicted caused serious "bodily [and] mental harm to members" of the group. Moreover, it seems likely that the ferocity of the attack was limited only by the means available to the attackers (passenger jets used as missiles). Were nuclear bombs at hand, one suspects that they would be used against civilian populations in the US, and perhaps elsewhere. This brings us close to the Convention requirement that genocidal acts be "committed with intent to destroy, in whole or in part, a national . . . group" (i.e., US Americans).

There was thus, at least, a palpable genocidal impetus and intent in 9/11 – one that could yet result in fully-fledged genocide. Only the coming decades will enable us to place the attacks in proper perspective: to decide whether they stand as isolated and discrete events and campaigns, or as opening salvos in a systematic campaign of genocide. Daniel Jonah Goldhagen goes too far in describing "Political Islam" as "currently the one expressly, publicly, and unabashedly genocidal major political movement." It is not a unified movement, nor are its adherents uniformly violent in their programs and actions, as al-Qaeda is. But certain strands of political Islam do evince "eliminationist civilizations' hallmark features: tyrannical regimes, eliminationist-oriented leaders, transformative eschatological visions, populaces brimming with eliminationist beliefs and passions, a sense of impunity, and eliminationism at the center of its normal political repertoire and existing practice."[131]

Structural and institutional violence

In the 1960s, peace researchers such as Johan Galtung began exploring the phenomenon of "structural violence": destructive relations embedded in social and economic systems. Some commentators argue that certain forms of structural and institutional violence are genocidal, "deliberately inflicting on [a designated] group conditions of life calculated to bring about its physical destruction in whole or in part," in the language of the UN Convention. For example, the Indian scholar and activist Vandana Shiva has described "the globalization of food and agriculture systems" under neoliberal trade regimes as "equivalent to the ethnic cleansing of the poor, the peasantry, and small farmers of the Third World. . . . Globalization of trade in agriculture implies genocide."[132] Jean Ziegler, the UN Special Rapporteur on the Right to Food, stated in October 2005: "Every child who dies of hunger in today's world is the victim of assassination," and referred to the *daily* death by starvation of 100,000 people as a "massacre of human beings through malnutrition."[133] My own work on gender and genocide (see Chapter 13) explores "gendercidal institutions" such as female infanticide and even maternal mortality, suggesting that they are forms of gender-selective mass killing, hence genocidal.

Much of structural violence is diffuse, part of the "background" of human relations. It is accordingly difficult to ascribe clear agency to phenomena such as racism, sexism, and other forms of discrimination. International relations scholar Kal Holsti rejects global-systemic visions of structural violence, like Galtung's, as "just too fuzzy," and evincing a tendency to "place all blame for the ills of the Third World on the first one." In Holsti's view, this overlooks the essential role of many Third World leaders and elites in the suffering and violence experienced by their populations. "It also fails to account for many former Third World countries that today have standards of living and welfare higher than those found in many 'industrial' countries."[134]

These points are well taken. Nonetheless, in my opinion, genocide studies should move to incorporate an understanding of structural and institutional violence as genocidal mechanisms. If our overriding concern is to prevent avoidable death and suffering, how can we shut our eyes to "the Holocaust of Neglect" that malnutrition, ill-health, and structural discrimination impose upon huge swathes of humanity?[135] Are we not in danger of "catching the small fry and letting the big fish loose," as Galtung put it?[136]

Moreover, when it comes to human institutions, it is not necessarily the case that responsibility and agency are impossible to establish. Consider the neoliberal economic policies and institutions that shape the destinies of much of the world's poor. Economist Jeffrey Sachs played a key role in designing the "structural adjustment" measures imposed by the World Bank and International Monetary Fund (IMF) around the Third World and former Soviet bloc. He later turned against such prescriptions, commenting in 2002 that they had "squeezed [targeted] countries to the point where their health systems are absolutely unable to function. Education systems are broken down, and *there's a lot of death associated with the collapse of public health and the lack of access to medicine.*"[137] In such cases, as Holsti has pointed out, "distinct agents with distinct policies and identifiable consequences" may be discerned, and moral and legal responsibility may likewise be imputed.[138]

In a recent essay on the structural genocide question, I argue that a claim of genocide related to structural and institutional forms of violations was *most* sustainable where evidence of debility and death as a result of the event or phenomenon in question is strong; where the causal chain is direct rather than indirect, and agency centralized and individualized rather than decentralized or diffuse; where actors' awareness of the impact of their policies is high; and where a meaningful measure of voluntary agency[139] among victims is lacking. I argue in the same essay that a discourse of genocide and structural/institution violence "deserves to be taken seriously, and moved closer to the mainstream of genocide studies."[140] Among other things, as historian Norbert Finzsch has suggested, it could serve as a useful corrective to the fact that "genocides in modern history tend to be perceived as chronologically limited occurrences that punctuate time, rather than as repetitive and enduring processes."[141]

IS GENOCIDE EVER JUSTIFIED?

This question may provoke a collective intake of breath.[142] Examining ourselves honestly, though, most people have probably experienced at least a twinge of sympathy with those who commit acts that some people consider genocidal. Others have gone much further, to outright *celebration* of genocide (see, e.g., Chapter 3). Is any of this justifiable, morally or legally?

In one sense, genocide clearly *is* justified – that is, people often seek to justify it. Perhaps the most common strategy of exculpation and celebration is a utilitarian one, applied most frequently in the case of indigenous peoples (Chapter 3). These populations have been depicted stereotypically as "an inertial drag on future agendas,"[143] failing to properly exploit the lands they inhabit and the rich resources underfoot.[144] A latent economic potential, viewed through the lens of the Protestant work ethic and a capitalist hunger for profit, is held to warrant confiscation of territories, and marginalization or annihilation of their populations.

Those subaltern populations sometimes rose up in rebellion against colonial authority, and those rebellions frequently evoke sympathy – though occasionally they have taken a genocidal form. To the cases of Upper Peru (Bolivia) in the late eighteenth century, and the Caste War of Yucatán in the nineteenth, we might add the revolution in the French colony of Saint-Domingue that, in 1804, created Haiti as the world's first free black republic. This was a revolt not of indigenous people, but of slaves. It succeeded in expelling the whites, albeit at a devastating cost from which Haiti never fully recovered. As in Bolivia and Yucatán, rebellion and counter-rebellion assumed the form of unbridled race war. Yet this particular variant finds many sympathizers. The great scholar of the Haitian revolution, C.L.R. James, described in the 1930s "the complete massacre" of Saint-Domingue's whites: "The population, stirred to fear at the nearness of the counter-revolution, killed all [whites] with every possible brutality." But James's appraisal of the events excused the race war on the grounds of past atrocities and exploitation by whites. Acknowledging that the victims were defenseless, James lamented only the damage done to the souls of the killers, and their future political culture:

> The massacre of the whites was a tragedy; *not for the whites*. For these old slave-owners, those who burnt a little powder in the arse of a Negro, who buried him alive for insects to eat . . . and who, as soon as they got the chance, began their old cruelties again; for these there is no need to waste one tear or one drop of ink. *The tragedy was for the blacks and the Mulattoes* [who did the killing]. It was not policy but revenge, and revenge has no place in politics. *The whites were no longer to be feared*, and such purposeless massacres degrade and brutalise a [perpetrator] population, especially one which was just beginning as a nation and had had so bitter a past. . . . Haiti suffered terribly from the resulting isolation. Whites were banished from Haiti for generations, and the unfortunate country, ruined economically, its population lacking in social culture, had its inevitable difficulties doubled by this massacre.[145]

Bolivia, Mexico, and Haiti are all examples of what Nicholas Robins and I call *subaltern genocide*, or "genocides by the oppressed."[146] In general, genocidal assaults that contain a morally plausible element of revenge, retribution, or revolutionary usurpation are less likely to be condemned, and are often welcomed. Allied fire-bombing and nuclear-bombing of German and Japanese cities, which Leo Kuper and other scholars considered genocidal, are often justified on the grounds that "they started it" (that is, the German and Japanese governments launched mass bombings of civilians before the Allies did). The fate of ethnic-German civilians in Czechoslovakia, Poland, and other Central European countries at the end of the Second World War, and in its aftermath, likewise attracted little empathy until recent times – again because, when it came to mass expulsions of populations and attendant atrocities, the Germans too had "started it." The quarter of a million Serbs expelled from the Krajina and Eastern Slavonia regions of Croatia in 1995 (Chapter 8) now constitute the largest refugee population in Europe; but their plight evokes no great outrage, because of an assignation of collective guilt to Serbs for the Bosnian genocide. (The trend was evident again after the 1999 Kosovo war, when Serb civilians in the province were targeted for murder by ethnic Albanian extremists.)[147]

Even the September 11, 2001 terrorist attacks on the World Trade Center and Pentagon, which could be considered genocidal massacres (see pp. 45–47), secured the equivocal or enthusiastic support of hundreds of millions of people worldwide.

Americans were deemed to have gotten what was coming to them after decades of US imperial intervention. A similar vocabulary of justification and celebration may be found among many Arabs, and other Palestinian supporters, after massacres of Jewish civilians in Israel.

Apart from cases of subaltern genocide, the defenders and deniers of some of history's worst genocides often justify the killings on the grounds of *legitimate defensive or retributory action against traitors and subversives*. The Turkish refusal to acknowledge the Armenian genocide (Chapter 4) depicts atrocities or "excesses" as the inevitable results of an Armenian rebellion aimed at undermining the Ottoman state. Apologists for Hutu Power in Rwanda claim the genocide of 1994 was nothing more than the continuation of "civil war" or "tribal conflict"; or that Hutus were seeking to pre-empt the kind of genocide at Tutsi hands that Hutus had suffered in neighboring Burundi (Chapter 9). Sympathizers of the Nazi regime in Germany sometimes present the invasion of the USSR as a pre-emptive, defensive war against the Bolshevik threat to Western civilization (Box 6a). Even the Nazis' demonology of a Jewish "cancer" and "conspiracy" resonated deeply with millions of highly educated Germans at the time, and fuels Holocaust denial to the present, though as a fringe phenomenon.

All these cases of denial need to be rejected and confronted (see Chapter 14). *But are there instances when genocide may occur in self-defense?* The Rome Statute of the International Criminal Court abjures criminal proceedings against "the person [who] acts reasonably to defend himself or herself or another person or . . . against an imminent and unlawful use of force, in a manner proportionate to the degree of danger to the person or the other person or property protected." Citing this, William Schabas has noted that "reprisal and military necessity are not formally prohibited by international humanitarian law." However, "reprisal as a defense must be proportional, and on this basis its application to genocide would seem inconceivable."[148] But Schabas has a tendency, in defending his "hard" and predictably legalistic interpretation of the UN Convention, to use terms such as "inconceivable," "obviously incompatible," "totally unnecessary," "definitely inappropriate." Sometimes these may close off worthwhile discussions, such as: What is the acceptable range of responses to genocide? Can genocidal counter-assault be "proportional" in any meaningful sense?

A large part of the problem is that the plausibility we attach to reprisals and retribution frequently reflects our political identifications. We have a harder time condemning those with whom we sympathize, even when their actions are atrocious. Consciously or unconsciously, we distinguish "worthy" from "unworthy" victims.[149] And we may be less ready to label as genocidal the atrocities that our chosen "worthies" commit. We will return to this issue at the close of the book, when considering personal responsibility for genocide prevention.

FURTHER STUDY

Alex Alvarez, *Governments, Citizens, and Genocide: A Comparative and Interdisciplinary Approach*. Bloomington, IN: Indiana University Press, 2001. A sharp and tautly-written analysis from a sociological and criminological perspective. See also *Genocidal Crimes*.

Paul Bartrop and Steven L. Jacobs, *Fifty Key Thinkers on the Holocaust and Genocide*. London: Routledge, 2010. Informative short essays on leading figures in Holocaust research and comparative genocide studies.

Frank Chalk and Kurt Jonassohn, *The History and Sociology of Genocide*. New Haven, CT: Yale University Press, 1990. Early and eclectic treatment, still widely read and cited.

John Cooper, *Raphael Lemkin and the Struggle for the Genocide Convention*. London: Palgrave Macmillan, 2008. The first full-length biography of Lemkin and his extraordinary campaign, competently handled.

Robert Gellately and Ben Kiernan, eds, *The Specter of Genocide: Mass Murder in Historical Perspective*. Cambridge: Cambridge University Press, 2003. One of the best edited volumes on the subject; diverse and vigorously written throughout.

Jonathan Glover, *Humanity: A Moral History of the Twentieth Century*. New Haven, CT: Yale University Press, 1999. Addresses genocide but ranges far beyond it; a central work of our time.

Daniel Jonah Goldhagen, *Worse Than War: Genocide, Eliminationism, and the Ongoing Assault on Humanity*. New York: Basic Books, 2009. Usefully situates genocide within a broader framework of "eliminationist" ideologies and strategies.

William L. Hewitt, ed., *Defining the Horrific: Readings on Genocide and Holocaust in the Twentieth Century*. Upper Saddle River, NJ: Pearson Education, 2004. Accessible, wide-ranging readings, ideal for undergraduate use.

Adam Jones, ed., *New Directions in Genocide Research*. London: Routledge, 2011. Highlights contributions from the new generation of genocide scholars.

Ben Kiernan, *Blood and Soil: A World History of Genocide and Extermination from Sparta to Darfur*. New Haven, CT: Yale University Press, 2007. Immense in scope and detail: the magnum opus by the director of Yale University's Genocide Studies Program.

Leo Kuper, *Genocide: Its Political Use in the Twentieth Century*. Harmondsworth: Penguin, 1981. The foundational text of comparative genocide studies, still in print.

Raphael Lemkin, *Key Writings of Raphael Lemkin on Genocide*. Compiled by PreventGenocide.org, http://www.preventgenocide.org/lemkin. Online selection of Lemkin's core work on genocide, much of which remains unpublished.

Mark Levene, *Genocide in the Age of the Nation State, Vol. 1: The Meaning of Genocide* and *Vol. 2: The Rise of the West and the Coming of Genocide*. London: I.B. Tauris, 2005. The richest, most nourishing, most mind-expanding work of genocide studies – and there are still two volumes to go.

Michael Mann, *The Dark Side of Democracy: Explaining Ethnic Cleansing*. Cambridge: Cambridge University Press, 2005. Sprawling study of modernity and "murderous ethnic cleansing."

Manus I. Midlarsky, *The Killing Trap: Genocide in the Twentieth Century*. Cambridge: Cambridge University Press, 2005. Fine study from a political-science perspective, emphasizing the contingency of genocidal processes.

Samantha Power, *"A Problem from Hell": America and the Age of Genocide*. New York: Basic Books, 2002. Power's multiple award-winning work focuses on the US response to various genocides.

John Quigley, *The Genocide Convention: An International Law Analysis*. London: Ashgate, 2006. Stimulating analysis of the Convention, especially provocative on framings of genocidal intent.

Nicholas A. Robins and Adam Jones, eds, *Genocides by the Oppressed: Subaltern Genocide in Theory and Practice*. Bloomington, IN: Indiana University Press, 2009. How, when, and why oppressed populations may adopt genocidal strategies against their oppressors.

Richard L. Rubenstein, *The Age of Triage: Fear and Hope in an Overcrowded World*. Boston, MA: Beacon Press, 1983. Groundbreaking study of the elimination of unwanted populations.

Martin Shaw, *What is Genocide?* Cambridge: Polity Press, 2007. Thoughtful reexamination of what, exactly, genocide "destroys."

Dinah Shelton, ed., *Encyclopedia of Genocide and Crimes Against Humanity* (3 vols). Detroit, MI: Macmillan Reference, 2005. Massive, admirably inclusive work; a standard reference.

Dan Stone, ed., *The Historiography of Genocide*. London: Palgrave Macmillan, 2008. Wide-ranging compilation examining core themes of the genocide studies literature.

Samuel Totten, William S. Parsons, and Israel W. Charny, eds, *A Century of Genocide: Critical Essays and Eyewitness Accounts* (3rd edn). New York: Routledge, 2008. Unparalleled collection of analyses and testimonies.

Samuel Totten and Paul R. Bartrop, eds, *The Genocide Studies Reader*. London: Routledge, 2009. A comprehensive selection of essays from the literature – a useful companion to this volume for graduate courses.

Hannibal Travis, *Genocide in the Middle East: The Ottoman Empire, Iraq, and Sudan*. Durham, NC: Carolina Academic Press, 2010. Broader in scope than its title suggests: one of the most meticulously documented and up-to-date of the major histories of genocide.

Eric D. Weitz, *A Century of Genocide: Utopias of Race and Nation*. Princeton, NJ: Princeton University Press, 2003. Cogent overview, with case studies paralleling some in this volume.

Benjamin Whitaker, *Revised and Updated Report on the Question of the Prevention and Punishment of the Crime of Genocide* (The Whitaker Report). ECOSOC (United Nations), July 2, 1985, available in full at http://www.preventgenocide.org/prevent/UNdocs/whitaker. A significant attempt to rethink and revise the UN Genocide Convention.[150]

NOTES

1 Leo Kuper, *Genocide: Its Political Use in the Twentieth Century* (Harmondsworth: Penguin, 1981), p. 9.

2 Frank Chalk and Kurt Jonassohn, *The History and Sociology of Genocide: Analyses and Case Studies* (New Haven, CT: Yale University Press, 1990), p. 64. Ronald Wright has cited archaeological evidence suggesting that the destruction of the Neanderthal population of Western Europe, roughly 25,000 years ago, "may have been the first genocide. Or, worse, *not* the first – merely the first of which evidence survives. It may follow from this that we are descended from a million years of ruthless victories, genetically predisposed by the sins of our fathers to do likewise again and again. . . . A bad smell of extinction follows *Homo sapiens* around the world." Wright, *A Short History of Progress* (Toronto: Anansi Press, 2004), pp. 25, 37.

3 Quoted in Chalk and Jonassohn, *The History and Sociology of Genocide*, p. 58. Notably, when Troy did finally fall, women and girl children were spared extermination, and instead abducted as slaves (Israel Charny, ed., *The Encyclopedia of Genocide* [Santa Barbara, CA: ABC-CLIO, 1999], p. 273). See the discussion of gender and genocide in Chapter 13.

4 Chalk and Jonassohn, *The History and Sociology of Genocide*, p. 28.

5 Helen Fein, *Genocide: A Sociological Perspective* (London: Sage, 1993), p. 26.

6 Karen Armstrong, *A History of God*; quoted in Roy F. Baumeister, *Evil: Inside Human Violence and Cruelty* (New York: W.H. Freeman, 1999), p. 171. For other examples of Old Testament genocide, see Chalk and Jonassohn, *The History and Sociology of Genocide*, pp. 62–63; Eric D. Weitz, *A Century of Genocide: Utopias of Race and Nation* (Princeton, NJ: Princeton University Press, 2003), p. 18, citing Joshua's "destruction by the edge of the sword [of] all in the city [of Jericho], both men and women, young and old, oxen, sheep, and donkeys."

7 "Genocide, God, and the Bible," http://stripe.colorado.edu/~morristo/genocide.html.

8 Mark Levene, *Genocide in the Age of the Nation State, Vol. 1: The Meaning of Genocide* (London: I.B. Tauris, 2005), p. 151.

9 Cited in Louis W. Cable, "The Bloody Bible," *Freethought Today*, June/July 1997. http://ffrf.org/legacy/fttoday/1997/june_july97/cable.html. See also the numerous examples of "God-ordered genocide" cited in Bill Moyers, "9/11 and the Sport of God," CommonDreams.org, September 9, 2005, http://www.commondreams.org/views05/0909-36.htm.

10 Numbers 31, Revised Standard Edition, quoted in Daniel Chirot and Clark McCauley, *Why Not Kill Them All? The Logic and Prevention of Mass Political Murder* (Princeton, NJ: Princeton University Press, 2006), pp. 29–30. For more on religion and genocide, see Chapter 15.

11 Ben Kiernan, "The First Genocide: Carthage, 146 BC," *Diogenes*, 203 (2004), pp. 27–39.

12 Andrew Bell-Fialkoff writes that the First Crusade (1096–99) left "a trail of blood and destruction, throughout the Rhine and the Moselle valleys, as well as in Prague and Hungary. Entire communities, perhaps tens of thousands of people in all, were wiped out. The Crusade culminated in a wholesale massacre of all non-Christians in Jerusalem." Bell-Fialkoff, *Ethnic Cleansing* (New York: St. Martin's Griffin, 1999), p. 13.

13 Eric S. Margolis, *War at the Top of the World: The Struggle for Afghanistan, Kashmir, and Tibet* (New York: Routledge, 2001), p. 155. In Hannibal Travis's summary: "After 1200 CE, Genghis Khan led a campaign through Asia that destroyed millions of lives and many ancient cities. In Beijing in 1219, the Mongols slaughtered thousands of people and set the city ablaze, causing it to burn for a month. . . . In present-day Konye-Urgench in Turkmenistan, then called Gurganj, a contingent from Genghis Khan's

army, with 100,000 Mongols in all, killed over a million people, in house-to-house fighting that burned large sections of the city. . . ." For his part, Genghis Khan's grandson, Hulagu Khan, "reached Baghdad in the 1250s and massacred 100,000 to two million people there, seizing enormous amounts of gold and treasure, destroying libraries, and soiling and ruining mosques. Mesopotamia's irrigation system was severely damaged, leaving a legacy of dependency on imported food that would have catastrophic consequences during U.N. sanctions in the 1990s." Travis, *Genocide in the Middle East: The Ottoman Empire, Iraq, and Sudan* (Durham, NC: Carolina Academic Press, 2010), pp. 167–68. On the UN sanctions, see pp. 44–45.

14 See Reynald Secher, *A French Genocide: The Vendée,* trans. George Holoch (Notre Dame, IN: University of Notre Dame Press, 2003); Mark Levene, "The Vendée – A Paradigm Shift?," ch. 3 in Levene, *Genocide in the Age of the Nation State, Vol. 2: The Rise of the West and the Coming of Genocide* (London: I.B. Tauris, 2005), pp. 103–61. This section also draws on Adam Jones, "Why Gendercide? Why Root-and-Branch? A Comparison of the Vendée Uprising of 1793–94 and the Bosnian War of the 1990s," *Journal of Genocide Research,* 8:1 (2006), pp. 9–25. For an interesting reportage of travel in the Vendée region, including sites connected with the genocide, see Anthony Peregrine, "France: Vengeance on the Vendée," *The Telegraph,* August 18, 2009. http://www.telegraph.co.uk/travel/destinations/europe/france/6048204/France-Vengeance-on-the-Vendee.html

15 Cited in Alain Gérard, *«Par principe d'humanité . . .» La Terreur et la Vendée* (Paris: Librairie Arthème Fayard, 1999), p. 295.

16 Cited in Arno J. Mayer, *The Furies: Violence and Terror in the French and Russian Revolutions* (Princeton, NJ: Princeton University Press, 2000), p. 353.

17 In the estimation of France's greatest historian, Jules Michelet; quoted in Mayer, *The Furies,* p. 325.

18 Quoted in Secher, *A French Genocide,* p. 132.

19 Mayer, *The Furies,* p. 340.

20 Michael R. Mahoney, "The Zulu Kingdom as a Genocidal and Post-genocidal Society, c. 1810 to the Present," *Journal of Genocide Research,* 5:2 (2003), p. 263.

21 Chalk and Jonassohn, *The History and Sociology of Genocide,* p. 223.

22 Ibid., pp. 224–25, citing Eugene Victor Walter, *Terror and Resistance: A Study of Political Violence.*

23 Mahoney, "The Zulu Kingdom," p. 254.

24 Chalk and Jonassohn, *The History and Sociology of Genocide,* pp. 224–25.

25 Mahoney, "The Zulu Kingdom," p. 255.

26 See PreventGenocide.org, "A Crime without a Name," http://www.preventgenocide.org/genocide/crimewithoutaname.htm.

27 John Cooper, *Raphael Lemkin and the Struggle for the Genocide Convention* (London: Palgrave Macmillan, 2008), p. 213.

28 Ibid., p. 24.

29 Samantha Power, *"A Problem from Hell": America and the Age of Genocide* (New York: Basic Books, 2002), p. 20.

30 Lemkin quoted in Power, *"A Problem from Hell,"* p. 20.

31 Lemkin quoted in Travis, *Genocide in the Middle East,* p. 28.

32 Lemkin quoted in Power, *"A Problem from Hell,"* p. 21.

33 "Of particular interest to Lemkin were the reflections of George Eastman, who said he had settled upon 'Kodak' as the name for his new camera because: 'First. It is short. Second. It is not capable of mispronunciation. Third. It does not resemble anything in the art and cannot be associated with anything in the art except the Kodak.'" Power, *"A Problem from Hell,"* pp. 42–43.

34 Lemkin, *Axis Rule in Occupied Europe,* p. 79.

35 On this point, see Ward S. Churchill, "Genocide by Any Other Name: North American Indian Residential Schools in Context," in Jones, ed., *Genocide, War Crimes and the West,* p. 80.

36 Stephen Holmes, "Looking Away," *London Review of Books*, November 14, 2002 (review of Power, *"A Problem from Hell"*).

37 According to Helen Fein, Lemkin's "examples of genocide or genocidal situations include: Albigensians, American Indians, Assyrians in Iraq, Belgian Congo, Christians in Japan, French in Sicily (*c.* 1282), Hereros, Huguenots, Incas, Mongols, the Soviet Union/Ukraine, [and] Tasmania." Fein, *Genocide: A Sociological Perspective*, p. 11. Lemkin's study of Tasmania has been edited for publication: see Raphael Lemkin, "Tasmania," edited by Ann Curthoys, *Patterns of Prejudice*, 39:2 (2005), pp. 170–96 (and Curthoys's Introduction, pp. 162–69).

38 William A. Schabas, *Genocide in International Law* (Cambridge: Cambridge University Press, 2000), p. 14.

39 As supplied in W. Michael Reisman and Chris T. Antoniou, eds, *The Laws of War: A Comprehensive Collection of Primary Documents on International Laws Governing Armed Conflict* (New York: Vintage Books, 1994), pp. 84–85.

40 Martin Shaw, *What is Genocide?* (Cambridge: Polity, 2007), p. 22.

41 L.J. van den Herik concurs that "it is not likely that genocidal acts other than killing – sub (b) to (e) – will be perceived as genocide when they are committed outside a context of mass killing." Van den Herik, *The Contribution of the Rwanda Tribunal to the Development of International Law* (Leiden: Martinus Nijhoff Publishers, 2005), p. 146.

42 Cited in Steven R. Ratner and Jason S. Abrams, *Accountability for Human Rights Atrocities: Beyond the Nuremberg Legacy* (2nd edn) (Oxford: Oxford University Press, 2001), pp. 30, 32.

43 Schabas, *Genocide in International Law*, p. 140.

44 See Beth Van Schaack, "The Crime of Political Genocide: Repairing the Genocide Convention's Blind Spot," *Yale Law Journal*, 106 (1997), pp. 2259–91.

45 Schabas, *Genocide in International Law*, pp. 175, 178.

46 For a survey of the early legal literature, see David Kader, "Law and Genocide: A Critical Annotated Bibliography," *Hastings International and Comparative Law Review*, 11 (1988).

47 See my "Filmography of Genocide and Crimes Against Humanity" at http://www.genocidetext.net/gaci_filmography.htm.

48 Christopher Rudolph, "Constructing an Atrocities Regime: The Politics of War Crimes Tribunals," *International Organization*, 55: 3 (Summer 2001), p. 659. Rudolph cites Kenneth Abbott and Duncan Snidal, who "define 'hard' legalization as legally binding obligations characterized by high degrees of obligation, precision, and delegation, and define 'soft' legalization as a more flexible manifestation characterized by varying degrees along one or most of these same dimensions."

49 In this context, it is worth noting the verdict of the ICTR that the law of genocide "did not include a requirement that the perpetrator be a State official. Hence, individuals connected to non-State actors, such as the *Interahamwe* [genocidal militia] and RTLM [extremist radio station], and other persons not affiliated with the government, such as businessmen, who had all played a major role in the preparation, organization and execution of the genocide, could also be held responsible for genocide" (see Chapter 9). Van den Herik, *The Contribution of the Rwanda Tribunal*, p. 269.

50 Mark Levene also stresses that *"it is the perpetrator, not the victim (or bystander) who defines the group"* (emphasis in original). Levene, *Genocide in the Age of the Nation State, Vol. 1*, p. 79. Patrick Wolfe contends that a property like "race cannot be taken as given. It is made in the targeting." Wolfe, "Structure and Event: Settler Colonialism, Time, and the Question of Genocide," in A. Dirk Moses, ed., *Empire, Colony, Genocide: Conquest, Occupation, and Subaltern Resistance in World History* (New York: Berghahn Books, 2008), p. 111. According to Scott Straus, "Genocide is not carried out against a group bounded by essential internal properties. Rather, genocide is carried out against a group that the perpetrator *believes* has essential properties . . . however fictive such a belief may be." Straus quoted in Levene, *Genocide, Vol. 1*, p. 87.

51 Irving Louis Horowitz, *Taking Lives: Genocide and State Power* (4th edn) (New Brunswick, NJ: Transaction Publishers, 1996), p. 265. Benjamin Whitaker, in his mid-1980s reevaluation of the Genocide Convention for the UN, likewise contended that "in part" should mean a "reasonably significant number, relative to the total of the group as a whole, or else a significant section of a group such as its leadership." Quoted in John Quigley, *The Genocide Convention: An International Law Analysis* (London: Ashgate, 2006), p. 141.

52 Drost quoted in Curthoys and Docker, "Defining Genocide," p. 22.

53 Steven Katz, *The Holocaust in Historical Context, Vol. 1: The Holocaust and Mass Death before the Modern Age* (New York: Oxford University Press, 1994), p. 131.

54 "Annan's Nobel Speech in Oslo," *The New York Times*, December 11, 2001.

55 Chile Eboe-Osuji, "Rape as Genocide: Some Questions Arising," *Journal of Genocide Research*, 9: 2 (2007), pp. 262–63. Eboe-Osuji adds: "This mischief was especially evident during the Rwandan genocide, when the US government refused to acknowledge that a genocide was in progress, for fear of being impelled to do something about it, while semantically acknowledging that 'acts of genocide' (rather than genocide) were occurring."

56 On the Marsh Arabs, see Joseph W. Dellapenna, "The Iraqi Campaign against the Marsh Arabs: Ecocide as Genocide," *Jurist*, January 31, 2003. http://jurist.law.pitt.edu/forum/forumnew92.php

57 See the full text of the declaration at http://www.un.org/esa/socdev/unpfii/en/drip.html.

58 Reporters Without Borders, "Media Allowed to Use Kurdish Language But Still Forbidden to Discuss Kurdish Issues Freely," November 20, 2009. http://www.rsf.org/Media-allowed-to-use-Kurdish.html

59 See Ilan Pappé, "The Memoricide of the Nakba," ch. 10 in Pappé, *The Ethnic Cleansing of Palestine* (Oxford: Oneworld, 2006), pp. 225–34; Jonathan Cook, "Memoricide in the West Bank," Counterpunch.org, March 10, 2009, http://www.counterpunch.org/cook03102009.html.

60 Shaw, *What is Genocide?*, pp. 34, 106, 156. Emphasis in original.

61 Daniel Feierstein, "Political Violence in Argentina and Its Genocidal Characteristics," in Marcia Esparza, Henry R. Huttenbach and Daniel Feierstein, eds, *State Violence and Genocide in Latin America: The Cold War Years* (London: Routledge, 2010), p. 61.

62 Lemkin quoted in Cooper, *Raphael Lemkin*, p. 241.

63 A. Dirk Moses, "Empire, Colony, Genocide: Keywords and the Philosophy of History," in Moses, ed., *Empire, Colony, Genocide*, pp. 12, 15.

64 William A. Schabas, "Convention on the Prevention and Punishment of the Crime of Genocide," United Nations Treaty Collection, http://untreaty.un.org/cod/avl/ha/cppcg/cppcg.html.

65 Robert van Krieken, "Cultural Genocide in Australia," in Stone, ed., *The Historiography of Genocide* (London: Palgrave Macmillan, 2008), p. 131.

66 For a nuanced exploration of the applicability of the genocide framework to indigenous peoples' experiences, see Andrew Woolford, "Ontological Destruction: Genocide and Canadian Aboriginal Peoples," *Genocide Studies and Prevention*, 4: 1 (2009), pp. 81–97.

67 Cooper, *Raphael Lemkin*, p. 158.

68 John Quigley, *The Genocide Convention: An International Law Analysis* (London: Ashgate, 2006), p. 105.

69 CBC Digital Archives, "Fighting Words: Bill 101," http://archives.cbc.ca/politics/provincial_territorial_politics/topics/1297/.

70 Benoit Aubin, "Bill 101: 30 Years On," *The Canadian Encyclopedia*, August 13, 2007.

71 "The UN says ethnic cleansing is by genocide or forced migration. In black and white I guess Bill 101 fits pretty well" (post by Wheresmyneighbours, February 28, 2009, http://blog.fagstein.com/2009/02/24/journal-lockout-1-month). A March 31, 2009 post by blogger Steve Karmazenuk, apparently a disenchanted member of the provincial Liberal Party, assailed "Quebec's War on Anglos," alleging an "underreported and ongoing campaign of ethnic cleansing by attrition [which] has continued to be

ignored" by the Liberals (http://kspaceuniverse.blogspot.com/2009/03/message-to-anglo-community.html). Interestingly, the language of genocide has recently been revived on the other side of the language fence – reflecting francophone concerns over creeping Anglicization and bilingualism. In a TV interview in 2008, the writer Victor-Levy Beaulieu declared that "If all Quebec becomes bilingual, what awaits us is a slow genocide." Graeme Hamilton, "Lost in Translation: 30 Years On, Quebecers Are Still Hot about Bill 101," *National Post*, February 16, 2008.

72 Government of Canada Privy Council Office figures cited and supplemented in "English-Speaking Quebecker," Wikipedia, http://en.wikipedia.org/wiki/English-speaking_Quebecker. See also Garth Stevenson, *Community Besieged: The Anglophone Minority and the Politics of Quebec* (Montreal, PQ: McGill-Queen's University Press, 1999).

73 CBC News Online, "Language Laws in Quebec," March 30, 2005, http://www.cbc.ca/canada/story/2009/10/22/f-quebec-language-laws-bill-101.html.

74 CBC Digital Archives, "Fighting Words."

75 "A generation later, the language charter is widely accepted as an intrinsic part of Quebec's social fabric. Both anglos and francophones of moderate persuasion say the law has engendered an unprecedented era of social peace and easing of language tensions and fostered a cross-cultural communication between English and French Quebecers that has served as an important bridge between the storied 'two solitudes' of the bad old days." Hubert Bauch, "Bill 101 Paved Way for Peace," *The Gazette* (Montreal), August 25, 2007.

76 Kuper, *Genocide*, p. 166.

77 Ibid.

78 David Moshman, "Conceptions of Genocide and Perceptions of History," in Dan Stone, ed., *The Historiography of Genocide* (London: Palgrave Macmillan, 2008), p. 86.

79 Adam Jones, "Problems of Gendercide," in Jones, ed., *Gendercide and Genocide* (Nashville, TN: Vanderbilt University Press, 2004), p. 260.

80 Jeffrey Herf, *The Jewish Enemy: Nazi Propaganda during World War II and the Holocaust* (Cambridge, MA: The Belknap Press of Harvard University Press, 2006), pp. 150–51. For another important study of the "Judeo-Bolshevik" motif, see Lorna Waddington, *Hitler's Crusade: Bolshevism and the Myth of the International Jewish Conspiracy* (London: Tauris Academic Studies, 2007). Like Herf, Waddington contends that in Hitler's mind, "the scourge of Bolshevism had always been inextricably linked to the wider danger presented to Germany and the world by the machinations of international Jewry. That fact alone is indicative of the profound significance of anti-Bolshevism as a determinant of his political actions" (p. 210), and as a determinant of how the Jew was depicted in the Nazi *Weltanschauung* (world-view).

81 Nazi press report quoted in Herf, *The Jewish Enemy*, p. 189.

82 Mark Levene writes that for Hitler and the Nazis, "the international Jewish conspiracy" "operat[ed] through manifold, multi-layered forces of subversion and pollution, including Bolshevism, capitalism, cultural modernism, sexual contamination, racial emasculation and disease . . ." Levene, *Genocide in the Age of the Nation State, Vol. 1*, p. 69.

83 Nazi pamphlet quoted in Herf, *The Jewish Enemy*, p. 101. In fact, as Herf shows (p. 96), while at one point Jews constituted over a quarter of Bolshevik Central Committee members (around 1917), by 1939 (when World War Two erupted, supposedly at Jewish behest) it was roughly 10 percent. At no time did Jewish members of the Communist Party exceed around 5 percent of the total.

84 Peter Fritzsche, *Life and Death in the Third Reich* (Cambridge, MA: The Belknap Press of Harvard University Press, 2008), p. 196.

85 Saul Friedländer similarly notes that "on occupied Soviet territory . . . the extermination was first aimed at Jews as carriers of the Soviet system, then at Jews as potential partisans and finally as hostile elements living in territories ultimately destined for German colonization: The three categories merged of course into one." Friedländer, *The Years of*

Extermination: Nazi Germany and the Jews, 1939–1945 (New York: HarperCollins, 2007), p. 237.

86 Shaw, *What is Genocide?*, p. 117.

87 Karl A. Schleunes, *The Twisted Road to Auschwitz: Nazi Policy toward German Jews, 1933–1939* (Urbana, IL: University of Illinois Press, 1990); Browning's comment is in his back-cover endorsement.

88 Levene, *Genocide in the Age of the Nation State, Vol. 2*, p. 66; *Vol. 1*, p. 51. Donald Bloxham likewise issues "a plea for *normalisation* of the study of state-sponsored mass murder, for a recognition that it emerges, like many other governmental policies across a spectrum of regimes, often piecemeal, informed by ideology but according to shifts of circumstances." Bloxham, *Genocide, The World Wars, and the Unweaving of Europe* (London: Vallentine Mitchell, 2008), p. 38.

89 Benjamin Madley, "Patterns of Frontier Genocide 1803–1910: The Aboriginal Tasmanians, the Yuki of California, and the Herero of Namibia," *Journal of Genocide Research*, 6: 2 (June 2004), pp. 167–92.

90 Levene, *Genocide in the Age of the Nation State, Vol. 1*, p. 61.

91 A. Dirk Moses, "Empire, Colony, Genocide: Keywords and the Philosophy of History," in Moses, ed., *Empire, Colony, Genocide*, p. 29.

92 Scott Straus, *The Order of Genocide: Race, Power, and War in Rwanda* (Ithaca, NY: Cornell University Press, 2006), p. 12.

93 As the International Law Commission, "which drafts treaties for the UN General Assembly," analyzed the question of genocidal intent: "The prohibited acts enumerated in subparagraphs (a) to (e) [of the Genocide Convention] are *by their very nature conscious, intentional or volitional acts* which an individual could not usually commit without knowing that certain consequences were likely to result." Quoted in Quigley, *The Genocide Convention*, p. 91. Emphasis added.

94 Robert Gellately and Ben Kiernan contend similarly that under the prevailing international-legal understanding, "genocidal intent also applies to acts of destruction that are not the specific goal but are predictable outcomes or by-products of a policy, which could have been avoided by a change in that policy." Gellately and Kiernan, "The Study of Mass Murder and Genocide," in Gellately and Kiernan, eds, *The Specter of Genocide: Mass Murder in Historical Perspective* (Cambridge: Cambridge University Press, 2003), p. 15.

95 Quigley, *The Genocide Convention*, pp. 121–22.

96 In his "Proposed Convention on Prevention and Punishment of the Crime of Genocide," Churchill maps "gradations of culpability" for genocide onto domestic law's concept of "degrees" of homicide. He distinguishes among "(a) *Genocide in the First Degree*, which consists of instances in which evidence of premeditated intent to commit genocide is present. (b) *Genocide in the Second Degree*, which consists of instances in which evidence of premeditation is absent, but in which it can be reasonably argued that the perpetrator(s) acted with reckless disregard for the probability that genocide would result from their actions. (c) *Genocide in the Third Degree*, which consists of instances in which genocide derives, however unintentionally, from other violations of international law engaged in by the perpetrator(s). (d) *Genocide in the Fourth Degree*, which consists of instances in which neither evidence of premeditation nor other criminal behavior is present, but in which the perpetrator(s) acted with depraved indifference to the possibility that genocide would result from their actions and therefore [failed] to effect adequate safeguards to prevent it." Ward Churchill, *A Little Matter of Genocide: Holocaust and Denial in the Americas, 1492 to the Present* (San Francisco, CA: City Lights Books, 1997), pp. 434–35.

97 Alex Alvarez, *Governments, Citizens, and Genocide: A Comparative and Interdisciplinary Approach* (Bloomington, IN: Indiana University Press, 2001), p. 52.

98 On "reasonable foreseeability," see Tony Barta, "Sorry, and Not Sorry, in Australia: How the Apology to the Stolen Generations Buried a History of Genocide," *Journal of Genocide Research*, 10: 2 (2008), p. 208, citing work by Sarah Pritchard.

99 This part of the discussion draws on personal correspondence with John Quigley, February 13, 2010.

100 Alexander K.A. Greenawalt, "Rethinking Genocidal Intent: The Case for a Knowledge-based Interpretation," *Columbia Law Review*, 99: 8 (1999), p. 2269. Emphasis added.

101 *Akayesu* judgment quoted in Schabas, *Genocide in International Law*, p. 212. Emphasis added. Schabas considers this approach "definitely inappropriate in the case of genocide."

102 Quigley, *The Genocide Convention*, p. 114.

103 Van den Herik, *The Contribution of the Rwanda Tribunal*, p. 111.

104 For a superbly accessible introduction to the institution of Atlantic slavery, see Robert Harms, *The Diligent: A Voyage Through the Worlds of the Slave Trade* (New York: Basic Books, 2002).

105 After conducting a useful review of available sources, Matthew White concludes: "If we assume the absolute worst, a death toll as high as 60 million is at the very edge of possibility; however, the likeliest number of deaths would fall somewhere from 15 to 20 million." White, "Twentieth Century Atlas – Historical Body Count," http://users. erols. com/mwhite28/warstatv.htm. To arrive at such a total, one can begin with the figure of eleven to fifteen million slaves "shipped between the fifteenth and the nine-teenth century," cited in Hugh Thomas, *The Slave Trade: The Story of the Atlantic Slave Trade: 1440–1870* (New York: Touchstone, 1997), p. 862. (Thomas himself argues for an "approximate figure . . . [of] something like eleven million slaves, give or take 500,000.") A widely held view is that approximately 50 percent of those captured as slaves died before they were shipped from West African ports. To these eleven to fifteen million victims, one adds approximately two million more who died on the "middle passage" between Africa and the Americas, and an unknown but certainly very large number who perished after arrival, either during the brutal "seasoning" process or on the plantations.

106 Seymour Drescher, "The Atlantic Slave Trade and the Holocaust: A Comparative Analysis," in Alan S. Rosenbaum, ed., *Is the Holocaust Unique? Perspectives on Comparative Genocide* (Boulder, CO: Westview Press, 2001), pp. 97–117. See also Jeffrey Herf, "Comparative Perspectives on Anti-Semitism, Radical Anti-Semitism in the Holocaust and American White Racism," *Journal of Genocide Research*, 9: 4 (2007), pp. 575–600; and A. Dirk Moses, "The Fate of Blacks and Jews: A Response to Jeffrey Herf," *Journal of Genocide Research*, 10: 2 (2008), pp. 269–87.

107 Michael Ignatieff, "Lemkin's Word," *The New Republic*, February 26, 2001.

108 See, e.g., the Black American journalist Keith Richburg's controversial article, "American in Africa," in *Washington Post Magazine*, March 26, 1995, available online at http://www. washingtonpost.com/wp-srv/inatl/longterm/richburg/richbrg1.htm.

109 Orlando Patterson, *Slavery and Social Death: A Comparative Study* (Cambridge, MA: Harvard University Press, 1982), p. 164.

110 The fact that slavery in the United States was far less destructive of slaves' lives, compared to the Caribbean or Portuguese America (Brazil), is an important factor in weighing the applicability of the genocide framework to different slavery institutions in the Americas. Life for slaves in the US was a calvary; in French-controlled Haiti it was a holocaust. Recall, however, that millions of slaves died *en route* to West African ports and New World plantations. These rates do not seem to have been lower for slaves shipped to US destinations.

111 *We Charge Genocide: The Historic Petition to the United Nations for Relief from a Crime of the United States Government against the Negro People* (New York: International Publishers, 1970), p. xv.

112 The Ku Klux Klan was, and in a somewhat transformed guise still is, a white-supremacist organization based in the US South. It began as an armed militia in the post-Civil War era, and was responsible for many acts of terrorism and violent vigilantism against blacks. See Allen W. Trelease, *White Terror: The Ku Klux Klan Conspiracy and Southern Reconstruction* (Baton Rouge, LA: Louisiana State University Press, 1995); Stephen Budiansky, *The Bloody Shirt: Terror after the Civil War* (New York: Plume, 2008).

113 *We Charge Genocide*, p. 6.

114 Raphael Lemkin's response to the controversy was illuminating, and not in a way that reflects well on the founder of genocide studies. According to Ann Curthoys and John Docker, Lemkin "argued vehemently that the provisions of the Genocide Convention bore no relation to the US Government or its position vis-à-vis Black citizens." He was anxious that the charges not derail American ratification of his cherished Genocide Convention. Moreover, Lemkin was ardently wooing the Slavic and Baltic populations that had fallen under Soviet rule (and receiving significant funding from their usually self-appointed representatives). Thus we have his frankly craven comments to *The New York Times* on December 18, 1951, accusing Patterson and Robeson of being "un-American," and declaring that *We Charge Genocide* was a communist ploy to "divert attention from the crimes of genocide committed against Estonians, Latvians, Lithuanians, Poles and other Soviet-subjugated peoples." For Curthoys and Docker, his response raises "disturbing questions . . . concerning Lemkin and his attitudes to African American history and people: perhaps there was a fundamental lack of sympathy." Ann Curthoys and John Docker, "Defining Genocide," in Stone, ed., *The Historiography of Genocide*, pp. 19–20. In this respect, the authors contend, Lemkin was "conforming to a long tradition of European superiority and contempt towards Africa" (p. 21).

115 Eric Langenbacher, "The Allies in World War II: The Anglo-American Bombardment of German Cities," in Jones, ed., *Genocide, War Crimes and the West*, pp. 117–19. See also Howard Zinn, "Hiroshima and Royan," in William L. Hewitt, ed., *Defining the Horrific: Readings on Genocide and Holocaust in the Twentieth Century* (Upper Saddle River, NJ: Pearson, 2004), pp. 187–99. Zinn, a renowned dissident historian, was also a US veteran of the area-bombing campaign against Germany; the chapter relates some of his personal experiences.

116 See the description of the raid in Eric Markusen and David Kopf, *The Holocaust and Strategic Bombing: Genocide and Total War in the Twentieth Century* (Boulder, CO: Westview Press, 1995), pp. 175–80.

117 "I cannot accept the view that . . . the bombing, in time of war, of such civilian enemy populations as those of Hiroshima, Nagasaki, Hamburg, and Dresden does not constitute genocide within the terms of the [UN] convention." Kuper, *Genocide*, cited in Chalk and Jonassohn, *The History and Sociology of Genocide*, p. 24. Mary Kaldor also argues that "the indiscriminate bombing of civilians . . . creat[ed] a scale of devastation of genocidal proportions." Mary Kaldor, *New and Old Wars: Organized Violence in a Global Era* (Stanford, CA: Stanford University Press, 2001), p. 25.

118 "Was strategic bombing genocidal? Put bluntly, our answer is yes." Markusen and Kopf, *The Holocaust and Strategic Bombing*, p. 255; see the extended discussion at pp. 244–58. For a judgment of the area bombings of German and Japanese cities as "moral crimes," see A.C. Grayling, *Among the Dead Cities: The History and Moral Legacy of the WWII Bombing of Civilians in Germany and Japan* (New York: Walker & Company, 2006). On the atomic bombings of Hiroshima and Nagasaki, see Daniel Jonah Goldhagen, *Worse Than War: Genocide, Eliminationism, and the Ongoing Assault on Humanity* (New York: Basic Books, 2009), pp. 3–8, arguing that "the willful slaughter of more than a quarter of a million people, in full view of the world, should be universally recognized for what it was, causing the label '*mass murderer*' to be affixed to [President Harry] Truman's name . . . putting Truman and his deeds into the same broad categories of Hitler and the Holocaust, Stalin and the gulag, Pol Pot, Mao, Saddam Hussein, and Slobodan Milosevic and their victims," though "without judging them morally as being equivalent" (pp. 6, 8).

119 Taylor quoted in Chalk and Jonassohn, *The History and Sociology of Genocide*, p. 25.

120 Ronald Takaki, *Hiroshima: Why America Dropped the Atomic Bomb* (Boston, MA: Little, Brown, 1995), pp. 30, 153 (n. 3).

121 See, e.g., Brahma Chellaney, "No Rationalization for Nagasaki Attack," *The Japan Times*, August 10, 2005.

122 See Ramsey Clark, "Criminal Complaint against the United States and Others for Crimes against the People of Iraq (1996) and Letter to the Security Council (2001)," in Jones, ed., *Genocide, War Crimes and the West*, p. 271. The forum in question was the International Court on Crimes Against Humanity Committed by the UN Security Council on [*sic*] Iraq, held on November 16–17, 1996. For more on citizens' tribunals, see Chapter 15. Clark's phrase "for the purpose of" is not clearly supported by the evidence; an accusation of genocide founded on willful and malignant negligence is, for me, more persuasive.

123 For an argument along these lines, see John G. Heidenrich, *How to Prevent Genocide: A Guide for Policymakers, Scholars, and the Concerned Citizen* (Westport, CT: Praeger, 2001), pp. 101–3.

124 Quigley, *The Genocide Convention*, p. 204.

125 Albright on *60 Minutes*, May 12, 1996. She later disowned the comment.

126 Bonior quoted in "US Congressmen Criticise Iraqi Sanctions," BBC Online, February 17, 2000, http://news.bbc.co.uk/1/hi/world/middle_east/646783.stm.

127 Denis J. Halliday, "US Policy and Iraq: A Case of Genocide?," in Jones, ed., *Genocide, War Crimes and the West*, p. 264 (based on a November 1999 speech in Spain).

128 A useful definition of terrorism is offered by the US Congress: "any [criminal] activity that . . . appears to be intended (i) to intimidate or coerce a civilian population; (ii) to influence the policy of a government by intimidation or coercion; or (iii) to affect the conduct of a government by assassination or kidnapping." Quoted in Noam Chomsky, *9-11* (New York: Seven Stories Press, 2001), p. 16 (note).

129 For Kuper, genocidal massacres are "expressed characteristically in the annihilation of a section of a group – men, women and children, as for example in the wiping out of whole villages." Kuper, *Genocide*, p. 10.

130 See the H-Genocide discussion logs for September 2001, searchable at http://www.h-net.org/logsearch/. The posts cited here can be found in the archives for September 16, 2001 (Ronayne) and September 20 (Cribb).

131 Goldhagen, *Worse Than War*, pp. 490–91. Goldhagen defines "Political Islam" as a "phenomenon includ[ing] only Islamic-grounded *political* regimes, organizations, and initiatives that share . . . a common ideological foundation about Islam's *political* primacy or its need to systematically and politically roll back the West – a conviction that the fundamentally corrupt modern world must be refashioned, including by annihilating others" (p. 492). In addition to the terrorists of al-Qaeda, he cites established regimes such as Mahmoud Ahmadinejad's in Iran (see p. 521) and Omar al-Bashir's in Sudan (Box 9a).

132 Vandana Shiva, "War against Nature and the Peoples of the South," in Sarah Anderson, ed., *Views from the South* (San Francisco, CA: Food First Books, 2000), pp. 93, 113. See also Paul Farmer, "On Suffering and Structural Violence: A View from Below," in Nancy Scheper-Hughes and Philippe Bourgois, eds, *Violence in War and Peace* (London: Blackwell, 2004), pp. 281–89.

133 Ziegler quoted in "UN Expert Decries 'Assassination' By Hunger of Millions of Children," UN News Center, October 28, 2005. An assistant to Ziegler confirmed that the comments were "directly translated from the French," and added that in the past Ziegler had described the "world order" as "murderous" (Sally-Anne Way, personal communication, November 3, 2005). In a similar vein, Stephen Lewis, the UN Special Envoy for HIV/AIDS in Africa, stated of the global AIDS crisis: "This pandemic cannot be allowed to continue, and those who watch it unfold with a kind of pathological equanimity must be held to account. There may yet come a day when we have peacetime tribunals to deal with this particular version of crimes against humanity." Lewis quoted in Michael Mann, *Incoherent Empire* (London: Verso, 2005), p. 61.

134 Kal Holsti, personal communication, June 29, 2005.

135 See Henry Shue, *Basic Rights: Subsistence, Affluence, and U.S. Foreign Policy* (2nd edn) (Princeton, NJ: Princeton University Press, 1996), p. 207 (n. 17). I am citing Shue somewhat out of context: his phrase refers to specific historical events during the Second

World War, when "over 6 million Asians were . . . allowed to starve" under colonial (British and French) dominion. See also the discussion of imperial famines in Chapter 2. In his study of Belgian genocide in the Congo (see Chapter 2), Martin Ewans also refers to "genocide by neglect" in post-independence Africa, "with a massive, on-going loss of life . . . being treated in Europe [and elsewhere] with near total indifference." Ewans, *European Atrocity, African Catastrophe: Leopold II, the Congo Free State and its Aftermath* (London: RoutledgeCurzon, 2002), p. 252.

136 Galtung quoted in Joseph Nevins, *A Not-so-distant Horror: Mass Violence in East Timor* (London: RoutledgeCurzon, 2002), p. 252.

137 Sachs quoted in J. Tyrangiel, "Bono," *Time* (Latin American edition), March 4, 2002. Princeton professor Stephen F. Cohen has argued that the death toll exacted by the "nihilistic zealotry" of proponents of "savage capitalism" was *tens of millions in Russia alone* following the collapse of the Soviet Union: to US supporters of radical free-market policies there, "the lost lives of perhaps 100 million Russians seem not to matter, only American investments, loans, and reputations." See Cohen, *Failed Crusade: America and the Tragedy of Post-communist Russia* (New York: W.W. Norton, 2000), pp. 38, 50.

138 Holsti, personal communication, June 29, 2005.

139 The issue of "voluntarism" is pertinent, for example, in the case of tobacco sale and consumption. It kills millions of people each year around the world, and is strongly "pushed" by corporate actors; but it is also to a significant extent "pulled" by the voluntary (though also dependent) agency of the tobacco consumer.

140 Adam Jones, "Genocide and Structural Violence: Challenges of Definition, Prevention, and Intervention," forthcoming in Jones, ed., *New Directions in Genocide Research* (London: Routledge, 2011).

141 Norbert Finzsch, "'The Aborigines . . . Were Never Annihilated, and Still They are Becoming Extinct': Settler Imperialism and Genocide in Nineteenth-century America and Australia," in Moses, ed., *Empire, Colony, Genocide*, p. 253.

142 Ervin Staub does ask "Is mass killing ever justified?," but quickly answers in the negative, and even rejects the notion that "genocides and mass killings [are] ever 'rational' expressions of self-interest." Staub, *The Roots of Evil: The Origins of Genocide and Other Group Violence* (Cambridge: Cambridge University Press, 1989), pp. 11–12.

143 Levene, *Genocide in the Age of the Nation State, Vol. 2*, p. 8.

144 For example, this comment by "a British observer" of the genocide against Herero and Nama in German South West Africa (Chapter 3): "There can be no doubt, I think, that the war has been of an almost unmixed benefit to the German colony. Two warlike races have been exterminated, wells have been sunk, new water-holes discovered, the country mapped and covered with telegraph lines, and an enormous amount of capital has been laid out." Quoted in Mark Levene, "Why Is the Twentieth Century the Century of Genocide?," *Journal of World History*, 11: 2 (2000), pp. 315–16.

145 C.L.R. James, *The Black Jacobins: Toussaint L'Ouverture and the San Domingo Revolution* (2nd rev. edn) (New York: Vintage Books, 1989), pp. 373–74. Emphasis added.

146 "Subaltern genocide" and "genocides by the oppressed" are terms that Nicholas Robins and I coined in 2004, and deployed in our edited volume, *Genocides by the Oppressed: Subaltern Genocide in Theory and Practice* (Bloomington, IN: Indiana University Press, 2009).

147 Martin Shaw writes: "Groups are always to some extent actors, participants in conflict, as well as victims of it. . . . Liberal humanitarianism often finds it easiest to represent victim groups as pure victims – innocent civilian populations attacked by state or paramilitary power. Thus the West sees Iraqi Kurds and Kosova Albanians only as helpless civilians, not as groups that have supported political movements or guerrilla struggle. . . . Armed groups may even carry out mutually genocidal war, against each others' populations. In these situations, we need to recognize the complex patterns that make groups – and often individuals – both participants and victims, at different times." Shaw, *War and Genocide: Organized Killing in Modern Society* (Cambridge: Polity Press, 2003), p. 187.

148 Schabas, *Genocide in International Law*, p. 341.

149 The terms "worthy" and "unworthy" victims are deployed by Edward S. Herman and Noam Chomsky in *Manufacturing Consent: The Political Economy of the Mass Media* (New York: Pantheon, 1988).

150 In 1982, the Englishman Benjamin Whitaker was appointed Special Rapporteur by the UN's Economic and Social Council (ECOSOC) to revise a previously commissioned study on reform to the Genocide Convention. Whitaker's report was submitted in 1985 and "made a number of innovative and controversial conclusions . . . Whitaker wanted to amend the Convention in order to include political groups and groups based on sexual orientation, to exclude the plea of superior orders, to extend the punishable acts to those of 'advertent omission' and to pursue consideration of cultural genocide, 'ethnocide' and 'ecocide.'" Schabas, *Genocide in International Law*, p. 467. Whitaker's proposals so divided his sponsors that his report was tabled and never acted upon – in my view, an opportunity missed to substantially advance legal and scholarly understandings of genocide.

CHAPTER 2

State and Empire; War and Revolution

No study of genocide can proceed without attention to the four horsemen of the genocidal apocalypse, cited in this chapter's title. Tracing the connections between state-formation and empire-building; incorporating an understanding of war and revolution; and linking all these to genocidal outbreaks, is arguably genocide studies' single most fertile line of recent inquiry.

At the heart of these phenomena is the nation-state, contests over it, and resistance to it. Mark Levine's two-volume *Genocide in the Age of the Nation State* gives the game away in the title.[1] For Levene, and for many other scholars, the emergence of the modern nation-state represents a qualitative irruption in history, and the advent of a new form of genocide – perhaps even of "genocide" as such. Whether or not ancient leaders can be branded as *génocidaires* remains a matter of dispute. I did not hesitate to do so in Chapter 1. Yet however one chooses to classify the state violence inflicted over millennia, it is clear that it was common in the pre-modern age. Exterminatory mass violence, in short, is inseparable from the human record. And generally, it has been the agents of states and quasi-states – military and police formations, colonists, bureaucratic administrators – that have been the most prominent and *essential* perpetrators. Their systematic behavior in various locations over time is what helps to distinguish genocide – legally, practically, and historically – from other patterned and collective violence, like the "riots and pogroms" of Paul Brass's classic study (see Chapter 12).

The central emphasis on state and empire in recent key works of genocide studies pivots on the concepts of social ordering and "legibility," ethnonational collectivity, and racial hierarchy and "purity" that emerged from the Enlightenment and its multiple philosophical and scientific revolutions. The modern state developed into a bureaucratically complex and administratively capacious entity. As it did, it tried to impose a "legible" order upon social formations that were often patchwork and fragmented, from the state's Olympian perspective. Political scientist James C. Scott's *Seeing Like a State* shows how this produced not only ugly, hyper-rational architectural schemes (viz. Brasilia), but also a hubris that fueled, in turn, some of modernity's greatest catastrophes, such as Stalin's collectivization campaigns and Mao's "Great Leap Forward" (Chapter 5).[2]

Classical and modern states alike have coalesced and expanded through acts of imperialism and colonization. The growing emphasis on these processes in genocide studies, led by the European/Australasian school gathered in Dirk Moses's *Empire, Colony, Genocide* collection, has supplemented the previous focus on the atrocities of fascism and communism. The new agenda, for the first time, directs systematic attention to a third major genocidal "-ism" – colonialism – and to the imperial holocausts that Western and other countries unleashed on indigenous populations during the great waves of Western colonization (sixteenth to twentieth centuries). Most of this colonial expansion was capitalist or proto-capitalist in nature, certainly with regard to the most destructive institutions imposed on native peoples. Indeed, it was the gold and silver of the Spanish American mines, sustained by genocidal slave labor and circulated throughout Europe by indebted Spanish rulers, that helped to kick-start modern capitalism. These tendencies remain prominent today, in a post-colonial period in which capitalism reigns supreme as a system of economic organization and exploitation. The fact that the most powerful "neo-colonial" players continue to be self-proclaimed democratic exemplars, as they were in the eighteenth and nineteenth centuries, may undermine the "democratic peace" hypothesis that figured in some early formulations of genocide and genocide prevention (see further discussion in Chapter 12).

Incorporating a global-comparative perspective on the genocides of the last half-millennium has enabled important advances in the understanding of events central to the genocide studies field – such as the process of Ottoman imperial dissolution, *reciprocal* genocidal killing (during the "Unweaving" in the Balkans), and complex international jockeying that factored into the massive anti-Christian slaughters in Anatolia in 1915 and thereafter (Chapter 4). Perhaps surprisingly, it is the most iconic genocide of all, the Jewish Holocaust, that has benefited most from these new framings. Analysts from Raul Hilberg to Zygmunt Bauman and Götz Aly had emphasized the statist-bureaucratic dimension of the Holocaust. Daniel Feierstein has now expanded on this to suggest that the Nazi state's very self-conception, its "reading" of the German population, led it to fundamentally distrust and anathematize "cosmopolitan" and "stateless" elements – Jews and Roma/Gypsies above all. These were depicted as standing in opposition, not only to the *German* state, but to the very *idea* and *project* of a state. Moreover, thanks to the work of historians like Benjamin Madley, Jürgen Zimmerer, and Jan-Bart Gewald, we better perceive the link between the Nazis and earlier German imperialists – notably those who orchestrated the systematic mass murder of the Herero and Nama peoples of present-day Namibia in 1904–07 (see Chapter 3). In the wake of seminal studies by (among others) historians Karel Berkhoff, Wendy Lower, and Mark Mazower, we also have for the first time a clear sense of the imperial contours and character of Nazi policies, in the occupied east above all (Poland, Belorussia, Ukraine, Russia).[3] We see how this empire was imagined, "sold" to Germans, and administered along traditional Western colonial lines – in part as a claiming or reclaiming of Germany's "place in the sun," following the failed imperial projects of previous decades.

If Germany's annihilation war in the east was fundamentally one of imperial conquest, then this points to war's role in enabling and justifying genocides throughout history. And as a vision of radical social revolution through titanic social engineering, it attests to the connection between genocide and the world-changing hubris that often underpins it – whether from a leftist-communist or rightist-capitalist direction. Such grand projects of social revolution, state-building, and political-imperial expansion inevitably generate resistance – and so, much of the warmaking of revolutionary and irredentist states becomes *counterinsurgent* violence. This dynamic is no less central to an understanding of war, revolution, and genocide for its involving, to some extent, a *reactive* stance and *retributive* policy on the state's part.

The present chapter addresses these "four horsemen" of genocide – state-building, imperialism/colonialism, war, and social revolution – and explores their interactions and interpenetrations. This paves the way for the exploration of genocide case-studies presented in Part 2 of the book.

THE STATE, IMPERIALISM, AND GENOCIDE

Imperialism is "a policy undertaken by a state to directly control foreign economic, physical, and cultural resources."[4] Colonialism is "a specific form of imperialism involving the establishment and maintenance, for an extended period of time, of rule over an alien people that is separate from and subordinate to the ruling power."[5]

Imperialism and colonialism are mapped into the DNA of the state, both in its classical and its modern guise. The units that we know as states or nation-states were generally created by processes of imperial expansion followed by *internal* colonialism.[6] The designated or desirable boundaries of the state were first imposed on coveted lands through imperialism, then actualized, rationalized, made "legible" and exploitable by the imposition of members of the dominant group or its surrogates upon adjacent or nearby territories and populations. The internal expansion of the state's capacities continued apace throughout the early modern period. Processes of turning *Peasants into Frenchmen*, to cite Eugen Weber – and into Germans, Britons, Americans, Soviets – could be evolutionary and benign, in Raphael Lemkin's view. But often, as in the Vendée case described in Chapter 1, the state's centralizing project was perceived as a mortal threat by other populations and power centers. The crushing of resistance to the statist-expansionist enterprise inevitably assumed a genocidal scale and character, and continues to do so.

The greatest relevance of the internal-colonialism concept is for indigenous populations worldwide. Native people occupy marginal positions both territorially and socially; their traditional homelands are often coveted by expanding state settlement from the center. Profits flow from periphery to core; the environment is ravaged. The result is the undermining and dissolution, often the destruction, of indigenous societies, accomplished by massacres, selective killings, expulsions, coerced labor, disease, and substance abuse. Other examples of internal colonialism in this book include the Chinese in Tibet (Chapter 5); Stalin's USSR vis-à-vis both the Soviet countryside and minority ethnicities (Chapter 5);[7] and Indonesia in East Timor (Chapter 7).

Genocide is further interwoven with colonialism in the phenomenon of *settler colonialism*. Here, the metropolitan power encourages or dispatches colonists to "settle" the territory. (In the British Empire, this marks the difference between settler colonies such as Canada, Australia, and New Zealand; and the Indian subcontinent, where just 25,000 Britons administered a vast realm.) Settler colonialism implies occupation of the land, and is often linked to genocide against indigenous peoples (and genocidally tinged rebellions against colonialism) (see Chapter 3). Settler colonies may also be born of expansionist and internal-colonialist projects close to the metropolitan core. The genocidal or near-genocidal campaigns against Ireland's and Scotland's native inhabitants from the sixteenth to nineteenth centuries,[8] for example, prompted the migration under massive duress of millions of Irish and Scottish to the British settler colonies and the United States. Likewise, the drive against "asocial" elements and political dissidents resulted in the transportation of tens of thousands of prisoners to the Australian penal colonies.[9] Ironically, it was sometimes representatives of these invaded and criminalized populations, thrust to the "sharp end" of colonial invasions, who proved energetic exponents and practitioners of genocide against indigenous populations.

Finally, we should expand upon the dimension of *neo-colonialism*. The concept is ambiguous and contested, but also useful. Under neo-colonialism, formal political rule is abandoned, while colonial structures of economic, political, and cultural control remain. The resulting exploitation may have genocidal consequences. Individual interventions with arguably genocidal consequences may be linked to prior colonial or quasi-colonial relationships (e.g., France in Rwanda before and during the 1994 genocide; Britain and the US in Iraq in 1991 and 2003). Many commentators also consider *structural violence* – that is, the destructive power residing in social and economic structures – to reflect neo-colonialism: the former colonial powers have maintained their hegemony over the formerly colonized ("Third") world, and immense disparities of wealth and well-being remain, producing "poorcide" in S.P. Udayakumar's framing (see p. 28).

The brief examination of genocide in classical and early modern times (Chapter 1) showed how frequently genocide accompanied imperial expansion and colonialism. In the modern era, the destruction of indigenous peoples has been a pervasive feature of these institutions, and is analyzed as a global phenomenon in Chapter 3. The communist tyrannies studied in Chapters 5 and 7 had a brazenly statist and imperial dimension, to be considered in its place. It remains here to provide an overview of some other key cases of genocide under colonial and imperial regimes in the past two centuries.

Imperial famines

"Famine crimes" or "genocidal famines" have increasingly drawn genocide scholars' attention.[10] The most extensively studied cases are Stalin's USSR (Chapter 5), Mao's China, and Ethiopia under the Dergue regime. Recently the North Korean case, in which up to two million people may have starved to death while the government remained inert, has sparked outrage (also explored in Chapter 5). The literature has focused strongly on cases of famine under dictatorial and authoritarian regimes. Influenced by Nobel Prize-winning economist Amartya Sen, who demonstrated that "there has never been a famine in a functioning multiparty democracy,"[11] this has produced groundbreaking case studies such as Robert Conquest's *The Harvest of Sorrow* (USSR) and Jasper Becker's *Hungry Ghosts* (China). The millions of dead in these catastrophes, from starvation and disease, form a substantial part of the indictment of communist regimes in the compendium, *The Black Book of Communism*.[12]

However, historian Mike Davis's *Late Victorian Holocausts* reminds us that liberal regimes have also been complicit in such crimes – extending far beyond the notorious example of the Great Hunger in 1840s Ireland.[13] Davis's subject is the epic famines of the later nineteenth and early twentieth centuries, linked both to nature (the El Niño phenomenon) and state policy, which devastated peasant societies from China to Brazil. He shares Sen's conviction that famines are not blows of blind fate, but "social crises that represent the failures of particular economic and political systems." Specifically, he asserts that "imperial policies towards starving 'subjects' were often the exact moral equivalents of bombs dropped from 18,000 feet."

India was largely free of famine under the Mogul emperors, but British administrators refused to follow the Mogul example of laying in sufficient emergency grain stocks. When famine struck, they imposed free-market policies that were nothing more than a "mask for colonial genocide," according to Davis. They continued ruinous collections of tax arrears, evincing greater concern for India's balance of payments than for "the holocaust in lives." When the British did set up relief camps, they were work camps, which "provided less sustenance for hard labor than the infamous Buchenwald concentration camp and less than half of the modern caloric standard recommended for adult males by the Indian government." The death-toll in the famine of 1897–98 alone, including associated disease epidemics, may have exceeded eleven million. "Twelve to 16 million was the death toll commonly reported in the world press, which promptly nominated this the 'famine of the century.' This dismal title, however, was almost immediately usurped by the even greater drought and deadlier famine of 1899–1902." In 1901, the leading British medical journal the *Lancet* suggested that "a conservative estimate of excess mortality in India in the previous decade . . . was 19 million," a total that "a number of historians . . . have accepted . . . as an order-of-magnitude approximation for the combined mortality of the 1896–1902 crisis."[14]

Overall, Davis argued that market mechanisms imposed in colonial (e.g., India) and neo-colonial contexts (e.g., China and Brazil) inflicted massive excess mortality. "There is persuasive evidence that peasants and farm laborers became dramatically more pregnable to natural disaster after 1850 as their local economies were violently incorporated into the world market. . . . Commercialization went hand in hand with

Figure 2.1 "The Famine in India – Natives Waiting for Relief in Bangalore." Engraving in *The Illustrated London News*, 1877. In subjugated India and Ireland in the nineteenth century, British imperialists pioneered the "faminogenic" catastrophes of the modern period, with famine relief sacrificed to the laws of the market or, in the Stalinist and Maoist cases, the drive for communist utopia (see Chapter 5). In all these cases, the ruling regimes *exported* foodstuffs on a large scale throughout the famines.

Source: Scanned from the original October 20, 1877 issue of *The Illustrated London News*, in the author's collection.

pauperization."[15] He explicitly linked colonial and neo-colonial relations to the economic structures and policies that devastated once-thriving economies, and produced the "Third World" of the post-colonial era.

The Congo "rubber terror"

Thanks to novelist Joseph Conrad's *Heart of Darkness*, published early in the twentieth century, the murderous exploitation of the Congo by Belgium's King Leopold has attained almost mythic status.[16] However, not until the publication of Adam Hochschild's *King Leopold's Ghost*, at the end of the last century, did contemporary audiences come to appreciate the scale of the destruction inflicted on the Congo, as well as the public outcry at the time that produced one of the first truly international campaigns for human rights.

Conrad's novella was based on a river voyage into the interior of the Congo, during which he witnessed what he called "the vilest scramble for loot that ever disfigured the history of human conscience and geographical exploration."[17] The territory that became the so-called Congo Free State was, and remains, immense (see Map 9a.1 in Box 9a). In 1874, King Leopold commissioned British explorer Henry Stanley to secure for the monarch a place in the imperial sun. By 1885, Leopold had established the Congo as his personal fief, free of oversight from the Belgian parliament. Ivory was the prize he first hungered for, then rubber as the pneumatic tire revolutionized road travel. To muster the forced labor (*corvée*) needed to supply these goods, Leopold's agents imposed a reign of terror on African populations.

The result was one of the most destructive and all-encompassing *corvée* institutions the world has known. It led to "a death toll of Holocaust dimensions," in Hochschild's estimation,[18] such that "Leopold's African regime became a byword for exploitation and genocide."[19] Male rubber tappers and porters were mercilessly exploited and driven to death. A Belgian politician, Edmond Picard, encountered a caravan of conscripts:

> Incessantly, we met these porters . . . black, miserable, their only clothing a horrible dirty loincloth . . . most of them sickly, their strength sapped by exhaustion and inadequate food, which consisted of a handful of rice and stinking dried fish, pitiable walking caryatids . . . organised in a system of human transport, requisitioned by the State with its irresistible *force publique* [militia], delivered by chiefs whose slaves they are and who purloin their pay . . . dying on the road or, their journey ended, dying from the overwork in their villages.[20]

The precipitous population decline during Leopold's rule remains astonishing. Hochschild accepted the conclusions of a Belgian government commission that "the population of the territory had 'been reduced by half.'" "In 1924," he added, "the population was reckoned at ten million, a figure confirmed by later counts. This would mean, according to the estimates, that during the Leopold period and its immediate aftermath the population of the territory dropped by approximately ten million people."[21] During this time, the region was also swept by an epidemic of

Figure 2.2   Imperial genocide: the wealth of the Congo, gathered by forced labor, is siphoned off by Belgian King Leopold.

Source: Scanned from Martin Evans, *European Atrocity, African Catastrophe*. Original source unknown.

sleeping sickness, "one of the most disastrous plagues recorded in human history."[22] However, as with indigenous peoples elsewhere, the impact of disease was exacerbated by slavery and privation, and vice versa: "The responsibility for this disaster is no less Leopold's because it was a compound one."[23] And the demographic data presented by Hochschild demonstrated a shocking under-representation of adult males in the Congolese population, indicating that genocide claimed millions of lives.[24] "Sifting such figures today is like sifting the ruins of an Auschwitz crematorium," wrote Hochschild. "They do not tell you precise death tolls, but they reek of mass murder."[25]

The only bright side to this, "one of the most appalling slaughters known to have been brought about by human agency,"[26] was an international protest movement, led by Joseph Conrad, Sir Arthur Conan Doyle – author of the Sherlock Holmes stories – and the Irishman Roger Casement. The Association spread across Europe and North America, and sponsored investigative exposés of Leopold's Congo.[27] All of this increased pressure on King Leopold to subject his territory to outside oversight. Finally, in 1908, Leopold agreed to sell his enormous fief to the Belgian government. Subsequent parliamentary monitoring appears to have substantially reduced mortality, though the "rubber terror" only truly lapsed after the First World War.

Belgium remained the colonial power in the territory until 1960, when it handed over the Congo to the pro-Western dictator, Mobutu Sese Seko. Early in the twenty-first century, the Congo is again torn apart by genocide, amidst the most destructive military conflict since the Second World War – a grim echo of the killing that rent the region under Leopold's rule (see Box 9a).

The Japanese in East and Southeast Asia

Japanese imperialism, founded on invasions of Korea and Taiwan in the late nineteenth century, grew by leaps and bounds under the military regime established during the 1930s. Domestic persecution of communists and other political opponents merged with aggressive expansion. In 1931, the Japanese invaded the mineral-rich Chinese region of Manchuria, setting up the puppet state of Manchukuo the following year.

In 1937, Japan effectively launched the Second World War, invading China's eastern seaboard and key interior points. The campaign featured air attacks that killed tens of thousands of civilians and even more intensive atrocities by troops on the ground. The occupation of the Chinese capital, Nanjing, in December 1937 became a global byword for war crimes. Japanese forces slaughtered as many as 200,000 Chinese men of "battle age," and raped tens of thousands of women and children – often murdering and mutilating their victims thereafter (see Chapter 13). "There are executions everywhere," wrote John Rabe, a German businessman who witnessed the atrocities of the "Rape of Nanjing," and worked indefatigably to save civilian lives (see p. 409). "You hear of nothing but rape. . . . The devastation the Japanese have wreaked here is almost beyond description."[28] Over the course of the Japanese occupation (1937–45), "nearly 2,600,000 unarmed Chinese civilians" were killed, together with half a million to one million prisoners of war.[29]

In December 1941, Japan coordinated its surprise attack on the US Pacific Fleet at Pearl Harbor with a lightning invasion of Southeast Asia. This brought the Philippines, Malaya (peninsular Malaysia), Singapore, and Indonesia under its direct rule. (Satellite control was established in Indochina, in collusion with the Vichy French regime.) Large-scale summary killings of civilians, death marches of Asian and European populations, and atrocities against Allied prisoners-of-war all figured in the postwar war-crimes trials (Chapter 15). The Japanese also imposed a *corvée* labor system, one of the worst in modern history, throughout the occupied territories. Not only did the notorious Burma–Thailand railroad kill 16,000 of the 46–50,000 Allied

Figure 2.3 Furious at popular resistance to their conquests, Japanese forces used captured Chinese prisoners-of-war as targets for bayonet practice, while others stood and enjoyed the spectacle. As many as 200,000 Chinese men, and tens of thousands of women, were murdered during the "Rape of Nanjing" in 1937–38.

Source: www.nanking-massacre.com.

Figure 2.4 Chinese American author Iris Chang revived the story of the Nanjing atrocities for contemporary readers with her powerful 1997 book, *The Rape of Nanking*. Tragically, Chang, who was plagued by depression, committed suicide in November 2004 at the age of 36. A bronze sculpture of her is today found in the Nanjing Massacre Memorial Hall in China (see http://en.wikipedia.org/wiki/File:Iris_chang.jpg).

Source: Jimmy Estimada/Courtesy Ying-Ying Chang/www.irischangmemorialfund.net.

prisoners forced to work on it, but "as many as 100,000 of the 120,000 to 150,000 Asian forced laborers may have died . . . ."[30] The trafficking of Asian women for prostitution (the so-called "comfort women") formed an integral part of this forced-labor system. Regionwide, the death-toll of *corvée* laborers probably approached, or even exceeded, one million. Both the "comfort women" and male forced laborers have in recent years petitioned the Japanese government for acknowledgment and material compensation, with some success but also much stonewalling (see Chapter 14).[31]

Like their Nazi counterparts, the Japanese believed themselves to be superior beings. Subject races were not considered "subhuman" in the Nazi fashion, but they were clearly regarded as inferior, and were usually assigned a helot status in the "Greater Asian Co-Prosperity Sphere." Japanese fantasies of racial supremacy also led to a Nazi-style preoccupation with genocidal technologies, reflected most notably in the biological warfare program and gruesome medical experiments. Unit 731 in Manchuria produced chemical and biological weapons that were tested on prisoners-of-war and civilians, and deployed throughout the war theater. In China, according to Japanese historian Yuki Tanaka,

> In Zhejiang province, biological weapons were used six times between September 18 and October 7, 1940. . . . Around the same time 270 kilograms of typhoid, paratyphoid, cholera, and plague bacteria were sent to Nanjing and central China for use by Japanese battalions on the battlefield. . . . After the outbreak of World War II, the Japanese continued to use biological weapons against the Chinese. They sprayed cholera, typhoid, plague, and dysentery pathogens in the Jinhua area of Zhejiang province in June and July 1942. . . . It is [also] well known that Unit 731 used large numbers of Chinese people for experiments. Many Chinese who rebelled against the Japanese occupation were arrested and sent to Pingfan where they became guinea pigs for Unit 731. . . . When they were being experimented on, the [subjects] were transferred from the main prison to individual cells where they were infected with particular pathogens by such means as injections or being given contaminated food or water. . . . After succumbing to the disease, the prisoners were usually dissected, and their bodies were then cremated within the compound.[32]

In an ironic outcome from which Nazi scientists also benefited, after the Second World War the participants in Unit 731 atrocities were granted immunity from prosecution – so long as they shared their knowledge of chemical and biological warfare, and the results of their atrocious experiments, with US authorities (see Chapter 15).[33]

The US in Indochina

With the possible exception of the French war to retain Algeria (1958–62), no imperial intervention in the twentieth century provoked as much dissent and political upheaval in the colonial power as the US's long war in Vietnam. And in the post-World War Two period, none was so destructive.

A French attempt in 1945–54 to reconquer Vietnam was defeated by a nationalist guerrilla movement under Ho Chi Minh and his military commander, Vo Nguyen Giap. The country was divided between a Chinese client regime in the North and a US client regime in the South. Under the Geneva agreements of 1954, this was supposed to be temporary. But recognizing that Ho would likely win nationwide elections scheduled for 1956, Ngo Dinh Diem's regime refused to hold them. After 1961, the US stepped up direct military intervention. In 1965, hundreds of thousands of US troops occupied the country to combat the South Vietnamese guerrillas (Viet Cong), as well as regular North Vietnamese forces infiltrating down the "Ho Chi Minh Trail" through southern Laos and eastern Cambodia.

About seven million tons of bombs and other munitions were dropped on North and (especially) South Vietnam during the course of the war. *This was more than was dropped by all countries in all theaters of the Second World War.* The bombing was combined with the creation of a network of "model villages" in the South Vietnamese countryside, kept under close US and South Vietnamese military observation.

Beyond these villages, essentially concentration camps, large swathes of the countryside were liable to be designated as "free-fire zones," in which anyone living was assumed to be an enemy. Populations who resisted evacuation risked annihilation from the air and massacre by US and South Vietnamese ground forces. The most infamous such event was the My Lai massacre – a four-hour-long rampage by US troops on March 16, 1968, in the village of Son My and its constituent hamlets of My Lai, My Khe, and Co Luy in Quang Ngai province. Infuriated by guerrilla attacks, US troops of Charlie Company, 1st Battalion slaughtered, raped, and wreaked material destruction.[34] The My Lai memorial plaque today lists 504 victims. A handful of troops resisted orders to kill, and genuine rescuers emerged – most heroically Lt.-Col. Hugh Thompson, Jr., who witnessed the killing from his helicopter, landed, and interposed himself between fleeing villagers and their would-be murderers, ordering his men to fire on the US forces if they advanced (see pp. 407–09). An extensive official cover-up of the massacre was mounted, until investigative reporter Seymour Hersh blew the lid off the case in articles for the *St. Louis Post-Dispatch* in November 1969.[35] An investigation was launched, but only one perpetrator – Lt. William Calley – was convicted. After a couple of years of house arrest, he was pardoned by President Richard Nixon. Calley lived thereafter in obscurity, until he emerged in 2009 to publicly apologize for his crimes.[36] Research by investigative reporters from the *Toledo Blade* and other publications has established that My Lai was no isolated incident. Rather, massacres were common for US forces fighting to "pacify" the south, after the Viet Cong/North Vietnamese "Tet Offensive" of 1968 rocked US popular support of the war to its foundations.[37]

Figure 2.5 The My Lai massacre of March 16, 1968, was the largest, but far from the only, genocidal massacre inflicted during the US imperial "pacification" of South Vietnam in 1968–69. Ronald K. Haeberle, an army photographer, captured this image of Vietnamese children and women rounded up in My Lai hamlet, seconds before they were gunned down by US troops. According to an army publicist accompanying the photographer (*LIFE*, December 5, 1969), "Haeberle jumped in to take a picture of the group of women. The picture shows the thirteen-year-old girl hiding behind her mother, trying to button the top of her pyjamas. When they noticed Ron, they left off and turned away as if everything was normal. Then a soldier asked, 'Well, what'll we do with 'em?' 'Kill 'em,' another answered. I heard an M60 go off, a light machine-gun, and when we turned all of them and the kids with them were dead."

Source: Ronald K. Haeberle/US Army/Wikimedia Commons.

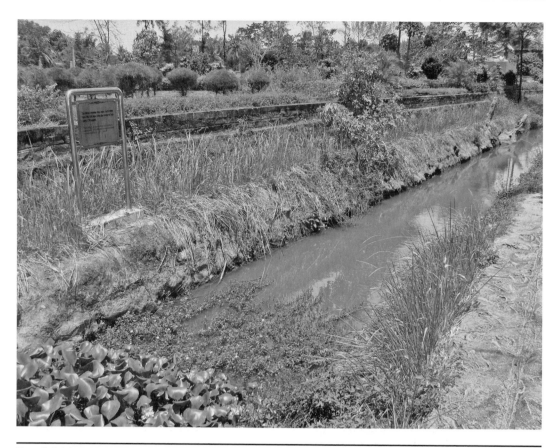

Figure 2.6 The irrigation ditch in My Lai hamlet where 170 Vietnamese villagers were gathered and slaughtered by US soldiers, now part of the My Lai massacre memorial site and museum (see also Figure 14.2, p. 503).

Source: Author's photo, July 2009.

In 1970, Nixon widened the war, stepping up the "secret" bombing of neighboring Cambodia on a scale that is only now being recognized (and fueling the rise of the genocidal Khmer Rouge; see Chapter 7). Extensive areas of Laos, notably the Plain of Jars and the Bolaven Plateau, were subjected to saturation bombing that killed their inhabitants or terrorized them into flight. The bombing continued until 1973, when a peace agreement was signed and most US soldiers withdrew from South Vietnam. Two years later, North Vietnamese forces invaded and conquered South Vietnam.

The human cost of the war to the US was some 58,000 soldiers killed. In Indochina, the toll was catastrophic. Somewhere between two million and five million Indochinese died, mostly at the hands of the US and its allies. In addition, the massive application of chemical warfare, aimed primarily at defoliating the countryside of forest cover in which guerrilla forces could hide, poisoned the soil and food chain.[38] "The lingering effects of chemical warfare poisoning continue to plague the health of adult Vietnamese (and ex-GIs) while causing increased birth defects. Samples of soil, water, food and body fat of Vietnamese continue to the present day to reveal dangerously elevated levels of dioxin." An estimated "3.5

million landmines and 300,000 tons of unexploded ordnance [UXO]" still litter the countryside, killing "several thousand" Vietnamese every year – at least 40,000 since the war ended in 1975.[39] Laos, too, is laced with UXO; hundreds of rural residents are killed and maimed annually, particularly younger children.[40]

The international revulsion that the Indochina war evoked led to the creation, in 1966, of an informal International War Crimes Tribunal under the aegis of the British philosopher Bertrand Russell. The Russell Tribunal panelists were "unanimous in finding the US guilty for using illegal weapons, maltreating prisoners of war and civilians, and aggressing against Laos." Most controversially, "there was a unanimous vote of guilty on the genocide charge."[41] A leading figure in this "citizens' tribunal" (see Chapter 15) was the French philosopher Jean-Paul Sartre, who wrote "On Genocide," an essay that made "a striking case for regarding the American war in Vietnam as genocide legally and conceptually."[42] Those fighting the war, Sartre argued, were "*living out* the only possible relationship between an overindustrialized country and an underdeveloped country, that is to say, a genocidal relationship implemented through racism."[43] Genocide scholar Leo Kuper likewise called the war genocidal, a verdict also rendered *prima facie* by the human rights and international law theorist, Richard Falk.[44] Fresh revelations of the extent of the genocidal massacres in South Vietnam in 1968–69, and of the true scale of the bombing of Cambodia, will likely bolster such assessments.[45]

The Soviets in Afghanistan

Soviet intervention in Afghanistan was a continuation of the historic Russian drive for influence and control along the imperial periphery. Severely mauled by the Nazi invasion during the Second World War, the Soviets thereafter established authoritarian police states in Eastern Europe, with forays beyond, notably in Asia and Africa.

Within the Soviet empire, governance strategies varied. In Central and Eastern Europe, with the exception of postwar East Germany and the Hungarian uprising of 1956 (in which some 25,000 were killed), Soviet imperial power did not produce large-scale killing. Afghanistan was different. Years of growing Soviet influence culminated in the establishment of a Soviet client government in Kabul in April 1978. In 1979, a reign of terror inflicted by President Hafizullah Amin further destabilized Afghan society. Finally, in December 1979, 25,000 Soviet troops invaded to "restore stability." Amin, who had outlived his usefulness, was killed at the outset of the invasion, and replaced by a more compliant Soviet proxy, Babrak Karmal. Occupying forces rapidly swelled to around 85,000.

The occupation spawned an initially ragtag but, with US assistance, increasingly coherent Islamist-nationalist resistance, the *mujahedin*. Osama bin Laden began his trajectory as a foreign volunteer with the *mujahedin*, as did others who would later wage war on the West. The Soviets responded with collective atrocity. In "a ferocious scorched-earth campaign that combined the merciless destructiveness of Genghis Khan's Mongols with the calculated terrorism of Stalin,"[46] the Soviets inflicted massive civilian destruction, recalling the worst US actions in Indochina. According to Afghanistan specialist Rosanne Klass,

Figure 2.7   Soviet troops round up young Afghan men in a counterinsurgency sweep in 1985. The fate of the men is unknown, but such sweeps were typically accompanied by harsh interrogation or torture, and widespread summary execution. Such measures are the norm when imperial powers seek, sometimes by genocidal means, to cow and subjugate a restive population (see Chapter 13). The Soviets repeated them in the campaign against the population of Chechnya in the 1990s and 2000s (Box 5a). In central respects, Russia's wars in Chechnya were racist acts of vengeance against Muslim populations, fueled by the humiliating defeat in Afghanistan. As many as two million people were killed during the decade-long Soviet occupation of the country (1979–89).

Source: Wikimedia Commons.

From January 1980 on . . . the Soviets made genocide a coherent, systematic policy. . . . Soviet and local communist forces targeted the rural civilian population, not the armed resistance. . . . Operational patterns (particularly air attacks) indicated a systematic effort to depopulate selected areas on an ethnic basis. . . . Overall Soviet strategy focused on emptying out the predominantly Pashtun areas, thereby altering the ethnic makeup of Afghanistan. . . . Thousands of very young children were (often forcibly) sent to the USSR and Eastern Europe for ten years for preparatory indoctrination; few if any have returned.

Air attacks through the southern and eastern provinces methodically killed hundreds of thousands and resulted in the mass exodus of millions, creating a depopulated no-man's-land in large areas along the Afghanistan–Pakistan border. In addition to the bombings, which reached their peak in 1986, the Soviets used terror – chemical weapons, weapons targeting children, gruesome localized atrocities, and the destruction of crops, orchards, animals, food supplies, and water sources – to empty out whole districts.[47]

Aerial bombing never assumed the saturation levels of Indochina. But once the Soviets realized that a genuinely popular insurgency had taken root, aerial attacks became collective and indiscriminate in their targeting. A former Soviet fighter pilot, Alexander Rutskoi, related during a conversation on the war in Chechnya in the 1990s (Box 5a) his view "that Russia should use the same approach he had employed in Afghanistan: 'A *kishlak* [village] fires at us and kills someone. I send a couple of planes and there is nothing left of the *kishlak*. After I've burned a couple of *kishlaks* they stop shooting.'"[48] As US atrocities in Vietnam mirrored the "Indian wars" of the past,[49] there are clear echoes in the Afghanistan campaign of Russia's ruthless wars of imperial expansion against Muslim minorities in the nineteenth century.

Ground-level counterinsurgency campaigns in Vietnam produced genocidal massacres at My Lai and elsewhere. Much the same occurred in the Soviets' Afghan war, in which the imperial strategy, according to Jeri Laber and Barnett Rubin, was "to spread terror in the countryside so that villagers will either be afraid to assist the resistance fighters who depend on them for food and shelter or be forced to leave." Benjamin Valentino described the mass-murderous consequences:

> Executions often were carried out with extreme savagery and in full public view, presumably to further intimidate the population. Since the Soviets generally lacked the information necessary to identify guerrilla supporters on an individual basis, they often slaughtered entire villages, including women and children. Two defectors from the Soviet army claimed that these atrocities were not merely the actions of out-of-control troops. In a typical operation, rather, "an officer decides to have a village searched to see if there are any rebels in it. . . . What usually happens is we found a cartridge or a bullet. The officers said: 'This is a bandit village; it must be destroyed.'. . . The men and young men are usually shot right where they are. And the women, what they do is try to kill them with grenades."[50]

"Conservative estimates put Afghan deaths at 1.25 million, or 9 percent of the population, with another three-quarters of a million wounded."[51] Some five million Afghans fled to Pakistan and Iran – one of the largest refugee flows in history.[52]

The Afghanistan–Vietnam comparison explored in these passages has often been advanced, but sometimes with attention to alleged differences between the two. In a well-known article for the *Denver Journal of International Law and Policy*, sociologist Helen Fein undertook to examine whether either or both cases constituted genocide. Her verdict on Vietnam was that while "repeated and substantive charges of war crimes . . . appear well-founded," the charge of "genocide . . . simply [is] not supported by the acts cited." In the Soviet case, however, Fein catalogued "repeated and substantive charges of 'depopulation,' massacre, deliberate injury, forced transfer of the children of Afghanis, and occasional charges of genocide." Combined, they "sustain[ed] a prima facie charge of genocide as well as charges of war crimes."[53]

One may disagree with Fein's gentler judgment about US conduct in Indochina (which featured bombing on a scale and of an intensity never matched in Afghanistan, for example). But it is hard to dispute the validity of the genocide framework for this instance of Soviet imperialism.

IMPERIAL ASCENT AND DISSOLUTION

Empires are most destructive in their waxing and waning phases. The onset of empire is often marked by vigorous imperial violence, much of which derives from – and is sometimes a desperate response to – the resistance of indigenous populations which may remain unvanquished, even against all technological and epidemiological odds.

Once consolidated, however, empires probably tend toward at least the measure of accommodation necessary for stable exploitation – the physical preservation of subject peoples, sometimes even their flourishing. In his rich study of the rise and decline of empires, and the skein of genocide woven through it, Mark Levene argued that "colonial genocides made no obvious sense," because empires have "inbuilt, usually self-interested and self-regulatory mechanisms for the avoidance of exterminatory conflict with subject peoples . . . " These include "political policies and administrative practices" that "at least allow[ed] their diverse peoples to co-exist with one another, often even where this involved widely divergent cultures, not to mention social and economic habits."[54]

When that order breaks down, and especially when multiethnic empires begin to dissolve in intercommunal strife, genocide rears anew. Now it is fueled and exacerbated by fear, even terror, at the encirclement, besieging, and looming collapse of the imperial order. When the heart of the empire is under threat of conquest, partition, and extinction, as with Constantinople and Vienna during the waning days of the Ottoman and Austro-Hungarian empires, the imperial backlash may be especially violent. When those empires experienced "relatively stable conditions" and "did not feel threatened," "ethnographic diversity . . . remained tenable." But "take away this stability and the most immediate and likely effect was a much more pronouncedly aggressive state ethnic policy with particularly dire consequences . . . "[55]

An essential element here is the perception of *diminution, humiliation,* and *dispossession*. From a psychopathological perspective, no context is more toxic, no fuel more combustible. We consider fear and humiliation more closely – along with the subaltern desires for vengeance that they engender – in Chapter 10's discussion of psychological perspectives on genocide.

These tendencies also shape the aftermath of empire – sometimes for centuries. Memories of past dispossessions become inextricably bound up with a sense of victimization, and the contemporary need for violent redress of perceived wrongs. For Levene, this is one of the features that may partly explain a specifically German *Sonderweg* (special path) to the Holocaust:

> The German example may help identify a particular type of state with the potentiality for genocide not so much on the basis of whether it is labeled as authoritarian, revolutionary, ethnically stratified or whatever . . . so much as one which suffers from what one might call a chronic 'strong' state–'weak' state syndrome. . . . Such states seem to have what one might only describe as a collective inferiority complex: that is, of a conviction shared by policy makers, opinion formers and possibly significant sections of their general population that

the position which they believe *ought* to be theirs in terms of international status is forever being denied or blocked off to them.[56]

This mentality pervaded not only Nazi actions, but the Ottoman empire's destruction of its Christian minorities (Chapter 5), the Khmer Rouge genocide in Cambodia in the 1970s (Chapter 7), and the Serb victimization narrative that fuelled the Bosnian genocide of the 1990s (Chapter 8).[57] A final example displaying this trajectory of genocidal ascent and genocidal decline is the Russian/Soviet/Chechen experience (Chapter 5 and Box 5a). The frequently exterminatory violence of tsarist Russia's conquest of the Caucasus, from the late 1820s to the 1860s, was followed by a measure of stability in the final decades of the tsarist empire, and sporadic stability – to the extent that any population enjoyed it – under Soviet and early Stalinist rule. But when the Stalinist regime felt itself mortally threatened in 1941–42, particularly in the peripheral areas conquered by its tsarist forebears, the uprooting was again epic in scale and the violence again mass-murderous, for Chechens and for other minority peoples besides. And the tendency can be traced to the contemporary period, with the wars-unto-genocide launched by the Yeltsin and Putin regimes against rebellious Chechnya (Box 5a). The pathological excesses of the violence reflect a post-Soviet Russia reduced and vulnerable, stripped of its quasi-colonies in eastern Europe and central Asia, and obsessed with holding onto minority-dominated territories on the fringes of the shrunken empire.

GENOCIDE AND WAR

> War's special trick is to push to incandescence the *imaginaire* of fear . . . It is "them" or "us." In the name of this security dilemma, everything becomes justifiable.
>
> Jacques Sémelin

If state formation, imperialism, war, and social revolution are genocide's "four horsemen," then war and genocide might be described as Siamese twins. The intimate bond between the two is evident from the twentieth-century record alone. All three of the century's "classic" genocides – against Armenians in Turkey, Jews in Nazi-occupied Europe, and Tutsis in Rwanda – occurred in a context of civil and/or international war. The wartime context is only a necessary, not a sufficient, explanation; but as historian Christopher Fettweis asked of the Jewish Holocaust, "Should one be surprised that the most destructive war in history was accompanied by one of the most dramatic instances of violence against civilians?"[58] A perceptive scholar of the relationship, Martin Shaw, considered genocide to be an offshoot of "degenerate" warfare, with its large-scale targeting of civilian populations.[59]

The line between "legitimate" war and genocide is hard to draw. Still, most genocide scholars acknowledge intimate connections between the two, and many rank war as genocide's greatest single enabling factor. "Thank God that now, during wartime, we have a whole series of opportunities that would be closed off to us in peacetime," Nazi leader Joseph Goebbels exulted in his diary in March 1942, as the machinery of full-scale Holocaust geared up around him.[60]

Figure 2.8 War seems always to have been waged, and glorified, in human history. It often assumes a genocidal character, physically annihilating and supplanting "enemy" populations. A frieze from the ruins of the ninth-century Angkor civilization in Cambodia vividly depicts the violence of much premodern warmaking.

Source: Courtesy Griselda Ramírez.

Figure 2.9 The collective struggle and sacrifice of war serve to bolster intracommunal bonds and heighten fear and suspicion of designated enemies. Through acts of memorialization, wars bind new generations to nationalist projects. Nowhere is this strategy more pivotal than in post-Soviet Russia, where the epic losses to the Nazis in World War Two (see Box 6a) nurture a sense of national pride and solidarity, and counter ethnic and class divisions. Here, visitors enter a museum exhibition on the war in Kazan, capital of Tatarstan, Russian Federation (for more on this unique city, see pp. 584–85).

Source: Author's photo, May 2008.

What are these points of connection between war and genocide?

- *War accustoms a society to violence.* Large portions of the male population may be drawn into institutions, the prime purpose of which is to inflict violence. Much of the remaining population is cast in various productive and reproductive roles. Nearly all adults are therefore complicit in the war machine. The boundaries between legality and criminality erode. Psychological and social inhibitions diminish, often to be replaced by blood-lust.

- *War increases the quotient of fear and hatred in a society.* "War creates a type of mass psychosis to which societies at peace cannot relate."[61] Both soldiers and civilians live in dread of death. Propaganda emphasizes the "traitor within": "Know that the person whose throat you do not cut now will be the one who will cut yours," warned Hutu intellectual Ferdinand Nahimana before the outbreak of the Rwandan genocide against Tutsis and moderate Hutus in 1994.[62] Fear fuels hatred of the one allegedly responsible for the fear, and dependence on the authority that pledges deliverance from the threat. The ideology of militarism inculcates "a condition of slavish docility" and "stolid passivity" throughout the militarized society.[63] Societies grow more receptive to state vigilance and violence, as well as to suspensions of legal and constitutional safeguards. Dissidence threatens unity and stability, and provokes widespread loathing and repression.

- *War eases genocidal logistics.* With the unified command of society and economy, it is easier to mobilize resources for genocide. State power is increasingly devoted to inflicting mass violence. (Indeed, the state itself, "evolving as it did within the crucible of endless rounds of combat, served initially as a more efficient apparatus to fight wars.")[64] For example, the wartime marshalling of rail and freight infrastructure was essential to the "efficient" extermination of millions of Jews, and others, in the Nazi death camps. Much of that infrastructure was built and/or maintained by forced laborers captured as spoils, another regular phenomenon in wartime.

Figure 2.10 Wartime propaganda often dehumanizes the enemy, promoting fear and hatred. A US recruiting poster from World War One (adapting an image previously used in Britain) depicts Germany as a slavering ape coming ashore in America, wielding a club labeled "Kultur" (culture), an innocent maiden (Lady Liberty?) crooked in his arm.

Source: H.R. Hopps (artist)/Wikimedia Commons.

- *War provides a smokescreen for genocide.*[65] "That's war" becomes the excuse for extermination. Traditional sources of information, communication, and denunciation are foreclosed or rigidly controlled. "Journalism is highly restricted, and military censorship prevents the investigation of reported atrocities. The minds of nations and of the international community are on other issues in time of war."[66]

- *War fuels intracommunal solidarity and intercommunal enmity.* Many who experienced the wars of the twentieth century recalled them with mingled pain and pleasure. Few had ever before considered themselves citizens swept up in a common cause. Most soldiers experienced "a new kind of community held together by common danger and a common goal,"[67] which forged the most enduring friendships of their lives. In general, war "exaggerates nationalistic impulses as populations come together under outside threats. . . . During conflict group identities are strengthened as the gap between 'us' and 'them' is magnified, and individuals increasingly emphasize their solidarity with the threatened group."[68] As psychologist David Barash put it succinctly: "In enmity, there is unity."[69] "What is France if not as defined against England or Germany? What is Serbia if not as defined against Germany or Croatia?"[70] Solidarity may coalesce around a dominant ethnicity within the society, prompting the anathematizing of Other-identified minorities.

- *War magnifies humanitarian crisis.* Refugee flows – whether of internally or internationally displaced peoples – may destabilize the society at war, and others around it. War complicates or prevents the provision of humanitarian assistance. Millions may starve to death beyond the reach of aid agencies, as in Congo's messy and multifaceted wars (Box 9a). "New wars" (see Chapter 12) may come to feed on war-related humanitarian assistance, which can also buttress genocidally inclined state authorities, as in Rwanda in the early 1990s.[71]

- *War stokes grievances and a desire for revenge.* Large numbers of Serbs were spurred to support Slobodan Milosevic's ultranationalist option by the collective memory of genocide committed against Serbs during World War Two. Fewer Germans would have supported Hitler or the Nazis (Chapter 6) without an abiding sense of grievance generated by the 1919 Versailles Treaty. Cambodia's Khmer Rouge (Chapter 7) would have enjoyed less popular support if years of American bombing had not terrorized, enraged, and displaced much of the country's peasant population.

It would be comforting to think that democratic societies are immune to these responses. Yet when liberal societies are under stress, as during the present "war on terror," they can slide toward genocidal mindsets, motifs and sometimes policies. In the first edition of this book, I cited comments on a rightwing blog (The Anti-Idiotarian Rottweiler) posted in the wake of the May 2004 execution, by slow decapitation, of an American journalist in Iraq. I suggested that the statements, of the exterminate-all-the-brutes variety, "exposed a brazenly genocidal discourse."[72] In November 2009, the UK *Guardian* reported that after the shooting rampage at Fort Hood, Texas, by an American Muslim army officer who shouted "Allahu Akhbar!" ("God is great!" in Arabic) as he fired, websites "filled with hate mail questioning [US Muslims'] loyalty."[73] I suspected that the Anti-Idiotarian Rottweiler might have something to say on the matter, and indeed it did. Its contributors were also vocal about a news item that followed immediately after Major Nadil Malik Hasan's atrocity at Fort Hood: the announcement that accused al-Qaeda mastermind Khaled Sheik Muhammed would be tried for the 9/11 attack (see pp. 45–47) in New York City, the main attack site. A quite representative sample of the posted comments follows (there were also a few tentatively liberal responses):

Define "win" [in the "war on terror"]? Okay, how's this: Make the enemy . . . fear you at a genetic level and never ever want to go anywhere near you for a thousand years or more. You use Genghis Khan level brutality. Men, women, children, young, old, sick or well, you erase them. You scrape the Earth and salt it. They want to go to allah, you help them in every way possible. They behead a journalist, we destroy a city. And by destroy I mean down to the cockroaches in their sewers. . . . Absolute total decimation. That is the only thing these barbarians truly understand.

(DJ Allyn, November 16, 2009)

Extermination, root and branch, to the third generation. Plow and salt the ground followed by the blood of swine. . . . They [Muslims] are a festering pustule everywhere they go. They will *not* "assimilate," not ever. They are instructed by the unHoly Quran to convert, or destroy, the whole world. There is no such thing as a permanent peace treaty with them . . .

(LC Jon Imperial Hunter, November 11 and 12, 2009)

I honestly do not see any other option to deal with these mutant freaks save overwhelming, make-them-shit-the-diapers-on-both-ends violence. Coddling them does not work. They are using our own morality against us. . . . Sometimes, the only MORAL and RIGHT thing to do is to unleash the beast. . . . It is time to stand up to them and kick their ass, like it was done to the filthy Nazis.

(Princess Natasha, November 16, 2009)

As for the shitstain in question [Major Hasan]. He again proves my point that American Muslims are Muslims first, and Americans a distant second. They should all be deported back to whatever goat-molesting shithole they came from.

(LC Beaker, November 6, 2009)[74]

To be fair to impressively multicultural America (see further discussion in Chapter 16), there were no serious acts of vigilante violence against Muslims in the aftermath of either Major Hasan's atrocity or the New York trial announcement – indeed, notably few after 9/11. But the rhetoric just cited reminds us of the genocidal potential lurking in *all* societies. The comments are representative and generic; there is nothing uniquely American about them. They are not even especially sadistic, compared to other examples that could be cited from the same "discussion" on the same website. Some posts have a timeless air, reminiscent of the proclamations of Assyrian kings or Mongol emperors as they prepared to embark on genocidal war and empire-building. (Note the references to classical precedents – Genghis Khan; the ancient sowing of destroyed cities with salt.)

But if something in war's extremism is timeless, something is also distinctively modern, and this merits exploration.

The First World War and the dawn of industrial death

In July 1916, my grandfather, Alfred George Jones (1885–1949), a British volunteer soldier, arrived on the Somme farmlands of the western front in France. This terrain had just witnessed the most massive and disastrous Allied offensive of the First World War. On July 1, commemorated as the "Black Day" of the British Army, an offensive by 100,000 troops produced 60,000 Allied casualties *in a single day*, including 20,000 killed. The image of British troops walking at a parade-ground pace, bayonets fixed, across the gently rolling landscapes of the Somme, and directly into German machine-gun fire, is iconic: "the Somme marked the end of an age of vital optimism in British life that has never been recovered"[75] (see Figures 2.11 and 2.12).

Figure 2.11   Alfred George Jones (1885–1949), the author's grandfather, a British First World War veteran. The photo appears to have been taken shortly after he volunteered for service, in time to be drawn into the maelstrom of the Battle of the Somme in July 1916.

Source: Author's collection.

Figure 2.12   An iconic image of the twentieth century: soldiers go "over the top" at the Battle of the Somme on July 1, 1916 – the "Black Day of the British Army." The soldier at right has already been shot and fallen into the barbed wire of the Allied trenchline. Nearly a century later, the Somme still symbolizes the futility of modern war, and the impersonal, industrialized mass killing that would reach its apogee with the Nazi Holocaust (see Chapter 6 and Box 6a).

Source: Imperial War Museum, London.

My grandfather was thrown into the meat-grinder that followed, which claimed 630,000 Allied casualties and a similar number of Germans over four-and-a-half months. A sapper in the Royal Engineers, he was blown up and buried for three days by an artillery shell in "no man's land" (a term that has since become a metaphor of the social and cultural dislocation wrought by the First World War). He was discovered by chance. Shell-shocked, he was shipped to England to convalesce. The experience triggered epileptic attacks that haunted him to the end of his days; but he survived to father my father. Thus, for better or worse, you hold this book in your hands because someone stumbled across my grandfather in no man's land nearly a century ago, during the definitive war of modern times.[76]

The crisis caused by the "Great War" derived from its combination of industrial technology and physical immobility. As millions of tons of munitions were unleashed, soldiers cowered in trenches that trembled or collapsed from the bombardments, and that between assaults were a wasteland of mud, rats, and corpses. Ten million soldiers died on all sides – a previously unimaginable figure, and one that left a gaping and traumatic hole where a generation of young men should have been. For sociologist Martin Shaw,

The slaughter of the trenches was in many ways the definitive experience of modern mass killing, seminal to virtually all the mass killing activities of the twentieth century. The massacre of conscripts was a starting-point for the development of each of the other strands. As the soldier-victims were mown down in their hundreds of thousands in the Somme and elsewhere, they provided a spectacle of mass death that set the tone for a century. . . . All the main paradigms of twentieth-century death were already visible in this first great phase of total war.[77]

Adolf Hitler spent four years in the trenches of the western front (see Figure 2.13). He had been swept up in nationalist euphoria at the war's outbreak – there is a photograph of a Munich crowd celebrating the declaration of war, in which Hitler's face may be seen, rapt with enthusiasm. As a soldier, he fought bravely, receiving the Iron Cross Second Class. He was nearly killed in an Allied gas attack that left him blind and hospitalized – the prone, powerless position in which he first heard of the "humiliating" armistice Germany had accepted. (For more on genocide and humiliation, see Chapter 10.) In the war's aftermath, Hitler joined millions of demobilized soldiers struggling to find a place in postwar society. His war-fueled alienation, and his nostalgic longing for the solidarity and comradeship of the trenches, marked him for life.

The Bolshevik Revolution in Russia, which spawned large-scale killing under Vladimir Lenin and epic slaughter under Joseph Stalin (Chapter 5), is inconceivable

Figure 2.13   The failed Austrian artist Adolf Hitler volunteered to fight in World War One, and discovered his destiny. He is pictured (at left) with fellow soldiers of Germany's 16th Bavarian Unit. Hitler won honors for bravery and was incapacitated in a gas attack, receiving the news of Germany's surrender in 1918 as he lay prone on his hospital bed. The experience – the intensity of "total war," the camaraderie and solidarity of the front lines, the humiliation of injury and surrender – stayed with Hitler for the rest of his life.

Source: The William Bremen Jewish Heritage Museum, Atlanta, GA.

without the trauma of the war. The conflict also directly sparked genocide against the Christian minorities of the Ottoman realm (see Chapter 4). The genocide was carried out on the grounds of military "self-defense" against minority groups accused of seeking to subvert the Ottoman state, in alliance with a historic enemy (Russia). Genocidal logistics, particularly transport, were greatly facilitated by the requisites of wartime emergency.

The Second World War and the "barbarization of warfare"

The European theater of the Second World War consisted of two quite different conflicts. In the west, Nazi occupation authorities were more disciplined and less brutal, though not where Jews or partisans were concerned. In the east, and in the Balkans to the south, crimes against humanity were the norm. Genocide featured prominently among them.

The heart of the eastern war was primarily the struggle between Nazi-led forces and the Soviet people.[78] Soviet armies were dealt a massive blow by the German *Blitzkrieg* (lightning-war) of June to December 1941, which pushed all the way to the suburbs of Moscow. There ensued a titanic struggle between two totalitarian systems – the largest and most destructive military conflict in history. For Hitler, according to historian Omer Bartov, it was from the start "an ideological war of extermination and enslavement":

> Its goal was to wipe out the Soviet state, to enslave the Russian people after debilitating them by famine and all other forms of deprivation, systematically to murder all "biological" and political enemies of Nazism, such as the Jews, the Gypsies [Roma], members of the Communist Party, intellectuals, and so forth, and finally to turn western Russia into a German paradise of "Aryan" colonizers served by hordes of Slav helots.[79]

Reflecting this racial animus and political extremism, the restraints that generally governed German troops in the West – the preservation of prisoners-of-war, a degree of respect for civilian lives and property – were abandoned from the outset. "This struggle must have as its aim the demolition of present Russia and must therefore be conducted with unprecedented severity," declared Panzer Group Colonel-General Hoepner before the invasion. "Both the planning and the execution of every battle must be dictated by an iron will to bring about a merciless, total annihilation of the enemy. Particularly no mercy should be shown toward the carriers of the present Russian-Bolshevik system."[80]

The result was a "demodernization" of the eastern front from 1941 to 1945, and a concomitant "barbarization of warfare," to cite historian Omer Bartov's term. Amidst physical travails, primitive conditions, and endless harassment by partisans, troops turned readily to atrocity. They were granted a "license to murder disarmed soldiers and defenseless civilians," and often carried out the task with an indiscriminate enthusiasm that transported them beyond the limited controls established by the army.

The Soviet stance towards the German invader could also be blood-curdling. The poet Ilya Ehrenburg penned a leaflet for circulation among Soviet frontline troops titled simply, "Kill": "The Germans are not human beings. From now on the word 'German' is for us the worst imaginable curse. . . . We shall kill. If you have not killed at least one German a day, you have wasted that day."[81]

Thus conditioned, when Soviet troops reached German soil in East Prussia they unleashed a campaign of mass rape, murder, and terror against German civilians, who were overwhelmingly children and women. The campaign of gang rape, which Stalin notoriously dismissed as the Soviet soldier "having fun with a woman," is seared into the German collective memory.[82] As many as two million German women were sexually assaulted: "it was not untypical for Soviet troops to rape every female over the age of twelve or thirteen in a village, killing many in the process."[83] However, whatever else may be said, Soviet ideology lacked a strong racist component. Perhaps as a result, after months of rape and killing, the regime finally imposed on the Soviet client-state of East Germany was much less malevolent a "new order" than Slavs experienced under Nazi rule.

Barbarization was also evident in the war in the Pacific, which pitted the US, UK, China, and their allies against Japanese occupation forces. In his *War Without Mercy*, historian John Dower examined the processes of mutual demonization and bestialization by the US and Japanese polities. These processes both conditioned and reflected the broader popular hostility in wartime. The American public's view of the Japanese enemy was conveyed in a poll taken in December 1944, in which, according to Gary Bass, "33 percent of Americans wanted to destroy Japan as a country after the war, 28 percent wanted to supervise and control Japan – and fully 13 percent wanted to kill *all* Japanese people."[84] Among soldiers consulted in both the Pacific and European theatres in 1943–44, between 42 percent (Pacific) and 67 percent (Europe) considered "wiping out the whole Japanese nation" as the most desirable option.[85]

GENOCIDE AND SOCIAL REVOLUTION

> It is on a blank page that the most beautiful poems are written.
>
> Mao Zedong, Chinese revolutionary leader

Revolutions are sudden, far-reaching, and generally violent transformations of a political order. Social revolutions, which go beyond a change of political regime to encompass transformations of the underlying class structure, are particularly wrenching.

Beginning with the English Civil War of 1648, the American Revolution of 1776, and the French Revolution of 1789, the modern era has witnessed an escalating series of such transformations. Revolution has been closely linked to struggles for national independence, as well as to attempts to engineer fundamental changes in the social order. The uprisings against the crumbling Ottoman Empire in the early twentieth century provided the template for the century's national liberation struggles. These coalesced as a comprehensive movement for decolonization following the Second World War.

The Soviet Revolution of 1917, which grew out of the chaos and privation of the First World War, epitomized the Marxist–Leninist variant of social-revolutionary strategy. This strategy viewed "all history [as] the history of class struggle" (to cite Marx and Engels's *Communist Manifesto*). Under the influence of Vladimir Lenin, it stressed the role of a vanguard party in dragging the workers and peasants to liberation, kicking and screaming if necessary (as it indeed proved to be).[86] Social-revolutionary struggle in the early part of the twentieth century also took a fascist form, as in Mussolini's Italy and Hitler's Germany.[87] Fascism found its shock troops among workers and the *lumpenproletariat* (lower social orders and riffraff). Its peasant following was also considerable. Nevertheless, its base resided in the lower-middle class, and featured an alliance – or marriage of convenience – with traditional, conservative sectors.

Both communist and fascist variants of revolution are highly militarized. This reflects the clandestine organizing and cell-based struggle of revolutionary strategy, as well as the need to crush counter-revolutionary opposition before, during, and after the revolution. It also attests to the conviction of some revolutionaries that the world should share in their victory, or be subjugated by it. As Martin Shaw noted,

> *revolution itself . . . increasingly took the form of war*, particularly guerrilla war . . . Revolutionaries pursued armed struggle not as a conclusion to political struggle, but as a central means of that struggle from the outset. Likewise, established power has used force not merely to defeat open insurrection, but to stamp out revolutionary forces and terrorize their actual or potential social supporters. As revolution became armed struggle, counter-revolution became counter-insurgency. In this sense there has been a radical change in the character of many revolutionary processes.[88]

Research into the Turkish and Nazi revolutions produced a key work of comparative genocide studies, political scientist Robert Melson's *Revolution and Genocide* (1996), which summarized the linkage as follows:

1. Revolutions created the conditions for genocidal movements to come to power.
2. Revolutions made possible the imposition of radical ideologies and new orders that legitimated genocide.
3. The social mobilization of low status or despised groups [e.g., in struggles for national liberation] helped to make them targets of genocide.
4. Revolutions leading to wars facilitated the implementation of genocide as a policy of the state.[89]

While revolution, especially social revolution, may take a genocidal form, so too may counter-revolution. This book contains numerous instances of revolutions that spawned genocides (Turkey's against Christian minorities, Lenin's and Stalin's terrors, the Nazis, the Khmer Rouge in Cambodia, "Hutu Power" in Rwanda). Yet it includes even more cases in which colonial and contemporary state authorities sought to stamp out "revolutionary" threats through genocide. The Germans in Southwest

Africa (Chapter 2), the Chinese in Tibet (Chapter 5), West Pakistan in East Pakistan/ Bangladesh (Box 8a), Serbia in Kosovo, Russia in Chechnya (Box 5a), and Sudan in Darfur (Box 9a) – all fit the pattern, as does the Guatemalan army's rampage against Mayan Indians in the 1970s and 1980s (Box 3a). In all cases, once war is unleashed, the radicalization and extremism of organized mass violence, described previously, come to dominate the equation.

THE NUCLEAR REVOLUTION AND "OMNICIDE"

> Total war is no longer only between all members of one national community and all those of another: it is also total because it will very likely set the whole world up in flames.
>
> Jean-Paul Sartre, *On Genocide*

As revolutions in the social and political sphere represent dramatic irruptions of new actors and social forces, so technological revolutions transform the world and human history. This was the case prior to the First World War, when scientific knowledge, wedded to an industrial base, facilitated the mass slaughter of 1914–18. An even more portentous transformation was the nuclear revolution – the discovery that the splitting (and later the fusion) of atoms could unleash unprecedented energy, and could be directed towards military destruction as well as peaceful ends. Atomic bombs had the power to render conventional weapons obsolete, while "the destructive power of the hydrogen bomb was as revolutionary in comparison with the atomic bomb as was the latter to conventional weaponry."[90]

The invention of nuclear weapons, first (and fortunately last) used in war at Hiroshima and Nagasaki in August 1945, transformed civilization to its very roots. "In a real way we all lead something of a 'double life,'" wrote psychologists Robert Jay Lifton and Eric Markusen. "We are aware at some level that in a moment we and everyone and everything we have ever touched or loved could be annihilated, and yet we go about our ordinary routines as though no such threat exists."[91] In his classic cry for peace, social critic Jonathan Schell described *The Fate of the Earth* as being "poised on a hair trigger, waiting for the 'button' to be 'pushed' by some misguided or deranged human being or for some faulty computer chip to send out the instruction to fire. That so much should be balanced on so fine a point . . . is a fact against which belief rebels."[92]

Lifton and Markusen compared the mindset of Nazi leaders and technocrats with those managing nuclear armories today. Both cultures reflected deep, sometimes hysterical preoccupations with "national security," which could be employed to depict one's own acts of aggression as pre-emptive. Both involved professionals whose specialization and distancing from the actuality of destruction helped them to inflict or prepare to inflict holocaust. A dry, euphemistic language rendered atrocity banal. Both mindsets accepted megadeath as necessary:

> With [nuclear] deterrence, there is the assumption that we must be prepared to kill hundreds of millions of people in order to prevent large-scale killing, to cure

the world of genocide. With the Nazis, the assumption was that killing all Jews was a way of curing not only the Aryan race but all humankind. Involvement in a therapeutic mission helps block out feelings of the deaths one is or may be inflicting.[93]

Whatever the parallels, the immensity of modern nuclear weapons' destructive power was beyond Hitler's wildest fantasies. Scholars coined the term "omnicide" – total killing – to describe the extinction that nuclear arms could impose: not only on humans, but on the global ecosystem and all complex life forms, with the possible exception of the cockroach. Nuclear weapons are the one threat that can make past and present genocides seem small.

Younger readers of this book may find such comments melodramatic. They will lack direct memories of the "balance of terror" and the (il)logic of "mutually assured destruction" that pervaded the Cold War. These spawned a degree of fear and mass psychosis that marked for life many of those who lived under it, including myself. Antinuclear sentiment sparked moves towards a prohibition regime (see Chapter 12), built around arms control treaties between the superpowers and monitoring the peaceful use of nuclear energy. This left the situation still extremely volatile, as populations across the Western world recognized in the 1980s: they staged the largest protest demonstrations in postwar European and North American history.

Figure 2.14   Another iconic image: the mushroom cloud of the first atomic bomb ever used against human beings; Hiroshima, Japan, August 6, 1945.

Source: Wikimedia Commons.

Figure 2.15   A victim of the atomic blast at Hiroshima, her skin burned in the pattern of the kimono she was wearing at the time of the explosion.

Source: Wikimedia Commons.

Since that time, immediate tensions have subsided. Few today feel themselves under the perpetual shadow of the mushroom cloud; but, arguably, this reflects no diminution of the threat. Thousands of missiles remain in the armories of the major nuclear powers – enough to destroy the world many times over. While a number of nuclear or proto-nuclear powers have abandoned their programs (South Africa, several former Soviet republics, Brazil, Argentina), other states have joined the nuclear club, including India, Pakistan, and North Korea. At least one "conflict dyad" seems capable of sparking a nuclear holocaust on short notice: that of India and Pakistan. These countries have fought four wars since 1947, and seemed poised for a fifth as recently as 2001.

In another way, too, the nuclear threat has multiplied, despite promising recent developments in the Russian–American relationship.[94] The Soviet collapse left thousands of missiles in varying states of decay, and often poorly guarded.[95] They made attractive targets for *mafiosi* and impoverished military officers seeking the ultimate black-market payoff. The client might be a rogue state or terrorist movement that would have little compunction about using its prize against enemies or "infidels." The next chapter of the nuclear saga thus remains to be written. It is possible that it will be a genocidal, even omnicidal one.

FURTHER STUDY

Omer Bartov, *Hitler's Army: Soldiers, Nazis, and War in the Third Reich*. New York: Oxford University Press, 1992. Brief, seminal study; see also Bartov's *The Eastern Front, 1941–45*.

Iris Chang, *The Rape of Nanking*. New York: Penguin, 1998. Account of Japan's genocidal massacres and mass rape in China in 1937–38.

Mike Davis, *Late Victorian Holocausts: El Niño Famines and the Making of the Third World*. New York: Verso, 2001. Influential exploration of how early capitalist economics in the colonial world combined with environmental stresses to inflict mass death.

John Dower, *War Without Mercy: Race and Power in the Pacific War*. New York: Pantheon, 1986. Analyzes the racism of both the US and Japanese war efforts, and its transformation into peaceful cooperation after 1945.

Barbara Ehrenreich, *Blood Rites: Origins and History of the Passions of War*. New York: Metropolitan Books, 1997. Intriguing interpretation of warfare as a vestige of human beings' prehistoric struggle against predators.

Marcia Esparza, Henry R. Huttenbach, and Daniel Feierstein, eds, *State Violence and Genocide in Latin America: The Cold War Years*. London: Routledge, 2010. The first volume to systematically explore genocide in a modern Latin American context; focuses on the "dirty wars" and genocides of the 1970s and '80s, along with the US imperial role.

J. Glenn Gray, *The Warriors: Reflections on Men in Battle*. Omaha, NB: University of Nebraska Press, 1998. Evocation of the soldier's soul, first published in 1959.

Fred Halliday, *Revolution and World Politics: The Rise and Fall of the Sixth Great Power*. Durham, NC: Duke University Press, 1999. Global overview by a leading scholar of revolutions.

Alan Kramer, *Dynamic of Destruction: Culture and Mass Killing in the First World War*. Oxford: Oxford University Press, 2007. How the First World War served as a precursor and prototype for the mass slaughters of the twentieth century.

Benjamin Lieberman, *Terrible Fate: Ethnic Cleansing in the Making of Modern Europe*. Chicago, IL: Ivan R. Dee, 2006. Moving, highly readable account of state formation and imperial collapse in Europe, and the human destruction it wrought.

Robert Jay Lifton and Eric Markusen, *The Genocidal Mentality: Nazi Holocaust and Nuclear Threat*. New York: Basic Books, 1990. Compares the mindset of Nazi leaders and functionaries with that of their counterparts in the nuclear age.

Eric Markusen and David Kopf, *The Holocaust and Strategic Bombing: Genocide and Total War in the Twentieth Century*. Boulder, CO: Westview Press, 1995. Excellent analysis of points of sociological and psychological crossover.

Arno J. Mayer, *The Furies: Violence and Terror in the French and Russian Revolutions*. Princeton, NJ: Princeton University Press, 2000. Epic study of two epochal revolutions.

Robert Melson, *Revolution and Genocide: On the Origins of the Armenian Genocide and the Holocaust*. Chicago, IL: University of Chicago Press, 1996. The interweaving of war, revolution, and genocide.

Jean-Paul Sartre and Arlette El Kaïm-Sartre, *On Genocide*. Boston, MA: Beacon Press, 1968. Sartre's controversial essay, set alongside evidence of US crimes in Vietnam.

Jonathan Schell, *The Fate of the Earth and the Abolition*. Stanford, CA: Stanford University Press, 2000. Two key works on nuclearism, now in a combined edition; see also *The Seventh Decade: The New Shape of Nuclear Danger*.

Martin Shaw, *War and Genocide: Organized Killing in Modern Society*. Cambridge: Polity Press, 2003. The best introduction to the subject.

Yukiko Tanaka, *Hidden Horrors: Japanese War Crimes in World War II*. Boulder, CO: Westview Press, 1997. Examines biological experiments, sexual enslavement, and atrocities against prisoners-of-war.

Benjamin A. Valentino, *Final Solutions: Mass Killing and Genocide in the 20th Century*. Ithaca, NY: Cornell University Press, 2004. Nuanced study of the insurgency–counterinsurgency dynamic in many genocidal campaigns; also strong on revolutionary ideologies and "communist mass killings."

NOTES

1 Mark Levene, *Genocide in the Age of the Nation State, Vol. 1: The Meaning of Genocide* and *Vol. 2: The Rise of the West and the Coming of Genocide* (London: I.B. Tauris, 2005).

2 James C. Scott, *Seeing Like A State: How Certain Schemes to Improve the Human Condition Have Failed* (New Haven, CT: Yale University Press, 1998).

3 Karel C. Berkhoff, *Harvest of Despair: Life and Death in Ukraine under Nazi Rule* (Cambridge, MA: Harvard University Press, 2004); Wendy Lower, *Nazi Empire-Building*

and the Holocaust in Ukraine (Chapel Hill, NC: The University of North Carolina Press, 2004); Mark Mazower, *Hitler's Empire: How the Nazis Ruled Europe* (New York: Penguin, 2008).

4 Leonard Seabrooke, "Imperialism," in Martin Griffiths, ed., *Encyclopedia of International Relations and Global Politics* (London: Routledge, 2005), p. 398.

5 Ripon College, "Important Concepts in Global Studies," originally at http://www.ripon. edu/academics/global/concepts.html (link now defunct).

6 The term was first deployed by leading Marxist theoreticians such as Lenin and Gramsci. The most prominent treatment of the theme is that of Michael Hechter, who built his analysis around the English conquest of the "Celtic Fringe" (Scotland, Wales, and Ireland). See Hechter, *Internal Colonialism: The Celtic Fringe in British National Development, 1536–1966* (Berkeley, CA: University of California Press, 1975).

7 This is the interpretation advanced by Lynne Viola in *The Unknown Gulag*: "The peasantry would serve as an internal colony for Soviet economic development. . . . The countryside became a foreign country to be invaded, occupied, and conquered." She cites a fascinating speech by the Soviet dictator, Joseph Stalin (see Chapter 5), to the Communist Party Central Committee in July 1928, which is worth reproducing at length for the insights it offers into state-building, internal colonialism, and genocidal processes:

> In capitalist countries industrialization was usually based not only on internal accumulation but also on the plundering of other countries, the plundering of colonies or vanquished countries, or on substantial loans from abroad. . . . Our country differs from the capitalist countries . . . in that it cannot and must not engage in the plundering of colonies or in the plundering of other countries in general. Therefore this path is closed to us. But our country doesn't have loans from abroad either. Consequently, this path is closed to us as well. In that case what is left for us? One choice is left: to develop industry, to industrialize the country on the basis of internal accumulation [*n.b.* effectively, internal colonialism]. . . . But where are the sources of this accumulation? . . . There are two such sources: first, the working class, which creates valuable output and moves industry forward; and second, the peasantry.
>
> The situation in our country with regard to the peasantry in this case is the following: it pays the state not only ordinary taxes, direct and indirect, but it also pays relatively high prices for goods from industry – that is first of all – and it doesn't receive the full value of the prices of agricultural products – that is second of all. This is an additional tax on the peasantry in the interests of developing industry, which serves the whole country, including the peasantry. This is something like a 'tribute,' something like a surtax, which we are forced to take temporarily in order to sustain and further develop the current rate of industrial growth. . . . This situation, needless to say, is unpleasant. But we would not be Bolsheviks if we papered over this fact and closed our eyes to the fact that, unfortunately, our industry and our country cannot manage without this additional tax on the peasantry.

> Viola, *The Unknown Gulag: The Lost World of Stalin's Special Settlements*
> Oxford: Oxford University Press, 2007, pp. 15, 32.

8 On Ireland, see Ben Kiernan, "The English Conquest of Ireland, 1565–1603," in Kiernan, *Blood and Soil: A World History of Genocide and Extermination from Sparta to Darfur* (New Haven, CT: Yale University Press, 2007), pp. 169–212; Robbie McVeigh, "'The Balance of Cruelty': Ireland, Britain and the Logic of Genocide," *Journal of Genocide Research*, 10: 4 (December 2008), pp. 541–61. According to Hannibal Travis, after the manipulated famine of the 1840s, "An Irish official accused the British prime minister of having 'smitten and offered up as a holocaust' a total of a 'million and a half Irish people.' The lord lieutenant of Ireland in 1849 condemned Parliament for pursuing a cold, calculating 'policy of extermination.'" Hannibal Travis, *Genocide in the Middle East: The Ottoman Empire, Iraq, and Sudan* (Durham, NC: Carolina Academic Press,

2010), p. 142. The usage in this early context of the modern-seeming language of "holocaust" and "extermination" is interesting (see more on "extermination" in Chapter 15).

9 A readable popular account is Robert Hughes, *The Fatal Shore: The Epic of Australia's Founding* (New York: Vintage, 1988).

10 For an overview of the literature and law surrounding "famine crimes," see David Marcus, "Famine Crimes in International Law," *The American Journal of International Law*, 97 (2003), pp. 245–81. See also Rhoda E. Howard-Hassmann, "Genocide and State-Induced Famine: Global Ethics and Western Responsibility for Mass Atrocities in Africa," *Perspectives on Global Development and Technology*, 4: 3–4 (2005), pp. 487–516.

11 Amartya Sen, *Development as Freedom* (New York: Anchor, 1999), p. 168. Sen's 1977 study of the 1943–45 famine in colonial Bengal, in which some three million Indians died, prompted Henry Shue to coin his famous phrase, "the Holocaust of Neglect." Sen, "Starvation and Exchange Entitlements: A General Approach and Its Application to the Great Bengal Famine," *Cambridge Journal of Economics*, 1:1 (1977), pp. 33–59; Shue, *Basic Rights: Subsistence, Affluence, and U.S. Foreign Policy* (2nd edn) (Princeton, NJ: Princeton University Press, 1996), p. 207 (n. 17).

12 Stéphane Courtois *et al.*, *The Black Book of Communism: Crimes, Terror, Repression* (Cambridge, MA: Harvard University Press, 1999).

13 See Cecil Woodham-Smith, *The Great Hunger: Ireland 1845–1849* (London: Hamish Hamilton, 1962).

14 Mike Davis, *Late Victorian Holocausts: El Niño Famines and the Making of the Third World* (London: Verso, 2001), pp. 158, 174.

15 Davis, *Late Victorian Holocausts*, pp. 15, 22, 37–38, 152, 287–88, 290. Eric Hobsbawm has also pointed out that colonial policy during the Indian famines occurred against a backdrop of Britain's "virtual destruction . . . of what had been a flourishing domestic and village industry which supplemented the rural incomes" across India, but which competed with British products. This "deindustrialization made the peasant village itself more dependent on the single, fluctuating fortune of the harvest," and correspondingly more vulnerable when famine struck. Hobsbawm, *The Age of Revolution, 1789–1848* (London: Abacus, 1994), p. 201.

16 The influence of Conrad's novella continues to the present, entrenching a notion of Congo, in Daniel Magnowski's words, "as being beyond anyone's help. . . . The idea of a dark, savage place resonates deeply in the Western psyche, to the point at which violence has become the expected national trait of Congo, and the country a canvas upon which the worst excesses of depravity have been painted." Magnowski, "'Cursed' Congo Still Shocks and Fascinates," Reuters dispatch, November 21, 2008.

17 Joseph Conrad, "Geography and Explorers," in Conrad, *Last Essays* (London: J.M. Dent & Sons, 1926), p. 25.

18 Adam Hochschild, *King Leopold's Ghost* (Boston, MA: Houghton Mifflin, 1998), p. 4. A potent two-hour television documentary, *Congo: White King, Red Rubber, Black Death* (dir. Peter Bate, 2003), was streaming on Google Videos (http://video.google.com/) at the time of publication.

19 Martin Ewans, *European Atrocity, African Catastrophe: Leopold II, the Congo Free State and its Aftermath* (London: RoutledgeCurzon, 2002), p. 3.

20 Quoted in Ewans, *European Atrocity, African Catastrophe*, pp. 112–13. Caryatids are (female) figures in the columns of Greek architecture, "used as pillar[s]" to support friezes and other stonework (*The Concise Oxford Dictionary*).

21 Hochschild, *King Leopold's Ghost*, p. 233.

22 Neal Ascherson, *The King Incorporated: Leopold the Second and the Congo* (London: Granta, 1999), p. 251.

23 Ascherson, *The King Incorporated*, p. 9.

24 For more on the gendering of the catastrophe, see Adam Jones/Gendercide Watch, "Case Study: *Corvée* (Forced) Labour," http://www.gendercide.org/case_corvee.html.

25 Hochschild, *King Leopold's Ghost*, p. 232. Nor were the Belgians the only imperial power to inflict genocidal atrocities on Congo: according to Hochschild (p. 280), French rule in "their" part of the Congo resulted in population losses also approaching 50 percent in the most afflicted regions.

26 Ascherson, *The King Incorporated*, p. 9.

27 See also E.D. Morel's influential contribution, *Red Rubber: The Story of the Rubber Slave Trade Which Flourished on the Congo for Twenty Years, 1890–1910* (Manchester: The National Labour Press, 1920).

28 John Rabe, *The Good Man of Nanking: The Diaries of John Rabe*, trans. John E. Woods (New York: Alfred A. Knopf, 1998), pp. 76–77, 134. Notoriously, the *Japan Advertiser* of December 7, 1937 related the "friendly contest" held between two Japanese sub-lieutenants "to see which of them will first fell 100 Chinese in individual sword combat" (i.e., the execution of Chinese male non-combatants).

> [Toshiaki] Mukai has a score of 106 and his rival [Takeshi Noda] has dispatched 105 men, but the two contestants have found it impossible to determine which passed the 100 mark first. Instead of settling it with a discussion, they are going to extend the goal by 50. . . . Mukai's blade was slightly damaged in the competition. He explained that this was the result of cutting a Chinese in half, helmet and all. The contest was 'fun,' he declared, and thought it a good thing that both men had gone over the 100 mark without knowing that the other had done so.
>
> (quoted p. 283)

29 R.J. Rummel, *Death by Government* (New Brunswick, NJ: Transaction Publishers, 1997), pp. 146, 151.

30 Ibid., p. 150.

31 For in-depth treatments of Japanese forced prostitution in the occupied territories, see Yuki Tanaka, *Japan's Comfort Women: The Military and Involuntary Prostitution During War and Occupation* (London: Routledge, 2002); George L. Hicks, *The Comfort Women: Japan's Brutal Regime of Enforced Prostitution in the Second World War* (New York: W.W. Norton, 1997). See further discussion in the context of memory issues and redress claims in Chapter 14.

32 Yukiko Tanaka, *Hidden Horrors: Japanese War Crimes in World War II* (Boulder, CO: Westview Press, 1997), pp. 137–38. A good, brief introduction to Japanese crimes is Laurence Rees, *Horror in the East: Japan and the Atrocities of World War II* (Cambridge, MA: Da Capo Press, 2002).

33 See Sheldon H. Harris, *Factories of Death: Japanese Biological Warfare, 1932–45 and the American Cover-Up* (rev. edn) (London: Routledge, 2001).

34 The most detailed account of the massacre is Michael Bilton and Kevin Sim, *Four Hours in My Lai* (New York: Penguin, 1992). The wrenching TV documentary of the same name can be searched on YouTube, and makes clear also the resulting trauma (in one case, to the point of self-destruction) for many of the guilt-ridden soldier-perpetrators.

35 Hersh's original dispatches on the My Lai massacre are compiled at http://www.pierretristam.com/Bobst/library/wf-200.htm.

36 In August 2009, in a speech to his local Kiwanis Club in Columbus, Georgia, Calley made his first public comment on the massacre: "There is not a day that goes by that I do not feel remorse for what happened that day in My Lai. I feel remorse for the Vietnamese who were killed, for their families, for the American soldiers involved and their families. I am very sorry." See "Calley Apologizes for Role in My Lai Massacre," Associated Press dispatch on MSNBC.com, August 21, 2009, http://www.msnbc.msn.com/id/32514139/ns/us_news-military.

37 See the account by *Toledo Blade* journalists Michael Sallah and Mitch Weiss, based on their Pulitzer Prize-winning reportage: *Tiger Force: A True Story of Men and War* (New York: Back Bay Books, 2006); and Deborah Nelson, *The War Behind Me: Vietnam Veterans Confront the Truth about US War Crimes* (New York: Basic Books, 2008).

In 2001, the former US Senator and Navy Seal, Bob Kerrey, confessed his involvement in one such massacre of civilians. See Douglas Valentine, "Bob Kerrey, CIA War Crimes, and the Need for a War Crimes Trial," Counterpunch.org, May 17, 2001, http://www.counterpunch.org/valentine.html. Valentine's earlier book, *The Phoenix Program* (Authors Guild, 2000), analyzes the post-Tet "pacification" atrocities, and is also essential. For a discussion of remarkably similar acts by US forces during the Korean War, only recently unearthed, see Charles J. Hanley, Sang-Hun Choe, and Martha Mendoza, *The Bridge at No Gun Ri: A Hidden Nightmare from the Korean War* (New York: Henry Holt & Company, 2001). For an argument that "the No Gun Ri incident . . . may be the tip of the iceberg in regards [*sic*] to the matter of mass killings committed by US and South Korean troops during the Korean War," citing "more than sixty cases of mass killing committed by US troops, by shooting, bombing, strafing or other means," see Dong Choon Kim, "Forgotten War, Forgotten Massacres: The Korean War (1950–1953) as Licensed Mass Killings," *Journal of Genocide Research*, 6: 4 (2004), pp. 523–44. As Kim notes (p. 531), "In every aspect of the war – America's use of napalm, indiscriminate bombing, and the shooting of 'voiceless' civilians of the Third World, the Korean War preceded the Indochina War in many tragic ways." See also Geoffrey Cain, "Is Time Running Out to Dig Up S. Korea's Mass Graves?," *Time*, November 27, 2009, http://www.time.com/time/world/article/0,8599,1943075,00.html.

38 Martha Ann Overland, "Agent Orange Poisons New Generations in Vietnam," *Time*, December 19, 2009, http://www.time.com/time/world/article/0,8599,1948084,00.html.

39 S. Brian Willson, "Bob Kerrey's Atrocity, the Crime of Vietnam and the Historic Pattern of US Imperialism," in Adam Jones, ed., *Genocide, War Crimes and the West: History and Complicity* (London: Zed Books, 2004), pp. 167–69.

40 As I learned on a visit to the Plain of Jars in summer 2009, one treads gingerly on narrow paths cleared by the dedicated workers of the Mines Advisory Group (MAG), even in areas at the heart of Laos's attempt to revive a tourist economy. To ramble away from the path is to risk death or disfigurement – nearly four decades after the bombing assault climaxed. See the website of the Mines Advisory Group (MAG), http://www.maginternational.org, and that of the organization devoted to crafting prosthetic limbs for UXO victims in Laos, the Cooperative Orthotic and Prosthetic Enterprise (COPE), http://www.copelaos.org.

41 Arthur Jay Klinghoffer, "International Citizens' Tribunals on Human Rights," in Adam Jones, ed., *Genocide, War Crimes and the West: History and Complicity* (London: Zed Books, 2004), p. 355.

42 Ann Curthoys and John Docker, "Defining Genocide," in Dan Stone, ed., *The Historiography of Genocide* (London: Palgrave Macmillan, 2008), p. 25.

43 Jean-Paul Sartre, "On Genocide," in Jean-Paul Sartre and Arlette El Kaïm-Sartre, *On Genocide* (Boston, MA: Beacon Press, 1968), p. 82.

44 "In the Vietnam War the use of bombing tactics and cruel weapons against the civilian population appears to me to establish a prima facie case of genocide against the United States." Richard Falk, writing in 1968; quoted in Arthur Jay Klinghoffer and Judith Klinghoffer, *International Citizens' Tribunals: Mobilizing Public Opinion to Advance Human Rights* (New York: Palgrave, 2002), p. 235 (n. 26).

45 See the discussion of recent findings on the bombing of Cambodia on p. 287.

46 Eric Margolis, *War at the Top of the World: The Struggle for Afghanistan, Kashmir, and Tibet* (New York: Routledge, 2001), p. 18.

47 Rosanne Klass, "Afghanistan," in Israel W. Charny *et al.*, eds, *The Encyclopedia of Genocide*, Vol. 2 (Santa Barbara, CA: ABC-CLIO, 2000), pp. 48–49. Benjamin Valentino's summary of Soviet scorched-earth strategies is succinct: "In regions of high guerrilla activity, Soviet forces systematically burned crops and dwellings, reducing vast swaths of territory to wasteland. Soviet aircraft employed incendiary weapons, including napalm and phosphorus cluster munitions, to burn crops from the air. Entire herds of livestock were slaughtered or confiscated. Irrigation systems were intentionally destroyed,

rendering agriculture in Afghanistan's arid climate all but impossible. Some reports suggest that Soviet forces deliberately poisoned village grain stores and water supplies. Houses and agricultural fields were heavily mined. By 1984 these tactics and the ensuing exodus of the rural population resulted in a 75 to 80 percent decline in agricultural production compared to pre-1979 levels." Valentino, *Final Solutions: Mass Killing and Genocide in the 20th Century* (Ithaca, NY: Cornell University Press, 2004), p. 224. As with the US "free-fire zones" in Vietnam, or the Mayan highlands of Guatemala during the military's campaign of "scorched communists" (Box 3a), this is precisely the kind of coordinated campaign to deliberately inflict "conditions of life calculated to bring about [the] physical destruction" of a group that is referenced in Article 2(c) of the UN Genocide Convention.

48 Ibid., p. 222.

49 As explored by Richard Drinnon in *Facing West: The Metaphysics of Indian Hating and Empire Building* (New York: Schocken Books, 1990).

50 Valentino, and Laber and Rubin quoted, in ibid., pp. 221–22.

51 Gregory Feifer, *The Great Gamble: The Soviet War in Afghanistan* (New York: HarperPerennial, 2009), p. 4.

52 Boulouque, "Communism in Afghanistan," p. 717.

53 Helen Fein, "Discriminating Genocide from War Crimes: Vietnam and Afghanistan Reexamined," *Denver Journal of International Law and Policy*, 22: 1 (1993), p. 61. Hannibal Travis also refers to "the genocidal war between Soviet and Afghan communist forces and the fundamentalist insurgents backed by the Western and wider Islamic worlds." Travis, *Genocide in the Middle East*, p. 385.

54 Levene, *Genocide in the Age of the Nation State, Vol. 2*, pp. 217, 232, 274.

55 Ibid., pp. 223–24. Many scholars, including Levene, Omer Bartov, and Jacques Sémelin, have also drawn attention "to those geographic zones situated at the crossroads of empires": "These buffer zones between two worlds, between two or more empires, would indeed appear fragile, if not uncontrollable. The melting-pot situation whereby populations mix and mingle constitutes a factor of uncertainty and of potential risk of violence, whether on the part of some community groups or of neighboring nations" – particularly, I would add, when empires feel especially vulnerable. Sémelin, *Purify and Destroy: The Political Uses of Massacre and Genocide* (New York: Columbia University Press, 2007), p. 118.

56 Levene, *Genocide in the Age of the Nation State, Vol. 1*, pp. 186–87.

57 On the Serb case, see David B. MacDonald, "From Jasenovac to Srebrenica: Subaltern Genocide and the Serbs," in Nicholas A. Robins and Adam Jones, eds, *Genocides by the Oppressed: Subaltern Genocide in Theory and Practice* (Bloomington, IN: Indiana University Press, 2009), pp. 103–21.

58 Christopher J. Fettweis, "War as Catalyst: Moving World War II to the Center of Holocaust Scholarship," *Journal of Genocide Research*, 5: 2 (2003), p. 225.

59 "Genocide can be regarded as a particular form of modern warfare, and an extension of the more common form of *degenerate* war," which "involves the deliberate and systematic extension of war against an organized armed enemy to war against a largely unarmed civilian population. . . . Therefore, the best way of making sense of genocide is to see it as *a distinctive form of war.*" Martin Shaw, *War and Genocide: Organized Killing in Modern Society* (Cambridge: Polity Press, 2003), p. 5.

60 Goebbels quoted in Jeffrey Herf, *The Jewish Enemy: Nazi Propaganda during World War II and the Holocaust* (Cambridge, MA: The Belknap Press of Harvard University Press, 2006), p. 149.

61 Fettweis, "War as Catalyst," p. 228.

62 Sémelin, *Purify and Destroy*, p. 172.

63 Barbara Ehrenreich, *Blood Rites: Origins and History of the Passions of War* (New York: Metropolitan Books, 1997), pp. 180–81.

64 Alex Alvarez, *Governments, Citizens, and Genocide: A Comparative and Interdisciplinary Approach* (Bloomington, IN: Indiana University Press, 2001), p. 68.

65 I am grateful to Benjamin Madley for this insight.

66 Norman M. Naimark, *Fires of Hatred: Ethnic Cleansing in Twentieth-century Europe* (Cambridge, MA: Harvard University Press, 2001), p. 187.

67 George L. Mosse, quoted in Ehrenreich, *Blood Rites*, p. 183.

68 Alvarez, *Governments, Citizens, and Genocide*, p. 68.

69 Barash quoted in Michael Shermer and Alex Grobman, *Denying History: Who Says the Holocaust Never Happened and Why Do They Say It?* (Berkeley, CA: University of California Press, 2002), p. 93.

70 Ehrenreich, *Blood Rites*, p. 196.

71 Peter Uvin, *Aiding Violence: The Development Enterprise in Rwanda* (West Hartford, CT: Kumarian Press, 1998).

72 Quoted in Adam Jones, *Genocide: A Comprehensive Introduction* (first edition) (London: Routledge, 2006), pp. 50–51.

73 Ewen MacAskill, "Fort Hood Backlash Feared," *The Guardian Weekly*, November 13, 2009.

74 Quoted passages from The Anti-Idiotarian Rottweiler (http://nicedoggie.net/), November 2009 archives, http://nicedoggie.net/2009/index.php/archives/date/2009/11. All typography as in the original.

75 John Keegan, *The First World War* (New York: Vintage, 1998), p. 299.

76 In 1989, I walked the Somme battlefields; the experience is described, with accompanying photos, in Adam Jones, "No Man's Land," *The Gazette* (Montreal), December 11, 1989 (available at http://adamjones.freeservers.com/nomans.htm).

77 Shaw, *War and Genocide*, p. 172. According to Lance Morrow, "Trench warfare prefigured the fatal industrialism of the Nazi death camps: there cling to the gray, corpse-littered wastelands of World War I something of the same atmosphere: individual life stripped of meaning, dignity, all life and all death rendered purposeless, and reduced to absolute metaphysical insignificance." Morrow, *Evil: An Investigation* (New York: Basic Books, 2003), p. 47.

78 A good overview of the Soviet side of the German–Soviet conflict is Richard Overy, *Russia's War* (London: Penguin, 1997). See also Catherine Merridale, *Ivan's War: Life and Death in the Red Army, 1939–1945* (New York: Picador, 2007); Antony Beevor, *Stalingrad: The Fateful Siege, 1942–1943* (London: Penguin, 1999); John Erickson's two-volume study, *The Road to Stalingrad* and *The Road to Berlin* (New Haven, CT: Yale University Press, 1999); British diplomat Alexander Werth's towering memoir, *Russia at War, 1941–1945* (New York: Carroll & Graf, 1999); and for a revisionist account of Stalin's capacities as military and national leader, Geoffrey Roberts, *Stalin's Wars: From World War to Cold War, 1939–1953* (New Haven, CT: Yale University Press, 2006).

79 Omer Bartov, *Germany's War and the Holocaust: Disputed Histories* (Ithaca, NY: Cornell University Press, 2003), p. 7.

80 Omer Bartov, *Hitler's Army: Soldiers, Nazis, and War in the Third Reich* (New York: Oxford University Press, 1992), p. 129.

81 Ehrenburg quoted in Alfred-Maurice de Zayas, *A Terrible Revenge: The Ethnic Cleansing of the East European Germans, 1944–1950* (New York: St. Martin's Press, 1994), p. 34.

82 Stalin quoted in Milovan Djilas, *Wartime* (New York: Harvest, 1980), p. 435.

83 Norman M. Naimark, *The Russians in Germany: A History of the Soviet Zone of Occupation, 1945–1949* (Cambridge, MA: The Belknap Press, 1995), pp. 72, 133; see also pp. 235–50 on the postwar uranium mining that killed thousands of German workers.

84 Gary Paul Bass, *Stay the Hand of Vengeance: The Politics of War Crimes Tribunals* (Princeton, NJ: Princeton University Press, 2000), p. 198.

85 Daniel Chirot and Clark McCauley, *Why Not Kill Them All? The Logic and Prevention of Mass Political Murder* (Princeton, NJ: Princeton University Press, 2006), p. 216.

86 Karl Marx and Friedrich Engels, *The Communist Manifesto* (London: Penguin, various editions).

87 Fascism "is closely associated with imperialism, militarism and nationalism. The logic of belief in racial superiority leads to policies of conquest, domination and even elimination of lesser races." Graham Evans and Richard Newnham, *The Penguin Dictionary of International Relations* (London: Penguin, 1999), p. 168.

88 Shaw, *War and Genocide*, p. 29.

89 Robert Melson, *Revolution and Genocide: On the Origins of Armenian Genocide and the Holocaust* (Chicago, IL: University of Chicago Press, 1996), p. 18.

90 Eric Markusen and Matthias Bjørnlund, "Hiroshima: Culmination of Strategic Bombing, Beginning of the Threat of Nuclear Omnicide," paper prepared for the symposium "Terror in the Sky: Indiscriminate Bombing from Hiroshima to Today," Hiroshima Peace Institute, August 2, 2003.

91 Robert Jay Lifton and Eric Markusen, *The Genocidal Mentality: Nazi Holocaust and Nuclear Threat* (New York: Basic Books, 1990), p. 38.

92 Jonathan Schell, *The Fate of the Earth and the Abolition* (Stanford, CA: Stanford University Press, 2000), p. 182.

93 Lifton and Markusen, *The Genocidal Mentality*, p. 226.

94 Andre De Nesnera, "US and Russia Close to an Arms Control Agreement," VAOnline.com, December 18, 2009.

95 See Terrence Henry, "Russia's Loose Nukes," *The Atlantic Monthly*, December 2004, pp. 74–75.

PART 2 CASES

CHAPTER 3

Genocides of Indigenous Peoples

INTRODUCTION

This chapter considers the impact of European invasion upon diverse indigenous peoples. Vast geographic, temporal, and cultural differences exist among these cases, but there are important common features in the strategies and outcomes of genocide.[1]

To grasp this phenomenon, we must first define "indigenous peoples." The task is not easy. Indeed, both in discourse and in international law, the challenge of definition remains a "complex [and] delicate" one, in anthropologist Ronald Niezen's appraisal.[2] Nevertheless, there are "some areas of general consensus among formal attempts at definition," well captured in a 1987 report by the UN Special Rapporteur on indigenous issues, José Martínez Cobo:

> Indigenous communities, peoples and nations are those which, having a historical continuity with pre-invasion and pre-colonial societies that developed on their territories, consider themselves distinct from other sectors of the society now prevailing in those territories, or parts of them. They form at present nondominant sectors of society and are determined to preserve, develop and transmit to future generations their ancestral territories and their ethnic identity, as the basis of their continued existence as peoples, in accordance with their own cultural patterns, social institutions and legal systems.[3]

By this definition, "indigenous" peoples are inseparable from processes of colonialism and imperialism that consigned the previously dominant population of a colonized territory to a marginal status.[4] A nexus of indigenous identity and structural subordination is generally held to persist today.

The political and activist components of the indigenist project are also clear from Martínez Cobo's definition. Indigenous peoples proclaim the validity and worth of their cultures, languages, laws, religious beliefs, and political institutions; they demand respect and political space. Increasingly, they have mobilized to denounce the genocides visited upon them in the past and demand their rights in the present. In large part thanks to the growth of international governmental and nongovernmental organizations, notably the United Nations system, these mobilizations have assumed a global character. This is analyzed further in the section on "Indigenous revival," below.

COLONIALISM AND THE DISCOURSE OF EXTINCTION

The histories of indigenous peoples cannot be understood without reference to imperialism and colonialism, examined in the previous chapter. In general, though not overlooking the counterexample of Atlantic slavery, the destruction of indigenous peoples was less catastrophic in cases of "empire lite," where foreign settlement was mostly limited to coastal settlements, and networks of trade and exploitation were predominantly in the hands of native satraps. Correspondingly, policies of extermination and/or exploitation unto death were most pronounced in areas where Europeans sought to conquer indigenous territories and both displace and supplant their native populations. The focus here is on this latter variant, known as "settler colonialism."

Three ideological tenets stand out as justifying and facilitating European conquest, "pacification," and "settlement." The first, most prominent in the British realm (especially the United States, Canada, and Australasia), was a *legal-utilitarian* justification, according to which native peoples had no right to territories they inhabited, owing to their "failure" to exploit them adequately. As Benjamin Madley has pointed out, this translated in Australasia to the fiction of *terra nullius*, i.e., that the territories in question had no original inhabitants in a legal sense; and, in America, to the similar concept of *vacuum domicilium*, or "empty dwelling."[5] The second tenet, most prominent in Latin America, was a religious ideology that justified invasion and conquest as a means of saving native souls from the fires of hell. The third, more diffuse, underpinning was a *racial-eliminationist* ideology. Under the influence of the most modern scientific thinking of the age, world history was viewed as revolving around the inevitable, sometimes lamentable supplanting of primitive peoples by more advanced and "civilized" ones. This would be engineered through military confrontations between indigenous peoples and better-armed Europeans, and "naturally," through a gradual dying-off of the native populations. "Genocide began to be regarded as the inevitable byproduct of progress," as literary scholar Sven Lindqvist observed – even if its perpetrators and supporters grew misty-eyed in the process.[6]

A sophisticated study of this pervasive ideology of inevitable extinction is Patrick Brantlinger's *Dark Vanishings*. Brantlinger pointed to the remarkable "uniformity . . . of extinction discourse," which pervaded the speech and writings of "humanitarians, missionaries, scientists, government officials, explorers, colonists, soldiers, journalists, novelists, and poets." Extinction discourse often celebrated the destruction of native peoples, as when the otherwise humane author Mark Twain wrote that the North American Indian was "nothing but a poor, filthy, naked scurvy vagabond, whom to exterminate were a charity to the Creator's worthier insects and reptiles."[7] Often, though, the discourse was more complex and ambivalent, including nostalgia and lament for vanishing peoples. English naturalist Alfred Russel Wallace, who shared credit with Charles Darwin for the theory of natural selection, wrote:

> The red Indian in North America and in Brazil; the Tasmanian, Australian, and New Zealander in the southern hemisphere, die out, not from any one special cause, but from the inevitable effects of an unequal mental and physical struggle. The intellectual and moral, as well as the physical qualities of the European are superior; the same powers and capacities which have made him rise in a few centuries from the condition of the wandering savage . . . to his present state of culture and advancement . . . enable him when in contact with the savage man, to conquer in the struggle for existence, and to increase at the expense of the less adapted varieties in the animal and vegetable kingdoms, – just as the weeds of Europe overrun North America and Australia, extinguishing native productions by the inherent vigor of their organization, and by their greater capacity for existence and multiplication.[8]

Several features of extinction discourse are apparent here, including the parallels drawn with natural biological selection, and the claims of racial superiority imputed to northern peoples. Yet it is interesting that Wallace depicted the European conquerors as analogous to "weeds . . . overrun[ning] North America and Australia," rather than as representatives of a noble race. Wallace was in fact an "anti-imperialist and anti-capitalist";[9] hence his critical edge. But like some contemporary observers (several of whom are cited in the section on "Denying genocide, celebrating genocide," below), Wallace found little difficulty in reconciling the extermination of native peoples with his progressive political views.

There is a close link between extinction discourse and the more virulent and systematically hateful ideologies that fueled the Nazi Holocaust in Europe (Box 6a). The Nazis, wrote Lindqvist, "have been made sole scapegoats for ideas of extermination that are actually a common European heritage."[10] We should also note the interaction of extinction discourse with ideologies of modernization and capitalist development, which created "surplus or redundant population[s]," in genocide scholar Richard Rubenstein's phrase. As Rubenstein explained in his *Age of Triage*, these ideologies produced destructive or genocidal outcomes in European societies as well, as with the colonial famines of the nineteenth century, or the Holocaust.[11] Ironically, this modernizing ideology also resulted in the migration – as convicts or refugees from want, political persecution, and famine – of millions of "surplus" Europeans to the New World. In Australia and the United States, among other locations, these settlers would become key, often semi-autonomous instruments of genocide against indigenous peoples.

THE CONQUEST OF THE AMERICAS

> The reader may ask himself if this is not cruelty and injustice of a kind so terrible that it beggars the imagination, and whether these poor people would not fare far better if they were entrusted to the devils in Hell than they do at the hands of the devils of the New World who masquerade as Christians.
>
> Bartolomé de las Casas, Spanish friar, 1542

> I have been looking far,
> Sending my spirit north, south, east and west.
> Trying to escape death,
> But could find nothing,
> No way of escape.
>
> Song of the Luiseno Indians of California

The European holocaust of indigenous peoples in the Americas may have been the most extensive and destructive genocide ever. Ethnic studies scholar Ward Churchill has called it "unparalleled in human history, both in terms of its sheer magnitude and its duration."[12] Over nearly five centuries, and perhaps continuing to the present, wide-ranging genocidal measures have been imposed.[13] These include:

- genocidal massacres;
- biological warfare, using pathogens (especially smallpox and plague) to which the indigenous peoples had no resistance;[14]
- spreading of disease via the "reduction" of Indians to densely crowded and unhygienic settlements;
- slavery and forced/indentured labor, especially though not exclusively in Latin America,[15] in conditions often rivaling those of Nazi concentration camps;
- mass population removals to barren "reservations," sometimes involving death marches *en route*, and generally leading to widespread mortality and population collapse upon arrival;
- deliberate starvation and famine, exacerbated by destruction and occupation of the native land base and food resources;
- forced education of indigenous children in white-run schools, where mortality rates sometimes reached genocidal levels.

Spanish America

The Spanish invasion, occupation, and exploitation of "Latin" America began in the late fifteenth century, and resulted, according to American studies scholar David Stannard, in "the worst series of human disease disasters, combined with the most extensive and most violent program of human eradication, that this world has ever seen."[16] The tone was set with the first territory conquered, the densely populated Caribbean island of Hispaniola (today the Dominican Republic and Haiti). Tens of thousands of Indians were exterminated: the Spanish "forced their way into native

Figure 3.1   After invading Hispaniola, the Spanish enslaved the population and inflicted systematic atrocities, like the severing of limbs depicted here, upon natives who failed to deliver sufficient gold to the Spaniards. In two or three decades, the indigenous population of Hispaniola was exterminated. The carnage sparked outrage in Europe, resulting in some stylized but otherwise accurate contemporary representations, like this (sixteenth-century?) rendering.

Source: Wikimedia Commons.

Figure 3.2   A detail of Diego Rivera's mural "La Gran Tenochtitlán" (1945), depicting the grandeur and social complexity of the pre-conquest Aztec capital. (Tenochtitlán is today's Mexico City; Rivera's mural, of which this is only a small section, occupies a wall of the presidential palace, just a few meters from the ruins of the Aztec main temple.) The accomplishments of indigenous societies – in engineering, agriculture, and urban sanitation, for example – often far outstripped those of early-modern Europe. But indigenous military technologies were no match for European ones. Moreover, some American societies – like the Aztecs, Mayans, and Iroquois – appear themselves to have waged war-unto-genocide, whether prior to or following European contact. In the Aztec case, this provoked neighboring Indian nations to join with the Spanish conquistadors, and supply most of the foot-soldiers who finally besieged and overthrew "the great Tenochtitlán."

Source: Diego Rivera/Courtesy James Kiracofe.

settlements," wrote eyewitness Bartolomé de las Casas, "slaughtering everyone they found there, including small children, old men, [and] pregnant women."[17] Those men not killed at the outset were worked to death in gold mines; women survivors were consigned to harsh agricultural labor and sexual servitude. Massacred, sickened, and enslaved, Hispaniola's native population collapsed, "as would any nation subjected to such appalling treatment"[18] – declining from as many as eight million people at the time of the invasion to a scant *20,000* less than three decades later.[19] African slaves then replaced native workers, and toiled under similarly genocidal conditions.

Rumors of great civilizations, limitless wealth, and populations to convert to Christianity in the Aztec and Inca empires lured the Spanish on to Mexico and Central America. Soon thereafter, assaults were launched against the Inca empire in present-day Peru, Bolivia, and Ecuador. The Incas constituted the largest empire in the world, but with their leader Atahuallpa captured and killed, the empire was decapitated, and quickly fell. "It is extremely difficult now to grasp the beliefs and

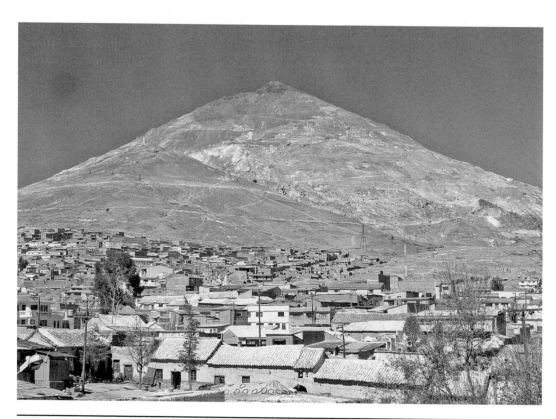

Figure 3.3 The Cerro Rico overlooking Potosí, Bolivia. Following the discovery of silver in the mid-sixteenth century, this mountain largely paid for the profligacy and foreign wars of the Spanish Crown for some two hundred years. Millions of Indians and some African slaves were forced to work in horrific conditions, making the Cerro possibly the world's single biggest graveyard: anywhere from one million to eight million forced laborers perished in the mines, or from silicosis and other diseases soon after. By some estimates, the mines killed seven out of every ten who worked there. Time for a Potosí holocaust museum, perhaps?

Source: Author's photo, 2005.

motives of the Conquistadores [conquerors] as they cheated, tortured, burnt, maimed, murdered and massacred their way through South and Meso-America, causing such ferocious destruction that their compatriot Pedro de Ciéza de Léon complained that 'wherever Christians have passed, conquering and discovering, it seems as though a fire has gone, consuming.'"[20] A holocaust it indeed proved for the Indians enslaved on plantations and in silver mines. Conditions in the mines – notably those in Mexico and at Potosí (see Figure 3.3) and Huancavelica in Upper Peru (Bolivia) – resulted in death rates matching or exceeding those of Hispaniola. According to Stannard, Indians in the Bolivian mines had a life expectancy of three to four months, "about the same as that of someone working at slave labor in the synthetic rubber manufacturing plant at Auschwitz in the 1940s."[21] In the contemporary testimony of Fray Toribio de Motolinía, "The Indians that died in the mines produced such a stench that it caused the plague . . . for about half a square league you could hardly walk without stepping on dead bodies or on bones; and so many birds and ravens came to eat that they greatly shadowed the sun, and many towns were depopulated."[22]

Only in the mid-sixteenth century did the exterminatory impact of Spanish rule begin to wane. A *modus vivendi* was established between colonizers and colonized, featuring continued exploitation of surviving Indian populations, but also a degree of autonomy for native peoples. It survived until the mid-nineteenth century, when the now-independent governments of Spanish America sought to implement the economic prescriptions then popular in Europe. This resulted in another assault on "uneconomic" Indian landholdings, the further erosion of the Indian land base and impoverishment of its population, and the "opening up" of both land and labor resources to capitalist transformation. Meanwhile, in both South America and North America, expansionist governments launched "Indian wars" against native nations that were seen as impediments to economic development and progress. The campaigns against Araucana Indians in Chile and the Querandí in Argentina form part of national lore in these countries. Only relatively recently have South American scholars and others begun to examine such exterminations under the rubric of genocide.[23]

The United States and Canada

The first sustained contact between Europeans and the indigenous peoples of North America developed around the whaling industry that, in the sixteenth century, began to cross the Atlantic in search of new bounty. Whaling crews put ashore to process the catch, and were often welcomed by the coastal peoples. Similarly, when the Pilgrims arrived at Plymouth Rock, Massachusetts, in 1608, their survival through the first harsh winters was due solely to the generosity of Indians who fed them and trained them in regional agriculture. The settlers, though, responded to this amity with contempt for the "heathen" Indians. In addition, as more colonists flooded into the northeastern seaboard of the future United States, they brought diseases that wreaked havoc on Indian communities, leading to depopulation that paved the way for settler expansion into the devastated Indian heartlands.

BOX 3.1 BUFFY SAINTE-MARIE, "MY COUNTRY 'TIS OF THY PEOPLE YOU'RE DYING"

Figure 3.4 Cree Canadian singer Buffy Sainte-Marie in concert. Sainte-Marie exemplified the North American Indian cultural and political revival of the 1960s and 1970s. Her 1965 song, "My Country 'Tis of Thy People You're Dying," was likely the first engagement with American Indian genocide in North American popular culture. It still stands as one of the most powerful and poetic statements on the subject.

Source: Courtesy www.creative-native.com.

My Country 'Tis of Thy People You're Dying

By Buffy Sainte-Marie

From *Little Wheel Spin and Spin* (1965)

Now that your big eyes are finally opened
Now that you're wondering, "How must they feel?"
Meaning them that you've chased across America's movie screens
Now that you're wondering, "How can it be real?"
That the ones you've called colorful, noble and proud
In your school propaganda,
They starve in their splendor.
You've asked for our comment I simply will render
My country 'tis of thy people you're dying.

Now that the longhouses "breed superstition"
You force us to send our children away
To your schools where they're taught to despise their traditions
Forbid them their languages, then further say
That American history really began
When Columbus set sail out of Europe and then stress

That the nations of leeches that conquered this land
Were the biggest and bravest and boldest and best.
And yet where in your history books is the tale
Of the genocide basic to this country's birth?
Of the preachers who lied? How the Bill of Rights failed?
How a nation of patriots returned to their earth?
And where will it tell of the Liberty Bell
As it rang with a thud
Over Kinzua mud[24]
And of brave Uncle Sam in Alaska this year?
My country 'tis of thy people you're dying.

Hear how the bargain was made for the West,
With her shivering children in zero degrees.
"Blankets for your land" – so the treaties attest,
Oh well, blankets for land, that's a bargain indeed.
And the blankets were those Uncle Sam had collected
From smallpox-diseased dying soldiers that day.
And the tribes were wiped out and the history books censored,
A hundred years of your statesmen say it's better this way.
And yet a few of the conquered have somehow survived,
Their blood runs the redder though genes have paled.
From the Grand Canyon's caverns to craven sad hills
The wounded, the losers, the robbed sing their tale.
From Los Angeles County to upstate New York
The white nation fattens while others grow lean;
Oh the tricked and evicted they know what I mean.
My country 'tis of thy people you're dying.

The past it just crumbled; the future just threatens;
Our life blood is shut up in your chemical tanks.
And now here you come, bill of sale in your hands
And surprise in your eyes, that we're lacking in thanks
For the blessings of civilization you've got us,
The lessons you've taught us, the ruin you've wrought us
Oh see what our trust in America's brought us.
My country 'tis of thy people you're dying.

Now that the pride of the sires receives charity,
Now that we're harmless and safe behind laws.
Now that my life's to be known as your heritage,
Now that even the graves have been robbed.
Now that our own chosen way is your novelty.
Hands on our hearts we salute you your victory:

Choke on your blue white and scarlet hypocrisy.
Pitying your blindness; how you never see
That the eagles of war whose wings lent you glory,
Were never no more than buzzards & crows,
Pushed some wrens from their nest; stole their eggs; changed their story;
The mockingbird sings it, it's all that she knows.
"Ah what can I do?," say a powerless few
With a lump in your throat and a tear in your eye
Can't you see how their poverty's profiting you?
My country 'tis of thy people you're dying.

Lyrics reprinted by permission of Buffy Sainte-Marie[25]

According to demographer Russell Thornton, disease was "without doubt . . . the single most important factor in American Indian population decline,"[26] which in five centuries reduced the Indian population of the present-day United States from between seven and ten million (though anthropologist Henry Dobyns has estimated as many as eighteen million) to *237,000* by the end of the nineteenth century.[27] Smallpox was the biggest killer: uncounted numbers of Indians died as did O-wapa-shaw, "the greatest man of the Sioux, with half his band . . . their bodies swollen, and covered with pustules, their eyes blinded, hideously howling their death song in utter despair."[28] At least one epidemic was deliberately spread, by British commander Lord Jeffery Amherst in 1763. Amherst ordered a commanding officer in 1763: "You will Do well to try to Inoculate the Indians [with smallpox] by means of Blanketts, as well as to try Every other method that can serve to extirpate this Execrable Race."[29] It is likely that other attempts were made to infect Indian populations with the pox, according to Norbert Finzsch, though their "success" is harder to determine.[30] Cholera, measles, plague, typhoid, and alcoholism also took an enormous toll. Other, often interlocking factors included "the often deliberate destructions of flora and fauna that American Indians used for food and other purposes,"[31] whether as a military strategy or simply as part of the exploitation of the continent's resources. An example of both was the extermination of the bison, which was hunted into near extinction. Perhaps sixty million buffalo roamed the Great Plains before contact. ". . . By 1895 there were fewer than *1,000* animals left," and the ecocidal campaign (see p. 26) "had not only driven [the Indians] to starvation and defeat but had destroyed the core of their spiritual and ceremonial world."[32]

Genocidal massacres were also prominent. According to Thornton, though direct slaughter was a subsidiary cause of demographic decline, it was decisive in the trajectories of some Indian nations "brought to extinction or the brink of extinction by . . . genocide in the name of war."[33] Perhaps the first such instance in North America was the Pequot War (1636–37) in present-day Connecticut, when Puritan settlers reacted to an Indian raid by launching an extermination campaign.[34] This "created a precedent for later genocidal wars,"[35] including that targeting Apaches in the 1870s. "As there has been a great deal said about my killing women and children," the civilian scout leader King Woolsey wrote to military authorities,

"I will state to you that we killed in this Scout 22 Bucks [males] 5 women & 3 children. We would have killed more women but [did not] owing to having attacked in the day time when the women were at work gathering Mescal. It sir is next to impossible to prevent killing squaws in jumping a rancheria [settlement] even were we disposed to save them. For my part I am frank to say that I fight on the broad platform of *extermination*."[36]

Perhaps most infamous was Colonel John Chivington's command to his volunteer soldiers, in November 1864 at Sand Creek, Colorado, to "kill and scalp all, little and big." Children could not be exempted, Chivington declared, because "Nits make lice."[37] The ensuing massacre prompted a government inquiry, at which Lieutenant James Connor testified:

> I did not see a body of man, woman or child but was scalped, and in many instances their bodies were mutilated in the most horrible manner – men, women and children's privates cut out, &c; I heard one man say that he cut out a woman's private parts and had them for exhibition on a stock . . . I also heard of numerous instances in which men had cut out the private parts of females and stretched them over their saddle-bows and wore them over their hats . . . .[38]

Recalling this rampage, US President Theodore Roosevelt would call it "as righteous and beneficial a deed as ever took place on the frontier."[39]

As noted above, killing was just one of a complex of genocidal strategies that were intended to result in the elimination of Indian peoples from the face of the earth. The Yuki Indians, for example, were subjected to one of the clearest and fastest genocides of a native nation in US history. The Yuki, numbering perhaps 20,000, inhabited territory in northern California. With the seizure of California and other Mexican territories in 1847, the Yuki fell under US control. The following year, the California Gold Rush began. It proved "probably the single most destructive episode in the whole history of Native/Euro-American relations."[40] Ranchers and farmers flowed in and, among many other atrocities, murdered Yuki men and stripped the communities of children and women, taking the former for servants and the latter for "wives" and concubines. The Yuki land base was expropriated and the "natives' food supply . . . severely depleted." Settler depredations received state sanction in 1859, when California governor John B. Weller "granted state commissions to companies of volunteers that excelled in the killing of Indians." The volunteers were dispatched to "Indian country," despite warnings from Army officers that they would "hunt the Indians to extermination." They proceeded to slaughter "all the Indians they encountered regardless of age or sex"; their actions were legitimized *post facto* by the state legislature's awarding of wages for their genocidal work. The combination of "kidnapping, epidemics, starvation, vigilante justice, and state-sanctioned mass killing" virtually annihilated the Yuki, reducing their numbers from the original 20,000 to about 3,500 in 1854, and *168* by 1880.[41] Special Treasury Agent J. Ross Browne subsequently wrote:

> In the history of the Indian race, I have seen nothing so cruel or relentless as the treatment of those unhappy people by the authority constituted by law for their

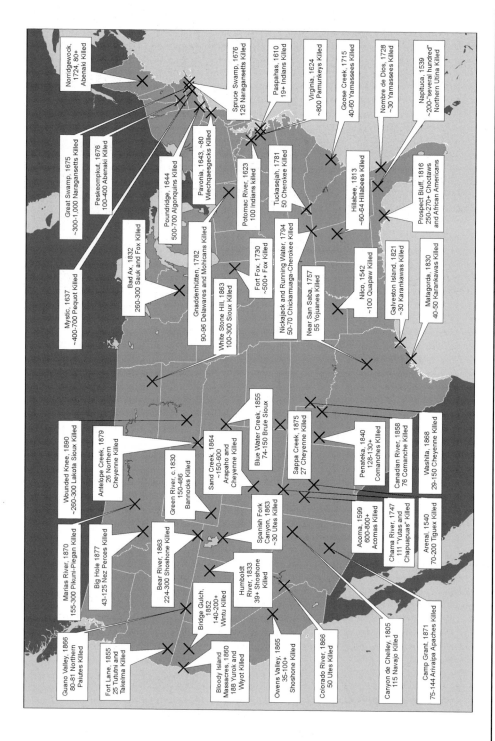

Map 3.1 Historian Benjamin Madley, a postdoctoral fellow at Dartmouth College, has published prizewinning investigations of systematic violence against Native Americans in the continental United States. This map, his latest (early 2010), is based on archival research and locates fifty massacres from North American colonial and post-colonial history.

Source: Courtesy and copyright Benjamin Madley.

Figure 3.5   US soldiers load the corpses of Indian victims of the Wounded Knee massacre for burial in mass graves, December 1890.

Source: Smithsonian Institution National Archives.

protection. Instead of receiving aid and succor they have been starved and driven away from the Reservations and then followed into the remote hiding places where they have sought to die in peace, cruelly slaughtered until that [*sic*] a few are left and that few without hope.[42]

James Wilson has likewise called this "a sustained campaign of genocide," and has argued that "more Indians probably died as a result of deliberate, cold-blooded genocide in California than anywhere else in North America."[43]

Other genocidal strategies

Forced relocations of Indian populations often took the form of genocidal death marches, most infamously the "Trails of Tears" of the Cherokee nation and the "Long Walk" of the Navajo, which killed between 20 and 40 percent of the targeted populations *en route*.[44] The "tribal reservations" to which survivors were consigned exacted their own toll through malnutrition and disease.

Then there were the so-called "residential schools," in which generations of Indian children were incarcerated after being removed from their homes and families. The schools operated until recent times; the last one in the US was closed in 1972. In an account of the residential-school experience, titled "Genocide by Any Other Name," Ward Churchill describes the program as the linchpin of assimilationist aspirations . . . in which it was ideally intended that every single aboriginal child would be removed from his or her home, family, community, and culture at the earliest possible age and held for years in state-sponsored "educational" facilities, systematically decultured, and simultaneously indoctrinated to see her/his own heritage – and him/herself as well – in terms deemed appropriate by a society that despised both to the point of seeking as a matter of policy their utter eradication.[45]

As Churchill has pointed out, the injunction in the UN Genocide Convention against "forcibly transferring children of the [targeted] group to another group" qualifies this policy as genocidal – and in Australia, where a similar policy was implemented, a government commission found that it met the Convention's definition of genocide (see further below). In addition, there was much that was genocidal in the operation of the North American residential schools apart from the "forcible transfer" of the captive native children. Crucially, "mortality rates in the schools were appalling from the outset," resulting in death rates – from starvation, disease, systematic torture, sexual predation,[46] and shattering psychological dislocation – *that matched or exceeded the death rates in Nazi concentration camps.* In Canada, for example, the 1907 "Bryce Report," submitted by the Indian Department's chief medical officer,

revealed that of the 1,537 children who had attended the sample group of facilities since they'd opened – a period of ten years, on average – 42 per cent had died of "consumption or tuberculosis," either at the schools or shortly after being discharged. Extrapolating, Bryce's data indicated that of the 3,755 native children then under the "care" of Canada's residential schools, 1,614 could be expected to have died a miserable death by the end of 1910. In a follow-up survey conducted in 1909, Bryce collected additional information, all of it corroborating his initial report. At the Qu'Appelle School, the principal, a Father Hugonard, informed Bryce that his facility's record was "something to be proud of" since "only" 153 of the 795 youngsters who'd attended it between 1884 and 1905 had died in school or within two years of leaving it.[47]

The experience of the residential schools reverberated through generations of native life in Canada and the US. Alcoholism and substance abuse are now increasingly understood to reflect the "worlds of pain" inflicted by residential schooling, and the traumas that Indians in turn inflicted on their own children. Churchill wrote of a "Residential School Syndrome" (RSS) studied in Canada, which

includes acutely conflicted self-concept and lowered self-esteem, emotional numbing (often described as "inability to trust or form lasting bonds"), somatic disorder, chronic depression and anxiety (often phobic), insomnia and nightmares, dislocation, paranoia, sexual dysfunction, heightened irritability and tendency to fly into rages, strong tendencies towards alcoholism and drug addiction, and suicidal behavior.[48]

AUSTRALIA'S ABORIGINES AND THE NAMIBIAN HEREROS

The cases of the aboriginal populations of British-colonized Australia and German-colonized Namibia further illuminate the fate of indigenous peoples worldwide. In both instances, decades of denial gave way, at the twentieth century's close, to a greater readiness to acknowledge the genocidal character of some colonial actions.

Genocide in Australia

In 1788, the "First Fleet" of British convicts was dumped on Australian soil. Over the ensuing century-and-a-half, the aboriginal population – estimated at about 750,000 when the colonists arrived – was reduced to just 31,000 by 1911. As in North America, the colonists did not arrive in Australia with the explicit intention of exterminating the Aborigines. The destruction inflicted on Australian Aborigines instead reflected a concatenation of ideologies, pressures, and circumstances. Arriving whites were aghast at the state of the Aborigines, and quickly determined that they were (1) barely, if at all, human[49] and (2) largely useless. Aboriginal lands, however, were coveted, particularly as convicts began to be freed (but not allowed to return to England) and as new waves of free settlers arrived. As the Australian colonial economy came to center on vast landholdings for sheep-raising and cattle-grazing, expansion into the interior brought colonists into ever-wider and more conflictive contact with the Aborigines. Through direct massacre – "at least 20,000 aborigines, perhaps many more, were killed by the settlers in sporadic frontier skirmishes throughout the nineteenth century and lasting into the late 1920s"[50] – Aborigines were driven away from areas of white colonization and from their own sources of sustenance. When they responded with raids on the settlers' cattle stocks, colonists "retaliated" by "surround[ing] an aborigine camp at night, attack[ing] at dawn, and massacr[ing] men, women, and children alike."[51]

Formal colonial policy did not generally favor genocidal measures. Indeed, the original instructions to colonial Governor Arthur Phillip were that he "endeavour by every means in his power to open an intercourse with the natives and to conciliate their goodwill, requiring all persons under his Government to live in amity and kindness with them." But these "benign utterances of far-away governments" contrasted markedly with "the hard clashes of interest on the spot."[52] Colonial officials often turned a blind eye to atrocities against the Aborigines, and failed to intervene effectively to suppress them. The most murderous extremes were reached in Queensland, where a state militia – effectively a death squad – was "given carte blanche to go out and pursue 'niggers' far into the bush and indiscriminately shoot them down – often quite regardless of whether a particular tribal group had been responsible for an alleged wrongdoing or not – with the rape of cornered women inevitably being one unofficially sanctioned perk of these operations."[53] Historian Henry Reynolds estimated between 8,000 and 10,000 Aborigines murdered in Queensland from 1824 to 1908.[54]

Legal discrimination, and the imposition of broader "social death" measures, buttressed these frequent genocidal massacres. Until the late nineteenth century, no

Aborigine was allowed to give testimony in a white man's court, rendering effective legal redress for dispossession and atrocity a practical impossibility. Moreover, extinction discourse took full flight, with the British novelist Anthony Trollope, for example, writing in the 1870s that the Aborigines' "doom is to be exterminated; and the sooner that their doom is accomplished, – so that there can be no cruelty [!], – the better will it be for civilization."[55]

The combination of clashes between colonists and natives, disease, and extermination campaigns was strikingly similar to the North American experience. The destruction of the aboriginal population of the island of Tasmania is often cited as a paradigmatic colonial genocide. The 3,000–15,000 native inhabitants were broken down by the usual traumas of contact, and survivors were dispatched (in a supposedly humanitarian gesture) to barren Flinders Island.[56] There "they died, if not directly from observable neglect, bad conditions and European illness, then from alcohol-assisted anomie, homesickness and the pointlessness of it all. Tellingly, there were few and ultimately no births on the island to make up for deaths."[57]

The destruction was so extensive that many observers contended that the island's aboriginals had been completely annihilated. This appears to have been true for full-blooded aboriginals, one of the last of whom, a woman named Truganini (Figure 3.6), died in 1876. It ignored, however, aboriginals of mixed blood, thousands of whom live on today.[58]

As was true for indigenous peoples elsewhere, the twentieth century witnessed not only a demographic revival of the Australian Aborigines but – in the latter half of the century – the emergence of a powerful movement for land rights and restitution. Subsequently, this movement's members worked to publicize the trauma caused by the kidnapping of aboriginal children and their placement in white-run institutional "homes." These were strikingly similar, in their underlying (assimilationist) ideology, rampant brutality, and sexual predation, to the "residential schools" imposed upon North American Indians. In response to growing protest about these "stolen generations" of aboriginal children (the title of a landmark 1982 book by Peter

Figure 3.6 Truganini (also known as Trugernanner) (1812–76) was often described as the last of the full-blooded aboriginal population of Tasmania, though in fact several may have outlived her. "Before she was eighteen, her mother had been killed by whalers, her first fiancé died while saving her from abduction, and in 1828, her two sisters, Lowhenunhue and Maggerleede, were abducted and taken to Kangaroo Island, off South Australia and sold as slaves." ("Trugernanner," http://en.wikipedia.org/wiki/Trugernanner.) Truganini was one of the approximately 200 Aborigines removed to Flinders Island off the Tasmanian coast, where most died from disease between 1833 and 1847. After her death in 1876, Truganini's skeleton was displayed by the Royal Society of Tasmania. Only in 1976 were her remains removed and cremated; fragments of her skin and hair housed in the Royal College of Surgeons, UK, were returned for burial in Tasmania in 2002. The date of the photo is uncertain.

Source: Anton Brothers/Wikimedia Commons.

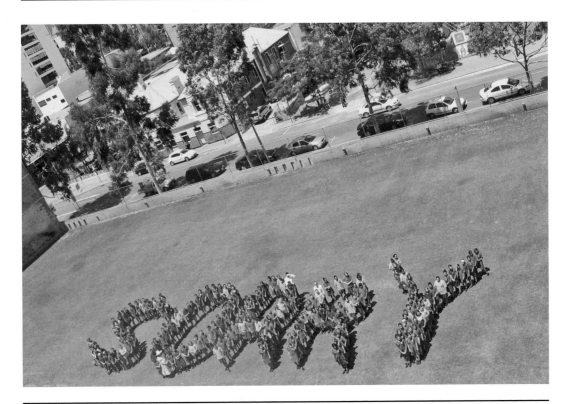

Figure 3.7   February 8, 2008: Children at a school in Perth, Australia, join forces to spell out "Sorry," shortly before the country's prime minister issued a formal apology to the "Stolen Generations" of aboriginal children. A national "Sorry Day," expressing remorse for Australia's treatment of its indigenous population, has become a national institution since it was first launched in 1998.

Source: Courtesy Mark Binns/Flickr.

Read),[59] a national commission of inquiry was struck in 1995. Two years later it issued *Bringing Them Home*, which stated that Australia's policy of transferring aboriginal children constituted genocide according to the UN Convention definition. This claim provoked still-unresolved controversy (and the report's co-author later abjured the term).[60] The Australian Prime Minister at the time, John Howard, denounced the "black armband" view of his country's history (that is, a focus on negative elements of the Australian and aboriginal experience). However, although many voices were raised in public fora and Australian media generally supported Howard's rejectionist stance, the report ensured that "the dreaded 'g' word is firmly with us," as Colin Tatz wrote. "Genocide is now in the vocabulary of Australian politics, albeit grudgingly, or even hostilely."[61]

In February 2008, incoming Labour prime minister Kevin Rudd declared as his government's first act of parliament: "We apologise for the laws and policies of successive parliaments and governments that have inflicted profound grief, suffering and loss on these our fellow Australians. . . . For the pain, suffering and hurt of these stolen generations, their descendants and for their families left behind, we say sorry."[62]

The Herero genocide

It is now widely acknowledged that the first genocide of the twentieth century was committed by German colonial forces in their near-extermination of the Herero nation in present-day Namibia, which took place during the century's first decade.[63]

The pattern of colonial invasion and occupation that provoked the Herero uprising was a familiar one. Drawn by the opportunities for cattle ranching, some 5,000 Germans had flooded into the territory by 1903. Colonists' deception, suasion, and violent coercion pushed the Hereros into an ever-narrower portion of their traditional landholdings. In 1904, the Hereros rose up against the Germans. Declaring, "Let us die fighting rather than die as a result of maltreatment, imprisonment, or some other calamity,"[64] Herero paramount chief Samuel Maharero led his fighters against military outposts and colonists, killing about 120 Germans. This infuriated the German leader Kaiser Wilhelm II, who responded by dispatching the hardline Lt.-Gen. Lothar von Trotha. Von Trotha was convinced that African tribes "are all alike. They only respond to force. It was and is my policy to use force with terrorism and even brutality. I shall annihilate the revolting [rebellious] tribes with rivers of blood and rivers of gold. Only after a complete uprooting will something emerge."[65]

After five months of sporadic conflict, about 1,600 German soldiers armed with machine guns and cannons decisively defeated the Hereros at the Battle of Waterberg.[66] After vanquishing the Hereros, the German Army launched a "mass orgy of killing":

> Not only were there repeated machine gunnings and cannonades, but Herero men were slowly strangled by fencing wire and then hung up in rows like crows, while young women and girls were regularly raped before being bayoneted to death. The old, the sick, the wounded were all slaughtered or burnt to death. Nor were children spared, one account describing how men, women and children were corralled into a high thorn and log enclosure before being "doused with lamp oil and burnt to a cinder."[67]

Survivors fled into the Omahake desert. Von Trotha then issued his notorious "annihilation order" (*Vernichtungsbefehl*). In it, he pledged that "within the German borders every Herero, with or without a gun, with or without cattle, will be shot. I will no longer accept women and children [as prisoners], I will drive them back to their people or I will let them be shot at."[68] The order remained in place for several months, until a domestic outcry led the German Chancellor to rescind it. A contemporary account described Hereros emerging from the desert "starved to skeletons with hollow eyes, powerless and hopeless."[69] They were then moved to concentration camps. "A continuing desire to destroy the Hereros played a part in the German maintenance of such lethal camp conditions," wrote Benjamin Madley; he noted elsewhere that "according to official German figures, of 15,000 Hereros and 2,200 Namas incarcerated in camps, some 7,700 or 45 percent perished."[70] (In October 1904, another tribal nation, the Namas, also rose up in revolt against German rule and was crushed, with approximately half the population killed. Many scholars thus refer to the genocide of the Hereros and Namas.)

Figure 3.8   Famished Hereros after emerging from the Omahake desert in Namibia, c. 1907.

Source: Ullstein Bilderdienst, Berlin/Wikimedia Commons.

Figure 3.9   Conditions in the Shark Island concentration camp inflicted death tolls on Hereros and Namas that were comparable to Nazi slave labor camps. Today the island is a tourist campsite.

Source: Dr. Klaus Dierks/www.klausdierks.com.

A comparative and global-historical approach to genocide allows us to perceive important connections between campaigns of mass killing and group destruction that are widely separated in time and space. Scholarship on the genocide against the Hereros provides an excellent example. It is increasingly acknowledged that it paved the way, in important respects, for the prototypical mass slaughter of that century – Nazi mass murder (Chapter 6 and Box 6a). As summarized by Madley:

> The Herero genocide was a crucial antecedent to Nazi mass murder. It created the German word *Konzentrationslager* [concentration camp] and the twentieth century's first death camp. Like Nazi mass murder, the Namibian genocides were premised upon ideas like *Lebensraum* [living space], annihilation war [*Vernichtungskrieg*], and German racial supremacy. Individual Nazis were also linked to colonial Namibia. Hermann Goering, who built the first Nazi concentration camps, was the son of the first governor of colonial Namibia. Eugen Fischer, who influenced Hitler and ran the institute that supported Joseph Mengele's medical "research" at Auschwitz, conducted racial studies in the colony. And Ritter von Epp, godfather of the Nazi party and Nazi governor of Bavaria from 1933–1945, led German troops against the Herero during the genocide.[71]

Following the independence of Namibia in 1990 (from South Africa, which had conquered the territory during the First World War), survivors' descendants called on Germany to apologize for the Herero genocide, and provide reparations. In August 2004 – the centenary of the Herero uprising – the German development-aid minister, Heidemarie Wieczorek-Zeul, attended a ceremony at Okakarara in the region of Otjozondjupa, where the conflict had formally ended in 1906. The minister eloquently stated that:

A century ago, the oppressors – blinded by colonialist fervour – became agents of violence, discrimination, racism and annihilation in Germany's name. The atrocities committed at that time would today be termed genocide – and nowadays a General von Trotha would be prosecuted and convicted. We Germans accept our historical and moral responsibility and the guilt incurred by Germans at that time. And so, in the words of the Lord's Prayer that we share, I ask you to forgive us.[72]

Of Wieczorek-Zeul's declaration, Jürgen Zimmerer wrote: "To my knowledge it is the first and only apology by a high-ranking member of the government of a former colonial power referring to genocide for colonial crimes."[73] Moves were afoot early in 2010 to offer millions of euros in reparations in the form of German development aid aimed at traditionally Herero regions of Namibia.

DENYING GENOCIDE, CELEBRATING GENOCIDE

> I celebrated Thanksgiving in an old-fashioned way. I invited everyone in my neighborhood to my house, we had an enormous feast, and then I killed them and took their land.
>
> Jon Stewart, US comedian

Denial is regularly condemned as the final stage of genocide (see Chapter 14). How, then, are we to class the mocking or *celebrating* of genocide? These are sadly not uncommon responses, and they are nowhere more prominent than with regard to genocides of indigenous peoples.

Among most sectors of informed opinion in the Americas – from Alaska to Tierra del Fuego – the notion that indigenous peoples experienced genocide at the hands of their white conquerors is dismissed and derided.[74] In a September 2001 post to the H-Genocide academic mailing list, Professor Alexander Bielakowski of the University of Findlay engaged in what seemed outright genocidal denial, writing that "if [it] was the plan" to "wipe out the American Indians . . . the US did a damn poor job following through with it."[75] This is a curious way to describe the annihilation of up to 98 percent of the indigenous population of the United States over three centuries. The fine British historian Michael Burleigh took a similarly flippant jab in his book *Ethics and Extermination*, scoffing at notions of "the 'disappearance' of the [Australian] Aboriginals or Native Americans, some of whose descendants mysteriously seem to be running multi-million dollar casinos."[76] How can a tiny Indian elite be considered representative of the poorest, shortest-lived ethnic minority in the US and Canada?

Celebrations of indigenous genocide also have no clear parallel in mainstream discourse. Thus one finds prominent essayist Christopher Hitchens describing protests over the Columbus quincentenary (1992) as "an ignorant celebration of stasis and backwardness, with an unpleasant tinge of self-hatred." For Hitchens, the destruction of Native American civilization was simply "the way that history is made, and to complain about it is as empty as complaint about climatic, geological or tectonic shift." He justified the conquest on classic utilitarian grounds:

It is sometimes unambiguously the case that a certain coincidence of ideas, technologies, population movements and politico-military victories leaves humanity on a slightly higher plane than it knew before. The transformation of part of the northern part of this continent into "America" inaugurated a nearly boundless epoch of opportunity and innovation, and thus *deserves to be celebrated with great vim and gusto*, with or without the participation of those who wish they had never been born.[77]

The arrogance and contempt in these comments are echoed in the pervasive appropriation of Indian culture and nomenclature by North American white culture. Note, for example, the practice of adopting ersatz Indian names and motifs for professional sports teams. James Wilson has argued that calling a Washington, DC football franchise the "Redskins" is "roughly the equivalent of calling a team 'the Buck Niggers' or 'the Jewboys.'"[78] Other acts of appropriation include naming gas-guzzling vehicles (the Winnebago, the Jeep Cherokee) after Indian nations, so that peoples famous for their respectful custodianship of the environment are instead associated with technologies that damage it. This is carried to extremes with the grafting of Indian names onto weaponry, as with the Apache attack helicopter and the Tomahawk cruise missile. In Madley's opinion, such nomenclature "casts Indians as threatening and dangerous," subtly providing "a post-facto justification for the violence committed against them."[79]

COMPLEXITIES AND CAVEATS

Several of the complicating factors in evaluating the genocide of indigenous peoples have been noted. Prime among them is the question of intent.

Specific intent (see pp. 37–38) is easy enough to adduce in the consistent tendency towards massacre and physical extermination, evident from the earliest days of European conquest of the Americas, Africa, Australasia, and other parts of the world. Yet in most or perhaps all cases, this accounted for a minority of deaths among the colonized peoples.

The forced-labor institutions of Spanish America also demonstrated a high degree of specific intent. When slaves are dying in large numbers, after only a few months in the mines or on the plantations, and your response is not to improve conditions but to feed more human lives into the inferno, this is direct, "first-degree" genocide (in Ward Churchill's conceptualizing; see Chapter 1, note 96). The mechanisms of death were not appreciably different from those of many Nazi slave-labor camps.

Disease was the greatest killer. Here, specific intent arguably prevailed only in the direct acts of biological warfare against Indian nations. More significant was a general genocidal intent, with disease tolls greatly exacerbated by malnutrition, overwork, and outright enslavement.[80] In some cases, though, entire Indian nations were virtually wiped out by pathogens before they had ever set eyes on a European. In addition, many of the connections between lack of hygiene, overcrowding, and the spread of disease were poorly understood for much of the period of the attack on indigenous peoples. Concepts of second- and third-degree genocide might apply here, if one supports Churchill's framing.

Further complexity arises in the agents of the killing. Genocide studies emphasizes the role of the state as the central agent of genocide, and one does find a great deal of state-planned, state-sponsored, and state-directed killing of indigenous peoples. In many and perhaps most cases, however, the direct perpetrators of genocide were colonial *settlers* rather than authorities. Indeed, colonists often protested the alleged lack of state support and assistance in confronting "savages." To the extent that policies were proposed to halt the destruction of native peoples, it was often those in authority who proposed them, though effective measures were rarely implemented. Measures were taken, as at Flinders Island, to "protect" and "preserve" aboriginal groups, but these often *contributed* to the genocidal process. As Colin Tatz has pointed out, "nowhere does the [Genocide] Convention implicitly or explicitly rule out intent with *bona fides*, good faith, 'for their own good' or 'in their best interests.'"[81]

Helpful here might be historian Patrick Wolfe's notion of a "logic of elimi-nation,"[82] and Tony Barta's influential concept of the "genocidal *society* – as distinct from a genocidal state." This is defined as a society "in which the whole bureaucratic apparatus might officially be directed to protect innocent people but in which a whole race is nevertheless subject to remorseless pressures of destruction inherent in the very nature of the society."[83] The nature of settler colonialism, in other words, made conflict with native peoples, and their eventual large-scale destruction, almost inevitable. As Mark Levene has phrased it, while benevolent intentions sometimes existed, "the problem was that these good intentions were at odds with the very colonial project itself." Whenever push came to shove, "the 'Anglo' state always ultimately sided with the interests of capital, property and development, whatever the murderous ramifications."[84] State authorities, though they might occasionally have decried acts of violence against natives, were above all concerned with ensuring that

Figure 3.10   Nahua victims of a sixteenth-century smallpox epidemic in Mexico, with the distinctive vomiting and spotted appearance of the infected.

Source: Nahua artist in the *Florentine Codex* compiled by Fray Bernardino de Sahagún in the sixteenth century/Wikimedia Commons.

the colonial or post-colonial endeavor succeeded. As one British House of Commons committee reported in the 1830s, "Whatever may have been the injustice of this encroachment [on indigenous lands], there is no reason to suppose that either justice or humanity would now be consulted by receding from it."[85] If the near-annihilation of the indigenous population nonetheless resulted, this was sometimes lamented (perhaps with romantic and nostalgic overtones, as described in Brantlinger's *Dark Vanishings*), but it was never remotely sufficient to warrant the cancellation or serious revision of the enterprise.[86]

A few other ambiguous features of genocides against indigenous peoples may be cited. First, the prevailing elite view of history has tended to underestimate the role of the millions of people who migrated from the colonial metropole to the "New World." These settlers and/or administrators were critical to the unfolding of the genocides, not only through the diseases they carried, but (notably in Australasia) through the massacres they authorized and implemented.[87] It should not be forgotten, however, that many of them were fleeing religious persecution or desperate material want. Think of the millions of Irish who abandoned their homeland during the Great Hunger of 1846–48, or the English convicts shipped off for minor crimes to penal colonies in the Antipodes. Settlers and administrators often suffered dreadful mortality rates. As with the indigenous population, death usually resulted from exposure to pathogens to which they had no resistance. To cite an extreme example, "it is said that 6,040 died out of the total of 7,289 immigrants who had come to Virginia by February, 1625, or around 83 percent."[88] Elsewhere, "tropical maladies turn[ed] assignments to military stations, missions, or government posts into death watches."[89]

Finally, we should be careful not to romanticize indigenous peoples and their precontact societies. To limit the discussion to the Americas: it was broadly true that genocide, and war unto genocide, featured only rarely. War among North American Indian communities (excluding present-day Mexico) was generally "farre lesse bloudy and devouring than the cruell Warres of Europe," as one European observer put it.[90] But there were notable exceptions. According to genocide scholars Daniel Chirot and Clark McCauley, "Before widespread contact with the Europeans, warfare among the stateless societies of [the North American northwest], ranging from Puget Sound through the coasts of British Columbia and into the Alaskan panhandle, was frequent and bloody, with exterminations of whole tribes, except for those taken as slaves, not uncommon."[91] Aboriginal slavery institutions could also be genocidal; of the Indians of the same northwest coastal region, sociologist Orlando Patterson has written that "*nothing in the annals of slavery*" can match them "for the number of excuses a master had for killing his slaves and the sheer sadism with which he destroyed them."[92] Post-contact warfare also assumed a virulent form, as with the Iroquois territorial expansion of the sixteenth and seventeenth centuries, which anthropologist Jeffrey Blick has studied as a case of genocide.[93]

Mass violence seems to have been more pervasive among the native populations of Central America and Mexico, at least during certain periods. In the classic era of Mayan civilization (600–900 CE), war seems to have been waged with frequency and sometimes incessantly; many scholars now link endemic conflict to the collapse of the great Mayan cities, and the classical civilization along with it. The Aztecs of

Mexico, meanwhile, warred to capture prisoners for religious sacrifice, sometimes thousands at a time, at their great temple in Tenochtitlán. The Aztecs so ravaged and alienated surrounding nations that these subjects enthusiastically joined with invading Spanish forces to destroy them.

Collaboration with the colonizing force, often arising from and exacerbating the tensions of indigenous international relations, was quite common throughout the hemisphere.[94] Soon Indians, too, became participants in genocidal wars against other Indian nations – and sometimes against members of the colonizing society as well. Reference has already been made (Chapter 1) to *subaltern genocide*, in which oppressed peoples adopt genocidal strategies against their oppressors. Latin America offers several examples, studied in detail by historian Nicholas Robins in *Native Insurgencies and the Genocidal Impulse in the Americas*.[95] The millenarian "Great Rebellion" in Upper Peru (Bolivia) in the 1780s explicitly aimed to slaughter or expel all white people from the former Inca realm. In Mexico's Yucatán peninsula in the mid-nineteenth century, Mayan Indians rose to extirpate the territory's whites or drive them into the sea.[96] In both cases, the genocidal project advanced some distance before the whites launched a successful (and genocidal) counter-attack. I believe we can sympathize with the enormous and often mortal pressure placed upon indigenous peoples, while still recognizing that a genocidal counter-strategy sometimes resulted.

INDIGENOUS REVIVAL

As the Guatemala case study (Box 3a) demonstrates, assaults on indigenous peoples – including genocide – are by no means confined to distant epochs. According to Ken Coates, "the era from the start of World War II through to the 1960s . . . [was] an era of unprecedented aggression in the occupation of indigenous lands and, backed by the equally unprecedented wealth and power of the industrial world, the systematic dislocation of thousands of indigenous peoples around the world."[97] In many regions, invasions and occupations by colonists and corporations, seeking to exploit indigenous lands and resources, continues. And in the "developed world" – Canada, the US, Australasia – the situation of indigenous peoples "is as deplorable as in the very poorest [parts] of the third world."[98] Measured in life expectancy, malnutrition, vulnerability to infectious disease, and many other basic indices, indigenous peoples in most of the countries they inhabit are the most marginalized and deprived of all.[99]

No less than in past periods, however, invasion, deprivation, and attempted domination have fueled indigenous resistance. In recent decades, this has assumed the new form of a *global* indigenous mobilization. The "indigenous revival" is linked to decolonization. It also reflects the development of human-rights philosophies and legislation – particularly in the period following the Second World War, when numerous rights instruments were developed (including the UN Genocide Convention). Decolonization brought to fruition the pledges of self-determination that had featured in the charter of the League of Nations, but had withered in the face of opposition from colonial powers. But this was liberation from domination by external colonial forces. As Niezen has pointed out, the horrors of the Nazi era in Europe "contributed to a greater receptiveness at the international level to measures for the protection of minorities," given the increasing recognition "that states could not always be relied upon to protect their own citizens, that states could even pass laws to promote domestic policies of genocide."[100] At the same time as this realization was gaining ground, so was an acceptance among the diverse colonized peoples that they were members of a global indigenous class. The United Nations, which in 1960 declared self-determination to be a human right, became a powerful forum for the expression of indigenous aspirations, particularly with the creation in 1982 of a Working Group on Indigenous Populations in the UN Economic and Social Council (ECOSOC). Attending a session of the working group, Australian aboriginal representative Mick Dodson described his dawning recognition that "We were all part of a world community of Indigenous peoples spanning the planet; experiencing the same problems and struggling against the same alienation, marginalisation and sense of powerlessness."[101]

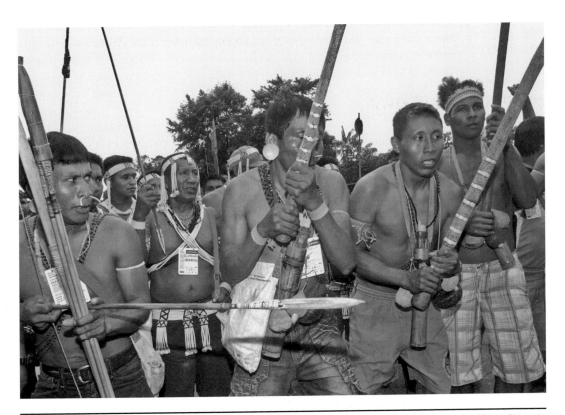

Figure 3.11 Belém, Brazil, January 2009: men from a coalition of Indian groups stage a protest against health conditions in their communities. Centuries after the initial rounds of Western conquest and genocide, indigenous groups remain among the shortest-lived and most economically impoverished populations in their respective nation-states. But recent decades have witnessed mounting resistance to these conditions, part of the global resurgence and revitalization of indigenous societies and identities.

Source: Fabio Rodrigues Pozzebom/Agência Brasil/Wikimedia Commons.

An event of great significance in the Western hemisphere was the first Continental Indigenous International Convention, held in Quito, Ecuador in July 1990, and "attended by four hundred representatives from 120 indigenous nations and organizations."[102] Simultaneously, the number of non-governmental organizations (NGOs) grew exponentially, so that by 2000 the UN High Commissioner for Human Rights could cite some 441 organizations of indigenous peoples world-wide. And indigenous peoples in many parts of the world strove to use the "master's tools" – the educational and legal systems of the dominant society – to reclaim the lands, political rights, and cultural autonomy stripped from them by their colonial conquerors.

At the national level, the impact of these movements is increasingly far-reaching. In the United States, an ever-greater number of individuals are choosing to self-identify as Native Americans,[103] and more and more native nations are petitioning for federal recognition; an "Indigenous Peoples' Day" has supplanted Columbus Day in some US cities. In Latin America, the impact has been more dramatic still. Indigenous peoples in Ecuador and Bolivia have "converged in mass mobilizations, breathtaking in their scale and determination," that overthrew governments and ushered in "a new revolutionary moment in which indigenous actors have acquired the leading role," led by current president Evo Morales.[104] In Mexico on January 1, 1994, indigenous peoples in the poverty-stricken southern state of Chiapas rose up in revolt against central authorities – the so-called Zapatista rebellion – protesting the disastrous impact on the native economy of cheap, subsidized corn exports from the US under the recently signed North American Free Trade Agreement (NAFTA). The Zapatistas have since established substantial local autonomy in their zone of control.

On September 13, 2007, nearly nine in ten member states of the United Nations General Assembly voted in favor of the UN Declaration on the Rights of Indigenous Peoples. The document expressed its concern "that indigenous peoples have suffered from historic injustices as a result of, *inter alia* [among other things], their colonization and dispossession of their lands, territories and resources, thus preventing them from exercising, in particular, their right to development in accordance with their own needs and interests. . ." In refutation of these imperial strategies, the declaration emphasized that:

> Indigenous peoples have the right to the full enjoyment, as a collective or as individuals, of all human rights and fundamental freedoms as recognized in the Charter of the United Nations, the Universal Declaration of Human Rights and international human rights law. . . . Indigenous peoples and individuals are free and equal to all other peoples and individuals and have the right to be free from any kind of discrimination, in the exercise of their rights, in particular that based on their indigenous origin or identity. . . . Indigenous peoples have the right to self-determination. By virtue of that right they freely determine their political status and freely pursue their economic, social and cultural development. . . . Indigenous peoples, in exercising their right to self-determination, have the right to autonomy or self-government in matters relating to their internal and local affairs, as well as ways and means for financing their autonomous functions. . . .

Indigenous peoples have the right to maintain and strengthen their distinct political, legal, economic, social and cultural institutions, while retaining their right to participate fully, if they so choose, in the political, economic, social and cultural life of the State.[105]

Despite the historic nature of the declaration, there were some notable holdouts among UN member states. Not surprisingly, the most prominent opponents – the only ones voting against the declaration – were delegates of countries responsible for some of the most brazen acts of colonial invasion and dispossession: the United States, Canada, New Zealand, and Australia.[106]

FURTHER STUDY

Patrick Brantlinger, *Dark Vanishings: Discourse on the Extinction of Primitive Races, 1800–1930*. Ithaca, NY: Cornell University Press, 2003. Examines European attitudes towards "primitive" races and their extinction.

Dee Brown, *Bury My Heart at Wounded Knee: An Indian History of the American West*. New York: Owl Books, 2001. First published in 1971, and still a classic introduction to the native North American experience.

Bartolomé de las Casas, *A Short Account of the Destruction of the Indies*. London: Penguin, 1992. First published in 1552: a Spanish friar's unrelenting description of colonial depredations in the Americas.

Alfred A. Cave, *The Pequot War*. Amherst, MA: University of Massachusetts Press, 1996. Definitive work on the Pequot genocide.

Ward Churchill, *A Little Matter of Genocide: Holocaust and Denial in the Americas, 1492 to the Present*. San Francisco, CA: City Lights Books, 1997. Forceful and well-documented polemic, with attention to genocide as a legal and academic concept.

Ken S. Coates, *A Global History of Indigenous Peoples: Struggle and Survival*. Basingstoke: Palgrave Macmillan, 2004. A solid introduction, especially good on the Second World War and the postwar era.

Mark Cocker, *Rivers of Blood, Rivers of Gold: Europe's Conquest of Indigenous Peoples*. New York: Grove Press, 2001. Comprehensive survey, ranging from the Americas to Africa and Australasia.

Mary Crow Dog with Richard Erdoes, *Lakota Woman*. New York: HarperPerennial, 1991. Rich memoir by a Native American activist.

Richard Drinnon, *Facing West: The Metaphysics of Indian Hating and Empire Building*. New York: Schocken Books, 1990. The racist ideology underlying US wars against American Indians, Filipinos, and Indochinese.

Jan-Bart Gewald, *Herero Heroes: A Socio-political History of the Herero of Namibia, 1890–1923*. Athens, OH: Ohio University Press, 2001. Study of the Herero genocide and its aftermath.

Francis Jennings, *The Invasion of America: Indians, Colonialism, and the Cant of Conquest*. New York: W.W. Norton, 1975. Early, widely cited account of the formative period of white–Indian interaction in North America.

Sven Lindqvist, *"Exterminate All the Brutes": One Man's Odyssey into the Heart of Darkness and the Origins of European Genocide*. New York: The New Press, 1996. Epigrammatic meditation on the links between colonialism and Nazi genocide.

MariJo Moore, ed., *Genocide of the Mind: New Native American Writing*. New York: Thunder's Mouth Press/Nation Books, 2003. Soul-searching reflections by native writers.

Alan Moorehead, *The Fatal Impact: The Invasion of the South Pacific, 1767–1840*. New York: HarperCollins, 1990. First published in 1966, this remains a moving introduction to the devastation of Pacific indigenous peoples.

A. Dirk Moses, ed., *Genocide and Settler Society: Frontier Violence and Stolen Indigenous Children in Australian History*. New York: Berghahn Books, 2004. Seminal collection of essays.

Ronald Niezen, *The Origins of Indigenism: Human Rights and the Politics of Identity*. Berkeley, CA: University of California Press, 2003. The growth of contemporary indigenous identities and movements.

Nicholas Robins, *Native Insurgencies and the Genocidal Impulse in the Americas*. Bloomington, IN: Indiana University Press, 2005. Groundbreaking study of Indian millenarian movements that adopted genocidal strategies against the European invader.

David E. Stannard, *American Holocaust: The Conquest of the New World*. New York: Oxford University Press, 1992. Perhaps the most enduring of the works published for the Columbus quincentenary.

Russell Thornton, *American Indian Holocaust and Survival: A Population History since 1492*. Norman, OK: University of Oklahoma Press, 1990. Foundational text on the demographic impact of European conquest and colonization.

James Wilson, *The Earth Shall Weep: A History of Native America*. New York: Atlantic Monthly Press, 1998. Fine overview of the native experience in North America.

Ronald Wright, *Stolen Continents: The "New World" Through Indian Eyes*. Boston, MA: Houghton Mifflin, 1993. Examines the conquest throughout the Western hemisphere from the perspective of its victims.

Geoffrey York, *The Dispossessed: Life and Death in Native Canada*. London: Vintage UK, 1990. Harrowing journalistic account of poverty and cultural dislocation among Canada's native peoples.

NOTES

1 For concise overviews, see Robert K. Hitchcock and Tara M. Twedt, "Physical and Cultural Genocide of Various Indigenous Peoples," in Samuel Totten *et al.*, eds, *Century of Genocide: Eyewitness Accounts and Critical Views* (New York: Garland Publishing, 1997), pp. 372–407; and Elazar Barkan, "Genocides of Indigenous Peoples: Rhetoric of Human Rights," in Robert Gellately and Ben Kiernan, eds, *The Specter of Genocide: Mass Murder in Historical Perspective* (Cambridge: Cambridge University Press, 2003), pp. 117–40.

2 Ronald Niezen, *The Origins of Indigenism: Human Rights and the Politics of Identity* (Berkeley, CA: University of California Press, 2003), p. 18.

3 Quoted in ibid., p. 20.

4 However, some have criticized definitions that emphasize colonialism as being too Eurocentric, denying agency to indigenous peoples, and overlooking imperial conquests by non-Western societies. See, e.g., Ken S. Coates, *A Global History of Indigenous Peoples: Struggle and Survival* (Basingstoke: Palgrave Macmillan, 2004), pp. 8–9.

5 See Benjamin Madley, "Patterns of Frontier Genocide, 1803–1910: The Aboriginal Tasmanians, the Yuki of California, and the Herero of Namibia," *Journal of Genocide Research*, 4: 2 (2004), p. 168.

6 Sven Lindqvist, *"Exterminate All the Brutes": One Man's Odyssey into the Heart of Darkness and the Origins of European Genocide* (New York: The New Press, 1996), p. 123.

7 Twain quoted in Patrick Brantlinger, *Dark Vanishings: Discourse on the Extinction of Primitive Races, 1800–1930* (Ithaca, NY: Cornell University Press, 2001), p. 10. Twain's complete essay on "The Noble Red Man," originally published in *The Galaxy* in 1870, is available on the Web at http://www.twainquotes.com/Galaxy/187009c. html.

8 Wallace quoted in Brantlinger, *Dark Vanishings*, pp. 185–86. President Andrew Jackson, one of the great tormentors of indigenous populations in US history, noted that "humanity has often wept over the fate of the aborigines of this country," and indeed, "to follow to the tomb the last of [this] race and to tread on the graves of extinct nations excite melancholy reflections. But," Jackson declared, "true philanthropy reconciles the mind to these vicissitudes as it does the extinction of one generation to make room for another." Jackson quoted in A. Dirk Moses, "Empire, Colony, Genocide: Keywords and the Philosophy of History," in Moses, ed., *Empire, Colony, Genocide: Conquest, Occupation, and Subaltern Resistance in World History* (New York: Berghahn Books, 2008), p. 19.

9 Brantlinger, *Dark Vanishings*, p. 186.

10 Lindqvist, *"Exterminate All the Brutes,"* p. 9.

11 Richard L. Rubenstein, *The Age of Triage: Fear and Hope in an Overcrowded World* (Boston, MA: Beacon Press, 1983), p. 1.

12 Ward Churchill, *A Little Matter of Genocide: Holocaust and Denial in the Americas, 1492 to the Present* (San Francisco, CA: City Lights Books, 1997), p. 97.

13 Russel Lawrence Barsh points to the concentration of Indians on "reservations" (a system that "undoubtedly brought chronic malnutrition to a great proportion of North America's indigenous population"), destruction of forests, and denial of access to clean water as additional factors promoting high Indian mortality (his analysis concentrates on the later nineteenth century). See Barsh, "Ecocide, Nutrition, and the 'Vanishing Indian,'" in Pierre L. van den Berghe, ed., *State Violence and Ethnicity* (Niwot, CO: University Press of Colorado, 1990), pp. 224, 231, 239.

14 See Elizabeth A. Fenn, "Biological Warfare in Eighteenth-century North America: Beyond Jeffery Amherst," *The Journal of American History*, 86: 4 (March 2000), pp. 1552–80.

15 On the North American variant, see Tony Seybert, "Slavery and Native Americans in British North America and the United States: 1600 to 1865," http://www.slavery inamerica.org/history/hs_es_indians_slavery.htm.

16 David E. Stannard, *American Holocaust: The Conquest of the New World* (New York: Oxford University Press, 1992), p. 54.

17 Bartolomé de las Casas, *A Short Account of the Destruction of the Indies* (London: Penguin, 1992), p. 15. Raphael Lemkin praised las Casas for efforts that "went much beyond the ordinary ecclesiastic opposition to genocide in the Indies; he preached a doctrine of humanitarianism which was actually beyond the values of his own time." Quoted in John Docker, "Are Settler-Colonies Inherently Genocidal?," in Moses, ed., *Empire, Colony, Genocide*, p. 92. However, whether las Casas was truly "beyond the values" of his era is questionable, since others advanced similar values

– sometimes in an even more rigorous way. While las Casas did accept the basic right of Spain to occupy territories in the Americas and incorporate their populations, his contemporary Francesco de Vitoria (1485–1546) rejected this utterly: "it is clear . . . that the Spaniards, when they first sailed to the land of the barbarians [*sic*], carried with them no right at all to occupy their countries." The contributions of Hugo Grotius (1583–1645) and Samuel von Pufendorf (1632–1694) are also vital in demonstrating that far from being a universally held norm, a sophisticated contemporary critique of Western imperialism existed. For a cogent discussion, see Andrew Fitzmaurice, "Anticolonialism in Western Political Thought: The Colonial Origins of the Concept of Genocide," in Moses, ed., *Empire, Colony, Genocide*, pp. 55–80 (Vitoria quoted p. 58).

18 De las Casas, *A Short Account*, p. 24.

19 James Wilson, *The Earth Shall Weep: A History of Native America* (New York: Atlantic Monthly Press, 1998), p. 34.

20 Ibid., p.35.

21 Stannard, *American Holocaust*, p. 89.

22 Toribio de Motolinía quoted in Luis N. Rivera, *A Violent Evangelism: The Politics and Religious Conquest of the Americas* (Louisville, KY: Westminster/John Knox Press, 1992), p. 170. Thanks to Tanya Nelson for this source.

23 See, e.g., Álvaro Kaempfer, "Lastarria, Bello y Sarmiento en 1844: Genocidio, historiografía y proyecto nacional," *Revista de Crítica Literaria Latinoamericana*, 32: 63–64 (2006), pp. 9–24; Florencia Roulet, "Genocidio en las Pampas. Crónica de una polémica abortada," Argentina Indymedia, February 11, 2005, http://argentina.indymedia.org/news/2005/02/264061.php.

24 On the forced relocation of Seneca Indians to flood land for the Kinzua Dam project in Pennsylvania, see Joy A. Bilharz, *The Allegany Senecas and Kinzua Dam: Forced Relocation through Two Generations* (Lincoln, NE: University of Nebraska Press, 1998).

25 See also the essay on Buffy Sainte-Marie's song by Ward Churchill, "'A Bargain Indeed,'" in Adam Jones, ed., *Evoking Genocide: Scholars and Activists Describe the Works That Shaped Their Lives* (Toronto, ON: The Key Publishing House Inc., 2009), pp. 18–22.

26 Russell Thornton, *American Indian Holocaust and Survival: A Population History since 1492* (Norman, OK: University of Oklahoma Press, 1987), p. 44.

27 Churchill, *A Little Matter of Genocide*, p. 97.

28 Testimony cited in Thornton, *American Indian Holocaust and Survival*, p. 95.

29 Amherst quoted in Ben Kiernan, *Blood and Soil: A World History of Genocide and Extermination from Sparta to Darfur* (New Haven, CT: Yale University Press, 2007), p. 245.

30 See Norbert Finzsch, "'[. . .] Extirpate or Remove That Vermine': Genocide, Biological Warfare, and Settler Imperialism in the Eighteenth and Early Nineteenth Century," *Journal of Genocide Research*, 10: 2 (2008), pp. 215–32.

31 Thornton, *American Indian Holocaust and Survival*, p. 51.

32 Wilson, *The Earth Shall Weep*, p. 283; see also Coates, *A Global History*, p. 128.

33 Thornton, *American Indian Holocaust and Survival*, p. 95.

34 On the Pequot War and its genocidal core, see Alfred A. Cave, *The Pequot War* (Amherst, MA: University of Massachusetts Press, 1996); Michael Freeman, "Puritans and Pequots: The Question of Genocide," *New England Quarterly*, 68 (1995), pp. 278–93; "'We Must Burn Them,'" ch. 13 in Francis Jennings, *The Invasion of America: Indians, Colonialism, and the Cant of Conquest* (New York: W.W. Norton, 1975), pp. 202–27.

35 Wilson, *The Earth Shall Weep*, p. 94.

36 Karl Jacoby, *Shadows at Dawn*, quoted in Tim Morrison, "A Massacre Explained," *Time*, Monday, November 24, 2008, http://www.time.com/time/arts/article/0,8599, 1861448,00.html. Emphasis in original.

37 Chivington quoted in Michael Mann, *The Dark Side of Democracy: Explaining Ethnic Cleansing* (Cambridge: Cambridge University Press, 2005), p. 98.

38 Connor quoted in Wilson, *The Earth Shall Weep*, p. 274. See also the description in Mark Levene, *Genocide in the Age of the Nation State, Vol. 2: The Rise of the West and the Coming of Genocide* (London: I.B. Tauris, 2005), pp. 93–94.

39 Roosevelt quoted in Paul R. Bartrop, "Punitive Expeditions and Massacres: Gippsland, Colorado, and the Question of Genocide," in A. Dirk Moses, ed., *Genocide and Settler Society: Frontier Violence and Stolen Indigenous Children in Australian History* (New York: Berghahn Books, 2004), p. 209.

40 Wilson, *The Earth Shall Weep*, p. 228.

41 These figures were provided by Benjamin Madley, a leading authority on the Yuki genocide. See Madley's article, "California's Yuki Indians: Defining Genocide in Native American History," *The Western Historical Quarterly*, 39: 3 (2008), pp. 303–32.

42 Frank Chalk and Kurt Jonassohn, *The History and Sociology of Genocide* (New Haven, CT: Yale University Press, 1990), pp. 197–99.

43 Wilson, *The Earth Shall Weep*, pp. 228, 231.

44 "The Trail Where They Cried," translated from Cherokee (Coates, *A Global History*, p. 185). For a detailed account, see John Ehle, *Trail of Tears: The Rise and Fall of the Cherokee Nation* (New York: Doubleday, 1988).

45 Ward Churchill, "Genocide by Any Other Name: North American Indian Residential Schools in Context," in Adam Jones, ed., *Genocide, War Crimes and the West: History and Complicity* (London: Zed Books, 2004), p. 87.

46 Canada's Ministry of National Health and Welfare cited evidence in 1993 that "100% of the children at some [residential] schools were sexually abused between 1950 and 1980" (*The Globe and Mail*); in the United States a "wall of silence" still surrounds this subject. Churchill, "Genocide by Any Other Name," pp. 104–5.

47 Ibid., p. 97. See also Debora Mackenzie, "Canada Probes TB 'Genocide' in Church-Run Schools," *New Scientist*, May 5, 2007. Andrew Woolford's judgment is notable: "Tuberculosis was rampant through many residential schools until the 1940s, and reports suggest that the staff at these schools did little to help the infected children. Susceptibility to this and other diseases was increased by the poor nutrition and inadequate clothing provided to students. In addition, there are reports of students' being required to bunk with others who were infected. With death tolls from tuberculosis reaching as high as 50% in some schools, any claim that this was simply 'natural' is exposed as disingenuous at best." Woolford, "Ontological Destruction: Genocide and Canadian Aboriginal Peoples," *Genocide Studies and Prevention*, 4: 1 (April 2009), pp. 90–91.

48 Churchill, "Genocide by Any Other Name," pp. 105–6.

49 "Whites spoke of Aborigines as 'horribly disgusting,' lacking 'any traces of civilization,' 'constituting in a measure the link between the man and the monkey tribe,' or 'undoubtedly in the lowest possible scale of human nature, both in form and intellect.'" Madley, "Patterns of Frontier Genocide," p. 169.

50 Mann, *The Dark Side of Democracy*, p. 80.

51 Ibid., p. 81.

52 Colin Tatz, "Genocide in Australia," AIATSIS Research Discussion Papers No. 8, 1999, http://www.kooriweb.org/gst/genocide/tatz.html.

53 Levene, *Genocide in the Age of the Nation State, Vol. 2*, p. 75.

54 Reynolds cited in Ben Kiernan, *Blood and Soil: A World History of Genocide and Extermination from Sparta to Darfur* (New Haven, CT: Yale University Press, 2007), p. 308.

55 Trollope quoted in Mark Cocker, *Rivers of Blood, Rivers of Gold: Europe's Conquest of Indigenous Peoples* (New York: Grove Press, 2001), p. 178.

56 Benjamin Madley, "From Terror to Genocide: Britain's Tasmanian Penal Colony and Australia's History Wars," *Journal of British Studies*, 47 (2008), p. 78 (fn. 7).

57 Levene, *Genocide in the Age of the Nation State, Vol. 2*, p. 42. The exterminatory character of the Flinders system was acknowledged in 1999 by the Tasmanian Premier, Jim Bacon, who referred to the Wybalenna concentration camp as "a site of genocide." Quoted in Madley, "Patterns of Frontier Genocide," p. 175. Madley added (p. 176): "From the outset, British authorities knew that conditions on Flinders Island were lethal. Inaction despite clear warnings and high mortality rates suggests that population decline was government policy, or was considered preferable to returning the survivors to their homes. . . . In 1836 the commander of Launceston visited Flinders Island and warned that if conditions were not improved, 'the race of Tasmania . . . will . . . be extinct in a quarter of a century.' . . . Still, the government did not address the issues contributing to mortalities. In fact, they operated Flinders Island with virtually no policy amendments for over a decade, until closing the reserve in 1847. The colonial government may not have planned to kill large numbers of Aborigines on Flinders Island, but they did little to stop mass death when they were clearly responsible for it."

58 Madley, "From Terror to Genocide," p. 104.

59 Peter Read, *The Stolen Generations: The Removal of Aboriginal Children in NSW, 1883–1969* (Sydney: Government Printer, 1982); revised edition available on the Web at http://www.daa.nsw.gov.au/publications/StolenGenerations.pdf.

60 "With hindsight, I think it was a mistake to use the word genocide . . . once you latch onto the term 'genocide,' you're arguing about the intent and we should never have used it." Sir Ronald Wilson, quoted in Robert van Krieken, "Cultural Genocide in Australia," in Dan Stone, ed., *The Historiography of Genocide* (London: Palgrave Macmillan, 2008), p. 130. For more on the international law surrounding forcible child transfer, see Kurt Mundorff, "Other Peoples' Children: A Textual and Contextual Interpretation of Article 2(e) of the Genocide Convention," *Harvard International Law Journal*, 50: 1 (2009), pp. 61–127.

61 Colin Tatz, *With Intent to Destroy: Reflecting on Genocide* (London: Verso, 2003), p. xvi.

62 "Text of Australian Prime Minister Kevin Rudd's Apology to Aborigines," *The Hindu*, February 13, 2008. http://www.thehindu.com/nic/auspmapology.htm.

63 For a solid overview, see Jon Bridgman and Leslie J. Worley, "Genocide of the Hereros," ch. 1 in Totten *et al.*, eds, *Century of Genocide*, pp. 3–40.

64 Maharero quoted in Mark Levene, *Genocide in the Age of the Nation State, Vol. 2: The Rise of the West and the Coming of Genocide* (London: I.B. Tauris, 2005), p. 248.

65 Von Trotha quoted in Jon Bridgman, *The Revolt of the Hereros* (New York: Berkeley, 1981), pp. 111–12.

66 Benjamin Madley, "From Africa to Auschwitz: How German South West Africa Incubated Ideas and Methods Adopted and Developed by the Nazis in Eastern Europe," *European Historical Quarterly*, 35: 3 (2005), p. 430.

67 Levene, *Genocide in the Age of the Nation State, Vol. 2*, p. 234.

68 Von Trotha quoted in Jan-Bart Gewald, "Imperial Germany and the Herero of Southern Africa: Genocide and the Quest for Recompense," in Jones, ed., *Genocide, War Crimes and the West*, p. 61.

69 Quoted in Gewald, "Imperial Germany and the Herero," p. 62.

70 Madley, "Patterns of Frontier Genocide," p. 188; Madley, "From Africa to Auschwitz," p. 181.

71 Benjamin Madley, personal communication, September 30, 2005.

72 Wieczorek-Zeul quoted in Jürgen Zimmerer, "Colonial Genocide: The Herero and Nama War (1904–08) in German South West Africa and Its Significance," in Stone, ed., *The Historiography of Genocide*, p. 323. See also Andrew Meldrum, "German Minister Says Sorry for Genocide in Namibia," *The Guardian*, August 16, 2004, http://www.guardian.co.uk/print/0,3858,4993918-103532,00.html. An excellent BBC documentary on the genocide of the Hereros and Namas, *Genocide and the Second Reich*, can be viewed on YouTube beginning at http://www.youtube.com/watch?v=Jg4 MKIUi34w.

73 Zimmerer, "Colonial Genocide," p. 323.

74 In academia, the denialist position is associated with scholars such as Steven Katz, Guenter Lewy, William Rubinstein, and (in Australia) Keith Windschuttle.

75 Alexander Bielakowski, post to H-Genocide, September 26, 2001; see my response of the same date in the H-Genocide archives, http://h-net.msu.edu/cgi-bin/logbrowse.pl?trx= lmandlist=H-Genocide.

76 Michael Burleigh, *Ethics and Extermination: Reflections on Nazi Genocide* (Cambridge: Cambridge University Press, 1997), p. 181.

77 Christopher Hitchens, "Minority Report," *The Nation*, October 19, 1992, emphasis added. Hitchens's "vulgar social Darwinism, with its quasi-Hitlerian view of the proper role of power in history" is effectively pilloried in David E. Stannard's essay, "Uniqueness as Denial: The Politics of Genocide Scholarship," in Alan S. Rosenbaum, ed., *Is the Holocaust Unique? Perspectives on Comparative Genocide* (2nd edn) (Boulder, CO: Westview Press, 2001), pp. 245–90 (on Hitchens, p. 248).

   A personal confession: I identified with such viewpoints until a couple of decades ago, when I was slapped rudely awake by Geoffrey York's book *The Dispossessed: Life and Death in Native Canada* (London: Vintage UK, 1990). I now believe that this outlook represented a deep failure of moral imagination on my part. Probably, it was grounded in the same factors that seem to inform the comments of Hitchens and others: ignorance; cultural hubris; and discomfort at acknowledging genocide perpetrated by one's "own" people.

78 Wilson, *The Earth Shall Weep*, p. xx.

79 Benjamin Madley, personal conversation, August 16, 2005.

80 See Tzvetan Todorov, *The Conquest of America: The Question of the Other* (New York: Harper Perennial, 1992), pp. 135–38. Ben Kiernan argues that "Whether genocide accounted for more or fewer deaths than other causes is irrelevant . . . Nor should larger, unplanned tragedies like epidemics obscure lesser crimes, even if unconnected, that lead to the extinction of a population also ravaged by disease. In other words, it is possible neither to convict microbes of genocide nor to present their great destruction as a defense exhibit for perpetrators." Kiernan, *Blood and Soil: A World History of Genocide and Extermination from Sparta to Darfur* (New Haven, CT: Yale University Press, 2007), p. 35.

81 Tatz, *With Intent to Destroy*, p. 99.

82 Patrick Wolfe, "Structure and Event: Settler Colonialism, Time, and the Question of Genocide," in Moses, ed., *Empire, Colony, Genocide*, p. 102.

83 Tony Barta, "Relations of Genocide: Land and Lives in the Colonization of Australia," in Isidor Wallimann and Michael N. Dobkowski, eds., *Genocide and the Modern Age: Etiology and Case Studies of Mass Death* (Westport, CT: Syracuse University Press, 2000), p. 240.

84 Levene, *Genocide in the Age of the Nation State, Vol. 2*, p. 44. He adds (p. 78) in the Australian context: "What had begun as a seemingly benign, implicitly anti-genocidal native policy thus became not just a *failed* policy but actually took on its reverse nightmare image; the very logic of non-negotiable, not to say accelerated, land seizure and conquest in the face of aboriginal resistance inevitably forcing Crown colonial good intentions into a cul-de-sac from which they could only be extricated through explosions of extreme, exterminatory violence."

85 Quoted in Ann Curthoys, "Genocide in Tasmania," in Moses, ed., *Empire, Colony, Genocide*, p. 233.

86 Another sophisticated analysis of the issues of agency and intent is A. Dirk Moses, "An Antipodean Genocide? The Origins of the Genocidal Moment in the Colonization of Australia," *Journal of Genocide Research*, 2:1 (2000), pp. 89–106.

87 For example – to cite a case where colonial administrators have often been credited with seeking to prevent or impede genocide against indigenous peoples – the Lieutenant Governor of Tasmania, Sir George Arthur, imposed martial law in the territory in 1828.

He called for "the most energetic measures on the part of the settlers themselves," though adding that "the use of arms is in no case to be resorted to until other measures for driving them off have failed." As Benjamin Madley notes, "Martial law made killing Aborigines legal until they had all been 'driven off,' resulting, within a year of the issuing of the decree, in the slaughter of over two-thirds of Tasmania's Aboriginal population." Madley, "Patterns of Frontier Genocide," p. 174.

88 Thornton, *American Indian Holocaust and Survival*, p. 69.

89 Coates, *A Global History*, p. 132.

90 Roger Williams, quoted in Wilson, *The Earth Shall Weep*, p. 55. Writes G.B. Nash: "The nature of pre-contact Indian war was far different than the wars known in Europe, both in duration and in scale of operations. Unlike the Europeans, Native Americans could not conceive of total war that was fought for months or even years, that did not spare non-combatants, and that involved the systematic destruction of towns and food supplies. Wars among Indians were conducted more in the manner of short forays, with small numbers of warriors engaging the enemy and one or the other side withdrawing after a few casualties had been inflicted." Quoted in Jeffrey P. Blick, "Genocidal Warfare in Tribal Societies as a Result of European-induced Culture Conflict," *Man*, New Series, 23:4 (1988), p. 658. See also "Savage War," ch. 9 in Jennings, *The Invasion of America*, pp. 146–70, pointing (among other things) to the extent to which Europeans themselves imported methods of warfare that were subsequently depicted as "savage" customs.

91 Daniel Chirot and Clark McCauley, *Why Not Kill Them All? The Logic and Prevention of Mass Political Murder* (Princeton, NJ: Princeton University Press, 2006), pp. 113–14.

92 Orlando Patterson, *Slavery and Social Death: A Comparative Study* (Cambridge, MA: Harvard University Press, 1982), p. 191.

93 Jeffrey P. Blick, "The Iroquois Practice of Genocidal Warfare (1534–1787)," *Journal of Genocide Research*, 3: 3 (2001), pp. 405–29.

94 See, e.g., Laura E. Matthew and Michel R. Oudijk, eds., *Indian Conquistadors: Indigenous Allies in the Conquest of Mesoamerica* (Norman, OK: University of Oklahoma Press, 2007).

95 Nicholas Robins, *Native Insurgencies and the Genocidal Impulse in the Americas* (Bloomington, IN: Indiana University Press, 2005).

96 See Nelson Reed, *The Caste War of Yucatan* (Stanford, CA: Stanford University Press, 1964).

97 Coates, *A Global History*, pp. 226–27. See also the case of the Aché Indians of Paraguay, described in one of the early treatises of genocide studies: Richard Arens, *Genocide in Paraguay* (Philadelphia, PA: Temple University Press, 1976), perhaps most cited today for the epilogue by Jewish Holocaust survivor Elie Wiesel.

98 Levene, *Genocide in the Age of the Nation State, Vol. 2*, p. 99.

99 For example, Ward Churchill notes that US Indians in the contemporary era "incur by far the lowest annual and lifetime incomes of any group . . . and the highest rates of infant mortality, death by malnutrition, exposure, and plague disease. Such conditions produce the sort of endemic despair that generates chronic alcoholism and other forms of substance abuse among more than half the native population – factors contributing not only to further erosion in physical health but to very high accident rates – as well as rates of teen suicide up to 14.5 times the national average. . . . 'Genocidal' is the only reasonable manner in which to describe the imposition, as a matter of policy, of such physiocultural effects upon any target group." Churchill, *A Little Matter of Genocide*, pp. 247–48. Conditions among Australian aboriginals are strikingly similar: this group "ended the twentieth century at the very top, or bottom, of every social indicator available." See the statistics cited in Tatz, *With Intent to Destroy*, pp. 104–5. In Australia, "the standard of health of Aborigines lags almost 100 years behind that of other Australians, with some indigenous people still suffering from leprosy, rheumatic heart

disease and tuberculosis, according to a report for the World Health Organisation. The report said that Aborigines and Torres Strait Islanders, which make up about 2.5% of Australia's population, have an average life expectancy 17 years below their fellow countrymen. The average age of death for Aboriginal men in some parts of New South Wales is 33." Barbara McMahon, "Aboriginal Health '100 Years Behind' Other Australians," *The Guardian*, May 1, 2007, http://www.guardian.co.uk/world/2007/may/01/australia. barbaramcmahon.

100 Niezen, *The Origins of Indigenism*, p. 40.

101 Quoted in ibid., p. 47.

102 Elazar Barkan, *The Guilt of Nations: Restitution and Negotiating Historical Injustices* (New York: W. W. Norton, 2000), p. 161.

103 For a survey of the trend, see Jack Hitt, "The Newest Indians," *New York Times Magazine*, August 21, 2005.

104 "Bolivia Fights Back: An Introduction," and Forrest Hylton and Sinclair Thomson, "Insurgent Bolivia," both in *NACLA Report on the Americas*, November to December 2004, pp. 14–15.

105 "United Nations Declaration on the Rights of Indigenous Peoples," adopted by General Assembly Resolution 61/295, September 13, 2007, http://www.un.org/esa/socdev/unpfii/en/drip.html.

106 Haider Rizvi, "UN Adopts Historic Statement on Native Rights," CommonDreams.org, September 14, 2007, http://www.commondreams.org/archive/2007/09/14/3831.

BOX 3A THE GENOCIDE OF GUATEMALA'S MAYANS

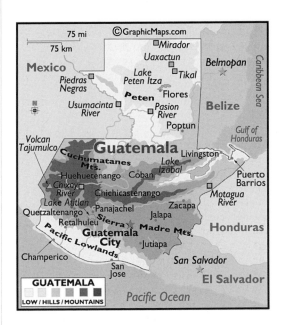

Guatemala's Mayans are the inheritors of one of the world's great civilizations, which erected the temple complexes of Tikal, Copán, Palenque, and Chichen Itzá (the last three lying just outside Guatemala's present-day boundaries, in Honduras and Mexico). The causes of the collapse of these civilizations, and the reversion of their monuments to the jungle, remain something of an enigma. But what is known suggests that two hugely destructive institutions in the West – war and environmental despoliation – were far from unknown to indigenous civilizations in the Americas. While (and in part because) growing populations placed great strain on available land and resources, patterns of Mayan warfare seem to have grown increasingly uncompromising –

Map 3A.1 Guatemala. The mountainous sierra zone is the heartland of Mayan culture and settlement, and was devastated in the genocide of 1981–83.

Source: Map provided by WorldAtlas.com.

perhaps exterminatory and genocidal, as for the Aztecs of the valley of Mexico several centuries later (see pp. 127–28).

After the collapse of classical Mayan culture, descendent populations gravitated toward the Guatemalan sierra and other mountainous regions, such as Chiapas in southern Mexico.[1] The Mayan region experienced one of the most savage of all sixteenth-century conquistador campaigns, when Pedro de Alvarado arrived to lay the territories waste and claim them for the Spanish crown. In his *Brief Account of the Destruction of the Indies*, the Spanish friar and Indian advocate, Bartolomé de las Casas, wrote of Alvarado's rampage through Guatemala that his forces

> plundered and ravaged an area of more than a hundred leagues by a hundred leagues that was among the most fertile and most heavily peopled on earth, killing all the leaders among the native population and, with all men of military age dead, reducing the survivors to the Hell of slavery. . . . As this very butcher himself was quite accurately to record in writing, there were more people in this region than in the whole of the kingdom of Mexico. Yet, in this same area, he and his brothers, together with their comrades-in-arms, were responsible for the deaths of more than four or five million souls over the fifteen or sixteen years, from 1524 to 1540. Nor is the butchery and destruction over, for those natives who have survived so far will soon perish in the same ways as have all the others in the region.[2]

Mark Levene aptly notes that what these conquistadors "did in mass murder was quite equal to the accomplishment of *Einsatzgruppen* [killing] units operating in the Russian borderlands of 1941–2" (see the discussion of the "Holocaust by Bullets" on pp. 239–40 and pp. 514–16).[3] Unlike the Arawaks of Hispaniola or the Beothuks of Newfoundland,[4] the Mayans were not hounded to complete extinction. But along with the other Indians of Mesoamerica, they experienced the most calamitous demographic collapse in recorded history. Las Casas's casualty estimate is far from untenable, given the densely-woven populations that inhabited much of the isthmus at the time of the conquest. And his prediction that the "same ways" of extermination and enslavement would be employed against Mayan populations in the future was prescient.

One important legacy of Spanish colonialism in Mesoamerica was the advent of a *ladino* (Hispanic) culture which, since *ladino* was a cultural rather than racial identification, gradually eroded and supplanted the native culture. Another crucial legacy, which afflicts neighboring El Salvador as well, was the glaringly unequal division of land and wealth resulting from the parceling up of conquered territories into vast *latifundias* (plantations), worked by armies of dragooned Indians. Mayan populations were squeezed to the point of bare subsistence and beyond, occupying tiny plots in inaccessible areas, so they would be forced to enter the cash economy in planting and harvest seasons, toiling in abominable conditions. During the great coffee boom of the nineteenth century, highland Indians were both pressed into forced labor and coerced into debt peonage – with the debts often passed down for generations.[5] In the twentieth century, they were transported in cattle trucks to the lowland *fincas* (plantations) that grew crops, especially cotton, for export. It was in such conditions that the global symbol of the Guatemalan Mayans, Rigoberta Menchú, labored alongside her family as a child, and lost two of her brothers to the *fincas* – one to malnutrition, the other to pesticide poisoning. Menchú would go on to be awarded the Nobel Peace Prize in 1992, the quincentenary of Columbus's invasion of the Americas.[6]

In 1944, Guatemala was ruled by Jorge Ubico, the latest in a long line of dictators. But an impetus for change was building, inspired both by the decolonization movements of the era and by US president Franklin Roosevelt's proclamation of "Four Freedoms" to guide the postwar era (freedom of speech and religion; freedom from want and fear). That same year, 1944, the first democratic wave crested with the deposing of Ubico and the election of a reformist government under Juan José Arévalo. He was succeeded in 1950 by an even more energetic reformer, Jacobo Arbenz, who introduced measures aimed at dissolving Guatemala's institutions of privilege and inequality, and sparking a *capitalist* modernization of the country. Fatefully, among Arbenz's decrees was the nationalization of the United Fruit Company – which enjoyed intimate access to the upper level of the Eisenhower administration in the US. The company was compensated, but based on the declared tax-value of its

Figure 3A.1   The awarding of the Nobel Peace Prize in 1992 to Rigoberta Menchú, a Quiché Indian from the highlands of Guatemala, symbolized the increased recognition of indigenous people's experiences worldwide. Menchú lost several family members to the state-sponsored genocide that swept Guatemala in the late 1970s and early 1980s; her autobiography, *I, Rigoberta Menchú* (see Further Study) is a classic of modern Latin American literature and indigenous advocacy. Menchú is shown at a speaking appearance at the University of Utah, Salt Lake City, in January 2009.

Source: Edgar Zuniga, Jr./Flickr.

immense and unproductive holdings. This was of course the lowest possible amount. Confronted by such a flagrant refusal of a formerly client regime to play its assigned role in US hemispheric designs, the Eisenhower administration declared Arbenz a dangerous communist – pointing to the "evidence" of four communist representatives out of 51 in Congress, along with a handful of sub-cabinet appointees.

The years 1944–54 are known as the "Ten Years of Spring" in Guatemala. They marked the only time in the country's post-colonial history where genuine attention was paid to the needs of the vast majority of the population. But they were about to be foreclosed, and followed by a genocidal winter.

On June 18, 1954, a force scarcely 150 strong – led by Castillo Armas, a military officer on the CIA payroll – "invaded" Guatemala from Honduras. There they paused, while the CIA organized a campaign of propaganda aimed at spreading terror of an impending foreign assault. The plan worked. Arbenz's nerve broke, and he was carted off to exile in his underclothes.[7] Armas and his military cronies took over and, with extensive US assistance, launched a counterinsurgency campaign against Arbenz's supporters and other opposition. Eventually, young officers rebelled against the dictatorial new order, forming the nucleus of a guerrilla group that fled the cities for the guerrilla redoubt of the highlands. The army's extermination campaign against them, this time conducted in close coordination with the US military, killed thousands of mostly Mayan civilians, at the same time as it routed the guerrilla insurgency.

Yet nothing had changed politically. By the end of the 1970s, populations were boiling over in Guatemala, as in nearby El Salvador and Nicaragua.[8] Trade-union mobilization swept the cities, while in the Mayan sierra, a *ladino*-led but mostly Indian force, the Guerrilla Army of the Poor (EGP), launched a fresh insurrection. The response of the Guatemalan army and security forces between 1978 and 1983 – with critical political, economic, and military support from the United States and Israel[9] – was probably the worst holocaust unleashed in the Americas in the twentieth century.

"Though their official targets were left-wing guerrillas," writes Patrick Brantlinger, "the army and the death squads tortured, raped, and killed indiscriminately, massacring entire Mayan villages in a patently genocidal campaign . . ."[10] In just six years, peaking under the regime of General Efraín Ríos Montt in 1982–83, some 440 Indian villages were obliterated. The author, visiting the ravaged highlands of Quiché province in 1987, found the scorched foundations of peasant dwellings still scattered across the landscape, and most of the remaining Mayan population locked up in "settlements" that seemed little more than concentration camps. Russell Schimmer's research for Yale University's Genocide Studies Program, which uses remote sensing technologies to detect changes to vegetation and land use caused by genocidal outbreaks, found signs of extensive destruction and despoliation in Quiché's "Ixil Triangle," where the most merciless scorched-earth measures were imposed. ("We have no scorched-earth policy," Ríos Montt notoriously declared after a meeting with President Reagan in Honduras. "We have a policy of scorched communists.")[11]

At least 200,000 and as many as 250,000 people, mostly Mayan, were massacred, often after torture. The barbarism was fully comparable to the early phase of Spanish colonization under Pedro de Alvarado half a millennium earlier. It involved acts of "extreme cruelty . . . such as the killing of defenseless children, often by beating them against walls or throwing them alive into pits where the corpses of adults were later thrown; the amputation of limbs; the impaling of victims; the killings of persons by covering them in petrol and burning them alive," all part of "military operations directed towards the physical annihilation" of opposition forces.

Such was the verdict of the Historical Clarification Commission (CEH), established after the United Nations brokered a peace agreement between the Guatemalan government and guerrilla forces in 1996.[12] The Commission's final report on the atrocities of the 1970s and '80s, released in February 1999, ascribed responsibility for fully 93 percent of them to the government and its paramilitary allies. Most of the atrocities, it found, "occurred with the knowledge or by the order of the highest authorities of the State." Finally, and crucially, the Commission declared, on the basis of its survey of four regions of the Mayan zone, that

> the acts committed with the intent to destroy, in whole or in part, numerous groups of Mayans were not isolated acts or excesses committed by soldiers who were out of control, nor were they the result of possible improvisation by mid-level Army command. With great consternation, the CEH concludes that many massacres and other human rights violations committed against these groups obeyed a higher, strategically planned policy, manifested in actions which had a logical and coherent sequence. . . . In consequence, the CEH concludes that agents of the State of Guatemala, within the framework of counterinsurgency operations carried out between 1981 and 1983, committed acts of genocide against groups of Mayan people which lived in the four regions analysed. This conclusion is based on the evidence that, in light of Article II of the Convention on the Prevention and Punishment of the Crime of Genocide, the killing of members of Mayan groups occurred (Article II.a), serious bodily or mental harm was inflicted (Article II.b) and the group was deliberately subjected to living conditions calculated to bring about its physical destruction in whole or in part (Article II.c). The conclusion is also based on the evidence that all these acts were committed "with intent to destroy, in whole or in part," groups identified by their common ethnicity, by reason thereof, whatever the cause, motive or final objective of these acts may have been (Article II, first paragraph).[13]

Since the ceasefire, the return of the tens of thousands of refugees who had fled to southern Mexico and elsewhere,[14] and the release of the Clarification Commission's report, measures have been instituted to bolster Mayan rights.[15]

In 1996, for example, 21 Mayan tongues were formally recognized by the state as official languages. Education in these languages is more widely available than previously. Exhumations and reburials, of the kind depicted in Victoria Sanford's book *Buried Secrets*,[16] have brought a measure of closure to thousands of indigenous families. And in December 2009, Col. Marco Antonio Sanchez was found guilty of the forcible disappearance of eight people during the war and genocide, and sentenced to 53 years in prison. It was the first such conviction ever rendered by a Guatemalan court, and human rights organizers expressed their hope that the trial would serve as a "test case" for future prosecutions.[17]

As for the profound disparities of wealth and land ownership that spawned rebellion in the first place, they seem only to have deepened, and are now some of the worst in the world.[18] According to Inter-American Development Bank statistics, cited by *NotiCen Report* in 2007, "Guatemala has surpassed Brazil as the most unequal country in Latin America. . . . Most of these impoverished people are indigenous and campesinos [peasants]. . . . Two-thirds of Guatemala's children, 2,700,000 of them, live in poverty, a poverty that will follow them all their lives in the form of decreased life expectancy and health outlook."[19]

Also generating deep concern is the skyrocketing male violence – principally against other males, but increasingly against women[20] – that prevails in "postwar" Guatemala. In this respect, the traumatized land stands as emblematic of many post-genocide societies[21] – awash with arms, drugs, and gangs; with military and security forces still rampaging as off-duty death squads, though now against "socially deviant" elements (street children, drug dealers and gang members, homosexuals and transvestites); pervaded by extreme *machismo* that fuels an epidemic of rape-murders of young women. And in Guatemala's Congress, reelected in September 2007, sits Efraín Ríos Montt – the former genocidal general and putative president of Guatemala during the worst of the genocide, taking full advantage of his congressional immunity. His hardline Guatemalan Republican Front (FRG) has been a prominent player in postgenocide politics. This, too, is not untypical of highly traumatized societies. One of their regular aspects, reflecting often spiraling levels of crime and social violence, is the appeal of "law and order" candidates. Frequently, like Ríos Montt and his ilk, they were once representatives of organs and institutions that pursued genocidal policies against political dissenters and indigenous populations.

FURTHER STUDY

Greg Grandin, *The Last Colonial Massacre: Latin America in the Cold War*. Chicago, IL: University of Chicago Press, 2004. A reflective historical study not only of modern Guatemala, but of the period of state terror around the hemisphere.

Guatemala: Memory of Silence: Report of the Commission for Historical Clarification, February 1999. Available online at http://shr.aaas.org/ guatemala/ceh/report/ english/toc.html.

Jim Handy, *Gift of the Devil: A History of Guatemala*. Toronto, ON: Between the Lines, 1984. Now dated, but a very readable introduction to Guatemala from the Spanish conquest to the onset of the genocide.

Ételle Higonnet, ed., *Quiet Genocide: Guatemala 1981–1983*, trans. Marcie Mersky. New Brunswick, NJ: Transaction Publishers, 2009. Analyzes modern Guatemala through a lens of genocide and crimes against humanity.

Michael McClintock, *The American Connection, Vol. 2: State Terror and Popular Resistance in Guatemala*. London: Zed Books, 1985. Detailed exposé of the Guatemalan terror-state, including "The Question of Genocide"; see also volume 1, *State Terror and Popular Resistance in El Salvador*.

Rigoberta Menchú with Elisabeth Burgos-Débray, *I, Rigoberta Menchú: An Indian Woman in Guatemala*. New York: Verso, 1987. Memoir, by the Nobel Peace Prize-winner, of her family's experience in the genocide against Mayan Indians.

Daniel Wilkinson, *Silence on the Mountain: Stories of Terror, Betrayal, and Forgetting in Guatemala*. Boston, MA: Houghton Mifflin Company, 2002. Explores the historical roots and human consequences of the Guatemalan genocide.

Ronald Wright, *Time Among the Maya: Travels in Belize, Guatemala, and Mexico*. New York: Viking, 1989. A politically astute travelogue through the Mayan heartland.

NOTES

1   It was in Chiapas, as noted, that the Spanish friar Bartolomé de las Casas centered his efforts to preserve the Indian population; the city of San Cristóbal de las Casas bears his name. It was also in Chiapas that modern oppression and marginalization of Mexico's Mayan Indian population erupted in the Zapatista uprising of January 1, 1994 – the same date that the North American Free Trade Agreement was scheduled to come into effect, which many Indian communities saw as a mortal threat to their subsistence-agricultural economy.

2   Bartolomé de las Casas, *A Short Account of the Destruction of the Indies*, trans. Nigel Griffin (London: Penguin, 1991), pp. 61–62.

3   Mark Levene, *Genocide in the Age of the Nation State, Vol. 2: The Rise of the West and the Coming of Genocide* (London: I.B. Tauris, 2005), p. 12.

4   On the extermination of the Indians of Hispaniola, see las Casas, *A Short Account*, pp. 18–25; David Stannard, *American Holocaust: The Conquest of the New World* (New York: Oxford University Press, 1992), pp. 62–75. On the Beothuks, see Frederick W. Rowe, *Extinction: The Beothuks of Newfoundland* (Toronto, ON: McGraw-Hill Ryerson, 1977); Arthur Grenke, *God, Greed, and Genocide: The Holocaust through the Centuries* (New Academic Publishing, 2005), pp. 170–73.

5   See Jim Handy, *Gift of the Devil: A History of Guatemala* (Toronto, ON: Between the Lines, 1984); Julio C. Cambranes, *Coffee and Peasants in Guatemala* (South Woodstock, VT: CIRMA/Plumsock Mesoamerican Studies, 1985); Adam Jones, *Guatemala Insurgent: Roots of Rebellion from the Rise of the Coffee Economy to the Present Day* (unpublished manuscript, University of British Columbia, 1989; available from the author).

6   Rigoberta Menchú with Elisabeth Burgos-Debray, *I, Rigoberta Menchú: An Indian Woman in Guatemala* (New York: Verso, 1987), chs. 4, 7. Menchú's autobiography is a classic of indigenous literature, though controversy has attended some of the personal history that Menchú recounts – a notable case of the struggle over history and memory examined in Chapter 14. For an overview, see Arturo Arias, ed., *The Rigoberta Menchú Controversy* (Bloomington, MN: Minnesota University Press, 2001).

7   The coup, and its prelude and aftermath, have been well studied as a paradigmatic case of US intervention. The fullest account is Stephen C. Schlesinger and Stephen Kinzer, *Bitter Fruit: The Story of the American Coup in Guatemala*, expanded edn (Cambridge, MA: Harvard University Press, 1999). See also Richard H. Immerman, *The CIA in Guatemala: The Foreign Policy of Intervention* (Austin, TX: University of Texas Press, 1982), and, on the aftermath, Stephen M. Streeter, *Managing the Counterrevolution: The United States and Guatemala, 1954–1961* (Athens, OH: Ohio University Press, 2000).

8   Nicaragua would experience a seizure of power by leftist revolutionaries, the Sandinistas, in 1979, prompting another Reagan administration-sponsored terrorist campaign, spearheaded by the so-called *Contras* (counter-revolutionaries). An estimated 20,000–30,000 Nicaraguan civilians were killed before the war wound down later in the 1980s, and the Sandinistas were voted out of power in 1990. As for El Salvador in the late 1970s and 1980s, it has not yet been studied as a case of genocide, and should be, if political groups (real or imagined) are included in the framing. See Americas Watch, *El Salvador's Decade of Terror: Human Rights since the Assassination of Archbishop Romero* (New Haven, CT: Yale University Press, 1991), and *New York Times* correspondent Raymond Bonner's devastating exposé, *Weakness and Deceit: US Policy and El Salvador* (New York: Times Books, 1984). The emblematic genocidal massacre of the war, inflicted by the US-trained Atlacatl battalion at the village of El Mozote in December 1981 – and followed by a US-engineered cover-up – is memorably described by Mark Danner in *The Massacre at El Mozote: A Parable of the Cold War* (New York: Vintage, 1994).

9   On the US role during the peak years of the genocide, see Michael McClintock, *The American Connection, Vol. 2: State Terror and Popular Resistance in Guatemala* (London: Zed Books, 1985). Of President Ronald Reagan, who directly sponsored the "anti-communist" campaigns of terrorism and extermination in Central America, Robert Parry wrote that he "found virtually every anti-communist action justified, no matter how brutal. From his eight years in the White House, there is no historical indication that he was troubled by the bloodbath and even genocide that occurred in Central America during his presidency, while he was shipping hundreds of millions of dollars in military aid to the implicated forces." Parry, "Reagan and Guatemala's Death Files," in William L. Hewitt, ed., *Defining the Horrific: Readings on Genocide and Holocaust in the Twentieth Century* (Upper Saddle River, NJ: Pearson Education, 2004), p. 247; available online at http://www.consortiumnews. com/1999/052699a1.html. On the basis of the US orchestration of genocide in El Salvador and Nicaragua (c. 100,000 killed), and also considering the "fundamental political support" (McClintock, p. 199) that his government extended to Guatemala

and other atrocious regimes throughout Latin America, there are grounds to regard Reagan as the single worst purveyor of mass atrocity in the western hemisphere during the twentieth century. Very little of this surfaced in the nauseating encomiums to Reagan in the US media following his death in 2004.

An indirect aspect of US support to Guatemala and El Salvador, under both Reagan and his predecessor Jimmy Carter, was the drafting of key clients – Israel and South Korea – to fill gaps in military and "security" assistance, especially when the US Congress restricted direct aid. Of Israel's involvement in arming and training the genocidal forces in Guatemala, serving both the Carter and Reagan administrations in this proxy role, the Israeli scholar Benjamin Beit-Hallahmi wrote: "What is unique [in the Central American mass murders of the twentieth century] is the extent to which those who carried out the deliberate policies of endless killings have proclaimed their indebtedness to Israel, as the source not only of their hardware, but of their inspiration." According to *The Washington Post*, not only did Israel train Guatemalan *génocidaires*, but "Israeli advisers – some official, others private – helped Guatemalan internal security agents hunt underground rebel groups." Beit-Hallahmi, *The Israeli Connection: Who Israel Arms and Why* (New York: Pantheon Books, 1987), pp. 79, 81. See also McClintock, *The American Connection, Vol. 2*, pp. 192–96. Israel was likewise instrumental in arming the military and security forces who perpetrated genocide, by this book's anchoring definition (p. 24), in next-door El Salvador in the 1970s and early 1980s. "During the 1970s, 80 percent of arms imports to El Salvador came from Israel, but after the United States resumed sales in 1980, Israel became only its second largest supplier" (Beit-Hallahmi, p. 85).

10 Patrick Brantlinger, reviewing recent books on Guatemala in *Journal of Genocide Research*, 11: 4 (2009), p. 531. Two important chapter-length treatments of the genocide are Victoria Sanford, "*¡Si Hubo Genocidio en Guatemala!* Yes! There Was Genocide in Guatemala," in Dan Stone, ed., *The Historiography of Genocide* (London: Palgrave Macmillan, 2008), pp. 543–76; and Marc Drouin, "Understanding the 1982 Guatemalan Genocide," in Marcia Esparza, Henry R. Huttenbach, and Daniel Feierstein, eds, *State Violence and Genocide in Latin America* (London: Routledge, 2010), pp. 81–104.

11 Ríos Montt quoted in Daniel Wilkinson, *Silence on the Mountain: Stories of Terror, Betrayal, and Forgetting in Guatemala* (Durham, NC: Duke University Press, 2004), p. 327. Ríos Montt's press secretary, Francisco Bianchi, also notoriously stated: "The Indians were subversives, right? And how do you fight subversion? Clearly you had to kill the Indians because they were collaborating with subversion. And then they would say, 'You're massacring innocent people.' But they weren't innocent. They had sold out to subversion." Quoted in McClintock, *The American Connection, Vol. 2*, p. 258.

12 For an overview of the Historical Clarification Commission's work, and the truth and reconciliation process in Guatemala more generally, see Anita Isaacs, "Truth and the Challenge of Reconciliation in Guatemala," in Joanna R. Quinn, ed., *Reconciliation(s): Transitional Justice in Postconflict Societies* (Montreal, QC: McGill-Queen's University Press, 2009), pp. 116–46. Genocide was also the verdict of an important human rights report on Guatemala issued while the slaughter was still underway: Craig W. Nelson and Kenneth I. Taylor, *Witness to Genocide: The Present Situation of Indians in Guatemala* (London: Survival International, 1983).

13 All quotes from *Guatemala: Memory of Silence: Report of the Commission for Historical Clarification*, February 1999. Available online at http://shr.aaas.org/guatemala/ceh/report/english/toc.html.

14 On the plight of the refugees, see Beatriz Manz, *Refugees of a Hidden War: The Aftermath of Counterinsurgency in Guatemala* (Albany, NY: State University of New York Press, 1988).

15 For an overview of decades of Mayan activism on this front, see Edward F. Fischer and R. McKenna Brown, *Maya Cultural Activism in Guatemala* (Austin, TX: University of Texas Press, 1996).

16 Victoria Sanford, *Buried Secrets: Truth and Human Rights in Guatemala* (New York: Palgrave Macmillan, 2003).

17 Stephen Gibbs, "Guatemala Colonel Given 53 Years for Civil War Crime," BBC Online, December 5, 2009, http://news.bbc.co.uk/2/hi/americas/8396691.stm.

18 In 2005, the United Nations Human Development Report ranked Guatemala seventh worst in the world for income inequality, just behind Brazil. These seem to be the most recent figures available: see the Human Development Report 2009's summary of Guatemala at http://hdrstats.undp.org/en/countries/country_fact_sheets/cty_fs_GTM.html.

19 "Hardly a Dent in Guatemalan Poverty, as Wealth Distribution Becomes World's Worst," *NotiCen: Central American & Caribbean Affairs*, October 4, 2007, http://goliath.ecnext.com/coms2/gi_0199-7031276/HARDLY-A-DENT-IN-GUATEMALAN.html. See also "Malnutrition in Guatemala: A National Shame," *The Economist*, August 27, 2009, noting that "in parts of rural Guatemala, where the population is overwhelmingly of Mayan descent, the incidence of child malnutrition reaches 80%."

20 On the *feminicidio* (femicide/feminicide) in Guatemala, see Victoria Sanford, *Guatemala: Del Genocidio al Feminicidio* (Guatemala City: F&G Editores, 2008); the stark documentary, *Guatemala: Killer's Paradise* (National Film Board of Canada, 2006), available on YouTube; and Sanford's essay on this film, "Images of Impunity," in Adam Jones, ed., *Evoking Genocide: Scholars and Activists Describe the Works That Shaped Their Lives* (Toronto, ON: The Key Publishing House Inc., 2009), pp. 210–14. See also the broader discussion of gender and genocide in Chapter 13.

21 See Alessandro Preti, "Guatemala: Violence in Peacetime – A Critical Analysis of the Armed Conflict and the Peace Process," *Disasters*, 26: 2 (2002), pp. 99–119.

CHAPTER 4

The Ottoman Destruction of Christian Minorities

They hate the Christians.

Charlotte Kechejian, survivor of the Armenian genocide

INTRODUCTION

The murder of over a million Armenians in Turkey between 1915 and 1923 presaged Adolf Hitler's even more gargantuan assault on European Jews in the 1940s. However, for decades, the events were almost forgotten. War crimes trials – the first in history – were held after the Allied occupation of Turkey, but were abandoned in the face of Turkish opposition. In August 1939, as he prepared to invade western Poland, Hitler mused to his generals that Mongol leader "Genghis Khan had millions of women and men killed by his own will and with a gay heart. History sees in him only a great state builder." And in noting his instructions to the Death's Head killing units "to kill without mercy men, women and children of Polish race or language," Hitler uttered some of the most resonant words in the history of genocide: "*Who, after all, talks nowadays of the annihilation of the Armenians?*"[1]

Fortunately, Hitler's rhetorical question cannot sensibly be asked today – except in Turkey. Over the past four decades, a growing movement for apology and restitution has established the Armenian catastrophe as one of the three canonical genocides of the twentieth century, alongside the Holocaust and Rwanda. However, a variant of Hitler's question *could* still obtain: who, today, talks of the genocides of the *other* Christian minorities of the Ottoman realm, notably the Assyrians (including Chaldeans, Nestorians, and Syrian/Syriac Christians)[2] and the Anatolian and Pontian Greeks?*

Historian Hannibal Travis, who has done more than any other scholar to bring the Assyrian catastrophe into mainstream genocide studies, notes that at the time of the anti-Christian genocides, "newspapers in London, Paris, New York, and Los Angeles regularly reported on the massacres of Assyrians living under Ottoman occupation." According to Travis, the attention the Assyrians received was such, and so intertwined with the Armenian atrocities, that when Raphael Lemkin pondered early versions of what would become his "genocide" framework, he had two main instances in mind: the Armenian holocaust, and a renewed round of anti-Assyrian persecutions, this time in post-Ottoman Iraq in 1933.[3]

As for the Anatolian, Thracean, and Pontian Greeks, they had been vulnerable ever since their linguistic brethren in the Greek mainland had become the first to successfully fling off Ottoman dominion – with numerous atrocities committed on both sides. This marked the beginning of the "Great Unweaving" that dismantled the Ottoman empire, and sent terrorized and humiliated Muslim refugees fleeing toward the Constantinople and the Anatolian heartland. By the beginning of the First World War, a majority of the region's ethnic Greeks still lived in present-day Turkey, mostly in Thrace (the only remaining Ottoman territory in Europe, abutting the Greek border), and along the Aegean and Black Sea coasts. They would be targeted both prior to and alongside the Armenians of Anatolia and the Assyrians of Anatolia and Mesopotamia.

For these reasons, while the events of the 1914–22 period have long been depicted in terms of the Armenian genocide and its aftermath, one is justified in portraying it instead as a unified campaign against all the empire's Christian minorities. This does greater justice to minority populations that have generally been marginalized in the narrative. The approach mirrors the discourse and strategizing of the time. Sultan Abdul Hamid II lamented "the endless persecutions and hostilities of the *Christian* world" as a whole.[4] Historian Donald Bloxham refers to "a general anti-Christian chauvinism" in which Christians "were cast as collective targets."[5] The German ambassador to the Ottoman empire, Baron Hans Freiherr von Wangenheim, described the regime's "internal enemies" as "local Christians."[6]

A "Christian genocide" framing acknowledges the historic claims of the Assyrian and Greek peoples, and the movements now stirring for recognition and restitution among Greek and Assyrian diasporas. It also brings to light the quite staggering cumulative death toll among the various Christian groups targeted. In Thea Halo's estimation, "Armenian deaths were estimated at 1.5 million. According to figures compiled by the Greek government in collaboration with the Patriarchate, of the 1.5 million Greeks of Asia Minor – Ionians, Pontians, and Cappadocians –

---

* Anatolia is the "Asian" region of Turkey, extending east from the Bosphorus Strait, which bisects the city of Istanbul. The major populations of "Anatolian Greeks" include those along the Aegean coast and in Cappadocia (central Anatolia), but not the Greeks of the Thrace region west of the Bosphorus. In a geographical sense, Anatolia technically includes the Pontus region along the Black Sea coast, but the Pontian Greeks are culturally and historically such a distinct community that I designate them separately.

Figure 4.1   The genocide of the Christian populations of present-day Turkey produced "the first international human rights movement in American history," according to poet and genocide scholar Peter Balakian. The campaign spearheaded by the American Committee for Relief in the Near East, symbolized by this contemporary poster, raised an astounding $116 million between 1915 and 1930 – equivalent to over a billion dollars today. Nearly two million refugees benefited from the assistance.

Source: Wikimedia Commons.

approximately 750,000 were massacred and 750,000 exiled. Pontian deaths alone totaled 353,000."[7] As for the Assyrian victims, the Assyrian delegation to the Paris Peace Conference cited a figure of 250,000 killed, a figure which has been accepted by Hannibal Travis and David Gaunt, arguably the two leading scholars of the Assyrian genocide.[8]

A broader framing also encourages attention to vulnerable Christian populations in the region *today* – most notably in Iraq, home to the descendants of the Assyrian populations targeted in earlier rounds of persecution and genocide. I return to the movements for recognition at the end of this chapter, and address the present-day vulnerabilities of Christian minorities in Box 4a, "Iraq: Liberation and Genocide."[9]

ORIGINS OF THE GENOCIDE

Three factors combined to produce the genocide of Christian minorities: (1) the decline of the Ottoman Empire, which provoked desperation and humiliation among Turkey's would-be revolutionary modernizers, and eventually violent reaction;[10] (2) Christians' vulnerable position in the Ottoman realm; and (3) the First World War, which confronted Turkey with attack from the west (at Gallipoli) and invasion by the Russians in the northeast. Significant as well was the Turkish variant of racial hygiene theory, echoing many motifs familiar from the subsequent Nazi period in Europe. According to Vahakn Dadrian, "measures for the better 'health' of the national body, [and for] 'eugenic improvements' of the race" were actively promoted.[11] Young Turk racial theory, according to Ben Kiernan, connected the Turks with the heroic Mongols, and contrasted them with inferior and untrustworthy Greeks, Armenians, and Jews.[12]

In Chapter 10, I argue that *humiliation* is one of the greatest psychological spurs to violence, including mass violence and genocide. Theories of Turkish racial superiority certainly provided a salve for the psychic wounds inflicted by the almost unbroken string of humiliations that constituted Ottoman history in its final decades. Indeed, the empire had been in decline ever since its armies were repulsed from the gates of Western Europe, at Vienna in 1688. "As well as the loss of Greece and effectively Egypt, in the first twenty-nine years of the nineteenth century alone the empire had lost control of Bessarabia, Serbia, Abaza, and Mingrelia." In 1878, the empire "cede[d] ownership of or genuine sovereignty over . . . Bosnia, Herzegovina, Bulgaria, Kars, Ardahan, and Cyprus," with "the losses of that year alone comprising one-third of Ottoman territory and 20 per cent of the empire's inhabitants."[13]

The human toll of this "Great Unweaving," from Greece's independence war in the early nineteenth century to the final Balkan wars of 1912–13, was enormous. Hundreds of thousands of Ottoman Muslims were massacred in the secessionist drive: Bloxham argued that "in the years up to the First World War, Muslims were the primary victims of violence in the region by state and sub-state Christian actors working in the name of nationalist liberation and self-determination for their ethnoreligious group."[14] Hundreds of thousands more were expelled as refugees from the former imperial periphery to the heartland, where most festered in poverty, and many yearned for revenge. According to Taner Akçam, "it was precisely those people who, having only recently been saved from massacre themselves, would now take a central and direct role in cleansing Anatolia of 'non-Turkish' elements."[15]

The situation within the shrinking empire was ripe for nativist backlash, and when it occurred, Ottoman Armenians were the targets. They are an ancient people who, by the late nineteenth century, constituted the largest non-Muslim population in eastern Anatolia.[16] In the 1870s and 1880s, Armenian nationalist societies began to form – part of a broader "'Armenian Renaissance' (*Zartonk*) that gained momentum from the middle of the nineteenth century on."[17] Like the small number of Armenian political parties that mobilized later, they demanded full equality within the empire, and occasionally appealed to outside powers for protection and support. These actions aroused the hostility of Muslim nationalists, and eventually prompted a violent backlash. Suspicions were heightened by the advent, in the 1870s and 1880s, of a small number of Armenian revolutionary societies that would later carry out robberies and acts of terrorism against the Ottoman state.

With the Ottomans' hold over their empire faltering, foreign intervention increasing, and Armenian nationalists insurgent, vengeful massacres swept across Armenian-populated territories. Between 1894 and 1896, "the map of Armenia in Turkey went up in flames. From Constantinople to Trebizond to Van to Diyarbekir, and across the whole central and eastern plain of Anatolia, where historic Armenia was lodged, the killing and plunder unfolded."[18] Vahakn Dadrian, the leading historian of the Armenian genocide, considered the 1894–96 massacres "a test case for the political feasibility, if not acceptability by the rest of the world, of the enactment by central authorities of the organized mass murder of a discordant nationality."[19] The killings were, however, more selective than in the 1915–17 conflagration, and central state direction more difficult to discern. According to Bloxham, the main role was played by "Muslim religious leaders, students, and brotherhoods," though many ordinary Muslims, especially Kurds, also participated.[20] Between 80,000 and 200,000 Armenians were killed.[21]

In the first few years of the twentieth century, outright collapse loomed for the Ottoman empire. In 1908, Bulgaria declared full independence, Crete's parliament proclaimed a union with Greece, and the Austro-Hungarian empire annexed Bosnia and Herzegovina. Italy seized Libya in 1912. The following year, Albania and Macedonia seceded. Summarizing these disasters, Robert Melson noted that "out of a total area of approximately 1,153,000 square miles and from a population of about 24 million, by 1911 the Turks had lost about 424,000 square miles and 5 million people";[22] and by 1913, only a narrow strip of European territory remained in their grasp.

In 1908, the tottering Ottoman sultanate was overthrown in the Young Turk revolution, led by a group of modernization-minded military officers. Christian minorities joined with other Ottoman peoples in welcoming the transformations. In the first blush of post-revolutionary enthusiasm, "a wave of fraternal effusions between Ottoman Christians and Muslims swept the empire."[23] It seemed there was a place for all, now that despotism had been overthrown. Indeed, Christians (together with Jews and other religious minorities) were now granted full constitutional rights.

Unfortunately, as with many revolutionary movements, the new Ottoman rulers (grouped under the Committee of Union and Progress, CUP) were split into liberal-democratic and authoritarian factions. The latter was guided by a "burgeoning ethnic nationalism (still informed by Islam) blended with a late-imperial paranoid chauvinism";[24] its leading ideologist was Ziya Gökalp, whose "pan-Turkism was bound up in grandiose romantic nationalism and a 'mystical vision of blood and race.'"[25] "Turks," declared Gökalp, "are the 'supermen' imagined by the German philosopher Nietzsche . . . New life will be born from Turkishness."[26] Within the CUP, amidst "economic and structural collapse, the vision of a renewed empire was born – an empire that would unite all Turkic peoples and stretch from Constantinople to central Asia. This vision, however, excluded non-Muslim minorities."[27]

In January 1913, in the wake of the shattering Balkan defeats of the previous year, the extremist CUP launched a coup against the moderates and took power. The new ruling triumvirate – Minister of Internal Affairs Talat Pasha; Minister of War Enver Pasha; and Minister of the Navy Jemal Pasha – quickly established a *de facto* dictatorship. Under the so-called Special Organization of the CUP that they directed, this trio would plan and oversee the genocides of the Christian minorities, with the Special Organization's affiliates in the Anatolia region serving as ground-level organizers.[28]

WAR, DEPORTATION, AND MASSACRE

The Ottoman genocide of Christians has long been depicted as starting in April 1915, when with Allied invaders on the doorstep in the Dardanelles, the Ottoman authorities rounded up Armenian notables, and the CUP's "final solution" to the

Armenian "problem" was implemented. If we speak of systematic, generalized destruction of a Christian population, either through direct murder or through protracted death marches, this may be true. Armenians, moreover, had been targeted for a premonitory wave of killings in 1909.[29] But the multipronged holocaust that swept the Ottoman realm during World War One was most directly presaged by violence not against Armenians, but against Greeks. It erupted in mid-1914, even before the outbreak of the war, with "group persecution" directed by the CUP against the "Ottoman Greeks living along the Aegean littoral," in Matthias Bjørnlund's account.[30] Historian Arnold Toynbee described a campaign of "general" attacks in which

> entire Greek communities were driven from their homes by terrorism, their houses and land and often their moveable property were seized, and individuals were killed in the process. . . . The terror attacked one district after another, and was carried on by "chetté" bands, enrolled from the Rumeli refugees [i.e., Muslim populations "cleansed" from the Balkans by Christian terror] as well as from the local population and nominally attached as reinforcements to the regular Ottoman gendarmerie.[31]

This was almost precisely the pattern that would be followed in the 1915 extermination campaign against all Christian minorities, only with a starker emphasis on direct killing.[32] US ambassador Henry Morgenthau cited testimony from his Turkish informants that they "had expelled the Greeks so successfully that they had decided to apply the same method toward all the other races in the empire."[33] Again the looting and destruction would be voracious; again the "Rumeli refugees," the most humiliated and dispossessed of the population, would be encouraged to avenge themselves on Christians; again the *chetés* would be mobilized for genocidal service under gendarmerie control.

When those "other races" were targeted in the full-scale genocide of 1915, the Aegean Greeks would again be among those exposed to the same process of concentration, deportation, and systematic slaughter as the Armenians and Assyrians. Of this second and more far-reaching wave of anti-Christian policies, Morgenthau wrote that the Ottoman authorities

> began by incorporating the Greeks into the Ottoman army and then transforming them into labor battalions using them to build roads in the Caucasus and other scenes of action. These Greek soldiers, just like the Armenians, died by thousands from cold, hunger, and other privations . . . The Turks attempted to force the Greek subjects to become Mohammadans; Greek girls . . . were stolen and taken to Turkish harems and Greek boys were kidnapped and placed in Muslim households . . . Everywhere, the Greeks were gathered in groups and, under the so-called protection of Turkish gendarmes, they were transported, the larger part on foot, into the interior.[34]

Alfred Van der Zee, Danish consul in the port city of Smyrna, reported in June 1916:

A reign of terror was instituted and the panic stricken Greeks fled
could to the neighbouring island of Mitylene. Soon the mover
Kemer, Kilissekeuy, Kinick, Pergamos and Soma. Armed *bashi*[
irregular troops] attacked the people residing therein, lifted the cattle, drove u....
from their farms and took forcible possession thereof. The details of what took
place [are] harrowing, women were seduced, girls were ravished, some of them
dying from the ill-treatment received, children at the breast were shot or cut down
with their mothers.[35]

That same year, 1916, Ottoman deputy Emanuel Emanuelidi Efendi announced that
some "550,000 [Greeks] . . . were killed."[36] By this point, the slaughter had spread
to the Armenian population; to the Assyrians of southeast Anatolia and Mesopotamia
(present-day Iraq); and to the Pontian Greek population of the Black Sea coast. We
will consider the experiences of these groups in turn.

THE ARMENIAN GENOCIDE

It appears that a campaign of race extermination is in progress under a pretext of reprisal
against rebellion.

Ambassador Morgenthau to the US Secretary of State, July 16, 1915

As with the other Christian minorities, war catalyzed the onset of mass murder against
the Armenians of the Ottoman empire. As early as December 1914 or January 1915,
a special conference of the CUP issued a "strictly confidential" document ordering
its agents to "close all Armenian Societies, and arrest all who worked against the
Government at any time among them and send them into the provinces such as
Bagdad or Mosul [i.e., in the distant eastern corner of the empire], *and wipe them
out either on the road or there.*" Measures were to be implemented "to exterminate all
males under 50, priests and teachers, leav[ing] girls and children to be Islamized,"
while also "kill[ing] off" all Armenians in the army.[37] This was essentially a blueprint
for the genocide that followed.

In April 1915, just as the Allies were about to mount their invasion of the
Dardanelles, the Turkish army launched an assault on Armenians in the city of Van,
who were depicted as traitorous supporters of the Russian enemy. In scenes that have
become central to Armenian national identity, the Armenians of Van organized a
desperate resistance that succeeded in fending off the Turks for weeks. Eventually,
the resistance was crushed, but it provided the "excuse" for genocide, with the stated
justification of removing a population sympathetic to the Russian army. As one Young
Turk, Behaeddin Shakir, wrote to a party delegate early in April: "It is the duty of all
of us to effect on the broadest lines the realization of the noble project of wiping out
of existence the Armenians who have for centuries been constituting a barrier to the
Empire's progress in civilization."[38]

On April 24, in an act of "eliticide" in Constantinople and other major
cities, hundreds of Armenian notables were rounded up and imprisoned. The great
majority were subsequently murdered, or tortured and worked to death in isolated
locales. (To the present, April 24 is commemorated by Armenians around the

world as "Genocide Memorial Day.") This was followed by a coordinated assault on Armenians throughout most of the Armenian-populated zone; a few coastal populations were spared, but would be targeted later.

The opening phase of the assault consisted of a gendercide against Armenian males. Like the opening eliticide, this was aimed at stripping the Armenian community of those who might mobilize to defend it. Throughout the Armenian territories, males of "battle age" not already in the Ottoman Army were conscripted. In Ambassador Morgenthau's account, Armenians "were stripped of all their arms and transformed into workmen," then worked to death. In other cases, it "became almost the general practice to shoot them in cold blood."[39] By July 1915, some 200,000 Armenian men had been murdered,[40] reducing the remaining community "to a condition of near-total helplessness, thus an easy prey for destruction."[41]

The CUP authorities turned next to destroying the surviving Armenians. A "Temporary Law of Deportation" and "Temporary Law of Confiscation and Expropriation" were passed by the executive.[42] Armenians were told that they were to be transferred to safe havens. However, as Morgenthau wrote, "The real purpose of the deportation was robbery and destruction; it really represented a new method of massacre. When the Turkish authorities gave the orders for these deportations, they were merely giving the death warrant to a whole race; they understood this well, and, in their conversations with me, they made no particular attempt to conceal the fact."[43] Modern bureaucratic structures and communications technologies, especially the railroad and telegraph, were critical to the enterprise.

Figure 4.2 A Danish missionary, Maria Jacobsen, took this photo of Armenian men in the city of Harput being led away for mass murder on the outskirts of town, May 1915.

Source: Courtesy Karekin Dickran's Danish-Armenian archive collection.

The pattern of deportation was consistent throughout the realm, attesting to its central coordination.[44] Armenian populations were called by town criers to assemble in a central location, where they were informed that they would shortly be deported – a day to a week being the time allotted to frantically gather belongings for the journey, and to sell at bargain-basement prices whatever they could. In scenes that prefigured the Nazi deportation of Jews, local populations eagerly exploited Armenians' dispossession. "The scene reminded me of vultures swooping down on their prey," wrote US Consul Leslie Davis. "It was a veritable Turkish holiday and all the Turks went out in their gala attire to feast and to make merry over the misfortunes of others. . . . [It was] the opportunity of a lifetime to get-rich-quick."[45]

Looting and pillaging were accompanied by a concerted campaign to destroy the Armenian cultural heritage. "Armenian monuments and churches were dynamited, graveyards were plowed under and turned into fields of corn and wheat, and the Armenian quarters of cities were torn down and used for firewood and scrap, or occupied and renamed."[46] The Armenian population was led away on foot – or in some cases dispatched by train – to the wastelands of the Deir el-Zor desert in distant Syria, in conditions calculated to kill tens of thousands *en route*.

Kurdish tribespeople swooped down to pillage and kill, but the main strike force mobilized for mass killing was the *chétés*, bands of violent convicts who had been active since the 1914 "cleansings" of the Aegean Greeks, and were now released from prison to exterminate Armenians and other Christians. The genocide's organizers believed that using such forces "would enable the government to deflect responsibility. For as the death tolls rose, they could always say that 'things got out of control,' and it was the result of 'groups of brigands.'"[47]

Figure 4.3 Armenian children and women suffered systematic atrocities during the deportations; the minority that reached refuge were often on the verge of death from starvation, wounds, and exhaustion.

Source: Maria Jacobsen/Courtesy Karekin Dickran's Danish-Armenian archive collection.

Attacks on the surviving children, women, and elderly of the deportation caravans gave rise to hellish scenes. "The whole course of the journey became a perpetual struggle with the Moslem inhabitants," wrote Morgenthau:

> Such as escaped . . . attacks in the open would find new terrors awaiting them in the Moslem villages. Here the Turkish roughs would fall upon the women, leaving them sometimes dead from their experiences or sometimes ravingly insane. . . . Frequently any one who dropped on the road was bayoneted on the spot. The Armenians began to die by hundreds from hunger and thirst. Even when they came to rivers, the gendarmes [guards], merely to torment them, would sometimes not let them drink.[48]

"In a few days," according to Morgenthau,

> what had been a procession of normal human beings became a stumbling horde of dust-covered skeletons, ravenously looking for scraps of food, eating any offal that came their way, crazed by the hideous sights that filled every hour of their existence, sick with all the diseases that accompany such hardships and privations, but still prodded on and on by the whips and clubs and bayonets of their executioners.[49]

In thousands of cases, children and women were kidnapped and seized by villagers; the women were kept as servants and sex-slaves, the children converted to Islam and raised as "Turks." One young male survivor described his group being gathered together in a field while word went out to the local population: "Whoever wants a woman or child, come and get them." "Albert said that people came and took whomever they wanted, comparing the scene to sheep being sold at an auction."[50]

BOX 4.1 ONE WOMAN'S STORY: ESTER AHRONIAN

Ester Ahronian remembered her childhood in the Anatolian town of Amasia as idyllic. "In the center of our courtyard we had a large mulberry tree with the sweetest mulberries I ever tasted. I would lie under the thick branches and reach up for handfuls of soft berries. Sometimes they fell off the branches onto my face and eyes. The cool, sweet juice ran down my cheeks into my ears. . . . I believed with all my heart that my world would never change. Nothing bad could ever happen to me."

But in May 1915, dark rumors began reaching Amasia – rumors of persecution of the Ottoman empire's Armenian population. One day, returning from school, Ahronian witnessed a young Armenian man being dragged to the town's central square and hanged. By the end of the month, "the streets were crowded with soldiers carrying rifles with fixed bayonets," and a Turkish leader of the town announced that all able-bodied Armenian males were to present themselves to the authorities. "I watched from my window as groups of men gathered daily in the street. Then, bunches of twenty or thirty were marched out of the city by the soldiers." "As soon as they are outside the city limits they will kill them and come back for more," a neighbor declared.

Shortly after, Ester observed a group of Turkish soldiers approaching an Armenian church. She "watched as a soldier threw a lit torch into an open window. The other soldiers laughed and shouted, 'Let's see your Christian God save you now. You will roast like pigs.' Then the screaming began . . ." Her father was taken away to detention by Turkish forces – never to be seen again. In the face of the mounting persecution, some Armenian girls agreed to be married to Muslim men, "promis[ing] never to speak the Armenian language or practice Christianity again." But Ester refused, and instead joined one of the caravans leaving Amasia as the town was emptied of its Christian population. "*Aksor* – the deportation word everyone in town was whispering. What did it mean? What would it be like?"

She soon learned. "We were only a half hour out of town when a group of Kurds charged down from the mountains and attacked the first group at the front of the caravan." The soldiers allegedly guarding them joined, instead, in the slaughter and pillage. "Then the soldiers came for the girls. The prettiest ones were taken first." Ester's grandmother clad her in baggy garb and smeared her with mud and raw garlic, and she was momentarily spared.

Her caravan "passed a deep pit by the side of the road filled with the naked bodies of young and old men." Another attack by soldiers: "Wagons were overturned. The sound of bullets filled the air. . . . Around us lay the dead and near-dead." Pausing by a river, she watched bodies and parts of bodies floating by. Almost comatose with trauma and exhaustion, she was seized by Kurds who thought she had expired; they stripped her and threw her "into a wagon filled with naked dead bodies. I lay there, not moving under the pile of rotting flesh." She was dumped with the bodies over a cliff. An elderly Armenian woman, disguising her ethnicity in order to work for Kurds, rescued her, and offered her a life-saving proposition: to toil as a domestic with a Muslim notable, Yousouf Bey, and his family. "Yes, if they'll have me, I'll work for them," Ester agreed.[51]

In Yousouf Bey's home, she overheard Turks boasting of their massacre of Armenians. She was told that when she had recovered from her ordeal, she would be married off to a Muslim. She entreated Yousouf Bay to release her. He agreed to send her to an orphanage in the city of Malatya – but before doing so, he drugged her and raped her, brutally taking her virginity. "It was his parting gift to me."

At the orphanage, "once a week, Turks came and took their pick of the girls. They chose as many as they wanted for cooks, field workers, housekeepers, or wives. Like slaves, no one asked any questions. No one had any choice." She was claimed by Shamil, a teenage Muslim boy, and forced to marry him. In Shamil's poor household, "three times a day we faced Mecca and chanted Muslim prayers." When she was discovered in possession of a cherished crucifix, Shamil whipped her until blood flowed.

Finally seizing her opportunity, Ester fled and took refuge with the Bagradians, one of the few Armenian families allowed to survive – they were blacksmiths, deemed essential laborers by the Turks. Finally, she was able to make her way back to her hometown of Amasia. "A heavy silence hung over the streets like a dark cloud. . . . I was returning to the scene of a violent crime." Approaching her house, she found it occupied by a Turkish woman. "You have no rights," the woman tells her. "I'm leaving, so you can have your house back but I'm taking everything in it with me. If you make a fuss, I'll have you arrested." Hunkering down there, she discovered that "those Armenian families that remained in the city spoke only Turkish. All the Armenian churches were boarded up and stood as empty shadows against the clear sky."

She was befriended by Frau Gretel, the wife of a distant relative. Eventually, the war ended; but in 1920 a new wave of killings of Armenians descended. "Escape with us to America," Gretel implored her, and she consented. "The only thing I brought with me to America was my memory – the thing I most wanted to leave behind." Ester forged a new life on the east coast of the US, living to the ripe age of 98. Resident in an old-age home, she finally opened up to her daughter, Margaret, about her experiences during the genocide of Anatolia's Christian population. She disclaimed any feeling of hatred for her Turkish persecutors: "Hatred is like acid, it burns through the container. You must let go of bad memories." Margaret published her mother's recollections several years after Ester's death, in 2007.[52]

For those not abducted, the death marches usually meant extermination. Morgenthau cited one convoy that began with 18,000 people and arrived at its destination with 150. The state of most survivors was such that they often died within days of reaching refuge. J.B. Jackson, the US consul in Aleppo, Syria, recounted eyewitness descriptions of

> over 300 women [who] arrived at Ras-el-Ain, at that time the most easterly station to which the German–Baghdad railway was completed, entirely naked, their hair flowing in the air like wild beasts, and after travelling six days afoot in the burning sun. Most of these persons arrived in Aleppo a few days afterwards, and some of them personally came to the Consulate and exhibited their bodies to me, burned to the color of a green olive, the skin peeling off in great blotches, and many of them carrying gashes on the head and wounds on the body as a result of the terrible beatings inflicted by the Kurds.[53]

By 1917, between half and two-thirds of Ottoman Armenians had been exterminated. Large-scale massacres continued. In the final months of the First World War, Turkey crossed the Russian frontier and occupied sizable parts of Russian Armenia. There, according to Dadrian, "the genocidal engine of destruction unleashed by the Young Turk Ittihadists was once more activated to decimate and destroy the other half of the Armenian population living beyond the established frontiers of Turkey. . . . According to Soviet and Armenian sources, in five months of Turkish conquest and occupation about 200,000 Armenians of the region perished."[54] Meanwhile, "Armenians attacked civilian populations in Turkish towns and villages, massacring civilians and doing as much damage as they could. Having survived genocide, some of the Armenian irregulars were attempting to avenge the atrocities of 1915."[55]

THE ASSYRIAN GENOCIDE

In his careful research, beginning with a groundbreaking article in *Genocide Studies and Prevention* and continuing through his meticulous 2010 study of *Genocide in the Middle East*, Hannibal Travis has shown that the targeting of the Assyrians was fully comparable to that of the Armenians, in scale, strategy, and severity – and was recognized as such at the time it was inflicted. "The Assyrian genocide," he wrote, is "indistinguishable in principle from the Armenian genocide, despite being smaller in size":

> Starting in 1914 and with particular ferocity in 1915 and 1918, Ottoman soldiers and Kurdish and Persian militia subjected hundreds of thousands of Assyrians to a deliberate campaign of massacre, torture, abduction, deportation, impoverishment, and cultural and ethnic destruction. Established principles of international law outlawed this campaign of extermination before it was embarked upon, and ample evidence of genocidal intent has surfaced in the form of admissions by Ottoman officials. Nevertheless, the international community has been hesitant to recognize the Assyrian experience as a form of genocide.[56]

The foundation for the campaign against the Assyrians was an October 1914 edict from the Interior Ministry that the Assyrian population of the Van region should "depart." In June 1915, it was the same region that served as a flashpoint for both the Armenian and Assyrian mass killings, and the suffering of the Assyrian Christians was, as Travis says, "indistinguishable" from that of the Armenians. As David Gaunt describes the slaughter,

> The degree of extermination and the brutality of the massacres indicate extreme pent-up hatred on the popular level. Christians, the so-called *gawur* infidels, were being killed in almost all sorts of situations. They were collected at the local town hall, walking in the streets, fleeing on the roads, at harvest, in the villages, in the caves and tunnels, in the caravanserais [travelers' inns], in the prisons, under torture, on the river rafts, on road repair gangs, on the way to be put on trial. There was no specific and technological way of carrying out the murders like the Nazis'

extermination camps. A common feature was that those killed were unarmed, tied up, or otherwise defenseless. All possible means of killing were used: shooting, stabbing, stoning, crushing, throat cutting, throwing off of roofs, drowning, decapitation. Witnesses talk of seeing collections of ears and noses and of brigands boasting of their collections of female body parts.[57]

Joseph Naayem, an Assyro-Chaldean priest, received firsthand reports from the town of Sa'irt (also known as Seert) in Bitlis province. Assyro-Chaldean deaths in Sa'irt were later estimated as numbering 7,000 to 8,000 – with massacres of Chaldeans substantially adding to the toll.[58] Naayem cited testimony that the "chettés" (Ottoman criminal gangs) had gathered Sa'irt's men, marched them to the valley of Zeryabe, and massacred them. Women and girls were then set upon.[59] An Ottoman officer, Raphael de Nogales, described the aftermath:

> The ghastly slope was crowned by thousands of half-nude and still bleeding corpses, lying in heaps, or interlaced in death's final embrace. . . . Overcome by the hideous spectacle, and jumping our horses over the mountains of cadavers, which obstructed our passage, I entered Siirt with my men. There we found the police and the populace engaged in sacking the homes of the Christians. . . . I met various sub-Governors of the province . . . who had directed the massacre in person. From their talk I realized at once that the thing had been arranged the day before . . . Meanwhile I had taken up my lodging in a handsome house belonging to Nestorians, which had been sacked like all the rest. There was nothing left in the way of furniture except a few broken chairs. Walls and floors were stained with blood.[60]

Ambassador Morgenthau's account of the destruction of the Christian minorities asserted that the "same methods" of attack were inflicted on the Assyrians ("Nestorians" and "Syrians," as he called them) as on Armenians and Greeks. "The greatest crime of all ages," as he called it in a missive to the White House, was "the horrible massacre of helpless Armenians *and Syrians.*"[61]

A British officer based in Persia, Sir Percy Sykes, later suggested that if the Assyrians had not fled in terror to northern Persia, they would have experienced "extermination at the hands of Turks and Kurds."[62] But as many as 65,000 died from exhaustion, malnourishment, and disease en route to refuge in Persia, or after their arrival.[63] The suffering of Assyrians in Mesopotamia (Iraq) was no less.[64] All told, "about half of the Assyrian nation died of murder, disease, or exposure as refugees during the war," according to Anglican Church representatives on the ground. "Famine and want were the fate of the survivors, whose homes, villages, churches and schools were wiped out."[65] The remnants of the Assyrian population of southeastern Anatolia crossed into Mesopotamia, then under British control, and settled in refugee camps there. The British brought no resolution to their plight, though a civil commissioner of the time acknowledged it was "largely of our own creation and a solution has been made more difficult by our own action, or rather inaction."[66] It is in that zone of present-day Iraq that their descendants have been exposed to new rounds of persecution, "ethnic cleansing," and genocidal killing, as described in Box 4a.

THE PONTIAN GREEK GENOCIDE

Approximately 350,000 Pontian Greeks are believed to be among the Christian minorities slaughtered between 1914 and 1922. The Turks began targeting the millennia-old community along the Black Sea coast as early as 1916. Their extermination therefore long predated the renewed killings and persecutions of the post-World War One period, accompanying the Greek invasion of Anatolia. Missionary testimony cited by George Horton in his account of the late-Ottoman genocides, *The Blight of Asia*, dated the onset of "the Greek deportations from the Black Sea" to January 1916:

> These Greeks came through the city of Marsovan by thousands [reported a missionary], walking for the most part the three days' journey through the snow and mud and slush of the winter weather. Thousands fell by the wayside from exhaustion and others came into the city of Marsovan in groups of fifty, one hundred and five hundred, always under escort of Turkish gendarmes. Next morning these poor refugees were started on the road and destruction by this treatment was even more radical than a straight massacre such as the Armenians suffered before.[67]

BOX 4.2 ONE WOMAN'S STORY: SANO HALO

Figure 4.4   Sano Halo (seated at left), aged 100, takes her oath of honorary Greek citizenship at the Greek consulate in New York City, June 11, 2009.[68] Sano is accompanied by her daughter Thea Halo, who told Sano's story of surviving the Pontian Greek genocide in her book *Not Even My Name*. Thea, who received honorary Greek citizenship alongside her mother, was a prime mover in a 2007 resolution by which the International Association of Genocide Scholars (IAGS) formally recognized the Greek and Assyrian genocides alongside the Armenian one.

Source: Costas Euthalitsidis/Courtesy Thea Halo.

Once Sano was Themía: like so many survivors of genocide, she has been stripped of her name along with the life she was born into, in the Pontian Greek-dominated region along the Black Sea coast, in 1909.

"We never thought that one day we would be forced to leave our paradise," Sano related in her daughter Thea's memoir, *Not Even My Name*. "Our history went back too far to believe that, and we had survived invasion after invasion for 3,000 years. By the time of Alexander the Great's short rule between 336 and 323 BC, Greeks had already been living in Asia Minor, or Ionia as they called it, for over 800 years. . . . Pontus flourished as a great commercial and educational center. After decades of war, the Romans finally conquered the kingdom of Pontus in 63 BC. But the Greek culture continued to have great influence. The conquered gave culture to the conqueror."

During the First World War, Halo's mountain village was not attacked, but her father was one of the many Greek men swept up by the notorious labor battalions, or *Amele Tabourou*. He managed to escape, and conveyed a chilling report to his family: "The camps are cold and full of vermin. We're worked day and night without enough food to eat or a decent place to sleep or wash. In some camps the Greeks are just left to die with nothing at all. Even when the war was still being fought, the Turks left the Greeks behind to be killed without arms to defend themselves or food to eat. I think that's what they want, for all of us to die."

When Themía and her family were finally swept up in the carnage, in 1921–22, the campaign bore the same genocidal hallmarks of massacre and death march that had been deployed against diverse Christian populations during the war period. Themía and her family were launched on a march that lasted "for seven to eight months from the frigid mountainous regions of the north through the desertlike plains of the south without concern for food, water, or shelter." The landscape changed from green to "jagged cliffs and parched, coarse earth . . . The sun beat down on us all day . . . " After four months, Themía's "shoes wore out completely. Walking through this barren land with bare feet was like walking on pitted glass. The food we had brought was also gone. Each day brought another death, another body left to decompose on the side of the road. Some simply fell dead in their tracks. Their crumpled bodies littered the road like pieces of trash flung from a passing cart, left for buzzards and wolves."[69]

To save her from starvation, Themía's mother left her with an Assyrian family in the south of Turkey, where she received the Kurdish name Sano. After she ran away, an Armenian family took Themía in and brought her to Aleppo, Syria. There she was presented to Abraham, an Assyrian Christian who had emigrated to America twenty years before. She agreed to marry him, beginning a new life across the oceans and surviving to the present day. In 2000, her daughter Thea published Sano's story, based in part on a journey that mother and daughter made to the Pontian village of Sano's youth. In 2009, on her centennial birthday, Sano was granted honorary Greek citizenship (see Figure 4.4).

Figure 4.5 "Weeding Out the Men: All men of military age were torn away from their wives and children and led away in groups for deportation to the interior" (original caption). Image from the Pontian Greek genocide – the date is given as 1915; the precise location is uncertain.

Source: George Horton, *The Blight of Asia* (1926)/Pontian.info.[70]

As the Paris Peace Negotiations ground on in 1919, the victorious Allies invited Greece, which had joined their side in 1917, to occupy the city of Smyrna on Turkey's Aegean coast. A large Greek community still resided there, even after the 1914–15 "cleansings," and by the end of the war, the Christian population of the city had been swelled by Armenian and Assyrian refugees. The 1920 Treaty of Sèvres, though never implemented, formally recognized Greece's intervention.

The problems associated with the decision to dispatch Turkey's historic enemy to occupy a major city and stretch of Turkish coastline were compounded by the further failure to specify how far the Greek zone of occupation extended. The result was a violent occupation of Smyrna in 1919, with the Greeks and fellow Christians inflicting atrocities while "pacifying" the city and expanding into surrounding areas. This was followed by an opportunistic invasion of the Anatolian heartland.[71] Ill-judged, abjured by the Allies, increasingly unpopular with the Greek population and its soldiers, this invasion was also accompanied by atrocities and destruction, in proclaimed vengeance for the wartime genocides of Greeks and other Christians. The atrocities and the strategic nature of the invasion appeared to "put the very survival of any Turkish state in question," wrote historian Benjamin Lieberman. ". . . With the Greek invasion there was no obvious end in sight, no boundary to fall back on, and no security for a new Turkey. Many Turks saw their nation threatened by nothing less than extermination."[72]

Turkish fury and vengefulness ignited a further genocidal explosion against Anatolian Greeks, including Pontians, before the Greek army was finally driven from Turkish soil at Smyrna in 1922. The Near East Relief committee (see Figure 4.1) described 30,000 Pontian Greek refugees in flight from their homes in 1922, with some 14,000 killed, and noted that "the Turkish authorities were frank in their statements that it was the intention to have Greeks die and all of their actions . . . seem to fully bear this statement out," including forcing the deportees to march through "severe snow storms" while doing "practically everything within [their] power to prevent any relief."[73]

An estimate of the Pontian Greek death toll at all stages of the anti-Christian genocide is about 350,000; for all the Greeks of the Ottoman realm taken together, the toll surely exceeded half a million, and may approach the 900,000 killed that a team of US researchers found in the early postwar period. Most surviving Greeks were expelled to Greece as part of the tumultuous "population exchanges" that set the seal on a heavily "Turkified" state. Apart from an anti-Greek pogrom in Istanbul in 1955 (the culmination of a series that reduced the Greek population from 297,788 in 1924 to fewer than 3,000 today),[74] only the restive Kurdish minority remained to challenge ethnic-Turkish hegemony within the new state boundaries. The Kurds, accordingly, were mercilessly repressed from the 1930s to the 1980s, a story that lies beyond the bounds of this account.[75]

AFTERMATH: ATTEMPTS AT JUSTICE

Turkey's defeat in the First World War, and the subsequent collapse and occupation of the Ottoman Empire, offered surviving Armenians an opportunity for national self-determination. In 1918, an independent Republic of Armenia was declared in the southwestern portion of Transcaucasia, a historically Armenian territory that had been under Russian sovereignty since the early nineteenth century. US President Woodrow Wilson was granted the right to delimit a new Armenian nation, formalized at the Treaty of Sèvres in 1920. Later that year, Wilson supervised the drawing of boundaries for independent Armenia that included parts of historic Ottoman Armenia in eastern Turkey.

Turkey, however, staged a rapid political recovery following its abject military defeat. The new leader, Mustafa Kemal (known as Ataturk, "father of the Turks"), repelled the Greek invasion through the bloody and indiscriminate countermeasures as described above; renounced the Sèvres Treaty; and in a secret gathering, declared it "indispensable that Armenia be annihilated politically and physically."[76] The Kemalist forces invaded, and reconquered six of the former Ottoman provinces that had been granted to independent Armenia under Sèvres. What remained of Armenia was swallowed up by the new Soviet Union. Following a brief period of cooperation with Armenian nationalists, the Soviets took complete control in 1921, and Armenia was incorporated into the Transcaucasian Soviet Federated Socialist Republic (TSFSR) in 1922. A separate Armenian Soviet Socialist Republic was created in 1936. Greeks had nearly all been killed or expelled, and surviving Assyrian populations were clustered outside Anatolia, under British mandatory control in Mesopotamia. The stage was set for the rebirth of Turkish nationalism and the resuscitation of Turkish statehood.

In the interim (1918–20) between the Ottoman collapse and the ascendancy of the Ataturk regime, and at the insistence of the Allies (who, as early as 1915, with

Figure 4.6   Mustafa Kemal, known as Ataturk – "father of the Turks" – in the early 1920s. After the crushing defeat of the First World War, he used his common touch and charisma to rally the Turks to expel foreign occupiers and restore Anatolia as the heartland of a post-Ottoman state. Ataturk modernized and secularized Turkish society, and established the country as an influential and strategic player in international politics. But the Turkish ethnonationalism that he both mobilized and catalyzed has proved to be a volatile quantity. It led to further massacres of Christians in the early Kemalist period, and the marginalization and persecution of the country's large Kurdish minority thereafter. And it impeded Turks' honest engagement with their country's past, including the genocides of the First World War period. Turks are, of course, hardly alone in such nationalistic/patriotic hubris and selective readings of history. See Chapters 2, 10, 14, and 16 for examples and further discussion.
Source: Wikimedia Commons.

an eye on the postwar dismemberment of the Turkish heartland, had accused the Young Turk rulers of "crimes against humanity"), the Turkish government – at British insistence, and in the hope of winning more favorable terms from the Allies at the Paris Peace Conference – held a remarkable series of trials of those accused of directing and implementing the Armenian genocide.

In April 1919, the Court pronounced that "the disaster visiting the Armenians was not a local or isolated event. It was the result of a premeditated decision taken by a central body . . . and the immolations and excesses which took place were based on oral and written orders issued by that central body."[77] Over a hundred former government officials were indicted, and a number were convicted, with Talat, Enver, and a pair of other leadership figures sentenced to death in absentia. After three relatively minor figures were executed, nationalist sentiment in Turkey exploded, greatly strengthening Ataturk's revolution. The British Foreign Office reported that "not one Turk in a thousand can conceive that there might be a Turk who deserves to be hanged for the killing of Christians"[78] – and in the face of that opposition and Allied pandering, the impetus for justice began to waver. "Correspondingly the sentences grew weaker, as the court refrained from handing down death sentences, finding most of the defendants only 'guilty of robbery, plunder, and self-enrichment at the expense of the victims.'"[79]

Eventually, in a tactic duplicated by Serbs in Bosnia-Herzegovina decades later (Chapter 8), Ataturk took dozens of British hostages from among the occupying forces. For Britain, which had decided some time earlier that the best policy was "cutting its losses," this was the final straw.[80] Anxious to secure the hostages' release, and to placate the new Turkish regime, the British freed many of the Turks in its custody. In July 1923, the Allies signed the Treaty of Lausanne with the Turks, which made no mention of the independent Armenia pledged at Sèvres. It was an "abject, cowardly and infamous surrender," in the estimation of British politician Lloyd George.[81]

Denied formal justice, Armenian militants settled on a vigilante version. All three of the main organizers of the genocide were assassinated: Talat Pasha in Berlin in 1921, at the hands of Soghomon Tehlirian, who had lost most members of his family in the genocide; Enver Pasha while leading an anti-Bolshevik revolt in Turkestan in 1922 (in an ambush "led by an Armenian Bolshevik officer");[82] and Jemal Pasha, by Armenians in Tiflis in 1922.

THE DENIAL

In 1915, the Allies staged an attempted invasion of Turkey at Gallipoli. During nine months of attacks launched from the narrow ribbon of beach they occupied, up precipitous cliffs and through thorny gullies, the Allies sought fruitlessly to reach the straits.[83] Fierce Turkish resistance stopped every thrust. In the end the Allies withdrew, having suffered tens of thousands of casualties, mostly from disease. Today, their carefully tended cemeteries dot the landscape, as do those where a similar number of Turkish casualties are buried.

It is likely that if the Gallipoli campaign had succeeded, the genocide against the Armenians would not have occurred. But it did – unless, that is, you shared the views of the author of a guidebook to the battlefields, available at souvenir shops in Çannakale across the Straits. According to this text, the Armenians were "privileged subjects of the Ottoman Empire [who] had been disloyal during the war, having crossed the [Russian] border, joined the Russian Army, and fought against the Turks":

Furthermore, they were hoarding arms for a movement to set up an independent Armenian state in Turkey. They had staked their future on the victory of the Allies and, like the Greeks, gloated over every Turkish reverse in the war. They were rich, and many of them handled commerce throughout the empire. In effect, they were a fifth column inside the country. . . . The leaders were punished with death and the rest put on the road to the south of the empire, to Syria and Mesopotamia [Iraq], in order to reduce the Armenian population near the Russian border. This event would later be introduced to the world as the so-called "Turkish massacre" and be turned into negative propaganda against the modern Republic of Turkey by the Armenian diaspora.[84]

For the guidebook's author, the death and destruction inflicted on the Armenians did not constitute genocide or even "massacre"; it was a necessary and morally justi-fiable response to the machinations of Armenian rebels. In espousing these views, moreover, the author was simply reflecting the general, indeed semi-official Turkish attitude towards the Armenian genocide.

This is classic genocide denial, force-fed to an international community by a sustained government campaign. As Bloxham summarized, Turkey has "written the Armenians out of its history books, and systematically destroyed Armenian archi-tecture and monuments to erase any physical traces of an Armenian presence." Moreover, "Armenian genocide denial is backed by the full force of a Turkish state machinery that has pumped substantial funding into public-relations firms and American university endowments to provide a slick and superficially plausible defence of its position."[85] In these efforts (analyzed in comparative context in Chapter 14), Turkey has been greatly assisted by its alliance with the US.[86] For the US, Turkey was critically important in the "containment" of the Soviet Union during the Cold War. Today, it is seen as a secular bulwark against Muslim-fundamentalist ferment in the Middle East. Accordingly, US military leaders, as well as "security"-minded politicians, have played a key role in denial of the genocide.[87] The close US–Turkish relationship means that Turkish studies in the United States is well-funded, not only through Turkish government sources, but thanks to the large number of contractors (mainly arms manufacturers) who do business with Turkey.

In recent years, however, the denial efforts of the Turkish government and its supporters have met with decreasing success. "Today, twenty countries, most of them

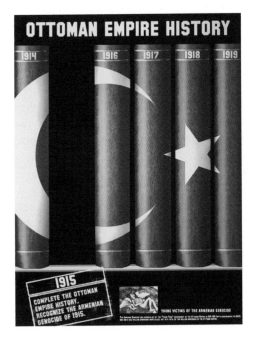

Figure 4.7 1915: the missing volume of Ottoman history. Poster by Yervant Herian.

Source: Courtesy Yervant Herian/ www.armeniangenocide posters.org.

in Europe, acknowledge the Armenian Genocide, as do the European Parliament, the United Nations, and the International Association of Genocide Scholars."[88] The most prominent national-level action was a 1998 resolution by the French National Assembly: a single sentence reading, "France recognizes the Armenian genocide of 1915."[89] This was passed over strong Turkish objections and threats of economic reprisals against French companies doing business with Turkey. In April 2004, the Canadian House of Commons voted to recognize "the death of 1.5 million Armenians between 1915 and 1923 as a genocide . . . and condemn this act as a crime against humanity."[90]

The United States still held out. After numerous abortive initiatives, the House of Representatives seemed poised in October 2000 to acknowledge the Armenian tragedy as genocide, and condemn its perpetrators. However, "minutes before the House was due to vote" on the measure, "J. Dennis Hastert, the speaker, withdrew the resolution . . . citing President Clinton's warnings that a vote could harm national security and hurt relations with Turkey, a NATO ally." President-to-be Barack Obama expressed his support on the campaign trail for formal recognition of the Armenian genocide, including the proposed congressional resolution, while campaigning in 2008: "As a US Senator, I have stood with the Armenian American community in calling for Turkey's acknowledgement of the Armenian Genocide." But as president, he has refrained from issuing a presidential declaration on the subject – as he pledged to do – and he carefully avoided using the word "genocide" during his April 2009 visit to Turkey.[91]

One reason cited for Obama's demurral was the sensitive question of Turkish–Armenian relations, which reached a kind of resolution in October 2009 with the signing in Zurich of an accord to re-establish diplomatic and economic relations between the two countries, severed since the 1990s crisis over the Armenian-majority zone of Nagorno-Karabakh in Azerbaijan. This set aside the genocide recognition issue, merely establishing a joint "impartial historical commission" to examine the issue. For some Armenians in the diaspora, and others, this suggested that the factual status of the genocide still had to be determined: the International Association of Genocide Scholars president, William Schabas, responded with a declaration that "acknowledgement of the Armenian Genocide must be the starting point of any 'impartial historical commission,' not one of its possible conclusions."[92] The keen observer of international affairs, Gwynne Dyer, pointed to how the genocide was being "remembered" differently (see Chapter 14) by the two main Armenian branches:

> The most anguished protests came from the Armenian diaspora – eight million people living mainly in the United States, France, Russia, Iran and Lebanon. There are only three million people living in Armenia itself, and remittances from the diaspora are twice as large as the country's entire budget, so the views of overseas Armenians matter. Unfortunately, their views are quite different from those of the people who actually live in Armenia. For Armenians abroad, making the Turks admit that they planned and carried out a genocide is supremely important. Indeed, it has become a core part of their identity. For most of those who are still in Armenia, getting the Turkish border re-opened is a higher priority.[93]

In Turkey itself, the picture is mixed. The international community was shocked by the assassination of Hrant Dink, a Turkish newspaper editor of Armenian background who had published widely on the Armenian genocide and Turkish–Armenian reconciliation. After years of death threats, Dink was gunned down in the streets of Istanbul in January 2007; his assassin was a 17-year-old Turkish nationalist. Other prominent figures who have spoken about the genocide, including the Nobel Prize-winning author Orhan Pamuk, have likewise been hounded, threatened, and prosecuted (as was Dink, three times) for "insulting Turkishness."[94]

On the other hand, notable cracks have appeared in the façade of denial. In extraordinary scenes after Dink's killing, some two hundred thousand Turkish mourners marched in his funeral procession: "cries of *Hepimiz Ermeniz* ('We are all Armenians!') [sounded] in the throats of tens of thousands of Turks."[95] This new sense of solidarity was evident in the brave scholarship of Taner Akçam and others, and relatedly in the move towards rapprochement with the country's Kurdish minority. In 2008, a quartet of Turkish intellectuals – Ahmet Insel, Baskin Oran, Ali Bayramoglu, and Cengiz Aktar – risked the wrath of the state, and nationalist vigilantes, by issuing a "public apology" for the Armenian genocide, in which the signatories declared:

> My conscience does not accept the insensitivity showed to and the denial of the Great Catastrophe that the Ottoman Armenians were subjected to in 1915. I reject this injustice and for my share, I empathise with the feelings and pain of my Armenian brothers. I apologise to them.[96]

Despite such dramatic gestures, "history," according to the Turkish writer Sechuk Tezgul, was still "waiting for that honest Turkish leader who will acknowledge his ancestors' biggest crime ever, who will apologize to the Armenian people, and who will do his best to indemnify them, materially and morally, in the eyes of the world."[97]

Recognition of the genocides of the other Christian populations of the Ottoman realm has also proceeded incrementally. In an announcement which ran counter to a tendency toward an "exclusivity of suffering,"[98] the Armenian National Committee of America (ANCA) "join[ed] with Pontian Greeks – and all Hellenes around the world – in commemorating . . . the genocide initiated by the Ottoman Empire and continued by Kemalist Turkey against the historic Greek population of Pontus along the southeastern coast of the Black Sea." "We join with the Hellenic American community in solemn remembrance of the Pontian Genocide, and in reaffirming our determination to work together with all the victims of Turkey's atrocities to secure full recognition and justice for these crimes," said ANCA's director, Aram Hamparian. By 2007, a number of US states, including Florida, New York, New Jersey, Massachusetts, and Pennsylvania, had also passed formal acts of recognition.

A more recent initiative was spearheaded in the International Association of Genocide Scholars (IAGS). A resolution was placed before the IAGS membership to recognize the Greek and Assyrian/Chaldean components of the Ottoman genocide against Christians, alongside the Armenian strand of the genocide (which the IAGS had already formally acknowledged). The result, passed emphatically in December 2007 despite not inconsiderable opposition, was a resolution which I co-drafted, reading as follows:

WHEREAS the denial of genocide is widely recognized as the final stage of genocide, enshrining impunity for the perpetrators of genocide, and demonstrably paving the way for future genocides;

WHEREAS the Ottoman genocide against minority populations during and following the First World War is usually depicted as a genocide against Armenians alone, with little recognition of the qualitatively similar genocides against other Christian minorities of the Ottoman Empire;

BE IT RESOLVED that it is the conviction of the International Association of Genocide Scholars that the Ottoman campaign against Christian minorities of the Empire between 1914 and 1923 constituted a genocide against Armenians, Assyrians, and Pontian and Anatolian Greeks.

BE IT FURTHER RESOLVED that the Association calls upon the government of Turkey to acknowledge the genocides against these populations, to issue a formal apology, and to take prompt and meaningful steps toward restitution.[99]

In my view, the initiative typified one of the more positive aspects of genocide studies: the opportunity to help in resuscitating long-forgotten or marginalized events for a contemporary audience; in acknowledging the victims and survivors of the genocide; and in exposing accepted framings and discourses to critical reexamination. Such processes themselves represent a kind of "humanitarian intervention" – primarily in the realms of history and memory, but also in contemporary crises, by highlighting the plight of vulnerable descendant populations today.

FURTHER STUDY

Taner Akçam, *A Shameful Act: The Armenian Genocide and the Question of Turkish Responsibility.* New York: Metropolitan Books, 2006. Based on intensive archival research in Turkish sources, the story of the planning, perpetration, and aftermath of the Armenian holocaust. See also *From Empire to Republic: Turkish Nationalism and the Armenian Genocide.*

Peter Balakian, *The Burning Tigris: The Armenian Genocide and America's Response.* New York: HarperCollins, 2003. The best overview of the genocide and the US humanitarian response; see also *Black Dog of Fate* (memoir).

Donald Bloxham, *The Great Game of Genocide: Imperialism, Nationalism, and the Destruction of the Ottoman Armenians.* Cambridge: Cambridge University Press, 2005. Excellent on the international machinations surrounding the "Armenian question." See also *Genocide, the World Wars and the Unweaving of Europe.*

Sébastien de Courtois, *The Forgotten Genocide: Eastern Christians, The Last Arameans,* trans. Vincent Aurora. Piscataway, NJ: Gorgias Press, 2004. One of the very few studies of the destruction of Assyrian/Syriac communities under the Ottomans.

Vahakn N. Dadrian, *The History of the Armenian Genocide: Ethnic Conflict from the Balkans to Anatolia to the Caucasus.* Providence, RI: Berghahn Books, 1995. Background to the genocide.

Marjorie Housepian Dobkin, *Smyrna 1922: The Destruction of a City*. New York: Newmark Press, 1998 (reprint). A standard though somewhat partisan account of one of the last spasms of war and "cleansing" in the Ottoman period.

David Gaunt, *Massacres, Resistance, Protectors: Muslim-Christian Relations in Eastern Anatolia during World War I*. Piscataway, NJ: Gorgias Press, 2006. Exhaustive survey of the mass violence in this little-studied corner of the empire.

Thea Halo, *Not Even My Name*. New York: Picador, 2001. Moving account of a survivor of the Pontian Greek genocide – the author's mother (Sano Halo, still alive in 2010, aged 100; see Figure 4.4, p. 163).

Richard G. Hovannisian, ed., *The Armenian Genocide in Perspective*. New Brunswick, NJ: Transaction Publishers, 1986. Early collection, still in print and still a concise and lucid introduction.

Donald E. Miller and Lorna Touryan Miller, *Survivors: An Oral History of the Armenian Genocide*. Berkeley, CA: University of California Press, 1999. Focuses on the experiences of Armenian children.

Henry Morgenthau, *Ambassador Morgenthau's Story*. http://www.gwpda.org/wwi-www/morgenthau/MorgenTC.htm. Memoirs of the US Ambassador to Constantinople.

Ronald Grigor Suny, *Looking Toward Ararat: Armenia in Modern History*. Bloomington, IN: Indiana University Press, 1993. Examines the rise of Armenian nationalism, the genocide, and the subsequent politics of Soviet Armenia and the diaspora.

The Treatment of Armenians in the Ottoman Empire, 1915–16. http://net.lib.byu.edu/~rdh7/wwi/1915/bryce/. Text of the British "Blue Book" (published in 1916) on atrocities against the Armenians.

Speros Vryonis, Jr., *The Mechanism of Catastrophe: The Turkish Pogrom of September 6–7, 1955, and the Destruction of the Greek Community of Istanbul*. New York: Greekworks, 2007. Meticulous investigation of an anti-Greek pogrom in post-Kemalist Turkey.

NOTES

1 In German, *"Wer redet heute noch von der Vernichtung der Armenier?"* Hitler quoted in Ronnie S. Landau, *The Nazi Holocaust* (Chicago, IL: Ivan R. Dee, 1994), p. 15. On the documentary evidence for Hitler's statement, see Vahakn N. Dadrian, *The History of the Armenian Genocide: Ethnic Conflict from the Balkans to Anatolia to the Caucasus* (6th rev. edn) (New York: Berghahn Books, 2003), pp. 403–09.

2 I follow Travis in referring "to the Assyrians, Nestorians, Chaldeans, and Syrian/Syriac Christians collectively as Assyrians. All of them are descended from the indigenous inhabitants of Mesopotamia, southeastern Anatolia, and northwestern Persia; Persian, Greek, and Arab rulers, as well as Chaldean Patriarchs, Syrian/Syriac priests and monks, and their Armenian neighbors, have referred to all three groups together as 'Assyrians.'" Travis, *Genocide in the Middle East: The Ottoman Empire, Iraq, and Sudan* (Durham, NC: Carolina Academic Press, 2010), p. 237 (n. 2).

3 Travis, *Genocide in the Middle East*, p. 299. As Travis points out, the original title of the famous "Blue Book," the Allied compilation of documents on Turkish atrocities, was *Papers and Documents on the Treatment of Armenians and Assyrian Christians by the Turks, 1915–1916, in the Ottoman Empire and North-West Persia*. The phrase "and Assyrian Christians" was deleted prior to the book's publication in Britain, and all references to

anti-Assyrian atrocities were removed from the French version presented at the postwar Paris Peace Conference (*Genocide in the Middle East*, p. 253).

4 Taner Akçam, *A Shameful Act: The Armenian Genocide and the Question of Turkish Responsibility* (New York: Metropolitan Books, 2006), p. 43.

5 Donald Bloxham, *The Great Game of Genocide: Imperialism, Nationalism, and the Destruction of the Ottoman Armenians* (Cambridge: Cambridge University Press, 2005), p. 71.

6 Wangenheim quoted in Akçam, *A Shameful Act*, p. 121.

7 Thea Halo, *Not Even My Name* (New York: Picador USA, 2001), p. 131.

8 Hannibal Travis, personal communication, January 25, 2010. Travis notes that the estimate squares with that of David Gaunt, and also the figures submitted to the Paris Peace Conference shortly after the events.

9 For a useful overview of contemporary anti-Christian persecution and genocide, asserting that "Christians are now considered the most persecuted religious group around the world," see "Christianity's Modern-Day Martyrs," *Spiegel Online*, February 28, 2010, http://www.spiegel.de/international/world/0,1518,680349,00.html.

10 Throughout this chapter, for convenience, I refer to "Turkey" and "the Ottoman Empire" interchangeably.

11 Vahakn Dadrian, "Documentation of the Armenian Genocide in Turkish Sources," in Israel Charny, ed., *Genocide: A Critical Bibliographic Review*, Vol. 2 (New Brunswick, NJ: Transaction Publishers, 1991); Dadrian, "The Role of Turkish Physicians in the World War I Genocide of Ottoman Armenians," *Holocaust and Genocide Studies*, 1 (1986), pp. 172–75, 184.

12 Ben Kiernan, *Blood and Soil: A World History of Genocide and Extermination from Sparta to Darfur* (New Haven, CT: Yale University Press, 2009), p. 402.

13 Bloxham, *The Great Game of Genocide*, pp. 30–31.

14 Donald Bloxham, *Genocide, the World Wars and the Unweaving of Europe* (London: Vallentine Mitchell, 2008), p. 1. However, Hannibal Travis contests Bloxham's claim of a clear primacy of Muslim victims: it "seems to ignore the massacres of 200,000 to 450,000 Ottoman Christians, including 30,000 Armenians in the 1900s, 100,000 to 300,000 mostly Armenians in the 1890s, about 15,000 Armenians and Slavs in the 1870s, about 12,000 Maronites in Lebanon around 1860, and about 70,000 Greeks in the 1820s." Travis, personal communication, January 24, 2010. Justin McCarthy's revisionist study, *Death and Exile: The Ethnic Cleansing of Ottoman Muslims, 1821–1922* (Princeton, NJ: The Darwin Press, 1995), claims that during the period under consideration, "Five and one-half million Muslims died, some of them killed in wars, others perishing as refugees from starvation and disease" (p. 1).

15 Akçam, *A Shameful Act*, p. 87.

16 The shrinking of the empire meant that the Ottoman realm became more homogeneous, and the minority Christians of the realm (the Armenians, Assyrians, and Pontian Greeks) stood out more prominently. Whereas the Ottoman Empire had once been unusually diverse, cosmopolitan, and tolerant, its dissolution spurred those who yearned for an ethnically "pure" Turkish homeland. I am indebted to Benjamin Madley for this point.

17 Stephan Astourian, "The Armenian Genocide: An Interpretation," *The History Teacher*, 23: 2 (February 1990), p. 123.

18 Balakian, *The Burning Tigris*, p. 59.

19 Dadrian, *The History of the Armenian Genocide*, p. 151. Daniel Jonah Goldhagen points out that "the Turks' massive assault upon the Armenians from 1894 to 1896 would rightly be called the Armenian Genocide – had an even more massive mass murder and elimination not followed twenty years later." Daniel Jonah Goldhagen, *Worse Than War: Genocide, Eliminationism, and the Ongoing Assault on Humanity* (New York: Basic Books, 2009), p. 302.

20 Bloxham, *The Great Game of Genocide*, p. 55.

21 For analysis of the death-toll, see Dadrian, *The History of the Armenian Genocide*, pp. 153–57.

22 Melson quoted in Donald E. Miller and Lorna Touryan Miller, *Survivors: An Oral History of the Armenian Genocide* (Berkeley, CA: University of California Press, 1999), p. 47.

23 Astourian, "The Armenian Genocide," p. 129.

24 Donald Bloxham, personal communication, August 31, 2005.

25 Balakian, *The Burning Tigris*, p. 164.

26 Gökalp quoted in Akçam, *A Shameful Act*, p. 88.

27 Miller and Miller, *Survivors*, p. 39.

28 For example, Bahaeddin Sakir, who headed the Special Organization in the eastern Ottoman provinces, wrote in February 1915 of the CUP's decision that "the Armenians living in Turkey will be destroyed to the last. The government has been given ample authority. As to the organization of the mass murder, the government will provide the necessary explanations to the governors, and to the army commanders. The delegates of [the CUP] in their own regions will be in charge of this task." Cited in Astourian, "The Armenian Genocide," p. 139.

29 In April 1909, another massacre of Armenians occurred in the city of Adana, with similar killing campaigns occurring "all across Cilicia and around the Gulf of Alexandretta." However, "this time the new revolutionary government decided to act and prosecuted 34 Turks and 6 Armenians for their part in the communal strife." Andrew Bell-Fialkoff, *Ethnic Cleansing* (New York: St. Martin's Griffin, 1999), p. 150.

30 Matthias Bjørnlund, "The 1914 Cleansing of Aegean Greeks as a Case of Violent Turkification," *Journal of Genocide Research*, 10: 1 (2008), p. 42.

31 Toynbee quoted in Akçam, *A Shameful Act*, p. 105.

32 For an interpretation running somewhat counter to the one offered here, see Bloxham, *The Great Game of Genocide*, pp. 64, 164. Bloxham describes the policy adopted towards Ottoman Greeks from 1913 to 1916 as "a combination of population engineering and economic appropriation, using boycotts, murders, terrorization, and then deportation" (*The Great Game of Genocide*, p. 64). However, he argues that generalized killing of Greeks did not occur until 1921–22, following the Greek invasion and occupation of large parts of Turkey; and then it took place in the context of a "war of extermination" featuring comparably widespread atrocities against civilians by both Greek and Turkish forces.

33 Morgenthau quoted in Akçam, *A Shameful Act*, p. 111.

34 Morgenthau quoted in ibid., pp. 105–06.

35 Van der Zee quoted in Bjørnlund, "The 1914 Cleansing," p. 46.

36 Emanuelidi Efendi quoted in Akçam, *A Shameful Act*, p. 107.

37 CUP document cited in Kiernan, *Blood and Soil*, p. 408.

38 Shakir quoted in Ronald Grigor Suny, *Looking Toward Ararat: Armenia in Modern History* (Bloomington, IN: Indiana University Press, 1993), p. 112.

39 Henry J. Morgenthau, *Murder of a Nation*, http://www.gwpda.org/wwi-www/morgenthau/MorgenTC.htm.

40 Michael Mann, *The Dark Side of Democracy: Explaining Ethnic Cleansing* (Cambridge: Cambridge University Press, 2005), p. 148.

41 Dadrian, *The History of the Armenian Genocide*, p. 226.

42 Ibid., pp. 221–22.

43 Morgenthau, *Murder of a Nation*.

44 "Some regional variations notwithstanding," wrote Taner Akçam, "the expulsions and massacres proceeded in the same way everywhere and are well documented in American, British and German archival materials, missionary reports, and survivors' accounts. The very persistence of the pattern indicates central planning." Akçam, *A Shameful Act*, p. 174.

45 Davis quoted in Balakian, *The Burning Tigris*, p. 234.

46 Norman M. Naimark, *Fires of Hatred: Ethnic Cleansing in Twentieth-century Europe* (Cambridge, MA: Harvard University Press, 2001), p. 41.

47 Balakian, *The Burning Tigris*, pp. 182–83.
48 Morgenthau, *Murder of a Nation*.
49 Ibid.
50 Miller and Miller, *Survivors*, p. 110.
51 For an overview of this practice, see Ara Sarafian, "The Absorption of Armenian Women and Children into Muslim Households As a Structural Component of the Armenian Genocide," ch. 9 in Omer Bartov and Phyllis Mack, *In God's Name: Genocide and Religion in the Twentieth Century* (New York: Berghahn Books, 2001), pp. 209–21.
52 Margaret Ajemian Ahnert, *The Knock at the Door: A Journey through the Darkness of the Armenian Genocide* (New York: Beaufort Books, 2007). The quoted passages are drawn from pp. 10, 15, 88–89, 91, 117, 121, 138, 168, 176.
53 Miller and Miller, *Survivors*, p. 119.
54 Vahakn N. Dadrian, "The Comparative Aspects of the Armenian and Jewish Cases of Genocide: A Sociohistorical Perspective," in Alan S. Rosenbaum, ed., *Is the Holocaust Unique? Perspectives on Comparative Genocide* (Boulder, CO: Westview Press, 1998), pp. 127–28.
55 Balakian, *The Burning Tigris*, p. 320.
56 Ibid., p. 245. David Gaunt likewise contends that the CUP viewed "the Syriac groups in the Ottoman Empire . . . with the same degree of suspicion as they did the Armenians." Gaunt, *Massacres, Resistance, Protectors: Muslim–Christian Relations in Eastern Anatolia during World War I* (Piscataway, NJ: Gorgias Press, 2006), p. 122.
57 Gaunt, *Massacres, Resistance, Protectors*, p. 304.
58 Ibid., p. 252 (citing Arthur Beylerian, *Les Grandes Puissances: L'Empire Ottoman, et les Arméniens dans les archives françaises (1914–1918)* [New York: Holmes & Meier Publishers, 1983]), pp. 478–79; Viscount James Bryce and Arnold Joseph Toynbee, *The Treatment of Armenians in the Ottoman Empire, 1915–1916: Documents Presented to Viscount Grey of Fallodon* (ed. Ara Sarafian) (Reading: Taderon Press, 2000), p. 120.
59 Joseph Naayem, *Shall This Nation Die?* (New York: Chaldean Rescue, 1921), pp. 145–162.
60 Nogales quoted in Travis, *Genocide in the Middle East*, p. 248.
61 Morgenthau quoted in ibid., p. 257. Emphasis added.
62 Sykes quoted in Lt. Col. Ronald S. Stafford, "Iraq and the Problem of the Assyrians," *International Affairs*, March 1934, p. 182.
63 Christoph Baumer, *The Church of the East: An Illustrated History of Assyrian Christianity* (London: I.B. Tauris, 2006), p. 263. I am grateful to Hannibal Travis for bringing this source and the preceding one to my attention.
64 Stafford, *Iraq and the Problem of the Assyrians*, p. 177.
65 Travis, *Genocide in the Middle East*, p. 256.
66 Quoted in Ibid., p. 207.
67 Horton cited in Ibid., p. 287.
68 See also Nancy Kriz, "Greek Citizenship Bestowed upon 100-year-old Monroe Woman Who Survived the Pontic Greek Genocide," Atour.com, July 24, 2009, http://www.atour.com/~aahgn/news/20090724a.html.
69 Halo, *Not Even My Name*, pp. 98, 131, 135–36.
70 The image with its original caption appears online at http://members.fortunecity.com/fstav1/horton/deportations2_1915.jpg.
71 A British commission investigating the occupation of Smyrna and environs delivered a "verdict on Greek behavior during the offensive of 1921 [that] was damning in the extreme. The commissioners wrote of the 'burning and looting of Turkish villages' and the explosion of violence of Greeks and Armenians against the Turks . . . : 'There is a systematic plan of destruction and extinction of the Moslem population. This plan is being carried out by Greek and Armenian hands, which appear to operate under Greek instruction and sometimes even with the assistance of detachments of regular troops.'"

Norman M. Naimark, *Fires of Hatred: Ethnic Cleansing in Twentieth-Century Europe* (Cambridge, MA: Harvard University Press, 2001), p. 45.

72 Benjamin Lieberman, *Terrible Fate: Ethnic Cleansing in the Making of Modern Europe* (Chicago, IL: Ivan R. Dee, 2006), p. 123.

73 Quoted in Travis, *Genocide in the Middle East*, p. 290.

74 See Speros Vryonis, Jr., *The Mechanism of Catastrophe: The Turkish Pogrom of September 6–7, 1955, and the Destruction of the Greek Community of Istanbul* (New York: Greekworks, 2007), pp. 16, 565.

75 See Jonathan C. Randal, *After Such Knowledge, What Forgiveness? My Encounters with Kurdistan* (Boulder, CO: Westview Press, 1999).

76 Cited in Balakian, *The Burning Tigris*, p. 328. In a precursor to subsequent Turkish campaigns of genocide denial, Ataturk claimed that the Armenians killed were "victims of foreign intrigues" and guilty of abusing "the privileges granted them."

77 Quoted in Gary Jonathan Bass, *Stay the Hand of Vengeance: The Politics of War Crimes Tribunals* (Princeton, NJ: Princeton University Press, 2000), p. 127.

78 British Foreign Office dispatch quoted in Akçam, *A Shameful Act*, p. 294.

79 Balakian, *The Burning Tigris*, p. 341. For more on the trials, see Akçam, *A Shameful Act*, part 3; Vahakn Dadrian, "The Turkish Military Tribunal's Prosecution of the Authors of the Armenian Genocide," *Holocaust and Genocide Studies*, 11: 1 (1997).

80 Bass, *Stay the Hand of Vengeance*, p. 136.

81 Lloyd George quoted in Bass, *Stay the Hand of Vengeance*, p. 144.

82 Balakian, *The Burning Tigris*, p. 345.

83 See the photo galleries of the (beautiful) battlefield sites at http://adamjones.freeservers. com/turkey03-00.htm. Peter Weir's film, *Gallipoli*, is a fair depiction of events from the viewpoint of Australian soldiers.

84 Mustafa Aşkin, *Gallipoli: A Turning Point* (Çanakkale: Mustafa Aşkin, n.d.), p. 40.

85 Bloxham, *The Great Game of Genocide*, pp. 211, 228. See also Amy Magaro Rubin, "Critics Accuse Turkish Government of Manipulating Scholarship," *Chronicle of Higher Education*, October 27, 1995.

86 On the Turkish–Israeli relationship, see Yair Auron, *The Banality of Denial: Israel and the Armenian Genocide* (New Brunswick, NJ: Transaction Publishers, 2003). See also Robert Melson, "Responses to the Armenian Genocide: America, the Yishuv, Israel" (review article), *Holocaust and Genocide Studies*, 20: 1 (2006), pp. 103–111. It should be stressed that some Israeli scholars have persistently pressed the Israeli government to recognize the genocide. Israel Charny and Yehuda Bauer deserve special mention in this respect.

87 The trend began early on. Colby Chester, a retired US admiral, wrote in 1922 in the *New York Times Current History*: "The Armenians were moved from the inhospitable regions where they were not welcome and could not actually prosper but to the most delightful and fertile parts of Syria . . . where the climate is as benign as in Florida and California whither New York millionaires journey each year for health and recreation. . . . And all this was done at great expense of money and effort." Quoted in Balakian, *The Burning Tigris*, p. 376.

88 Peter Balakian, personal communication, September 11, 2005.

89 "French Parliament Recognises 1915 Armenian Genocide," Reuters dispatch, May 29, 1998. However, "the wording of the resolution was deliberately designed to remove any suggestion of the responsibility of the modern Turkish state for the genocide; indeed no perpetrator agency of any sort was recalled in the brief statement of recognition." Bloxham, *The Great Game of Genocide*, p. 224.

90 "Turkey Denounces Armenian Genocide Vote in Commons," CBC News, April 22, 2004 .

91 See Pierre Tristam, "Obama, Turkey and the Armenian Genocide," Pierre's Middle East Issues Blog, March 18, 2009; "Barack Obama Sidesteps Armenian Genocide Row on Trip to Turkey," *The Times*, April 6, 2009, http://www.timesonline.co.uk/tol/news/ world/europe/article6045165.ece.

92 "IAGS: Armenian Genocide Recognition Must Be Starting Point of Historical Commission, Not One of Its Possible Conclusions," PanArmenian.net, October 14, 2009, http://www.panarmenian.net/news/eng/?nid=37827.

93 Gwynne Dyer, "Ending the Debate on an Armenian Genocide," Straight.com, October 15, 2009, http://www.straight.com/article-264662/gwynne-dyer-ending-debate-armenian-genocide.

94 Alison Flood, "Pamuk 'Insult to Turkishness' Claims Return to Court," *The Guardian*, May 15, 2009, http://www.guardian.co.uk/books/2009/may/15/pamut-insult-turkishness-court (*n.b.* "pamut" as given). "Pamuk said in [a] February 2005 interview that '30,000 Kurds and a million Armenians were killed in these [Turkish] lands and nobody but me dares to talk about it.' He was charged and tried for 'public denigration of Turkish identity' under Article 301 of the penal code later that year, but the case was subsequently dropped in the wake of international outrage. However, . . . six people – including the nationalist lawyer Kemal Kerincsiz, who has filed cases in the past against Pamuk and the murdered journalist Hrant Dink, and who is currently detained in the Ergenekon trial – have been given leave to demand 36,000 lira (£15,000) in compensation from the celebrated author . . . . Their case, which claims personal damages arising from the 'insult' to Turkishness, has been rejected twice previously, but . . . the case will now be reassessed." In October 2009, the Turkish Supreme Court of Appeals upheld the ruling, and the case for damages against Pamuk proceeded. No further updates were available at the time of writing (March 2010) (thanks to Jill Mitchell for research assistance with this case).

95 Hratch Tchilingirian, "Hrant Dink and Armenians in Turkey," OpenDemocracy.net, February 23, 2007, http://www.opendemocracy.net/democracy-turkey/dink_armenian_4378.jsp.

96 Robert Tait, "Writers Risk Backlash with Apology for Armenian Genocide," *The Guardian*, December 8, 2008.

97 Tezgul quoted in Balakian, *The Burning Tigris*, p. 391.

98 Thea Halo, "The Exclusivity of Suffering: When Tribal Concerns Take Precedence over Historical Accuracy," unpublished research paper, 2004.

99 A facsimile of the resolution as passed is available at http://www.greek-genocide.org/iags_resolution.html.

BOX 4A IRAQ: LIBERATION AND GENOCIDE

Iraq is at the heart of one of the world's oldest civilizations, but the modern state was cobbled together in 1922 by British mandatory authorities, following the Ottoman empire's collapse. In the 1970s, one of the twentieth century's worst tyrants, Saddam Hussein, gradually seized power as the head of the secular Ba'th Party, and ruled with an iron fist until his overthrow in 2003. The first edition of this book included a case study of one of Saddam's worst atrocities – the 1987–88 "Anfal" campaign against Iraqi Kurds in the country's north. At least 50–100,000 Kurds, perhaps as many as 180,000, were exterminated by bombings, mass shootings, and poison gas attacks.[1] Just as Ottoman Armenians had been denounced as vassals of Russian imperialism, Saddam's Sunni Muslim-dominated regime depicted the Kurds as subversives allied with Iran. This case study has been moved to the book's website (see http://www.genocidetext.net/anfal.pdf), and provides another example of the kind of state-directed, insecurity-fuelled eruptions witnessed in the Ottomans' destruction of Christian

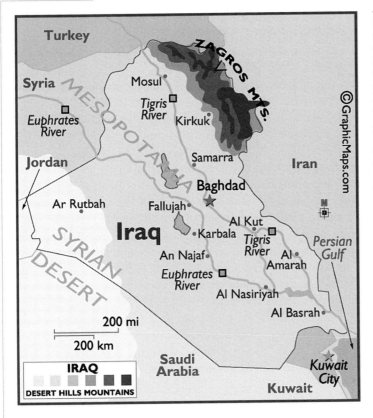

Map 4A.1   Iraq. While most of the violence since 2003 has been concentrated in the Tigris and Euphrates river valleys, the mountainous zone in the northeast witnessed Saddam Hussein's 1987–88 Anfal Campaign against Iraqi Kurds. As of 2010, conflict among Kurds, Arabs, and Turkmen was simmering in the oil-rich region around the city of Kirkuk.

Source: Map provided by WorldAtlas.com.

minorities, the holocaust of Guatemala's Mayans (Box 3a), and too many other historical cases to cite.

Saddam's campaign against the Kurds was renewed at the time of the 1991 Gulf War, and accompanied by mass atrocities against Shia Muslims (notably after the war concluded with Saddam still in power). To his murderous account must be added the hundreds of thousands of Iraqis, and even more Iranians – mostly youthful conscripts – killed by Iraq's invasion of a weakened post-revolutionary Iran, and the ensuing carnage of the First Gulf War (1980–88, with well over one million killed on both sides).

Saddam's regime fell before invading US and British forces in March 2003. He fled into hiding, but was captured in 2004; given something of a show-trial by the new Shia-dominated government; found guilty of genocide for the 1982 killing of 148 Shia at Dujail; and hanged on December 30, 2006.[2] Mystifying though it seems, however, what has transpired in Iraq since 2003 *has probably exacted a greater civilian toll than Saddam's depredations over the entire period of his rule.* Most of the casualties occurred in a paroxysm of intercommunal Shia–Sunni killing between 2005 and 2007. Among the other victims were Iraqi Christians, targeted as such, including descendants of the same Assyrian/Chaldean communities that suffered so greatly at Ottoman hands.

How many Iraqis were murdered and otherwise died violently in the post-2003 period remains a subject of intense and sometimes vituperative dispute. But a civilian toll in the many hundreds of thousands seems in keeping with the most systematic and consistent data. Indeed, according to those data, by 2007 when the most devastating wave of killing had subsided (at least temporarily), *over a million* Iraqis had died violently. As Joshua Holland noted at the time, it may well be that "the human toll exceeds the 800,000 to 900,000 believed killed in the Rwandan genocide in 1994, and is approaching the number (1.7 million) who died in Cambodia's infamous 'Killing Fields' during the Khmer Rouge era of the 1970s" (see Chapters 7 and 9).[3]

How did this happen? How did a supposed attempt to emancipate Iraqis from a dictator's rule descend into a new bloodbath? In substantial part, as already hinted, the answer lies in the bitter animosities built up between Sunni and Shia over the years of Saddam's rule – in particular, the marginalization of Shia, the demographic majority in Iraq, by minority Sunnis (notably Saddam's tribal clique, centered on the city of Tikrit). Greatly facilitating a descent into genocide, however, was the infamous absence of planning and preparation for occupation on the part of the US government under President George W. Bush. Within hours of the arrival of foreign forces in Baghdad, the Iraqi capital, the city had descended into chaos, with widespread looting and vigilantism. Moving to exploit the vacuum were Sunni militants, accompanied by terrorists of al-Qaeda, who launched increasingly devastating attacks on the US and British occupiers, United Nations personnel (including the assassination by truck-bomb of the UN special representative to Iraq, Sergio Vieira de Mello, in 2003), and mostly Shia civilians.

But Shia, too, had flooded into the power vacuum, exploiting their demographic weight to triumph in the first multiparty elections, in January 2005. With strong support from an unexpected pairing of US occupiers and the Shias' coreligionists in neighboring Iran, they established a stranglehold over key government ministries – in particular the Interior Ministry and its attached security forces.

As attacks were launched by Saddam loyalists and other terrorist elements within the disaffected Sunni community, the Shia-dominated government responded by organizing a network of death squads, suspiciously similar to the US-sponsored variety in Central America and elsewhere during the 1970s and 1980s.[4] The death squads were composed mostly of police officers (often in uniform), Interior Ministry paramilitaries, and forces led by the Shia "Mahdi army" of hardline cleric Moqtada al-Sadr. In 2005, they were unleashed, and by November of that year *The Los Angeles Times* was reporting "hundreds of bodies . . . discovered in rivers, garbage dumps, sewage treatment facilities and alongside roads and in desert ravines."[5] The UK *Independent* wrote that "bodies appear every week of men, and sometimes women, executed with their hands tied behind their backs. Some have been grotesquely mutilated with knives and electric drills before their deaths."[6]

The slaughter set the tone for the reciprocal genocidal carnage that engulfed Iraq in 2006–07. (A reason for the hesitancy of Western commentators to label what resulted as "genocide," apart from the usual timidity when Western regimes bear significant responsibility, was the fact that so much violence was tit-for-tat. But as noted in Chapter 1, neither the UN Genocide Convention definition of genocide, nor my preferred one, requires that one side exercise a monopoly or near-monopoly of violence.)

A turning point was the February 2006 bombing of a Shia shrine in the city of Samarra, apparently by Sunni terrorists. "In the three days after the bombing," wrote *The Independent*'s Patrick Cockburn, "some 1,300 people, mostly Sunni, were picked up on the street or dragged from their cars and murdered. . . . The scale of the violence is such that most of it is unreported."[7] *The Washington Post* described the "staring faces of the dead: men shot in the mouth, men shot in the head, men covered with blood, men with bindings twisted around their necks."[8] In May, Dahr Jamail reported the testimony of a doctor in Baghdad's main morgue:

> Yesterday we received 36 bodies from the police pickups. All of them are unknown, without IDs, and we don't have refrigerators to put them in since all of ours are completely full already. So we had to keep them on the ground. 12 of them were handcuffed, most of them received between 2 and 10 bullets, some many more than 10. . . . Most of them are between 20 to 30 years . . . This is the number that was brought directly to us in one day, plus there are the dead who are sent to the hospitals. . . . Since the shrine explosion [in Samarra], deaths have almost doubled. Daily, we receive between 70 to 80 bodies . . . within these 40 minutes that I've talked with you, we received 9 bodies. Nearly every morning the count will be doubled twice this number, for the police find them at night. Most are either found in the streets or killed without sending them to hospitals. Four days ago we received 24 bodies in just 2 hours.[9]

In October 2006, Peter Beaumont of the UK *Guardian* reported that "there are so many bodies that their disposal has become a problem of waste management."[10] No refuge was safe: by December, *The Sunday Times* was noting "mounting evidence that Shi'ite death squads are being encouraged to roam hospitals in search of fresh Sunni victims," including Sunni doctors found in the wards.[11] Sunni revenge attacks also targeted unknown but substantial numbers of Shia civilians.

On both sides, the overwhelming majority of those murdered were male, making Iraq unquestionably the worst political-military gendercide of the early twenty-first century.[12] "Every day, there are crowds of women outside weeping, yelling and flailing in grief," a Baghdad morgue worker told the Associated Press. "They're all looking for their dead sons and I don't know how the computer or we will bear up." The same dispatch noted that "the fear of leaving the bereaved without a corpse to bury is so strong that some Iraqi men now tattoo their names, phone numbers and other identifying information on their upper thighs, despite Islam's strict disapproval against such practices."[13]

Apart from inflicting revenge, the terror was designed to force whole populations to flee neighborhoods and communities where they had long coexisted peacefully with members of other ethnic groups. Baghdad, in particular, was transformed from a mostly bi-ethnic or multi-ethnic patchwork to demarcated zones where members of "enemy" groups risked immediate death if they entered. As in Rwanda in 1994, checkpoints – mostly Shia-staffed – were set up across the city to check motorists' and pedestrians' identity cards. Those with "enemy" names were pulled aside and either disappeared or summarily executed. It was this practice above all that prompted Samantha Power, author of "A Problem from Hell": America and the Age of Genocide (see Figure 1.2, p. 11), to label the killings as genocidal.[14]

By the end of 2007, the pattern of genocidal "cleansing" among Shias and Sunnis had spent itself. Once mixed neighborhoods were now mini-ethnocracies.[15] This seems to have been the major cause of the generally declining death rate from 2007 through to 2009. But it also appeared to spur a new round of murders and expulsions – this time of members of Iraq's ancient Christian communities.[16] In his 2010 volume *Genocide in the Middle East*, Hannibal Travis reported that

> hundreds of Christians have been targeted and killed based on such signifiers of "Christian" identity as doing the janitorial or translation work for multi-national forces or civilian contractors, operating convenience stores that sell alcohol, being women appearing in public with their faces or legs uncovered, for wearing fashionable Western haircuts or clothes, or listening to or selling Western music. Assyrian and other Christian children have been beheaded and in one case literally crucified. The leader of the Chaldean church in Turkey has stated that the current situation is worse than ever, with news reaching Istanbul every day of five or six more Chaldeans having been killed in Iraq. Women have suffered disfiguring acid attacks and frequent kidnapping in a climate of fundamentalist resurgence and a breakdown of government institutions. Christian women and girls became "virtual prisoners in their homes," with religious services at a halt and 30 Christian women kidnapped in a month.

"Under international law," Travis concluded, "Christians in Iraq could be suffering from an attempt or conspiracy to commit genocide."[17] Tens of thousands of them fled, joining a flow of exiled and internally-displaced Iraqis that had by then swelled to some *four million people*. This was probably the largest forced population movement of the new century (though Congo must also be considered – see Box 9a), and was the largest in the Middle East since the expulsion of hundreds of thousands of Palestinians from the nascent state of Israel in 1947–48.[18] Governments and aid agencies of neighboring countries, notably Jordan and Syria, were overwhelmed.[19] The refugees began to trickle back in 2008 – partly because violence seemed to be on the wane, and partly because their resources were running out. But though new displacements slowed, they did not entirely stop. At the outset of 2010 the UN High Commissioner for Refugees was still estimating over two million Iraqis internally displaced, living as refugees, or just returned.[20]

How many had died violently since 2003, and at whose hands? Estimates and interpretations have varied wildly. The lowest civilian death toll announced is the 95–103,000 civilian victims tabulated by the UK organization Iraq Body Count (www.iraqbodycount.org) as of January 2010. The organization acknowledges that its tally does not include the "many deaths that go unreported."[21] A survey by the Iraqi Ministry of Health, published in the *New England Journal of Medicine*, "found 151,000 deaths by violence as of June 2006."[22] The most systematic data, however, were those compiled in 2004 and 2006 by researchers from Baltimore's Johns Hopkins Bloomberg School of Public Health, and in 2008 by Opinion Research Business (ORB), a leading UK polling organization. Both employed sampling methodologies of the kind used to produce, for example, the similarly shocking but widely accepted figure of 5.7 million "excess deaths" in the Congolese conflict (Box 9a).[23] The Johns Hopkins researchers, in their 2004 report, offered the "hugely controversial" figure of 100,000 Iraqis killed as a result of the invasion – many if not most of whom probably died at the hands of US and British invaders.[24] But this scarcely compared with the furore surrounding the researchers' 2006 findings, published in the prestigious British medical journal *The Lancet*. They reported a likely *655,000 excess deaths*, overwhelmingly violent ones, to that point – some 500 a day, killing 2.5 percent of the entire Iraqi population. "In Baghdad, almost half of those interviewed reported at least one violent death in their household."[25] Fully 91 percent of those killed were males, the vast majority between the ages of 15 and 44.[26] How many could reasonably be classed as civilians, killed by both Allied forces and fellow Iraqis, will never be known. This author would be surprised if it were not a substantial majority, though those less willing to grant full civilian status to "battle-age" males might disagree (see Chapters 13 and 16).

The US and British governments predictably attacked the findings. So too did some scientists, though arguably without full knowledge of the survey methodology.[27] After a Freedom of Information request was filed in Britain, it was learned that Sir Roy Anderson, the Defence Ministry's chief scientific adviser, had described the *Lancet* study as "robust" and "employ[ing] methods that are regarded as close to 'best practice.'" A Department for International Development statistician in Great Britain also considered the methodology "tried and tested"; in fact, he suggested, it "should lead to an *underestimation* of the deaths in the war and early post-invasion period."[28]

The Johns Hopkins data were bolstered in 2008, when Opinion Research

Business (ORB) reported the results of its "face-to-face interviews" with 2,144 Iraqis in 15 out of the country's 18 provinces. According to ORB, *"approximately 1.03 million people had died as a result of the war"*; "20 percent of people [interviewed] had had at least one death in their household as a result of the conflict, rather than natural causes." Moreover, the three provinces not surveyed "included two of Iraq's more volatile regions – Kerbala and Anbar."[29] *The Los Angeles Times* reported that "48% of the victims were shot to death and 20% died as a result of car bombs, with other explosions and military bombardments blamed for most of the other fatalities."[30]

By early 2010, under the new Barack Obama administration, US forces were exiting Iraq, with many headed to the battleground of Afghanistan. As they did, violence was again on the increase, including devastating car-bombings by resurgent Sunni militias. In a worrying replay of the events of 2005–07, attacks were recorded "by men wearing Iraqi Army uniforms," "reviv[ing] the specter of the death squads" and "stirring concern at the highest levels of the Iraqi and American commands."[31] Looming as a fresh flashpoint was the long-simmering region around the city of Kirkuk, contested by Kurds, Turkmen, and Arabs. It seemed quite likely, therefore, that the decline in violence at decade's end marked an interregnum rather than an endpoint.

FURTHER STUDY

Gilbert Burnham, Riyadh Lafta, Shannon Doocy, and Les Roberts, "Mortality after the 2003 Invasion of Iraq: A Cross-sectional Cluster Sample Survey." *The Lancet*, October 11, 2006, http://brusselstribunal.org/pdf/lancet111 006.pdf.

The Human Cost of the War in Iraq: A Mortality Study, 2002–2006. Bloomberg School of Public Health, 2006, http://web.mit.edu/CIS/pdf/Human_Cost_ of_War.pdf.

NOTES

1 The most detailed account in English of the Anfal genocide is Human Rights Watch-Middle East, *Iraq's Crime of Genocide: The Anfal Campaign Against the Kurds* (New Haven, CT: Human Rights Watch/Yale University Press, 1995). On the current forensic investigations into the Anfal genocide, see Heather Pringle, "Witness to Genocide," *Archaeology*, 62: 1 (January–February 2009), http://www. archaeology.org/0901/etc/iraq. html; and Asso Ahmed, "Kurds in Search of Their Dead Meet Remains," *The Los Angeles Times*, November 30, 2008. See also Figure 11.3, p. 438.

2 See Michael J. Kelly, "The Anfal Trial against Saddam Hussein," *Journal of Genocide Research*, 9: 2 (2007), pp. 235–42. The title of Kelly's article is deliberately ironic: the Anfal-related charges against Saddam were dropped after his execution (rather than his execution being postponed until he could face them, or the trial

continuing posthumously). However, his cousin and henchman, Ali Hassan al-Majid ("Chemical Ali"), responsible for the gas attacks on Halabja and other Kurdish targets in 1988, was tried and, in June 2007, found guilty of genocide (as well as war crimes and crimes against humanity). He received three further death sentences for atrocities under Saddam, before finally being hanged in January 2010.

3 Joshua Holland, "Iraq Death Toll Rivals Rwanda Genocide, Cambodian Killing Fields," AlterNet.org, September 17, 2007, http://www.alternet.org/waroniraq/62728.

4 How significant a role the US played in organizing and training these death squads, which after all were ostensibly aimed at elements targeting US forces, remains unclear. For some limited insights, see Christopher Dickey, "Death-Squad Democracy," *Newsweek*, January 11, 2005, http://www.newsweek.com/id/47999; and Elizabeth DiNovella, "Salvador Option Surfaces Again," *The Progressive*, March 16, 2007, http://www.progressive.org/ blogressive/031507/amaya. Senior US officials at least maintained a respectful silence concerning the death squads' manifest links to the Iraqi government.

5 Solomon Moore, "Killings Linked to Shiite Squads in Iraqi Police Force," *The Los Angeles Times*, November 29, 2005. "The Death Squads," an up-close and stomach-churning documentary produced by Britain's Channel 4, can be searched on Google Videos (http://videos.google.com).

6 Kim Sengupta, "Raid on Torture Dungeon Exposes Iraq's Secret War," *The Independent*, November 16, 2005. See also Kim Sengupta, "The Dirty War: Torture and Mutilation Used on Iraqi 'Insurgents,'" *The Independent*, November 20, 2005; Dexter Filkins, "Sunnis Accuse Iraqi Military of Kidnappings and Slayings," *The New York Times*, November 29, 2005; Solomon Moore, "Killings Linked to Shiite Squads in Iraqi Police Force," *The Los Angeles Times*, November 29, 2005.

7 Patrick Cockburn, "Death Squads on the Prowl in a Nation Paralysed by Fear," *The Independent*, March 20, 2006, http://www.independent.co.uk/news/world/middle-east/death-squads-on-the-prowl-in-a-nation-paralysed-by-fear-470650.html.

8 Ellen Knickmeyer and Bassam Sebti, "Iraq's Deadly Surge Claims 1,300," *The Washington Post* (on MSNBC.com), February 27, 2006, http://www.msnbc.msn.com/ id/11597322.

9 Dahr Jamail, "'Reason for Their Death Is Known,'" Truthout.org, May 3, 2006, http:// www.truthout.org/article/dahr-jamail-reason-their-death-is-known.

10 Peter Beaumont, "Aura of Fear and Death Stalks Iraq," *The Guardian*, October 12, 2006, http://www.guardian.co.uk/world/2006/oct/12/iraq.peterbeaumont.

11 Hala Jaber, "Death Squads Roam Baghdad's Hospitals," *The Sunday Times*, December 3, 2006, http://www.timesonline.co.uk/tol/news/world/article658326.ece. See also Christian Berthelsen, "Iraqis Turn to Tattoos as Indelible IDs," *The Los Angeles Times*, April 20, 2007.

12 Gendercidal killings of women for alleged transgressions of Islamic morality were also reported, particularly in the southern city of Basra at the hands of "Propagation of Virtue and Prevention of Vice" squads set up by the Shia authorities controlling the city. See Yifat Susskind, "Who Is Killing the Women of Basra?," CommonDreams.org, January 10, 2008, http://www.commondreams.org/archive/2008/01/10/6287. "City officials reported on December 31 [2007] that 133 women were killed and mutilated last year, their bodies dumped in trash bins with notes warning others against 'violating Islamic teachings . . .' But ambulance drivers who are hired to troll the city streets in the early mornings to collect the bodies confirm what most residents believe: the actual numbers are much higher. The killers' leaflets are not very original. They usually accuse the women of being

prostitutes or adulterers. But . . . most of the women who have been murdered 'are PhD holders, professionals, activists, and office workers.' Their crime is not 'promiscuity,' but rather opposition to the transformation of Iraq into an Islamist state. That bloody transition has been the main political trend under US occupation." Thanks to Peter Prontzos for this source.

13 "Baghdad's Morgues Working Overtime," Associated Press dispatch on MSNBC.com, November 12, 2006, http://www.msnbc.msn.com/id/15690725. See also Hala Jabar, "The Accursed: Widows of Iraq's Torn-Apart Society," *The Sunday Times*, April 29, 2007, http://www.timesonline.co.uk/tol/news/world/iraq/article1719913.ece.

14 Power's comments were made at a talk on "Iraq's Collateral Damage" that I attended at Yale University on November 14, 2006. She was quoted around the same time as stating that "with Shi'ite and Sunni sub-groups already identifying and killing victims solely on the basis of their religious identity, 'genocidal intent' is already present in Iraq" (*Time*, November 29, 2006, cited in Travis, *Genocide in the Middle East*, p. 534).

15 "The streets [of Baghdad] are calmer now. The fighting between Shiites and Sunnis has largely ceased. But this is not a sign of normalcy in the Iraqi capital. It's fear that keeps the peace. Only an estimated 16 percent of the mainly Sunni families forced by Shiite militiamen and death squads to flee their homes have dared to return. It takes two sides to have a fight, and there's really only one side left in Baghdad after violence and fear turned parts of neighborhoods into ghost towns." Hamza Hendawi, "It's Fear That Keeps Baghdad's Peace," Associated Press dispatch on Yahoo! News, March 25, 2009.

16 See Preti Taneja, "Assimilation, Exodus, Eradication: Iraq's Minority Communities since 2003" (London: Minority Rights Group International, 2007), http://www.christians ofiraq.com/Full_Report.pdf.

17 Travis, *Genocide in the Middle East*, p. 537. In October 2008, Germany's *Der Spiegel* described the persecution of the Christian population of Mosul in the north of the country, apparently at the hands of Sunni militants: "Churches have been set on fire, and priests, doctors, engineers and businesspeople have been murdered. In March [2008], aides found the body of Archbishop Paulos Faraj Rahho on the outskirts of the city. A new series of killings that began in late September has already claimed 18 lives. To stop the Christians who are fleeing Mosul, their persecutors set up fake checkpoints along the roads leading out of the city. They are often robbed, beaten and even killed. In the Sadik neighborhood, masked men recently stopped a man with his child. When they saw a Christian name on his identification card, they shot the man on the spot. When the boy said the man they had just killed was his father, they shot him as well. Church members who have not yet fled are finding flyers in their apartments with a 'Warning to all Christians.' 'If you do not leave,' the flyers read, 'you will be slaughtered in three days.' These are not empty threats." Peter Wensierski and Bernhard Zand, "Christians on the Run in Iraq," *Der Spiegel Online*, October 30, 2008, http://www.spiegel.de/international/world/0,1518,587345,00.html. See also Deborah Haynes, "'We Are Killed Because We Are Christians,'" *The Times*, October 27, 2008, http://www.timesonline.co.uk/tol/news/ world/iraq/article5021028.ece; "Pope Condemns Christian Killings in Iraq, India," Associated Press dispatch on CNN.com, October 26, 2008.

18 Sudarsan Raghavan, "War in Iraq Propelling a Massive Migration," *The Washington Post*, February 4, 2007; Patrick Cockburn, "Iraqis Abandon Their Homes in Middle East's New Refugee Exodus," *The Independent*, January 29, 2007, http://www.independent.co. uk/news/world/middle-east/iraqis-abandon-their-homes-in-middle-easts-new-refugee-exodus-434561.html.

19 "UN Warns of Iraq Refugee Disaster," *BBC Online*, February 7, 2007, http://news. bbc. co.uk/2/hi/middle_east/6339835.stm.

20 "2010 UNHCR Country Operations Profile – Iraq," http://www.unhcr.org/cgi-bin/ texis/vtx/page?page=49e486426.

21 Haroon Siddiqui, "How Many Civilians Have Died?," *The Star* (Toronto), September 20, 2007.

22 John Tirman, "Right-Wingers Can't Cover Up Iraq's Death Toll Catastrophe," AlterNet.org, January 21, 2008, http://www.alternet.org/waroniraq/74263.

23 Jon Wiener, "Iraq: Counting the Dead," *The Nation*, January 17, 2007, http://www. thenation.com/blogs/notion/158153.

24 Sarah Boseley, "'655,000 Iraqis Killed Since Invasion,'" *The Guardian*, October 11, 2006, http://www.guardian.co.uk/world/2006/oct/11/iraq.iraq.

25 Holland, "Iraq Death Toll."

26 Boseley, "655,000 Iraqis Killed."

27 Sarah Boseley, "UK Scientists Attack Lancet Study over Death Toll," *The Guardian*, October 24, 2006, http://www.guardian.co.uk/Iraq/Story/0,,1930002, 00.html. "Sean Gourley and Professor Neil Johnson of the physics department at Oxford University and Professor Michael Spagat of the Economics Department of Royal Holloway, University of London, claimed the methodology of the study was fundamentally flawed by what they term 'main street bias' [i.e., focusing their sample on households situated along main streets, which were more likely to be targeted in bombings and other attacks]. But the lead author of the study [Gilbert Burnham] . . . said the researchers penetrated much further into residential areas than was clear from the *Lancet* paper. The notion 'that we avoided back alleys was totally untrue.' He added that 28% of households were in rural areas – which matches the population spread." The controversy has at least served as a fine primer on these increasingly prominent survey techniques and methodologies.

28 Anderson quoted in Owen Bennett Jones, "Lancet Was Right – Shock," *New Statesman*, April 2, 2007, http://www.newstatesman.com/society/2007/04/iraq-death-toll-lancet-survey. Emphasis added.

29 "Iraq Conflict Has Killed a Million Iraqis: Survey," Reuters dispatch, January 30, 2008. Emphasis added. "The margin of error in the survey, conducted in August and September 2007, was 1.7 percent, giving a range of deaths of 946,258 to 1.12 million."

30 Tina Susman, "Poll: Civilian Death Toll in Iraq May Top 1 Million," *The Los Angeles Times*, September 14, 2007. See also John Tirman, "Iraq's Shocking Human Toll," *The Nation* on AlterNet.org, February 2, 2009, http://www.alternet. org/story/123818.

31 Marc Santora, "In Iraq, 2 Attacks Raise Fears of Sectarianism," *The New York Times*, November 25, 2009, http://www.nytimes.com/2009/11/26/world/middle east/26iraq. html. It was of course questionable whether those "at the highest levels" in Iraq were truly "concerned," or rather active participants in the killing.

CHAPTER 5

Stalin and Mao

> Enemies are not people. We're allowed to do what we like with them. People indeed!
>
> Soviet secret police interrogator to Eugenia Ginzburg,
> in *Journey into the Whirlwind*

"No other state in history," wrote genocide scholar Richard Rubenstein, "has ever initiated policies designed to eliminate so many of its own citizens as has the Soviet Union."[1] His contention can be challenged. In absolute numbers, the death toll inflicted on the Chinese people by Mao Zedong's communists was significantly greater than the Soviet one. And per capita, Cambodia's Khmer Rouge government (see Chapter 7) devised policies that destroyed fully one-quarter of the country's population in less than four years. A striking feature of these cases is the links among them. Mao's communists were in many ways Stalin's protégés; the Sino-Soviet split of the late 1950s, which irretrievably sundered the world communist movement, reflected Mao's conviction that the Soviets had betrayed Stalin's great legacy. The Khmer Rouge, in turn, took its inspiration from both Stalinism and Maoism, but particularly from the latter's ultra-collectivism and utopianism.

The version of communism instituted in these three regimes was in central respects a perversion of the original doctrine, developed by Karl Marx and others in the nineteenth century. "Marxism" defines society and historical evolution in terms of social classes, inevitably unequal and opposed, and therefore destined for "class struggle." It posits that when the proletariat – the urban working classes created by modern capitalism – finally takes control of the commanding heights of the economy and political structure, the state will wither away, and a world without hierarchy will come into being, in which humans work according to their ability, and receive according to their need. This endpoint is distant and hazy in Marxist doctrine, however. And the twentieth-century movements that proclaimed themselves "Marxist" generally proved consummate statists and hierarchs. In Stalin's Soviet Union, communist China, and Cambodia under the Khmer Rouge, all those outside the party faithful (and eventually many of the faithful too) were labeled "enemies," denounced, humiliated, and destroyed. Moreover, notions of incremental advance toward communism were replaced by a hubristic conviction that paradise was just around the corner – if only the population could be induced to haul the state and economy toward it. Given that all three countries were predominantly agricultural, massive "collectivization" of the rural population was used to yoke them to their revolutionary task, and to support the headlong drive for urbanization and industrialization that figured so prominently in the Soviet and Chinese models.

The result, in all three cases, was ideological extremism and human destruction on a scale that beggars belief. Much of that destruction took the form of outright murder. But most victims were killed *indirectly*, through incarceration and forced labor, or manipulated famines. The famines were not planned as such, but they were the predictable result of regime policies, exacerbated by leaders' conscious refusal to intervene and ameliorate them. In that sense, genocidal intent may be discerned in both the direct and indirect forms of killing. And while in all three cases the majority of victims were drawn from the same ethnonational group as the perpetrators, a more "orthodox" genocidal targeting of ethnic minorities also featured. This chapter explores the Stalinist and Maoist cases with, as noted, the Khmer Rouge genocide examined separately in Chapter 7.

THE SOVIET UNION AND STALINISM

1917: The Bolsheviks seize power

The Bolshevik Revolution took place after centuries of dictatorship and underdevelopment in Russia, as well as the most destructive war to that point in European history (see Chapter 2). By 1917, Russian armies facing German and Austro-Hungarian forces had been pushed to the brink of collapse, and the Russian population confronted famine. Bread riots broke out in the capital, Petrograd (St. Petersburg). In the face of growing popular and elite opposition, Tsar Nicholas II abdicated, turning over power to a liberal-dominated provisional government under Alexander Kerensky. Fatefully, Kerensky's regime chose to continue the war. Russian forces crumbled in a poorly conceived military offensive. Hundreds of thousands of soldiers deserted. Across Russia's fertile regions, spontaneous seizures of land added to the chaos.

Poised to exploit the turmoil was Lenin's Bolshevik party. Lenin was a Russian of noble birth who had discovered Marxist socialism and agitated from exile for the overthrow of the tsarist regime. Spirited back to Russia on a sealed train by the German government, which saw Lenin (presciently) as a means of removing Russia from the war, Lenin and the Bolsheviks found themselves in a minority position *vis-à-vis* the leading socialist faction, the Mensheviks. Lenin improved Bolshevik fortunes by promising "Bread, Peace, Land." But the party was still a marginal force, almost non-existent outside the major cities, when Lenin launched a coup against the weak Kerensky regime.

After storming Petrograd's Winter Palace and seizing key infrastructure, the Bolsheviks found themselves in power – but with many predicting that their regime would last only weeks or months. To bolster their position and popular base, they quickly sued for peace with Germany and, in the Treaty of Brest-Litovsk (March 1918), gave up some of Russia's most fertile, resource-rich territories.

"There can be no revolution without counterrevolution," wrote historian Arno Mayer.[2] A potent counterrevolution now confronted the new "Soviet Union" (the "soviets" were workers' councils taken over by the Bolsheviks as a means of controlling Russia's working classes). "Whites" – anti-Bolshevist Russians – sought to overthrow the Bolshevik "Reds." Russia's former allies, notably Britain and the United States, were furious at Lenin's retreat from the First World War, and terrified at the prospect of socialist revolution spreading across Europe. With funding, arms, and tens of thousands of troops on the ground, they backed the Whites in a three-year struggle with the Bolshevik regime.

This civil war, one of the most destructive of the twentieth century, lasted until 1921 and claimed an estimated nine million lives on all sides. According to historian Alec Nove, "[its] influence . . . on the whole course of subsequent history, and on Stalinism, cannot possibly be overestimated. It was during the civil war that Stalin and men like Stalin emerged as leaders, while others became accustomed to harshness, cruelty, terror."[3] Red forces imposed "War Communism," an economic policy that repealed peasants' land seizures, forcibly stripped the countryside of grain to feed city dwellers, and suppressed private commerce. All who opposed these policies were "enemies of the people." "This is the hour of truth," Lenin wrote in mid-1918. "It is of supreme importance that we encourage and make use of the energy of mass terror directed against the counterrevolutionaries."[4] The Cheka, the first incarnation of the Soviet secret police (later the NKVD and finally the KGB), responded with gusto. Lenin and other Bolshevik leaders may have viewed mass terror as a short-term measure,[5] but its widespread use belies claims that it was Stalin's invention.

The civil war left the Reds victorious but the Soviet Union shattered. Famine had struck large areas of the country, and millions in rural areas were kept alive only through foreign, especially US, generosity.[6] Acknowledging reality – a capacity not yet extinguished among Bolsheviks – Lenin repealed the War Communism measures. He allowed peasants to return to the land, and instituted the so-called New Economic Policy (NEP). Under the NEP, market mechanisms were revived, and the economy was regenerated.

Weakened by an assassination attempt and a series of strokes, Lenin died in 1924, leaving the field open for an up-and-coming Bolshevik leader to launch his drive for absolute power.

Joseph Stalin was born Joseph Dzhugashvili in Gori, Georgia, in 1879. His Caucasian background, his abusive upbringing, and the years he spent in Russian Orthodox seminaries have all been linked to his personality and subsequent policies: "There has been too much cod-psychology about Stalin's childhood," cautioned Simon Sebag Montefiore in his Stalin biography, "but this much is certain: raised in a poor priest-ridden household, he was damaged by violence, insecurity and suspicion but inspired by the local traditions of religious dogmatism, blood-feuding and romantic brigandry."[7] In the pre-revolutionary period, the brigand led a series of bank robberies that brought him to the attention of high officials. It was at this time that Dzhugashvili adopted his party moniker, Stalin, meaning "Man of Steel." Captured by tsarist authorities, he endured two spells of exile in Siberia.

After the Bolsheviks seized power, Stalin was appointed General Secretary of the Communist Party in 1922. In itself, the post was an administrative one. But Stalin used it to build a power base and establish control over the party bureaucracy, while also earning a reputation as "a dynamic leader who had a hand in nearly all the principal discussions on politics, military strategy, economics, security and international relations."[8] When Lenin died in 1924, a struggle for supremacy pitted Stalin against his nemesis, Leon Trotsky, and a host of lesser figures. Stalin's victory was slow and hard-won, but by 1927 he and his allies had succeeded in expelling Trotsky from the party and, in 1929, from the country.[9]

By 1928, Stalin was entrenched as supreme Soviet leader. With world revolution a distant prospect, Stalin chose the course of "socialism in one country," which for him meant "a new programme of extremely – almost hysterically – rapid industrialization."[10] In this decision lay the seeds of two principal genocidal policies: the massive expansion of the Gulag, or prison, system, and the campaign against the peasantry, whose grain was needed to feed cities swelled by Stalin's crash industrialization program.

The two strategies intersected. By waging class warfare in the countryside, Stalin could expropriate the holdings of the wealthier (or less poor) peasants; conscript millions of them into forced labor on industrial projects; and also use the new bounty of prisoners to extract natural resources (especially gold and timber) that could be sold abroad for the hard currency needed to purchase industrial machinery and pay foreign advisors.

Collectivization and famine

Whatever their rhetorical claims to represent working people, the Soviet attitude toward peasants was one of thinly disguised contempt. "On the one hand they were the People incarnate, the soul of the country, suffering, patient, the hope of the future," wrote Robert Conquest, a leading historian of the Stalinist era. "On the other, they appeared as the 'dark people,' backward, mulish, deaf to argument, an oafish impediment to all progress."[11]

Of this group, it was the so-called "kulaks" who aroused the greatest Bolshevik hatred. The definition of "kulak" (the word means "fist," as in "tightfisted") was subject to terrifyingly random variations, and remained "abstract, unclear, and contested" throughout the life of the Stalinist regime.[12] In general, at least at the outset of the campaign, the kulaks were better-off peasants, perhaps only slightly better-off. Owning a cow or hiring a helper could be enough to get one labeled a kulak, with consequences that were often fatal, even in the earliest phase of Bolshevik rule. Lenin, for example, referred to kulaks as "avaricious, bloated, and bestial," spiders," "leeches," "vampires," and "the most brutal, callous, and savage exploiters."[13] "Merciless mass terror against the kulaks. . . . Death to them!" Lenin pronounced, before death took him as well.[14]

As was his habit, Stalin carried things to extremes. The definition of "kulak" grew ever more expansive: "As the state entered into what would be a protracted war with the peasantry," wrote historian Lynne Viola, "the kulak came to serve as a political metaphor and pejorative for the entire peasantry."[15] In January 1930, Stalin formally "approved the liquidation of kulaks as a class."[16] Bolshevik leader Mendel Khataevich then instructed Communist Party functionaries to "throw your bourgeois human-itarianism out the window" and "beat down the kulak agent wherever he raises his head. It's war – it's them or us. The last decayed remnant of capitalist farming must be wiped out at any cost."[17]

In a taste of the quota-fueled terror that would prevail later in the decade, Orlando Figes noted that "in some villages the peasants chose the 'kulaks' from their own number. They simply held a village meeting and decided who should go as a 'kulak' (isolated farmers, widows and old people were particularly vulnerable)."[18] "At least 10 million 'kulaks' were expelled from their homes and villages between 1929 and 1932." About 1.4 million were dispatched to the Gulag concentration-camp system (see next section) or attached forced-labor camps. The conditions under which they were transported frequently killed them before they arrived, including months spent "in primitive detention camps, where children and the elderly died like flies in the appalling conditions."[19] As for the "special settlements" themselves, they were generally established in remote and inhospitable northern regions – part of the regime's designs to open up the mineral- and timber-rich north, to which free laborers could not readily be lured. Virtually no preparations were made for their arrival, leading to mortality rates (15 percent in the Northern Territory of Siberia in 1930 alone)[20] that can be considered as genocide implemented through intentional negligence and wilful disregard for subsistence needs. Working conditions, especially in the timber camps, were themselves genocidal, as Viola wrote:

> The commandants and work bosses in charge of the special settlers viewed them as little more than a "muscle force" to be exploited mercilessly in order to fulfill the plan. In their minds, the kulak workforce was infinitely replenishable as a result of both the exile of entire families – [known as] labor reproductive units – and the continuing deportation of peasants through the first half of the 1930s. According to an official in the Northern Territory [of Siberia], "there was practically a directive that the sooner the special settlers die, the better."[21]

After the "kulaks" were destroyed or banished, the regime's agents scoured the newly collectivized countryside for grain to feed the cities. Often the tax imposed on peasants exceeded the amount that could be harvested. The result was widespread famine, not only in Ukraine, but in the Volga region, Kazakhstan, and other terri-tories afflicted by the twin evils of forced collectivization and grain seizures. Stalin and his associates cared little. In their minds, famine was the price of progress and national security; the Soviet Union would "develop," and buttress itself against a hostile world. Moreover, just as the British architects of nineteenth-century Irish and Indian famines

Figure 5.1 "Enemies of the Five Year Plan." The plan imposed collectivization on the Soviet countryside, with genocidal consequences. "This poster from 1929 attacks eight groups that were frequently scapegoated [in the USSR] (clockwise from top left): landlords, kulaks, journalists, capitalists, White Russians [supporters of the former tsarist regime], Mensheviks [factional opponents of the Bolsheviks], priests, and drunkards. ... The poem at the bottom of the poster was written by Demyan Bedny, one of Stalin's favorite poets. The poem harshly ridicules these members of the 'old order,' describing them as 'hounds that have not yet been caged.' The group is condemned for 'declaring war' on the Five-Year Plan because 'they understand that it will bring about their final destruction.'"

Source: Gareth Jones collection (www.garethjones.org); artwork by Viktor Deni; caption text from *Hoover Digest*, 1998: 3 (http://www.hoover.org/publications/digest/3532831.html).

had stockpiled and exported food throughout the crises (see Chapter 2), so did Stalin's Soviet Union. "While millions of peasants were dying of hunger," wrote Nicholas Werth, "the Soviet government was exporting 1,800,000 tons of cereals to honour its debts to Germany and to buy foreign machinery intended to make possible the accelerated industrialization plans. In that year of 1933, the state's strategic reserves, held in case of war, exceeded three million tons – a quantity more than sufficient to save millions of the starving populations."[22]

Then, as the crisis escalated, it appears that Stalin and his henchmen seized the opportunity to wreak havoc on Ukrainian nationalism, embedded as it was in peasant culture and society. Most scholars now reject Robert Conquest's initial assertion that Stalin *planned* the famine to this end.[23] But pre-planning is hardly necessary for a finding of genocide, and the results of intentional actions that aggravated the famine – the seizure of crops, seed grain, and livestock – were no less devastating than if they had been meticulously plotted in advance.[24] As collectivization spread, "a veritable crescendo of terror by hunger" descended on Ukraine and

Kazakhstan.[25] "A former activist" in Ukraine described the consequences, particularly for the most vulnerable:

> The most terrifying sights were the little children with skeleton limbs dangling from balloon-like abdomens. Starvation had wiped every trace of youth from their faces, turning them into tortured gargoyles; only in their eyes still lingered the reminder of childhood. Everywhere we found men and women lying prone, their faces and bellies bloated, their eyes utterly expressionless.[26]

The massive mortality was covered up by, among other measures, systematically expunging data from village records. In April 1934, for instance, secret instructions were issued to the Odessa region in Ukraine "to withdraw death registration books from village councils: for 1933 from all village councils without exception and for 1932 according to the list provided . . . To transfer the withdrawn village council registration books to the raion [district] executive committees for safekeeping as classified material."[27] For decades, it was possible to refer to the famine only with euphemisms like "food difficulties."

A credible estimate of excess deaths in the famine, across all regions of the USSR from 1930 to 1933, is 5.7 million[29] – approximately the number of European Jews killed by the Nazis, including those murdered indirectly by starvation and disease. Perhaps 3.9 million perished from unnatural causes in Ukraine between 1926 and 1937, mostly during what succeeding generations of Ukrainians have come to know as the *Holodomor*, or "hunger-extermination."[30] The overwhelmingly majority were ethnic Ukrainians, and for those who allow for notions of cultural genocide, the gutting of Ukrainian society's integrity and identity in the decades following the Holodomor could serve as a prime example. The lives of perhaps 1,450,000 Kazakhs were extinguished during the same period – almost unnoticed, then or since. Proportional to their population, this marks the Kazakhs as the national group that "suffered the most consequences of the 'revolution from above' in the rural sector."[31]

Figure 5.2 "Passers-by no longer pay attention to the corpses of starved peasants on a street" in Kharkov, Ukraine, during Stalin's "terror-famine" of 1932–33.[28]

Source: *Famine in the Soviet Ukraine 1932–1933: A Memorial Exhibition*, Widener Library, Harvard University/Wikimedia Commons.

The Gulag

As noted, hundreds of thousands of the "kulaks" deported during the collectivization drive were deposited in the Gulag prison system (the term "Gulag" was an acronym for administrative use). They joined other class enemies in a vast slave-labor network that had swelled to 2.4 million inmates by 1936[32] (see Map 5.1). Much of their labor was diverted to hare-brained schemes such as the White Sea Canal, which claimed tens of thousands of lives but fell into near-disuse after its completion.[33] In general, they were concentrated in climatically extreme environments, virtually devoid of infrastructure, which free workers shunned. Typical was the fate of "scores of thousands of prisoners, almost entirely peasants . . . thrown ashore at Magadan [in Siberia] in an ill-considered crash programme to exploit the newly discovered gold seams in the area." Conquest wrote that "whole camps perished to a man, even including guards and guard dogs"; "not more than one in fifty of the prisoners, if that, survived" their first year of incarceration in the remote region.[34]

It was these Siberian camps, devoted either to gold-mining or timber harvesting, that inflicted the greatest toll in the Gulag system. Such camps "can only be described as extermination centres," according to Leo Kuper.[35] The camp network that came to symbolize the horrors of the Gulag was centered on the Kolyma gold-fields, where "outside work for prisoners was compulsory until the temperature reached −50C and the death rate among miners in the goldfields was estimated at about 30 per cent per annum."[36] Apart from death by starvation, disease, accidents, and overwork, NKVD execution squads pronounced death sentences on a whim. In just one camp, Serpantinka, "more prisoners were executed . . . in the one year 1938, than the total executions throughout the Russian Empire for the whole of the last century of Tsarist rule."[37] The number of victims claimed by the Kolyma camps was between a quarter

Figure 5.3 Slave labor on Stalinist megaprojects like the White Sea Canal, pictured here in 1932, killed hundreds of thousands of "kulaks" and "enemies of the people."

Source: Government of the Russian Federation/Wikimedia Commons.

Map 5.1   A Russian map of the Gulag labor-camp system prepared by Memorial, a citizens' organization that works to document the crimes of the former USSR (see also Chapter 14, pp. 509–11). The map shows the reach of the Gulag "across the length and breadth of the Soviet Union, from the islands of the White Sea to the shores of the Black Sea, from the Arctic Circle to the plains of central Asia, from Murmansk to Vorkuta to Kazakhstan, from central Moscow to the Leningrad [St. Petersburg] suburbs." The major network in the northeast includes the Kolyma gold fields in Siberia, where some of the most murderous camps were located.

Source: Memorial/www.memo.ru.

of a million and over a million; in the today lightly populated region, "skeletons in frozen, shallow mass graves far outnumber the living."[38] Other names engraved on Russians' historical memory include Norilsk, "the centre of a group of camps more deadly than Kolyma"; and Vorkuta, with a regime characterized by "extravagant cold," "exhaustion," and a "starvation diet."[39]

Were the imprisoned multitudes in the Soviet Union *meant* to die? Can we speak of genocidal intent in that sense? The answer may vary according to location and historical-political context. The deaths in the northern camps of the Arctic Circle appear to have exhibited a high degree of genocidal intent, both specific and general (see pp. 37–39). The predominantly peasant and political prisoners were regularly depicted as subhuman or (in the case of "politicals") the most dangerous of enemies. At best, they were viewed as fodder for the mines and quarries and frozen forests. Since the most dangerous conditions imaginable were inflicted, tolerated, and perpetuated; since life expectancy in the camps was often measured in weeks and months; and since almost no measures were proposed or successfully introduced to keep prisoners alive, their fate seems no less genocidal than that of the American Indians worked and starved to death in the Spanish silver mines (Chapter 3).

However, unlike the Spanish mines or the Nazi death camps, conditions varied significantly across the vast Gulag system (apart from the worst of the war years, when privation reigned all across the USSR). Outside the Arctic camps, work regimes were less harsh and death rates far lower. Here, indeed – and even in Siberia after 1938–39 – high mortality rates could be viewed as undermining socialist production. While work regimes in the Nazi death camps were specifically designed to inflict mass murder, the intended function of the Soviet camps was primarily political and economic (though the Gulag never turned a profit). Camp commanders who impeded these functions by imposing an overly destructive regime could be sanctioned, even dismissed. Finally, at no point did the Soviets institute a "selection" process analogous to the Nazi ritual of dispatching older or weaker prisoners (along with children and pregnant women) for immediate slaughter. In fact, Soviet practice differed sharply.[40]

The Great Purge of 1937–38

> I am shot! – lightly clad. They judged me;
> The dull, featureless gun barrels carried out the sentence.
>
> Anatoly Potyekin

In 1934, the "kulaks" – at least, those who had survived incarceration in the Gulag – were joined by "terrorists," "saboteurs," and "provocateurs" arrested by the hundreds of thousands after the assassination of Leningrad Party chief Sergei Kirov. The Kirov murder "laid the foundation for a random terror without even the pretence of a rule of law."[41] Stalin used it as a launching pad for the great purge of 1937–38, in which 1,575,000 people were arrested, 1,345,000 sentenced, and at least 681,000 executed ("more than 85 percent of all the death sentences handed down during the entire Stalinist period").[42]

It is the purge of the Communist Party that many view as the zenith of Stalinist terror. However, as the Gulag's chronicler, Anne Applebaum, pointed out, this is misleading. Millions had already died – in famines, while undergoing deportation, in exile, and in camps – before Stalin turned against the "Old Bolsheviks" and their alleged legions of co-conspirators. The apex of the Gulag system actually came much later, after the Second World War. Moreover, as historians Orlando Figes and Lynne Viola have both noted, the largest category of victims in 1937–38 was not the communist elite, but "kulaks" in the "second dekulakization campaign" known as "mass operation 00447." Hundreds of thousands had fled the "special settlements," and Stalin regarded them with fear as a potential fifth column. The remaining "kulaks" were, Stalin declared in July 1937, "the primary ringleaders of all sorts of anti-Soviet and diversionary crimes both in the collective farms and the state farms and in transport and other branches of industry." By this time, according to Viola, "the appellation of kulak had lost any residual socioeconomic meaning . . . retaining only a political content that could be molded according to regime needs."[43] National minorities like Poles, depicted as spies and subversives, were also highly vulnerable.

In its way, though, the purge of the Communist Party displays better than any other event Stalin's ruthless megalomania and intense paranoia. The campaign began with moves against the "Right opposition," led by Nikolai Bukharin, which had questioned the crash-collectivization and crash-industrialization campaigns, and was now calling for a return to the New Economic Policy and reconciliation with the shattered peasantry. Three separate "show trials" targeted the opposition between 1936 and 1938, in which Bukharin and others were accused of conspiring with Trotskyite and foreign elements to sabotage communism in the Soviet Union. The evidence presented was almost non-existent, with convictions based on absurd confessions extracted through torture, threats against family members, and (bizarrely) appeals to revolutionary solidarity.[44]

The old guard was convicted almost *en bloc*, and usually sentenced to execution. "Of the 139 Central Committee members elected at the Seventeenth Party Congress in 1934, 102 were arrested and shot, and five more killed themselves in 1937–38."[45] The military, too, was ravaged: "of the 767 members of the high command . . . 412 were executed, 29 died in prison, 3 committed suicide, and 59 remained in jail."[46] This would have catastrophic consequences in the early stages of the Nazi–Soviet war of 1941–45, when the USSR's poorly-trained armies were vanquished and nearly annihilated by the German army.

Everyone who confessed named names (and more names, and still more names). Investigations and arrests snowballed; detention centers and execution lists were filled by quota.[47] Meanwhile, the prevailing paranoia meant that sabotage lurked around every corner, in every seemingly innocuous situation. According to the Soviet dissident Alexander Solzhenitsyn, "any adult inhabitant of this country, from a collective farmer up to a member of the Politburo, always knew that it would take only one careless word or gesture and he would fly off irrevocably into the abyss."[48] "Most of us didn't live in any real sense," wrote Nadezhda Mandelstam (eventually consigned to the Gulag) in her autobiography, *Hope Against Hope*. Instead, tens of millions of Soviet citizens "existed from day to day, waiting anxiously for something until the time came to die. . . . In the years of the terror, there was not a home in the country where people did not sit trembling at night, their ears straining to catch the murmur of passing cars or the sound of the elevator."[49]

Like careerists and *génocidaires* everywhere, NKVD officials and others in "the exterminating profession" were anxious to match, and if possible exceed, their commanders' expectations. If "enemies of the people" could not be found in sufficient numbers, individuals – overwhelmingly adult men – were rounded up, shot, or convicted under Article 58 and shipped off to the Gulag.[50]

The Great Purge ended only when it became clear that "at the rate arrests were going, practically all the urban population would have been implicated within a few months."[51] As usual, Stalin's underlings took the fall. The NKVD was purged, and its leader, Nikolai Yezhov, arrested and executed.[52] Stalin went on to preside over the eighteenth Party Congress in March 1939, proclaiming the accomplishments of the purge. Only 35 of the nearly 2,000 delegates who had attended the previous Party Congress were still around to celebrate with him.[53]

The war years

The 1939 Soviet invasion of Poland, following the signing of a non-aggression pact with Nazi Germany, brought with it atrocities that are still relatively little known. The exception is the mass murder, on Stalin's orders, of 20,000 Polish officers who were then buried in the Katyn forest.[54] This was only a small part of a wider Soviet campaign against the Polish nation. Apart from military officers, the campaign concentrated on destroying political leaders, professionals, intellectuals, and businesspeople. The war against the Ukrainian people was thus paralleled in Poland, and subsequently in the Baltic states, which the Soviets invaded and occupied in 1940.

The "eliticidal" character of the Soviets' Baltic campaign is conveyed by a list of those officially designated for arrest and deportation from Lithuania. According to Applebaum, the targets included members of "political parties; former members of the police or the prison service; important capitalists and bourgeoisie; former officers of the national armies; family members of all of the above; anyone repatriated from Germany; refugees from 'former Poland'; as well as thieves and prostitutes." However, this was not sufficient for one Soviet commissar, who added (in his words): "Esperantists [those speaking the 'universal language' of Esperanto]; philatelists; those working with the Red Cross; refugees; smugglers; those expelled from the Communist Party; priests and active members of religious congregations; the nobility, landowners, wealthy merchants, bankers, industrialists, hotel and restaurant owners."[55]

BOX 5.1 ONE MAN'S STORY: JANUSZ BARDACH

One of the millions of foreign victims of Stalinist terror was Janusz Bardach, a Jew whose family hailed from Odessa in Russia, but who grew to maturity in the Polish town of Wlodzimierz-Wolynski. There, Bardach experienced some of the discrimination meted out to Jews in Poland. (It would explode into murderous frenzy during the Nazi occupation, when many Poles eagerly helped the Nazis in their genocide against Jews.)[56] "In school I sensed that my classmates didn't truly accept me; I felt I was a stranger among them. Some called me names and made me feel that I couldn't live happily among Poles because I was Jewish."[57] But the family held fast amidst the anti-Jewish racism, which included commercial boycotts and harassment by government bureaucrats.

When the Nazis invaded Poland in September 1939, Bardach was dealt a "stinging reminder" of his outsider status: the Polish army declined Jews' offers to help defend the nation. Bardach joined the flight of military-age males to the east of the country. Having imbibed socialist influences in his adolescence, he was happy to encounter Soviet troops storming into eastern Poland (they were occupying the eastern half of the country, as agreed in the previous month's Nazi–Soviet pact). Bardach was convinced the Soviets would protect Jews like him from Nazi depredations: "I believed that the Soviet Union was a paradise for the oppressed, ruled by workers and peasants, and that the Red Army was the enforcer of social justice. I couldn't imagine them as my enemies." His joy only increased when he learned that his home town of Wlodzimierz-Wolynski would be just inside the Soviet occupation zone.

Bardach's faith in the Soviet revolution began to waver when he was forced to serve as a civilian witness accompanying a unit of the NKVD, the Soviet secret police, on a night-time raid of local homes. His brother, Jurek, was caught in the dragnet and badly beaten during interrogation; so when, in summer 1940, the Red Army announced a military draft of men of Bardach's age, he was dismayed, and sought to flunk the medical. But he was pronounced fit. He chose the tank corps, since it offered a term of four years' service instead of the usual five.

In June 1941, the Germans broke the Nazi–Soviet pact and invaded eastern Poland and the USSR. Bardach's thoughts turned to his family on the front lines. He himself was soon in mortal danger, however. Exhausted, with Soviet forces in headlong retreat, Bardach lost concentration at the helm of his T-34 tank. While traversing a river, he inadvertently left a hatch open, and the tank capsized.

For this, Bardach was sentenced to death. "I sat with my face in my hand, stunned by how quickly and easily the death sentence was pronounced." Then, nearly miraculously, an NKVD officer recognized his surname – the officer had grown up next to the Bardachs in Odessa! Bardach's sentence was commuted to ten years' hard labor.

He was sent to a way-station, Burepolom, in northwest Russia. *En route*, in a crowded and unsanitary cattle-car, he socialized with the *urkas* – the common criminals, with their own distinctive subculture. Most Gulag memoirs by Soviet intellectuals express a horror of the *urkas*. Many inmates reported savage treatment at their hands. But Bardach somehow established a rapport that lasted through his incarceration, and made of the *urkas* his allies, sometimes his friends.

The *urkas* told him about his ultimate destination, Kolyma. "There, it was said, the guards shot prisoners for sport or sent them to work without coats or boots and placed bets on how long it would take them to freeze to death." Bardach was terrified. "I had never done hard physical work, and the thought of spending ten years at it was terrifying . . . I had little chance of surviving."

At Burepolom, Bardach was set to tree-felling. "Starvation was routine," he recounted. "We weren't given enough food to sustain us throughout one day of hard work, let alone weeks and months. . . . At times I felt I could eat anything. . . . Gradually I learned that anything I could chew – even a leaf or fresh twig – gave the illusion of eating."

Bardach was then launched on an epic journey across the length of the Soviet Union, by railway car and "slave ship," to Kolyma – the harshest outpost of the Gulag. On arrival, he was "assigned to clear a new area of boulders, stones, roots, and shrubs." He learned crucial survival skills, especially the fine art of faking work by "creat[ing] the illusion of activity" and thereby marshaling his energy. Still, "the oppressive work regimen was a form of torture in itself. Sometimes I thought hacking the cement-hard soil with a wrought-iron crowbar was unbearable. I felt the limits of my endurance approaching . . . I still wanted to live, but I thought about injuring myself as so many other prisoners had done, hoping to win several days in the hospital, to be assigned to a lighter job, to be transferred to another camp."

The work proceeded even in the intense cold of the coldest populated region on the planet. "Touching a metal tool with a bare hand could tear off the skin, and going to the bathroom was extremely dangerous. A bout of diarrhea could land you in the snow forever." Disease was rife amid the hard labor, minimal nutrition, and squalid living conditions. Bardach came down with scurvy, and was sent to the hospital zone. There, another semi-miracle occurred. After successfully inflating his medical credentials (he had a year of medical training in prewar Poland), Bardach was granted a post as an orderly. He was released after the war, and returned home – only to discover that virtually his entire family had perished at Nazi hands.

Tens of thousands of people were executed, and hundreds of thousands more consigned to the Gulag, which now expanded to include camps in occupied territories.[58] When the Nazi–Soviet Pact collapsed and Germany invaded Soviet-occupied Poland in June 1941, fresh catastrophe descended. Forced into retreat, NKVD killing squads massacred many of those whom they had imprisoned on Polish territory. Legions of others were deported on foot, in scenes "hauntingly similar to the marches undertaken by the prisoners of the Nazi concentration camps four years later"[59] (see Chapter 6).

The tide turned in 1943, with the Soviet victories at Stalingrad and Kursk. By 1944, the Soviets were reinvading Poland and pushing into German territory in East Prussia. Some of the destruction wreaked upon German civilians by vengeful Soviet soldiers is discussed in Box 6a on "The Nazis' Other Victims." Notable here is the Gulag's expansion into Germany and other invaded lands (Romania, Bulgaria). In Germany, the so-called *spetslagerya* were sometimes established in former Nazi concentration camps. Again, Soviet policy aimed to undermine any national resistance to Soviet occupation. Inmates were predominantly "judges, lawyers, entrepreneurs, businessmen, doctors and journalists." Of the 240,000 incarcerated, over one-third – 95,000 people – perished in the *spetslagerya*, while camps in Romania were more deadly still.[60] In addition, as many as 760,000 Japanese prisoners were captured during the few days that the two countries were at war in August 1945, and dispatched to the Gulag, where tens of thousands died, predominantly during the 1945–46 winter.[61] The camp system in fact reached its apogee in 1950, well after the Second World War had ended.

Finally, in one of modern history's most tragic ironies, repatriated Soviet prisoners-of-war (Box 6a) were arrested *en masse* in the USSR on suspicion of collaboration with the Germans. Most were sentenced to long terms in the Gulag, with hundreds of thousands consigned to mine uranium for the Soviet atomic bomb. "Few survived the experience."[62] As Solzhenitsyn noted: "In Russian captivity, as in German captivity, the worst lot of all was reserved for the Russians."[63]

The destruction of national minorities

As already mentioned, Soviet belligerence toward any ethnic nationalism but the Russian produced a genocidal famine in Ukraine, whose people were the most powerful and resource-rich of those inclined toward autonomy or independence.[64] Both before and during the Second World War, suspicion of national minorities as potential "fifth columnists" led to their deportation from regions deemed vulnerable to foreign attack and occupation. Though the wartime deportations are reasonably widely known, historian Alexander Statiev has shown that the trend actually began several years before the outbreak of the conflict. The first to suffer were tens of thousands of Germans, Poles, Finns, and Iranians, among others. Subsequent measures included "the resettlement of all 171,781 Koreans . . . from the Far East to Central Asia in October 1937," which "initiated the deportations of entire ethnic groups."[65] They joined the kulaks in the catastrophic conditions of the "special settlements." The onset of the Second World War in 1939–40, and the Soviet occupation of the

Baltic states and eastern Poland, "triggered another series of deportations," of national elements deemed hostile and subversive. "About 400,000 Poles were exiled in 1940–41 . . . while 133,138 Germans were repatriated from Moldavia alone. In addition, in May and June 1941, the government banished 85,716 'socially dangerous elements,' mostly members of the titular majorities of the western republics."[66]

The shocking mortality rates among many of the prewar deportees means, according to Statiev, that when the Soviets initiated new rounds of deportations during the war, they "must have understood that in wartime their capacity to . . . [provide for] the accommodation and supply of exiles would be even more limited, which would result in far greater privations for the blacklisted minorities." Implicit here is a case for genocidal intent – constructive or general intent, rather than a specific and explicit exterminatory desire – in what followed, and indeed in much that had preceded it.[67]

After the German invasion of the Soviet Union in June 1941, Soviets of ethnic German origin in the Volga region, numbering well over a million, were a predictable target. Again depicted as potential saboteurs and subversives, some 1.2 million people were rounded up and deported from territories they had inhabited for centuries.[68] The Nazi offensive in the Caucasus and Crimea in 1942 spelled doom for a host of minorities there and in Soviet Central Asia. Accused of collaborating with the German invader, polyglot groups were rounded up by the NKVD and expelled from their homelands – generally under terrible conditions – and to desolate territories where agriculture was difficult and infrastructure nonexistent. "The seven peoples deported during the war were: Balkars, Chechens, Crimean Tatars,[69] Ingushi, Karachai, Kalmyks, and Meskhetians."[70] With the translocation went a systematic assault on the foundations of these minorities' cultures:

> For the first time, Stalin had decided to eliminate not just members of particular, suspect nationalities, or categories of political "enemies," but entire nations – men, women, children, grandparents. . . . After they had gone, the names of all of the deported peoples were eliminated from official documents – even from the *Great Soviet Encyclopædia*. The authorities wiped their homelands off the map, abolishing the Chechen-Ingush Autonomous Republic, the Volga-German Autonomous Republic, the Kabardino-Balkar Autonomous Republic, and the Karachai Autonomous Province. The Crimean Autonomous Republic was also liquidated, and Crimea simply became another Soviet province.[71]

The devastation of the Chechen nation was only one of many such atrocities, but it had especially fateful consequences. The Chechen genocide – Applebaum estimates that 78,000 Chechens died on transport trains alone[72] – resonates to the present day. The fierce Chechen struggle for independence in the 1990s and 2000s reflects memories of the genocide during the Second World War. The response of the post-Soviet Russian government was a new round of genocide, with tens of thousands of Chechens killed and hundreds of thousands more displaced as refugees (Box 5a).[73]

In the final months of his life, Stalin directed his paranoid zeal against a minority that so far had largely escaped targeting as such: Soviet Jews. Those arrested in the so-called "Doctors' Plot" in January 1953 were mostly Jewish, and it seemed the

Figure 5.4 A Russian woman brandishes a placard with a portrait of Joseph Stalin at a May 1st demonstration in Moscow, Russia, in 2007. Many Russians who survived Stalin's dictatorship remember it as a time of economic development, national unity, and patriotic pride. They yearn for the return of a "strong hand" amidst the social dislocation of the post-communist period.

Source: Yuri Kochetkov/EPA/Corbis.

arrests might presage a repeat of the Great Purge. But in March, the dictator died. Rapidly, a "thaw" spread through Soviet life. Over the following decade, the vast majority of Gulag prisoners were released, the "camp-industrial complex" was shut down, and many of the dead and still living were officially rehabilitated. Limited criticism was permitted of Stalin and the cult of personality, "the most grandiose in history,"[74] that surrounded him.

The thaw after Stalin's death peaked with his eventual successor, Nikita Khrushchev. A Ukrainian who had helped to consign millions of his fellow Ukrainians to death or the Gulag, Khrushchev nonetheless allowed something of the truth of life in the camps to be published for the first time, with Alexander Solzhenitsyn's 1961 novella *One Day in the Life of Ivan Denisovich*. But in 1964, Khrushchev was ousted for his failed brinkmanship during the Cuban Missile Crisis, and his disastrous agricultural policies. A new chill descended. When Solzhenitsyn completed his three-volume study of *The Gulag Archipelago*, he could publish it only abroad; and though the work won its author the Nobel Prize for literature, it led to his house arrest and forced exile. Only with a new and deeper thaw under Mikhail Gorbachev did a genuine reckoning with the Stalinist and Gulag legacies begin – although post-Soviet citizens have proven notably reluctant to revisit this aspect of the national past (see Chapter 14, pp. 508–11).

CHINA AND MAOISM

The ravages of Stalinism in the USSR were, if anything, outdone by the twentieth century's other leading Stalinist, Mao Zedong. Political scientist R.J. Rummel has estimated over *thirty-five million people* killed under Mao's rule, from 1949 through Mao's death in 1976. The carnage occurred, Rummel contended, for the same reason it occurred in the Soviet Union . . . In each case, Power was nearly absolute, the central tenets of Marxism the bible, high communist officials its priests, the Communist Party its church, and the achievement of the Marxist heaven – communism – the ultimate goal. In each country, the same classes – bourgeoisie, priests, landlords, the rich, and officers and officials of the previous regime – were sinful, enemies of the Good. Capitalists or their offspring were especially evil. The verdict for such class membership was often death.[75]

Like the Soviet Bolsheviks, the Chinese Communist Party began as a reaction to centuries of despotic rule. Like the Bolsheviks, most of the early Chinese communist leaders were well educated, generally prosperous individuals moved by the plight of the masses. Unlike the Bolsheviks, however, the Chinese communists recognized early on that the heart of China's revolutionary potential lay in the peasantry, the large majority of the population, rather than in the tiny urban proletariat, as Marxist orthodoxy dictated. In stark contrast to the Bolsheviks' seizure of power in St. Petersburg, which was essentially a coup by a marginal political force, in China the communists seized power after decades of patient mobilization and expansion in the countryside. Throughout, they were hounded – at times almost to extinction – by their opponents, notably Chiang Kai-shek's Nationalist Party (*Guomindang*, or KMT). This persecution, for which there is no real parallel in the Soviet case, spawned a mentality of paranoia and vengeful hatred toward all "class enemies."

In 1925, Chiang Kai-shek's forces inflicted a devastating massacre on CCP ranks – a moment that genocide scholar Ben Kiernan describes as a "watershed." Thereafter, as Haifeng regional party secretary Peng Pai declared, "We have to shift from sorrow to power. We are mad for merciless extermination of the enemy: we thirst for the last drop of the enemy's blood as compensation for our martyred comrades. . . . From now on we . . . must exterminate our enemy to the last."[76] When the communists retook Haifeng, they announced a "Workers-Peasants' Dictatorship" whose primary purpose was "the extermination of anti-revolutionaries": "All persons aiding the enemy and all reactionaries, such as corrupt officials, greedy bureaucrats, bully landowners, evil gentry, spies, propagandists, policemen, Peace Preservation corpsmen, messengers and tax collectors for the enemy, and all those who work in their offices must be seized and executed."[77]

When Chiang's Nationalists destroyed an abortive communist "commune" in Guangdong in 1927, Mao rose to the forefront of the movement. The killings initiated under his regime were initially selective, mostly targeting landlords whom peasants denounced as particularly brutal and exploitative. Both violence and land seizures were de-emphasized during the 1937–45 war against the Japanese, when the Communist Party formed a fragile common front with the Nationalists against the invader (see Chapter 3). Following the Japanese defeat, however, the Communists and Nationalists turned to their final confrontation, and extremism increased on both sides. By this time, the communists had established a state-within-a-state in Henan province. There, Mao fine-tuned the pattern of denunciation, public humiliation, and often murder of "spies" and "class enemies" that would become his regime's hallmark after 1949. "Bad landlords," in particular, were exposed to indiscriminate violence – and as with Stalin's targeting of so-called "kulaks," such a designation could be terrifyingly random. It was often filled by quota (10 percent of the population was an accepted norm), and often based on grudges and personal rivalries in the local community. "Those designated as targets were made to stand facing large crowds," which would "shout slogans while brandishing fists and farm tools. Village militants and thugs would then inflict physical abuse, which could range from making the victims kneel on broken tiles on their bare knees, to hanging them up by their wrists or feet, or beating them, sometimes to death, often with farm implements."[78] There was little danger that the functionaries organizing such proceedings would be punished. Indeed, they were encouraged to excel in their infliction of violence. "Without using the greatest force," Mao wrote in an essay titled "The Question of 'Going Too Far,'" "the peasants cannot possibly overthrow the deep-rooted authority of the landlords . . . To put it bluntly, it is necessary to create terror for a while in every rural area, or otherwise it would be impossible to suppress the activities of the counter-revolutionaries in the countryside or overthrow the authority of the gentry."[79]

According to Mao biographers Jung Chang and Jon Halliday, "Hundreds of thousands, possibly as many as a million, were killed or driven to suicide" during this period of communist expansion.[80] Yet it was only a foretaste of the terror that would sweep the countryside when the communists, having crushed Chiang's KMT and sent it into exile on Taiwan, declared a "People's Republic" on August 1, 1949. "China has stood up," Mao declared; now all enemies would be brought low. A radical land reform program was instituted at breakneck speed, and the main targets were again to be the Chinese equivalent of the kulaks – not just landlords, but any peasant accused of owning marginally more than his or her neighbor. As with Soviet collectivization under Stalin in 1929–30, large-scale resistance resulted as the communists pushed their "reform" program into the Chinese hinterland. According to political scientist Benjamin Valentino,

> In some regions, communist officials were assassinated and large-scale riots and armed rebellions erupted. CCP cadres were dispatched to the villages with orders to identify landlords and other village "exploiters" and confiscate virtually all of their land, animals, and personal possessions. In an effort to incite "class struggle," landlords were dragged in front of village meetings where cadres encouraged poor peasants to "speak bitterness" against them. The meetings often culminated in brutal beatings or executions.[81]

Presaging the Khmer Rouge's genocidal campaigns in Cambodia, this first post-1949 phase of Maoist repression also targeted "urban elites (especially the capitalists, the westernized intellectuals and the Christians), and even more the former Guomindang cadres, civilian as well as military, down to the lowest ranks."[82] Mao himself acknowledged that 800,000 people had been executed between 1949 and 1954,[83] while Valentino estimated that "between one million and four million people were probably killed" during roughly these years.[84] Many of them perished in the *lao-gai* (labor camps). At least 2.5 million "class enemies" were dispatched to the camps in this first period of national rule, and conditions there were no less murderous than in the Soviet Gulag which had served as their model. "To be sent to *lao-gai* meant being condemned to backbreaking labor in the most hostile wastelands and down the most contaminating mines, while being hectored and harassed incessantly."[85] Throughout Mao's reign, and especially in the 1960s, the camps accounted for a majority of those killed by the regime. Chang and Halliday estimate that "the number of people in detention in any one year under Mao has been calculated at roughly 10 million. It is reasonable to assume that on average 10 percent of these were executed or died of other causes."[86]

■ BOX 5.2 TIBET: REPRESSION AND GENOCIDE

Map 5.2   Chinese Tibet (the Tibet Autonomous Region), showing also the contours of historic Tibet and of significant Tibetan population today (especially in Qinghai). The plateau of Buddhist Tibetans, traditionally herders ruled over by a small religious-political elite, has been penetrated by Chinese roads and railways, and inundated by Han Chinese military and civilian personnel. Allegations of physical genocide against Tibetans center mostly on the period during the late 1950s and early 1960s, when Tibet was arguably the region hardest hit by the disastrous "Great Leap Forward," and when Tibetans were heavily overrepresented in often lethal slave-labor camps. Advocates of a concept of "cultural genocide" cite Tibet as a paradigmatic example.

Source: Wikimedia Commons.

In exploring Chinese policies toward Tibet, we must distinguish between two versions of Tibet that are often confused. Ethnic Tibet – the area in which self-identified Tibetans reside – covers more or less the area of the Tibetan plateau.[87] But it also includes the areas of Amdo and Kham (often referred to as "eastern Tibet"). These were traditionally controlled by warlords more beholden to the Han Chinese center than to the Tibetan authorities in central Tibet – with its capital at Lhasa, home to the supreme religious authority, the Dalai Lama. "Tibet" today is generally held – except by Tibetans – to refer to the Tibet Autonomous Region (TAR) declared by China in 1965. This constitutes barely half the territory of ethnic Tibet, while the more populous territories of "Outer Tibet" (including Amdo and Kham) are mostly divided between the Chinese provinces of Sichuan and Qinghai. Although home to about half of all ethnic Tibetans, these provinces are populated by a Han Chinese majority, and the demographic disparity is increasing.[88]

Historically, Tibet was the product of empire-building, and for 300 years (600–900 CE) was one of the most powerful states in Asia. Although Tibet's Buddhist lamas were pressured into a tribute relationship with the Mongol and Manchu emperors of China from the thirteenth to the twentieth century, not until 1911 was Tibet declared part of the Chinese state. The Nationalist regime that made the declaration could never enforce it, and from 1911 to 1950, "the Tibetan Government exercised internal and external freedom, which clearly demonstrated the country's independence."[89]

To justify their 1950 invasion, the communist Chinese government depicted pre-occupation Tibet as "a hell on earth ravaged by feudal exploitation," with rapacious monks oppressing impoverished peasants.[90] The true picture was more complex. Tibet was authoritarian, with a powerful monastic class that exacted high taxes from the laboring population. Supporters of Tibetan nationalism acknowledge that "traditional Tibetan society – like most of its Asian contemporaries – was backward and badly in need of reforms." But there was no hereditary rule. The supreme authority, the Dalai Lama, was chosen from the ordinary population as the reincarnation of his predecessor – an egalitarian strategy mirroring the upward mobility that life as a monk could provide. In addition, the system was not truly feudal: peasants "had a legal identity, often with documents stating their rights, and also had access to courts of law," including "the right to sue their masters."[91] Peasant holdings appear to have provided adequate subsistence, with crop failures and other agricultural emergencies offset by state reserves.

During the Nationalist era, as noted above, Tibet was claimed but not administered by China. That changed in 1949–50, after Mao's Communist Party took power in Beijing. With rationales that ranged from bringing civilization to the natives, to the need to counter moves by American "hegemonists," the Chinese invaded and partially occupied Tibet in October 1950. "Tibet's frantic appeals for help to the United Nations, India, Britain, and the United States were ignored, or rebuffed with diplomatic evasions. No nation was about to challenge the new People's Republic of China, which had some ten million men under arms, over the fate of an obscure mountain kingdom lost in the Himalayas."[92] The logistical difficulty of doing so would also have been nightmarish.

In May 1951, China imposed a punitive 17-Point Agreement on Tibet. It guaranteed Tibetan political, religious, and educational rights, but allowed the People's Liberation Army (PLA) to enter the territory, and gave the Chinese control over Tibetan foreign affairs.[93] The Chinese also enjoyed a free hand in the eastern Tibetan territories. They used it to impose communist measures such as collectivization of agriculture. Rebellion against the measures gradually swelled among the Tibetans of the east. The Chinese responded with greater violence, killing thousands of Tibetans and incarcerating tens of thousands under brutal conditions.

When rebellion reached central Tibet, in 1959, it sparked a general uprising that the Chinese rapidly suppressed. The Dalai Lama fled across the border into India, where he still resides in Dharamsala, presiding over a 20,000-strong Tibetan exile community.[94] The Chinese government then extended their regime of "struggle" against supposedly reactionary elements to Tibet. Communist cadres denounced, tortured, and frequently executed "enemies of the people." "These struggle sessions resulted in more than 92,000 deaths" out of a total Tibetan population of about six million people.[95] The killings may be seen as part of a genocidal strategy against Tibetans as a whole, but also as an "eliticide," targeting the better-educated and leadership-oriented elements among the Tibetan population.

After the 1959 uprising, a catastrophic toll was inflicted by the forced-labor camps of Qinghai and Sichuan, which swept up hundreds of thousands of Tibetans.[96] They were set to work extracting Tibet's minerals and building Chinese military infrastructure, especially roads and railways. Toiling at high, frozen altitudes and with minimal food rations, tens of thousands of Tibetans died in the first half of the 1960s, in conditions that rivaled the Soviet Gulag. According to Jean-Louis Margolin,

> it appears that very few people (perhaps as few as 2 percent) ever returned alive from the 166 known camps, most of which were [established] in Tibet or the neighboring provinces. Entire monastic communities were sent to the coal mines. Detention conditions on the whole appear to have been dreadful, with hunger, cold, or extreme heat the daily lot of the prisoners. There are as many tales of execution of prisoners refusing to renounce Tibetan independence as there are tales of cannibalism in prison during the Great Leap Forward. It was as though the entire population of Tibet . . . were suspects.[97]

The second Chinese campaign to devastate Tibet occurred during the "Great Proletarian Cultural Revolution," unleashed in 1966. Tibet was seen as a hotbed of "reaction" and "feudalism," and persecution and cultural destruction occurred there on a vast scale. "In the process, thousands of monks were slaughtered."[98]

Mao died in 1976, and the extremist phase of the Chinese revolution passed with him. The 1980s were marked by an opening up to the West which launched a remarkable transformation of China's economy and society, which continues today.

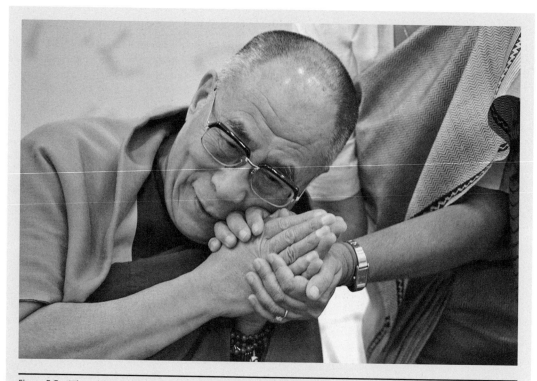

Figure 5.5   The 14th Dalai Lama, Tenzin Gyatso, attending the Hind Swaraj International Centenary Conference in Delhi, November 2009. The Dalai Lama has become the face of Tibetan nationalism and a leading exponent of Buddhism and nonviolence. The Tibetan government-in-exile which he leads has pursued an accommodationist line toward the Chinese government, rejecting violence while seeking autonomy within China, rather than full independence.

Source: Pankaj Mistry/www.pankajmistry.com.

This opening has been characterized by something of a softening of China's policies toward Tibetan national and cultural rights.[99] However, with increasing Han Chinese migration, Tibetans have become a minority in their capital of Lhasa – a trend only exacerbated in the 2000s by the opening of a new railway from central China to the Tibetan heartland.[100] Renewed ideological campaigns, such as the "Strike Hard" and "Spiritual Civilization" initiatives, have been aimed at the so-called "Dalai Clique" – notably representatives of the Tibetan religious institutions that have revived since the Cultural Revolution. Hundreds of monks and nuns have been arrested, and thousands more expelled from their institutions. Finally, "in a massive campaign that recalls the socialist engineering of an earlier era, the Chinese government has relocated some 250,000 Tibetans – nearly one-tenth of the population – from scattered rural hamlets to new 'socialist villages' . . . The broader aim seems to be remaking Tibet – a region with its own culture, language, and religious traditions – in order to have firmer political control over its population."[101]

Tibetan resistance continued beneath the surface, occasionally erupting in open revolt. In March 1989 there occurred "the largest anti-Chinese demonstration in

[Lhasa] since 1959."[102] It was met by crackdowns, mass roundups, and torture. Renewed protests in 2008 led to the deaths of dozens of demonstrators (and Tibetan vigilante attacks on Han Chinese). The repression prompted the Dalai Lama to accuse China of imposing a "rule of terror" in the territory, adding: "Whether intentionally or unintentionally, some cultural genocide is taking place . . . . [An] ancient nation with ancient cultural heritage is actually dying."[103] He deployed similar language in March 2010, accusing the Chinese government of seeking to "deliberately annihilate Buddhism."[104]

Overall, perhaps hundreds of thousands of Tibetans likely have died at Chinese hands since 1950, mostly in the decade following the 1959 invasion. The Tibetan government-in-exile estimates 1.2 million deaths, but Margolin calculated a death-toll "as high as 800,000 – a scale of population loss comparable to that in Cambodia under the Khmer Rouge" (see Chapter 7).[105]

As early as 1960, the International Commission of Jurists declared that there existed "a *prima facie* case that on the part of the Chinese, there has been an attempt to destroy the national, ethnical, racial and religious group of Tibetans by killing members of the group and causing serious bodily harm to members of the group. . . . These acts constitute the crime of genocide under the Genocide Convention of the United Nations of 1948."[106] Since then, supporters of Tibetan self-determination have frequently deployed a genocide discourse. For example, in 1998 Maura Moynihan of Refugees International argued that Tibet suffered "a grimly familiar, twentieth-century, state-sponsored genocide."[107] Such claims are hotly disputed by the Chinese government and its supporters.

Meanwhile, Tibet's government-in-exile has proposed realistic and moderate responses to Chinese occupation. A five-point plan that the Dalai Lama presented in a 1987 speech to the US Congress included the following:

1. Transformation of the whole of Tibet into a zone of peace.
2. Abandonment of China's population transfer policy which threatens the very existence of the Tibetan people.
3. Respect for the Tibetan people's fundamental human rights and democratic freedoms.
4. Restoration and protection of Tibet's natural environment and the abandonment of China's use of Tibet for the production of nuclear weapons and dumping of nuclear waste.
5. Commencement of earnest negotiations on the future status of Tibet and of relations between the Tibetan and Chinese people.[108]

The Dalai Lama has made it clear that Tibetans are willing to accept autonomy within China, rather than full independence. Such an arrangement seems remote, however, given China's ambitions for Tibet, and its growing military and colonizing presence.[109]

Gargantuan death tolls left Mao and most of his associates unfazed. Conscious that he was overlord of the most populous country on earth, confronting a superpower (the United States) armed with nuclear weapons, Mao was notorious for blasé statements that anticipated and accepted almost unimaginable hecatombs of dead in pursuit of political goals. "We are prepared to sacrifice 300 million Chinese for the victory of the world revolution," he declared on a visit to Moscow in 1957,[110] and in May 1958 he told the 8th Party Congress: "Don't make a fuss about a world war. At most, people die . . . Half the population wiped out – this happened quite a few times in Chinese history . . . It's best if half the population is left, next best one third."[111]

This world view, blended with Mao's desire to project China as the rightful leader of world communism, led to the greatest disaster of the Maoist period – the "Great Leap Forward" in 1958–61. The "Great Leap" was supposed to accomplish for China what Stalin had sought in the Soviet Union: to collectivize all agriculture and industrialize a peasant nation in short order. Stalin, at monumental human cost, achieved his goal. The Chinese "Leap," however, was an unmitigated economic and human disaster. "Mao proceeded by simply asserting that there was going to be an enormous increase in the harvest, and got the provincial chiefs to proclaim that their area would produce an astronomical output." When the harvest arrived, the chiefs, fearing for their jobs and probably their lives, duly "declare[d] that their areas had indeed produced fantastic crops."[112] The "surpluses" were a cruel fiction. But as under Stalin, they served as the basis for grain seizures that provoked mass famine – the worst in China's famine-plagued history, and according to Margolin, "probably the worst in the history of the world."[113] The famine claimed the lives of "an estimated 40 million people" in just three years;[114] Chang and Halliday report that in 1960 alone, no fewer than "22 million people died of hunger."[115] In a macabre touch, as

Figure 5.6   Mao Zedong (right) was an acolyte of Joseph Stalin. While Stalin was alive, the relationship between the world's two leading communist leaders was strong, as depicted in this Soviet propaganda poster. After the Soviet Union's "destalinization" process, Mao denounced the Soviets as "revisionists," and sought to take over leadership of the global communist movement – ambitions which contributed to the "Great Leap Forward" and mass famine of 1959–62.

Source: Wikimedia Commons.

the British had done throughout the Irish and Indian famines of the nineteenth century and as Stalin decreed during the 1930s, food was actually *exported* on a massive scale during the famine:

> Net grain exports, principally to the USSR, rose from 2.7 million tons in 1958 to 4.2 million in 1959, and in 1960 fell only to the 1958 level. In 1961, 5.8 million tons were actually imported, up from 66,000 in 1960, but this was still too little to feed the starving. Aid from the United States was refused for political reasons. The rest of the world, which could have responded easily, remained ignorant of the scale of the catastrophe.[116]

The arrangement apparently struck even the Soviets as perverse. In 1961, they offered "to suspend the repayment of the loans and to furnish emergency food deliveries." Mao, however, rejected the offer.[117]

The final paroxysm of Maoist violence was the "Great Proletarian Cultural Revolution" of 1966–76 (peaking, it seems, in 1968). This equivalent of the Stalinist purges was designed to "cleanse the class ranks" of remaining classical influences and counterrevolutionary elements. It produced some of the notorious images of suspects clad in dunce caps and paraded for public humiliation and violence. Lee Ta-ling, a former Red Guard, remembered seeing

> rows of teachers, about 40 or 50 in all, with black ink poured over their heads and faces so that they were now in reality a "black gang." Hanging on their necks were placards with words such as "reactionary academic authority so-and-so," "corrupt ringleader so-and-so," "class enemy so-and-so," "capitalist roader so-and-so"; all epithets taken from the newspapers. On each placard was a red cross, making the teachers look like condemned prisoners awaiting execution. They all wore dunce caps painted with similar epithets and carried dirty brooms, shoes, and dusters on their backs. Hanging from their necks were pails filled with rocks. . . . All were barefoot, hitting broken gongs or pots as they walked around the field crying out: "I am black gangster so-and-so." Finally, they all knelt down, burned incense, and begged Mao Zedong to "pardon their crimes." . . . Beatings and torture followed. I had never seen such tortures before: eating nightsoil [human waste] and insects, being subjected to electric shocks, being forced to kneel on broken glass, being hanged "like an airplane" by the arms and legs. . . . The heaviest blow to me that day was the killing of my most respected and beloved teacher, Chen Ku-teh.[118]

Tens of thousands apparently chose suicide over further persecution. In Beijing, for example, where "the cleansing of the class ranks resulted in the deaths of 3,731 people between January 1968 and May 1969 . . . more than 94 percent of the deaths [were] registered as suicide."[119]

Chang and Halliday estimated that "in the ten years from when Mao started the Purge until his death in 1976, at least 3 million people died violent deaths, and post-Mao leaders acknowledged that 100 million people, one-ninth of the entire population, suffered in one way or another."[120] Eventually the so-called "Red Guard"

Figure 5.7   Spectators look on as purge victims are paraded for public humiliation during the Cultural Revolution, the last bout of Maoist extremism before the dictator's 1976 death.

Source: University of Florida.

factions that Mao had mobilized began running out of targets and fighting among themselves. What had begun as "a massive pogrom against people of exploiting class background" became, in many areas, "a campaign of retribution and murder against factional rivals."[121]

The terror ended with Mao's death in 1976, at the age of 82. The "Gang of Four" (including Mao's wife, Jiang Qing), which had supervised the day-to-day logistics of his later-life derangements, was purged and incarcerated by reformists headed by Deng Xiaoping, who sought the equivalent of a "destalinization" campaign. However, China's revision of Maoism went only so far: to reveal all of Mao's crimes, genocidal and otherwise, would have risked undermining the government's claim to legitimacy. Deng Xiaoping, who had been suppressed under Mao's regime, provided the official formula: Mao was "seven parts good, three parts bad."[122] His portrait still hangs over the entrance to the imperial city on the edge of Tiananmen Square, and despite his "errors," he is still revered as the father of modern China.[123] One-party rule persists, bolstered by selective violence – notably the Tiananmen Square massacre of 1989, in which several thousand Chinese were slaughtered by government forces.[124] Resurgent nationalist protests on the Chinese periphery, in Tibet and in the Muslim-majority region of Xinjiang, have also been ruthlessly quashed.

BOX 5.3 NORTH KOREA AND "THE CLEANEST RACE"

The tyrannical and ultra-isolated nation of North Korea is one inheritor of Stalinist and Maoist patterns of rule. These include a "cult of personality" surrounding the family dictatorship that has run the country (into the ground) since the Second World War, political persecution, and widespread famine.[125] Unlike either of these models, however, North Korea also indulges in "explicit racial theorizing," including a "strident acclamation of Koreans as the world's 'cleanest' or 'purest' race."[126] The concern with purity (see the discussion of this psychological phenomenon in Chapter 10) is reflected in the regime's ultra-isolation from the rest of the world, and its suffocation of modernity in every area save military hardware.[127] The ideology, which also includes strong elements of paranoia and dependency, is examined in a groundbreaking 2010 work, *The Cleanest Race*, by B.R. Myers. One of Myers's insights is that to the extent the North Korean ideology is defined by its "race-based worldview," it may make "more sense to posit it on the extreme right than on the far left. Indeed, the similarity to the worldview of fascist Japan is striking."[128]

It was Japan that colonized Korea in the nineteenth century, and divided after the Second World War into northern and southern zones under different occupation regimes, Korea solidified into two opposing states. Conflict between them flared into open war – with Soviet, Chinese, and US backing – from 1950 to 1953. After a truce was agreed, North Korea, under its dictator and "Dear Leader" Kim Il Sung, became "the Hermit kingdom" – the most tightly sealed and secretive dictatorship in the world.

The fall of communism elsewhere changed nothing in North Korea. The Kim dynasty continued with the ascent of Kim Jong Il following his father's 1994 death. Privation and mass suffering increased after the fall of the Soviet Union and Chinese policy transformations dramatically cut foreign aid. The result, in 1994, was one of the worst famines in recent history, killing two to three million North Koreans. As international aid flooded in, the regime conducted a brutal "triage," denying food to those "not seen as critical to the survival of the state." "The corrupt cadres are stealing the food and selling it on the markets for their own profit while we starve," refugees told investigators.[129] As under Stalin, forced requisitions exacerbated the famine: "to feed the army, Kim Jong Il sent soldiers directly to the farms at harvest time to forcibly grab the harvest" and "did everything to prevent the population from finding alternative ways of feeding themselves." So wrote journalist Jasper Becker in his study *Rogue Regime*. While acknowledging that "genocide is normally interpreted to mean the mass killings of another race," Becker contended that "this too" – the death of millions through politically-manipulated famine – "is a form of genocide."[130]

In the face of the rampant starvation, North Koreans staged acts of resistance, including "protests, strikes, local uprisings, the sabotage of official buildings, and the murder of officials and their families."[131] The Kim regime, of course, viewed all such manifestations as "traitorous." Those not subjected to summary execution were dispatched to the North Korean version of the Gulag. Since its founding, successive North Korean regimes have operated a network of "special control institutions" (*Kwanliso*), some of them up to twenty miles long and half as wide. If they were not summarily shot, prisoners were forced into mortally dangerous slave labor. According to Young Howard, a South Korean activist working with the US National Endowment for Democracy:

> Prisoners are provided just enough food to be kept perpetually on the verge of starvation. They are compelled by their hunger to eat, if they can get away with it, the food of the labor-camp farm animals, as well as plants, grasses, bark, rats, snakes and anything remotely edible. In committing such desperate acts driven by acute hunger the prisoners simultaneously incur the extreme risk of being detected by an angry security guard and subjected to a brutal, on-the-spot execution. Not surprisingly, the prisoners are quickly reduced to walking skeletons after their arrival. All gulag survivors said they were struck by the shortness, skinniness, premature aging, hunchbacks, and physical deformities of so many of the inmates they saw upon arriving at the gulag. These descriptions parallel those provided by survivors of the Holocaust in infamous camps like Auschwitz.

In its 2007 report, *North Korea: A Case to Answer, A Call to Act*, issued in 2007, the nongovernmental organization Christian Solidarity Worldwide (CSW) contended that the conditions inflicted on prisoners had killed hundreds of thousands of inmates over the decades – with estimates ranging from 380,000 to over one million. This could qualify as both genocide and the crime against humanity of "extermination" (see p. 539). "The political prison camp policy," wrote CSW, "appears *calculated to cause the death of a large number of persons* who form a part of the population, namely those labelled as 'enemies' who suffer on account of their genuine or alleged political beliefs or other crimes."[132]

STALIN, MAO, AND GENOCIDE

Genocide scholars increasingly accept that the tyrannies of both Joseph Stalin and Mao Zedong produced "canonical" cases of genocide. But this is a relatively recent phenomenon – in large part because both Stalin's and Mao's violence was primarily inflicted upon *political* and *class* "enemies," and these groups lie outside the bounds of the UN Genocide Convention (see Chapter 1). As with the Cambodian case discussed in Chapter 7, however, there is now a greater awareness of the extent to which "traditional" groups were targeted for genocide (notably national minorities like the Chechens and Tibetans), as well as a greater willingness among scholars to incorporate political groups and social classes into a broad genocide framing.

In evaluating the Stalinist period, the application of a genocide framework to the Ukrainian famine (1931–32) remains a controversial subject of debate. But even some of those once skeptical of the label have shifted toward it. Nicholas Werth declined to render a verdict of genocide in his long chapter on Stalinist crimes for *The Black Book of Communism* in 1999. But by 2008, his position had shifted:

> A whole panoply of repressive measures was put in place, ranging from closure of shops to police questioning of any peasants trying to flee from their starving villages. Over and above this range of repressive measures, it is clear that Stalin, *from the end of the summer of 1932*, really had decided to worsen the famine that was beginning, to turn it into a weapon, to *extend it deliberately*. . . . Recent research has shown, without any doubt, that the Ukrainian case is quite specific, at least from the second half of 1932 onwards. On the basis of these new considerations, it seems to me legitimate to classify as genocide the totality of the actions taken by the Stalin regime to punish, by means of famine and terror, the Ukrainian peasantry.[133]

Lynne Viola similarly contended that "the famine was the natural conclusion of the disasters of collectivization, dekulakization, and merciless grain levies; it was minutely observed and publicly ignored by a regime and a dictator that viewed the peasantry as less than human, as raw material to be exploited to the maximum."[134]

Scholars of such calamities who accept the validity of a genocide framework, including this one, generally argue that *culpable negligence may constitute genocidal intent*, as Martin Shaw has suggested with specific reference to the Chinese famine in 1959–62: "If leaders know that their policies may lead (or are leading) to the social and physical destruction of a group, and fail to take steps to avoid (or halt) it – as Mao Zedong, for example, knew of the effects of the Great Leap Forward but continued his policies – then they come to 'intend' the suffering they cause and may similarly be guilty [of genocide]."[135]

Both Stalin and Mao, as we have seen, also targeted ethnic minorities like the Chechens in the Soviet Union (Box 5a) and Tibetans (Box 5.2, above). But it was in the targeting of "enemy" classes and political tendencies – whether real or imagined – that these regimes truly served as twentieth-century prototypes. By means of direct execution (and, especially in the Chinese case, by deliberately driving numerous victims to suicide), these regimes killed millions of innocent people. Though their image as a "socialist vanguard" for the world's oppressed waned long ago, the Stalinist and Maoist models survive in North Korea, which, ironically, seems to serve both present-day Russia and China as a useful buffer against democratic reform from abroad (see Box 5.3).

FURTHER STUDY

Stalin and Stalinism

Note: The Stalinist period in the USSR has become a classic study of dictatorship and political terror. The following is a small sample of works in English.

Martin Amis, *Koba the Dread: Laughter and the Twenty Million*. New York: Hyperion, 2002. British novelist's uneven but evocative study of Stalin's era and personality.

Anne Applebaum, *Gulag: A History*. London: Penguin, 2003. Winner of the Pulitzer Prize; an epic single-volume history of the Soviet forced-labor camps.

Robert Conquest, *The Harvest of Sorrow: Soviet Collectivization and the Terror-Famine*. New York: Oxford University Press, 1986. Conquest has retreated from his thesis that Stalin planned the famine of the early 1930s, but his groundbreaking work well conveys the scale and horror of the human destruction wreaked by collectivization.

Robert Conquest, *The Great Terror: A Reassessment*. New York: Oxford University Press, 1990. Updated version of Conquest's seminal 1960s study.

Stéphane Courtois *et al.*, *The Black Book of Communism: Crimes, Terror, Repression*, trans. Jonathan Murphy and Mark Kramer. Cambridge, MA: Harvard University Press, 1999. Massive indictment of communist regimes; includes Nicolas Werth's penetrating study of the USSR, "A State Against Its People."

R.W. Davies and Stephen G. Wheatcroft, *The Years of Hunger: Soviet Agriculture, 1931–1933*. Basingstoke: Palgrave Macmillan, 2004. Volume in the series "The Industrialisation of Soviet Russia"; usefully consulted alongside Conquest's *Harvest of Sorrow*.

Miron Dolot, *Execution by Hunger: The Hidden Holocaust*. New York: W.W. Norton, 1985. Memoir of the Ukrainian famine.

Orlando Figes, *The Whisperers: Private Life in Stalin's Russia*. New York: Henry Holt and Company, 2007. Searing portraits of life under Stalinist terror. See also *A People's Tragedy: A History of the Russian Revolution*.

Sheila Fitzpatrick, *Everyday Stalinism: Ordinary Life in Extraordinary Times: Soviet Russia in the 1930s*. Oxford: Oxford University Press, 1999. Individual perspectives on social transformations; see also *Stalin's Peasants: Resistance and Survival in the Russian Village after Collectivization*.

Eugenia Ginzburg, *Journey into the Whirlwind*. New York: Harvest, 2002. Account of arrest and the Gulag; see also the sequel, *Within the Whirlwind*.

Adam Hochschild, *The Unquiet Ghost: Russians Remember Stalin*. New York: Viking, 1994. Taut work on history and memory.

Halyna Hryn, ed., *Hunger by Design: The Great Ukrainian Famine and Its Soviet Context*. Cambridge, MA: Harvard University Press, 2008. Slender volume capturing the "state of the art" of Holodomor research.

Nadezhda Mandelstam, *Hope Against Hope*, trans. Max Hayward. New York: The Modern Library, 1999. Powerful, poetic recollections of Stalinist terror.

Simon Sebag Montefiore, *Stalin: The Court of the Red Tsar*. London: Phoenix, 2004. Montefiore's description of life in Stalin's "court" is gossipy but galvanizing.

Robert Service, *Stalin: A Biography*. Cambridge, MA: The Belknap Press, 2005. A very serviceable biography, though brisk with the human consequences of Stalin's rule.

Varlam Shalamov, *Kolyma Tales*. London: Penguin, 1994. Documentary-style short stories about the Kolyma camps, by a former inmate.

Alexander Solzhenitsyn, *The Gulag Archipelago, 1918–1956*. New York: HarperPerennial, 2002. Abridged one-volume version of Solzhenitsyn's classic three-volume study of the camp system.

Robert W. Thurston, *Life and Terror in Stalin's Russia, 1934–1941*. New Haven, CT: Yale University Press, 1996. Fine, somewhat revisionist social history.

Lynne Viola, *The Unknown Gulag: The Lost Worlds of Stalin's Special Settlements*. Oxford: Oxford University Press, 2007. Moving, intensively researched study of the "kulak" deportations during the period of Stalinist collectivization and political purges.

Chris Ward, ed., *The Stalinist Dictatorship* (2nd edn). London: Arnold, 1998. Comprehensive survey of the roots and functioning of the Stalinist system.

Mao, Maoism, and Tibet

Jasper Becker, *Hungry Ghosts: Mao's Secret Famine*. New York: Henry Holt, 1998. Describes the catastrophe of Mao's "Great Leap Forward," with particular attention to ethnic Tibetan suffering.

Central Tibetan Administration, *Tibet Under Communist China – Fifty Years*. Available at http://www.tibet.net/en/index.php?id=187&rmenuid=11. A detailed report by the Tibetan government-in-exile; partisan but well-researched, and reflecting the government's political moderation.

Jung Chang and Jon Halliday, *Mao: The Unknown Story*. New York: Anchor Books, 2005. Borders on caricature in places, but sobering and myth-shattering on many counts.

Mary Craig, *Tears of Blood: A Cry for Tibet*. Washington, DC: Counterpoint Press, 2000. Impassioned overview of Tibet under Chinese rule.

Roderick MacFarquhar, *Mao's Last Revolution*. Cambridge, MA: The Belknap Press of Harvard University Press, 2006. The most detailed treatment in English of the Cultural Revolution of 1966–76.

Jean-Louis Margolin, "China: A Long March into Night," in Courtois *et al.*, *The Black Book of Communism* (see Stalin and Stalinism, above), pp. 463–546. Detailed evaluation of Chinese communism's record.

Tsering Shakya, *The Dragon in the Land of Snows: A History of Modern Tibet Since 1947*. New York: Penguin Compass, 2000. "The first scholarly history of Tibet under Chinese occupation" (*Time*); fair-minded throughout.

North Korea

Christian Solidarity Worldwide, "North Korea: A Case to Answer, A Call to Act," 2007 report, http://dynamic.csw.org.uk/article.asp?t=report&id=35. Human rights report on the North Korean regime, with much firsthand testimony from escapees.

Jasper Becker, *Rogue Regime: Kim Jong Il and the Looming Threat of North Korea.* Oxford: Oxford University Press, 2005. Like the author's *Hungry Ghosts*, a readable overview of a despot's catastrophic rule.

B.R. Myers, *The Cleanest Race: How North Koreans See Themselves – and Why It Matters.* Brooklyn, NY: Melville House, 2009. Intriguing study of "North Korea's dominant ideology or worldview," extensively illustrated with samples of the regime's propaganda.

NOTES

1 Richard Rubenstein, *The Age of Triage: Fear and Hope in an Overcrowded World* (Boston, MA: Beacon Press, 1983), p. 19.
2 Arno J. Mayer, *The Furies: Violence and Terror in the French and Russian Revolutions* (Princeton, NJ: Princeton University Press, 2000), p. 45.
3 Alec Nove, *Stalinism and After* (London: George Allen & Unwin, 1975), p. 23.
4 Lenin quoted in Nicolas Werth, "A State Against Its People: Violence, Repression, and Terror in the Soviet Union," in Stéphane Courtois *et al.*, *The Black Book of Communism: Crimes, Terror, Repression*, trans. Jonathan Murphy and Mark Kramer (Cambridge, MA: Harvard University Press, 1999), p. 70.
5 Werth, no friend of Leninism, argues that "the use of terror as a key instrument in the Leninist political project had been foreseen during the outbreak of the civil war, and was intended to be of limited duration" ("A State Against Its People," p. 265).
6 "At the maximum, the American Relief Administration and its associated organizations were feeding over 10,400,000 mouths, and various other organizations nearly two million more, for a total of more than 12,300,000." Robert Conquest, *The Harvest of Sorrow: Collectivization and the Terror-Famine* (New York: Oxford University Press, 1986), p. 56. This must qualify as one of the most extraordinary and successful "humanitarian interventions" in history, saving millions of lives.
7 Simon Sebag Montefiore, *Stalin: The Court of the Red Tsar* (London: Phoenix, 2004), p. 27.
8 Robert Service, *Stalin: A Biography* (Cambridge, MA: The Belknap Press, 2005), p. 174.
9 In exile, Trotsky founded the "Fourth International" of the socialist movement, and became the most outspoken opponent of Stalin's policies. A Stalinist agent tracked him down and killed him in Mexico City in 1940.
10 Anne Applebaum, *Gulag: A History* (London: Penguin, 2004), p. 62.
11 Conquest, *The Harvest of Sorrow*, p. 19.
12 Lynne Viola, *The Unknown Gulag: The Lost World of Stalin's Special Settlements* (Oxford: Oxford University Press, 2009), p. 5.
13 Lenin quoted in *ibid.*, p. 110.
14 Lenin quoted in Montefiore, *Stalin: The Court of the Red Tsar*, p. 45.
15 Viola, *The Unknown Gulag*, p. 6.
16 Service, *Stalin: A Biography*, p. 267.
17 Khataevich quoted in Applebaum, *Gulag*, p. 515.
18 Figes, *The Whisperers*, p. 87.
19 See Werth, "A State Against Its People," p. 155, with an "estimate that approximately 300,000 deportees died during the process of deportation"; Figes, *The Whisperers*, p. 88.
20 Viola, *The Unknown Gulag*, p. 114.
21 Ibid., p. 91.
22 Nicholas Werth, "The Crimes of the Stalin Regime: Outline for an Inventory and

Classification" (trans. Mike Routledge), in Dan Stone, ed., *The Historiography of Genocide* (London: Palgrave Macmillan, 2008), p. 408.

23 See, for example, the judicious assessment of Andrea Graziosi: "Between the end of 1932 and the summer of 1933 [i.e., at the height of the famine], . . . Stalin and the regime he controlled and coerced . . . consciously executed, as part of a drive directed at breaking the peasantry, an anti-Ukrainian policy aimed at mass extermination and causing a genocide . . . whose physical and psychological scars are still visible today. . . . This genocide was the product of *a famine that was not willfully caused with such aim in mind, but was willfully maneuvered towards this end once it came about as the unanticipated result of the regime policies . . .*" Graziosi, "The Soviet 1931–1933 Famines and the Ukrainian Holodomor: Is a New Interpretation Possible, and What Would Its Consequences Be?," in Halyna Hryn, ed., *Hunger by Design: The Great Ukrainian Famine and Its Soviet Context* (Cambridge, MA: Harvard University Press, 2008), p. 11; emphasis added. See also the verdict of Nicolas Werth (p. 217).

24 This was Robert Conquest's assertion (*The Harvest of Sorrow*, p. 196), but is contested by R.W. Davies and Stephen G. Wheatcroft in *The Years of Hunger: Soviet Agriculture, 1931–1933* (Basingstoke: Palgrave Macmillan, 2004), pp. 440–41. Conquest himself has now abandoned a strongly "intentionalist" position.

25 Conquest, *The Harvest of Sorrow*, p. 224.

26 Testimony quoted in ibid., p. 245.

27 The document is reproduced and translated in Hryn, ed., *Hunger by Design*, pp. 44–45.

28 The phenomenon was evident as well during the famine conditions imposed by the Nazis on Jews in the ghettoes of the occupied territories (see Chapter 6). The Warsaw Ghetto's great chronicler, Emmanuel Ringelblum, described "an evident and terrible slackening of the sentiment of compassion. Walking through the streets, one passes children as emaciated as skeletons, barefoot and naked, who put out frozen-blue hands for alms – in vain. People have grown as hard and unfeeling as stones." Ringelblum, *Notes from the Warsaw Ghetto: The Journal of Emmanuel Ringelblum*, ed. and trans. Jacob Sloan (New York: Schocken, 1974), p. 225.

29 Davies and Wheatcroft, *The Years of Hunger*, p. 415. According to Werth, about four million of the victims were Ukrainian ("A State Against Its People," p. 167).

30 Sergei Maksudov, "Victory over the Peasantry," in Hryn, ed., *Hunger by Design*, pp. 92, 94.

31 Niccolò Pianciola, "The Collectivization Famine in Kazakhstan, 1931–1933," in Hryn, ed., *Hunger by Design*, p. 103.

32 Figes, *The Whisperers*, p. 208.

33 See Applebaum, *Gulag*, ch. 4.

34 Conquest, *The Harvest of Sorrow*, pp. 127–28.

35 Leo Kuper, *Genocide: Its Political Use in the Twentieth Century* (Harmondsworth: Penguin, 1981), p. 150.

36 Ibid.

37 Robert Conquest, *Kolyma: The Arctic Death Camps* (London: Methuen, 1978), p. 229.

38 Adam Hochschild, *The Unquiet Ghost: Russians Remember Stalin* (New York: Viking, 1994), p. xxv. "I asked four . . . researchers, who between them have written or edited more than half a dozen books on the *gulag*, what was the total Kolyma death toll. One estimated it at 250,000, one at 300,000, one at 800,000, and one at 'more than 1,000,000.' . . . We will probably never know the answer" (p. 237).

39 Kuper, *Genocide*, p. 150.

40 "I have not, it must be noted, found any memoirs describing 'selections' of the sort that took place in German death camps. That is, I have not read of regular selections which ended in weak prisoners being taken aside and shot. . . . Weak prisoners were not murdered upon arrival in some of the further-flung camps, but rather given a period of 'quarantine,' both to ensure that any illnesses they were carrying would not spread, and to allow them to 'fatten up,' to recover their health after long months in prison and terrible journeys." Applebaum, *Gulag*, p. 175.

41 Montefiore, *Stalin: The Court of the Red Tsar*, p. 151. Robert Conquest calls the Kirov killing "the crime of the century" because it became "the keystone of the entire edifice of terror and suffering by which Stalin secured his grip on the Soviet peoples." Robert Conquest, *The Great Terror: A Reassessment* (New York: Oxford University Press, 1990), p. 37.

42 Werth, "A State Against Its People," pp. 190, 264.

43 Viola, *The Unknown Gulag*, pp. 163, 165. Figes wrote that "By far the biggest of [the] mass campaigns was the 'kulak operation' instituted by the infamous Directive 00447: it accounted for half of all arrests (669,929) and more than half the executions (376,202) in 1937–38. Nearly all the victims were former 'kulaks' and their families who had recently returned from 'special settlements' and Gulag labour camps . . . " "As a result of the 'national operation' against the Poles, launched by Directive 00485 in August 1937, almost 140,000 people were shot or sent to labour camps by November 1938" (*The Whisperers*, p. 241). Overall, the "kulak" death toll during the 1930s was "roughly half a million" (Viola, *The Unknown Gulag*, p. 183).

44 The strength of appeals to solidarity and party unity in extracting confessions from the "Old Bolsheviks" was memorably captured in Arthur Koestler's 1940 novel, *Darkness at Noon* (New York: Bantam, 1984).

45 Figes, *The Whisperers*, p. 238.

46 Ibid., pp. 238–39.

47 The infamous Order 00447, also known as the "Kulak Eradication Program," established "for every region . . . initial quotas for those to be executed and for those to be imprisoned for 8–10 years. The quota for the Moscow region was 5,000 people to be shot and 30,000 incarcerated; for Leningrad, 4,000 and 10,000 respectively. Ukraine's quota was set at 8,000 to be shot and 20,800 incarcerated." Ben Kiernan, *Blood and Soil: A World History of Genocide and Extermination from Sparta to Darfur* (New Haven, CT: Yale University Press, 2007), p. 508.

48 Alexander Solzhenitsyn, *The Gulag Archipelago Two* (New York: Harper & Row, 1975), p. 633.

49 Nadezhda Mandelstam, *Hope Against Hope* (New York: Modern Library, 1999), pp. 322–23, 352.

50 See, e.g., Robert W. Thurston, *Life and Terror in Stalin's Russia, 1934–1941* (New Haven, CT: Yale University Press, 1996), pp. 79–80.

51 Conquest, *The Great Terror: A Reassessment*, p. 433.

52 In part to shift blame from Stalin, the purge became known subsequently as the *Yezhovshchina*, or "The Reign of Yezhov," in Werth's translation ("A State Against Its People," p. 184).

53 Conquest, *The Great Terror: A Reassessment*, p. 438.

54 The Nazis uncovered some 4,000 of the corpses during Operation Barbarossa in 1941. The Soviet regime accused them of spreading libels, and blamed the Nazis for the crime at the Nuremberg tribunal.

55 Applebaum, *Gulag*, pp. 382–83.

56 See Jan Gross, *Neighbors: The Destruction of the Jewish Community in Jedwabne, Poland* (Princeton, NJ: Princeton University Press, 2002).

57 Janusz Bardach, *Man is Wolf to Man: Surviving the Gulag* (Berkeley, CA: University of California Press, 1999). The quoted passages in this section are drawn from pp. xiii, 11, 19, 88, 106, 114, 133–34, 192, 204, 220, 231, and 233.

58 "The exploitation of this Gulag labour force became more intense during the war. In mines and logging camps, prisoners were driven to the brink of death to increase fuel supplies, while rations were reduced to the bare minimum required to keep them alive. In 1942, the rate of mortality in the Gulag labour camps was a staggering 25 per cent – that is, one in every four Gulag workers died that year." Figes, *The Whisperers*, p. 426.

59 Applebaum, *Gulag*, pp. 378–79.

60 Ibid., p. 410.

61 See the various prisoner totals and casualty estimates cited in "Japanese Prisoners of War in the Soviet Union," Wikipedia.org, http://en.wikipedia.org/wiki/Japanese_prisoners_of_war_in_the_Soviet_Union.

62 Ibid.

63 Alexander Solzhenitsyn, *The Gulag Archipelago One* (New York: Harper & Row, 1974), p. 240.

64 An earlier precedent, important for understanding Leninist–Stalinist continuity, is the genocide against the Don and Kuban Cossacks during the civil war of 1919 to 1920. According to Eric Weitz, "'Cossack' came to mean anti-Soviet, a synonym for 'enemy' that carried an implicit racialization of a group defined not even by ethnicity but by its special service relationship to the czarist state." The death-toll was 300,000 to 500,000 out of a population of three million. Eric D. Weitz, *A Century of Genocide: Utopias of Race and Nation* (Princeton, NJ: Princeton University Press, 2003), p. 69; see also Werth, "A State Against Its People," pp. 98–102.

65 Alexander Statiev, "Soviet Ethnic Deportations: Intent versus Outcome," *Journal of Genocide Research*, 11: 2–3 (2009), pp. 243–44.

66 Ibid., p. 244.

67 Ibid., p. 246. Statiev, however, bound by a highly restrictive definition of (specific) "intent," contends that the fact that the deportations did not constitute planned exterminations means that they do not constitute "a clear-cut case of genocide and any further discussion on whether the government committed genocide would be not only ideologically loaded but also sterile" (p. 260). I believe this gives short shrift to more flexible and encompassing understandings of genocidal intent. It also overlooks the legal definition of "extermination" as a crime against humanity, and its overlap with Article 2(c) of the Genocide Convention: that is, the infliction of conditions of life which it is known, or should be known, will cause the destruction of the designated groups in whole or in part. See further discussion on pp. 13 and 539.

68 Finnish speakers in the Karelia region of northwest Russia also suffered after the Finns, seeking to regain territories lost to Stalin in the winter war of 1939–40, joined the Nazi thrust into the Soviet Union.

69 On the Crimean Tatars, see Brian Glyn Williams, "Hidden Ethnocide in the Soviet Muslim Borderlands: The Ethnic Cleansing of the Crimean Tatars," *Journal of Genocide Research*, 4: 3 (2002), pp. 357–73.

70 Lyman H. Legters, "Soviet Deportation of Whole Nations: A Genocidal Process," ch. 4 in Samuel Totten *et al.*, *Century of Genocide: Eyewitness Accounts and Critical Views* (New York: Garland Publishing, 1997), pp. 112–35. See also Robert Conquest, *The Nation Killers: The Soviet Deportation of Nationalities* (London: Macmillan, 1970); Aleksander M. Nekrich, *The Punished Peoples: The Deportation and Tragic Fate of Soviet Minorities at the End of the Second World War*, trans. George Saunders (New York: Norton, 1978); and J. Otto Pohl, "Stalin's Genocide against the 'Repressed Peoples,'" *Journal of Genocide Research*, 2: 2 (June 2000), pp. 267–93.

71 Applebaum, *Gulag*, p. 388.

72 Ibid. According to Nicolas Werth, "Of the 608,749 people deported from the Caucasus, 146,892, or nearly 1 in 4, had died by 1 October 1948. . . . Of the 228,392 people deported from the Crimea, 44,887 had died after four years." Werth, "A State Against Its People," p. 223.

73 After Stalin's death, the remnants of some deported nationalities were allowed to return to their former territories, but the extinguished political units were not always revived.

74 Service, *Stalin: A Biography*, p. 592.

75 R.J. Rummel, *Death by Government* (New Brunswick, NJ: Transaction Publishers, 1994), p. 101.

76 Peng Pai quoted in Kiernan, *Blood and Soil*, p. 519.

77 Kiernan, *Blood and Soil*, p. 521.

78 Jung Chang and Jon Halliday, *Mao: The Unknown Story* (New York: Anchor Books, 2006), p. 309.

79 Mao quoted in Sudeep Chakravarti, *Red Sun: Travels in Naxalite Country* (New Delhi: Viking, 2008), p. 169.

80 Chang and Halliday, *Mao*, p. 311.

81 Benjamin Valentino, *Final Solutions: Mass Killing and Genocide in the 20th Century* (Ithaca, NY: Cornell University Press, 2004), p. 121.

82 Jean-Louis Margolin, "Mao's China: The Worst Non-Genocidal Regime?," in Dan Stone, ed., *The Historiography of Genocide* (London: Palgrave Macmillan, 2008), p. 453.

83 Kiernan, *Blood and Soil*, p. 529.

84 Margolin, "Mao's China," p. 453.

85 Chang and Halliday, *Mao*, p. 319.

86 Ibid.

87 Central Tibetan Administration (hereafter, CTA), *Tibet under Communist China – Fifty Years* (2001), http://www.tibet.net/en/index.php?id=187&rmenuid=11, p. 54.

88 The distinction between "Outer Tibet" and "Inner Tibet" was first made in the 1913–1914 Simla Conference and Convention, in which Tibet, China, and Britain participated. "Chinese suzerainty over the whole of Tibet was recognized but China engaged not to convert Tibet into a Chinese province. The autonomy of Outer Tibet was recognised and China agreed to abstain from interference in its internal administration which was to rest with Tibetans themselves. In Inner Tibet the central Tibetan Government at Lhasa was to retain its existing rights." George N. Patterson, "China and Tibet: Background to the Revolt," *The China Quarterly*, 1 (January–March 1960), p. 90.

89 Tsering Shakya, *The Dragon in the Land of Snows: A History of Modern Tibet since 1947* (New York: Penguin Compass, 2000), p. xxx.

90 Ibid., p. xxviii.

91 CTA, *Tibet under Communist China*, p. 130.

92 Eric S. Margolis, *War at the Top of the World: The Struggle for Afghanistan, Kashmir, and Tibet* (New York: Routledge, 2001), p. 195.

93 See the full text of the "Agreement of the Central People's Government and the Local Government of Tibet on Measures for the Peaceful Liberation of Tibet" at http://www.china-un.org/eng/gyzg/xizang/t424244.htm.

94 See Frank Morales, *The Revolt in Tibet* (New York: Macmillan, 1960).

95 CTA, *Tibet under Communist China*, p. 9.

96 Shakya refers to "areas where all able young men had been arrested and imprisoned, leaving the villages inhabited only by old people and women." *The Dragon in the Land of Snows*, p. 271.

97 Jean-Louis Margolin, "China: A Long March into Night," in Stéphane Courtois *et al.*, eds, *The Black Book of Communism: Crimes, Terror, Repression* (Cambridge, MA: Harvard University Press, 1999), p. 545.

98 "The Cultural Revolution and Its Legacy in Tibet," available at: cu/ccba/cear/issues/spring98/text-only/hennsidebar2.htm.

99 For an overview of this period, see Solomon M. Karmel, "Ethnic Tension and the Struggle for Order: China's Policies in Tibet," *Pacific Affairs*, 68 (Winter 1995–96), pp. 485–505.

100 See Anita Chang, "Group [the International Campaign for Tibet] Says Railway Threatens Tibet," Associated Press dispatch on Yahoo! News, February 27, 2008.

101 Tim Johnson, "China Orders Resettlement of Thousands of Tibetans," Realcities.com, May 6, 2007.

102 Shakya, *The Dragon in the Land of Snows*, p.430.

103 Tristan Stewart-Robertson, "80 People Dead in 'Cultural Genocide,'" *The Scotsman*, 17 March 2008. See also Isabel Hilton, "The World Is No Longer Looking – But Tibet's Plight Isn't Over," *The Independent*, March 10, 2009.

104 "China 'Annihilating Tibetan Buddhism,'" Associated Press dispatch in *The Sydney Morning Herald*, March 11, 2010, http://www.smh.com.au/world/china-annihilating-tibetan-buddhism-20100311-pzj2.html.

105 Margolin, "China," p.546.

106 Quoted in Shakya, *The Dragon in the Land of Snows*, p. 223; see the "ICJ Report on Tibet 1960."

107 Maura Moynihan, "Genocide in Tibet," *The Washington Post*, January 25, 1998. Tibetan nationalists have often alleged that China is guilty of another strategy of genocide under the terms of the UN Convention: preventing Tibetan births through forcible sterilization of Tibetan women. However, the evidence does not support this. See Melvyn C. Goldstein and Cynthia M. Beall, "China's Birth Control Policy in the Tibet Autonomous Region: Myths and Realities," *Asian Survey*, 31: 3 (March 1991), pp. 285–303.

108 See "The Five Point Peace Plan for Tibet, by His Holiness the Dalai Lama, Washington, DC, 21 September 1987," http:// www.freetibet.org/info/file/file3.html. The proposals were "further clarified" but "also developed . . . further" in the Dalai Lama's speech to European Parliament representatives in June 1988; for details, see Shakya, *The Dragon in the Land of Snows*, p. 423.

109 For an account of strategic rethinking now underway in the Tibetan exile community, see "Tibetans Meet to Rethink Autonomy," AlJazeera.net, November 17, 2008.

110 Chang and Halliday, *Mao*, p. 431.

111 Margolin, "Mao's China," p. 446.

112 Chang and Halliday, *Mao*, pp. 418–19.

113 Margolin, "China," p. 495.

114 Shakya, *The Dragon in the Land of Snows*, p. 262.

115 Chang and Halliday, *Mao*, p. 443.

116 Ibid. In 1958–59, according to Chang and Halliday, "Grain exports alone, almost exactly 7 million tons, would have provided the equivalent of over 840 calories per day for 38 million people – the difference between life and death. And this was only grain; it does not include the meat, cooking oil, eggs and other foodstuffs that were exported in very large quantities. Had this food not been exported (and instead distributed according to humane criteria), very probably not a single person in China would have had to die of hunger" (*Mao*, p. 430).

117 Margolin, "Mao's China," p. 459.

118 Lee quoted in Margolin, "China," p. 495.

119 Roderick MacFarquhar and Michael Schoenhals, *Mao's Last Revolution* (Cambridge, MA: The Belknap Press of Harvard University Press, 2006), p. 258.

120 Chang and Halliday, *Mao*, p. 536.

121 Walder quoted in MacFarquhar and Schoenhals, *Mao's Last Revolution*, p. 256.

122 Jonathan Watts, "China Must Confront Dark Past, Says Mao Confidant," *The Guardian*, June 2, 2005, http://www.guardian.co.uk/world/2005/jun/02/china.jonathanwatts. See also Andrew Jacobs, "China Is Wordless on Traumas of Communists' Rise," *The New York Times*, October 1, 2009 (60th anniversary of the victory of the communist revolution), http://www.nytimes.com/2009/10/02/world/asia/02anniversary.html.

123 See, e.g., Jonathan Watts, "Mao Casts Long Shadow Over China," *The Guardian*, May 16, 2006, http://www.guardian.co.uk/world/2006/may/16/china.jonathanwatts.

124 Robin Munro, "Remembering Tiananmen Square: Who Died in Beijing, and Why," *The Nation*, June 11, 1990, http://www.thenation.com/doc/19900611/munro.

125 This box text includes and adapts passages from Adam Jones, *Crimes Against Humanity: A Beginner's Guide* (Oxford: Oneworld, 2008), pp. 81–84.

126 B.R. Myers, *The Cleanest Race: How North Koreans See Themselves – and Why It Matters* (Brooklyn, NY: Melville House, 2010).

127 One of the more poignant images of the modern era is the nighttime contrast between the northern and southern states of the Korean peninsula, the latter lit up like a casino,

the former almost invisible. See, e.g., "Korea's Dark Half," Strange Maps, http://strangemaps.wordpress.com/2007/12/16/218-koreas-dark-half/.

128 Myers, *The Cleanest Race*, p. 15.

129 Andrew Natsios, "The Politics of Famine in North Korea," United States Institute of Peace report, 2 August 1999. http://www.usip.org/files/resources/sr990802.pdf

130 Jasper Becker, *Rogue Regime: Kim Jong Il and the Looming Threat of North Korea* (New York: Oxford University Press, 2006), pp. 32–33, 266.

131 Ibid., p. 36.

132 Christian Solidarity Worldwide, *North Korea: A Case to Answer, a Call to Act* (New Malden: Christian Solidarity Worldwide, 2007), p. 43. Emphasis added. The report can be downloaded in PDF format at http://dynamic.csw.org.uk/article.asp?t=report&id=35. See also Blaine Harden, "Escapee Tells of Horrors in North Korean Prison Camp," *The Washington Post*, December 11, 2008.

133 Werth, "The Crimes of the Stalin Regime," p. 415. Emphasis in original.

134 Viola, *The Unknown Gulag*, p. 133.

135 Martin Shaw, *What is Genocide?* (Cambridge: Polity, 2007), p. 85.

BOX 5A CHECHNYA

As discussed in Chapter 5, the people of Chechnya were among a number of nationalities accused of complicity with the Nazis during the Second World War, rounded up, and deported under murderous conditions to distant and barren lands. At least 390,000 Chechens – perhaps many more – were uprooted in this way. Fully a quarter of them died *en route* to their exile, and survivors faced a constant struggle against the elements and poor soils.[1] After Stalin's death, most of these populations were returned to their homelands. Yet bitter memories lingered, and they explain something of the extraordinary persistence of Chechen rebel forces in their war for independence.[2]

One must dig deeper for the roots of Chechen nationalism and its conflict with "Greater Russia." Chechens were at the forefront of efforts to resist Russian expansion during the mid-nineteenth century. For three decades after 1829, the expansionist tsarist state waged "almost unremitting warfare" in the Caucasus, with "hundreds upon hundreds of villages . . . razed, accompanied by terrorist reprisal and atrocity directed against their inhabitants."[3] When the North Caucasus was finally overwhelmed and incorporated into the empire, some 600,000 Caucasians – 100,000 of them Chechens – "were sent to the Ottoman Empire, where tens of thousands perished from starvation and disease."[4]

The Chechens rallied after the Bolshevik Revolution of 1917, but their aspirations for independence were doomed by renewed Russian (now Soviet) expansionism. The Bolsheviks occupied Chechnya, and in 1924 established the Chechen-Ingush Autonomous Region which Stalin would cancel in the 1940s.

The liberalizing wave that struck the Soviet Union and Eastern Europe in the late 1980s resulted in the breakup of the Soviet empire; but Chechnya was a federal unit of Russia, not a Soviet union republic. When Russian president

Boris Yeltsin took over from Soviet president Mikhail Gorbachev, he decided that no secession from Russia itself would be permitted. In the Chechen case, there were material considerations: a major oil pipeline ran through Chechnya, which was home to substantial petroleum resources of its own. Whoever controlled them was guaranteed a strategic presence in the region as a whole.

Russian policy reflected an ingrained racism towards Chechens. Chechnya had long been an "obsession" for the Russians, wrote journalist David Remnick: "an image of Islamic defiance, an embodiment of the primitive, the devious, the elusive." Chechens were seen as bumpkins and "black asses." "Yeltsin knew well that for many Russians the Chechens were nothing more than a tribe of 'thieving niggers.'"[5] The conflict can also be viewed in light of the Russian humiliation in the war against Afghanistan (1979–90; see Chapter 2). As Gregory Feifer noted in his 2009 history of that war, "the Kremlin calls the [Chechen] rebels 'bandits' and 'terrorists' – echoing the same words the Soviet Union used to describe the Afghan mujahideen [Islamic warriors] – and claims the conflict in Chechnya was part of the global war against terrorism."[6]

In 1991, the mercurial Chechen leader, Dzhokar Dudayev – previously a general in the Soviet air force – rebelled against Moscow and declared Chechnya independent. Under his rule, "Chechnya became an epicenter of financial scams

Map 5A.1   Chechnya

Source: Map provided by WorldAtlas.com.

and illegal trade in oil and contraband, and a safe haven for criminals from all over Russia," while violence against ethnic Russians in the territory rose alarmingly.[7]

The bombastic, alcoholic Yeltsin countered by seeking to undermine the Chechen regime from within.[8] When a Russian-led assault on Grozny, using Chechen forces opposed to Dudayev, ended in a shambles, the Russians reacted with fury. In December 1994, 40,000 Russian troops – mostly ill-trained conscripts – were sent into Chechnya. Yeltsin apparently believed the declaration of his defense minister, Pavel Grachev, that the territory could be conquered "in two hours by a single paratrooper regiment."[9] Two years later, Russian forces were still there.

The first assault on Grozny was disastrous. Russian tank columns and troop formations were torn apart by hit-and-run rebel attacks. The Russians responded with "the heaviest artillery bombardment that anyone had seen since the Second World War."[10] "Indiscriminate strikes became the preferred mode of warfare against a ground war the Russian armed forces were unfit to win."[11] Numerous towns and villages were pulverized. Tens of thousands of Chechen residents were killed, overwhelmingly civilians. In a grim irony, many of the victims were ethnic Russians who lacked the contacts in the countryside that allowed many Chechen Muslims to find refuge. When the Russians finally claimed control of Grozny in March, visiting journalists marveled at "the sheer scale of the destruction," with the city "not only in ruins but . . . destroyed [to] its very foundations." Even years later, the heart of the city remained "a desert scene of rubble and burnt-out buildings."[12]

To the extent that Russians discriminated in their killing, the strategy was predominantly gendercidal (see Chapter 13). "I killed a lot," a Russian soldier returned from Chechnya told Maura Reynolds of the *Los Angeles Times*:

> I wouldn't touch women or children, as long as they didn't fire at me. But I would kill all the men I met during mopping-up operations. I didn't feel sorry for them one bit. They deserved it. I wouldn't even listen to the pleas or see the tears of their women when they asked me to spare their men. I simply took them aside and killed them.[13]

In keeping with such strategies, mass round-ups and detentions of Chechen men were staged, with detainees passed through "filtration camps" run by the Russian military and FSB (formerly the KGB). Torture was frequent in the camps, and "disappearances" rampant.

All of this occurred in Europe; yet few Europeans, or others, raised their voices in protest. Russia, even in its post-Soviet incarnation, is a great power, and a nuclear one. European governments have been more interested in courting it and exploiting its immense resources than in criticizing "internal" practices, even genocidal ones. The response of the Clinton and Bush administrations was likewise "woefully late and pitifully restrained."[14]

Figure 5A.1   February 2000: Russian troops view a mass grave filled with executed Chechens, one of many that dotted the landscape during the brutal Chechen wars.

Source: Natalia Medvedeva/Wikimedia Commons.

Destructive as the war was, it was just the first round. In 1996, remarkably, rebel forces reoccupied Grozny, holding it for weeks against a sustained and again indiscriminate Russian counter-attack. For the Russian public, this was the final straw. Public opposition to the slaughter (albeit mainly to the deaths of Russian conscripts) drove Yeltsin's approval ratings to dismally low levels. The Russian media enjoyed their most brilliant moment since 1917, with press reports and TV investigations carefully documenting the Chechen chaos. Finally, Russian forces pulled out in defeat, leaving the territory still nominally part of Russia, but effectively in the hands of Chechen rebels and warlords.

With the economy and infrastructure virtually destroyed, Chechnya again lapsed into lawlessness. In September 1999, Yeltsin, now a lame duck, sent the troops back in. His policy was energetically continued and expanded by Vladimir Putin, who pungently pledged to "corner the bandits in the shithouse and wipe them out."[15] Putin calculated that a hard line on Chechnya would help him consolidate his power and appeal to voters in future elections.[16]

Under Putin, the Russian tactics of the previous conflict were revived, from indiscriminate bombardment to filtration camps. Again adult men were special targets. Human Rights Watch stated that "every adult Chechen male" was treated "as if he were a rebel fighter."[17] Chechen women were also assaulted and raped on an increasing scale.[18]

Once again, Russian forces became mired in an intractable guerrilla war. As the quagmire deepened, Putin sought to indigenize the war. "Chechenization" became the new buzzword, and achieved some success from the Russian perspective. As this book went to press, a measure of coerced stability prevailed under a young, carefully groomed former rebel, Ramzan Kadyrov, whose strategy was to "get down and dirty, fighting – and winning – Chechen style":

> Those methods have been simple, violent and effective. At their core is the so-called Kadyrovtsy, a private irregular army of close to 10,000 former rebels who wear US military fatigues and black T shirts with a portrait of their leader Ramzan. Their violence is less indiscriminate than the Russians' – instead of emptying whole quarters of villages in search of guerrillas, for instance, Kadyrov's men target single households – but more extreme. Tactics commonly include kidnapping family members as a way of persuading outlaws to give themselves up, according to the human rights group Memorial.[19]

The tactics also appear to include targeted killing of young men, also a long-established aspect of the "Chechen style." A defector, Umar Israilov – subsequently murdered – "described many brutal acts by Mr. Kadyrov and his subordinates, including executions of illegally detained men" and the sodomizing "by a prominent police officer" of "another prisoner," who was then "at Mr. Kadyrov's order put to death."[20] Freedom House in 2009 selected Kadyrov's regime as one of the most repressive in the world – one of only two substate territories, along with Tibet, so designated.[21]

As for the rebels, their own actions, within Chechnya and beyond, grew more indiscriminately violent and terroristic. In 2004 alone, hundreds of schoolchildren died in the town of Beslan in neighboring Ingushetia, when Russian forces stormed a school seized by rebels. Two civilian passenger planes downed by female Chechen rebels – the so-called "Black Widows"[22] – added to the casualty count. The toll among Chechen civilians, though, was much greater – probably approaching 100,000 as of early 2005, though killings have been selective since then. Evaluating Russia's overall record, Chechnya specialist Matthew Evangelista considered it "plausible" that Russia had "violated the Genocide Convention for 'acts committed with intent to destroy, in whole or in part, a national, ethnical, racial, or religious group.'"[23] In 2001, the US Holocaust Memorial Museum's Committee on Conscience "placed Chechnya on its Genocide Alert list, which had been created to sound warnings of potential genocides"; it remained there as of early 2010.[24]

If Russian repression has remained a constant theme, so has the "mixture of eager complicity and mute acquiescence" that the outside world has displayed.[25] After September 11, 2001, Putin's regime positioned itself as an ally in the "war on terror" and a partner in the new globalized economy. This provided camouflage and justification for Russia's campaign against Chechen Muslims, as it does under Putin's successor, Dimitry Medvedev. As Lindsey Hilsum has written, "Chechnya is a shameful example of western leaders refusing to confront another government on human rights abuses and war crimes because, in the end, strategic and political issues matter more. Chechnya is complex and dangerous and miserable, and we just don't care enough to try to make a difference."[26]

FURTHER STUDY

Arkady Babchenko, *One Soldier's War*. New York: Grove Press, 2008. Grim memoir by a Russian soldier who fought in both Chechen wars.

Matthew Evangelista, *The Chechen Wars: Will Russia Go the Way of the Soviet Union?* Washington, DC: Brookings Institution Press, 2002. Astute political analysis, with a chapter on "War Crimes and Russia's International Standing."

Carlotta Gall and Thomas de Waal, *Chechnya: Calamity in the Caucasus*. New York: New York University Press, 1998. Journalistic account of the first Chechen war.

Emma Gilligan, *Terror in Chechnya: Russia and the Tragedy of Civilians in War*. Princeton, NJ: Princeton University Press, 2010. The best study of the human rights dimension of the second Chechen war and its aftermath.

Human Rights Watch, *Swept Under: Torture, Forced Disappearances, and Extrajudicial Killings during Sweep Operations in Chechnya*. February 2002. Available at http://www.hrw.org/en/reports/2002/02/02/swept-under. HRW report on atrocities in the renewed war against Chechens.

Anna Politkovskaya, *A Small Corner of Hell: Dispatches from Chechnya*. Chicago, IL: University of Chicago Press, 2003. Account by a Russian investigative journalist, assassinated in 2006. See also *A Dirty War: A Russian Reporter in Chechnya*.

NOTES

1 On the struggle to survive after deportation, see Michela Pohl, "'It Cannot Be That Our Graves Will Be Here': The Survival of Chechen and Ingush Deportees in Kazakhstan, 1944–1957," *Journal of Genocide Research*, 4: 3 (2002), pp. 401–30.

2 See Birgit Brauer, "Chechens and the Survival of Their Cultural Identity in Exile," *Journal of Genocide Research*, 4: 3 (2002), pp. 387–400.

3 Mark Levene, *Genocide in the Age of the Nation State, Vol. 2: The Rise of the West and the Coming of Genocide* (London: I.B. Tauris, 2005), p. 299.

4 Tony Wood, "The Case for Chechnya," *New Left Review*, 30 (November–December 2004), p. 10.

5 David Remnick, *Resurrection: The Struggle for a New Russia* (New York: Vintage, 1998), pp. 266, 271. Likewise, during the second Chechen war, "Chechens were dehumanized with racially bigoted language that depicted the enemy as 'blacks' (*chernye*), 'bandits' (*banditi*), 'terrorists' (*terroristi*), 'cockroaches' (*tarakany*), and 'bedbugs' (*klopi*)" – all terms familiar to a student of genocidal propaganda. Emma Gilligan, *Terror in Chechnya: Russia and the Tragedy of Civilians in War* (Princeton, NJ: Princeton University Press, 2010), p. 6.

6 Gregory Feifer, *The Great Gamble: The Soviet War in Afghanistan* (New York: HarperPerennial, 2009), p. 276.

7 Nabi Abdullaev, "Chechnya Ten Years Later," *Current History* (October 2004), p. 332.

8 President Dudayev was assassinated by a Russian missile in April 1996; his successor, Aslan Maskhadov, was killed in March 2005.

9 Grachev quoted in Remnick, *Resurrection*, p. 278.

10 Carlotta Gall and Thomas de Waal, *Chechnya: Calamity in the Caucasus* (New York: New York University Press, 1998), p. 219.

11 Gilligan, *Terror in Chechnya*, p. 26.

12 Ibid., p. 227.

13 Maura Reynolds, "War Has No Rules for Russian Forces Battling Chechen Rebels," *The Los Angeles Times*, September 17, 2000.

14 Gilligan, *Terror in Chechnya*, p. 26.

15 Remnick, *Resurrection*, p. 284.

16 See the trenchant analysis of Putin's policies, and their underlying motivations, in Wood, "The Case for Chechnya," pp. 27–31.

17 Human Rights Watch cited in Geoffrey York, "Russians Accused of Executing Chechens," *The Globe and Mail*, February 14, 2000.

18 See "Serious Violations of Women's Human Rights in Chechnya," Human Rights Watch backgrounder, January 2002, http://www.hrw.org/en/news/2002/01/09/russian-federation-serious-violations-womens-human-rights-chechnya.

19 Owen Mathews and Anna Nemtsova, "Ramzan's World," *Newsweek*, September 25, 2006, http://www.newsweek.com/id/45665. See also Valery Dzutsev, "Moscow Sees Chechnya's Kadyrov as a Silver Bullet for the North Caucasus," Jamestown.org, May 22, 2009. For a further flavor of Kadyrov's tactics, see the Human Rights Watch report, "'What Your Children Do Will Touch Upon You': Punitive House-Burning in Chechnya," July 2, 2009, http://www.hrw.org/en/reports/2009/07/02/what-your-children-do-will-touch-upon-you.

20 C.J. Chivers, "Slain Exile Detailed Chechen Ruler's Systematic Cruelty," *The New York Times*, January 31, 2009, http://www.nytimes.com/2009/02/01/world/europe/01torture.html.

21 Freedom House, "Freedom in the World 2009: Freedom Retreats for Third Year" (press release), January 12, 2009.

22 See Chris Stephen, "The Black Widows of Chechnya," *The Scotsman*, September 17, 2004, http://news.scotsman.com/chechnya/The-Black-Widows-of-Chechnya.2564759.jp.

23 Matthew Evangelista, *The Chechen Wars: Will Russia Go the Way of the Soviet Union?* (Washington, DC: Brookings Institution Press, 2002), p. 142; see also p. 177. Emma Gilligan echoes the judgment, writing: "If we look at the conflict in Chechnya from the vantage point of the 1948 UN Convention on the Prevention and Punishment of the Crime of Genocide, the acts committed by the Russian armed forces might well be framed under article 2 of the convention." Gilligan, *Terror in Chechnya*, p. 9.

24 Gilligan, *Terror in Chechnya*, p. 1; see also United States Holocaust Memorial Museum, "Who Is at Risk? Chechnya, Russia," http://www.ushmm.org/genocide/take_action/atrisk/region/chechnya-russia/. As justification for the alert, the USHMM cited the "past persecution of Chechens as a people," "the demonization of Chechens as a group within Russian society," and "the level of violence directed against Chechen civilians by Russian forces."

25 Wood, "The Case for Chechnya," p. 36.

26 Lindsey Hilsum, "The Conflict the West Always Ignores," *New Statesman*, January 26, 2004.

CHAPTER 6

The Jewish Holocaust

INTRODUCTION

The genocide of European Jews – which many scholars and others call simply "the Holocaust"[1] – "is perhaps the one genocide of which every educated person has heard."[2] Between 1941 and 1945, five to six million Jews were systematically murdered by the Nazi regime, its allies, and its surrogates in the Nazi-occupied territories.[3] Yet despite the extraordinary scale and intensity of the genocide, its prominence in recent decades was far from preordained. The Second World War killed upwards of fifty million people in all, and attitudes following the Nazi defeat tended to mirror those during the war, when Western leaders and publics generally refused to ascribe special urgency to the Jewish catastrophe. Only with the Israeli capture of Adolf Eichmann, the epitome of the "banality of evil" in Hannah Arendt's famous phrase, and his trial in Jerusalem in 1961, did the Jewish *Shoah* (catastrophe) begin to entrench itself as the paradigmatic genocide of human history. Even today, in the evaluation of genocide scholar Yehuda Bauer, "the impact of the Holocaust is growing, not diminishing."[4]

This impact is expressed in the diverse debates about the Holocaust. Among the questions asked are: How could the systematic murder of millions of helpless individuals have sprung from one of the most developed and "civilized" of Western states? What are the links to European anti-semitism? How central a figure was Adolf Hitler in the genesis and unfolding of the slaughter? What part did "ordinary men" and "ordinary Germans" play in the extermination campaign? How extensive was Jewish resistance? What was the role of the Allies (notably Britain, France, the USSR, and the United States), both before and during the Second World War, in abandoning

Jews to destruction at Nazi hands? And what is the relationship between the Jewish Holocaust and the postwar state of Israel? This chapter addresses these issues in its later sections, while also alighting on the debate over the alleged "uniqueness" of the *Shoah*.

ORIGINS

Until the later nineteenth century, Jews were uniquely stigmatized within the European social hierarchy, often through stereotypical motifs that endure, in places, to the present.[5] Medieval Christianity "held the Jews to violate the moral order of the world. By rejecting Jesus, by allegedly having killed him, the Jews stood in defiant opposition to the otherwise universally accepted conception of God and Man, denigrating and defiling, by their very existence, all that is sacred. As such, Jews came to represent symbolically and discursively much of the evil in the world."[6] Jews – especially male Jews – were reviled as "uprooted, troublesome, malevolent, shiftless" (see pp. 488–90).[7]

The Catholic Church, and later the Protestant offshoot founded by the virulently anti-semitic Martin Luther, assailed Jews as "thirsty bloodhounds and murderers of all Christendom."[8] The most primitive and powerful myth was the so-called "blood

Figure 6.1   Jews were scapegoated and persecuted by many Christian regimes and populations in Europe. A medieval manuscript depicts a mass burning of Jews in 1349 as "punishment" for supposedly colluding with demonic forces to bring the Black Death (bubonic plague) to European shores.

Source: H.H. Ben-Sasson, ed., *A History of the Jewish People*/Wikimedia Commons.

Figure 6.2   The Nazis revived and vigorously inculcated anti-semitic stereotypes. This front page of the propaganda newspaper *Der Stürmer* (*The Attacker*) depicts innocent Aryan womanhood being ritually murdered (*Ritualmord*) and drained of blood by the demonic Jewish male.

Source: St. Brendan School Network.

libel": the claim that Jews seized and murdered Gentile children in order to use their blood in the baking of ceremonial bread for the Passover celebration.[9] Fueled by this and other fantasies, anti-Jewish *pogroms* – localized campaigns of violence, killing, and repression – scarred European Jewish history. At various points, Jews who refused to convert to Christianity were also rounded up and expelled, most notoriously from Spain and Portugal in 1492.[10]

The rise of modernity and the nation-state recast traditional anti-semitism in new and contradictory guises. (The term "anti-semitism" is a product of this era, coined by the German Wilhelm Marr in 1879.) On one hand, Jews were viewed as *enemies* of modernity. Cloistered in the cultural isolation of ghetto (to which previous generations had consigned them), they could never be truly part of the nation-state, which was rapidly emerging as the fulcrum of modern identity.[11] On the other hand, for sectors suspicious of or threatened by change, Jews were seen as dangerous *agents* of modernity: as key players in oppressive economic institutions; as urban, cosmopolitan elements who threatened the unity and identity of the *Volk* (people).

It would be misleading, however, to present European history as one long campaign of discrimination and repression against Jews. For several centuries Jews in Eastern Europe "enjoyed a period of comparative peace, tranquility and the flowering of Jewish religious life."[12] They were even more prominent, and valued, in Muslim Spain. Moreover, ideologies of nationalism sometimes followed the liberal "melting-pot" motif exemplified by the United States. Those Jews who sought integration with their societies could be accepted. The late nineteenth and early twentieth centuries are seen as something of a golden age for Jews in France, Britain, and Germany, even while some two-and-a-half million Jews were fleeing pogroms in tsarist Russia.

Germany was widely viewed as one of the more tolerant European societies; Prussia, the first German state to grant citizenship to its Jews, did so as early as 1812. How, then, could Germany turn first to persecuting, then to slaughtering, nearly two-thirds of the Jews of Europe? Part of the answer lies in the fact that, although German society was in many ways tolerant and progressive, German politics was never liberal or democratic, in the manner of both Britain and France.[13] Moreover, German society was deeply destabilized by defeat in the First World War, and by the imposition of a humiliating peace settlement at Versailles in 1919. Germany was forced to shoulder full blame for the outbreak of the "Great War." It lost its overseas colonies, along with some of its European territories; its armed forces were reduced to a fraction of their former size; and onerous reparations were demanded. "A tidal wave of shame and resentment, experienced even by younger men who had not seen military service, swept the nation," wrote Richard Plant. "Many people tried to digest the bitter defeat by searching furiously for scapegoats."[14] These dark currents ran beneath the political order, the Weimar Republic, established after the war. Democratic but fragile, it presided over economic chaos – first, the hyperinflation of 1923, which saw the German mark slip to 4.2 trillion to the dollar, and then the widespread unemployment of the Great Depression, beginning in 1929.

The result was political extremism. Its prime architect and beneficiary was the NSDAP (the National Socialist or "Nazi" party), founded by Adolf Hitler and sundry alienated colleagues. Hitler, a decorated First World War veteran and failed artist from Vienna, assumed the task of resurrecting Germany and imposing its hegemony on all Europe. This vision would lead to the deaths of tens of millions of people. But it was underpinned in Hitler's mind by an epic hatred of Jews – "these black parasites of the nation," as he called them in *Mein Kampf* (My Struggle), the tirade he penned while in prison following an abortive coup attempt in 1923.[15]

As the failed *putsch* indicated, Hitler's path to power was far from direct. By 1932, he seemed to many to have passed his peak. The Nazis won only a minority of parliamentary seats in that year's elections; more Germans voted for parties of the Left than of the Right. But divisions between the Socialists and Communists made the Nazis the largest single party in the Reichstag, and allowed Hitler to become Chancellor in January 1933.

Once installed in power, the Nazis proved unstoppable. Within three months, they had seized "total control of [the] German state, abolishing its federalist structure, dismantling democratic government and outlawing political parties and trade unions." The Enabling Act of March 23, 1933 gave Hitler "*carte blanche* to terrorize and neutralize all effective political opposition."[16] Immediately thereafter, the Nazis' persecutory stance towards Jews became plain. Within a few months, Jews saw their businesses placed under Nazi boycott; their mass dismissal from hospitals, the schools, and the civil service; and public book-burnings of Jewish and other "degenerate" works. The Nuremberg Laws of 1935 stripped Jews of citizenship and gave legal shape to the Nazis' race-based theories: intermarriage or sexual intercourse between non-Jews and Jews was prohibited.

With the Nuremberg edicts, and the threat of worse measures looming, increasing numbers of Jews fled abroad. The abandonment of homes and capital in Germany meant penury abroad – the Nazis would allow only a fraction of one's wealth to be exported. The unwillingness of the outside world to accept Jewish refugees meant that many more Jews longed to leave than actually could. Hundreds of those who remained committed suicide as Nazi rule imposed upon them a "social death."[17]

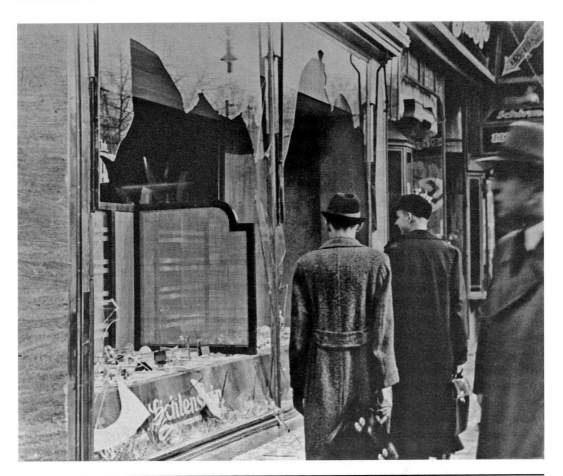

Figure 6.3 "Germans pass by the broken shop window of a Jewish-owned business that was destroyed during Kristallnacht," Berlin, November 10, 1938. While many Germans strongly supported the Nazis' anti-semitic policies, many also bridled at the violence of the "Night of Broken Glass," and the "un-German" disorder it typified. The Nazis monitored public opinion carefully, and such sentiments prompted them, when the time came to impose a "final solution of the Jewish problem," to "outsource" the mass extermination process to the occupied territories in Poland and the USSR.

Source: United States Holocaust Memorial Museum/National Archives and Records Administration.

The persecution mounted further with the *Kristallnacht* (Night of Broken Glass) on November 9–10, 1938, "a proto-genocidal assault"[18] that targeted Jewish properties, residences, and persons. Several dozen Jews were killed outright, billions of deutschmarks in damage was inflicted, and some 30,000 male Jews were rounded up and imprisoned in concentration camps. Now attempts to flee increased dramatically, but this occurred just as Hitler was driving Europe towards crisis and world war, and as Western countries all but closed their frontiers to Jewish would-be emigrants.

"ORDINARY GERMANS" AND THE NAZIS

In recent years, a great deal of scholarly energy has been devoted to Hitler's and the Nazis' evolving relationship with the German public. Two broad conclusions may be drawn from the work of Robert Gellately, Eric Johnson, and David Bankier – and also from one of the most revelatory personal documents of the Nazi era, the diaries of Victor Klemperer (1881–1960). (Klemperer was a Jew from the German city of Dresden who survived the Nazi period, albeit under conditions of privation and persecution, thanks to his marriage to an "Aryan" woman.)

The first insight is that Nazi rule, and the isolation of the Jews for eventual expulsion and extermination, counted on a broad wellspring of popular support. This was based on Hitler's pledge to return Germany to social order, economic stability, and world-power status. The basic thesis of Gellately's book, *Backing Hitler: Consent and Coercion in Nazi Germany*, is that "Hitler was largely successful in getting the backing, one way or another, of the great majority of citizens." Moreover, this was based on the anathematizing of whole classes of citizens: "the Germans generally turned out to be proud and pleased that Hitler and his henchmen were putting away certain kinds of people who did not fit in, or who were regarded as 'outsiders,' 'asocials,' 'useless eaters,' or 'criminals.'"[19]

Victor Klemperer's diaries provide an "extraordinarily acute analysis of the day-to-day workings of German life under Hitler" and "a singular chronicle of German society's progressive Nazification."[20] Klemperer oscillated between a conviction that German society had become thoroughly Nazified, and the ironic conviction (given his expulsion from the body politic) that the Germany he loved would triumph. "I certainly no longer believe that [the Nazi regime] has enemies inside Germany," he wrote in May 1936. "The majority of the people is content, a small group accepts Hitler as the lesser evil, no one really wants to be rid of him. . . . And all are afraid for their livelihood, their life, all are such terrible cowards." Yet as late as March 1940, with the Second World War well underway, "I often ask myself where all the wild anti-Semitism is. For my part I encounter much sympathy, people help me out, but fearfully of course." He noted numerous examples of verbal contempt, but also a surprising number of cases where colleagues and acquaintances went out of their way to greet him warmly, and even police officers who accorded him treatment that was "very courteous, almost comically courteous." "Every Jew has his Aryan angel," one of his fellow inmates in an overcrowded communal house told him in 1941. But by then Klemperer had been stripped of his job, pension, house, and typewriter; he would shortly lose his right to indulge even in his cherished cigarettes. In September 1941, he was forced to put on a yellow Star of David identifying him as a Jew. It left him feeling "shattered": nearly a year later, he would describe the star as "torture – I can resolve a hundred times to pay no attention, it remains torture."[21] Hundreds of miles to the east, the program of mass killing was gearing up, as Klemperer and other Jews – not to mention ordinary Germans – were increasingly aware.

If Jews came to be the prime targets of Nazi demonization and marginalization, they were not the only ones, and for some years they were not necessarily the main ones. Communists (depicted as closely linked to Jewry) and other political opponents, handicapped and senile Germans, homosexuals, Roma (Gypsies), Polish intellectuals, vagrants, and other "asocial" elements all occupied the attention of the Nazi authorities during this period, and were the victims of "notorious achievements in human destruction" exceeding the persecution of the Jews until 1941.[22] Of these groups, political opponents (especially communists) and the handicapped and senile were most at risk of extreme physical violence, torture, and murder. "The political and syndical [trade union] left," wrote Arno Mayer, "remained the principal target of brutal repression well past the time of the definitive consolidation of the new regime in July–August 1934."[23] In the slaughter of the handicapped, meanwhile, the Nazis first "discovered that it was possible to murder multitudes," and that "they could easily recruit men and women to do the killings."[24] Box 6a explores the fate of political oppositionists and the handicapped under Nazi rule in greater detail.

THE TURN TO MASS MURDER

> I also took part in the day before yesterday's huge mass killing [of Jews in Belorussia] . . . When the first truckload [of victims] arrived my hand was slightly trembling when shooting, but one gets used to this. When the tenth load arrived I was already aiming more calmly and shot securely at the many women, children and infants. . . . Infants were flying in a wide circle through the air and we shot them still in flight, before they fell into the pit and into the water. Let's get rid of this scum that tossed all of Europe into the war . . .
>
> Walter Mattner, a Viennese clerk recruited for service in the *Einsatzgruppen* during the "Holocaust by Bullets"; letter to his wife (!), October 5, 1941

Between the outbreak of the Second World War in September 1939 and the onset of full-scale extermination in mid-1941, the Nazis were busy consolidating and confining the Jews under their control. The core policy in the occupied territories of the East was *ghettoization*: confinement of Jews in overcrowded neighborhoods of major cities. One could argue that with ghettoization came genocidal intent: "The Nazis sought to create inhuman conditions in the ghettos, where a combination of obscene overcrowding, deliberate starvation . . . and outbreaks of typhus and cholera would reduce Jewish numbers through 'natural wastage.'"[25] Certainly, the hundreds of thousands of Jews who died in the ghettos are numbered among the victims of the Holocaust.

In the two years following the German invasion of the Soviet Union on June 22, 1941, some 1.8 million Jews were rounded up and murdered, mostly by point-blank rifle fire, in what the Catholic priest Patrick Desbois has dubbed "the Holocaust by bullets." (For more on Desbois's activism and on this phase of the Holocaust, see Chapter 14.) The direct genocidal agents included the so-called *Einsatzgruppen*, four death-squad battalions – some 3,000 men in all – who followed behind the regular German army.[26] They were accompanied by SS formations and police units filled out with middle-aged recruits plucked from civilian duty in Germany – such as the "ordinary men" of Reserve Police Battalion 101, studied by both historian Christopher Browning and political scientist Daniel Goldhagen (see "Further Study"; Figures 6.10–6.11). Most of the killings occurred before the machinery of industrial killing was erected in the death camps of occupied Poland in spring 1942. They continued mercilessly thereafter, hunting down the last Jews still in flight or hiding. Bruno Mayrhofer, a German gendarme in Ukraine, reported that

> On 7 May 1943, 21.00 hours, following a confidential report [*n.b.* probably by a Ukrainian collaborator], 8 Jews, that is 3 men, 2 women and 3 children were flushed out of a well-camouflaged hole in the ground in an open field not far from the post here, and all of them were ["]shot while trying to escape["]. This case concerned Jews from Pohrebyshche who had lived in this hole in the ground for almost a year. The Jews did not have anything else in their possession except their tattered clothing. . . . The burial was carried out immediately on the spot.[27]

The role of the regular German army, or *Wehrmacht*, in this eruption of full-scale genocide was noted at the Nuremberg trials of 1945–46 (see Chapter 15). However, in part because the Western allies preferred to view the *Wehrmacht* as gentlemanly opponents, and subsequently because the German army was reconstructed as an ally by both sides in the Cold War, a myth was cultivated that the *Wehrmacht* had acted "honorably" in the occupied territories. Scholarly inquiry has now demonstrated that this is "a wholly false picture of the historical reality."[28] Permeated to the core by the Nazis' racist ideology, the *Wehrmacht* was key to engineering the mass murder of

Figure 6.4 Soviet Jews gathered in a ravine prior to their mass execution by *Einsatzgruppen* killing units during the "Holocaust by Bullets," 1941–42.

Source: Instytut Pamieci Narodowej/US Holocaust Memorial Museum.

3.3 million Soviets seized as prisoners-of-war (see Box 6a).[29] The *Wehrmacht* was also central to the perpetration of the Jewish Holocaust. The *Einsatzgruppen*, wrote Hannah Arendt, "needed and got the close cooperation of the Armed Forces; indeed, relations between them were usually 'excellent' and in some instances 'affectionate' (*herzlich*, literally 'heartfelt'). The generals . . . often lent their own men, ordinary soldiers, to assist in the massacres."[30] A great many soldiers "felt drawn to the killing operations . . . standing around as spectators, taking photographs, and volunteering to be shooters."[31] As SS Lieutenant-Colonel Karl Kretschmer wrote home in September 1942: "Here in Russia, wherever the German soldier is, no Jew remains."[32]

Even such intensive slaughter, however, could not eliminate European Jewry in a "reasonable" time. Moreover, the intensely intimate character of murder by gunfire, with human tissue and brain matter spattering onto the clothes and faces of the German killers, began to take a psychological toll. The difficulty was especially pronounced in the case of murders of children and women. While it was relatively easy for executioners to persuade themselves that adult male victims, even unarmed civilians, were dangerous and deserved their cruel fate, the argument was harder to make for people traditionally viewed as passive, dependent, and helpless.[33]

To reduce this stress on the killers, and to increase the logistical efficiency of the killing, the industrialized "death camp" with its gas chambers was moved to the fore. Both were refinements of existing institutions and technologies. The death camps grew out of the concentration-camp system the Nazis had established upon first taking power in 1933, while killings by gas were first employed in 1939 as part of the "euthanasia" campaign that was such a vital forerunner of the genocide of the Jews. (It was wound down, in fact, at the precise point that the campaign against European Jews turned to root-and-branch extermination.) Gas chambers allowed for the desired psychological distance between the killers and their victims: "It was the gas that acted, not the man who pulled the machine-gun trigger."[34]

Principally by this means, nearly one million Jews were killed at Auschwitz – a complex of three camps and numerous satellites, of which Auschwitz II (Birkenau) operated as the main killing center. Zyklon B (cyanide gas in crystal form) was overwhelmingly the means of murder at Auschwitz. Nearly two million more Jews died by gas, shootings, beatings, and starvation at the other "death camps" in occupied Poland, which were distinguished from the vastly larger Nazi network of concentration camps by their core function of extermination. These death camps were Chelmno (200,000 Jews slaughtered); Sobibor (260,000); Belzec (500,000); Treblinka (800,000, mostly from the Polish capital Warsaw); and Majdanek (130,000).[35]

It would be misleading to distinguish too sharply between the "death camps," where gas was the normal means of extermination, and the broader network of camps where "destruction through work" (the Nazis' term) was the norm.[36] Killings of Jews reached exterminatory levels in the latter institutions as well. As Daniel Goldhagen has argued, "after the beginning of 1942, the camp system in general was lethal for Jews," and well over a million died outside the death camps, killed by starvation, disease, and slave labor.[37] Perhaps 500,000 more, in Raul Hilberg's estimate, succumbed in the Jewish ghettos, themselves a kind of concentration camp. Finally, tens of thousands died on forced marches, often in the dead of winter, as Allied forces closed in.[38]

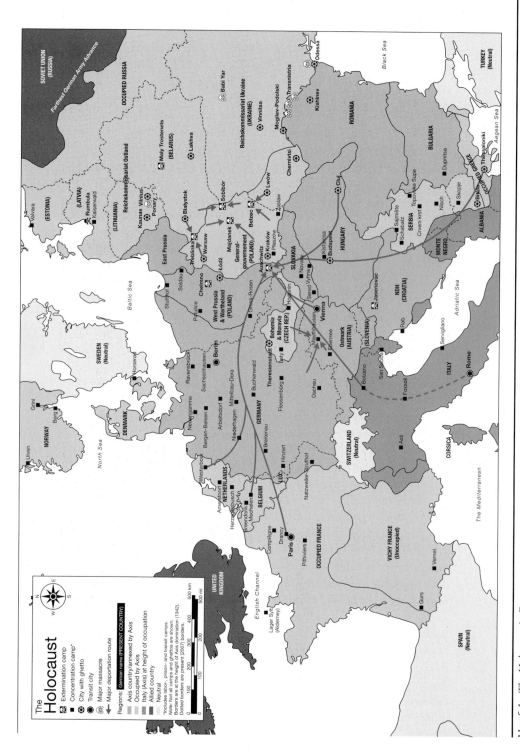

Map 6.1 The Holocaust in Europe

Source: Map by Dennis Nilsson/Wikimedia Commons.

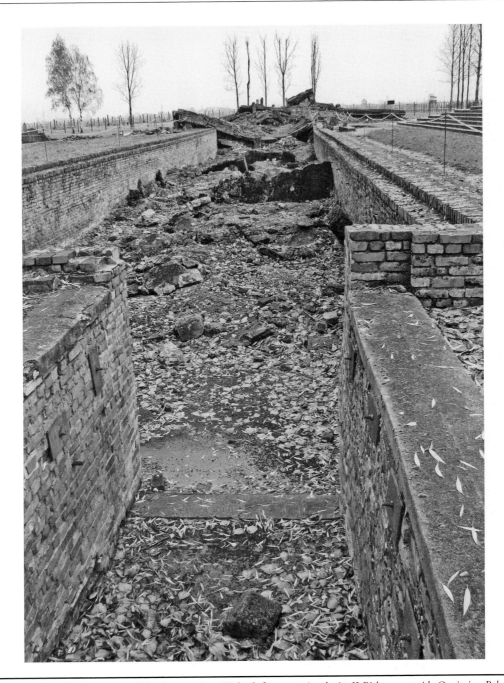

Figure 6.5   The haunting ruins of the Crematorium III death factory at Auschwitz II-Birkenau outside Oswiecim, Poland, dynamited by the Nazis just before the camp was liberated by Soviet soldiers in January 1945. The view is looking down the steps which victims, mostly Jews transported from all over Europe, were forced to tread en route to the undressing room within. They were then murdered in an underground gas chamber (at top left, not clearly visible), and cremated in ovens under the (now-collapsed) roof-and-chimney complex at the rear. More than one million children, women, and men – overwhelmingly Jews, but also Roma/Gypsies and Soviet prisoners-of-war – were murdered at Auschwitz-Birkenau. The site has become synonymous with the Jewish Holocaust and modern genocide.

Source: Author's photo, November 2009.

Figures 6.6–6.9 Four indelible images of the Jewish Holocaust. *Top left:* A Jewish man is murdered by pistol fire at a death pit outside Vinnytsia, Ukraine, during the "Holocaust by Bullets" of 1941–42. *Top right:* Near Novgorod, Russia, in 1942, a German soldier takes aim at civilian victims in the killing fields; the rifles of other members of the execution squad are partially visible at left (note also the victim – wounded? killed? – lying by the soldier's right foot). *Bottom left:* After the Warsaw Ghetto uprising of January–May 1943, Jewish survivors are rounded up for transport and extermination. *Bottom right:* In the final stages of the Holocaust, the death factories worked overtime to "process" victims, above all Jews, even when this diverted resources from the Nazi war effort. A member of a *Sonderkommando* corpse-disposal unit in Auschwitz II-Birkenau (see Figure 6.5) surreptitiously photographed the burning of the bodies of gassed victims, probably Jews from the last major genocidal roundup in Hungary, in an open pit near Crematorium V (May 1944).

Source: Wikimedia Commons.

Notoriously, the extermination system continued to function even when it impeded the war effort. In March 1944, the Nazis intervened to occupy Hungary as a bulwark against advancing Soviet forces. Adolf Eichmann promptly arrived to supervise the rounding up for slaughter of the country's Jews. Thousands were saved by the imaginative intervention of Swedish diplomat Raoul Wallenberg (see Chapter 10). But some 400,000 were packed off to be gassed at Auschwitz-Birkenau and other death camps – despite the enormous strain this imposed on the rail system and the Nazis' dwindling human and material resources. It seemed that the single-minded devotion to genocidal destruction outweighed even the Nazis' desire for self-preservation.

BOX 6.1 ONE WOMAN'S STORY: NECHAMA EPSTEIN

Nechama Epstein was a Polish Jew from Warsaw who was just 18 years old when she "and her family were herded into the city's ghetto together with 350,000 other Jews."[39] One of the few survivors of the Auschwitz death camp, she was interviewed after the war by David P. Boder, an American psychologist who published a book entitled *I Did Not Interview the Dead*. However, Boder chose not to include his conversation with Epstein; her testimony did not see the light of day until it was excerpted in Donald Niewyk's chapter for the *Century of Genocide* anthology. Her account, Niewyk noted, "reveals a remarkable breadth of experiences, including survival in ghettos, slave labor camps, and extermination centers."[40]

Epstein described the grim privations of life in the Warsaw ghetto – the very ghetto that would rise up so heroically against the Germans in early 1943, and be crushed. "It was very bad," she remembered. "We had nothing to sell any more. Eight people were living on a kilo of beets a day. . . . We did not have any more strength to walk. . . . Every day there were other dead, small children, bigger children, older people. All died of a hunger death."

Epstein was caught up in the mass round-up of Jews to be shipped to the extermination center at Treblinka in September 1942. Packed into a single cattle-car with 200 other Jews, she passed an entire night before the train began to move: "We lay one on top of the other. . . . One lay suffocating on top of another. . . . We could do nothing to help ourselves. And then real death began." Tormented by thirst and near-asphyxiation, Jews struggled with each other for a snatch of air or any moisture. "Mothers were giving the children urine to drink."

Some enterprising prisoners managed to saw a hole in the cattle-car, and Epstein, among others, leapt out. With the help of a Polish militia member, she found her way to the Miedryrzec ghetto, where she passed the next eight months. "Every four weeks there were new deportations." The first of these she survived by hiding in an attic and eating raw beets. "I did not have anything to drink. The first snow fell then, so I made a hole in the roof and pulled in the hand a little snow. And this I licked. And this I lived on."

Her luck ran out at the time of the last deportation. She was led away, to a transport and apparently her doom, on "a beautiful summer day" in 1943. This time the destination was Majdanek, another of the extermination centers in occupied Poland. There, "We were all lined up. There were many who were shot [outright]. . . . The mothers were put separately, the children separately, the men separately, the women separately. . . . The children and the mothers were led to the crematory. All were burned. . . . We never laid eyes on them again."

She spent two months at Majdanek. "I lived through many terrible things. We had nothing to eat. We were so starved. . . . The food consisted of two hundred grams of bread a day, and a little soup of water with nettles." A German SS woman entered the barracks every day "at six in the morning . . . beating everybody."

In July 1943, Epstein was shipped off to Auschwitz. By good fortune, she was consigned to a work camp rather than to immediate extermination in the Birkenau gas chambers. "We worked carrying stones on barrows, large stones. To eat they did not give us. We were beaten terribly" by German women guards: "They said that every day they must kill three, four Jews." She fell sick, and survived her time in the hospital only by hiding from the regular round-ups that carted off ill inmates to the crematoria. "Christian women were lying there, so I climbed over to the Christians, into their beds, and there I always had the good fortune to hide."

In October, the entire sick-ward was emptied. "There was a girl eighteen years old, and she was crying terribly. She said that she is still so young, she wants to live. . . . [But] nothing helped. They were all taken away." When she emerged from the ward, she saw the Auschwitz crematory burning in the night: "We saw the entire sky red [from] the glow of the fire. Blood was pouring on the sky." But Epstein again survived the selection for the Birkenau extermination center. She was sent back to Majdanek, where she witnessed SS and Gestapo killers forcing male inmates to dig mass graves, then lining up hundreds of female inmates to be shot. Over the course of a further eight months at Majdanek, she remained among the handful of inmates – several hundred only – spared gassing and cremation.

Epstein was eventually sent to a forced-labor center: Plaszow, near Krakow (the same camp featured in Steven Spielberg's film *Schindler's List*). By late 1944, the Soviets were approaching Plaszow. "We were again dragged away. I was the second time taken to Auschwitz." After that, she was dispatched to Bergen-Belsen; then to Aschersleben in Germany proper, where she labored alongside Dutch, Yugoslav, and French prisoners-of-war.

American forces were now closing in from the West. Epstein was conscripted into a death march alongside 500 other inmates. "Only women. Two hundred fell en route." At last, after a march of more than 250 kilometers, she reached Theresienstadt in Czechoslovakia. This had long served as a "model" detention facility for the Nazis – the only one to which Red Cross representatives were admitted. "We were completely in tatters. . . . We were very dirty. . . . We were badly treated. We were beaten. They screamed at us. 'Accursed swine! You are filthy. What sort of people are you?'" Epstein and her fellow inmates now looked like the "subhumans" the Germans had been indoctrinated to expect.

On the very last day of the European war, May 8, 1945, Theresienstadt was liberated by Russian forces. "We didn't believe it. . . . We went out, whoever was able. . . . We went out with great joy, with much crying. . . .

"But now there began a real death. People who had been starved for so many years. . . . The Russians had opened all the German storehouses, all the German stores, and they said, 'Take whatever you want.' People who had been badly starved, they shouldn't have eaten. . . . And the people began to eat, to eat too much, greedily. . . . Hundreds of people fell a day. . . . People crawled over the dead." Typhus broke out. But Epstein survived. She returned to Warsaw, married, and emigrated to Palestine.

DEBATING THE HOLOCAUST

Many of the central themes of the Nazis' attempted destruction of European Jews have served as touchstones for the broader field of comparative genocide studies. No other genocide has generated remotely as much literature as the Holocaust, including thousands of books and essays. It is important, therefore, to explore some major points of debate, not only for the insights they give into the events described in this chapter, but for their relevance to genocide studies as a whole.

Intentionalists vs. functionalists

The core of the debate over the past two decades has revolved around a scholarly tendency generally termed "intentionalist," and a contrasting "functionalist" interpretation. Intentionalists, as the word suggests, place primary emphasis on the *intention* of the Nazis, from the outset, to eliminate European Jews by means that eventually included mass slaughter. Such an approach emphasizes the figure of Adolf Hitler and his monomaniacal zeal to eliminate the Jewish "cancer" from Germany and Europe. ("Once I really am in power," Hitler allegedly told a journalist as early as 1922, "my first and foremost task will be the annihilation of the Jews.")[41] Necessary as well was the anti-semitic dimension of both Nazi ideology and European history.

This fueled the Nazis' animus against the Jews, and also ensured there would be no shortage of "willing executioners" to do the dirty work.

The functionalist critique, on the other hand, downplays the significance of Hitler as an individual. It "depicts the fragmentation of decision-making and the blurring of political responsibility," and emphasizes "the disintegration of traditional bureaucracy into a crooked maze of ill-conceived and uncoordinated task forces," in Colin Tatz's summary.[42] Also stressed is the evolutionary and contingent character of the campaign against the Jews: from legal discrimination, to concentration, to mass murder. In this view, "what happened in Nazi Germany [was] an unplanned 'cumulative radicalization' produced by the chaotic decision-making process of a polycratic regime and the 'negative selection' of destructive elements from the Nazis' ideological arsenal as the only ones that could perpetually mobilize the disparate and otherwise incompatible elements of the Nazi coalition."[43]

This sometimes acrimonious debate gave way, in the 1990s, to a recognition that the intentionalist and functionalist strands were not irreconcilable. "Both positions in the debate have a number of merits and demerits; both ultimately reflect different forms of historical explanation; and the ground between them is steadily narrowing in favour of a consensus which borrows elements from both lines of argument."[44] The raw material for Nazi genocide was present from the start, but required a host of historically contingent features to actualize and maximize it. Michael Shermer and Alex Grobman propose the term "intentional functionalism" to capture this interplay of actors and variables.[45]

Jewish resistance

The depiction of Jews as having gone meekly to their deaths was first advanced by Raul Hilberg in his 1961 treatise *The Destruction of the European Jews*, and was then enshrined by Hannah Arendt in her controversial account of *Eichmann in Jerusalem*. Both Hilberg and Arendt noted the close pre-war coordination between the Jewish Agency (which sought to promote Jewish immigration to Palestine) and the Nazi authorities.[46] They also stressed the role of the Jewish councils (*Judenräte*), bodies of Jews delegated by the Nazis to oversee the ghettos and the round-ups of Jewish civilians. "The whole truth," as Arendt summarized it, was that without Jewish leadership and organization, the Jewish people would have suffered "chaos and plenty of misery" at Nazi hands, "but the total number of victims would hardly have been between four and a half and six million people."[47]

While it may be true that "the salient characteristic of the Jewish community in Europe during 1933–1945 was its step-by-step adjustment to step-by-step destruction,"[48] research has undermined this depiction of Jewish passivity and complicity. Scholars have described how, under horrific circumstances, Jews found ways to resist: going into hiding; struggling to preserve Jewish culture and creativity; and even launching armed uprisings. (The Warsaw ghetto uprising which peaked in April–May 1943, and the mass escape from the Sobibor death camp in October 1943, are the most famous of these rebellions against the Nazis.)[49] Large numbers of Jews also joined the armed forces of the Allies, or fought as partisans behind German lines.

On balance, "it is pure myth that the Jews were merely 'passive,'" wrote Alexander Donat in his memoir *The Holocaust Kingdom*:

> The Jews fought back against their enemies to a degree no other community anywhere in the world would have been capable of were it to find itself similarly beleaguered. They fought against hunger and starvation, against disease, against a deadly Nazi economic blockade. They fought against murderers and against traitors within their own ranks, and they were utterly alone in their fight. They were forsaken by God and by man, surrounded by hatred or indifference. Ours was not a romantic war. Although there was much heroism, there was little beauty – much toil and suffering, but no glamour. We fought back on every front where the enemy attacked – the biological front, the economic front, the propaganda front, the cultural front – with every weapon we possessed.[50]

Moreover, to the extent that Jews did *not* mount an effective resistance to their extermination, it is worth noting – as Daniel Goldhagen does – that "millions of Soviet POWs, young military men with organization, and leadership, and initial vigor, died passively in German camps [see Box 6a]. If these men, whose families were not with them, could not muster themselves against the Germans, how could the Jews be expected to have done *more*?"[51]

The Allies and the churches: Could the Jews have been saved?

The genocide against European Jews *could* have been avoided, argues the historian Yehuda Bauer, just as the Second World War itself might never have occurred – "had the Great Powers stopped Nazi Germany when it was still weak." But at this point, "nobody knew that a Holocaust was even possible, because nobody knew what a Holocaust was; the Germans had not decided on anything like it in the 1930s."[52] The Allies, haunted by the carnage of the First World War, sought accommodation ("appeasement") rather than confrontation.

The Evian Conference of July 1938, held in a French town on Lake Geneva, brought together representatives of Western countries to address the Jewish plight. In retrospect, and even at the time, it offered the best chance to alleviate the plight of German Jews, through the simple expedient of opening up Western borders to Jewish refugees. But instead, the West ducked its responsibility. In Germany, Hitler could barely conceal his delight. The rejection of the Jews not only further humiliated Jews themselves, but highlighted the hypocrisy of the West's humanitarian rhetoric.

Turning to the period of full-scale genocide against the Jews, it seems clear that details of the killing operations were known to the Allies early on. For example, radio communications of the Nazi Order Police were intercepted, alluding to mass murder during the "Holocaust by Bullets." But the Allies were observing from a distance, with Germany at the height of its power on the European continent. The sheer speed of the slaughter also militated against meaningful intervention. "From mid-March 1942 to mid-February 1943," that is, in less than a year, "over one-half the victims of the Jewish Holocaust . . . lost their lives at the hands of Nazi killers."[53]

It may be argued that the inclusion of targets such as Auschwitz's gas chambers and crematoria in the Allied bombing campaign, along with key transport points for Jews, could have disrupted the Nazi killing machine. The case is especially cogent for the later stages of the war, as with the genocide of the Hungarian Jews in 1944–45 (when the USSR might also have been able to intervene). But on pre-war evidence, it is hard to believe that, if more effective military measures could have been found, the Allies would have placed saving Jews higher on the list of military priorities – or that doing so would have made much difference.

The role of the Christian churches has also been scrutinized and criticized. Pope Pius XII's placating of the Nazi regime in Germany, and his silence on the persecution of the Jews, are notorious.[54] While "the Holy See [Vatican] addressed numerous protests, demands, and inquiries *via diplomatic channels* both regarding the situation of Catholics in Poland and about the killing of the mentally ill . . . *Not one such diplomatic intervention dealt with the overall fate of the Jews.*" Regarding the fate of "non-Aryans in the territories under German authority," Pius wrote to a German bishop who had protested deportations of Jews: "Unhappily, in the present circumstances, We cannot offer them effective help other than through Our prayers."[55]

Within Germany, the churches did virtually nothing to impede the genocide and indeed strove not to notice it, thereby facilitating it. The Nazis at numerous points demonstrated a keen sensitivity to public opinion, including religious opinion – protests from German churches were partly responsible for driving the "euthanasia" campaign underground after 1941. But such protests were not forthcoming from more than a handful of principled religious voices. When it came to defending co-parishioners whom the Nazis deemed of Jewish origin, "both Church and Church members drove away from their community, from their churches, people with whom they were united in worship, as one drives away mangy dogs from one's door."[56]

The most successful examples of resistance to Hitler's genocidal designs for European Jewry came from a handful of Western and Northern European countries that were either neutral or under relatively less oppressive occupation regimes.[57] Here, sometimes, extension of the killing campaign could impose political costs that the Nazis were not willing to pay. The most vivid display of public opposition swept up virtually the entire adult population of Denmark, led by the royal family. When the Nazis decreed the imposition of the Jewish yellow star, non-Jewish Danes adopted it in droves as well, as a powerful gesture of solidarity. The regulation was rescinded. Subsequently, Danes arranged for the evacuation of the majority of the country's Jews to neutral Sweden, where they lived through the rest of the war (see Chapter 10). Sweden, meanwhile, saved "about half of Norwegian Jewry and almost all of the Danish Jews," and in 1944

> involved herself more heavily in the heart of Europe, particularly in Budapest, where, along with Switzerland, Portugal, and the Vatican, the Swedish legation issued "protective passports," established safe houses, and generally attempted to restrain the German occupants and their Hungarian puppets from killing more Jews on Hungarian soil in the final hours of the war. Upon the liberation of Jews in concentration camps in the spring of 1945, Sweden accepted thousands of victims for medical treatment and rehabilitation.[58]

Willing executioners?

Just as scholars have demonstrated increased interest in "micro-histories" of public opinion under the Nazis, and the role of ordinary German citizens in accepting and sustaining the regime, so have questions been raised about the role of different sectors of the German population in the genocide. After decades of research by Raul Hilberg and many others, it is a truism that not only German social and economic elites, but all the professions (up to and including the clergy, as we have seen), were corrupted or compromised by the Nazi state. In Michael Burleigh's words, an "understanding of the process of persecution [on racial grounds] now includes greater awareness of the culpable involvement of various sections of the professional intelligentsia, such as anthropologists, doctors, economists, historians, lawyers and psychiatrists, in the formation and implementation of Nazi policies."[59] For such figures, "the advent of the Nazi regime was coterminous with the onset of 'boom' conditions. No one asked or compelled these academics and scientists actively to work on the regime's behalf. Most of them could have said no. In fact, the files of the regime's many agencies bulge with their unsolicited recommendations."[60]

What of the genocidal participation of ordinary Germans? This subject has spawned the most vigorous debate in Holocaust studies over the past decade, though the illumination has not always matched the heat generated.

At the heart of the controversy was the publication, in 1992 and 1996 respectively, of Christopher Browning's *Ordinary Men: Reserve Police Battalion 101 and the Final Solution in Poland*, and Daniel Goldhagen's *Hitler's Willing Executioners: Ordinary Germans and the Holocaust*. Both scholars examined the same archives on Reserve Police Battalion 101, which consisted overwhelmingly of Germans drafted from civilian police units (often too old for regular military service). The records described in detail the battalion's killings of helpless, naked Jewish civilians in occupied Poland during 1941–42, and the range of reactions among group members.

In interpreting the records, Browning acknowledged the importance of "the incessant proclamation of German superiority and incitement of contempt and hatred for the Jewish enemy." But he also stressed other factors: "conformity to the group," that is, peer pressure; the desire for praise, prestige, and advancement; and the threat of marginalization and anathematization in highly dangerous wartime circumstances. He referred to "the mutually intensifying effects of war and racism. . . . Nothing helped the Nazis to wage a race war so much as the war itself."[61]

Goldhagen, dismissing Browning's work, advanced instead an essentially mono-causal thesis. The Jewish Holocaust was the direct outgrowth of "eliminationist" anti-semitism, which by the twentieth century had become "common sense" for Germans. By 1941, "ordinary Germans easily became genocidal killers . . . [and] did so even though they did not have to." They "kill[ed] Jews willingly and often eagerly,"[62] though Goldhagen did recognize the importance of Nazi leaders in activating and channeling the anti-semitic impulse.

With the controversy now cooled, it is easier to appreciate the significance of "the Goldhagen debate."[63] Goldhagen did counter a trend toward bloodless analysis and abstract theorizing in studies of the Jewish catastrophe. In addition, by achieving mass popularity, Goldhagen's book, like Samantha Power's *"A Problem from Hell"* (2002),

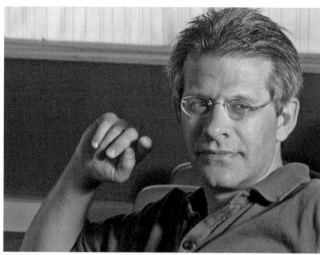

Figures 6.10 and 6.11   The exchange between Christopher Browning (left), author of *Ordinary Men* (1992), and Daniel Jonah Goldhagen, author of *Hitler's Willing Executioners* (1996), centered on the motivations of "ordinary" German killers of Jews during the Holocaust. Was "eliminationist anti-semitism" the central factor, as Goldhagen argued? Or was it secondary to peer pressure and masculine bonding in wartime, as Browning suggested? The result was a defining – and continuing – debate in Holocaust and genocide studies.

Sources: *The Gazette*, University of North Carolina (Browning); JTN Productions (Goldhagen).

broke down the usual wall between scholarship and public debate. However, the core elements of Goldhagen's thesis – that there was something unique about German anti-semitism that spawned the Holocaust; that Germans were only too ready to leap to bloodthirsty murder of Jews – have been decisively countered. Not only was anti-semitism historically stronger in countries other than Germany, but the virulence of its expression during the Second World War in (for example) Lithuania and Romania exceeded that of Germany. The Nazis, as noted above, were reluctant to confront "ordinary Germans" with bloody atrocity, though according to Saul Friedländer, "recent historical research increasingly turns German ignorance of the fate of the Jews into a mythical postwar construct."[64] Nor could they rely on a widespread popular desire to inflict cruelty on Jews as the foundational strategy for implementing their genocide.

Israel, the Palestinians, and the Holocaust

Occasionally an experience of great suffering has been recognized as warranting creation or recognition of a homeland for the targeted group. Such was the case with East Timor (Box 7a), born from Indonesian occupation and genocide. The Kurdish protected zone and *de facto* state in northern Iraq may also qualify (Box 4a), together with the widespread recognition of Kosovo's declaration of independence from Serbia in 2008. But no case is as dramatic as that of Israel in the wake of the Second World War. The dream of the Zionist movement founded in the nineteenth century, to establish a Jewish homeland in Palestine through mobilization and mass immigration, became a reality in the postwar period, as Britain abandoned its territorial mandate over Palestine, and Arabs and Jews fought over the territory. "Anti-Zionism in the Jewish community collapsed, and a consensus that Jewry, abandoned during the war, had to have a home of its own crystallized overnight."[65] Jewish survivors of Nazi genocide provided Palestine with a critical mass of Jewish immigrants and, in the decades following the declaration of the Israeli state on May 15, 1948, Israel received tens of billions of dollars from the Federal Republic of Germany as reparations for the Holocaust of the Jews.

To a significant degree, successive Israeli governments have relied on the Holocaust as a touchstone of Jewish experience and national identity, and have used the threat of another genocide of the Jews to justify military and security policies.[66] Israeli prime minister Benjamin Netanyahu, for example, commemorated the country's Holocaust Remembrance Day on April 21, 2009, by asserting that "only a matter of a few decades after the Holocaust, new forces have arisen that openly declare their intention to wipe the Jewish state off the face of the earth," a reference to statements allegedly made in 2005 by Iranian President Mahmoud Ahmadinejad (see p. 521). Netanyahu added: "Holocaust deniers cannot commit another Holocaust against the Jewish people. This is the state of Israel's supreme obligation." Deputy Prime Minister Silvan Shalom claimed that "what Iran is trying to do right now" – a reference to the country's nuclear program – "is not far away at all from what Hitler did to the Jewish people just 65 years ago."[67]

Palestinians and their supporters, for their part, have tended to adopt the genocide framework as well – but to attract attention to the Palestinian cause. They have sought to draw parallels between Israel's repressive policies and those of the Nazis against Jews. Often such comparisons have seemed hysterical and/or counterproductive;[68] but sometimes they have resonated. Notable was Israeli general (later prime minister) Ariel Sharon's dispatching of Christian Phalangist militia to the Palestinian refugee camps of Sabra and Shatila, during the Israelis' 1982 invasion of Lebanon. This led predictably to the *Einsatzgruppen*-style massacre of thousands of Palestinian civilians, as Israeli troops stood by. Renewed denunciations, employing the language of genocide and crimes against humanity, were issued after Israel imposed a ruinous blockade on the Gaza Strip, still in place at the time of writing (March 2010). The blockade was described as a "genocidal policy" by Israeli historian Ilan Pappé.[69] It prompted Richard Falk, subsequently the UN Human Rights Council's monitor for Israel-Palestine, to write in 2007 that Israeli strategies toward Gaza were reminiscent of Nazi ghettoization policies toward Jews, displaying "a deliberate intention . . . to subject an entire human community to life-endangering conditions of utmost cruelty."[70] In December 2008, Israel launched a massive assault on the Gaza Strip, killing many hundreds of Palestinian civilians and laying waste to large swathes of the territory. In the estimation of UN investigator Judge Richard Goldstone, this "deliberately disproportionate attack" was "designed to punish, humiliate and terrorize a civilian population, radically diminish its local economic capacity both to work and to provide for itself, and to force upon it an ever-increasing sense of dependency and vulnerability."[71]

Is the Jewish Holocaust "uniquely unique"?

Few historical and philosophical issues have generated such intense scholarly debate in genocide studies as the question of Holocaust uniqueness. On one level, it is clearly facile. As Alex Alvarez put it: "All genocides are simultaneously unique and analogous."[72] The question is whether the Jewish Holocaust is *sui generis* – that is, "uniquely unique."[73]

In genocide studies, a well-known exponent of the uniqueness thesis is Steven Katz, who devoted his immense tome *The Holocaust in Historical Context, Vol. 1* to arguing that the Jewish Holocaust was "phenomenologically unique by virtue of the fact that never before has a state set out, as a matter of intentional principle and actualized policy, to annihilate physically every man, woman, and child belonging to a specific people."[74] The Nazi campaign against the Jews was the only true genocide, as Katz defined the term (see p. 18; recall that my own preferred definition of genocide reworks Katz's).

Other scholars have argued against the uniqueness hypothesis. Historian Mark Levene has pointed to an "obvious contradiction": "while, on the one hand, the Holocaust has come to be commonly treated as the yardstick for all that might be described as 'evil' in our world, on the other, it is . . . a subject notably cordoned off and policed against those who might seek to make connections [with other genocides]."[75] Writer and poet Phillip Lopate has likewise argued that claims of uniqueness tend to bestow "a sort of privileged nation status in the moral honor roll."[76] This claim of privilege then carries over to "the Jewish state," Israel, helping to blunt criticism of its treatment of the Palestinians.[77]

My own view should be clearly stated: the Jewish Holocaust was *not* "uniquely unique." On no major analytical dimension – speed, scale, scope, intensity, efficiency, cruelty, ideology – does it stand alone and apart. If it is unique in its mix of these ingredients, so too are most of the other major instances of mass killing in their own way.[78] I also believe that uniqueness proponents, like the rest of us, were severely shaken by the holocaust in Rwanda in 1994 (see Chapter 9). The killing there proceeded much faster than the slaughter of the Jews; destroyed a higher proportion of the designated victim group (some 80 percent of Rwandan Tutsis versus two-thirds of European Jews); was carried out by "a chillingly effective organizational structure that would implement the political plan of genocide more efficiently than was achieved by the industrialized death camps in Nazi Germany";[79] and – unlike the Jewish catastrophe – featured active participation by a substantial portion of the general population. Was Rwanda, then, "uniquely unique"? The claim seems as tenable as in the case of the Jewish Holocaust – but in both cases, a nuanced comparative framework is preferable.[80]

The Jews *were* unique as a target of the Nazis. "In the end," wrote Raul Hilberg, ". . . the Jews retained their special place."[81] According to Omer Bartov,

> It was *only* in the case of the Jews that there was a determination to seek out every baby hidden in a haystack, every family living in a bunker in the forest, every woman trying to pass herself off as a Gentile. It was only in the case of the Jews that vast factories were constructed and managed with the sole purpose of killing

trainload after trainload of people. It was only in the case of the Jews that huge, open-air, public massacres of tens of thousands of people were conducted on a daily basis throughout Eastern Europe.[82]

Lastly, the Jewish Holocaust holds a unique place in genocide studies. Among all the world's genocides, it alone produced a scholarly literature that spawned, in turn, a comparative discipline. Specialists on the subject played a central role in constituting the field and its institutions, such as the International Association of Genocide Scholars (IAGS) and the *Journal of Genocide Research*: "Genocide studies is really the outgrowth of the study of the Holocaust," as sociologist Thomas Cushman has noted; according to historian Dan Stone, "for good or ill," the Holocaust "has provided many of the theoretical frameworks and research strategies for analyzing other genocides."[83]

Still, there is no denying that the Holocaust has been significantly de-centered from comparative genocide studies since the emergence of the post-Lemkin research agenda in the 1970s and 1980s. In introducing the third edition of his edited collection *Is the Holocaust Unique?* (2009), Alan S. Rosenbaum acknowledged that

> since [my] initial conception of this project some fifteen years ago, the center of gravity for the once-intense debate about the overall arguable claim for the significant uniqueness of the Holocaust may gradually but perceptibly be shifting. . . . It is not that the Holocaust is considered by most responsible or fair-minded scholars as any less paradigmatic, but rather [that] as the Holocaust recedes into history and other genocidal events occur, its scope and dimensions may naturally be better understood in the context of a broader genocide studies investigation.[84]

FURTHER STUDY

Note: No genocide has generated remotely as much scholarly attention as the Nazis' Holocaust against the Jews. The following is a bare sampling of core works in English; others are cited in subsequent chapters.

Irving Abella and Harold Troper, *None is Too Many: Canada and the Jews of Europe, 1933–1948*. Toronto, ON: Key Porter Books, 2002. Canada's shameful treatment of Jewish would-be refugees from Germany and Nazi-occupied Europe; one facet of the West's abandonment of the Jews.

Götz Aly, *"Final Solution": Nazi Population Policy and the Murder of the European Jews*. London: Arnold, 1999. Aly's "functionalist" argument stresses the role of Nazi bureaucrats confronted with problems of population management in the occupied territories. See also *Hitler's Beneficiaries: Plunder, Racial War, and the Nazi Welfare State*.

Omer Bartov, *Germany's War and the Holocaust: Disputed Histories*. Ithaca, NY: Cornell University Press, 2003. Essays by the principal scholar of the *Wehrmacht's* war on the eastern front; see also *Hitler's Army*.

Donald Bloxham, *The Final Solution: A Genocide*. Oxford: Oxford University Press,

2009. A nuanced and fluidly written comparative treatment, by one of genocide studies' most dynamic younger scholars.

Christopher Browning, *Ordinary Men: Reserve Police Battalion 101 and the Final Solution in Poland*. New York: Perennial, 1993. Based on some of the same archival sources as Goldhagen's *Hitler's Willing Executioners* (see below), but emphasizes group dynamics in addition to anti-semitism. See also *The Origins of the Final Solution: The Evolution of Nazi Jewish Policy, September 1939–March 1942*.

Avraham Burg, *The Holocaust is Over, We Must Rise from Its Ashes*. London: Palgrave Macmillan, 2008. Critical examination of the use and misuse of the Holocaust in contemporary Israeli society.

Michael Burleigh and Wolfgang Wippermann, *The Racial State: Germany 1933–1945*. Cambridge: Cambridge University Press, 1991. How Nazi racial ideology inspired genocidal policy.

Lucy S. Dawidowicz, *The War Against the Jews, 1933–1945*. New York: Bantam, 1986 (reissue). Dawidowicz's 1975 work is now generally seen as too "intentionalist" in its interpretation of the Judeocide. But it is still in print and widely read.

Alexander Donat, *The Holocaust Kingdom*. New York: Holocaust Library, 1978. Classic memoir of ghetto and death camp, sensitively told and translated.

Saul Friedländer, *The Years of Extermination: Nazi Germany and the Jews, 1939–1945*. New York: HarperCollins, 2007. Friedländer's work won the Pulitzer Prize, and has been praised for integrating firsthand testimonies with the historical and archival record. See also *Nazi Germany and the Jews, Volume I: The Years of Persecution, 1933–1939*.

Peter Fritzsche, *Life and Death in the Third Reich*. Cambridge, MA: Harvard University Press, 2008. Up-close, galvanizing account of daily life in Germany as the Nazi Holocaust was unleashed on Central and Eastern Europe.

Robert Gellately, *Backing Hitler: Consent and Coercion in Nazi Germany*. Oxford: Oxford University Press, 2001. Argues that ordinary Germans generally supported Nazi policies, often exhibiting enthusiasm beyond the call of duty.

Daniel J. Goldhagen, *Hitler's Willing Executioners: Ordinary Germans and the Holocaust*. New York: Vintage, 1997. Controversial book ascribing a monocausal explanation for the genocide, rooted in Germans' visceral hatred of the Jews.

Jan T. Gross, *Fear: Anti-Semitism in Poland after Auschwitz*. New York: Random House, 2007. How murderous pogroms of Jews continued in Poland after the fall of the Third Reich. See also *Neighbors: The Destruction of the Jewish Community in Jedwabne, Poland*.

Jeffrey Herf, *The Jewish Enemy: Nazi Propaganda during World War II and the Holocaust*. Cambridge, MA: The Belknap Press of Harvard University Press, 2006. Eye-opening study of the Nazi conception of Jews as political threats ("Judeo-Bolsheviks") above all else.

Raul Hilberg, *The Destruction of the European Jews* (3rd edn), 3 vols. New Haven, CT: Yale University Press, 2003. Massive, meticulous study of the bureaucracy of death.

Adolf Hitler, *Mein Kampf* (My Struggle), trans. Ralph Mannheim. Boston, MA: Houghton Mifflin, 1943. First published in 1925–26; lays out Hitler's vision of German destiny, as well as his virulent anti-semitism.

Eric A. Johnson and Karl-Heinz Reuband, *What We Knew: Terror, Mass Murder, and Everyday Life in Nazi Germany: An Oral History*. New York: Basic Books, 2005. Rich study based on interviews with German-Jewish Holocaust survivors.

Ian Kershaw, *The Nazi Dictatorship: Problems and Perspectives of Interpretation* (4th edn). London: Arnold, 2000. Overview of, and contribution to, scholarly debates about the nature of the Nazi regime.

Victor Klemperer, *I Will Bear Witness: A Diary of the Nazi Years*, 2 vols. New York: Modern Library, 1999, 2001. An essential document of the twentieth century: the testimony of a German Jewish professor who survived the entire Nazi era. See also *The Lesser Evil: The Diaries of Victor Klemperer, 1945–59*; and *The Language of the Third Reich: LTI – Lingua Tertii Imperii: A Philologist's Notebook*.

Ronnie S. Landau, *The Nazi Holocaust*. Chicago, IL: Ivan R. Dee, 1994. A good, accessible primer on the origins and course of the Jewish catastrophe.

Primo Levi, *Survival in Auschwitz*. New York: Touchstone, 1996. Haunting account of a year and a half in the Nazi death camp; see also *The Drowned and the Saved*.

Wendy Lower, *Nazi Empire-Building and the Holocaust in Ukraine*. Durham, NC: University of North Carolina Press, 2005. How Nazism exposed its imperial and genocidal nature most nakedly in the occupied territories of the East.

David B. MacDonald, *Identity Politics in the Age of Genocide: The Holocaust and Historical Representation*. London: Routledge, 2008. How non-Jews have deployed the language and motifs of the Holocaust to highlight their own and others' victimization.

Peter Novick, *The Holocaust in American Life*. Boston, MA: Mariner, 2000. Myth-shattering investigation of the Holocaust's evolving interpretations, and its emergence as a unifying force in American Jewish life.

Alan S. Rosenbaum, ed., *Is the Holocaust Unique? Perspectives on Comparative Genocide*, 3rd edn. Boulder, CO: Westview Press, 2009. Important and controversial essays, including some significant new ones for this edition.

Ron Rosenbaum, *Explaining Hitler: The Search for the Origins of His Evil*. New York: Perennial, 1999. Quest for the essence of the malignancy that was Hitler.

Shlomo Venezia, *Inside the Gas Chambers: Eight Months in the Sonderkommando of Auschwitz*. Cambridge: Polity, 2009. Astonishing testimony of a Greek Jew forced to serve in the gas chambers and crematoria of the Nazis' most destructive death camp.

NOTES

1   In religious usage, a "holocaust" is "a sacrificial offering wholly consumed by fire in exaltation of God" (Arno J. Mayer, *Why Did the Heavens Not Darken? The "Final Solution" in History* [New York: Pantheon, 1988], p. 16). However, in the twentieth century, this was supplanted by a secular usage, in which "holocaust" designates "a wide variety of conflagrations, massacres, wars, and disasters." See Jon Petrie's fascinating etymological study, "The Secular Word HOLOCAUST: Scholarly Myths, History, and 20th Century Meanings," *Journal of Genocide Research*, 2: 1 (2000), pp. 31–64.

2   Donald L. Niewyk, "Holocaust: The Jews," in Samuel L. Totten *et al.*, eds, *Century of Genocide: Eyewitness Accounts and Critical Views* (New York: Garland Publishing, 1997), p. 136. The figure of 5.1 to 5.4 million killed is used by the US Holocaust Museum; see

Peter Balakian, *The Burning Tigris: The Armenian Genocide and America's Response* (New York: HarperCollins, 2003), p. 195.

3 Statistics cited in Michael Shermer and Alex Grobman, *Denying History: Who Says the Holocaust Never Happened and Why Do They Say It?* (Berkeley, CA: University of California Press, 2002), p. 174. Saul Friedländer also estimates "between five and six million Jews . . . killed" in the Holocaust: Friedländer, *The Years of Extermination: Nazi Germany and the Jews, 1939–1945* (New York: HarperCollins, 2007), p. 662.

4 Yehuda Bauer, *Rethinking the Holocaust* (New Haven, CT: Yale University Press, 2001), p. xi.

5 See Marvin Perry and Frederick M. Schweitzer, eds, *Antisemitic Myths: A Historical and Contemporary Anthology* (Bloomington, IN: Indiana University Press, 2008).

6 Daniel Jonah Goldhagen, *Hitler's Willing Executioners: Ordinary Germans and the Holocaust* (New York: Vintage, 1997), pp. 37–38. For a detailed study of the progressive demonization of the Jews, see Steven T. Katz, "Medieval Antisemitism: The Process of Mythification," ch. 6 in Katz, *The Holocaust in Historical Context, Vol. 1: The Holocaust and Mass Death before the Modern Age* (Oxford: Oxford University Press, 1994), pp. 225–316. However, as Mark Levene has pointed out to me, there was also a sense in which medieval Christianity *needed* the Jews – "for its own Christological endtime" and teleological myth. It may thus have been constrained from launching a full-scale genocidal assault on them. Levene, personal communication, August 26, 2005.

7 Colin Tatz, *With Intent to Destroy: Reflecting on Genocide* (London: Verso, 2003), p. 44.

8 Luther quoted in Raul Hilberg, *The Destruction of the European Jews* (3rd edn), Vol. 1 (New Haven, CT: Yale University Press, 2003), p. 13.

9 The most infamous anti-semitic tract of modern times is the *Protocols of the Elders of Zion* (1903), a pamphlet that is now generally held to have been devised by the Tsar's secret police in pre-revolutionary Russia, but which purported to represent the ambitions and deliberations of a global Jewish conspiracy against Christian civilization. For the complete text of the *Protocols*, and a point-by-point refutation, see Steven Leonard Jacobs and Mark Weitzman, *Dismantling the Big Lie: the Protocols of the Elders of Zion* (Jersey City, NJ: Ktav Publishing House, 2003 – *n.b.* the centenary of the *Protocols*). For a consideration of its bizarrely enduring influence, see Evan Derkacz, "Again With the 'Jewish Conspiracy,'" AlterNet.org, April 11, 2006. http://www.alternet.org/story/34812.

10 Nor is the institution of the anti-semitic pogrom unknown even in post-World War Two Europe, as Jan T. Gross's sterling study, *Fear: Anti-Semitism in Poland After Auschwitz: An Essay in Historical Interpretation*, (New York: Random House, 2006) makes clear.

11 In addition, for exponents of biological anti-semitism (a nineteenth-century invention), Jews came to be viewed as *innately* at odds with Western-Christian civilization. Religious conversion could no longer expunge their Jewishness – which helps explain why this option was denied to Jews under Nazi rule. My thanks to Benjamin Madley for this point.

12 Ronnie S. Landau, *The Nazi Holocaust* (Chicago, IL: Ivan R. Dee, 1994), p. 44.

13 In the case of France, strong arguments have been made that anti-semitism was far more widespread and virulent, in elite and popular opinion, than was true in Germany. But "in France – unlike Germany – whatever the strength of antisemitic feeling on the streets, in the bars and in the universities, political power always remained in the hands of the liberal republicans, a government which never endorsed political antisemitism" (Landau, *The Nazi Holocaust*, p. 63). However, when dictatorial government and "eliminationist anti-semitism" (Daniel Goldhagen's term) *were* imposed in France from 1940 to 1944 – under direct Nazi occupation and under the Vichy puppet regime – the authorities and a key section of the population cooperated enthusiastically in the transport for mass execution of the Jews.

14 Richard Plant, *The Pink Triangle: The Nazi War against Homosexuals* (New York: Owl Books, 1988), p. 23.

15 Adolf Hitler, *Mein Kampf* (My Struggle), trans. Ralph Mannheim (Boston, MA: Houghton Mifflin, 1943), p. 562.

16 Landau, *The Nazi Holocaust*, pp. 317, 122.

17 See Orlando Patterson, *Slavery and Social Death: A Comparative Study* (Cambridge, MA: Harvard University Press, 1982), and the discussion in Goldhagen, *Hitler's Willing Executioners*, pp. 168–70.

18 Goldhagen, *Hitler's Willing Executioners*, p. 141. A recent book treatment is Alan E. Steinweis, *Kristallnacht 1938* (Cambridge, MA: The Belknap Press of Harvard University Press, 2009). For an excellent short analysis, see Leonidas E. Hill, "The Pogrom of November 9–10, 1938 in Germany," in Paul R. Brass, ed., *Riots and Pogroms* (Washington Square, NY: New York University Press, 1996), pp. 89–113.

19 Robert Gellately, *Backing Hitler: Consent and Coercion in Nazi Germany* (Oxford: Oxford University Press, 2001), p. vii.

20 Omer Bartov, *Germany's War and the Holocaust: Disputed Histories* (Ithaca, NY: Cornell University Press, 2003), p. 197.

21 Victor Klemperer, *I Will Bear Witness 1933–1941* (New York: The Modern Library, 1999), pp. 165, 329–30, 393, 422, 429; Klemperer, *I Will Bear Witness 1942–1945* (New York: The Modern Library, 2001), pp. 66, 71. Elisabeth Freund, a Jewish Berliner, also described the mixed but frequently sympathetic reaction that German Jews received from "Aryans" when forced to don the yellow star in September 1941: "I am greeted on the street with special politeness by complete strangers, and in the street car ostentatiously a seat is freed for me, although those wearing a star are allowed to sit only if no Aryan is still standing. But sometimes guttersnipes call out abusive words after me. And occasionally Jews are said to have been beaten up. Someone tells me of an experience in the city train. A mother saw that her little girl was sitting beside a Jew: 'Lieschen, sit down on the other bench, you don't need to sit beside a Jew.' At that an Aryan worker stood up, saying: 'And I don't need to sit next to Lieschen.'" Quoted in Friedländer, *The Years of Extermination*, p. 253.

    The important study by Eric A. Johnson and Karl-Heinz Reuband, *What We Knew: Terror, Mass Murder, and Everyday Life in Nazi Germany: An Oral History* (New York: Basic Books, 2005), further buttresses Klemperer's impression that anti-semitism was not widespread in Germany before 1933. Most German Jewish Holocaust survivors interviewed for the volume "stated that they and their families had felt well accepted and integrated in German society. Only a few believed that anti-Semitism was especially prevalent in Germany before the Nazi takeover in January 1933." However, and again meshing with Klemperer's documentation of a swiftly darkening situation, "the figures show that after Hitler took power in 1933, the once positive relations between Jews and non-Jews deteriorated. Whereas over two-thirds of the survivors' families before 1933 had friendly relations with non-Jews in their communities, after 1933 nearly two-thirds had relations that the survivors described as clearly worse or even hostile . . . Very few Jewish families in any German communities after 1933 maintained friendly associations with non-Jews . . . Even more disturbing, 22 percent of the survivors . . . suffered physical beatings from German civilians, and this was nearly three times the percentage of those who suffered beatings from Nazi policemen or other officials . . ." (pp. 269, 273, 279). While one-third of survivors "received significant help and support from non-Jewish German civilians during the Third Reich," it was also the case that "about two-thirds could not find a single German willing to help them, and one can only wonder about the Jews who did not survive" (p. 283).

22 Christopher R. Browning, *The Path to Genocide: Essays on Launching the Final Solution* (Cambridge, MA: Cambridge University Press, 1992), p. ix.

23 Mayer, *Why Did the Heavens Not Darken?*, pp. 114, 116–17.

24 Michael Burleigh, "Psychiatry, German Society and the Nazi 'Euthanasia' Programme," in Omer Bartov, ed., *The Holocaust: Origins, Implementation, Aftermath* (London: Routledge, 2000), p. 70.

25 Landau, *The Nazi Holocaust*, pp. 154–55. In his memoir of the Warsaw ghetto, Alexander Donat gives a figure for half a million ghetto internees as "27,000 apartments in an area of 750 acres, with six or seven persons to a room" (Donat, *The Holocaust Kingdom*

[Washington, DC: Holocaust Library, 1999], p. 24). A famous portrait of life in the Warsaw ghetto in 1941, conveying the hardship and horror of ghetto life, is provided by the photographs taken by a German army officer, Heinrich Jost. See Gunther Schwarberg, *In the Ghetto of Warsaw: Photographs by Heinrich Jost* (Göttingen: Steidl Publishing, 2001).

26 See Richard Rhodes, *Masters of Death: The SS-Einsatzgruppen and the Invention of the Holocaust* (New York: Alfred A. Knopf, 2002).

27 Mayrhofer quoted in Wendy Lower, *Nazi Empire-Building and the Holocaust in Ukraine* (Durham, NC: University of North Carolina Press, 2005), pp. 133–34.

28 Omer Bartov, *Germany's War and the Holocaust: Disputed Histories* (Ithaca, NY: Cornell University Press, 2003), p. 14. See also the excellent two-part essay by Wolfgang Weber, "The Debate in Germany over the Crimes of Hitler's *Wehrmacht*," World Socialist Web Site, September 19–20, 2001, http://www.wsws.org/articles/2001/sep2001/wehr-s19.shtml and http://www.wsws.org/articles/2001/sep2001/wehr-s20.shtml.

29 A key "tipping point" for the Wehrmacht's "indiscriminate, systematic and wholesale resort to carnage" was the Commissar Order issued on June 6, 1941, which called for "Communist Party functionaries . . . to be identified . . . and murdered by the army either on the spot or in rear areas." "Effectively," notes Michael Burleigh, "the army was assuming the functions hitherto performed by the Einsatzgruppen, namely the killing of an entire group of people solely by virtue of their membership of that group and without formal process." Burleigh, *Ethics and Extermination: Reflections on Nazi Genocide* (Cambridge: Cambridge University Press, 1997), p. 67.

30 Hannah Arendt, *Eichmann in Jerusalem: A Report on the Banality of Evil* (New York: The Viking Press, 1965), p. 107.

31 Peter Fritzsche, *Life and Death in the Third Reich* (Cambridge, MA: The Belknap Press of Harvard University Press, 2008), p. 200.

32 Kretschmer quoted in Shermer and Grobman, *Denying History*, p. 185.

33 This gendered element of the slaughter is discussed further in Chapter 13.

34 Jacques Sémelin, *Purify and Destroy: The Political Uses of Massacre and Genocide* (New York: Columbia University Press, 2007), p. 276.

35 The statistics are drawn from Landau, *The Nazi Holocaust*.

36 Fritzsche, *Life and Death in the Third Reich*, p. 215.

37 "Whether the Germans were killing [Jews] immediately and directly in the gas chambers of an extermination camp or working and starving them to death in camps that they had not constructed for the express purpose of extermination (namely in concentration or 'work' camps), the mortality rates of Jews in camps was at exterminatory, genocidal levels and typically far exceeded the mortality rates of other groups living side by side with them. . . . The monthly death rate for Jews in Mauthausen [camp] was, from the end of 1942 to 1943, 100 percent. Mauthausen was not formally an extermination camp and, indeed, it was not for non-Jews, who at the end of 1943 all had a mortality rate below 2 percent." Goldhagen, *Hitler's Willing Executioners*, p. 173. For more on the Nazi system of forced and slave labor, see Wolf Gruner, *Jewish Forced Labor Under the Nazis: Economic Needs and Racial Aims, 1938–1944*, trans. Kathleen M. Dell'Orto (Cambridge: Cambridge University Press, 2006).

38 On the forced marches of Jews and other camp inmates, see "Marching to What End?," ch. 14 in Goldhagen, *Hitler's Willing Executioners*, pp. 355–71.

39 Niewyk, "Holocaust: The Jews," p. 150.

40 Ibid.; for Epstein's testimony, see pp. 150–70.

41 Hitler quoted in Gerald Fleming, *Hitler and the Final Solution* (Berkeley, CA: University of California Press, 1984), p. 17.

42 Tatz, *With Intent to Destroy*, p. 22.

43 Browning, *The Path to Genocide*, p. 86.

44 Michael Burleigh and Wolfgang Wippermann, *The Racial State: Germany 1933–1945* (Cambridge: Cambridge University Press, 1991), p. 96. Dan Stone likewise contends that "there are now very few historians who would take either an extreme intentionalist or an

extreme functionalist position, since most now recognize both that before 1941 or 1942 there was no clearly formulated blueprint for genocide and that a worldview built on mystical race thinking, especially anti-Semitism, lay at the heart of the regime." Stone, "The Holocaust and its Historiography," in Dan Stone, ed., *The Historiography of Genocide* (London: Palgrave Macmillan, 2008), p. 377.

45 Shermer and Grobman, *Denying History*, p. 213.

46 Hilberg, *The Destruction of the European Jews*, Vol. 1, pp. 139–40; Arendt, *Eichmann in Jerusalem*, pp. 59–60.

47 Arendt, *Eichmann in Jerusalem*, pp. 117–18, 125. See also the discussion in Hilberg, *The Destruction of the European Jews*, Vol. 1, pp. 218–22. "With the growth of the destructive function of the Judenräte, many Jewish leaders felt an almost irresistible urge to look like their German masters" (p. 219).

48 Raul Hilberg, *Perpetrators, Victims, Bystanders: The Jewish Catastrophe 1933–1945* (New York: Perennial, 1993), p. 170. In *The Destruction of the European Jews* (Vol. 2, p. 901), Hilberg referred to "masses of Jewish deportees, numb, fantasy-ridden, and filled with illusions, [who] reacted with mechanical cooperation to every German command" (the specific reference is to the Hungarian deportations of 1944).

49 See Richard Rashke, *Escape from Sobibor* (Champaign, IL: University of Illinois Press, 1995); Israel Gutman, *Resistance: The Warsaw Ghetto Uprising* (Boston, MA: Houghton Mifflin, 1998). Also notable was the doomed rebellion of the *Sonderkommando* (Jews selected to do the dirty work in the gas chambers and crematoria) at Auschwitz II-Birkenau in October 1944, and the Polish Jewish partisan movement led by the three Bielski brothers, depicted in the 2008 film *Defiance* (based on Nechama Tec, *Defiance: The True Story of the Bielski Partisans* [Oxford: Oxford University Press, 1994]).

50 Donat, *The Holocaust Kingdom*, p. 7.

51 Daniel Jonah Goldhagen, *Worse Than War: Genocide, Eliminationism, and the Ongoing Assault on Humanity* (New York: Basic Books, 2009), p. 133.

52 Bauer, *Rethinking the Holocaust*, p. 213.

53 Browning, *The Path to Genocide*, p. ix.

54 See John Cornwell, *Hitler's Pope: The Secret History of Pius XII* (New York: Penguin, 2008); Daniel Jonah Goldhagen, *A Moral Reckoning: The Role of the Catholic Church in the Holocaust and Its Unfulfilled Duty of Repair* (New York: Alfred A. Knopf, 2002).

55 Friedländer, *The Years of Extermination*, pp. 568, 572.

56 Reginald H. Phelps, quoted in Goldhagen, *Hitler's Willing Executioners*, p. 443.

57 In the case of Denmark, Saul Friedländer wrote: "The Germans had allowed a semi-autonomous Danish government to stay in place, and their own presence as occupiers was hardly felt. Hitler had decided on this peculiar course to avoid unnecessary difficulties in a country [that was] strategically important . . . 'racially related' to the community of Nordic peoples, and mainly an essential supplier of agricultural products . . .'" Friedländer, *The Years of Extermination*, p. 545.

58 Hilberg, *Perpetrators, Victims, Bystanders*, p. 258.

59 Burleigh, *Ethics and Extermination*, pp. 155, 164.

60 Burleigh and Wippermann, *The Racial State*, p. 51.

61 Christopher Browning, *Ordinary Men: Reserve Police Battalion 101 and the Final Solution in Poland* (New York: HarperPerennial, 1998), pp. 184, 186.

62 Goldhagen, *Hitler's Willing Executioners*, pp. 277, 446.

63 See Robert R. Shandley, ed., *Unwilling Germans? The Goldhagen Debate* (Minneapolis, MN: The University of Minnesota Press, 1998).

64 Friedländer, *The Years of Extermination*, p. 511. See Chapter 14 for further discussion of history and memory in Germany after the Second World War.

65 Hilberg, *Perpetrators, Victims, Bystanders*, p. 191. As Martha Minow comments, "The creation of Israel could be viewed as a kind of international reparation effort." Minow, *Between Vengeance and Forgiveness: Facing History after Genocide and Mass Violence* (Boston, MA: Beacon Press, 1998), p. 133.

66 See Idith Zertal, *Israel's Holocaust and the Politics of Nationhood* (Cambridge: Cambridge University Press, 2005).

67 "Israel Pledges to Protect Itself from 'New Holocaust' Threat Posed by Iran's Nuclear Programme," *Daily Telegraph*, April 21, 2009. Ahmadinejad's comments, made to a "World Without Zionism" conference in Tehran on October 26, 2005, were translated in many media as "Israel must be wiped off the map," suggesting the country and its population should be physically destroyed. However, this is disputed by, among others, Juan Cole, who claims a more accurate translation is: "This regime occupying Jerusalem must vanish from the page of time." In this reading, asserts Cole, "Ahmadinejad was not making a threat, he was quoting a saying of [Ayatollah] Khomeini and urging that pro-Palestinian activists in Iran not give up hope – that the occupation of Jerusalem was no more a continued inevitability than had been the hegemony of the Shah's government," overthrown in Iran in 1979. See Cole, "Informed Comment," May 3, 2006, http://www.juancole.com/2006/05/hitchens-hacker-and-hitchens.html.

68 See, e.g., "[Palestinian Authority president Mahmoud] Abbas: IDF [Israel Defense Forces] Action Worse than Holocaust," *The Jerusalem Post*, March 2, 2008; "Iran: Israeli Crimes Outstrip Holocaust," Reuters dispatch on Aljazeera.net, February 12, 2006.

69 Ilan Pappé, "Genocide in Gaza," *The Electronic Intifada*, September 2, 2006, http://electronicintifada.net/v2/article5656.shtml.

70 Richard Falk, "Slouching toward a Palestinian Holocaust," The Transnational Foundation for Peace and Future Research, June 29, 2007, http://www.transnational.org/Area_MiddleEast/2007/Falk_PalestineGenocide.html. A Red Cross report leaked in 2008 described a "progressive deterioration in food security for up to 70 per cent of Gaza's population" as a result of the Israeli siege, adding that "Chronic malnutrition is on a steadily rising trend and micronutrient deficiencies are of great concern." Quoted in Donald Macintyre, "Chronic Malnutrition in Gaza Blamed on Israel," *The Independent*, November 15, 2008. Former US president Jimmy Carter stated in 2008 that the Palestinian population of Gaza was being "starved to death," with caloric intakes lower than in the poorest African countries: "It's an atrocity what is being perpetrated as punishment on the people in Gaza. . . . I think it is an abomination that this continues to go on." Jonathan Wright, "Carter Calls Gaza Blockade a Crime and Atrocity," Reuters dispatch on Yahoo! News, April 18, 2008.

71 Goldstone report cited in Rory McCarthy, "UN Investigation Finds Evidence of War Crimes in Gaza Campaign," *The Guardian*, October 25, 2009.

72 Alex Alvarez, *Governments, Citizens, and Genocide: A Comparative and Interdisciplinary Approach* (Bloomington, IN: Indiana University Press, 2001), p. 14.

73 The phrase "uniquely unique" was first used by Alice L. Eckhardt and Roy Eckhardt; see Gunnar Heinsohn, "What Makes the Holocaust a Uniquely Unique Genocide?," *Journal of Genocide Research*, 2: 3 (2000), p. 430 (n. 95).

74 Katz, *The Holocaust in Historical Context*, p. 28.

75 Mark Levene, *Genocide in the Age of the Nation-State, Vol. 1: The Meaning of Genocide* (London: I.B. Tauris, 2005), p. 2.

76 Lopate, cited in Helen Fein, *Genocide: A Sociological Perspective* (London: Sage Publications, 1993), p. 52.

77 A recent polemic charges that a "Holocaust industry" has been created to win financial concessions from banks, industrial enterprises, and others who profited from the Jewish catastrophe. See Norman G. Finkelstein, *The Holocaust Industry: Reflections on the Exploitation of Jewish Suffering* (new edn) (New York: Verso, 2003).

78 As David Moshman put it: "True, the Holocaust is phenomenologically distinct from every other genocide, but so is every other genocide distinct from every other. Every genocide is unique, and the Holocaust is no exception." Moshman, "Conceptions of Genocide and Perceptions of History," in Stone, ed., *The Historiography of Genocide*, p. 72.

79 Nicholas Wheeler, *Saving Strangers: Humanitarian Intervention in International Society* (Oxford: Oxford University Press, 2000), p. 212.

80 Interestingly, Vol. 2 of Steven Katz's *The Holocaust in Historical Context*, which was supposed to apply his uniqueness thesis to twentieth-century cases of mass killing, was scheduled for publication some years ago, but has yet to appear. I have often wondered whether Katz hit an insuperable roadblock in applying his uniqueness thesis to the Rwandan genocide, which occurred the same year his first volume was published.

81 Hilberg, *The Destruction of the European Jews*, Vol. 3, p. 1075.

82 Bartov, *Germany's War and the Holocaust*, p. 106.

83 Thomas Cushman, "Is Genocide Preventable? Some Theoretical Considerations," *Journal of Genocide Research*, 5: 4 (2003), p. 528; Dan Stone, "Introduction," in Stone, ed., *The Historiography of Genocide*, p. 2. Interestingly, the fate of the Jews was not primary in Raphael Lemkin's framing of genocide in his 1944 book, which first propounded the concept. Martin Shaw has written: "For Lemkin (although himself Jewish and absolutely concerned about the horrors inflicted on the Jews), Nazi genocide was never exclusively or primarily an anti-Jewish campaign; that was not the standard against which other Nazi persecutions were measured. On the contrary, his book aimed to demonstrate (by placing on record translations of Nazi laws in the occupied countries) how comprehensively, against a range of subject peoples, the Nazis had attempted to destroy the existence of nations, their well-being, institutions and ways of life." Shaw, *What is Genocide?* (Cambridge: Polity, 2007), pp. 20–21.

84 Alan S. Rosenbaum, "Introduction to the Third Edition," in Rosenbaum, ed., *Is the Holocaust Unique? Perspectives on Comparative Genocide* (Boulder, CO: Westview Press, 2009), p. 21. Martin Shaw goes further: "In order to understand other genocides . . . the imperative is not to compare them with the Holocaust – which as a specific episode was necessarily unique in many respects – but to interpret them in terms of a coherent general conception. We don't need a standard that steers all discussion towards a maximal concept of industrial extermination, a standard that distorts even the Nazi genocide against the Jews. We do need a coherent, generic, sociological concept of genocide that can make sense of a range of historical experiences." Shaw, *What is Genocide?*, p. 45.

BOX 6A THE NAZIS' OTHER VICTIMS

While most people associate Nazi genocide with the Jewish Holocaust, a plethora of other victim groups accounted for the majority of those killed by the Nazis. Only in 1942 did the mass murder of Jews come to predominate, as historian Christopher Browning pointed out:

> If the Nazi regime had suddenly ceased to exist in the first half of 1941, its most notorious achievements in human destruction would have been the so-called euthanasia killing of seventy to eighty thousand German mentally ill and the systematic murder of the Polish intelligentsia. If the regime had disappeared in the spring of 1942, its historical infamy would have rested on the "war of destruction" against the Soviet Union. The mass death of some two million prisoners of war in the first nine months of that conflict would have stood out even more prominently than the killing of approximately one-half million Jews in that same period.

"Ever since," wrote Browning, the Jewish Holocaust "has overshadowed National Socialism's other all-too-numerous atrocities."[1] It does so in this book as well. Yet it is important to devote attention, however inadequate, to the Nazis' other victims.

PRE-WAR PERSECUTIONS AND THE "EUTHANASIA" CAMPAIGN

Communists and socialists

The first Nazi concentration camp was located at Dachau, near Munich. Opened in March 1933 – two months after the Nazis seized power – its stated purpose was "to concentrate, in one place, not only all Communist officials but also, if necessary, the officials of . . . other Marxist formations who threaten the security of the state."[2] Bolshevism was as central to Hitler's *Weltanschauung* (worldview) as anti-semitism, embodying the decadent modernist tendencies that he loathed. In fact, Hitler's ideology and geopolitical strategy are best seen as motivated by a hatred of "Judeo-Bolshevism," and a conviction that the Nazis' territorial ambitions in Central and Eastern Europe could be realized only through victory over "the Marxist-cum-Bolshevik 'octopus' and the Jewish world conspiracy."[3]

One can distinguish between pre-war and wartime phases of the campaign against communists and socialists. In the pre-war stage, these sectors dominated the security policies of the Reich. They were the major targets of state violence and incarceration in camps; Jews-as-Jews were not targeted for substantial physical violence or imprisonment until *Kristallnacht* in 1938, by which time the German Left had been crushed. Communists, socialists, and other Left-oppositionists were also purged from public institutions in a manner very similar to Jews.[4] Historian Arnold Sywottek estimates that the Gestapo murdered in excess of 100,000 communists during the twelve years of the Third Reich.[5]

After the occupation of western Poland in September–October 1939, and especially with the invasion of eastern Poland and the Soviet Union in June 1941, the struggle against bolshevism became bound up with the Nazis' ambition to enslave and exterminate the Slavic "subhuman." "What the Bolsheviks are must be clear to anybody who ever set sight upon the face of a Red Commissar," declared an article in the Nazi military paper, *Mitteilungen für die Truppe* (Information for the Troops), as the invasion of the Soviet Union was launched in June 1941. "Here no theoretical explanations are necessary anymore. To call beastly the traits of these people, a high percentage of whom are Jews, would be an insult to animals. . . . In these Commissars we see the uprising of subhumans against noble blood."[6] As this quotation suggests, the Nazis' ideological struggle against communists and socialists became intertwined with the national and military struggle with the USSR; the threat of ethnic swamping by "barbarians from the East"; and the assault on European Jewry.

Asocials and undesirables

The Nazis' quest for racial purity and social homogeneity meant that "asocial" elements were to be annihilated or, in some cases, reformed. An effective study of this phenomenon is Robert Gellately's book on Nazism and German public opinion, *Backing Hitler*. Considered asocial was "anyone who did not participate as a good citizen and accept their social responsibilities." Among the groups harassed and punished were men seen as "shirking" paid work, or otherwise congenitally prone to unemployment or vagabondage.[7] Gellately describes a "special action" organized by Nazi police chief Heinrich Himmler in March 1937 "to arrest 2,000 people out of work":

> The instruction was to send to concentration camps, those who "*in the opinion of the Criminal Police*" were professional criminals, repeat offenders, or habitual sex offenders. The enthusiasm of the police was such that they arrested not 2,000, but 2,752 people, only 171 of whom had broken their probation. Police used the event as a pretext to get rid of "problem cases." Those arrested were described as break-in specialists (938), thieves (741), sex offenders (495), swindlers (436), robbers (56), and dealers in stolen goods (86). Only 85 of them [3 percent] were women.[8]

According to Gellately, "A recurrent theme in Hitler's thinking was that in the event of war, the home front would not fall prey to saboteurs, that is, anyone vaguely considered to be 'criminals,' 'pimps,' or 'deserters'." The result was that "asocial" men, along with some women accused of involvement in the sex trade or common crimes, were confined in "camps [that] were presented as educative institutions . . . places for 'race defilers, rapists, sexual degenerates and habitual criminals'" (quoting an article in *Das Schwarze Korps* newspaper). Although "these camps were nothing like the death camps in the eastern occupied territories, the suffering, death, and outright murder in them was staggering."[9]

Just as Jews and bolshevism blurred in the Nazis' ideology, it is important to recognize the overlap among asocials, Jews, and Roma (Gypsies). It was a cornerstone of the Nazi demonization of Jews that they were essentially a parasitic class, incapable of "honest" work and thus driven to usury, lazy cosmopolitanism, and criminality. Likewise, perhaps the *core* of the Nazi racial hatred of Roma lay in their stereotypical depiction as shiftless and inclined to criminal behavior. The genocidal consequences of these stereotypes are examined in the "Other Holocausts" section, below.

Homosexual men

For all the promiscuous hatreds of Adolf Hitler, "homophobia was not one of his major obsessions,"[10] and Hitler does not seem to have been the moving force behind the Nazi campaign against gay men. (Lesbian women were never systematically targeted or arrested.)[11] Rather, that dubious honor goes to the owlish Heinrich Himmler, supreme commander of the SS paramilitary force, "whose loathing of homosexuals knew no bounds."[12] As early as 1937, in a speech to the SS academy at Bad Toelz, Himmler pledged: "Like stinging nettles we will rip them [homosexuals] out, throw them on a heap, and burn them. Otherwise . . . we'll see the end of Germany, the end of the Germanic world." Later he would proclaim to his Finnish physiotherapist, Dr. Felix Kersten:

> We must exterminate these people root and branch. Just think how many children will never be born because of this, and how a people can be broken in nerve and spirit when such a plague gets hold of it. . . . The homosexual is a traitor to his own people and must be rooted out.[13]

As these comments suggest, the reviling of gays was linked to Nazi beliefs surrounding asocial and "useless" groups, who not only contributed nothing productive to the body politic, but actively subverted it. Gay males – because they chose to have sex with men – "were self-evidently failing in their duty to contribute to the demographic expansion of the 'Aryan-Germanic race,' at a time when millions of young men had perished in the First World War."[14] Just as Roma and (especially) Jews were deemed parasites on German society and the national economy, so were gays labeled "as useless as hens which don't lay eggs" and "sociosexual propagation misfits."[15] (They did, however, have their uses: among some conquered peoples, homosexuality was to be encouraged, since it "would hasten their degeneracy, and thus their demise.")[16]

Richard Plant's study of the Nazi persecution of gays, *The Pink Triangle*, estimated the number of men convicted for homosexual "crimes" from 1933 to 1944 to be "between 50,000 and 63,000, of which nearly 4,000 were juveniles."[17] In the concentration camps that were the destiny of thousands of them, their "fate . . . can only be described as ghastly."[18] Like the Jews, they were forced to wear a special badge (the pink triangle of Plant's title), were referred to contemptuously as *Mannweiber* ("manwives"), and were segregated from their fellow prisoners, who often joined in the derision and brutalization. An inmate at Dachau reported that "the prisoners with the pink triangle did not live very long; they were quickly and systematically exterminated by the SS."[19] According to Konnilyn Feig, they found themselves "tormented from all sides as they struggle[d] to avoid being assaulted, raped, worked, and beaten to death."[20] Gay men were also among the likeliest candidates for medical experiments. At no point was support and solace likely from relatives or friends, because of the shame and stigma attaching to their "crimes." Plant estimates that the large majority of homosexuals consigned to concentration camps perished there – some 5,000 to 15,000 men.[21]

Jehovah's Witnesses and religious dissidents

If gays were dragged into the Nazi holocaust by their "traitorous" reluctance to contribute to Germany's demographic revival, Jehovah's Witnesses – already anathematized as a religious cult by the dominant Protestant and Catholic religious communities – were condemned for refusing to swear loyalty to the Nazi regime and to serve in the German military. In April 1935 the faith was formally outlawed, and later that year the first 400 Jehovah's Witnesses were consigned to the Sachsenhausen concentration camp. By 1939 the number incarcerated there and in other prisons and camps had ballooned to 6,000.

When war broke out in September 1939, the Witnesses' rejection of military service aroused still greater malevolence. Only a few days after the German invasion of Poland, a believer who refused to swear loyalty to the regime, August Dickmann, was executed by the Gestapo "in order to set an example."[22] In all, "Over the course of the dictatorship, as many as 10,000 members of the community were arrested, with 2,000 sent to concentration camps, where they were treated dreadfully and as many as 1,200 died or were murdered."[23]

In a curious twist, however, a positive stereotype also arose around the Witnesses. They came to be viewed in the camps as "industrious, neat, and tidy, and uncompromising in [their] religious principles." Accordingly,

> the SS ultimately switched to a policy of trying to exploit [the Witnesses'] devotion to duty and their reliability. . . . They were used as general servants in SS households or put to work in small Kommandos [work teams] when there was a threat that prisoners might escape. In Ravensbrück [women's concentration camp], they were showcased as "exemplary prisoners," while in Niederhagen, the only camp where they constituted the core population, they were put to work on renovations.[24]

As for mainstream religion, in general the Nazis distrusted it, preferring their own brand of mysticism and *Volk*-worship. Their desire not to provoke unrest among the general population, or (before the war) international opposition, limited their campaign against the main Protestant dominations and the large Catholic minority in Germany. No such restraint obtained in occupied Poland, however, where leading Catholic figures were swept up in the campaign of eliticide against the Polish intelligentsia. At home, as the war turned against Germany, religious dissidents of all stripes came to be hounded, imprisoned, and killed. The best-known case is that of the Protestant pastor Dietrich Bonhoeffer, who declaimed against the Nazi regime from his pulpit, and was hanged in Flossenburg concentration camp shortly before the war ended. His *Letters and Papers from Prison* has become a classic of devotional literature.[25]

The handicapped and infirm

As with every other group the Nazis targeted, the campaign against the handicapped and infirm exploited a popular receptiveness based on long-standing patterns of discrimination and anathematization in European and Western culture. An offshoot of the Western drive for modernity was the development of a science of eugenics, taking both positive and negative forms: "Positive eugenics was the attempt to encourage increased breeding by those who were considered particularly fit; negative eugenics aimed at eliminating the unfit."[26] The foci of this international movement were Germany, Great Britain, and the United States (the US pioneered the use of forced sterilization against those considered "abnormal").[27] In Germany in the 1920s, treatises by noted legal and medical authorities railed against those "unworthy of life" and demanded the "destruction" of disabled persons in institutions. This was not murder but "mercy death."[28] Such views initially received strong public backing, even among many relatives of institutionalized patients.[29]

Once in power, the Nazis intensified the trend. Within a few months, they had promulgated the Law for the Prevention of Hereditarily Diseased Progeny, beginning a policy that by 1945 had led to the forced sterilization of some 300,000 people. The Marriage Health Law followed in 1935, under which Germans seeking to wed were forced to provide medical documentation proving that they did not carry hereditary conditions or afflictions. If they could not so demonstrate, the application was rejected.[30]

In the two years prior to the outbreak of the Second World War, Hitler and other Nazi planners began paving the way for the collective killing of disabled infants and children, then of adults. Hitler used the "fog of war" to cover the implementation of the campaign (the authorization, personally signed by Hitler on September 8, 1939, was symbolically backdated to September 1 to coincide with the invasion of Poland). "An elaborate covert bureaucracy"[31] was established in a confiscated Jewish property at Tiergartenstrasse 4 in Berlin, and "Aktion T-4" – as the extermination program was dubbed – moved into high gear. The program's "task was to organise the registration, selection, transfer and murder of a previously calculated target group of 70,000 people, including chronic schizophrenics, epileptics and long-stay patients."[32] All were deemed *unnutze Esser*, "useless eaters" – surely one of the most macabre phrases in the Nazi vocabulary. In the end, the plan was overfulfilled. Among the victims were an estimated 6,000 to 7,000 children, who were starved to death or administered fatal medication. Many adults were dispatched to a prototype gas chamber.[33]

At every point in the chain of death, the complicity of nurses, doctors, and professionals of all stripes was enthusiastic. Yet as the scope of the killing widened, the general population (and Germany's churches) proved more ambivalent, eventually leading to open protest. In August 1941, "Aktion T-4" was closed down in Germany. But a decentralized version continued in operation until the last days of the war, and even beyond (the last victim died on May 29, 1945, under the noses of Allied occupiers). Meanwhile, the heart of the program – its eager supervisors and technicians – was bundled east, to manage the extermination of Jews and others in the death camps of Treblinka, Belzec, and Sobibor in Poland. Thus, "the euthanasia program was the direct precursor of the death factories – ideologically, organizationally, and in terms of personnel."[34]

Predictably, then, mass murder in the eastern occupied territories also targeted the handicapped. "In Poland the Germans killed almost all disabled Poles . . . The same applied in the occupied Soviet Union."[35] With the assistance of the same *Einsatzgruppen* death squads who murdered hundreds of thousands of Jews in the first year of the war, some 100,000 people deemed "unworthy of life" were murdered at a single institution, the Kiev Pathological Institute in Ukraine.[36] In all, perhaps a quarter of a million handicapped and disabled individuals died to further the Nazis' fanatical social-engineering scheme.

Figure 6A.1 A farmer took this clandestine photo of smoke billowing from the crematorium chimney of the Schloss Hartheim killing complex in Germany, as Aktion (Operation) T-4 – the mass murder of the handicapped – was underway in 1940–41. Hartheim was one of six main facilities for the Nazi "euthanasia" campaign, which served as a trial run for the Holocaust, including the use of gas chambers to kill victims.

Source: Wolfgang Schuhmann/United States Holocaust Memorial Museum.

OTHER HOLOCAUSTS

The Slavs

The ethnic designation "Slav" derives from the same root as "slave," and that is the destiny to which Nazi policies sought to consign Poles, Russians, Ukrainians, White Russians (Belorussians), and other Slavic peoples. "The Slavs are a mass of born slaves, who feel the need of a master," Hitler declared, making clear his basically colonialist fantasies for the east: "We'll supply the Ukrainians with scarves, glass beads and everything that colonial peoples like."[37]

But if they were primitive and contemptible, the Slavic "hordes" were also dangerous and expansionist – at least when dominated and directed by Jews (i.e., "Judeo-bolsheviks"). It may be argued that the confrontation with the Slavs was inseparable from, and as central as, the campaign against the Jews. Consider the words of Colonel-General Hoepner, commander of Panzer Group 4 in the invasion of the Soviet Union, on sending his troops into battle:

> The war against the Soviet Union is an essential component of the German people's struggle for existence. It is the old struggle of the Germans against the Slavs, the defense of European culture against the Muscovite-Asiatic flood, the warding off of Jewish Bolshevism. This struggle must have as its aim the demolition of present Russia and must therefore be conducted with unprecedented severity. Both the planning and the execution of every battle must be dictated by an iron will to bring about a merciless, total annihilation of the enemy.[38]

The first victims of the anti-Slav genocide were, however, Polish. Hitler's famous comment, "Who, after all, talks nowadays of the annihilation of the Armenians?" (see Chapter 4), is often mistaken as referring to the impending fate of Jews in Nazi-occupied territories. In fact, Hitler was speaking just before the invasion of Poland on September 1, 1939, referring to commands he had issued to "kill without pity or mercy all men, women, and children of Polish descent or language. Only in this way can we obtain the living space we need."[39] Richard Lukas is left in little doubt of Nazi plans:

> While the Germans intended to eliminate the Jews before the end of the war, most Poles would work as helots until they too shared the fate of the Jews. . . . The conclusion is inescapable that had the war continued, the Poles would have been ultimately obliterated either by outright slaughter in gas chambers, as most Jews had perished, or by a continuation of the policies the Nazis had inaugurated in occupied Poland during the war – genocide by execution, forced labor, starvation, reduction of biological propagation, and Germanization.

Others dispute the claim that non-Jewish Poles were destined for annihilation. Nonetheless, as Lukas notes, "during almost six years of war, Poland lost 6,028,000 of its citizens, or 22 percent of its total population, the highest ratio of losses to population of any country in Europe." Nearly three million of the murdered Poles were Jews, but "over 50 percent . . . were Polish Christians, victims of prison, death camps, raids, executions, epidemics, starvation, excessive work, and ill treatment."[40] Six million Poles were also dispatched to toil in Germany as slave-laborers. The Soviets' depredations during their relatively brief occupation of eastern Poland (September 1939 to June 1941), and again after 1944, also contributed significantly to the death-toll (see Chapter 5).

As for the Slavs of Ukraine, Russia, and other parts of the Soviet Union, their suffering is legendary. A commonly cited estimate is that *about twenty-seven million* Soviet citizens died. The disproportionate number of militarized male victims would have "catastrophic . . . demographic consequences" for decades after, with women of the relevant age groups outnumbering men by two or even three to one.[41] But two-thirds of the victims – *about eighteen million people* – were civilians.[42] Exploitation of Slavs as slave laborers was merciless and genocidal. According to historian Catherine Merridale, "At least three million [Soviet] men and women (one famous Russian source gives a figure of over five million) were shipped off to the Reich to work as slaves. Many of these – probably more than two million – were worked so hard that they joined Europe's Jews in the death camps, discarded by the Reich for disposal like worn-out nags sent to the abattoir."[43]

Titanic Soviet sacrifices, and crushing military force, proved key to Nazi Germany's defeat, with the other Allies playing important supporting roles. Between the German invasion of the USSR in June 1941 and the D-Day invasion of France in June 1944, some 80 percent of German forces were deployed in the East, and the overwhelming majority of German military casualties occurred there. As Yugoslav partisan leader Arso Jovanovic put it at the time: "Over there on the Eastern front – that's the real war, where whole divisions burn up like matchsticks" – and millions of civilians along with them.[44]

Soviet prisoners-of-war

"Next to the Jews in Europe," wrote Alexander Werth, "the biggest single German crime was undoubtedly the extermination by hunger, exposure and in other ways of . . . Russian war prisoners."[45] Yet the murder of at least 3.3 million Soviet POWs is one of the least-known of modern genocides; there is still no full-length book on the subject in English. It also stands as one of the most intensive genocides of all time: "a holocaust that devoured millions," as Catherine Merridale acknowledges.[46] The large majority of POWs, some 2.8 million, were killed in just eight months of 1941–42, a rate of slaughter matched (to my knowledge) only by the 1994 Rwanda genocide.[47]

The Soviet men were captured in massive encirclement operations in the early months of the German invasion, and in gender-selective round-ups that occurred in the newly occupied territories. All men between the ages of 15 and 65 were deemed to be prisoners-of-war, and liable to be "sent to the rear." Given that the Germans, though predicting victory by such epic encirclements, had deliberately avoided making provisions for sheltering and feeding millions of prisoners, "sent to the rear" became a euphemism for mass murder.

"Testimony is eloquent and prolific on the abandonment of entire divisions under the open sky," wrote Alexander Dallin:

> Epidemics . . . decimated the camps. Beatings and abuse by the guards were commonplace. Millions spent weeks without food or shelter. Carloads of prisoners were dead when they arrived at their destination. Casualty figures varied considerably but almost nowhere amounted to less than 30 percent in the winter of 1941–42, and sometimes went as high as 95 percent.[48]

A Hungarian tank officer who visited one POW enclosure described "tens of thousands of Russian prisoners. Many were on the point of expiring. Few could stand on their feet. Their faces were dried up and their eyes sunk deep into their sockets. Hundreds were dying every day, and those who had any strength left dumped them in a vast pit."[49] German guards took their amusement by "throwing a dead dog into the prisoners' compound," citing an eyewitness

Figure 6A.2 Soviet prisoners-of-war await their fate in Nazi captivity, summer or autumn 1941.
Source: Hulton-Deutsch Collection/Corbis.

Figure 6A.3 Mass grave of Soviet prisoners, 1941–42. "The photos . . . were found by chance during a search action. They are from the widow of a member of *Landesschützenbataillon* 432, which guarded the Dulag [= *Durchgangslager*, transit camp for POWs] 121 in Gomel . . . The photo in all probability shows a scene from the huge mass dying of the prisoners of war" (holocaustcontroversies. blogspot.com).

Source: Klaus-Michael Mallmann *et al.*, eds, *Deutscher Osten 1939–1945: Der Weltanschauungskrieg in Photos und Texten* (Darmstadt: Wissenschaftliche Buchgesellschaft, 2003).

account: "Yelling like mad, the Russians would fall on the animal and tear it to pieces with their bare hands. . . . The intestines they'd stuff in their pockets – a sort of iron ration."[50] Cannibalism was rife. Nazi leader Hermann Goering joked that "in the camps for Russian prisoners of war, after having eaten everything possible, including the soles of their boots, they have begun to eat each other, and what is more serious, have also eaten a German sentry."[51]

Hundreds of thousands of Soviet prisoners were sent to Nazi concentration camps, including Auschwitz, which was originally built to house and exploit them. Thousands died in the first tests of the gas chamber complex at Birkenau. Like the handicapped and Roma, then, Soviet POWs were guinea-pigs and stepping-stones in the evolution of genocide against the Jews. The overall estimate for POW fatalities – 3.3 million – is probably low. An important additional group of victims consists of Soviet soldiers, probably hundreds of thousands, who were killed shortly after surrendering.

In one of the twentieth century's most tragic ironies, the two million or so POWs who survived German incarceration were arrested upon repatriation to the USSR, on suspicion of collaboration with the Germans. Most were sentenced to long terms in the Soviet concentration camps, where tens of thousands died in the final years of the Gulag (see Chapter 5).

The Romani genocide (*Porrajmos*)

Perhaps more than any other group, the Nazi genocide against Romani (Gypsy) peoples* parallels the attempted extermination of European Jews. Roma were subjected to virulent racism in the centuries prior to the Holocaust – denounced as dirty, alien, and outside the bonds of social obligation. (Ironically, the Roma "were originally from North India and belonged to the Indo-Germanic speaking, or as Nazi racial anthropologists would have it, 'Aryan' people.")[52]

The grim phrase "lives undeserving of life," which most people associate with Nazi policy towards the handicapped and the Jews, was coined with reference to the Roma in a law passed only a few months after Hitler's seizure of power. Mixed marriages between Germans and Roma, as between "Aryan" Germans and Jews, were outlawed in 1935. The 1935 legislation against "hereditarily diseased progeny," the cornerstone of the campaign against the handicapped, specifically included Roma among its targets.

Figure 6A.4 Roma interned in the Nazis' Belzec death camp in Poland. Of all demographic groups in Europe, the Roma and Sinti – long known as "Gypsies" – were probably the only ones destroyed in the Nazi holocaust in about the same proportion as European Jews. Roma and Sinti remain vulnerable across much of Europe, from Ireland in the west (where they are known as "Travellers") to Romania in the east. They are widely depicted as a shiftless and/or criminal element, and are liable to discrimination, harassment, and vigilante violence.[53]

Source: United States Holocaust Memorial Museum.

* The term "Gypsy" has derogatory connotations for some, and is now often substituted by Roma/Romani, a practice I follow here.

In July 1936, more than two years prior to the first mass round-up of Jewish men, Romani men were dispatched in their hundreds to the Dachau concentration camp outside Munich. (The measures were popular: Michael Burleigh noted "the obvious glee with which unwilling neighbours and local authorities regarded the removal of Sinti and Roma from their streets and neighbourhoods.")[54] While Hitler decreed a brief moratorium on anti-Jewish measures prior to the 1936 Berlin Olympics, raids were conducted in the vicinity of Berlin to capture and incarcerate Roma.

"On Combating the Gypsy Plague" was the title of a 1937 polemic by Heinrich Himmler, taking a break from his fulminations on homosexuals and Jews. It "marked the definitive transition from a Gypsy policy that was understood as a component of the extirpation of 'aliens to the community' . . . to a persecution *sui generis*."[55] The following year, the first reference to an *endgültige Lösung der Zigeunerfrage*, a "total solution" to the Romani "question," appeared in a Nazi pronouncement.[56] A thousand more Roma were condemned to concentration camps in 1938.

A few months after the outbreak of the Second World War, some 250 Romani children at Buchenwald became test subjects for the Zyklon-B cyanide crystals later used to exterminate Jews. In late 1941 and early 1942, about 4,400 Roma were deported from Austria to the death camp at Chelmno, where they were murdered in the mobile gas vans then being deployed against Jews in eastern Poland and the Soviet Union.[57] Up to a quarter of a million more perished in *Einsatzgruppen* executions, "legitimised with the old prejudice that the victims were 'spies.'"[58]

In December 1942, Himmler decreed that Roma be deported to the most notorious of the death camps, Auschwitz-Birkenau. There they lived in a "family camp" (so named because Romani families, unlike Jewish ones, were not broken up), while the Nazi authorities decided what to do with them. A camp doctor who spoke with psychologist Robert Jay Lifton described conditions in the Romani barracks as "extraordinarily filthy and unhygienic even for Auschwitz, a place of starving babies, children and adults."[59] Those who did not die from privation, disease, or horrific medical experiments were finally consigned to the gas chambers in August 1944. In all, "about 20,000 of the 23,000 German and Austrian Roma and Sinti deported to Auschwitz were killed there."[60]

When the toll of the camps is combined with *Einsatzgruppen* operations, the outcome in terms of Romani mortality rates was not very different from the Jewish Holocaust. From a much smaller population, the Roma lost between 500,000 and 1.5 million of their members in the catastrophe that they call the *Porrajmos* ("Devouring"). While the lower figure is standard, Romani scholar Ian Hancock argues that it is "grossly underestimated," failing to recognize the extent to which Romani victims of (for example) the *Einsatzgruppen* death squads were designated as "partisans" or "asocials," or assigned other labels that tended to obscure ethnic identity.[61] When to the camp victims are added the huge numbers of Roma – perhaps more than perished in the camps – who "were murdered in the fields and forests where they lived,"[62] the death toll may well match that of the Armenian genocide.

Until recent years, however, the *Porrajmos* has been little more than a footnote in histories of Nazi mass violence. In part, this reflects the fact that Roma constituted a much smaller proportion of the German and European population than did Jews – about 0.05 percent. In addition, most Roma before and after the Second World War were illiterate, and thus unable to match the outpouring of victims' testimonies and academic analyses by Jewish survivors and scholars. Finally, and relatedly, while anti-semitism subsided dramatically after the war, Roma continued to be marginalized and stigmatized by European societies, as they remain today.

The result, in historian Sybil Milton's words, was "a tacit conspiracy of silence about the isolation, exclusion, and systematic killing of the Roma, rendering much of current Holocaust scholarship deficient and obsolete."[63] Even in contemporary Europe, Roma are the subject of violence and persecution; in a 2009 essay, Hancock declared that "anti-Gypsyism is at an all-time high."[64] Only since the late 1970s has a civil-rights movement, along with a body of scholarly literature, arisen to confront discrimination and to memorialize Romani suffering during the Nazi era.

Germans as victims

For decades after the end of the Second World War, it was difficult to give voice to German suffering in the war. Sixty years after the war's end, it is easier to accept claims that the Germans, too, should be numbered among the victims of Nazism – and victims of Nazism's victims.

Predictably, the debate is sharpest in Germany itself (see further discussion in Chapter 14). Two books published in 2003 symbolized the new visibility of the issue. A novel by Nobel Prize-winning author Günter Grass, *Im Krebsgang* (*Crabwalk*), centers on the twentieth century's worst maritime disaster: the torpedoing of the *Wilhelm Gustloff* by a Soviet submarine, as the converted liner attempted to carry refugees (and some soldiers) from East Prussia to the German heartland, ahead of advancing Soviet armies. Nine thousand people died. In addition, a revisionist historian, Jörg Friedrich, published *Brandstätten* (*Fire Sites*), a compendium of grisly, never-before-seen archival photographs of German victims of Allied fire-bombing (see Chapter 14).[65]

Estimates of the death-toll in the area bombing of German cities "range from about 300,000 to 600,000, and of injuries from 600,000 to over a million." The most destructive raids were those on Hamburg (July 27–28, 1943) and Dresden, "the German Hiroshima" (February 13, 1945).[66] Both strikes resulted in raging fire-storms that suffocated or incinerated almost all life within their radius. As discussed in Chapter 1, various genocide scholars have described these and other aerial bombardments as genocidal.

Among the estimated eight million German soldiers killed on all fronts during the war were those who died as prisoners-of-war in the Soviet Union. Many German POWs were executed; most were sent to concentration camps where, like their Soviet counterparts, they died of exposure, starvation, and additionally overwork. "In all, at least one million German prisoners died out of the 3,150,000 [captured] by the Red Army," and this does not reflect those summarily shot before they could be taken prisoner.[67] In one of the most egregious cases, of 91,000 Sixth Army POWs seized following the German surrender at Stalingrad in 1943, only 6,000 survived to be repatriated to Germany in the 1950s.[68]

A final horror inflicted on German populations was the reprisal killing and mass expulsion of ethnic Germans from the Soviet Union and Eastern Europe, often from territories their forebears had inhabited for centuries. As early as September 1939, in the opening weeks of the Nazi invasion of Poland, an estimated 60,000 ethnic Germans were allegedly murdered by Poles.[69] With the German army in retreat across the eastern front in 1944–45, large numbers of Germans fell prey to the vengeful atrocities of Soviet troops (notably in East Prussia) and local populations (especially in Poland and Czechoslovakia). Some twelve to fourteen million ethnic Germans were uprooted, of whom about two million perished. Much of this occurred after the war had ended, under the aegis of Allied occupation authorities, as the philosopher Bertrand Russell noted in an October 1945 protest letter:

> In Eastern Europe now mass deportations are being carried out by our allies on an unprecedented scale, and an apparently deliberate attempt is being made to exterminate millions of Germans, not by gas, but by depriving them of their homes and of food, leaving them to die by slow and agonizing starvation. This is not done as an act of war, but as a part of a deliberate policy of "peace."[70]

Moreover, an agreement reached among the Allies at the Yalta Conference (February 1945) "granted war reparations to the Soviet Union in the form of labor services. According to German Red Cross documents, it is estimated that 874,000 German civilians were abducted to the Soviet Union." They suffered a higher casualty rate even than German prisoners-of-war, with some 45 percent dying in captivity.[71]

FURTHER STUDY

Michael Berenbaum, ed., *A Mosaic of Victims: Non-Jews Persecuted and Murdered by the Nazis*. New York: New York University Press, 1990. Wide-ranging collection.

Michael Burleigh, *Ethics and Extermination: Reflections on Nazi Genocide*. Cambridge: Cambridge University Press, 1997. Essays on themes including "euthanasia," the German–Soviet war, and the racial state.

Henry Friedlander, *The Origins of Nazi Genocide: From Euthanasia to the Final Solution.* Chapel Hill, NC: University of North Carolina Press, 1995. Traces the evolution of the Nazi killing machine from the initial targeting of disabled and handicapped Germans to the mass slaughter of Jews and Roma.

Robert Gellately and Nathan Stoltzfus, eds, *Social Outsiders in Nazi Germany.* Princeton, NJ: Princeton University Press, 2001. Examines the Nazi campaign against "unwanted populations."

Gerhard Hirschfeld, ed., *The Policies of Genocide: Jews and Soviet Prisoners of War in Nazi Germany.* Boston, MA: Allen & Unwin, 1986. The links between the fate of the Jews and the Soviet prisoners.

Norman M. Naimark, *The Russians in Germany: A History of the Soviet Zone of Occupation, 1945–1949.* Cambridge, MA: The Belknap Press, 1995. Especially strong on atrocities against German women and workers under Soviet occupation.

Richard Plant, *The Pink Triangle: The Nazi War against Homosexuals.* New York: Owl, 1986. The persecution and killing of homosexuals, described by a refugee of the Nazi regime.

Alexander B. Rossino, *Hitler Strikes Poland: Blitzkrieg, Ideology, and Atrocity.* Lawrence, KS: University Press of Kansas, 2003. First-rate survey of the Nazi rampage in Poland, which served as a trial run for the war against the Soviet Union.

Martin K. Sorge, *The Other Price of Hitler's War: German Military and Civilian Losses Resulting from World War II.* Westport, CT: Greenwood Press, 1986. Concise account of German suffering in the war.

Frederick Taylor, *Dresden: Tuesday, February 13, 1945.* New York: HarperCollins, 2004. In-depth study of the Allied fire-bombing of the historic German city.

Alfred-Maurice de Zayas, *A Terrible Revenge: The Ethnic Cleansing of the East European Germans, 1944–1950.* New York: St. Martin's Press, 1994. The atrocities against ethnic Germans, ably cataloged.

NOTES

1 Christopher R. Browning, *The Path to Genocide: Essays on Launching the Final Solution* (Cambridge: Cambridge University Press, 1992), p. ix.

2 Heinrich Himmler's announcement of Dachau's opening, quoted in Arno J. Mayer, *Why Did the Heavens Not Darken? The Final Solution in History* (New York: Pantheon, 1988), p. 125.

3 Mayer, *Why Did the Heavens Not Darken?*, pp. 107–8.

4 According to Dominique Vidal, approximately 150,000 communists and left-leaning social democrats were incarcerated in concentration camps between 1933 and 1939. Vidal, "From 'Mein Kampf' to Auschwitz," *Le Monde diplomatique*, October 1998.

5 Sywottek estimate cited in Adam LeBor and Roger Boyes, *Seduced by Hitler: The Choices of a Nation and the Ethics of Survival* (New York: Barnes & Noble, 2000), p. 69.

6 Quoted in Saul Friedländer, *The Years of Extermination: Nazi Germany and the Jews, 1939–1945* (New York: HarperCollins, 2007), pp. 134–35.

7 "The 'work-shy' were [defined as] males medically fit to work, but who (without good reason) refused jobs on two occasions, or quit after a short time." Robert Gellately, *Backing Hitler: Consent and Coercion in Nazi Germany* (Oxford: Oxford University Press, 2001), p. 98.

8 Ibid., p. 96.

9 Ibid., pp. 60, 63, 68, 70.

10 Geoffrey J. Giles, "The Institutionalization of Homosexual Panic in the Third Reich," in R. Gellately and J. Stoltzfus, eds, *Social Outsiders in Nazi Germany* (Princeton, NJ: Princeton University Press, 2001), p. 233.

11 "Lesbians were not subjected to formal persecution in the Third Reich, despite the fact that some zealous legal experts demanded this. . . . In a state which extolled manly, martial roughness, lesbians were less of a threat to the regime than men who subverted its crude stereotypes of 'normal' male behaviour." Michael Burleigh and Wolfgang Wippermann, *The Racial State: Germany 1933–1945* (Cambridge: Cambridge University Press, 1991), p. 268.

12 Richard Plant, *The Pink Triangle: The Nazi War against Homosexuals* (New York: Owl Books, 1988), p. 62.

13 Himmler quoted in ibid., pp. 89, 99.

14 Michael Burleigh, *Ethics and Extermination: Reflections on Nazi Genocide* (Cambridge: Cambridge University Press, 1997), p. 162.

15 Quoted in Plant, *The Pink Triangle*, p. 102.

16 Ibid., p. 99.

17 Ibid., p. 149.

18 Quoted in ibid., p. 166.

19 Saul Friedländer, *Nazi Germany and the Jews, Volume 1: The Years of Persecution, 1933–1939* (New York: HarperCollins, 1997), p. 206.

20 Konnilyn Feig, "Non-Jewish Victims in the Concentration Camps," in Michael Berenbaum, ed., *A Mosaic of Victims: Non-Jews Persecuted and Murdered by the Nazis* (New York: New York University Press, 1990), p. 163.

21 Plant, *The Pink Triangle*, p. 154.

22 Gellately, *Backing Hitler*, p. 75.

23 Ibid. For Web links and a bibliography on the persecution and killings of Jehovah's Witnesses, see "A Teacher's Guide to the Holocaust: Jehovah's Witnesses," http://fcit.coedu.usf.edu/holocaust/people/VictJeho.htm.

24 Wolfgang Sofsky, *The Order of Terror: The Concentration Camp*, trans. William Templer (Princeton, NJ: Princeton University Press, 1999), pp. 122–23.

25 Dietrich Bonhoeffer, *Letters and Papers from Prison* (New York: Touchstone, 1997). See also the United States Holocaust Memorial Museum page on Bonhoeffer's life and work at http://www.ushmm.org/museum/exhibit/online/bonhoeffer/.

26 Henry Friedlander, "The Exclusion and Murder of the Disabled," in Gellately and Stolzfus, eds, *Social Outsiders in Nazi Germany*, p. 146.

27 "Between 1907 and 1939, more than 30,000 people in twenty-nine [US] states were sterilized, many of them unknowingly or against their will, while they were incarcerated in prisons or institutions for the mentally ill." See "Handicapped: Victims of the Nazi Era, 1933–1945," *A Teacher's Guide to the Holocaust*, http://fcit.coedu.usf.edu/ people/USHMMHAN.HTM.

28 Friedlander, "The Exclusion and Murder of the Disabled," p. 147.

29 An opponent of such views, Ewald Meltzer, the director of Katherinenhof juvenile asylum in Saxony, decided in 1925 "to carry out a poll of the views on 'euthanasia' held by the parents of his charges. To his obvious surprise, some 73 per cent of the

162 respondents said that they would approve 'the painless curtailment of the life of [their] child if experts had established that it is suffering from incurable idiocy.' Many of the 'yes' respondents said that they wished to offload the burden represented by an 'idiotic' child, with some of them expressing the wish that this be done surreptitiously, in a manner which anticipated later National Socialist practice." Burleigh, *Ethics and Extermination*, p. 121.

30 Recall that under the UN Convention definition of genocide, preventing births within a group may be considered genocidal.

31 Burleigh, *Ethics and Extermination*, p. 123.

32 Ibid.

33 See "'Wheels Must Roll for Victory!' Children's 'Euthanasia' and 'Aktion T-4,'" ch. 3 in Michael Burleigh, *Death and Deliverance: 'Euthanasia' in Germany c. 1900–1945* (London: Pan Books, 1994), pp. 97–127.

34 Sofsky, *The Order of Terror*, p. 243. Peter Fritzsche also points to the connections between the "euthanasia" campaign and the Holocaust that would erupt shortly after: "Figuring out by trial and error the various stages of the killing process, from the identification of patients to the arrangement of special transports to the murder sites to the killings by gas in special chambers to the disposal of the bodies, and mobilizing medical experts who worked in secret with a variety of misleading euphemisms to conceal their work . . . the Nazis built important bureaucratic bridges that would lead to the extermination of Jews and Gypsies." Fritzsche, *Life and Death in the Third Reich* (Cambridge, MA: The Belknap Press of Harvard University, 2008), p. 118.

35 Friedlander, "The Exclusion and Murder of the Disabled," p. 157.

36 Friedlander, *The Origins of Nazi Genocide*, p. 142.

37 Hitler quoted in Jürgen Zimmerer, "The Birth of the *Ostland* out of the Spirit of Colonialism: A Postcolonial Perspective on the Nazi Policy of Conquest and Extermination," *Patterns of Prejudice*, 39: 2 (2005), p. 202. Raphael Lemkin recognized the colonialist core of the Nazi enterprise: "Hitler's plan covered the Poles, the Serbs, the Russians, the Frenchmen. . . . The main purpose of the Nazis was a commission of a G[enocide] against nations in order to get hold of their territory for colonisation purposes. This was the case of the Poles, and the Russians and the Ukrainians." Quoted in A. Dirk Moses, "Empire, Colony, Genocide: Keywords and the Philosophy of History," in Moses, ed., *Empire, Colony, Genocide: Conquest, Occupation, and Subaltern Resistance in World History* (New York: Berghahn Books, 2008), p. 21.

38 Quoted in Omer Bartov, *Hitler's Army: Soldiers, Nazis, and War in the Third Reich* (New York: Oxford University Press, 1992), p. 129.

39 Heinrich Himmler, tasked with engineering the destruction of the Polish people, parroted Hitler in proclaiming that "all Poles will disappear from the world. . . . It is essential that the great German people should consider it as its major task to destroy all Poles." Hitler and Himmler quoted in Richard C. Lukas, "The Polish Experience during the Holocaust," in Berenbaum, ed., *A Mosaic of Victims*, p. 89.

40 Lukas, "The Polish Experience," p. 90.

41 Orlando Figes, *The Whisperers: Private Life in Stalin's Russia* (New York: Metropolitan Books, 2007), p. 457.

42 Anthony Beevor, *Stalingrad* (New York: Viking Press, 1998), p. 428.

43 Catherine Merridale, *Ivan's War: Life and Death in the Red Army, 1939–1945* (New York: Picador, 2006), p. 291.

44 Quoted in Milovan Djilas, *Wartime* (New York: Harvest, 1980), p. 73. Omer Bartov has written: "It was in the Soviet Union that the Wehrmacht's back was broken long before the Western Allies landed in France, and even after June 1944

it was in the East that the Germans continued to commit and lose far more men. . . . By the end of March 1945 the *Ostheer*'s [German eastern front] casualties mounted to 6,172,373 men, or double its original manpower on 22 June 1941, a figure which constituted fully four-fifths of the [Germans'] total losses . . . on all fronts since the invasion of the Soviet Union." Bartov, *Hitler's Army*, pp. 29, 45. Alec Nove points out that more Russians died in the German siege of Leningrad alone (1941–43) "than the total of British and Americans killed from all causes throughout the war." Nove, *Stalinism and After* (London: George Allen & Unwin, 1975), p. 93.

45 Alexander Werth, *Russia at War, 1941–45* (New York: Carroll & Graf, 1999), p. 634.

46 Merridale, *Ivan's War*, p. 149.

47 If the upper-end estimates for those killed in Bangladesh genocide of 1971 are accurate (three million; see Box 8a), this might also match the intensiveness of Rwanda and the genocide against Soviet POWs.

48 Alexander Dallin, *German Rule in Russia, 1941–45: A Study of Occupation Policies* (2nd edn) (London: Macmillan, 1981), pp. 414–15; Omer Bartov, *The Eastern Front, 1941–45: German Troops and the Barbarization of Warfare* (Basingstoke: Macmillan, 1985), p. 110.

49 Quoted in Werth, *Russia at War*, pp. 635–36.

50 Merridale, *Ivan's War*, p. 290.

51 Goering quoted in Dallin, *German Rule in Russia*, p. 415.

52 Burleigh and Wippermann, *The Racial State*, p. 116.

53 See, e.g., Anna Porter, "Fascism: The Next Generation," *The Globe and Mail*, May 9, 2009; "Bottom of the Heap," *The Economist*, June 21, 2008.

54 Burleigh, *Ethics and Extermination*, p. 167.

55 Michael Zimmermann, "The National Socialist 'Solution of the Gypsy Question,'" ch. 7 in Ulrich Herbert, ed., *National Socialist Extermination Policies: Contemporary German Perspectives and Controversies* (New York: Berghahn Books, 2000), p. 194.

56 Sybil H. Milton, "'Gypsies' as Social Outsiders in Nazi Germany," in Gellately and Stoltzfus, eds, *Social Outsiders in Nazi Germany*, p. 222.

57 Friedländer, *The Years of Extermination*, p. 317.

58 Burleigh and Wippermann, *The Racial State*, p. 125.

59 Robert Jay Lifton, *The Nazi Doctors: Medical Killing and the Psychology of Genocide* (New York: Basic Books, 1986), p. 161 (the quoted passage is Lifton's paraphrase).

60 Milton, "'Gypsies' as Social Outsiders," p. 226.

61 Ian Hancock, "Responses to the Porrajmos: The Romani Holocaust," in Alan S. Rosenbaum, ed., *Is the Holocaust Unique? Perspectives on Comparative Genocide*, 3rd edn. (Boulder, CO: Westview Press, 2009), p. 86.

62 Sybil Milton, "Holocaust: The Gypsies," in Samuel Totten *et al.*, eds, *Century of Genocide* (New York: Garland Publishing, 1997), p. 188.

63 Ibid., p. 92.

64 Hancock, "Responses to the Porrajmos."

65 Günter Grass, *Crabwalk*, trans. Krishna Winston (New York: Harvest, 2004); Jörg Friedrich, *Brandstätten* (Berlin: Propylaen, 2003).

66 Eric Langenbacher, "The Allies in World War II: The Anglo-American Bombardment of German Cities," in Adam Jones, ed., *Genocide, War Crimes and the West: History and Complicity* (London: Zed Books, 2004), p. 118. See also Hermann Knell's study of the lesser-known attack on Würzburg in March 1945, *To Destroy a City: Strategic Bombing and Its Human Consequences in World War II* (Cambridge, MA: Da Capo Press, 2003).

67 S.P. MacKenzie, "The Treatment of Prisoners in World War II," *Journal of Modern History*, 66:3 (September 1994), p. 511.

68 Beevor, *Stalingrad*, p. 430.
69 Martin K. Sorge, *The Other Price of Hitler's War: German Military and Civilian Losses Resulting from World War II* (Westport, CT: Greenwood Press, 1996), p. 89.
70 Russell cited in Alfred-Maurice de Zayas, *A Terrible Revenge: The Ethnic Cleansing of the East European Germans, 1944–1950* (New York: St. Martin's Press, 1994), p. 111.
71 De Zayas, *A Terrible Revenge*, p.116.

CHAPTER 7

Cambodia and the Khmer Rouge

ORIGINS OF THE KHMER ROUGE

A prevalent view of Cambodia prior to the upheavals of the late 1960s and 1970s was of a "gentle land," with peaceful Buddhist authorities presiding over a free and relatively prosperous peasantry. This picture is far from false. Indeed, Cambodia was abundant in rice, and peasant landownership was comparatively common. But the stereotype overlooks a darker side of Cambodian history and culture: absolutism, a politics of vengeance, and a frequent recourse to torture. "Patterns of extreme violence against people defined as enemies, however arbitrarily, have very long roots in Cambodia," acknowledged historian Michael Vickery.[1] Anthropologist Alex Hinton pointed to "a Cambodian model of disproportionate revenge" – "a head for an eye," in the title of his seminal essay on the subject – which was well entrenched by the time the Khmer Rouge communists took power in 1975.[2]

This is not to say that "a tradition of violence" determined that the Khmer Rouge (KR) would rule. In fact, until relatively late in the process, the movement was a marginal presence. Neither, though, was the Khmer Rouge an outright aberration. Certainly, the KR's emphasis on concentrating power and wielding it in tyrannical fashion was in keeping with Cambodian tradition. "Absolutism . . . is a core element of authority and legitimacy in Cambodia," wrote David Roberts.[3] As for the supposedly pacific nature of Buddhism, the religion that overwhelmingly predominated in Cambodia, Vickery denounced it as "arrant nonsense." "That Buddhists may torture and massacre is no more astonishing than that the Inquisition burned people or that practicing Catholics and Protestants joined the Nazi SS."[4]

Another element of Cambodian history and politics is an aggressive nostalgia for past glories. Cambodia under the Angkor Empire, which peaked from the twelfth to the fourteenth centuries, was a powerful nation, incorporating sizable territories that today belong to neighbors. It extended to the South China Sea, and included southern regions of Vietnam as well as parts of present-day Laos, Thailand, and Burma. At the height of its power, forced laborers built the great temples of Angkor Wat, the world's largest religious complex. Ever since, including for the Khmer Rouge, Angkor Wat has served as Cambodia's national symbol.

Cambodian nationalists harked back constantly to these halcyon days, and advanced irredentist claims with varying degrees of seriousness. Most significantly, the rich lands of today's southern Vietnam were designated Kampuchea Krom, "Lower Cambodia" in nationalist discourse – though they have been part of Vietnam since at least 1840. This rivalry with Vietnam, and a messianic desire to reclaim "lost" Cambodian territories, fueled Khmer Rouge fanaticism. The government led by the avowedly anti-imperialist Communist Party of Cambodia (the official name of the KR) proved as xenophobic and expansionist as any regime in modern Asian history.

By the nineteenth century, Cambodia's imperial prowess was long dissipated, and the country easily fell under the sway of the French. On the pretext of creating a buffer between their Vietnamese territories, British-influenced Burma, and independent Siam (Thailand), the French established influence over the court of King Norodom. The king, grandfather of Prince Norodom Sihanouk who would rule during the KR's early years, accepted protectorate status. He eventually became little more than a French vassal.

As elsewhere in their empire, France provoked nationalist sentiments in Cambodia – through economic exploitation and political subordination, but also through the efforts of French scholars who worked to "'recover' a history for Cambodia." This project bolstered "Khmer pride in their country's heritage," providing "the ideological foundation of the modern drive for an expression of an independent Khmer nation."[5]

Another French contribution to Khmer nationalism was the awarding of academic scholarships to Cambodians for study in Paris. In the 1950s, the French capital was likely the richest environment for revolutionary ferment anywhere in the world. The French Communist Party, which had led the resistance to Nazi occupation, emerged as a powerful presence in postwar politics. In earlier years, Paris had nurtured nationalists from the French colonies, including Vietnam's Ho Chi Minh. The Paris of the 1950s likewise provided a persecution-free environment in which revolutionaries from the Global South could meet and plot. Among the beneficiaries were most of the leaders of the future Khmer Rouge,[6] including:

- Saloth Sar, who subsequently took the name Pol Pot, "Brother Number One" in the party hierarchy, and became Prime Minister of Democratic Kampuchea during the KR's period in power;
- Khieu Samphan, later President of Democratic Kampuchea (DK);
- Son Sen, DK's deputy Prime Minister and Minister of Defense and Security;

- Ieng Sary, deputy Prime Minister in charge of foreign affairs during the DK period;
- his wife, Ieng (Khieu) Thirith, Minister of Social Action for the DK regime.[7]

In retrospect, Khmer Rouge fanaticism was fueled by some of the ideological currents of the time. The French Communist Party was in its high-Stalinist phase, supporting campaigns against "enemies of the people." Intellectuals like Frantz Fanon, another denizen of Paris at the time, espoused the view "that only violence and armed revolt could cleanse the minds of Third World peoples and rid them of their colonial mentalities."[8]

The 1950s and 1960s were a period of nationalist ferment throughout the Global South. The government of Prince Norodom Sihanouk was positioning itself as an anti-colonialist, politically neutral force in Southeast Asia. Sihanouk was a leader of the Non-Aligned Movement that burst onto the world stage at the Bandung Conference in 1955.

Many returning students flocked to the Indochinese Communist Party, which united communist movements in Vietnam and Cambodia. Tensions soon developed between the two wings, however. Cambodians like Pol Pot felt they "had to carry excrement for the Vietnamese," according to Khieu Thirith.[9] Following the 1954

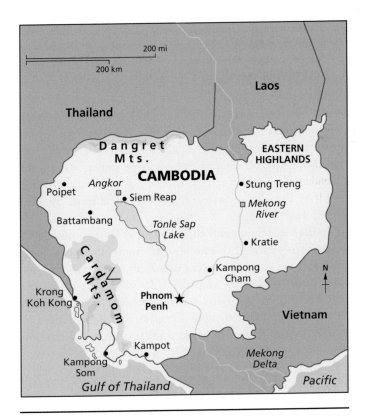

Map 7.1 Cambodia

Source: Map provided by WorldAtlas.com.

Vietnamese victory over the French at Dien Bien Phu, and the signing of the Geneva Accords, the Vietnamese withdrew from Cambodia. As they did, they split the Cambodian party membership by transferring some 1,000 cadres to Vietnam, leaving another 1,000 in Cambodia – including Pol Pot and the future core leadership of the Khmer Rouge. This would have fateful consequences when returning cadres who had spent their formative period in Vietnam were targeted by the KR for extermination, together with all ethnic Vietnamese in Cambodia (or within reach on the other side of the border). In the case of Vietnamese remaining in Cambodia, the destruction was *total*.

In 1966, Sihanouk, whose police had been quietly implementing a campaign of "government murder and repression" against communists in the countryside,[10] launched a crackdown on members of the urban left whom he had not fully co-opted. Khieu Samphan and Hou Youn were forced underground. Not the least of the party's problems was its estrangement from Hanoi. The North Vietnamese regime chose to support the neutralist and anti-imperialist Sihanouk, rather than aid a rebellion by its Cambodian communist "brothers." Hanoi valued Sihanouk as a bulwark against US domination of Southeast Asia, and therefore as an ally in the Vietnamese national struggle. By contrast, Pol Pot's new Cambodian communist leadership considered Sihanouk a US lapdog. It decided to abandon political activity in the city for armed struggle in remote parts of the countryside, where the Khmer Rouge could nurture its revolution beyond Sihanouk's reach.

WAR AND REVOLUTION, 1970–75

How did Cambodia's communists, politically marginal throughout the 1960s, manage to seize national power in 1975? The explanation, according to Cambodia specialist David Chandler, lies in a combination of "accidents, outside help, and external pressures. . . . Success, which came slowly, was contingent on events in South Vietnam, on Vietnamese communist guidance, on the disastrous policies followed by the United States, and on blunders made by successive Cambodian governments."[11]

After the US invasion of South Vietnam in 1965, conflict spilled into Cambodia. Supplies from the North Vietnamese government, destined for the guerrillas of the National Liberation Front in the south, moved down the "Ho Chi Minh Trail" through Laos and eastern Cambodia. US bombing of the trail, including areas inside Cambodia, pushed Vietnamese forces deeper into Cambodia, until they came to control significant territory in border areas. The Vietnamese, prioritizing their own liberation struggle, urged restraint on their Cambodian communist allies. But in 1970, as war spread across Cambodia, the extension of Vietnamese power provided a powerful boost for the Khmer Rouge, including vital training. In the early 1970s, the Vietnamese forces were inflicting far more damage on Cambodian government forces than was the KR.

The Vietnamese occupation of Cambodian border areas provoked two major responses from the United States, both central to what followed. First, in 1970, came

US support for a coup against Prince Sihanouk, whom the US saw as a dangerous socialist and neutralist. He was replaced by Lon Nol, Sihanouk's former right-hand man and head of the armed forces, a religious fanatic who believed that "Buddhist teaching, racial virtues, and modern science made the Khmers invincible."[12] (Clearly, extreme chauvinism in Cambodia was not an invention of Democratic Kampuchea.) Lon Nol duly repaid his benefactors by inviting the US and South Vietnam to launch an invasion of Cambodian territory which lasted for three months.[13]

The significance of this action was outweighed by a second US response: the escalation, from 1970, of the saturation bombing campaign first launched against Vietnamese border sanctuaries in Cambodia in 1969. The campaign climaxed in 1973, a year that saw *a quarter of a million tons* of bombs dropped on Cambodia in just six months. This was one-and-a-half times as much high explosive as the US had unleashed on Japan during the whole of the Second World War – a country with which it was at least formally at war.

The impact was devastating. "We heard a terrifying noise which shook the ground," one villager recalled; "it was as if the earth trembled, rose up and opened beneath our feet. Enormous explosions lit up the sky like huge bolts of lightning."[14] After bombing raids, "villagers who happened to be away from home returned to find nothing but dust and mud mixed with seared and bloody body parts."[15] Moreover, the assault effectively destroyed the agricultural base of an agrarian nation – more effectively, in fact, than Stalin had with his collectivization drive against the Soviet peasantry (Chapter 5). "The amount of acreage cultivated for rice dropped from six million at the beginning of the war to little more than one million at the end of the bombing campaign," wrote Elizabeth Becker.[16] Malnutrition was rampant, and mass starvation was kept at bay only by food aid from US charitable organizations. (This should be borne in mind when the aftermath of the Khmer Rouge victory is considered, below.)[17]

In the first edition of this book, I wrote that "the US bombing of a defenseless population" was "probably genocidal in itself," and unquestionably (quoting Michael Vickery) "one of the worst aggressive onslaughts in modern warfare." This was based on the best available estimate: that "between 1969 and 1973, more than half a million tons of munitions" had been unleashed on Cambodia. Data revealed since publication have decisively recast our understanding of the bombing campaign. According to Taylor Owen and leading Cambodia scholar Ben Kiernan, systematic analysis of US Air Force statistics shows that "from October 4, 1965, to August 15, 1973, the United States dropped far more ordnance on Cambodia than was previously believed: *2,756,941 tons' worth*, dropped in 230,516 sorties on 113,716 sites."[18] A simultaneous discovery was that "the bombing began four years earlier than is widely believed," in 1965. The 1970–73 assaults accounted for a tonnage of munitions more than *four times greater* than previously recognized.

In *The Pol Pot Regime* (1996), Kiernan estimated the death toll inflicted by the bombing at between 50,000 and 150,000. He acknowledged in the wake of his subsequent research with Owen, however, that this was based upon an extrapolation from the tonnage then believed to have been dropped on civilian Cambodians. If that tonnage now needed to be revised upward substantially, Kiernan stated that the death toll, too, might need to be reassessed. This could bring total casualties closer to the jaw-dropping figure of 600,000 proposed by Christopher Hitchens in *The Trial of Henry Kissinger* (2001).[19]

The US bombing of the Cambodian rural population was also the most important factor in bringing the genocidal Khmer Rouge to power. "Civilian casualties in Cambodia drove an enraged populace into the arms of an insurgency that had enjoyed relatively little support until the bombing began, setting in motion . . . the rapid rise of the Khmer Rouge, and ultimately the Cambodian genocide," wrote Owen and Kiernan.[20] One KR leader who defected, Chhit Do, eloquently captured the political impact of the bombardment:

> Every time after there had been bombing, [the Khmer Rouge guerrillas] would take the people to see the craters, to see how big and deep the craters were, to see how the earth had been gouged out and scorched. . . . The ordinary people . . . sometimes literally shit in their pants when the big bombs and shells came. . . . Their minds just froze up and they would wander around mute for three or four days. Terrified and half-crazy, the people were ready to believe what they were told. . . . That was what made it so easy for the Khmer Rouge to win the people over. . . . It was because of their dissatisfaction with the bombing that they kept on cooperating with the Khmer Rouge, joining up with the Khmer Rouge, sending their children off to go with them.[21]

"This is not to say that the Americans are responsible for the genocide in Cambodia," as social critic Michael Ignatieff noted. "It is to say that a society that has been pulverised by war is a society that is very susceptible to genocide."[22]

Under the Paris Peace Accords of 1973, Vietnamese forces left Cambodia, but the focus of military opposition to the Lon Nol regime had already shifted to the Khmer Rouge. Buoyed by Vietnamese arms and training, they were now a hardened force – at least a match for poorly motivated and half-starved government conscripts. The KR moved rapidly to besiege Phnom Penh and other cities. Meanwhile, in the areas of the countryside already under their control, they implemented the first stage of their distinctive – and destructive – revolutionary ideology.

A GENOCIDAL IDEOLOGY

In their jungle camps, the Khmer Rouge developed the philosophy that would guide their genocidal program and turn Cambodia "into our time's arguably most murderous, brutal, inhuman small country."[23] Let us consider the basic elements of this world view, and its consequences from 1975 to 1979:

- *Hatred of "enemies of the people."* Like many communist revolutionaries of the twentieth century – notably those in the USSR and China – the KR exhibited a visceral hatred of the revolution's enemies. As with Lenin–Stalin and Mao Zedong, too, "enemies" were loosely defined. They could be members of socioeconomic classes. The Khmer Rouge targeted the rich/ bourgeoisie;

professionals (including those who returned from abroad to help the new regime); "imperialist stooges" (collaborators with the US and its client regime in Phnom Penh); and the educated class. In effect, this swept up most urbanites. Enemies could also be designated on ethnic grounds. Just as Stalin waged genocide against the people of Ukraine and the Caucasus, so the Khmer Rouge exterminated ethnic Vietnamese, Chinese, Muslim Chams – in fact, almost every ethnic minority in Cambodia. (Even geographically defined Khmers were targeted for annihilation, such as those from southern Vietnam or the "traitorous" Eastern Zone in 1978.) The enemy could also be religious believers seen to be out of step with the KR pseudo-religion that now ruled the roost.

Lastly, enemies could be purged on the basis of supposed subversion or betrayal of the revolution from within. Stalin's purges of the Soviet Communist Party (Chapter 5) would be matched and exceeded, relative to population and party membership, by the Khmer Rouge's attacks on internal enemies.

- *Xenophobia and messianic nationalism.* As noted, the KR – in tandem with other Cambodian nationalists – harked back to the Angkor Empire. As is standard with nationalism, territorial claims reflected the zenith of power in the nation's past. Pol Pot and his regime apparently believed in their ability to reclaim the "lost" Cambodian territories of Kampuchea Krom in southern Vietnam. Territorial ambitions were combined with a fear and hatred of ethnic Vietnamese, seen both as Cambodia's historical enemy and the betrayer of Cambodian communism. The desire was imputed to Vietnamese to conquer Cambodia and destroy its revolution – a paranoid vision that harmonized with the Khmer Rouge's narcissistic sense of Cambodia as "the prize other powers covet."[24]

Racism and xenophobia produced an annihilationist ideology that depicted Cambodia's ethnic Vietnamese minority as a deadly internal threat to the survival of the Khmer nation. Khmer Krom from the historically Cambodian territories of southern Vietnam were targeted with similar venom. Finally, the xenophobia led to repeated Cambodian invasions of Vietnamese territory in 1977 and 1978. These eventually sparked the Vietnamese invasion that overthrew the regime.

- *Peasantism, anti-urbanism, and primitivism.* Like the Chinese communists, but unlike the Soviets, the Khmer Rouge gleaned most of their support from rural rather than urban elements. Peasants were the guardians of the true and pure Cambodia against alien, cosmopolitan city-dwellers. However, the Khmer Rouge vision of the peasantry was misguided from the first. As Ben Kiernan pointed out, the DK regime attacked the three foundations of peasant life: religion, land, and family. The KR rejected the peasants' attachment to Buddhist religion; imputed to peasants a desire for agricultural collectivization that was alien to Cambodia; revived the hated *corvée* (forced labor); and sought to destabilize and dismantle the family unit.

The primitivist dimension of Khmer Rouge ideology seems to have been influenced by the tribal peoples among whom KR leaders lived in Cambodia's eastern jungles. These people, in particular the Khmer Loeu (highland Khmer), provided indispensable refuge and sustenance for the party in its nascent period. "Pol Pot and Ieng Sary . . . claimed later to have been inspired by the spirit of people who had no private property, no markets, and no money. Their way of life and their means of production corresponded to the primitive communist phase of social evolution in Marxist thinking," and likely influenced the KR decision to abandon the market and the money economy.[25] Soldiers from the highland tribes played an important role in the KR's final campaign to crush the Lon Nol regime, but increasingly fell victim to the genocide against ethnic minorities under DK (see below).[26]

A bizarre aspect of KR primitivism was the conviction that no natural challenge was insuperable, no scientific accomplishment unattainable, if peasant energies and know-how were tapped. "The young are learning their science from the workers and peasants, who are the sources of all knowledge," declared Radio Phnom Penh.[27] "Formerly to be a pilot required a high school education – twelve to fourteen years," declared another classic piece of propaganda. "Nowadays, it's clear that political consciousness is the decisive factor. . . . As for radar, we can learn how to handle it after studying for a couple of months."[28] Not surprisingly, the Khmer Rouge air force never amounted to much.

In Mao Zedong's "Great Leap Forward," an almost identical mentality had produced catastrophic outcomes (see Chapter 5). Undeterred, the DK regime announced that an even more impressive "*Super* Great Leap Forward" would be initiated in Cambodia. Like Mao's experiment, the Super Great Leap would be about self-sufficiency. Foreign help was neither desirable nor required, and even the Chinese model was dismissed. Indeed, the country would be all but sealed off from the outside world.[29]

- *Purity, discipline, militarism.* Like the Nazis, the Khmer Rouge expressed their racism through an emphasis on racial purity. Like the Soviets and Chinese, purity was also defined by class origin, and by an unswerving loyalty to revolutionary principle and practice. Self-discipline was critical. It demonstrated revolutionary ardor and self-sacrifice. In most revolutions of Left and Right, rigorous discipline has spawned an ideology of chaste sexuality – though this was not necessarily realized in practice. There is little question that the Khmer Rouge presided over a regime of "totalitarian puritanism"[30] perhaps without equal in the twentieth century. Among other things, "any sex before marriage was punishable by death in many cooperatives and zones."[31]

Discipline among revolutionaries also buttresses the inevitable military confrontation with the counter-revolution. Ben Kiernan and Chanthou Boua consider militarism to be *the* defining feature of Khmer Rouge rule, reflected in "the forced evacuation of the cities, the coercion of the population into economic programmes organized with military discipline, the heavy reliance on the armed forces rather than civilian cadres for administration, and the almost total absence of political education or attempts to explain administrative decisions in a way that would win the psychological acceptance of the people affected by them."[32]

Some of the ironies and contradictions of Khmer Rouge ideology should be noted. Despite their idealization of the peasants, no senior Khmer Rouge leader was of peasant origin. Virtually all were city-bred intellectuals. Pol Pot came from the countryside, but from a prosperous family with ties to the Royal Court in Phnom Penh. As noted earlier, the core leadership belonged to a small, privileged intellectual class able to study overseas on government scholarships. These racist chauvinists, opposed to any foreign "interference" including aid, were by background among the most "cosmopolitan" Cambodians in history. The genocide they inflicted on intellectuals and urban populations in general, as well as on hundreds of thousands of peasants, was hypocritical as well as indelibly brutal.

A POLICY OF "URBICIDE," 1975

Throughout world history, human civilization has meant urbanization (the Latin *civitas* is the etymological root of both "city" and "civilization"). "Cities," wrote Daniel Jonah Goldhagen, "are the principal sites of modernity, of economic productivity, of technological productivity."[33] They are also, as political scientist Allan Cooper noted in *The Geography of Genocide*, sites of "hybridity" and cultural mixing. Cooper considered genocide a "fundamentally anti-city" phenomenon, pointing to the regularity with which genocidal perpetrators focus their assaults on urban environments, seeking to destroy them as symbols of group identity and social modernity.[34] Such campaigns are often accompanied by depictions of cities as cesspools of corruption and of foreign-affiliated cliques, requiring "cleansing" and "purifying" by genocidal agents.

These "deliberate attempts at the annihilation of cities as mixed physical, social, and cultural spaces"[35] constitute *urbicide*.[36] The term was originally popularized in the Serbo-Croatian language, by Bosnian architects, to describe the Serb assault on Sarajevo and the Croat attack on Mostar during the Balkan wars of the 1990s (see pp. 334–35). There are numerous historical precedents. A classical example is the Roman siege and obliteration of Carthage (see Chapter 1). Significantly, this was preceded by an ultimatum that the Carthaginians abandon their city for the countryside. When the ultimatum failed to produce the desired results, the Romans made plain their opposition to Carthage *as a city*. They razed it to rubble, and consigned the surviving population to slavery around the known world.

Apart from the Balkans case, contemporary examples of urbicide include the Nazi assaults on Leningrad and Stalingrad during the Second World War; the Syrian assault on the rebellious city of Hama in 1982; and the Russian obliteration of Grozny in Chechnya (1994–95). There are few more vivid instances, however, than the policy imposed by the Khmer Rouge on Phnom Penh and other cities in March 1975. "For most of the people in Cambodia's towns what happened during those few days literally overturned their lives."[37]

Within hours of arriving in the capital, the Khmer Rouge set about rounding up its two million residents and deporting them to the countryside. Bedraggled caravans of deportees headed back to their old life (in the case of refugees from rural areas) or to a new one of repression and privation (for urbanites). Similar scenes occurred in other population centers nationwide. Without damage to a single building, whole cities were destroyed.

To residents, the Khmer Rouge justified the deportations on the grounds that the Americans were planning bombing attacks on Cambodian cities. (Given recent history, this was not an inconceivable prospect.) To an international audience – on the rare occasions when KR leaders bothered to provide rationales – the urbicide was depicted as a humanitarian act. With the end of the US aid that had fed swollen city populations, albeit inadequately, "the population had to go where the food was," in the words of Ieng Sary.[38] But this excuse faltered in light of the KR's obstinate emphasis on self-sufficiency. Most revealingly, foreign donations of food and other aid went unsolicited, and were rejected when offered. And there is no doubting the murderous destructiveness of the forced marches themselves, in which "the Khmer Rouge intentionally killed and drove to death many tens of thousands of people, perhaps as many as 400,000 people."[39]

After the urbicide, and for the remainder of the DK period, Phnom Penh and other cities remained ghost towns. They were inhabited by only a skeleton crew of KR leaders, cadres, and support staff. The countryside thus served as the backdrop for the Khmer Rouge assault on Cambodia's culture and people.

"BASE PEOPLE" VS. "NEW PEOPLE"

The peasantry, the base of Khmer Rouge support, were depicted as "base" people (*neak moultanh*). Deported city-folk were "new" people (*neak thmey*), late arrivals to the revolution. In a sense, though, all of Cambodia was new and revolutionary in the Khmer Rouge conception. The year 1975 was declared "Year Zero" – a term that evokes the nihilistic core of KR policies.

The reception that awaited new people varied significantly, in ways that decisively affected their survival chances. Some reports attested to a reasonably friendly welcome from peasants. In other cases, the peasants – who had suffered through the savage US bombing campaign and the violence and upheaval of civil war – felt the newcomers had received a just comeuppance. This feeling was bolstered by the preferential treatment the base people received from most KR authorities. Srey Pich Chnay, a Cambodian former urbanite, described his experiences to Kiernan and Boua in 1979:

> The Khmer Rouge treated the peasants as a separate group, distributing more food to them than to the city people, and assigning them easier tasks (usually around the village), whereas the city people almost always worked in the fields. Sometimes the peasants, as well as the Khmer Rouge themselves, would say to the newcomers, "You used to be happy and prosperous. Now it's our turn."[40]

The memoir of Loung Ung, who was a young girl in the KR period, conveyed the tension of this confrontation between different worlds, and the experience, unfamiliar to an urbanite, of finding herself despised:

> The new people are considered the lowest in the village structure. They have no freedom of speech, and must obey the other classes. The new people . . . cannot farm like the rural people. They are suspected of having no allegiance to the Angkar [i.e., the KR leadership] and must be kept under an ever-watchful eye for signs of rebellion. They have led corrupt lives and must be trained to be productive

workers. To instill a sense of loyalty . . . and break what the Khmer Rouge views as an inadequate urban work ethic, the new people are given the hardest work and the longest hours.[41]

There is the flavor here of *subaltern genocide*, a "genocide by the oppressed" against those seen as oppressors, and indeed the anthropologist and Cambodia specialist Alex Hinton has explored the KR period in these terms.[42] Michael Vickery argued that the DK period was characterized *above all* by the revolutionary terror of the peasantry against urbanites and the intellectual/professional classes: "It is certainly safe to assume that [KR leaders] did not foresee, let alone plan, the unsavory developments of 1975–79. *They were petty-bourgeois radicals overcome by peasant romanticism.*"[43]

However, there are difficulties with this framing. One, as Kiernan has pointed out, is that Vickery's informants were predominantly *non*-peasants, poorly placed to describe the dynamics of a peasant revolution. Another is that, as we have seen, power was centralized in a leadership that was overwhelmingly urban and intellectual. Even at the regional and local level, where KR cadres with a peasant background were more likely to hold sway, there is little evidence that their policies *responded* to a groundswell of peasant resentment. Rather, they reflected instructions and frameworks supplied by the center, with subaltern animosities channeled into genocidal duties. "By 1977," wrote Kiernan, "the DK system was so tightly organized and controlled that little spontaneous peasant activity was possible,"[44] but there was no shortage of peasant involvement – and eager, virulently hostile involvement too – in the genocide against designated class enemies.

CAMBODIA'S HOLOCAUST, 1975–79

Our brothers and sisters of all categories, including workers, peasants, soldiers, and revolutionary cadres have worked around the clock with soaring enthusiasm, paying no attention to the time or to their fatigue; they have worked in a cheerful atmosphere of revolutionary optimism.

Radio Phnom Penh broadcast under the KR

There were no laws. If they wanted us to walk, we walked; to sit, we sat; to eat, we ate. And still they killed us. It was just that if they wanted to kill us, they would take us off and kill us.

Cham villager interviewed by Ben Kiernan

In Cambodia between 1975 and 1978, the KR's genocidal ideology found full expression. The result was one of the worst genocides, relative to population, in recorded history. In less than four years – mostly in the final two – mass killing swept the Cambodian population. In part it resulted from direct KR murders of anyone perceived as an enemy. Internal purges reached a crescendo in 1977–78, claiming hundreds of thousands of lives. Even more significant, though, were the indirect killings through privation, disease, and ultimately famine. These swelled the death-toll to an estimated 1.7 to 1.9 million, out of a population estimated at just under eight million in April 1975. Between 21 and 24 percent of the entire Cambodian population died in the short period under discussion.[45]

Most scholars accept that "complex regional and temporal variations" were evident under the KR.[46] Temporally, life in many regions appears to have been spartan but tolerable for most of the first two years of KR rule. State terror had yet to descend with full force. Thousands of executions certainly accompanied the forced evacuations of Phnom Penh and other cities, and more took place in the countryside, but there are also accounts of moderate and reasonable Khmer Rouge cadres.

Then things changed. "Most survivors of DK agree that living conditions (that is, rations, working hours, disruptions to family life, and the use of terror) deteriorated sharply in 1977." Chandler pointed to three reasons for the shift: "the regime's insistence on meeting impossible agricultural goals at a breakneck pace"; growing leadership paranoia about "plots"; and, further fueling that paranoia, the mounting conflict with Vietnam.[47] The most exterminatory period was probably the final one: in 1978, prior to Vietnam's successful invasion in December. The repression visited upon the Eastern Zone over the preceding months had turned it into a graveyard, with up to a quarter of a million people killed.[48]

The extent of regional variation in Democratic Kampuchea is one of the most hotly debated aspects of the KR regime. Michael Vickery has argued that "almost no two regions were alike with respect to conditions of life":

> The Southwestern and Eastern Zones, the most important centers of pre-1970 communist activity, were the best organized and most consistently administered, with the East, until its destruction in 1978, also providing the more favorable conditions of life, in particular for "new" people. In contrast, the West, the Northwest, except for [the region of] Damban 3, and most of the North-Center, were considered "bad" areas, where food was often short, cadres arbitrary and murderous, and policy rationales entirely beyond the ken of the general populace.[49]

Other scholars, however, emphasize the "unchanging character" and "highly centralized control" that marked KR rule.[50] Central direction was certainly evident in the establishment and operation of three key genocidal institutions: the forced-labor system, the mass executions, and the internal purge.

BOX 7.1 ONE WOMAN'S STORY: MOLYDA SZYMUSIAK

"Work, rain, hunger. It was the hunger that tormented us the most: all we could think of was finding something to appease the gnawing of our stomachs. I was fifteen years old."

Molyda Szymusiak (the name she was given by her adoptive Polish parents) grew up as a privileged member of Cambodian society – the daughter of a prominent member of the government that battled the Khmer Rouge until the guerrillas seized power in Phnom Penh on April 17, 1975. "Suddenly we heard cheering and triumphant cries: 'Kampuchea [revolutionary Cambodia] is free!' . . . Down the center of the pavement, in single file, were marching kids in black pants and jackets, their guns on their shoulders, wearing sandals made out of pieces of tires. Without a word or a smile, they stared straight ahead."

Along with the entire urban population of Phnom Penh, Molyda and her family were rounded up and ordered out of the city – allegedly for only "two or three days." She had been warned before the exodus to keep her class origins absolutely secret: a sympathetic Khmer Rouge soldier told her, "Never say that you are of bourgeois origin or that you have had any trade other than a manual one. All such people will be liquidated."

The family headed east along the Mekong river, following Route Number 1. Finding temporary refuge in a rural village, "Our mothers went to work in the fields. Father was sent to help demolish the pagoda, breaking down the walls, and decapitating the Buddhas" – part of the Khmer Rouge's "Year Zero" project to strip Cambodians of their past and traditional culture.

Molyda had never worked a day in her life. Now, under the watchful eye of her Khmer Rouge overlords, she planted rice and dried out green branches for firewood. "Learn," a villager told her, "or you won't survive." "It was forbidden to eat three times a day, since rice had to be economized until the next harvest. It was forbidden to use perfume, or to keep items that came from the city . . . It was forbidden to wear colored skirts. . . . Everything we had been used to had been turned upside down."

Exhausted, ravaged by hunger and malaria, the family was shifted from worksite to worksite, moving west to the area around Lake Sap. On one such journey, Molyda caught a glimpse of what would become infamous as the "killing fields" of the Khmer Rouge. Collecting water from a pond, "we saw hands sticking up from the surface, and swollen corpses floating a bit farther on; severed heads and hands were piled up on the bank. . . . There were dozens of corpses strewn every which way at the water's edge, and a stomach-turning stench."

Hunger turned to starvation. "A baby was dying over at our neighbor's . . . The child's mother suggested to my mother that they eat the baby when it died. 'If you don't denounce me, I'll give you half.'" The would-be cannibal was discovered with the remains of her infant in the cooking pot. She "was led away, never to be seen again in the village."

Molyda's father, saving his meager rations to divide among the family, eventually succumbed on the same day as her Aunt Nang. Her mother died soon after: "Now

I was alone." But no mourning was permitted. Molyda was told she was now a "Daughter of Pol Pot," and owed all to the glorious revolution. She was put to road-building – a "useless and exhausting task," since basic engineering principles were ignored. No matter: she was exhorted by Khmer Rouge who "shouted slogans of triumph and encouragement: 'Let's forge ahead! The Angkar [supreme revolutionary authority] is watching us! We love our country!'"

"I vomited, I was cold, I was burning up" with sickness, but the Khmer Rouge mocked her: "So, you're sick? . . . You know we have no use for sick people here. Perhaps you'll get better if we put you in a bag!" – suffocation being the preferred method of execution, to preserve bullets. But the threats ceased to frighten her: "We'd spent so much time with death we weren't afraid of it anymore."

Denunciations and brutal interrogations isolated those who came from privileged or otherwise suspect backgrounds. Molyda witnessed "a group of about fifty people herded along . . . Their wrists were tied in front or behind their backs with cords of red nylon. . . . They began screaming and wailing: they understood that they wouldn't receive even the pretense of a trial. . . . Prisoners and their torturers followed one another out under the orange trees until nightfall. . . . In a corner of the courtyard a man was being beaten to death. His screams flew up to the sky, shattered, and rained down on me like hail battering my skull. Farther away, a column of people was beginning to move toward the grove concealing the gaping mass grave."

She was saved only by the Vietnamese invasion, which pushed the Khmer Rouge into jungle hideouts in the west of the country. Amidst the chaos and breakdown of authority, Molyda and her fellow laborers made their way along mine-laden trails to the Thai border, where she found refuge at the Kao I Dang camp. Eventually she and two cousins were flown to France, where they were adopted by Jan and Carmen Szymusiak, themselves refugees from communist-ruled Poland. "We have been most fortunate in the love and understanding of our adoptive parents," Molyda wrote in her autobiographical account, *The Stones Cry Out*.[51] But "the years of slavery, fear, and starvation have left their mark deep within us."

- *Forced labor* imposed a work regime that was unprecedented in modern Cambodia. Both base people and new people arose before dawn and were allowed to rest only after dark.[52] Food was distributed exclusively in communal kitchens, and after the 1975–76 interlude there was almost never enough. What could be harvested was mostly confiscated by KR cadres. The population could not buy extra supplies: money and markets were outlawed. They could not supplement rations with produce from their own plots, since private property was banned. They could not engage – legally, at least – in traditional foraging for alternative food sources. Any attempt to do so was seen as "sabotaging" the work effort, and was severely punished. They could not even draw upon networks of family solidarity and sharing. Although the KR never banned the family per se, they invigilated and eroded it by various means.[53]

Those who fell sick from overwork and malnutrition, or from the malaria that spread across Cambodia when the KR decided to refuse imports of pesticide, had little hope of treatment. Medicine was scarce, and usually reserved for the KR faithful. In addition, former urban residents from the Southwestern Zone, one of six main administrative zones in the DK, were again relocated to the Northwestern Zone. Some 800,000 people were dumped in the northwest with desperately inadequate provisions. Perhaps 200,000 died of starvation, or in the mass killings that descended in 1978 when cadres imported from the Southwestern Zone imposed a new round of purges (described below).

- *Mass executions.* These were conducted against "class enemies," on the one hand, and ethnic minorities on the other. Suspect from the start, "new people" were the most likely Khmer victims of such atrocities. Frequently, entire families would be targeted. "The Khmer Rouge actually had a saying . . . which encouraged such slaughter: 'To dig up grass, one must also dig up the roots' (*chik smav trauv chik teang reus*). . . . This phrase meant that cadres 'were supposed to "dig up" the entire family of an enemy – husband, wife, kids, sometimes from the grandparents down – so that none remained . . . to kill off the entire line at once so that none of them would be left to seek revenge later, in turn.'"[54] A witness, Bunhaeng Ung, described one such execution:

> Loudspeakers blared revolutionary songs and music at full volume. A young girl was seized and raped. Others were led to the pits where they were slaughtered like animals by striking the backs of their skulls with hoes or lengths of bamboo. Young children and babies were held by the legs, their heads smashed against palm trees and their broken bodies flung beside their dying mothers in the death pits. Some children were thrown in the air and bayoneted while music drowned their screams. . . . At the place of execution nothing was hidden. The bodies lay in open pits, rotting under the sun and monsoon rains.[55]

These were the "killing fields" made infamous by the 1985 film of the same name (Box 7.2). How many died in such executions is uncertain, but it was doubtless in the hundreds of thousands.

- *Violent internal purges* were a feature of KR insurgent politics well before the revolutionary victory. But after Democratic Kampuchea was established, the leadership's paranoia increased, and the zeal for purges with it. Pol Pot declared before a party audience in 1976 that "a sickness [exists] inside the party": "As our socialist revolution advances . . . seeping more strongly into every corner of the party, the army and among the people, we can locate the ugly microbes."[56] The language was strikingly similar to that employed by Stalin's henchmen against "enemies of the people" in the 1930s.

During the DK period, two major regional purges occurred. Both were carried out by Ta Mok, nicknamed "The Butcher" for his efforts. The first, as noted above, occurred in 1977–78 in the Northwestern Zone. The second, more of a

Figure 7.1   A cell in the Tuol /Sleng S-21 detention and torture center in Phnom Penh, Cambodia. Some 20,000 prisoners passed through S-21; only six are known to have survived. When Vietnamese forces liberated Phnom Penh early in 1979, they discovered days-old corpses still shackled to this and other bedframes in the facility – the last victims of S-21.

Source: Author's photo, July 2009.

Figure 7.2   Victims of Khmer Rouge purges, after incarceration and interrogation at Tuol Sleng and other centers, were executed in the "killing fields," now key memorial sites of the Cambodian genocide.

Source: Greg Vassie/Flickr.

"conventional military suppression campaign,"[57] was launched in May 1978 against the sensitive Eastern Zone bordering Vietnam. The east, "the heartland of Khmer communism," was the best-administered zone in the country; but the Phnom Penh authorities viewed its residents and cadres as "Khmer bodies with Vietnamese minds."[58] The campaign pushed the Eastern Zone into open rebellion against the center, and finally into the arms of Vietnam. Eastern Zone rebels would give a "Cambodian face" to the Vietnamese invasion at the end of the year, and to the People's Republic of Kampuchea which it established.

Tens of thousands of victims of these and other purges passed through KR centers established for interrogation, torture, and execution. The most notorious was Tuol Sleng in the capital, codenamed "S-21," where an estimated 14,000 prisoners were incarcerated during the KR's reign. Only *ten* are known to have survived.[59] Now a Museum of Genocide in Phnom Penh, Tuol Sleng was one of many such centers across Democratic Kampuchea (see Figures 7.1, 7.5, 7.6).

As in Mao's China and Stalin's USSR, the purges fed on themselves, and undermined the capacity of the revolution to resist its enemies. Just as Stalin's purges of the Soviet military and bureaucracy increased the country's vulnerability to Nazi invasion, the Khmer Rouge killing sprees paved the way for Vietnam's rapid conquest of Cambodia in 1978.

GENOCIDE AGAINST BUDDHISTS AND ETHNIC MINORITIES

Early commentaries on Khmer Rouge atrocities emphasized the targeting of class and political enemies. Subsequent scholarship, especially by Ben Kiernan, has revealed the extent to which the KR also engaged in genocidal targeting of religious groups and ethnic minorities.

Cambodian Buddhism suffered immensely under the genocide: "the destruction was nearly complete, with more devastating consequences for Cambodia than the Chinese attack on Buddhism had had for Tibet" (Chapter 5).[60] Religious institutions were emptied, often obliterated. Monks were sent to the countryside or executed. "Of the sixty thousand Buddhist monks, only three thousand were found alive after the Khmer Rouge reign; the rest had either been massacred or succumbed to hard labor, disease, or torture."[61]

A patchwork of ethnic minorities, together constituting about 15 percent of the population, was exposed to atrocities and extermination. Local Vietnamese were most virulently targeted. Kiernan offers the stunning estimate that *fully 100 percent of ethnic Vietnamese perished under the Khmer Rouge*.[62] The Muslim Chams were despised for their religion as well as their ethnicity. "Their religion was banned, their schools closed, their leaders massacred, their villages razed and dispersed."[63] Over one-third of the 250,000 Chams alive in April 1975 perished under DK.[64]

As for Cambodia's Chinese population, it was concentrated in the cities, and it is sometimes hard to distinguish repressive action based on racial hatred from repression against the urbanite "new people." Regardless, in DK this group "suffered the worst disaster ever to befall any ethnic Chinese community in Southeast Asia."[65] Only half the Chinese population of 430,000 at the outset of Khmer Rouge rule survived to see its end.

The grim tale of minority suffering under the Khmer Rouge does not end there. "The Thai minority of 20,000 was reportedly reduced to about 8,000. Only 800 families survived of the 1,800 families of the Lao ethnic minority. Of the 2,000 members of the Kola minority, 'no trace . . . has been found.'"[66]

BOX 7.2 CAMBODIA: KILLING FIELDS AND *THE KILLING FIELDS*

Figure 7.3   Dith Pran (left), the journalist whose odyssey under the Khmer Rouge inspired the 1984 film *The Killing Fields*, poses with Haing S. Ngor, himself a survivor of the Cambodian genocide, who won an Oscar for his performance as Dith in the film. The two were photographed on a joint return to Phnom Penh in 1986.

Source: Magnum Photos/Steve McCurry.

In the early 1980s, Cambodia/Kampuchea struck most Westerners, if it struck them at all, as a somehow undifferentiated humanitarian crisis. *The Killing Fields*, a British film directed by Roland Joffé and released in 1984, changed all that. "In a matter of months," wrote Elizabeth Becker, "*The Killing Fields* catapulted Cambodia from Cold War politics to mass culture. Black-pajamaed Khmer Rouge joined the brown-shirted Nazis as recognizable villains of the twentieth century. The term killing fields became part of the American vocabulary."[67] It remains so today, as a generic descriptor for the mass gravesites that symbolize atrocity zones worldwide.

The Killing Fields is arguably the greatest dramatic film about genocide, though votes for *Schindler's List* will be counted. It tells the story of Dith Pran (pictured at left in Figure 7.3), who worked as an assistant and translator for *New York Times* journalist Sydney Schanberg during and after the fall of Phnom Penh to the Khmer Rouge in April 1975. Sending his family to safety in the US, Dith stayed behind. On one occasion, he risked his life to save Schanberg's and that of two cohorts, including Al Rockoff (see Figure 7.4), threatened with execution by Khmer Rouge cadres. When Schanberg and other foreigners took refuge in the French embassy, Dith was forced to leave, and began a journey to the heart of the "killing fields." (It was Dith, in fact, who coined that iconic term to describe his ordeal.)[68]

The Killing Fields follows Dith as he is drafted as a forced laborer, reduced to a filthy, malnourished state, and forced to witness the depravities of the Khmer Rouge regime up close. Dith's trajectory was depicted by Haing S. Ngor (at right in Figure 7.3) – himself a Cambodian refugee and genocide survivor. Ngor's performance would win him an Academy Award for Best Supporting Actor; he told his personal story of suffering and survival in a memoir, *A Cambodian Odyssey* (1987). Tragically, Ngor, who had endured four years under the Khmer Rouge, was killed in a street hold-up in Los Angeles in February 1996. For his part, after his successful escape from Cambodia and reunion with Schanberg, Dith Pran rejoined the staff of *The New York Times* as a photographer, and became a regular speaker on genocide prevention. He died of pancreatic cancer in March 2008.

In 2009, on my first visit to Phnom Penh, I was introduced to none other than Al Rockoff, the US photojournalist played by John Malkovich in *The Killing Fields*. Over a couple of drinks, Rockoff (see Figure 7.4) derided the movie for portraying him as failing to "fix" a passport image for Dith Pran, thus guaranteeing Dith's expulsion from the French embassy. It never happened, Rockoff insisted; he would never be so amateurish. But he allowed that the heart-stopping scene in which he, Schanberg, British journalist Jon Swain, and Dith are detained and nearly gunned down by the Khmer Rouge captured events very much as they had unfolded. It was one of several

Figure 7.4 Al Rockoff, *Killing Fields* photojournalist (John Malkovich's character), at a Mexican cantina in Phnom Penh, Cambodia.

Source: Author's photo, May 2009.

occasions during the Indochina wars when Rockoff nearly died prematurely. He is currently working on a photo project documenting the lives of Cambodians in peacetime.

In his memoir, Haing Ngor wrote that until *The Killing Fields* came out, "relatively few people knew what had happened in Cambodia during the Khmer Rouge years – intellectuals and Asia experts had, maybe, but not the general public. The film put the story of those years in terms that everybody could understand."[69] As such, it remains a classic instance of a cultural product becoming so intertwined with the events it describes that it can be difficult for the layperson to separate them. How many people, one wonders, have mistaken the survivor and original inspiration Dith Pran for Haing Ngor, the survivor who immortalized him on film?

AFTERMATH: POLITICS AND THE QUEST FOR JUSTICE

On December 25, 1978, 150,000 Vietnamese soldiers, accompanied by 15,000 Cambodian rebels and air support, crossed the border of Democratic Kampuchea and seized Phnom Penh in two weeks. The Khmer Rouge leadership fled to sanctuaries in western Cambodia and across the border in Thailand.[70] It used these for the next decade-and-a-half as it fought to return to power at the head of a coalition of forces opposed to Vietnamese occupation. (Prince Sihanouk, who had spent most of the DK years under *de facto* house arrest in Phnom Penh, served as figurehead for the coalition from 1982.) Meanwhile, former KR leaders, the rebels from the Eastern Zone, were appointed as Vietnamese surrogates to run the new People's Republic of Kampuchea (PRK). While Heng Samrin was appointed president, real power eventually fell into the hands of his former subordinate in the Eastern Zone, Hun Sen.

Throughout the 1980s, in one of the twentieth century's "more depressing episodes of diplomacy,"[71] the Western world moved from branding the Khmer Rouge as communist monsters to embracing them as Cambodia's legitimate representatives. At the United Nations, the US led a push to grant Cambodia's General Assembly seat to the anti-Vietnamese coalition dominated by the Khmer Rouge. Why this Orwellian flip-flop? US hostility to Vietnam was still pronounced after the US defeat of 1975. An enemy of Vietnam was America's friend, regardless of its sanguinary past. In the words of US Secretary of State Henry Kissinger, speaking to the Thai Foreign Minister Chatichai Choonhavan a few months after the Khmer Rouge takeover:

> We are aware that the biggest threat to Southeast Asia at the present time is North Vietnam . . . Cambodia [is] a barrier to the Vietnamese. . . . You should . . . tell the Cambodians that we will be friends with them. They are murderous thugs, but we won't let that stand in our way.[72]

Thus one witnessed the anomalous sight, throughout the 1980s, of genocidal communists receiving some of their firmest backing from Washington, DC. China was

Figure 7.5 and 7.6   Two photos of victims of "S-21," the Tuol Sleng torture and execution center in Phnom Penh, today a Museum of Genocide. Only ten inmates out of 14,000 are known to have survived incarceration at Tuol Sleng. The Khmer Rouge carefully registered and photographed the prisoners; today, these images serve as valuable documentation of the Cambodian genocide.

Source: Author's photos of Tuol Sleng museum display, May 2009.

also an important player – as it had been throughout the Khmer Rouge years in power, despite KR pledges to make Cambodia "self-sufficient."

In October 1991, with the Cold War at an end, the Comprehensive Political Settlement of the Cambodian Conflict was signed in Paris. Vietnamese forces had left the country in 1989. The United Nations stepped in to supervise the peace process. It launched UNTAC, the UN Transitional Authority in Cambodia, "the single most ambitious field operation in [UN] history" to that point.[73] However, the path to national elections in 1993 was fraught with difficulties. The Khmer Rouge boycotted the vote, and stepped up military attacks.

Ultimately, in May 1993, elections were held, but they did not produce the results Hun Sen desired. Voters gave a plurality of votes to Prince Ranariddh, son of Norodom Sihanouk. Hun Sen, the "great survivor of Cambodian politics,"[74] then used his control over Cambodia's key institutions to strong-arm Ranariddh into accepting a coalition government. By 1997, Hun Sen had tired of the arrangement. He launched what was in essence a *coup d'état*, re-establishing himself as the supreme authority. The absolutist strain in Cambodian politics was proving difficult to shake, especially against a backdrop of economic and social breakdown.

The campaign to bring surviving Khmer Rouge leaders to justice proceeded, albeit haltingly.[75] The project was marginalized throughout the 1980s by US and communist Chinese opposition. The 1998 death of Pol Pot in his jungle exile, apparently from natural causes, further hampered the process, as did messy wrangling between the United Nations and the Cambodian government over the nature and composition of any tribunal. In June 2003, the two parties finally reached agreement. The Cambodian tribunal would include "international jurists, lawyers and judges [who] will occupy key roles as the co-prosecutor, co-investigating judge and two out of five trial court judges, and must be a party to conviction or exoneration of any accused."[76] This "mixed tribunal" constituted an interesting new legal institution to try genocide cases.

It was this tribunal, based only a short distance from the Cheung Ek "killing fields" site outside Phnom Penh, that was functioning when I visited in May 2009 (see the further discussion of the "mixed tribunals" in Chapter 15). The first of five leadership figures to be tried (though, in this case, for crimes against humanity and war crimes, not genocide) was Kaing Guek Eav, "Comrade Duch" (pronounced "Doik"), former commander of the infamous Tuol Sleng/S-21 killing center which appears on the cover of this book. Duch, "a wiry, compact man, expressionless, his silver hair combed tidily to the side,"[77] took occasional notes as his lawyers wrangled over procedure. He showed emotion, according to observers, only when he was taken to the Cheung Ek site where so many of S-21's prisoners were taken for execution. Duch was reportedly "moved to tears" by the experience, "especially . . . when he stood before a tree with a sign describing how executioners disposed of child victims by bashing their heads against its trunk."[78]

Figure 7.7 Kaing Guek Eav, alias "Duch", the first senior Khmer Rouge figure to be placed on trial before the Extraordinary Chamber of the Cambodian Courts (ECCC) – the innovative "mixed tribunal" established for the Cambodian genocide. Duch was the commander of the notorious Tuol Sleng/S-21 prison and torture complex in Phnom Penh, depicted on the cover of this book and on pp. 298 and 303.

Source: AP Photo/Heng Sinith.

Apart from this episode, Duch remained stolid, even brazen – petitioning the court in his closing hearing for release based on time served, for example. Evidence in his trial concluded in November 2009; deliberations were still underway at the time of writing. Scheduled to appear next was Khieu Samphan, the 78-year-old former head of state under the Khmer Rouge. Khieu had always denied knowledge of the atrocities committed by the regime, declaring that he became aware of them only after viewing a documentary on S-21 in 2003.[79]

By this point, the tribunal's operations were running more than $100 million over budget. The cost of the proceedings, together with the advanced age of the defendants, allegations of political interference,[80] and the fact that the foreign (especially Chinese and US) role in the genocide was ignored, evoked ambivalence in Cambodia. The majority of Cambodians, after all, were born after the Khmer Rouge were toppled from power – while many current leaders, notably Prime Minister Hun Sen, were themselves Khmer Rouge functionaries until breaking with the movement and joining in its overthrow. For survivors of the genocide, however, the priority was swift justice. "If the process of the trial continues to be too slow, then the aging former Khmer Rouge leaders will die before facing trial," said Yin Kean, a nun in her seventies who joined hundreds of others in a 2007 demonstration protesting the numerous delays in the proceedings. "I wish to see these leaders taken to court soon so that they will reveal who is responsible for the deaths of Cambodians under their regime."[81]

FURTHER STUDY

Denise Affonço, *To the End of Hell: One Woman's Struggle to Survive Cambodia's Khmer Rouge*, trans. Margaret Burn and Katie Hogben. London: Reportage Press, 2007. Memoir of forced labor and privation, with introductions by Jon Swain and David Chandler.

Elizabeth Becker, *When the War Was Over: Cambodia and the Khmer Rouge Revolution*. New York: Public Affairs, 1998. The most accessible overview of the Khmer Rouge years.

David P. Chandler, *The Tragedy of Cambodian History: Politics, War and Revolution since 1945*. New Haven, CT: Yale University Press, 1991. Fine short history.

Tom Fawthrop and Helen Jarvis, *Getting Away with Genocide? Cambodia's Long Struggle against the Khmer Rouge*. London: Pluto Press, 2004. Justice in post-genocide Cambodia.

Evan R. Gottesman, *Cambodia after the Khmer Rouge: Inside the Politics of Nation Building*. New Haven, CT: Yale University Press, 2003. Political change and continuity after the genocide.

Alexander Laban Hinton, *Why Did They Kill? Cambodia in the Shadow of Genocide*. Berkeley, CA: University of California Press, 2005. Insightful anthropological analysis, also drawing on social and existential psychology.

Ben Kiernan, *The Pol Pot Regime: Race, Power and Genocide in Cambodia under the Khmer Rouge*, 3rd edn. New Haven, CT: Yale University Press, 2008. Detailed study of the Khmer Rouge years; a sequel to *How Pol Pot Came to Power*.

Haing Ngor with Roger Warner, *A Cambodian Odyssey*. New York: Macmillan, 1987. Memoir by the Cambodian doctor and genocide survivor who won an Oscar for playing Dith Pran in *The Killing Fields* (see p. 300–02).

William Shawcross, *Sideshow: Kissinger, Nixon and the Destruction of Cambodia* (rev. edn). New York: Cooper Square Press, 2002. The US air war against Cambodia and its role in bringing the Khmer Rouge to power.

Philip Short, *Pol Pot: Anatomy of a Nightmare*. New York: Henry Holt and Company, 2004. The most detailed biography of "Brother Number One" in the Khmer Rouge regime.

Loung Ung, *First They Killed My Father: A Daughter of Cambodia Remembers*. New York: HarperCollins, 2000. Memoir of a Chinese-Cambodian girl who lived through the genocide.

Michael Vickery, *Cambodia 1975–1982*. Boston, MA: South End Press, 1984. Revisionist study, arguing for an emphasis on local/regional dynamics of Khmer Rouge rule.

NOTES

1 Michael Vickery, *Cambodia 1975–1982* (Boston, MA: South End Press, 1984), p. 7.

2 Alexander Laban Hinton, "A Head for an Eye: Revenge in the Cambodian Genocide," in Hinton, ed., *Genocide: An Anthropological Reader* (Malden, MA: Blackwell, 2002), pp. 254–85. See also Hinton, *Why Did They Kill? Cambodia in the Shadow of Genocide* (Berkeley, CA: University of California Press, 2005).

3 David W. Roberts, *Political Transition in Cambodia, 1991–1999: Power, Elitism and Democracy* (New York: St. Martin's Press, 2001), p. 205.

4 Vickery, *Cambodia 1975–1982*, p. 9.

5 Elizabeth Becker, *When the War Was Over: Cambodia and the Khmer Rouge Revolution* (New York: Public Affairs, 1998), p. 37.

6 "Khmer Rouge" (Red Khmers) is actually a label applied derisively to the CPK by Cambodian President Norodom Sihanouk.

7 Two other members of the core KR group would hold important regional posts under DK. These were Mok, who would serve as party secretary in the DK's Southwest Zone, and carry out a vicious purge of the Northwest Zone in 1977; and Ke Pauk, a key military leader who directed the Kampuchean army to genocidal ends. A more independent member of the Paris group, Hou Youn, was purged and killed in 1975, at the dawn of the DK era, apparently for his opposition to the forced evacuation of Phnom Penh. Ke Pauk died of natural causes in February 2002. The seminal study of the origins of Cambodian communism is Ben Kiernan, *How Pol Pot Came to Power: Colonialism, Nationalism, and Communism in Cambodia, 1930–1975* (2nd edn) (New Haven, CT: Yale University Press, 2004).

8 Frank Chalk and Kurt Jonassohn, *The History and Sociology of Genocide* (New Haven, CT: Yale University Press, 1990), p. 400.

9 Khieu Thirith quoted in Becker, *When the War Was Over*, p. 75.

10 Becker, *When the War Was Over*, p. 87.

11 David P. Chandler, *The Tragedy of Cambodian History: Politics, War, and Revolution since 1945* (New Haven, CT: Yale University Press, 1991), p. 108.

12 Ibid., p. 205.

13 The coup, invasion, and subsequent bombing campaign are memorably described in William Shawcross, *Sideshow: Kissinger, Nixon, and the Destruction of Cambodia* (rev. edn) (New York: Cooper Square Press, 2002).

14 Quoted in Taylor Owen and Ben Kiernan, "Bombs Over Cambodia," *The Walrus*, October 2006, http://www.walrusmagazine.com/articles/2006.10-history-bombing-cambodia.

15 Samantha Power, *"A Problem from Hell": America and the Age of Genocide* (New York: Basic Books, 2002), p. 94.

16 Becker, *When the War Was Over*, p. 17.

17 In the view of genocide scholar Leo Kuper, "the [Khmer Rouge] government of Kampuchea [Cambodia] had every justification for its indictment of American imperialists. . . . They had left the new rulers with a most desperate food crisis and the overwhelming task of immediately restoring the cultivation of rice in a war-shattered country. They bear a heavy responsibility for many of the subsequent developments under the revolutionary government." Kuper, *Genocide: Its Political Use in the Twentieth Century* (Harmondsworth: Penguin, 1981), p. 159.

18 Owen and Kiernan, "Bombs Over Cambodia."

19 Ben Kiernan, personal conversations; Kiernan, *The Pol Pot Regime: Race, Power, and Genocide in Cambodia under the Khmer Rouge, 1975–79*, 2nd edn (New Haven, CT: Yale University Press, 2001); Christopher Hitchens, *The Trial of Henry Kissinger* (New York: Verso, 2002), pp. 25–43.

20 Owen and Kiernan, "Bombs Over Cambodia."

21 Chhit Do quoted in Power, *"A Problem from Hell,"* pp. 94–95.

22 Ignatieff quoted in *Crimes against Humanity*, documentary produced by the Imperial War Museum, London, December 2002 (from the official transcript supplied by the IWM).

23 Daniel Jonah Goldhagen, *Worse Than War: Genocide, Eliminationism, and the Ongoing Assault on Humanity* (New York: Basic Books, 2009), p. 123.

24 Becker, *When the War Was Over*, p. 304. According to Pol Pot, speaking in July 1975: "In the whole world, since the advent of the revolutionary war and since the birth of US imperialism, no country, no people, and no army has been able to drive the imperialists out to the last man and score total victory over them [as we have]." This was "a precious model for the world's people." Quoted in Kiernan, *The Pol Pot Regime*, p. 94.

25 Chandler, *The Tragedy of Cambodian History*, p. 175.

26 On the fate of the tribal peoples, see Kiernan, *The Pol Pot Regime*, pp. 302–9.

27 Cited in Chalk and Jonassohn, *The History and Sociology of Genocide*, p. 405.

28 Cited in Eric D. Weitz, *A Century of Genocide: Utopias of Race and Nation* (Princeton, NJ: Princeton University Press, 2003), p. 152.

29 "The borders were closed, foreign embassies and press agencies expelled, newspapers and television stations shut down, radios confiscated, mail and telephone use suppressed, the speaking of foreign languages punished." Kiernan, *The Pol Pot Regime*, p. 9.

30 Tom Fawthrop and Helen Jarvis, *Getting Away with Genocide? Cambodia's Long Struggle against the Khmer Rouge* (London: Pluto Press, 2004), p. 94.

31 Becker, *When the War Was Over*, p. 224.

32 Ben Kiernan and Chanthou Boua, *Peasants and Politics in Kampuchea, 1942–1981* (London: Zed Press, 1982), p. 239.

33 Daniel Jonah Goldhagen, *Worse Than War: Genocide, Eliminationism, and the Ongoing Assault on Humanity* (New York: Basic Books, 2009), p. 122.

34 Allan D. Cooper, *The Geography of Genocide* (Lanham, MD: University Press of America, 2009), p. 67. Provocatively, Cooper asserts a gender dimension to urbicide: for genocidal perpetrators, who generally adhere to a traditional patriarchal model of gender relations, "the city, in particular, becomes a female terrain marked by chaos and uncontrolled sexual license where patriarchal social controls are surrendered. And by female I really mean that which is not heterosexually male" (p. 73). See the discussion of gender and genocide in Chapter 13.

35 The quoted passage is drawn from a posted announcement of "an international and interdisciplinary academic workshop" entitled "Urbicide: The Killing of Cities," at the University of Durham, November 24–25, 2005.

36 See the discussion in Chapter 1, p. 29, and Stephen Graham, ed., *Cities, War, and Terrorism: Towards an Urban Geopolitics* (Oxford: Blackwell, 2004).

37 Chandler, *The Tragedy of Cambodian History*, p. 250.

38 Quoted in Chalk and Jonassohn, *The History and Sociology of Genocide*, p. 403.

39 Goldhagen, *Worse Than War*, p. 108.

40 Kiernan and Boua, *Peasants and Politics in Kampuchea*, pp. 345–46. Urban folk, for their part, "often found it impossible to accept that they had become the servants of dark, uneducated people." Chandler, *The Tragedy of Cambodian History*, p. 243.

41 Loung Ung, *First They Killed My Father: A Daughter of Cambodia Remembers* (New York: HarperCollins, 2000), p. 62.

42 Alexander Laban Hinton "Oppression and Vengeance in the Cambodian Genocide," ch. 4 in Nicholas A. Robins and Adam Jones, eds, *Genocides by the Oppressed: Subaltern Genocide in Theory and Practice* (Bloomington, IN: Indiana University Press, 2009), pp. 84–102.

43 Vickery, *Cambodia 1975–1982*, pp. 66, 286–87, emphasis added. Curiously, Vickery echoes these prejudices, describing Cambodian urbanites as "spoiled, pretentious, contentious, status-conscious at worst, or at best simply soft, intriguing, addicted to city comforts and despising peasant life" (p. 26).

44 Kiernan, *The Pol Pot Regime*, p. 212.

45 The statistics are of course subject to dispute. For calculations, see Ben Kiernan, "The Demography of Genocide in Southeast Asia: The Death Tolls in Cambodia, 1975–79, and East Timor, 1975–80," *Critical Asian Studies*, 35: 4 (2003), pp. 586–87.

46 Chandler, *The Tragedy of Cambodian History*, p. 265.

47 Ibid., pp. 270–71.

48 Hinton, *Why Did They Kill?*, p. 167.

49 Vickery, *Cambodia 1975–1982*, pp. 68–69, 86.

50 Chandler, *The Tragedy of Cambodian History*, p. 265.

51 Molyda Szymusiak, *The Stones Cry Out: A Cambodian Childhood, 1975–1980* (New York: Hill & Wang, 1986). The quoted passages are drawn from pp. 4, 15, 22, 25, 45, 55, 77, 95, 134, 145, 155–56, 162, 181, 245.

52 "1978 was the year of hardest work, night and day. We planted from 4 a.m. to 10 a.m., then ate a meal. At 1 p.m. we started again, and worked until 5 p.m., and then from 7 to 10 p.m. . . . There was not enough food, and foraging was not allowed." Testimony cited in Ben Kiernan, "The Cambodian Genocide – 1975–1979," in Samuel Totten *et al.*, eds, *Century of Genocide: Eyewitness Accounts and Critical Views* (New York: Garland Publishing, 1997), p. 359.

53 These included valuing children over parents (the young were the "blank slates" of the revolution); encouraging children to spy on their elders and report "suspicious activities" to KR cadres; and, in later stages, the outright seizure and sequestering of children to be raised and indoctrinated by party representatives.

54 Hinton, "A Head for an Eye," p. 273.

55 Ung quoted in Alexander Laban Hinton, *Why Did They Kill? Cambodia in the Shadow of Genocide* (Berkeley, CA: University of California Press, 2005), p. 168.

56 Pol Pot quoted in Kiernan, *The Pol Pot Regime*, p. 336.

57 Kiernan, "The Cambodian Genocide," pp. 338–39.

58 Ben Kiernan, "Genocidal Targeting: Two Groups of Victims in Pol Pot's Cambodia," in P. Timothy Bushnell *et al.*, eds, *State Organized Terror: The Case of Violent Internal Repression* (Boulder, CO: Westview Press, 1991), pp. 209, 212. In an echo of Nazi Germany's labeling of Jews with the Star of David, inhabitants of the Eastern Zone were outfitted with blue scarves (*kromar*) that allowed them to be easily identified and eliminated once deported from the zone (see pp. 213–18).

59 Statistics cited in Fawthrop and Jarvis, *Getting Away with Genocide?*, p. 245. On Tuol Sleng, see David Chandler, *Voices from S-21: Terror and History in Pol Pot's Secret Prison* (Berkeley, CA: University of California Press, 1999).

60 Becker, *When the War Was Over*, p. 254.

61 Sydney Schanberg, "Cambodia," in Hewitt, ed., *Defining the Horrific*, p. 261. Ironically, as Alexander Hinton notes, "the DK regime's glorification of asceticism, detachment, the elimination of attachment and desire, renunciation (of material goods and personal behaviors, sentiments, and attitudes), and purity paralleled prominent Buddhist themes that were geared toward helping a person attain greater mindfulness." Hinton, *Why Did They Kill?*, p. 197.

62 Kiernan, *The Pol Pot Regime*, p. 458.

63 Kiernan, "Genocidal Targeting," p. 218.

64 Kiernan, *The Pol Pot Regime*, p. 461.

65 Kiernan, "The Cambodian Genocide," p. 341.

66 Ibid., p. 342.

67 Becker, *When the War Was Over*, p. 459.

68 See Jon Swain, "War Reporter Jon Swain Pays Tribute to Dith Pran," *The Sunday Times*, April 6, 2008, http://www.timesonline.co.uk/tol/news/uk/article3688459.ece. See also Swain's vivid account of "The Fall of Phnom Penh" in his memoir *River of Time* (New York: Berkley Books, 1995), pp. 119–70.

69 Haing Ngor with Roger Warner, *A Cambodian Odyssey* (New York: Macmillan, 1987), p. 455.

70 On the Vietnam–Cambodia relationship during the Khmer Rouge era, and the Vietnamese invasion of 1978–79, see Nayan Chanda, *Brother Enemy: The War after the War* (New York: Collier, 1986).

71 Eric Hobsbawm, *The Age of Extremes: A History of the World, 1914–1991* (New York: Vintage Books, 1994), p. 451.

72 Kissinger quoted in Ben Kiernan, "Documentation Delayed, Justice Denied: The Historiography of the Cambodian Genocide," in Dan Stone, ed., *The Historiography of Genocide* (London: Palgrave Macmillan, 2008), p. 469.

73 Mats Berdal and Michael Leifer, "Cambodia," in James Mayall, ed., *The New Interventionism, 1991–1994: United Nations Experience in Cambodia, Former Yugoslavia and Somalia* (Cambridge: Cambridge University Press, 1996), p. 36.

74 Nicholas Wheeler, *Saving Strangers: Humanitarian Intervention in International Society* (Oxford: Oxford University Press, 2000), p. 84.

75 For an overview of the twisted course of justice in Cambodia, see "A Case Study: The Atrocities of the Khmer Rouge," Part III in Steven R. Ratner and Jason S. Abrams, *Accountability for Human Rights Atrocities in International Law: Beyond the Nuremberg Legacy*, 2nd edn (Oxford: Oxford University Press, 2001), pp. 267–328.

76 Fawthrop and Jarvis, *Getting Away with Genocide?*, p. 240.

77 Miriama Kamo, "Killing Fields Executioner Faces Justice," *The Independent*, March 13, 2009.

78 "Khmer Rouge Defendant Weeps at Site of Mass Graves," Associated Press dispatch in the *International Herald Tribune*, February 26, 2008, http://www.iht.com/articles/2008/02/26/asia/cambo.php.

79 Seth Mydans, "Khmer Rouge Leader Is Arrested," *The New York Times*, November 20, 2007, http://www.nytimes.com/2007/11/20/world/asia/20cambo.html. The others in custody and awaiting trial at the time of writing were Ieng Sary, Ieng Thirith, and Nuon Chea.

80 Seth Mydans, "Efforts to Limit Khmer Rouge Trials Decried," *The New York Times*, January 31, 2009, http://www.nytimes.com/2009/02/01/world/asia/01cambodia.html.

81 "Cambodians Seek Quick Genocide Trials," Associated Press dispatch on ABCNews.com, December 25, 2007.

BOX 7A EAST TIMOR

East Timor's road to independence began in the same year – 1975 – that the Khmer Rouge took power in Cambodia. For four years following the Indonesian invasion and occupation of East Timor in December, events in these two Southeast Asian lands moved in grim tandem. Both witnessed genocides as severe, in terms of proportion of population killed, as any since the Jewish Holocaust. The Khmer Rouge regime became a byword for ideological fanaticism and the brutal exercise of power, sparking international condemnation. In contrast, the genocide in East Timor was protested and publicized only by a small group of Timorese exiles, human rights activists, and concerned scholars.[1] In the 1990s, as Indonesian atrocities continued, the Timor solidarity movement grew. The global network it established was a key ingredient in confronting the final blast of Indonesian genocide, in 1999, aiming to overturn a pro-independence referendum result. East Timor thus offers an inspiring example of a genocide ended, in large part, by popular mobilization and protest.

East Timor owes its distinctiveness from the rest of the island of Timor, and the wider Indonesian archipelago, to its colonization by the Portuguese in the mid-seventeenth century. The division of the island between the Portuguese and Dutch was formalized in 1915. During the Second World War, the colonial regime gave way to Japanese occupation. This spawned the first large-scale resistance movement in East Timor, assisted by Australian troops. When Australia abandoned the territory, the Timorese were left at the mercy of the Japanese, who slaughtered an estimated 60,000 of them – 13 percent of the population. (Notably, some of the most powerful calls in the 1975–99 period for solidarity with East Timor came from Australian Second World War veterans, who recalled the solidarity the Timorese had shown them *in extremis*.)

After the war, the Dutch East Indies became the independent Republic of Indonesia. Portugal, meanwhile, re-established control over East Timor. But in April 1974, a left-wing military coup against the fascist government in Lisbon established a democratic government, leading Portugal to stage a rapid retreat from its overseas empire (including Angola and Mozambique). Indigenous political parties sprang up in East Timor, and elections for a National Constituent Assembly were set for 1976, with full independence anticipated three years later.

By 1975, the leading political force in the territory was Fretilin (the Revolutionary Front of Independent East Timor), which had established strong grassroots support throughout the countryside. In 1975, Fretilin won village-level elections over its main competitor, the Timorese Democratic Union (UDT). Disaffected UDT members, responding to Indonesian machinations, refused to accept the result. Their abortive coup was quickly crushed, with a death-toll of several thousand. The UDT leadership fled to Indonesia, and Fretilin issued a declaration of independence on November 28, 1975.

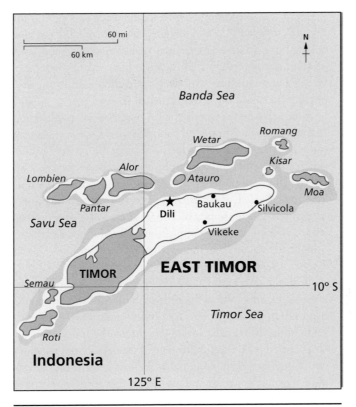

Map 7A.1 East Timor

Source: Map provided by WorldAtlas.com.

Just over a week later, on December 7 – after receiving the green light from visiting US president Gerald Ford and Secretary of State Henry Kissinger[2]– the Indonesians launched an invasion of East Timor by land, sea, and air. In the largest city, Dili, the Indonesian military murdered thousands of Timorese in mass executions. Fretilin forces were driven into the mountainous interior. Over the following years, tens of thousands of Timorese civilians would join them there, preferring isolation in harsh conditions to Indonesian violence and repression.

With Dili and secondary towns under their control, Indonesian forces fanned out across the territory. Massacres occurred almost everywhere they went. Families of suspected Fretilin supporters were killed along with the suspects themselves. In some cases, whole villages were exterminated. This strategy reached its apogee in the Aitana region in July 1981, where "a ghastly massacre . . . murdered everyone, from tiny babies to the elderly, unarmed people who were not involved in the fighting but were there simply because they had stayed with Fretilin and wanted to live freely in the mountains."[3] Perhaps 10,000 Timorese died in this killing spree.

The atrocities continued on a smaller scale throughout the 1980s. At Malim Luro in August 1983, for example, "after plundering the population of all their belongings, [Indonesian troops] firmly tied up men, women and children, numbering more than sixty people. They made them lie on the ground and then drove a bulldozer over them, and then used it to place a few centimetres of earth on top of the totally crushed corpses."[4]

Survivors of the rampages were confined to "model villages" invigilated by Indonesian soldiers and local paramilitaries. Disease, starvation, and forced labor caused many deaths. The territories not under full Indonesian control also suffered genocide. Indonesian forces launched repeated scorched-earth sorties; rained bombs on civilian populations; and imposed a strict blockade on Fretilin-held areas that led, as designed, to starvation. According to Timor specialist John Taylor, tens of thousands of Timorese died as a result of this war of "encirclements, bombing, uprooting of the population, malnutrition and generalized brutalities."[5] In total, an estimated 170,000 Timorese – "24 to 26 percent of East Timor's 1975 population" – died between 1975 and 1999.[6]

With the international community's acceptance of Indonesia's "new order,"[7] it seemed unlikely that the independence movement could survive, let alone triumph. In the 1990s, however, Indonesia's hold weakened. On November 12, 1991, some 270 civilians were slaughtered by Indonesian troops in Dili's Santa Cruz cemetery. Witnessed by several foreign observers, who managed to escape with film footage, the Dili massacre provoked the first substantial international outcry against genocide in East Timor. The territory's profile was raised further in 1996, when the Nobel Peace Prize was awarded to the leader of the East Timor Catholic Church, Carlos Filipe Ximenes Belo, and Fretilin's leader in exile, José Ramos Horta. Meanwhile, taking advantage of new Internet technologies, the international Timorese solidarity movement – spearheaded by the East Timor Action Network (ETAN) – organized demonstrations and lobbied governments to condemn Indonesian repression.

A dramatic transformation within Indonesia catalyzed the final independence drive. In 1998, with Indonesia suffering an economic crisis, General Suharto, the erstwhile military dictator, resigned and handed power to his vice-president, B.J. Habibie. Habibie stunned the world by announcing, in January 1999, that Indonesia was willing to "let East Timor go" if its people chose independence in a referendum. The United Nations, with Portugal taking the lead, rapidly organized a vote, scheduled for August 30.

Behind the scenes, the Indonesian military – which had amassed huge economic holdings in East Timor over the previous twenty-five years – prepared to sabotage the independence process. It relied on locally raised paramilitary forces (the so-called *ninjas*), overseen by the elite Kopassus army unit, to terrorize the population into voting to stay with Indonesia. In the prelude to the referendum, hundreds of Timorese, especially activist youth, were murdered by death squads or in local-level massacres.[8] Despite these atrocities, the UN fatefully chose to leave "security" in the hands of the Indonesian army.

The stage was thus set for the violence and destruction unleashed at the end of August 1999. Voting peacefully and in overwhelming numbers, 78.5 percent of Timorese opted for independence. The Indonesian military and its local allies swung immediately into action. As international observers looked on in horror, and the UN hunkered down in its headquarters, militia killed unknown numbers of Timorese. (A regularly cited figure is 1,500, but this may be a substantial undercount.)[9] Indonesian troops and local militias burned swathes of territory and whole city neighborhoods to the ground, in a campaign aimed at "the virtual demolition of the physical basis for survival in the territory."[10]

The UN then decided to evacuate staff from its Dili compound, and leave the terrified Timorese gathered there to their fate. This craven action was only avoided by an unprecedented staff rebellion against the edict (see Robinson, Further Study). Meanwhile, hundreds of thousands of demonstrators took to the streets in North America, Europe, and Australia, bringing sustained pressure to bear on their governments.[11] With memories of Rwanda and Bosnia (see Chapters 8 and 9) doubtless reverberating in his mind, UN Secretary-General Kofi Annan issued a strongly worded warning to Indonesia. The Clinton administration in the US also announced that it was prepared to suspend the military aid on which the Indonesian armed forces depended. The Australian government, for its part, offered to lead a stabilization force to occupy and patrol the territory. Faced with this concerted opposition, the Indonesian government backed down. Australian forces deployed in Dili on September 20; a week later, Indonesia ceded control to the international contingent.

East Timor became an independent nation two years later, in August 2001. The happy ending, however, was undermined by material and human devastation, spiraling unemployment, and social dislocation. Street violence waged by frustrated, demobilized members of the army and police, as well as by gangs and political factions, led Prime Minister José Ramos Horta to declare in 2007 that the country was still in a "fragile and precarious" state.[12]

Attempts to establish the truth of what had occurred during the mass violence of 1999 – and the quarter-century preceding it – were confounded by a lack of resources,[13] and by the reluctance of Indonesian and (more surprisingly) East Timorese authorities to pursue justice. *The Economist* reported in August 2004 that "of the 16 members of the Indonesian security forces and two East Timorese civilians who were indicted [by Indonesian courts], all the Indonesians have either been acquitted or freed on appeal," while the Timorese received light punishments.[14]

The most significant effort to document the atrocities throughout the period of Indonesian rule was launched by the UN-sponsored Commission for Reception, Truth and Reconciliation, established in 2001. The commission reported its findings to the East Timorese government in October 2005 – but the government "suppressed [them] for months," fearing destabilization of its relations with its huge neighbor and former occupier.[15] "Let us not waste time in kneeling ourselves before the wailing wall," declared President Xanana

Gusmão. "We must respect the courage of the Indonesians in accepting our independence and not disrupt their progress towards democratisation by demanding formal justice."[16]

The 2500-page report, as finally leaked to the media, was indeed explosive. The commission chose to deploy the language of "extermination" as a crime against humanity, rather than "genocide," to describe Indonesian actions – in part to encompass the indirect and structural forms of violence that accounted for a majority of the victims. (See further discussion of "extermination" and crimes against humanity legislation in Chapter 15, pp. 538–41.) But it pulled no punches in detailing the nature and extent of the crimes, finding that "the Indonesian military used starvation as a weapon to exterminate the East Timorese," killing "as many as 180,000 civilians" throughout its dominion over the territory. "Napalm and chemical weapons, which poisoned the food and water supply, were [also] used," and the report documented "a litany of massacres, thousands of summary executions of civilians and the torture of 8500 East Timorese – with horrific details of public beheadings, the mutilation of genitalia, the burying and burning alive of victims, use of cigarettes to burn victims, and ears and genitals being lopped off to display to families."[17]

The commission was also blunt in its assessment of the role played by the United States and Australia in supporting the invasion and turning a blind eye to the ensuing exterminations. US "political and military support [was] fundamental to the Indonesian invasion and occupation," the report's authors declared; the support arose from "a strategically-motivated desire to maintain a good relationship with Indonesia, whose anti-communist regime was seen as an essential bastion against the spread of communism."[18] As for Australia, the report accused the then-government of "contribut[ing] significantly to denying the people of Timor-Leste their right to self-determination before and during the Indonesian occupation," eager to preserve good relations with its powerful neighbor and to secure favorable terms in boundary negotiations over the oil-and gas-rich "Timor Gap."[19] The commissioners insisted that the two countries, along with Britain, France, and others who funded and armed Indonesia's military dictatorship, should pay reparations to the Timorese who died as a consequence. Predictably, the demand fell on deaf ears.

FURTHER STUDY

Peter Carey and G. Carter Bentley, eds, *East Timor at the Crossroads: The Forging of a Nation*. Honolulu, HI: University of Hawaii Press, 1995. Essays on the Timorese independence struggle.

Tim Fischer, *Seven Days in East Timor: Ballots and Bullets*. London: Allen & Unwin, 2000. Eyewitness account of the 1999 independence vote.

Matthew Jardine, *East Timor: Genocide in Paradise*. Berkeley, CA: Odonian Press, 1999. A succinct introduction.

Joseph Nevins, *A Not-so-distant Horror: Mass Violence in East Timor*. Ithaca, NY: Cornell University Press, 2005. Good on the post-1999 quest for justice.

Geoffrey Robinson, *"If You Leave Us Here, We Will Die": How Genocide Was Stopped in East Timor*. Princeton, NJ: Princeton University Press, 2010. The inspiring story, by a participant, of how rebellion in UN ranks helped to prompt a humanitarian intervention in 1999.

John G. Taylor, *East Timor: The Price of Freedom*. London: Zed Books, 2000. The best all-round study of the Indonesian occupation, with a useful chronology.

NOTES

1 Among the academic voices were Noam Chomsky and Edward S. Herman. In a 1979 study, they contrasted the outrage over Cambodian atrocities with the near-total media blackout on East Timor. Victims of the communist Khmer Rouge were "worthy victims," they wrote ironically, while the East Timorese – whose tormentor, Indonesia, was a valued Western ally – were deemed "unworthy," and thus consigned to oblivion. Chomsky and Herman, *The American Connection and Third World Fascism*, Vol. 1 of *The Political Economy of Human Rights* (Boston, MA: South End Press, 1979).

2 See the declassified documents posted by the National Security Archive on "Ford, Kissinger and the Indonesian Invasion, 1975–76," December 6, 2001, http://www.gwu.edu/~nsarchiv/NSAEBB/NSAEBB62/index2.html.

3 Source cited in John G. Taylor, *East Timor: The Price of Freedom* (London: Zed Books, 2000), p. 118. See also Taylor's fine chapter, "'Encirclement and Annihilation': The Indonesian Occupation of East Timor," in Robert Gellately and Ben Kiernan, eds, *The Specter of Genocide: Mass Murder in Historical Perspective* (Cambridge: Cambridge University Press, 2003), pp. 163–85.

4 Source cited in Taylor, *East Timor*, p. 103. Together with indiscriminate, "root-and-branch" massacres of this type, a pattern of gendercidal killings of males was also evident, as it would be after the independence referendum in 1999. For a detailed investigation, see Adam Jones/Gendercide Watch, "Case Study: East Timor, 1975–99," http://www.gendercide.org/case_timor.html, from which part of this box text is adapted.

5 Taylor, *East Timor*, p. 151.

6 Ben Kiernan, "The Demography of Genocide in Southeast Asia: The Death Tolls in Cambodia, 1975–79, and East Timor, 1975–80," *Critical Asian Studies*, 35: 4 (2003), p. 594, citing research by Gabriel Defert.

7 According to Joseph Nevins, "Although there were numerous and diverse reasons for the various countries' support for Jakarta, the principal rationale was simple: Indonesia was a populous country with great market potential and a very wealthy resource base and occupied a strategic location." Nevins, *A Not-so-distant Horror: Mass Violence in East Timor* (Ithaca, NY: Cornell University Press, 2005), p. 77.

8 Ibid., p. 83.

9 See, e.g., Ellen Nakashima, "For Survivors of E. Timor Massacres, Justice Still Elusive," *The Washington Post*, September 16, 2005. For an examination of the physical, eyewitness, and circumstantial evidence pertaining to the Timorese death-toll in 1999, see Jones/Gendercide Watch, "Case Study: East Timor."

10 Noam Chomsky, "East Timor Is Not Yesterday's Story," *ZNet*, October 23, 1999.

11 The fact that the Timor events followed closely on the war in Kosovo (March–June 1999), which *had* prompted Western intervention, added to the pressure on governments – an interesting case of "norm grafting" (see Chapter 12).

12 Lindsay Murdoch, "East Timor Asks for Help as Street Violence Escalates," *The Sydney Morning Herald*, February 14, 2007.

13 Only the most cursory investigation was launched into the atrocities inflicted before and after the independence vote. By contrast with the hundreds of forensic investigators dispatched to Kosovo after the 1999 war there (Chapter 8), fewer than a dozen were allotted to East Timor, and only for a short period. As a result, no clear picture of the scale of the Indonesian-directed killing has yet emerged. In 2008, however, internationally-sponsored forensic work began at mass graves containing the victims of the 1991 Santa Cruz massacre: see Susan Wellings, "Timor's Mass Graves to be Excavated," *The Sydney Morning Herald*, February 18, 2008.

14 "Above the Law," *The Economist*, August 14, 2004, available at http://www.etan.org/et2004/august/08-14/13above.htm.

15 Sian Powell, "UN Verdict on East Timor," *The Australian*, January 19, 2006. Progress was made, however, by the Serious Crimes Unit within East Timor, established with UN assistance. "This body has indicted some 375 people and secured more than 50 convictions. Most of those convicted are militiamen who say they were acting under the orders of the Indonesian armed forces. About 280 indictees remain at large in Indonesia. They include the Indonesian commander at the time, General Wiranto, for whom the unit has issued an arrest warrant," though the Timorese government (!) refused to forward it to Interpol. It is notable that all of the accusations and legal initiatives relate to the 1999 atrocities; even leading human rights organizations such as Amnesty International have avoided recommending prosecutions for the genocide committed against Timorese over the previous quarter-century (see Nevins, *A Not-so-distant Horror*, p. 165).

16 Gusmao quoted in Lindsay Murdoch, "Timor's Truth Time Bomb," *The Sydney Morning Herald*, February 13, 2006.

17 Powell, "UN Verdict."

18 Colum Lunch, "Report: US Arms Helped Indonesia Attack East Timor," *The Washington Post*, January 25, 2006.

19 "East Timor Report Scathing of Downer," Australian Associated Press dispatch in *The Sydney Morning Herald*, February 2, 2006.

CHAPTER 8

Bosnia and Kosovo

The dissolution of Yugoslavia in the early 1990s returned genocide to Europe after nearly half a century's absence. During those years, European states and the wider world looked on ineffectually as the multiethnic state of Bosnia-Herzegovina collapsed into genocidal conflict. The most extensive and systematic atrocities were committed by Serbs against Muslims, but clashes between Croats and Serbs, and between Muslims and Croats, claimed thousands of lives. The restive Serb province of Kosovo, with its ethnic-Albanian majority, was another tinder-box, though mass violence did not erupt there until Spring 1999.

ORIGINS AND ONSET

Yugoslavia, the federation of "Southern Slavs," was cobbled together from the disintegrated Ottoman Empire after the First World War. Fragile federations everywhere are prone to violence in times of crisis (see, e.g., Chapter 4, Box 4a, Chapter 5, Box 5a). For Yugoslavia, the crisis came in the Second World War, when the federation was riven by combined Nazi invasion and intercommunal conflict. Yugoslavia in fact became one of the most destructive theaters of history's most destructive war.[1] Under the German occupation regime in Serbia and the fascist Ustashe government installed by the Nazis in Croatia, most of Yugoslavia's Jewish population was exterminated. Hundreds of thousands of Croatian Serbs were rounded up by the Ustashe and slaughtered, most notoriously at the Jasenovac death camp.

Muslims in Bosnia mostly collaborated with the Nazis, earning them the enduring enmity of the Serb population. The Serbs themselves were divided between the

Chetniks, who supported the deposed royalist regime, and a partisan movement led by Josip Broz, known as Tito. Chetnik massacres and other atrocities prompted an equally murderous response from Tito's forces. After the partisans seized power in the Yugoslav capital, Belgrade, in the late stages of the war, thousands of Chetniks fled to neighboring countries. The Allies returned the majority of them to Yugoslavia to face summary punishment. Throughout 1945–46, Tito's forces killed tens of thousands of Chetniks and other political opponents.

The socialist state that Tito instituted, however, was liberal by the standards of Central and Eastern Europe. Yugoslavs enjoyed extensive freedom of movement: millions worked overseas, especially in Germany. The country gained a reputation not only for comparative openness, but for successful ethnic pluralism. Tito, a Croat, worked to ensure that no ethnic group dominated the federation. Political mobilization along ethnic lines was banned (resulting in a wave of detention and imprisonment in the 1970s, when Croatian leaders within the Yugoslav Socialist Party sought greater autonomy for Croatia).* State authorities worked hard to defuse ethnic tensions and generate an overarching Yugoslav identity, with some success.

But Tito died in May 1980, and the multinational federation rapidly unraveled amidst pervasive economic strife. The weak collective leadership faltered when confronted by an emerging generation of ethnonationalist politicians, most prominently Slobodan Milosevic in Serbia and Franjo Tudjman in Croatia. Tudjman, "a small-minded, right-wing autocrat,"[2] led a political movement – the HDZ – that explicitly revived Ustashe symbolism and rhetoric. He also allowed, and probably supervised, a campaign of harassment and violence against the large Serb population of the Krajina region. Serbs were dismissed from their jobs, allegedly to redress preferential treatment granted to them in the past. Worse would follow.

In Milosevic of Serbia, meanwhile, we see one of the most influential European politicians of the second half of the twentieth century – albeit a malign influence. This did not reflect any special talent or charisma. Rather, Milosevic was an *apparatchik* (child of the state-socialist system) who realized sooner than most that rousing nationalist passions was an effective way to exploit the Yugoslav upheavals for personal power.[3]

Milosevic sowed the seeds for genocide in April 1987, on a visit to the restive Albanian-dominated province of Kosovo. (Ironically, it was over Kosovo that the term "genocide" was first deployed in a contemporary Balkans context – by Serbs, to describe the fate that supposedly awaited their people at the hands of a swelling Albanian majority.)[4] Dispatched by Serb president Ivan Stambolic, his mentor, to hold talks with the local Socialist Party leadership, Milosevic was greeted by a rowdy outpouring of Serbs barely kept in check by police. Rocks were thrown, apparently as a provocation. The police reacted with batons. Milosevic was urged to calm the crowd. Instead, he told them: "No one should dare to beat you," "unwittingly coining a modern Serb rallying call."[5]

---

*Throughout this chapter and volume, I use "Croatian" and "Croat," "Serbian" and "Serb," to refer to the polity and ethnic group respectively.

Transformed by the ecstatic reaction to his speech, Milosevic forged ahead with his nationalist agenda. A few months later, in September 1987, he shunted aside his mentor, Ivan Stambolic, and took over the presidency. In 1989, Serbs initiated a repressive drive in Kosovo that ended the province's autonomy within Serbia, dismissed tens of thousands of Kosovars (ethnic Albanians) from their jobs, and made of Kosovo "one large militia camp . . . a squalid outpost of putrefying colonialism."[6] More than a hundred Kosovars were killed in the repression.[7] In retrospect, this was the key event that unraveled Yugoslavia. After the Kosovo crackdown, no ethnic group could feel safe in a Serb-dominated federation.

In 1991–92, Yugoslavia exploded into open war. On June 25, 1991, Croatia and Slovenia declared independence. A surreal ten-day war for Slovenia resulted in the withdrawal of the Yugoslav Army (JNA) and the abandonment of Yugoslav claims to the territory. Croatia, though, was a different matter. It included sizable Serb populations in Krajina (the narrow strip of territory running adjacent to the Dalmatian coast and bordering Serb-dominated areas of Bosnia-Herzegovina) and Eastern Slavonia.

Map 8.1   Bosnia and Herzegovina today (though Serbia and Montenegro are now separate states).

Source: Map provided by WorldAtlas.com.

Milosevic recognized the inevitability of Croatia's secession, but sought to secure territories in which Serbs were strongly represented for his "Greater Serbia." In December 1991, after several months of fighting, the Krajina Serbs declared independence from Croatia. Meanwhile, the world's attention was captured by the artillery bombardment of the historic port of Dubrovnik; less so by the far more severe JNA assault on Vukovar, which reduced the city to rubble and was followed by the genocidal massacre of some 200 wounded Croatian soldiers in their hospital beds.

The independence declarations by Slovenia and Croatia left multiethnic Bosnia-Herzegovina in an impossible position. As epitomized by its major city, Sarajevo – hitherto a model of ethnic tolerance – Bosnia was divided among Muslims, Serbs, and Croats. If it sought to secede, the result would surely be a secession by Bosnian Serbs in turn, to integrate "their" zone of Bosnia into Milosevic's Greater Serbia, while remaining within the federation meant enduring Serb domination. This was the scenario that played out when, in February 1992, the Muslim-dominated federation declared its independence from Yugoslavia.

Figure 8.1 The siege of the cosmopolitan city of Sarajevo became the focal point of the Bosnian war for the outside world, though the bulk of the killing occurred elsewhere. The siege and bombardment can also be considered an important contemporary case of *urbicide*, the destruction of an urban living space and its population as part of a broader genocidal strategy (see p. 29). FAMA International produced this map of the siege, showing the ring of Serb gun emplacements around the city, broken only by the UN airport zone at the bottom left. Enterprising Sarajevans dug a tunnel under the airport runway to connect their city with Bosnian government-held territory beyond. Today the tunnel is a tourist attraction.

Source: FAMA International/www.famainternational.com.

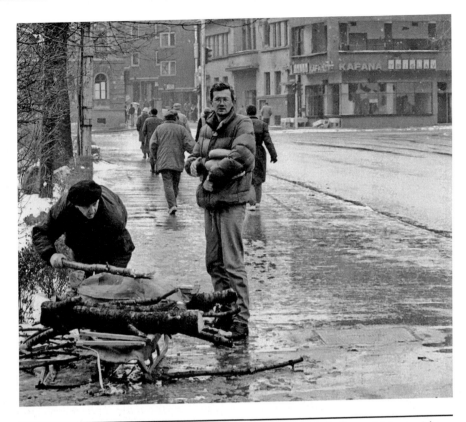

Figure 8.2 "Sarajevo siege life, winter of 1992–93. Collecting branches for firewood. Man on right cradles precious loaves of bread."

Source: Christian Maréchal/Wikimedia Commons.

In this atmosphere of pervasive fear and uncertainty, populations sought safety in ethnic exclusivity – as leaders, especially Milosevic and Tudjman, presumably anticipated. "Before, we shared the good times and the bad. . . . [Now,] we hardly wish anyone good-day or good-evening any more. Suddenly people have a different look about them, their faces have changed. For me it all happened in one day. It is indescribable."[8] So stated a Bosnian Muslim woman, recalling the breakdown of relations with her Croat neighbors.

Bosnia promptly became the most brutal battlefield of the Balkan wars. Serb gunners launched a siege and artillery bombardment of Sarajevo that evoked global outrage. Apart from killing thousands of civilians, they also staged a systematic campaign of urbicide, targeting the cultural repositories of the Bosnian Muslim and cosmopolitan Sarajevan civilizations:

> Serbs purposely shelled the major cultural institutions . . . as they sought not only to eliminate Bosniaks [Bosnian Muslims] from Bosnia but also to obliterate their communal and cultural existence's foundation. They first destroyed the Oriental Institute, burning the largest collection of Islamic and Jewish manuscripts in southeastern Europe, then the National Museum, and finally the National Library,

incinerating more than one million books, more than 100,000 manuscripts and rare books, and centuries of the country's historical records. For the artist Aida Musanovic, and certainly for other Sarajevans, seeing their principal cultural repository engulfed in flames and then having the smoke, ash, and wisps of burnt paper hovering over and raining down on their city, "was the most apocalyptic thing I'd ever seen."[9]

The attack on Sarajevo and its cultural landmarks also distracted international attention from the far greater killing elsewhere in Bosnia, especially in the industrialized east.[10] The Yugoslav army was ordered out, but left most of its weapons in the hands of Bosnian Serbs, who now constituted a formidable 80,000-man army. Bosnian Muslims, hampered by their land-locked territory and limited resources, were in most places rolled over by Serb forces. Then – from early 1993 – they found themselves fighting their Croatian former allies as well, in a war nearly as vicious as the Serb–Muslim confrontation. Not surprisingly, the Muslims responded by generating "a strident, xenophobic Muslim nationalism" mirroring that of their tormentors.[11] However, neither it nor its Croatian counterpart ever matched Serb nationalism in destructiveness. An in-depth United Nations report subsequently ascribed 90 percent of atrocities in Bosnia-Herzegovina to Serbs, and just 10 percent to Croats and Muslims combined.[12]

In August 1992, Western reporters broke the story of Serb-run concentration camps in Bosnia where Muslim males, and some females, were detained.[13] At Omarska, the grimmest of these camps, "there were routine and constant beatings; in the dormitories, on the way to and from the canteen or the latrines, all the time. The guards used clubs, thick electrical cable, rifle butts, fists, boots, brass knuckle-dusters, iron rods. . . . Every night, after midnight, the guards called out the names of one or more prisoners. These prisoners were taken out and beaten bloody, their bones often broken and their skin punctured."[14] Hundreds if not thousands died; Penny Marshall of ITN wrote that survivors were reduced to "various stages of human decay and affliction; the bones of their elbows and wrists protrude like pieces of jagged stone from the pencil thin stalks to which their arms have been reduced."[15] Such images, reminiscent of Nazi concentration camps, sparked an international uproar. Combined with revelations of mass executions and the rape of Bosnian-Muslim women, the camps spawned the first widespread use of the term "genocide" in a Balkans context.

GENDERCIDE AND GENOCIDE IN BOSNIA

The strategy of "ethnic cleansing," as it became known in Western media and public discussion, was intended not only to ensure military victory and the expulsion of target populations, but to establish the boundaries of a post-genocide territorial arrangement. As Laura Silber and Alan Little argue, "the technique . . . was designed to render the territory ethnically pure, and to make certain, by instilling a hatred and fear that would endure, that Muslims and Serbs could never again live together."[16]

Central to this policy was killing civilians, overwhelmingly men of "battle age." The war in Bosnia-Herzegovina offers one of the most vivid modern instances of gendercide, or gender-selective mass killing, discussed in a comparative context in Chapter 13. As with most cases of gendercide, the gender variable interacted with those of *age* and *community prominence* to produce a genocidal outcome in Bosnia (and again in Kosovo in 1999). Journalist Mark Danner described the *modus operandi* of Serb forces as follows:

1. *Concentration.* Surround the area to be cleansed and after warning the resident Serbs – often they are urged to leave or are at least told to mark their houses with white flags – intimidate the target population with artillery fire and arbitrary executions and then bring them out into the streets.
2. *Decapitation.* Execute political leaders and those capable of taking their places: lawyers, judges, public officials, writers, professors.
3. *Separation.* Divide women, children, and old men from men of "fighting age" – sixteen years to sixty years old.
4. *Evacuation.* Transport women, children, and old men to the border, expelling them into a neighboring territory or country.
5. *Liquidation.* Execute "fighting age" men, dispose of bodies.[17]

Throughout the Bosnian war, this strategy was systematically implemented – primarily, but not solely, by Serb military and paramilitary forces. The Srebrenica slaughter of July 1995 was by far the most destructive instance of gendercidal killing in the Balkans (brace yourself, then see Figure 13.2, p. 466); but there are dozens of more quotidian examples. Some are cited in a short section of the Helsinki Watch report, *War Crimes in Bosnia-Hercegovina*, covering the first and most murderous phase of the war:

In my village, about 180 men were killed. The army put all men in the center of the village. After the killing, the women took care of the bodies and identified them. The older men buried the bodies.

(Trnopolje)

The army came to the village that day. They took us from our houses. The men were beaten. The army came in on trucks and started shooting at the men and killing them.

(Prnovo)

The army took most of the men and killed them. There were bodies everywhere.

(Rizvanovici)

Our men had to hide. My husband was with us, but hiding. I saw my uncle being beaten on July 25 when there was a kind of massacre. The Serbs were searching for arms. Three hundred men were killed that day.

(Carakovo)[18]

The trend culminated in the genocidal slaughter of some 8,000 Bosnian Muslim men and boys, described in Box 8.1. In a tally supplied several years after the war and genocide ended, the International Committee of the Red Cross (ICRC) noted that of the thousands of Bosnians still registered as missing, "92% are men and 8% are women."[19]

As in Armenia in 1915, with community males murdered or incarcerated, Serb soldiers and paramilitaries were better able to inflict atrocities on remaining community members. Women, especially younger ones, were special targets. They were subject to rape, often repeatedly, often by gangs, and often in the presence of a father or husband. Typical was the testimony offered by "E.," just 16 years old:

> Several Chetniks arrived. One, a man around 30, ordered me to follow him into the house. I had to go. He started looking for money, jewelry and other valuables. He wanted to know where the men were. I didn't answer. Then he ordered me to undress. I was terribly afraid. I took off my clothes, feeling that I was falling apart. The feeling seemed under my skin; I was dying, my entire being was murdered. I closed my eyes, I couldn't look at him. He hit me. I fell. Then he lay on me. He did it to me. I cried, twisted my body convulsively, bled. I had been a virgin.
>
> He went out and invited two Chetniks to come in. I cried. The two repeated what the first one had done to me. I felt lost. I didn't even know when they left. I don't know how long I stayed there, lying on the floor alone, in a pool of blood.
>
> My mother found me. I couldn't imagine anything worse. I had been raped, destroyed and terribly hurt. But for my mother this was the greatest sorrow of our lives. We both cried and screamed. She dressed me.
>
> I would like to be a mother some day. But how? In my world, men represent terrible violence and pain. I cannot control that feeling.[20]

It was in the Bosnian context that the term "genocidal rape" was minted, stressing the centrality of sexual assaults of women to the broader campaign of "cleansing." It should be noted that men and adolescent boys were also sexually assaulted and tortured on a large scale in detention facilities such as Omarska and Trnopolje.[21]

THE INTERNATIONAL DIMENSION

If the caliber of the political leadership on all sides of the Balkan wars left much to be desired, the same may be said of international policy-making, beginning with Germany's machinations over Croatian and Slovenian independence. Animated by a vision of expanding economic and political influence, Germany – led by foreign minister Hans-Dietrich Genscher – pressed the rest of the European Union to support Yugoslavia's dissolution. The campaign was fiercely opposed by British representative Lord Carrington, whose plan to safeguard peace in the Balkans depended upon a carrot of recognition being extended only in return for guarantees of minority rights. Bosnian Muslim leader Alija Izetbegovic desperately tried to head off a German/EU declaration of support, while UN Secretary-General Perez de Cuellar warned Genscher that recognizing Croatia would unleash "the most terrible war" in Bosnia-Herzegovina.[22] The efforts were to no avail, and German/EU recognition was duly granted in May 1992. Many see this as an important spur to the genocide unleashed across Bosnia in ensuing months.

The pivotal role of the United States was characterized by vacillation on the independence issue, guided by a conviction that "we don't have a dog in this fight" (George Bush Sr.'s Secretary of State, James Baker, speaking in 1992). The besieging of Srebrenica and other Muslim-majority cities in Bosnia in spring 1993 prompted a US-led response to establish six "safe areas" under UN protection, but these were never effectively defended. When Srebrenica fell to the Serbs, it was "protected" by fewer than 400 Dutch peacekeepers, mostly lightly armed and under orders not to fire their weapons except in self-defense. Genocidal massacres of Bosnian Muslim men and boys were the predictable result. Suspicion has swirled that, mass atrocities aside, the US and EU were not unhappy to see the "safe areas" fall to the Serbs. (An unnamed US official stated at the time that "While losing the enclaves has been unfortunate for Bosnia, it's been great for us.")[23]

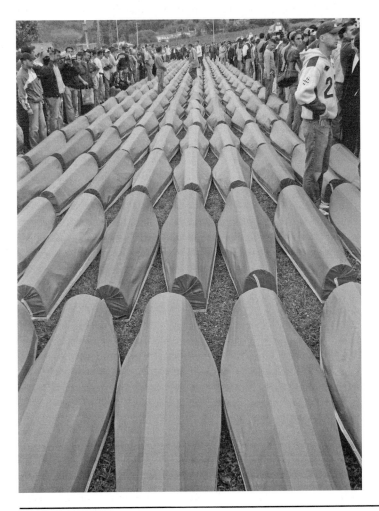

Figure 8.3   Coffins containing the exhumed remains of Srebrenica massacre victims are prepared for reinterment at the annual memorial ceremony in Potocari, Bosnia and Herzegovina, July 2007.

Source: Author's photo.

Figure 8.4   Bosnian Muslim women mourners at the Srebrenica reinterment ceremony depicted in Figure 8.3.

Source: Author's photo, July 2007.

BOX 8.1   ONE MAN'S STORY: NEZAD AVDIC

July 1995. For three years, the city of Srebrenica, with its majority Bosnian-Muslim population, had been one of the major conflict points of the war in Bosnia-Herzegovina. In April 1993, with Srebrenica on the verge of falling to Bosnian Serb forces, the United Nations oversaw the evacuation of children, women, and the elderly, while accepting Serb demands that no males of "battle age" be allowed to leave. It then declared Srebrenica a UN-protected "safe haven." This status held for a little over two years, overseen by first Canadian, then Dutch peacekeepers. The population experienced ever greater hunger and material deprivation. It also fell under the sway of Naser Oric, a Muslim paramilitary leader who organized murderous raids out of the enclave against Serb civilians in surrounding villages.[24]

Finally, on July 6 1995, the Bosnian Serbs decided to implement their "endgame."[25] Serb General Ratko Mladic promised his men a "feast": "There will be blood up to your knees."[26] The peacekeepers watched without firing a shot as the Serbs overcame light Bosnian-Muslim resistance and rounded up most of the population.

Understanding immediately that they were at mortal risk, thousands of "battle-age" men sought to flee through the surrounding hills to Muslim-controlled territory. Most were killed in the hills, or massacred *en masse* after capture. The men who remained behind, including elderly and adolescent males, were systematically separated from the children and women, who – as in 1993 – were allowed to flee in buses to safety. The captured males were trucked off to be slaughtered.

Nezad Avdic, a 17-year-old Bosnian Muslim, was among the intended victims. "When the truck stopped, we immediately heard shooting outside," he recalled. "The Chetniks [Serb paramilitaries] told us to get out, five at a time. I was in the middle of the group, and the men in front didn't want to get out. They were terrified, they started pulling back. But we had no choice, and when it was my turn to get out with five others, I saw dead bodies everywhere."

Avdic was lined up in front of a mass grave. "We stood in front of the Chetniks with our backs turned to them. They ordered us to lie down, and as I threw myself on the ground, I heard gunfire. I was hit in my right arm and three bullets went through the right side of my torso. I don't recall whether or not I fell on the ground unconscious. But I remember being frightened, thinking I would soon be dead or another bullet would hit. I thought it would soon be all over."

Lying among wounded men, "hear[ing] others screaming and moaning," Avdic maintained his deathlike pose. "One of the Chetniks ordered the others to check and see what bodies were still warm. 'Put a bullet through all the heads, even if they're cold.'" But his partner replied: "Fuck their mothers! They're all dead."[27]

They weren't. "I heard a truck leave," Avdic said. "I didn't know what to do. . . . I saw someone moving about ten metres away from me and asked, 'Friend, are you alive?'"

With his companion, Avdic managed to flee the scene after Serb forces departed. He was one of a tiny handful of survivors of a connected series of genocidal massacres that claimed more than 7,000 lives. This made Srebrenica the worst slaughter in Europe since the killings of political opponents by Yugoslav partisan forces after the Second World War. Srebrenica was also the crowning genocidal massacre of the Balkan wars of the 1990s – but not, unfortunately, the final one. The Serb assault on Kosovo, with its ethnic-Albanian majority, followed in 1999, with genocidal atrocities reminiscent of Srebrenica, though on a smaller scale.

The Americans and Europeans turned a blind eye to Croatia's rearmament, which violated the arms embargo formally imposed on all sides. The US also forged a "tacit agreement to allow Iran and other Moslem countries to expand covert arms supplies to the Bosnians."[28] A month after Srebrenica fell, the Croatians combined with Muslim forces to launch Operation Storm, a dramatic offensive against the Serb-held Krajina region.[29] Milosevic, once the Bosnian Serbs' ardent champion, now abandoned them, the better to present himself as a Balkans peacemaker, and secure the lifting of economic sanctions.

In a matter of days, the Croatian–Muslim offensive overran Krajina, resulting in "another biblical movement of people" as up to 200,000 Serbs fled to Serb-populated regions of Bosnia.[30] "Greater Serbia is in refugee convoys," commented a Belgrade

Figure 8.5   The Dayton Accords, reached in Dayton, Ohio in November 1995, brought an end to the war in Bosnia, establishing the unstable multiethnic state of Bosnia and Herzegovina. Shown at the official signing ceremony in Paris on December 14, 1995, are former Yugoslav president Slobodan Milosevic (seated third from left); to Milosevic's left, Bosnian prime minister Alija Izetbegovic; and past the assistant's outstretched arm, Croatian president Franjo Tudjman. All three leaders are now dead. While Izetbegovic bore a measure of responsibility for fueling intercommunal tensions in the prelude to the war, it was Tudjman and, above all, Milosevic who fomented the genocidal outbreak of the 1990s. Milosevic went on to order an assault on the Kosovar Albanian population of Kosovo in 1998–99. He died of a heart attack on March 11, 2006, while on trial for genocide, crimes against humanity, and war crimes at the International Criminal Tribunal for the Former Yugoslavia (ICTY) in The Hague, Netherlands (see Chapter 15).

Source: Brian Schlumbohm/US Air Force/Wikimedia Commons.

observer.[31] Croatian President Tudjman celebrated the expulsions, declaring that the country's Serbs had "disappeared ignominiously, as if they had never populated this land."[32] The Krajina *fait accompli* left in its wake Europe's largest refugee population, but it was welcomed by the West, especially the US.[33] In the aftermath, the Clinton government invited the warring parties to talks at Wright-Patterson Air Force Base in Dayton, Ohio. These resulted in the signing of a comprehensive peace agreement (the Dayton Accords) in November 1995, and the introduction of 60,000 NATO peacekeepers to oversee it.

An estimated 102,000 people had died in the Bosnian war and genocide, about 50 percent of them Muslim and 30 percent Serbs. "However, while Serb casualties were overwhelmingly among military personnel, Muslim casualties were evenly split between military and civilian, so that the great majority of civilian casualties were Muslims."[34] And there was still a final genocidal act to be inflicted on a Muslim population in pursuit of Greater Serbia – in Kosovo, the Serb province where Milosevic first unveiled his nationalist agenda.

KOSOVO, 1998–99

To counter the Serb police state imposed in 1989, a parallel political structure arose in Kosovar Albanian communities, built around the non-violent resistance movement led by Ibrahim Rugova. Remarkably, this parallel authority managed to preserve Albanian-language education and a semblance of social services for ethnic Albanians.

Eventually, after nearly a decade of "a system of apartheid that excluded the province's majority Albanian population from virtually every phase of political, economic, social, and cultural life,"[35] an armed guerrilla movement – the Kosovo Liberation Army (KLA) – launched attacks in 1997. Many KLA leaders desired the political union of Kosovo's Albanians with their "compatriots" across the border in Albania proper. Guerrilla war through 1998 and into 1999 resulted in the Serb killing of hundreds of ethnic-Albanian civilians, and the internal displacement of 200,000 more.

Milosevic now began to plot a decisive resolution of the Kosovo quandary. "In a long career, this would be his masterpiece, cleansing the Serb homeland of its Albanian interlopers in a matter of weeks."[36] US General Wesley Clark witnessed a "choleric" outburst by Milosevic against Kosovar Albanians in 1998. "We know how to deal with those murderers and rapists," Milosevic raged. "They are killers, killers of their own kind, but we know how to deal with them and have done it before. In 1946, in Drenica [in post-World War Two reprisals], we killed them all. . . . Well, of course, we didn't [kill them] all at once. It took several years." Clark described it as "like watching a Nuremberg rally."[37]

European countries sought to head off full-scale war, dispatching an observer team (the Kosovo Verification Commission) to monitor a ceasefire between the Serbs and the KLA. Both sides were guilty of violations, but Serb paramilitaries' mass murder of dozens of Kosovar men at the village of Racak (January 16, 1999) sparked the greatest protest. Abortive negotiations under Western auspices at Rambouillet, France, ended in impasse and acrimony. Pro-Serb commentators have accused Western countries, in league with the KLA, of stage-managing a crisis at Rambouillet in order to justify a quick military defeat to bring Milosevic into line.[38]

It did not transpire that way. On March 19, 1999, the Serbs launched "a massive campaign of ethnic cleansing, aimed not only at tipping the demographic balance [of Kosovo] in Belgrade's favor but also – by driving hundreds of thousands of desperate Albanians over the border into the fragile neighboring states of Macedonia and Albania – at threatening the Western allies with the destabilization of the entire Balkan peninsula."[39] The campaign reached its peak after March 24, when NATO began high-altitude bombing of Serb positions in Kosovo and other targets through-out Yugoslavia. This would remain NATO's exclusive, and ineffective, military tactic. The Allies seemed terrified of taking casualties, on the ground or in the air, and jeopardizing popular support for the war. They also assumed that Milosevic would quickly

Map 8.2   Kosovo.

Source: Map provided by WorldAtlas.com.

crumble in the face of Allied aerial assault. It proved "a colossal miscalculation," and there are grounds for arguing that the bombing in fact prompted an escalation of the Serb campaign. "NATO leaders, then, stand accused of exacerbating the very humanitarian disaster that their actions were justified as averting."[40]

The Serb assault on Kosovar Albanians bore many of the hallmarks of earlier Serb campaigns. Army units and paramilitary forces worked in close coordination to empty the territory of ethnic Albanians through selective acts of terror and mass murder. Gendercidal killing again predominated, as in the largest massacre of the war, at the village of Meja:

> Shortly before dawn on April 27, according to locals, a large contingent of Yugoslav army troops garrisoned in Junik started moving eastward through the valley, dragging men from their houses and pushing them into trucks. "Go to Albania!" they screamed at the women before driving on to the next town with their prisoners. By the time they got to Meja they had collected as many as 300 men. The regular army took up positions around the town while the militia and

paramilitaries went through the houses grabbing the last few villagers and shoving them out into the road. The men were surrounded by fields most of them had worked in their whole lives, and they could look up and see mountains they'd admired since they were children. Around noon the first group was led to the compost heap, gunned down, and burned under piles of cornhusks. A few minutes later a group of about 70 were forced to lie down in three neat rows and were machine-gunned in the back. The rest – about 35 men – were taken to a farmhouse along the Gjakove road, pushed into one of the rooms, and then shot through the windows at point-blank range. The militiamen who did this then stepped inside, finished them off with shots to the head, and burned the house down. They walked away singing.[41]

About 10,000 ethnic Albanians died during the war, along with some Serbs and Roma (Gypsies).[42] The killings were accompanied by the largest mass deportation of a civilian population in decades. Some 800,000 Kosovar Albanians were rounded up and expelled to Albania and Macedonia. Pictures of the exodus bolstered Western resolve, and the Allies began to discuss sending ground forces into the conflict.

In response to growing Allied resolve, Russian pressure, and perhaps the war-crimes indictment issued against him in late May 1999, Milosevic agreed to a ceasefire. The arrangement provided for the withdrawal of Serb forces from Kosovo, and the introduction of 18,000 NATO troops along with 3,500 UN police. These outside forces arrived quickly, but not rapidly – or resolutely – enough to prevent a round of revenge attacks by ethnic Albanians against Serb civilians in northern Kosovo. These prompted 150,000 Serbs to flee to the Serbian heartland, where they joined the 200,000 refugees still stranded by Operation Storm in 1995.

AFTERMATHS

The Dayton Accords brought peace to Bosnia-Herzegovina, and between Croatia and what was left of Yugoslavia. They also froze in place the genocidal "ethnic cleansing" of preceding years. The peace was the peace of the grave: in addition to the more than 100,000 people killed, an astonishing 1,282,000 were registered as internally displaced persons (IDPs).[43] Despite formal declarations that all IDPs should be allowed to return to their homes, in Bosnia the "ground reality . . . in many ways resembles *de facto* nationalist partition rather than a single, sovereign state. . . . The overwhelming majority of Bosnians, well over 90%, now live in areas that are largely homogeneous in the national sense."[44]

The new state of Bosnia-Herzegovina was administered by the Organization for Security and Cooperation in Europe (OSCE). Its High Representative had "far-reaching powers . . . extend[ing] well beyond military matters to cover the most basic aspects of government and state."[45] Over US$5 billion was pledged to "the largest per capita reconstruction plan in history,"[46] and tens of thousands of NATO troops arrived to police the peace. (In December 2004, NATO was replaced by a 7,000-strong European Union force, though most of the troops simply switched insignias.)

An important test of the post-Dayton era was the peace agreement between Croatia and rump Yugoslavia. In 2004, with Croatia pushing for membership in the European Union, the new Prime Minister Ivo Sanader shifted away from the extreme nationalism of Franjo Tudjman, who had died in 2001. After years of "insurmountable impediments" being placed in the way of Serbs attempting to return to their homes (according to Human Rights Watch), Sanader promised a more constructive approach. As the British newspaper *The Guardian* pointed out, however, he ran "little political risk" for doing so, "simply because so few Serbs are returning." While some 70,000 mostly elderly Serbs had accepted the offer, over 200,000 remained as refugees in Bosnia and Herzegovina along with Serbia.[47]

What of those who supervised and committed the atrocities? Many lived comfortably, protected by their ethnic communities and by the lackadaisical approach of NATO forces to rounding them up. But international justice did register some successes. The International Criminal Tribunal for the Former Yugoslavia (ICTY), established by the UN Security Council in May 1993, began proceedings at The Hague on May 16, 1996. Many greeted the tribunal with derision, viewing it as too little, too late. Nonetheless, by late 2004 the Tribunal had conducted fifty-two

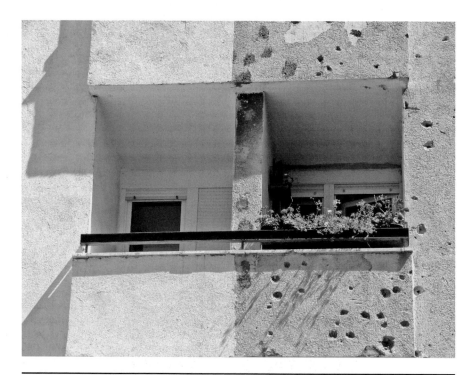

Figure 8.6   A half-restored, half bullet-pocked façade in Mostar, Bosnia and Herzegovina, symbolizes the divisions that remain among Bosnia's ethnic communities, after the Dayton Accords established a tenuous peace in 1995. Despite promising experiments in interethnic coexistence (including between Croats and Muslims in Mostar), the international commitment to Bosnia may now be waning, and worrisome signs have emerged of a resurgence of ethnic militancy – with Mostar again serving as an example (see p. 334).

Source: Author's photo, July 2007.

prosecutions and sentenced thirty individuals. Its greatest coup came on June 28, 2001, when former Yugoslav president Slobodan Milosevic was transported to The Hague to stand trial. (Milosevic had been toppled by a popular uprising in September 2000, after refusing to recognize unfavorable election results.) The successor government under Vojislav Kostunica saw surrendering Milosevic as the price of rejoining the international community (see further discussion in Chapter 16). Milosevic, charged with genocide for crimes in Bosnia-Herzegovina,[48] waged a spirited defense before the tribunal, but died in March 2006 before a verdict was reached.

Gradually, more of Milosevic's key partners in crime in Bosnia-Herzegovina have been brought to justice. Bosnian Serb commander, General Radislav Krstic, was captured and turned over to The Hague, where he was found guilty in August 2001 of the crime of genocide for his leading role in the carnage at Srebrenica. The biggest coup was the capture of Radovan Karadzic (see Figure 8.7), former prime minister of the Bosnian Serbs, in July 2008. At the time of writing, Karadzic's case was just reaching trial, and promised to be one of the setpiece international-legal showdowns of its time. Croatian, Bosnian Muslim, and Kosovar Albanian suspects also faced the tribunal – as with the 2001 indictment of Croatian General Ante Gotovina for atrocities committed in Krajina, and Kosovo Prime Minister Ranush Haradinaj, indicted by the tribunal in March 2005 on charges of "murder, rape and deportation of civilians."[49] (For more on the ICTY, see Chapter 15.)

Figure 8.7 Radovan Karadzic, a former psychiatrist, was prime minister of the breakaway Bosnian Serb republic throughout the war and genocide of the 1990s. Karadzic was captured in Serbia in July 2008 following a tipoff, and turned over to the International Criminal Tribunal for the Former Yugoslavia (ICTY). This photo was taken at his first court appearance before the tribunal in The Hague, Netherlands, in November 2009.

Source: Courtesy ICTY.

Another precedent-setting legal case was brought by the government of Bosnia and Herzegovina against Serbia and Montenegro (Montenegro left the federation in 2006) before the venerable International Court of Justice. The suit claimed compensation from Serbia for the genocide inflicted at Srebrenica. In a February 2007 decision that surprised many observers, the Court rejected the genocide charge, ruling

> that Bosnia and Herzegovina had not proved that the authorities in Belgrade had ordered the massacre, and indeed that "all indications are to the contrary: that the decision to kill the adult male population of the Muslim community of Srebrenica was taken by the VRS [Bosnian Serb Army] Main Staff, but without instructions from or effective control by" Serbia and Montenegro. For this reason, the [court] . . . found that Serbia had not committed genocide, incited the commission of genocide, conspired to commit genocide, or been complicit in the commission of genocide in Bosnia, but that it had violated the Genocide convention by failing to prevent genocide in Srebrenica and by not arresting general Ratko Mladic.[50]

On the ground in Bosnia and Herzegovina, there were indications in 2008–09 that an intercommunal truce was solidifying – but also that it was eroding. "Significant riots or civil disturbances are rare," wrote Valery Perry of the OSCE in a 2009 "survey of reconciliation processes." "Having experienced three and a half years of war, people prefer this cold peace. Yet a true peace awaits." Perry pointed to a still-toxic political atmosphere: one "in which all parties have defined politics as a zero-sum game," and in which "compromise is viewed as loss, and long-term possibilities are sacrificed for short-term gains." Moreover, "much of society remains dangerously politicized . . . Civil society is still very weak and has been unable to begin to effectively and consistently shape and determine the political agenda."[51]

As so often, the city of Mostar (see Figure 8.6) provided a litmus test. A triangular conflict there among Muslims, Serbs, and Croats had produced some of the fiercest fighting of the war. In the conflict's wake, a gradual remingling of the population began, as this author witnessed on a visit to Mostar in July 2007. It was acceptable for Croats to visit the Muslim side and vice versa, to shop, to stroll, to eat in restaurants. Along the shattered main strip of the city – still the single most war-damaged urban landscape I have ever seen, though I have not been to Grozny (Box 5a) – a unique experiment was thriving at the Mostar Gymnasium (high school). The Gymnasium was heavily damaged in the war, and after a lengthy spell in which only Croat students occupied a single floor of it, it became the only mixed public school in the city. As Nicole Itano of the *Global Post* noted, however, "even here, the integration only goes so far: there are two separate curricula for Croatian and Muslim students." Nevertheless, "sports, school activities and a few classes, such as technology, are combined," and students mingled relatively freely during recess and in other social contexts. Significant intercommunal flirting was also reported – always a good sign. On the third floor of the refurbished building, the institution that gave me my start in international life – the United World College network (www.uwc.org) – had set up its latest college promoting coexistence and mutual understanding. Graduates, including scholarship students from around the world, received internationally-recognized accreditation through the Swiss-based International Baccalaureate system.[52]

Yet the Gymnasium was an oasis in a city where the reconciliation process still seemed fragile. Informants who stated that either "side" could stroll freely on the other's territory also stressed that it would be unwise for out-group members to purchase property or otherwise establish residence on the "wrong" side of the river. In 2008, a politically significant clash broke out in Mostar over a football (soccer) game. Turkey and Croatia were playing in a tense quarter-final at the Euro 2008 championship. Mostar's Muslim population rooted publicly for the Turks; the city's Croats were predictably otherwise inclined. The result (of a match which Turkey won) was a fierce confrontation between "rival fans, who hurled rocks and bottles at each other," while "gunshots and car alarms could be heard as fans attacked cars and smashed nearby shop windows."[53]

It was entirely possible that, following a "decent interval," the ethnic cantons of Bosnia and Herzegovina would become independent countries, as other former Yugoslavian territories like Montenegro and Kosovo (see below) had done in the postwar period. This would place something of a seal on the genocidal "cleansings" of the 1990s. At the same time, one could imagine such a patchwork of smaller states being reabsorbed into larger associations, both continental and regional, which are a prominent feature of the European political landscape (see further discussion in Chapter 16). Such fragmentation might not, therefore, impede efforts to reestablish historic linkages across these sundered lands and traumatized populations. Symbolic in this respect was the reopening in 2010 of the Belgrade–Sarajevo train route, abandoned since the federation collapsed in the early 1990s. Younger travelers, in particular, expressed optimism that such linkages could overcome the chasms of the recent past. Twenty-one-year-old passenger Sasa Mehmedagic defined himself as "half-Muslim and half-Serb and . . . proud of it," adding: "I think young people realize that nationalism and racism are wrong because we are all from the same flesh." He and his friends "said they no longer wanted to be defined along ethnic or religious lines but viewed themselves simply as Bosnians. They believed that their people were ready to move beyond the ethnic divisions that led their parents' generation to war, they said, if their leaders stopped agitating for political gain."[54]

As for Kosovo, its trajectory since the first edition of this book was published in 2006 has been dramatic. With its declaration of independence on February 17, 2008, it succeeded East Timor as the world's newest independent state – at least for the 63 governments that had recognized it by early 2010.[55] While many observers, this one included, welcomed Kosovo's entry to the community of nations, concerns persisted over the fate of the now-stranded Serb minority, concentrated around Mitrovica in the north of the state. In March 2004, an anti-Serb pogrom in Kosovo had killed nineteen people and destroyed hundreds of Serb homes. Human Rights Watch criticized international forces for doing little to prevent or stop the violence: "In many cases, minorities under attack were left entirely unprotected and at the mercy of the rioters. . . . In too many cases, NATO peacekeepers locked the gates to their bases and watched as Serb homes burned."[56] How future such outbreaks would be quelled, with NATO peacekeepers even less inclined to intervene, was uncertain, and in late 2009 there were rumors that a territorial exchange was being discussed to allow

Serb-dominated areas to join the independent Republic of Serbia, with Kosovo compensated by another slice or slices of Serbian territory. Such an arrangement would likely require a revenue-sharing agreement or other compensation to Serbia for the loss of access to Kosovo's rich mineral deposits in the Serb-dominated zone. But it perhaps offered the best possibility of reconciling Serbia to the *fait accompli* of Kosovo's independence, ensuring a stable peace, and preserving the security of the Serb minority.

FURTHER STUDY

Fred Abrahams, Gilles Peress, and Eric Stover, *A Village Destroyed, May 14, 1999: War Crimes in Kosovo*. Berkeley, CA: University of California Press, 2001. Vivid photographic record and text.

Norman Cigar, *Genocide in Bosnia: The Policy of "Ethnic Cleansing."* College Station, TX: Texas A&M University Press, 1995. An early treatment in the genocide studies literature, still regularly cited.

Misha Glenny, *The Fall of Yugoslavia: The Third Balkan War* (3rd rev. edn). London: Penguin, 1996. Solid journalistic overview, best read alongside Silber and Little (see below).

Helsinki Watch, *War Crimes in Bosnia-Hercegovina, Vol. 2*. New York: Human Rights Watch, 1993. Detailed investigation of atrocities in the first phases of the Bosnian war.

Michael Ignatieff, *Virtual War: Kosovo and Beyond*. New York: Viking, 2000. Examines Kosovo in the context of modern media and military technologies.

Michael A. Innes, ed., *Bosnian Security after Dayton: New Perspectives*. London: Routledge, 2006. Useful collection examining the first decade of peacemaking (1995–2005) in Bosnia.

Robert D. Kaplan, *Balkan Ghosts: A Journey Through History*. New York: St. Martin's Press, 1993. Clichéd but influential survey of recent Balkan history.

Ivana Macek, *Sarajevo Under Siege: Anthropology in Wartime*. Philadelphia, PA: University of Pennsylvania Press, 2009. Anthropological study of life during the three-year siege of Bosnia's cosmopolitan capital.

Organization for Security and Cooperation in Europe (OSCE), *Kosovo/Kosova: As Seen, As Told*. Available at http://www.osce.org/item/17755.html. Detailed report on atrocities in Kosovo.

David Rohde, *Endgame: The Betrayal and Fall of Srebrenica, Europe's Worst Massacre Since World War II*. Boulder, CO: Westview Press, 1998. Heart-stopping account of the 1995 catastrophe.

Michael P. Scharf and William A. Schabas, *Slobodan Milosevic on Trial: A Companion*. New York: Continuum, 2002. Background to, and evaluation of, the case against the former Serbian dictator.

Louis Sell, *Slobodan Milosevic and the Destruction of Yugoslavia*. Durham, NC: Duke University Press, 2002. Incisive study of Milosevic's rise and fall.

Laura Silber and Allan Little, *The Death of Yugoslavia* (rev. edn). London: BBC Books, 1996. The best overview of the breakup of Yugoslavia.

Chuck Sudetic, *Blood and Vengeance: One Family's Story of the War in Bosnia*. London: Penguin, 1998. Intimate portrait of Bosnia in upheaval.

Ed Vulliamy, *Seasons in Hell: Understanding Bosnia's War*. New York: St. Martin's Press, 1994. Pulitzer Prize-winning reportage from the war zone.

NOTES

1 See Stevan K. Pavlowitch, *Hitler's New Disorder: The Second World War in Yugoslavia* (London: Hurst Publishers Ltd., 2008).

2 Misha Glenny, *The Fall of Yugoslavia* (3rd rev. edn) (London: Penguin, 1996), p. 86.

3 Of Milosevic, Louis Sell wrote, "Nationalism for him was just a tool. Milosevic dropped nationalism just as quickly when it became inconvenient to his efforts to cultivate the image of a peacemaker." Louis Sell, *Slobodan Milosevic and the Destruction of Yugoslavia* (Durham, NC: Duke University Press, 2002), p. 170. For insights into the roots of Serb nationalism, see Branimir Anzulovic, *Heavenly Serbia: From Myth to Genocide* (New York: New York University Press, 1999).

4 On the early deployment of the rhetoric of "genocide" in the Balkan wars, see Bette Denich, "Dismembering Yugoslavia: Nationalist Ideologies and the Symbolic Revival of Genocide," *American Ethnologist*, 21 (1994), pp. 367–90. In 1986, a declaration by the Serbian Academy of Sciences and Arts referred to "the physical, political, legal, and cultural genocide of the Serbian population of Kosovo" (quoted in Peter Ronayne, "Genocide in Kosovo," *Human Rights Review*, 5: 4 [July 2004], p. 59). Kosovo was additionally significant to Serbs as the site of "the Serbian Golgotha," a famous 1389 battle with the Ottoman armies that Serbs viewed as a heroic defeat, though most historians regard its outcome as inconclusive. See Michael Sells, "Kosovo Mythology and the Bosnian Genocide," ch. 8 in Omer Bartov and Phyllis Mack, eds, *In God's Name: Genocide and Religion in the Twentieth Century* (New York: Berghahn Books, 2001), pp. 180–205.

5 Laura Silber and Allan Little, *The Death of Yugoslavia* (rev. edn) (London: BBC Books, 1996), p. 37.

6 Glenny, *The Fall of Yugoslavia*, pp. 46, 67.

7 Sell, *Slobodan Milosevic*, p. 83.

8 Quoted in the film by Tone Bringa, *We Are All Neighbours*, cited in Jacques Sémelin, *Purify and Destroy: The Political Uses of Massacre and Genocide* (New York: Columbia University Press, 2007), p. 144.

9 Daniel Jonah Goldhagen, *Worse Than War: Genocide, Eliminationism, and the Ongoing Assault on Humanity* (New York: Basic Books, 2009), p. 142.

10 "Though Sarajevo grabbed the headlines, it was clear from the first day of the war that eastern Bosnia, with its hydroelectric dams, highways, and Muslim-majority population, was the key to the Serb leaders' plans to partition Bosnia." Chuck Sudetic, *Blood and Vengeance: One Family's Story of the War in Bosnia* (London: Penguin, 1998), p. 100. Silber and Little also note that "during the summer months of 1992 . . . the world's media concentrated almost exclusively on the siege and bombardment of [Sarajevo], even though much more decisive battles and campaigns were being waged elsewhere. . . . [This] suited Serb leaders very well." Silber and Little, *The Death of Yugoslavia*, p. 253.

11 Aside from the thousands of human casualties, the Muslim–Croat conflict claimed the famous bridge at Mostar, which mirrored Sarajevo with its Catholic, Greek Orthodox, and Muslim populations. The bridge was completely destroyed by Croatian shelling, rebuilt with international assistance, and reopened in 2004.

12 Cited in James Waller, *Becoming Evil: How Ordinary People Commit Genocide and Mass Killing* (Oxford: Oxford University Press, 2002), p. 262.

13 Among the reporters was Ed Vulliamy, who has given a detailed description of the camps and their discovery in his book *Seasons in Hell* (New York: St. Martin's Press, 1994).

14 David Hirsh, *Law against Genocide: Cosmopolitan Trials* (London: Glasshouse Press, 2003), pp. 66–67.

15 Marshall quoted in Silber and Little, *The Death of Yugoslavia*, p. 250.

16 Silber and Little, *The Death of Yugoslavia*, p. 245.

17 Mark Danner, "Endgame in Kosovo," *The New York Review of Books*, May 6, 1999, p. 8.

18 Helsinki Watch, *War Crimes in Bosnia-Hercegovina*, Vol. 2 (New York: Human Rights Watch, 1993), pp. 82–83.

19 International Committee of the Red Cross, "The Impact of Armed Conflict on Women," March 6, 2001, available at http://www.reliefweb.int/library/documents/2001/icrc-women-17oct.pdf.

20 Slavenka Draculic, "Rape After Rape After Rape," *The New York Times*, December 13, 1992.

21 For example, the most bestial of the camps, Omarska, held some 2,000 men and 33 to 38 women (Helsinki Watch, *War Crimes in Bosnia-Hercegovina*, p. 87).

22 Perez de Cuellar quoted in Glenny, *The Fall of Yugoslavia*, p. 164.

23 Quoted in Sell, *Slobodan Milosevic*, p. 234.

24 The raids were accompanied by "a horde of Muslim refugees, men and women, young and old, who were driven by hunger and, in many cases, a thirst for revenge. Thousands strong, these people would lurk behind the first wave of attacking soldiers and run amok when the defenses around Serb villages collapsed. Some of the refugees used pistols to do the killing; others used knives, bats, and hatchets. But most of them had nothing but their bare hands and the empty rucksacks and suitcases they strapped onto their backs. They came to be known as *torbari*, the bag people. And they were beyond [Naser] Oric's control." Sudetic, *Blood and Vengeance*, p. 157.

25 See David Rohde, *Endgame: The Betrayal and Fall of Srebrenica, Europe's Worst Massacre since World War II* (New York: Farrar, Straus and Giroux, 1997).

26 Quoted in Mark Danner, "The Killing Fields of Bosnia," *The New York Review of Books*, September 24, 1998 (citing reporting by Roy Gutman of *Newsday*).

27 Avdic's testimony is recounted in Jan Willem Honig and Norbert Both, *Srebrenica: Record of a War Crime* (London: Penguin, 1996), p. 62.

28 Sell, *Slobodan Milosevic*, p. 215.

29 See Mark Danner, "Operation Storm," *The New York Review of Books*, October 22, 1998.

30 Glenny, *The Fall of Yugoslavia*, p. 284.

31 Quoted in Benjamin Lieberman, *Terrible Fate: Ethnic Cleansing in the Making of Modern Europe* (Chicago, IL: Ivan R. Dee, 2006), p. 322.

32 Tudjman quoted in "Stormy Memories," *The Economist*, July 30, 2005.

33 Stated one European diplomat: "Until now at least the international community has been united in its condemnation of ethnic cleansing. Now it seems one of its members is openly supporting the mass movement of population by the most terrible force." Quoted in Glenny, *The Fall of Yugoslavia*, p. 285.

34 Robert M. Hayden, "Mass Killings and Images of Genocide in Bosnia, 1941–5 and 1992–5," in Dan Stone, ed., *The Historiography of Genocide* (London: Palgrave Macmillan, 2008), p. 487.

35 Sell, *Slobodan Milosevic*, p. 93.

36 Danner, "Endgame in Kosovo," p. 11.

37 Sell, *Slobodan Milosevic*, p. 269.

38 This is a common theme of the literature cited in Chapter 16, n. 30.

39 Sell, *Slobodan Milosevic*, p. 304.

40 Nicholas Wheeler, *Saving Strangers: Humanitarian Intervention in International Society* (Oxford: Oxford University Press, 2000), p. 269.

41 Sebastian Junger, "The Forensics of War," in Junger, *Fire* (New York: W.W. Norton, 2001), p. 158. Another reporter estimates that 500 men were killed in the Meja massacre: see Joshua Hammer, "On the Trail of Hard Truth," *Newsweek*, July 9, 2000.

42 The debate over the alleged "exaggeration" of Kosovar Albanian deaths was spirited after the war, and reflects, in Samantha Power's estimation, "the inescapable difficulty of accurately gauging the scale of atrocities while they are being committed." Power, *"A Problem from Hell": America and the Age of Genocide* (New York: Basic Books, 2002), p. 467. Power notes that the ICTY "has received reports that some 11,334 Albanians are buried in 529 sites in Kosovo alone"; moreover, "In 2001 some 427 dead Albanians from Kosovo were exhumed in five mass graves that had been hidden in Serbia proper. An additional three mass grave sites, containing more than 1,000 bodies, were found in a Belgrade suburb and awaited exhumation. Each of the newly discovered sites lies near Yugoslav army or police barracks" (pp. 471–72). For a critique of attempts to downplay genocide in Kosovo, mostly by my colleagues on the Left, see Adam Jones, "Kosovo: Orders of Magnitude," *IDEA: A Journal of Social Issues*, 5: 1 (July 2000), available at http://www.ideajournal.com/articles.php ?id=24.

43 Figures on dead and displaced from Rory Keane, *Reconstituting Sovereignty: Post-Dayton Bosnia Uncovered* (Burlington, VT: Ashgate, 2002), p. 69.

44 Sumantra Bose, *Bosnia after Dayton: Nationalist Partition and International Intervention* (London: Hurst & Co., 2002), pp. 22, 34.

45 David Chandler, *Bosnia: Faking Democracy after Dayton* (2nd edn) (London: Pluto Press, 1999), p. 43.

46 Bose, *Bosnia after Dayton*, p. 6.

47 Ian Traynor, "Croatia Builds Goodwill in Serb Villages," *The Guardian*, June 19, 2004.

48 Genocide was "curiously absent" from the charge-sheet for Milosevic's actions in Kosovo, "despite the fact that the arc of crime and atrocity in Kosovo seems to fit the Convention's legal definition quite neatly." Ronayne, "Genocide in Kosovo," p. 66.

49 "Ex-Kosovo PM Pleads Not Guilty to War Crimes," Reuters dispatch, March 14, 2005.

50 Hayden, "Mass Killings," p. 506.

51 Valery Perry, "A Survey of Reconciliation Processes in Bosnia and Herzegovina: The Gap between People and Politics," in Joanna R. Quinn, ed., *Reconciliation(s): Transitional Justice in Postconflict Societies* (Montreal, QC: McGill-Queen's University Press, 2009), pp. 226–28.

52 Nicole Itano, "Meet the Students at an Integrated Bosnian High School," *Global Post*, October 15, 2009, http://www.globalpost.com/dispatch/europe/091014/mostar-bosnia-high-school. I was a scholarship student at the United World College of South-East Asia in Singapore from 1979 to 1981, and credit it with much of the international consciousness I've displayed since. Readers of the relevant age range are strongly encouraged to apply (www.uwc.org).

53 "Bosnian Muslims and Croats Clash after Euro Match," Reuters dispatch, June 21, 2008. Nor were such clashes a new phenomenon. In 1998, after Croatia emerged as surprise victors in the quarter finals of the World Cup, a 25-year-old Muslim woman was killed, allegedly "by a stray bullet." Perhaps as a consequence, Mostar's Muslims did not miss a chance to retaliate against Croats, even when they had no direct investment in the results. A previous outbreak of interethnic rioting in Mostar, in 2006, erupted when "the town's Muslims supported *Brazil* in a World Cup match that saw the Croats lose 1–0" (emphasis added).

54 Nicholas Kulish, "Train Line Across the Balkans Restitches a Region," *The New York Times*, January 10, 2010, http://www.nytimes.com/2010/01/11/world/europe/11train. html.

55 See Dan Bilefsky, "Kosovo Declares Its Independence from Serbia," *The New York Times*, February 18, 2007, http://www.nytimes.com/2008/02/18/world/europe/18kosovo.html.

56 "UN and NATO Slammed over Kosovo," *BBC Online*, July 26, 2004, http://news.bbc.co.uk/2/hi/europe/3928153.stm.

BOX 8A GENOCIDE IN BANGLADESH, 1971

By some estimates, the mass killings in Bangladesh – at the time, East Pakistan – are on a par with the twentieth century's most destructive genocides. At least one million Bengalis, perhaps as many as three million,[1] were massacred by the security forces of West Pakistan, assisted by local allies. Yet the genocide remains almost unknown in the West. Only recently has its prominence increased slightly, as a result of a handful of educational and memorialization projects.[2]

Although it preceded events in the Balkans by two decades, the Bangladeshi genocide is usefully placed alongside the Bosnia and Kosovo case study. Both conflicts had at their core a militarized security threat; a crisis surrounding secession of federal units; and ethnic conflict. On a strategic and tactical level, both genocides featured strong elements of "eliticide" (destruction of the socioeconomic and intellectual elites of a target group – see p. 26), as well as the gendercidal targeting of adult and adolescent males (see Chapter 13).

The federation of East and West Pakistan was forged in the crucible of Indian independence in 1947–48. Most of India had been under British rule for two centuries. As independence loomed after the Second World War, two distinct political projects arose. One, associated with the century's leading proponent of non-violence, Mohandas (Mahatma) Gandhi, sought to keep India whole and prevent division along religious and ethnic lines. However, strong Hindu and Muslim nationalist movements, along with the departing British, pressed for the creation of two states – one Hindu-dominated (India), the other Muslim-dominated (Pakistan). This project triumphed, but not without cataclysmic violence. The partition of India in 1947 witnessed one of the greatest movements of peoples in modern times, as millions of Muslims fled India for Pakistan, and millions of Hindus moved in the other direction. Hundreds of thousands of people, perhaps over a million, were slaughtered on both sides.[3]

Not the least of Pakistan's post-independence difficulties was its division into two wings, separated by 1,200 miles of Indian territory and an ethnolinguistic gulf. West Pakistan, home to some 55 million people in 1971, was predominantly Urdu-speaking. The Bengali speakers of East Pakistan occupied only one-third of total Pakistani territory, but were the demographic majority – some 75 million people. Most were Muslim, but there was also a large Bengali Hindu minority (the Biharis) that was especially targeted during the genocide. Even Bengali Muslims were viewed as second-class citizens by the inhabitants of wealthier West Pakistan. Pakistani Lieutenant-General A.A.K. Niazi referred to the Ganges river plain – home to the majority of Bengalis and the largest city, Dhaka – as a "low-lying land of low, lying people." According to R.J. Rummel, "Bengalis were often compared with monkeys and chickens. . . . The [minority] Hindus among the Bengalis were as Jews to the Nazis: scum and vermin that [had] best be exterminated."[4]

Reacting to West Pakistan's persistent discrimination and economic exploitation,[5] a strong autonomy movement arose in the east, centered on the

Awami League of Sheikh Mujibur Rahman. The spark for the conflagration came in December 1970, with national elections held to pave the way for a transition from military rule. The Awami League won a crushing victory – 167 out of East Pakistan's 169 parliamentary seats. This gave the League a majority in the Pakistani parliament as a whole, and the right to form the next government. West Pakistani rulers, led by General Yahya Khan, saw this as a direct threat to their power and interests. After negotiations failed to resolve the impasse, Khan met with four senior generals on February 22, 1971, and issued orders to annihilate the Awami League and its popular base. From the outset, they planned a campaign of genocide. "Kill three million [Bengalis]," said Khan, "and the rest will eat out of our hands."[6]

On March 25, the genocide was launched. In an attempt to decapitate East Pakistan's political and intellectual leadership, Dhaka University – a center of nationalist agitation – was attacked. Hundreds of students were killed in what was dubbed "Operation Searchlight." Working from prepared lists, death squads roamed the streets. Perhaps 7,000 people died in a single night, 30,000 over the course of a week. The terror sparked an epic flight: "it was estimated that in April some thirty million people [!] were wandering helplessly across East Pakistan to escape the grasp of the military."[7] The 10–12 million-strong Hindu community of East Pakistan was also targeted *en bloc*; Hindus comprised most of the 10 million people who fled to India as refugees. This spurred increasing calls for Indian military intervention, which would have the added advantage – from India's perspective – of dismembering Pakistan. (The countries had already fought two full-scale wars by 1971; they were, and remain, poised for another one.) The surviving Awami League leadership moved quickly to declare a fully independent Bangladesh, and to organize a guerrilla resistance.

With the opening eliticide accomplished, the West Pakistani leadership moved to eradicate the nationalist base. As the election results suggested, this comprised the vast majority of Bengalis. Genocidal killing, however, followed a gendercidal pattern, with all males beyond childhood viewed as actual or potential guerrilla fighters. To produce the desired number of corpses, the West Pakistanis set up "extermination camps"[8] and launched a wave of gender-selective killing:

> The place of execution was the river edge [here, the Buriganga River outside Dhaka], or the shallows near the shore, and the bodies were disposed of by

Figure 8A.1 Bengali victims of genocide by Pakistani forces in Dhaka, 1971, most with their hands bound before execution.

Source: Articlesbase.com.

the simple means of permitting them to flow downstream. The killing took place night after night. Usually the prisoners were roped together and made to wade out into the river. They were in batches of six or eight, and in the light of a powerful electric arc lamp, they were easy targets, black against the silvery water. The executioners stood on the pier, shooting down at the compact bunches of prisoners wading in the water. There were screams in the hot night air, and then silence. The prisoners fell on their sides and their bodies lapped against the shore. Then a new bunch of prisoners was brought out, and the process was repeated. In the morning the village boatmen hauled the bodies into midstream and the ropes binding the bodies were cut so that each body drifted separately downstream.[9]

The West Pakistani campaign extended to mass rape, aimed at "dishonoring" Bengali women and undermining Bengali society. Between 200,000 and 400,000 women were attacked. "Girls of eight and grandmothers of seventy-five had been sexually assaulted," wrote feminist author Susan Brownmiller in her book, *Against Our Will: Men, Women and Rape*.[10] An unknown number of women were gang-raped to death, or executed after repeated violations.

The slaughter and other atrocities were ended by one of the rare instances of successful outside intervention in genocide.[11] Indian troops invaded in December 1971, vanquishing West Pakistani forces in a couple of weeks. The independence of Bangladesh was sealed, though at a staggering human cost.

In the blood-letting following the expulsion of the West Pakistani army, perhaps 150,000 people were murdered by independence forces and local vigilantes. Biharis who had collaborated with West Pakistani authorities were dealt with especially harshly.[12] Themes of the post-genocide era include the continued suffering and social marginalization of hundreds of thousands of Bengali rape victims, and the enduring impunity of the *génocidaires*. None of the leaders of the genocide has ever been brought to trial; they remain comfortably ensconced in Pakistan (the former West Pakistan) and other countries. In recent years, activists have worked to bring those leaders before an international tribunal, so far without success.

FURTHER STUDY

Rounaq Jahan, "Genocide in Bangladesh," in Samuel Totten *et al.*, eds, *Century of Genocide: Eyewitness Accounts and Critical Views*. New York: Garland Publishing, 1997. A rare treatment in the genocide-studies literature.

Anthony Mascarenhas, *The Rape of Bangla Desh*. Delhi: Vikas Publications, 1971. A decent enough overview; one takes what one can get in English on this little-studied subject.

Robert Payne, *Massacre*. London: Macmillan, 1973. Journalistic account of the genocide.

Richard Sisson and Leo Rose, *War and Secession: Pakistan, India, and the Creation of Bangladesh*. Berkeley, CA: University of California Press, 1990. Focuses on policy-making by leaders during the crisis.

NOTES

1 R.J. Rummel observes: "The human death toll over only 267 days was incredible. Just to give for five out of the eighteen districts some incomplete statistics published in Bangladesh newspapers or by an Inquiry Committee, the Pakistani army killed 100,000 Bengalis in Dacca, 150,000 in Khulna, 75,000 in Jessore, 95,000 in Comilla, and 100,000 in Chittagong. For eighteen districts the total is 1,247,000 killed. This was an incomplete toll, and to this day no one really knows the final toll," which Rummel estimates may have reached 3 million. Rummel, *Death by Government* (New Brunswick, NJ: Transaction Publishers, 1994), p. 331.

2 See in particular the Liberation War Museum Online at http://www.liberation warmuseum.org.

3 On partition, see Paul R. Brass, "The Partition of India and Retributive Genocide in the Punjab, 1946–47: Means, Methods, and Purposes," *Journal of Genocide Research*, 5: 1 (March 2003), pp. 71–101; Urvashi Butalia, *The Other Side of Silence: Voices from the Partition of India* (Durham, NC: Duke University Press, 2000); Yasmin Khan, *The Great Partition: The Making of India and Pakistan* (New Delhi: Penguin Books India, 2007).

4 Rummel, *Death by Government*, p. 335.

5 "The Bangladesh nationalist movement was also fueled by a sense of economic exploitation. Though jute, the major export earning commodity, was produced in Bengal, most of the economic investments took place in Pakistan. A systematic transfer of resources took place from East to West Pakistan creating a growing economic disparity and a feeling among the Bengalis that they were being treated as a colony by Pakistan." Rounaq Jahan, "Genocide in Bangladesh," ch. 10 in Samuel Totten *et al.*, eds, *Century of Genocide: Eyewitness Accounts and Critical Views* (New York: Garland Publishing, 1997), p. 292.

6 Quoted in Robert Payne, *Massacre* (London: Macmillan, 1973), p. 50.

7 Payne, *Massacre*, p. 48.

8 Leo Kuper, *The Prevention of Genocide* (New Haven, CT: Yale University Press, 1985), p. 47.

9 Payne, *Massacre*, p. 55. For more on the gendercidal character of the large majority of killings during the genocide, see Adam Jones/Gendercide Watch, "Case Study: Genocide in Bangladesh, 1971," http://www.gendercide.org/case_bangladesh.html, from which Box 8a is adapted.

10 Susan Brownmiller, *Against Our Will: Men, Women and Rape* (New York: Bantam, 1975), p. 83.

11 For a concise overview of the Indian intervention, see Nicholas J. Wheeler, "India as Rescuer? Order versus Justice in the Bangladesh War of 1971," ch. 2 in Wheeler, *Saving Strangers: Humanitarian Intervention in International Society* (Oxford: Oxford University Press, 2000), pp. 55–77. For a discussion of the role of the United States and then-secretary of state Henry Kissinger, see Suhail Islam and Syed Hassan, "The Wretched of the Nations: The West's Role in Human Rights Violations in the Bangladesh War of Independence," in Adam Jones, ed., *Genocide, War Crimes and the West: History and Complicity* (London: Zed Books, 2004), pp. 201–13.

12 During the genocide, Urdu-speaking Biharis in East Pakistan "joined the West Pakistanis in killing the Bengalis." This exposed them to retaliation from "Awami League supporters [who] also engaged in killing the West Pakistanis and Biharis in East Pakistan. A White Paper issued by the Pakistani government shows that the Awami League had massacred at least 30,000 Biharis and West Pakistanis," atrocious behavior that nonetheless does not match the systematic slaughter of Bengalis by the West Pakistanis and their Bihari allies. See Wardatul Akman, "Atrocities against Humanity during the Liberation War in Bangladesh: A Case of Genocide," *Journal of Genocide Research*, 4: 4 (2002), p. 549; also "The Right to Self Determination: The Secession of Bangladesh," ch. 4 in Kuper, *The Prevention of Genocide*, pp. 44–61.

CHAPTER 9

Apocalypse in Rwanda

INTRODUCTION: HORROR AND SHAME

The genocide that consumed the tiny Central African country of Rwanda from April to July 1994 was in some ways without precedent. The international law specialist John Quigley has called it "probably the most concentrated mass killing ever seen,"[1] and this in no way exhausts the holocaust's extraordinary and even unique aspects. In just twelve weeks, approximately one million people – overwhelmingly Tutsis, but also tens of thousands of Hutus opposed to the genocidal government – were murdered, primarily by machetes, clubs, and small arms. About 80 percent of victims died in a "hurricane of death . . . between the second week of April and the third week of May," noted Gérard Prunier. "If we consider that probably around 800,000 people were slaughtered during that short period . . . the daily killing rate was at least five times that of the Nazi death camps."[2]

While debate has raged over the extent of the complicity of "ordinary Germans" in the genocide against the Jews and others, the German killers were in uniform, and strict measures were taken to ensure that the civilian population did not witness the mass slaughter. In Rwanda, by contrast, the civilian Hutu population – men, women, and even children – was actively conscripted and comprised the bulk of *génocidaires*: "For the first time in modern history, a state succeeded in transforming the mass of its population into murderers."[3]

Despite noble pledges of "Never Again" following the Jewish Holocaust, the international community stood by while a million defenseless victims died. Numerous warnings of impending genocide were transmitted, and an armed United Nations "assistance mission" (UNAMIR), under the command of Canadian Major-General Roméo Dallaire, had been in place in the capital, Kigali, since October 1993. In what one UNAMIR officer would later refer to as an "act of total cowardice,"[4] well-armed foreign forces were flown in when the genocide broke out – but only to evacuate whites. In one notorious instance captured on video, at the Caraes Psychiatric Hospital in Ndera, Kigali prefecture, a few sobbing whites were evacuated while rapacious militia cruised just outside the gates, and hundreds of terrified Tutsi refugees begged the foreign troops for protection. "Solve your problems yourselves," shouted one soldier to the crowd, and left with his comrades. The Tutsis were massacred within hours of the troops' departure.[5]

With the expatriates safely removed, the UN Security Council turned its attention to withdrawing UNAMIR forces. A US State Department memorandum of April 14, 1994 instructed the US mission to the UN to "give highest priority to full, orderly withdrawal of all UNAMIR personnel as soon as possible."[6] On April 21, the Council voted to withdraw all but 270 of the 2,500-strong UNAMIR contingent. "In a clearly illegal act," General Dallaire and Brigadier General Henry Kwami Anyidoho, who commanded the Ghanaian contingent of the UN force, managed to defy the Council order and hold on to about 470 peacekeepers. Even these few were enough to save thousands of lives over the course of the genocide.[7]

On May 17, the UN Security Council would finally vote to dispatch 5,500 troops to Rwanda, "but authorizing a higher troop figure is not the same as actually finding the troops' contributors."[8] The troops did not arrive until after the genocide had ended. The United States spent long weeks bickering with the UN over the lease of ancient armored-personnel carriers. They, too, would not arrive until "after the genocide was over and they were stripped of machine guns, radio[s], tools, spare parts and training manuals. General Dallaire described them as tons of rusting metal."[9]

For all the lofty rhetoric of universal human rights, it seemed "Rwanda was simply too remote, too far, too poor, too little, and probably too black to be worthwhile," in the scathing assessment of human rights investigator Alison Des Forges.[10] General Dallaire, for his part, issued a blistering denunciation at the end of his tenure in 1994: "Although Rwanda and UNAMIR have been at the centre of a terrible human tragedy, that is not to say Holocaust, and although many fine words had been pronounced by all, including members of the Security Council, the tangible effort . . . has been totally, completely ineffective."[11]

In *Shake Hands with the Devil*, Dallaire echoed Des Forges' assessment: that the genocide displayed the "indifference, self-interest and racism" of the international community.[12] In March 2004, UN Secretary-General Kofi Annan offered a qualified apology for member states' unwillingness to confront the Rwandan catastrophe. "The international community failed Rwanda, and that must leave us always with a sense of bitter regret and abiding sorrow." Ten years after the slaughter, Annan asked: "Are we confident that, confronted by a new Rwanda today, we can respond effectively, in good time?" His response was sobering: "We can by no means be certain we would."[13]

BACKGROUND TO GENOCIDE

Understanding the human catastrophe that consumed Rwanda in 1994 requires attention to a host of complex factors. They include:

- the colonial and post-colonial history of the country, notably the politicization of Hutu and Tutsi ethnicities under Belgian rule and into the independence era that began in 1959;
- the authoritarian and tightly regulated character of the political system installed by the nation's post-independence rulers, including the second-class political status it assigned to Tutsis, fueling a Tutsi-led rebel movement based in Uganda;
- the role of outside actors, especially France, in financing and fueling Hutu extremism;
- the pervasive economic crisis in Rwanda, one of the world's poorest and most densely populated countries;
- the international factors that inhibited and occasionally encouraged humanitarian interventions in the first half of the 1990s.

As with the Balkan genocide (Chapter 8), foreign observers tended to view the Rwandan conflict as an expression of "ancient tribal hatreds." Until the twentieth century, however, "Hutus" and "Tutsis" did not constitute separate nations. It is hard even to describe them as distinct ethnicities, since they share the same language, territory, and religion. Rather, the two groups in the pre-colonial period may be viewed as *social castes*, based on material wealth. Broadly speaking, Tutsis were those who owned cattle; Hutus tilled the land and provided labor to the Tutsis. The designations were hardly arbitrary, and they indeed had a basis in physiognomic differences (see below). But they were fluid and permeable, as the Africa specialist Mahmood Mamdani notes: "The rare Hutu who was able to accumulate cattle and rise through the socioeconomic hierarchy could *kwihutura* – shed Hutuness – and achieve the political status of a Tutsi. Conversely, the loss of property could also lead to the loss of status, summed up in the Kinyarwanda word *gucupira*." These processes were "of little significance statistically," but "their social and political significance cannot be overstated."[14] Thus, "although Rwanda was definitely not a land of peace and bucolic harmony before the arrival of the Europeans, there is no trace in its precolonial history of systematic violence between Tutsi and Hutu as such."[15]

From its beginnings around the seventeenth century, the political organization of Rwandan society featured "centralised forms of political authority and . . . a high degree of social control," reflecting "the fact that the land is small, the population density is (and has always been) high and social interactions are constant, intense and value-laden."[16] This authoritarianism reached its apogee under the rule of Mwami Kigeri Rwabugiri (1860–1895), at which point traditional obligations of *corvée* labor came to be imposed on Hutus alone, "thereby polarizing the social difference between Hutu and Tutsi."[17]

In 1894, Germany established indirect suzerainty over Rwanda, coopting and taking over the pyramidal structure of political rule. The Germans gave way, after their defeat in the First World War, to Belgian colonial administration. The Belgians were the first to rigidly codify Hutu and Tutsi designations. In the divide-and-rule tradition, Tutsis became colonial favorites and protégés.[18] In part, this reflected the Tutsis' minority status – it is often easier for colonizers to secure the allegiance of a minority, which recognizes that its survival may depend on bonds with the imperial authority (see Chapter 12). It also derived from an egregious nineteenth-century contribution of the nascent discipline of anthropology. Early explorers of Central Africa, notably the Englishman John Hanning Speke, propounded the "Hamitic hypothesis." This depicted the Hutus as offspring of Ham, the black son of Noah, cursed by God and destined forever to serve as "hewers of wood and drawers of water"; and, by noble contrast, the Tutsi caste, descended from the Nilotic civilization of classical Egypt. As was typical of imperial racial theorizing, the mark of civilization was grafted on to physiognomic difference, with the generally taller, supposedly more refined Tutsis destined to rule, and shorter, allegedly less refined Hutus to serve.[19]

Under Belgian rule and afterwards, both Tutsis and Hutus were indoctrinated with this Hamitic hypothesis. It served both to justify Tutsi overlordship under the Belgian

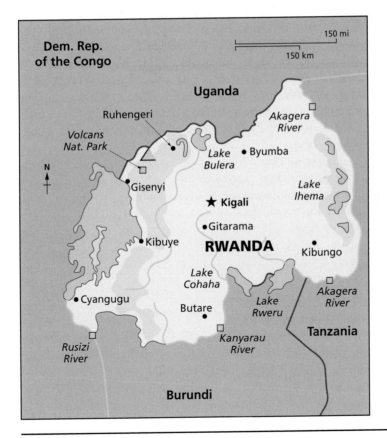

Map 9.1   Rwanda

Source: Map provided by WorldAtlas.com.

colonial power, and resentment and vengefulness among Hutu,[20] which would erupt first in the massacres of 1959–60 and culminate, in 1994, in full-scale genocide. In 1994, taller Hutus died at roadblocks because they were assumed to be Tutsis, whatever their identity cards said. And the corpses of thousands of Tutsi victims were dumped into the Nyabarongo river, which flowed into Lake Victoria, the source of the Nile – thus symbolically dispatching Tutsis back to their "Nilotic" origins (see Chapter 12 for more on the symbolic dimension of the Rwandan genocide).[21]

It was under the Belgians, too, that a new, racially segregated state, church, and education system was constructed. Tutsis were assigned a dominant role in each.[22] The symbol of the newly bureaucratized system was the distribution of identity cards defining every Rwandan as either Hutu, Tutsi, or Twa – the last of these a Pygmy ethnicity, constituting around 2 percent of the population. The institution of these identity cards was perpetuated by the post-colonial government, and in 1994 proved a key genocidal facilitator. At the thousands of roadblocks established across the country, carrying a Tutsi identity card meant a death sentence.

After the Second World War, with anti-colonial national liberation movements in ascendance, Belgian authorities performed a dramatic about-face. Pro-independence movements were springing up throughout the colonized world, and in Rwanda the Tutsis, having benefited from their positions of dominance in education and the state bureaucracy, moved to the forefront of the various anti-colonial initiatives. The Belgians, perceiving the threat – and perhaps also influenced by the democratizing tendency unleashed by the Second World War – switched their favor to the less-educated, less-threatening Hutu majority. This unleashed pent-up Hutu frustrations, and led to the first proto-genocidal massacres of Tutsis, claiming several thousand victims. Tens of thousands of Tutsis fled to neighboring Zaire, Tanzania, and especially Uganda, where the exiles formed an armed rebel movement and launched attacks into Rwanda.

Throughout the 1960s, remaining Rwandan Tutsis established a *modus vivendi* with the new Hutu-dominated order. Although almost totally frozen out of formal political power, they were not systematically expelled from other institutional spheres, such as schools and the Catholic Church; and under the rule of Hutu dictator Juvénal Habyarimana, who seized the presidency in a 1973 coup, their conditions improved.

But trouble was brewing just beneath the surface. Although Habyarimana projected a liberal image to attract foreign aid, his regime was dominated by the *akazu*, or "little house": "a tightly knit mafia" of Hutus from the north of Rwanda that coalesced around the figure of Habyarimana's wife, Agathe.[23] It was the *akazu* that, operating as "the 'invisible government' of Rwanda during Habyarimana's reign,"[24] gradually increased ethnic hatred against the Tutsis, encouraging a climate of fear and panic to forestall demands for democracy.

In 1987, Rwandan exiles in Uganda formed the Rwandan Patriotic Front, and in 1990 the RPF launched a military invasion of Rwanda.[25] This offensive had three crucial results. First, it brought immediate outside assistance to prop up the Habyarimana regime – from France, a country that had constructed its post-colonial role in Africa around support for *La Francophonie*, the network of French-speaking countries that Paris viewed as a bulwark against the "Anglo" influence typified by Uganda. French forces succeeded in stalling the RPF invasion, and they remained to train and advise the Hutu military and militias that would implement the 1994 genocide. Second, military conflict exacerbated the economic crisis in Rwanda. "Fragile at the start, the Rwandan economy . . . crumbled under the burden of the costs of war," wrote Alison Des Forges. "Living conditions worsened dramatically as per capita income that stood at US $320 in 1989 (nineteenth poorest in the world) fell to US $200 in 1993."[26] Third, the invasion, with its abuses and atrocities against Hutu civilians, contributed to a growing climate of fear among ordinary Hutus, already deeply anxious after genocidal massacres of Hutus in next-door Burundi by the Tutsi-dominated armed forces there.[27]

Invasion from without; economic crisis; growing domestic and international support for extremists – it is hard to imagine more propitious circumstances for genocide. Between 1990 and 1993, "a series of minipograms against Tutsi [took place] in different parts of the country," which in retrospect appear to be "rehearsals for the conflagration of 1994."[28] Perhaps 2,000 people were murdered. A UN Special Rapporteur, Bacre Waly Ndiaye, visited Rwanda in April 1993 and "decided that the word genocide was appropriate and that the Convention on the Prevention and Punishment of the Crime of Genocide of 1948 was applicable" to these killings. His superiors in Geneva warned him to avoid the term, but he used it nonetheless in his report, which was quickly buried ("Ndiaye said later that he might just as well have put the report in a bottle and thrown it into the sea").[29]

Exterminationist propaganda against Tutsis became commonplace in Rwanda. As early as December 1990, the infamous "Hutu Ten Commandments" were issued by the Hutu extremist paper *Kangura*; "The Hutu must be firm and vigilant against their common Tutsi enemy," read one of the commandments. In August 1993, the radio station RTLM (Radio-Télévision Libre des Mille Collines) began broadcasting, with funding from the Christian Democratic International.[30] RTLM transformed the staid Rwandan media, and fueled a hysterical fear of the threat posed by RPF forces and their "fifth column" inside Rwanda – the Tutsi minority, designated by RTLM as *inyenzi*, or "cockroaches." "The cruelty of the *inyenzi* is incurable," declared one broadcast; "the[ir] cruelty . . . can only be cured by their total extermination."[31]

Propaganda and militia killings reached a peak precisely when the Habyarimana regime was being pressured to respect its 1990 pledge to implement multiparty democracy and seek peace with the RPF. The Arusha Peace Accords of August 1993 guaranteed free elections in less than two years, to include the RPF, which had been allowed to install several hundred troops in Kigali. Some 2,500 foreign peacekeepers arrived to constitute the United Nations Assistance Mission for Rwanda (UNAMIR); their task was to monitor the ceasefire and the prelude to elections.

The Arusha Accords and the UNAMIR intervention proved to be the last straw for "Hutu Power" extremists. Genocide against the Tutsi minority would simultaneously eliminate the perceived constituency for the RPF; resolve the economic crisis through distribution of Tutsi land, wealth, and jobs; and bind the Hutu majority in genocidal complicity. The extremists imported hundreds of thousands of machetes in 1993–94; this weapon would become the symbol of the Rwanda genocide.

■ GENOCIDAL FRENZY[32]

At 8:30 p.m. on April 6, 1994, the plane carrying President Habyarimana back from talks in Tanzania was shot down as it neared Kigali airport – by either Hutu Power or RPF elements anxious to scuttle the Arusha peace process.[33] By 9:18, the Presidential Guard had begun to erect roadblocks around Kigali.

The following day, working from carefully prepared lists, soldiers and militias began murdering thousands of Tutsis and oppositionist Hutus. Crucially, ten Belgian peacekeepers protecting the moderate Prime Minister, Agathe Uwimiliyana, were seized, tortured, and murdered, along with Uwimiliyana herself. The murders prompted Belgium to withdraw its remaining forces from Rwanda. Over the heated protests of UNAMIR commander Dallaire, other countries followed suit. In the end, Dallaire would be left with "454 [peacekeepers] of all ranks, along with [one] dozen UN civilians" to stop perhaps the most explosive genocide in recorded history.[34] Foreign journalists also departed *en bloc*.

From the start, the extremist government capitalized on several factors that they appear to have known would limit outside opposition to the genocide. First, they played upon stereotypes of African "tribal conflict," depicting the killings as reciprocal excesses. Second, they seem to have realized that killing some foreign troops would scare away the remainder, with memories still fresh of the 1993 Battle of Mogadishu, when two dozen Pakistani troops and eighteen US Rangers died at the hands of Somali militias.[35] Third, the extremists benefited from the "blind commitment" of the French government to its Rwandan counterpart: "the Rwandese leadership kept believing that *no matter what it did*, French support would always be forthcoming. And it had no valid reasons for believing otherwise."[36] Lastly, the "Hutu Power" regime exploited the limited energy and resources of international media and public opinion where Africa was concerned, and the fact that media attention was overwhelmingly directed toward the inaugural free elections in South Africa.

Army and militia forces went street to street, block by block, and house to house, in Kigali and every other major city save Butare in the south (which resisted the genocidal impetus for two weeks before its prefect was deposed and killed, and replaced by a compliant *génocidaire*). Tutsis were dragged out of homes and hiding places and murdered, often after prolonged torture and rape. At the infamous roadblocks, those carrying Tutsi identity cards – along with some Hutus who were deemed to "look" Tutsi – were shot or hacked to death. Often the killers, whether drunk and willing or conscripted and reluctant, severed the Achilles' tendons of their victims to immobilize them. They would be left for hours in agony, until the murderers mustered the energy to return and finish them off. Numerous accounts exist of Tutsis paying to be killed by rifle bullets, rather than slowly and agonizingly with machetes and hoes.

In what can only be called "an incomprehensible scandal,"[37] the killings took place literally before the eyes of UNAMIR and other foreign forces, whose mandate and orders forbade them to intervene beyond saving white lives. As early as April 9, in the church at Gikondo in Kigali, a slaughter occurred that presaged the strategies to be followed in coming weeks – one that was witnessed by Polish nuns, priests, and UN military observers:

A Presidential Guard officer arrived and told the soldiers not to waste their bullets because the Interahamwe [Hutu Power militia] would soon come with machetes. Then the militia came in, one hundred of them, and threatening the [Polish] priests they began to kill people, slashing with their machetes and clubs, hacking arms, legs, genitals and the faces of the terrified people who tried to protect the children under the pews. Some people were dragged outside the church and attacked in the courtyard. The killing continued for two hours as the whole compound was searched. Only two people are believed to have survived the killing at the church. Not even babies were spared. That day in Gikondo there was a street littered with corpses the length of a kilometre. . . . The killing in Gikondo was done in broad daylight with no attempt to disguise the identity of the killers, who were convinced that there would be no punishment for their actions.[38]

The following day, April 10, the UN established contact with military observers in Gisenyi, the heartland of Hutu extremism, where mass killing had erupted three days earlier. The stunned observers described "total chaos" with "massacres everywhere," leaving tens of thousands of Tutsi corpses.[39] With such reports to hand, and the eyewitness testimony of observers in Gikondo, the UN and the international community were fully aware, within a few days of Habyarimana's death on April 6, that killing of a genocidal nature and on a genocidal scale was occurring in Rwanda. They did nothing to stop it, though there were more than enough troops on hand to suppress the killing in Kigali at the very least – and thousands more arrived in the early days of the genocide, albeit only to evacuate foreigners (and their pets), not to prevent genocidal killings of Tutsis.[40] Indeed, Security Council members – notably France and the US – would wrap themselves in knots during the ensuing weeks to avoid rendering an unambiguous verdict of genocide. "Be Careful," warned an internal memo following a May 1 meeting at the Pentagon. "Legal [department] at State [Department] was worried about this yesterday – Genocide finding could commit US government to actually do something."[41] Most notorious was the painfully awkward response by State Department spokeswoman Christine Shelly to reporters who sought to pin her down on the genocide question (reproduced from the official State Department transcript, mangled syntax included):

SHELLY: Based on the evidence we have seen from observations on the ground, we have every reason to believe that acts of genocide have occurred in Rwanda.
REPORTER: What's the difference between "acts of genocide" and "genocide"?

. . .

REPORTER: How many acts of genocide does it take to make genocide?
SHELLY: Alan, that's just not a question that I'm in a position to answer.
REPORTER: Well, is it true that you have specific guidance not to use the word "genocide" in isolation but always to preface it with these words "acts of"?
SHELLY: I have guidance which I try to use as best as I can. There are formulations that we are using that we are trying to be consistent of our use of. I don't have an absolute categorical prescription against something, but I have the definitions. I have phraseology which has been carefully examined and arrived at as

best as we can apply to exactly the situation and the actions which have taken place.. . . [42]

It seems evident, in retrospect, that the *génocidaires* were not only hoping for such a response, but were awaiting it before launching a full-scale slaughter. Linda Melvern's book *Conspiracy to Murder* conveys the sense of suspended animation in the first week of the genocide, while Hutu Power gauged international reactions to the opening wave of killing. When it became clear there would be no outside impediment, murder spread like a virus across the territories under extremist control. By April 23, Roméo Dallaire, on a journey north from the capital, was "pass[ing] over bridges in swamps that had been lifted by the force of the bodies piling up on the struts. We had inched our way through villages of dead humans. . . . We had created paths amongst the dead and half-dead with our hands. And we had thrown up even when there was nothing in our stomachs."[43]

Parish churches, along with schools and similar facilities, were soon piled thigh-high with the shot, hacked, and savaged corpses of the victims.[44] One such massacre,

Figure 9.1   David Blumenkrantz, working in neighboring Uganda at the time of the Rwandan genocide, captured this extraordinary image of victims' corpses pulled from Lake Victoria by Ugandan fishermen. Murdered Tutsis were often dumped into tributaries of the lake, which is the source of the Nile river. As explored by the anthropologist Christopher Taylor (see Chapter 11, p. 436), this was a means of symbolically expunging the Tutsis from Rwanda, and returning them to their supposedly foreign, "Nilotic" origins.

Source: Courtesy David Blumenkrantz.

in fact, may stand as the most concentrated ground-level slaughter of the twentieth century (by which I mean a mass killing inflicted in hours or days rather than months or years, and by means other than aerial bombing). On April 20, at the parish of Karama in Butare prefecture, "between thirty-five and forty-three thousand people died *in less than six hours*."[45] This was more than were killed in the Nazis' two-day slaughters of Jews outside Odessa and Kiev (at Babi Yar) in 1941, or in the largest single-day extermination spree in the gas chambers of Auschwitz-Birkenau.[46]

Tens of thousands of Tutsis sought sanctuary in schools, stadiums, and especially places of worship. But there was no sanctuary to be had. In fact, those encouraging them to seek it were usually *génocidaires* working to concentrate their victims for mass killing. Astonishingly, church figures across Rwanda played a leading role in legitimizing and even inflicting genocidal killing (although "many priests, pastors and nuns" also displayed "courage and compassion," hiding and protecting potential victims).[47]

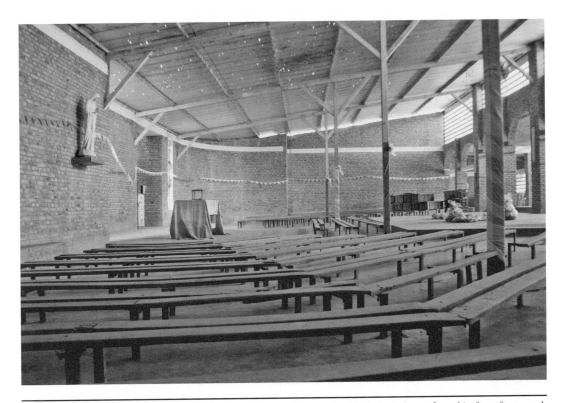

Figure 9.2   Tutsis were murdered *en masse* in Rwanda in part because they flocked to places of worship for refuge – such sanctuaries had been respected in past outbreaks of violence. In fact, both the Catholic and Anglican churches in Rwanda were deeply complicit in the genocide; Hutu priests, nuns, and lay workers often cooperated with the authorities and with *interahamwe* killers to target Tutsi members of their congregations. The Nyamata Memorial Site, shown here, is centered on a church and surrounding area where some 2,500 Tutsis were butchered in April 1994. "Government soldiers surrounded it and threw in grenades. After that, militiamen, many from the surrounding villages, entered the church with machetes, axes, even screwdrivers and hacked at the survivors."[48] The bodies were removed for burial; bullet holes are still visible in the roof. Many such massacre sites across Rwanda are now carefully maintained memorials to the holocaust that swept the country in 1994.

Source: Fanny Schertzer/Wikimedia Commons.

BOX 9.1 ONE WOMAN'S STORY: GLORIOSE MUKAKANIMBA

A Tutsi woman and mother of three, Gloriose Mukakanimba lived in the Rwandan capital of Kigali, where she ran a tailoring shop. On April 7, 1994, she witnessed the outbreak of the most intensive mass-killing spree in human history. Hutu militias – the so-called *interahamwe* ("those who fight together") – went door-to-door. They first targeted "prominent and rich people," Gloriose said, but quickly moved on to attack ordinary citizens: "They shot you just because you were a Tutsi. When they started using machetes, they didn't even bother to ask for ID cards. It was as if they had carried out a census; they knew you were a Tutsi."

Gloriose's home was one of those invaded. "Around 11:00 a.m. on Sunday [April 10] a large group of interahamwe came to our house. They tried to break the gate. They had difficulties with the gate so they cut through the hedge. They came in and started searching the house." After a while, they prepared to leave – but their leader arrived and ordered them "to go back in and kill." Her family was ordered outside. There, her husband, Déo Rutayisire, and her brother, Maurice Niyoyita, were hacked to death with machetes. Gloriose tried to flee with her 2-year-old daughter in her arms, but the child slipped from her grasp, "and I saw them cutting her up. I ran with all the strength I had."

While she desperately sought a place to hide, Gloriose was stunned to hear her neighbors calling out to the militia members: "Here she is, here she is!" "These were neighbors I had already considered friends, people I felt had been kind to me." Finally she found sanctuary in an abandoned house with an old vehicle parked adjacent. "The bonnet was open and it did not have an engine. I jumped right inside the bonnet and stayed there for about a day and a half." Militia scoured the house, coming close to the car where she was hiding. "I could feel them so near to me. I was terrified to death. I stopped myself from breathing."

When the interahamwe moved on, Gloriose begged for refuge from a neighbor who had been friendly with her sister. But the neighbor demanded that she leave. She decided to return to her house, only to run into an "ambush [that] had been set up for me." She was detained for a few hours, until the militia decided to execute her. An interahamwe "hit me with the machete. Fortunately it was dark and he could not see very well. He kept trying to aim for my neck but I instinctively put my hands over my neck. He kept hitting my hands, thinking it was my neck. After a while, I decided to let him think I was dead." Finally "they left, thinking they had finished their job."

Gloriose ran to hide in a water-filled ditch. But "some other militia saw me and went to tell my killers that they had not completed their job. The next morning, my killers came back, this time with guns and grenades." They shot and tossed grenades into the trench, but Gloriose was able to evade them. "It was a very long trench. This made it difficult for them to know my exact location because of course I kept moving."

Apparently believing she must have been killed by the fusillade, the militia again moved on. "I spent the night in the trench. The wounds in my arms were not only extremely painful but had come to smell. I decided to come out of the trench for fear that I would die there." She fled to the nearby residence of one of the few surviving Tutsi families in the area: "I found out that the husband had been an invalid for a long time; maybe that's why the killers let them live." Together with her rescuers, she joined a flood of Tutsis heading towards the lines of the rebel Rwandan Patriotic Front in Gitarama district.

On the verge of starvation, she and her companions finally stumbled on an RPF patrol. She was taken to a health center in the city of Rutare. There, her wounds were treated, and she was interviewed by researchers from African Rights, a London-based organization that would go on to publish the most detailed and harrowing account of the Rwandan genocide.[49]

In Kibuye prefecture, some 20,000 Tutsis had congregated at Gatwaro stadium. The stadium was surrounded by soldiers and militia, who began firing into the stadium and at anyone who sought to flee. Twelve thousand people died in a single day. Elsewhere in the prefecture, perhaps the most exterminatory killing of the genocide took place. "Entire Tutsi communities were wiped out with no witnesses left to tell what happened. From a population of 252,000 Tutsi in a 1991 census, by the end of June there were an estimated 8,000 left alive."[50]

Many Tutsis fled to high ground, such as Bisesero mountain in southwestern Rwanda. The "mountain of death" was the scene of unforgettable acts of resistance, as Tutsis sought desperately to fend off the attacks. A survivor, Claver Mbugufe, recalled:

There were constant attempts to kill the refugees at Bisesero. But we were always able to defend ourselves. Towards mid-May, when we were still in the grip of the interahamwe militia and their allies, they received enormous reinforcements. . . . Soldiers also came and set up a camp near Bisesero for three days, during which they killed many refugees. We spent the entire day running up and down. We tried to concentrate our defence in one area in order to break their stranglehold. We did everything possible to kill any one of them who stood in our way. Sometimes, we even managed to wrest guns from soldiers and policemen. We killed many of these aggressors.[51]

Despite such heroism, tens of thousands of people died at Bisesero in April and May. A series of other massacres, notably in Cyahindu prefecture, claimed over 10,000 victims at one time. Then there were the "death camps" such as those in the Kabgayi archbishopric, where "over thirty thousand terrified Tutsis" congregated.[52] Militia roamed freely through Kabgayi, selecting Tutsi men and boys for execution, and women and girls for rape. (The gendering of the Rwandan catastrophe is discussed further in Chapter 13.) This horror ended only when the Rwandan Patriotic Front captured Kabgayi on June 2.

Throughout, a remarkable feature of the genocide was its routinized character. The killings were "marked not by the fury of combat or paroxysms of mob violence, but by a well-ordered sanity that mirrored the rhythms of ordinary collective life."[53] Killers arrived for their duties at a designated hour, and broke off their murderous activities at five in the afternoon, as though clocking off.

Another signal feature, as noted above, was the involvement of ordinary Hutus in the slaughter. "Had the killing been the work of state functionaries and those bribed by them," wrote Mamdani, "it would have translated into no more than a string of massacres perpetrated by death squads. Without massacres by machete-wielding civilian mobs, in the hundreds and thousands, there would have been no genocide."[54] In a development perhaps unprecedented in the history of genocide, Hutu women flocked or were conscripted by the tens of thousands to participate in the killing of Tutsis and the stripping of corpses. To the extent that their violence was directed against Tutsi women,

> there appears to have been a kind of gendered jubilation at the "comeuppance" of Tutsi females, who had for so long been depicted in Hutu propaganda as Rwanda's sexual elite. Otherwise, the motivations for women's involvement as genocidal killers frequently paralleled those of Hutu men: bonds of ethnic solidarity . . . suasion and coercion by those in authority (including other women); the lure of material gain; and the intoxicating pleasure of untrammelled sadism.[55]

It is impossible to know how many of the killers, male and female, would have avoided their role if they could. It is clear, however, that hundreds of thousands of Hutus participated eagerly. "It was as if all the men, women and children had come to kill us," recalled one survivor.[56] Many were motivated by greed – the chance to loot Tutsi belongings and seize Tutsi land (see Chapter 10). And for those at the bottom of the social ladder, there was the unprecedented opportunity to exercise life-and-death power over others. Gérard Prunier captures this element vividly, noting that "social envy came together with political hatred to fire the . . . bloodlust":

> In Kigali the [militias] . . . had tended to recruit mostly among the poor. As soon as they went into action, they drew around them a cloud of even poorer people, a lumpenproletariat of street boys, rag-pickers, car-washers and homeless unemployed. For these people the genocide was the best thing that could ever happen to them. They had the blessings of a form of authority to take revenge on socially powerful people as long as these [victims] were on the wrong side of the political fence. They could steal, they could kill with minimum justification, they could rape and they could get drunk for free. This was wonderful. The political aims pursued by the masters of this dark carnival were quite beyond their scope. They just went along, knowing it would not last.[57]

It did not last – in part because the killers were running out of victims, but in larger part because the genocide distracted the Hutu Power regime from confronting RPF forces. Immediately following the outbreak of the genocide on April 6–7, the RPF contingent in Kigali had moved out of its barracks to establish control over several neighborhoods of the capital, thereby protecting thousands of Tutsis who would otherwise have faced certain death. Rwanda thus witnessed the surreal phenomenon of street battles in the heart of the capital, while the government was extending the holocaust to every corner of the countryside under its control. That control rapidly ebbed, however, as the RPF renewed its offensive. By mid-June, they had decisively defeated Rwandan government forces, which were pushed into a limited zone in the southwest of the country. The offensive was accompanied by large-scale revenge killings of Hutus in territory that RPF soldiers had overrun. Estimates of those killed range as high as 50,000, with many summary executions, particularly of "battle-age" Hutu men who were automatically assumed to have participated in the genocide.[58]

At this point, foreign forces finally staged a decisive intervention – but one that primarily benefited the *génocidaires*. On June 17, France proposed to the UN Security Council that French troops be sent to Rwanda under UN auspices. Four days later, thousands of French troops began assembling on the Rwandan border with Zaire – an indication of how rapidly a substantial intervention can be mounted when the political will exists.[59] On July 4, the RPF gained full control of the capital, Kigali; the following day, France, with UN approval in hand, established a "safe zone" in the southwest.

The French intervention, known as Opération Turquoise, may have saved many Tutsi lives. But protecting Tutsis was not the main purpose of the intervention. Rather, the operation was a continuation of the long-standing French support for the Hutu Power government. It permitted the orderly evacuation of nearly *two million* Hutus, including tens of thousands of *génocidaires*, to refugee camps in neighboring Zaire. As Gérard Prunier wrote, "the refugees moved to the camps in perfect order, with their *bourgmestres* and communal counsellors at their head. Inside the camps they remained grouped according to their *communes* of origin and under the control of the very political structure which had just been responsible for the genocide."[60]

This mass flow of refugees was highly visible to international media that gained access to the camps. The humanitarian crisis – especially outbreaks of cholera and other diseases that killed thousands of refugees – was something the international community could address with minimum risk. The Clinton government in the US, which had spent the period of the mass slaughter instructing its representatives to avoid using the word "genocide" and placing obstacle after obstacle in the path of intervention, now leapt into action. US troops arrived within days to begin distribution of water, supplies, and medical aid to the camps.

"Like a monstrous cancer, the camps coalesced, solidified and implanted themselves in the flesh of east Zaire."[61] Hutu extremists inflicted genocidal atrocities against Tutsis living in eastern Zaire and staged cross-border raids into Rwanda, prompting the newly installed RPF regime in Rwanda to launch operations in the region that themselves led to the deaths of thousands of civilians, together with hard-core *génocidaires*.[62] According to Christian Scherrer, "The export of genocide from

Rwanda is the main cause in the spread of conflict to the whole of the Central African region, and the chief reason for the unprecedented violence, intensity, and destructiveness of that conflict" – possibly the most murderous since the Second World War.[63] The complex war in the Democratic Republic of the Congo is examined in Box 10a.

AFTERMATHS

Early estimates of the death-toll in the Rwandan genocide were between 500,000 and 800,000, overwhelmingly Tutsis. Subsequent investigations have revised these mind-boggling figures upward. A detailed census in July 2000 cited 951,018 victims, but estimated the total death-toll at over a million. According to a subsequent report, "93.7% of the victims were killed because they were identified as Tutsi; 1% because they were related to, married to or friends with Tutsi; 0.8% because they looked like Tutsi; and 0.8% because they were opponents of the Hutu regime at the time or were hiding people from the killers."[64]

Since Hutu Power was crushed in Rwanda in July 1994, the country has faced a staggering task of material reconstruction, human recovery, restitution, and political reconciliation. Fleeing Hutus had stripped the country almost bare, down to the zinc roofing on houses. Nonetheless, the Tutsi-dominated regime scored notable successes. Economic production was restored to pre-1994 levels. Approximately 1.3 million Hutu refugees were repatriated from camps in Zaire (now the Democratic Republic of the Congo).

The basic orientation of the post-genocide government is clear: it is guided by "the conviction that power is the condition of Tutsi survival."[65] Its "Never Again" rallying cry can be interpreted as a pledge that never again will Hutus achieve dominance in Rwandan politics. "The reality," wrote Gérard Prunier in 1997, "is that the government is perceived by the average Hutu peasant as a foreign government."[66] The ambiguous success that the Rwandan regime claims is considered further in Chapter 16.

Mounting criticism of the RPF-dominated regime's authoritarianism has been accompanied by an increasingly skeptical appraisal, in the scholarly and other commentary on Rwanda over the past few years, of the actions of the RPF *during* the genocide, when its forces almost certainly massacred tens of thousands of Hutus in revenge for the scenes of carnage that their troops discovered as they advanced against the Hutu Power regime.

Roméo Dallaire, commander of the UNAMIR forces in Rwanda, was harsh in his assessment of RPF's performance before and during the genocide, condemning its "inability to see beyond [its] own self-interest" in his widely-read memoir, *Shake Hands with the Devil*. The RPF was "intransigent" and "relentlessly inflexible about any concessions that might have eased the tension in the country, both before the civil war broke out and later, when they had [government forces] on the run."[67] On April 18, ceasefire negotiations broke down, and the RPF resumed its advance toward Kigali; for Dallaire, "it was absolutely plain that [the RPF] didn't want a ceasefire." Meeting in early May with RPF commander (now Rwandan president) Paul Kagame, he records Kagame's "pragmatic" demeanor, "the complete portrait of the cool warrior," and quotes him as saying: "There will be many sacrifices in this war. If the [Tutsi] refugees have to be killed for the cause, they will be considered as having been part of the sacrifice." According to Dallaire, it was only one of "several points" at which Kagame "talked candidly . . . about the price his fellow Tutsis might have to pay for the cause."[68]

While serious attention to Tutsi/RPF abuses and atrocities was present at the outset in some human-rights commentary (see, e.g., Alison Des Forges's *Leave None to Tell the Story* [Figure 9.3]), and has gradually percolated into the scholarly literature, it has been notably absent in the quest for justice since 1994. In November 1994, the United Nations established the International Criminal Tribunal for Rwanda in Arusha, Tanzania. However, despite an impressive budget of US$1.8 billion, the tribunal launched proceedings only against alleged perpetrators of genocide against Tutsis and moderate Hutus (that is, no prosecutions were launched of post-1994 Rwandan government leaders for alleged involvement in RPF-inflicted atrocities against Hutus). It also proceeded excruciatingly slowly. The ICTR did not hear its first case until 1997, and nearly a dozen years later, with its mandate again extended so the backlog could be cleared, it fell prey to Gérard Prunier's scathing assessment that it "combined three different evils":

Figure 9.3 Alison Des Forges (1942–2009) was the very model of the genocide investigator. A longtime specialist in Africa's Great Lakes region, she was positioned as few others were to examine the aftermath of Rwanda's 1994 holocaust. The resulting Human Rights Watch report, *Leave None to Tell the Story* (1999 – see Further Study), stands as a classic of human-rights reporting and genocide research. In February 2009, at age 66, Des Forges was killed in the crash of a passenger jet near Buffalo.[69]

Source: Human Rights Watch, 2005.

It was an embodiment of the worst aspects of UN bureaucratic inefficiency; a muted, closed arena for jousting over all the unacknowledged political contradictions of the genocide; and a swamp of nepotistic and corrupt practices. . . . Whereas it had taken the Nuremberg Tribunal one year (from November 1945 to November 1946) to judge twenty-four Nazis and hang ten, the ICTR had managed to carry out only twenty procedures in ten years at a cost of around $700 million.[70]

A central purpose of the court, however, was to refine the law of genocide and crimes against humanity, and contribute to the growing body of case law that was rendering these concepts workable (or manifestly unworkable) for the first time.[71] One of the ICTR's convictions – that of Jean-Paul Akayesu in 1998 – was especially significant, with its "historic determination that systematic rape was a crime against humanity and that sexual violence constituted genocide in the same way as any other act." In another case, two former media officials of Rwandan "hate radio" were convicted of using media as genocidal instruments (see Chapter 15).[72]

In Rwanda itself, some 120,000 accused *génocidaires* languished for years in grim and sometimes murderous conditions in jail, while the country's shattered legal system sought to bring at least some to trial. Finally, in 2003, it was recognized that formal proceedings could never cope with the massive number of accused. Over 20,000 prisoners were released, and others were promised a reduction of sentences in return for confessions. The most interesting form of attempted justice was *gacaca*, or "on the grass," a traditional form of tribunal that sacrificed formal legal procedures and protections for speedy results and a focus on restorative rather than punitive justice (see Chapter 15). However, according to Amnesty International in 2009, thousands of those released from jail were subsequently rearrested, so that after a period of decline the prison population had increased again, to over 60,000. The majority remained "incarcerated on charges of participating in the genocide," more than a decade-and-a-half after that genocide ended.[73]

FURTHER STUDY

African Rights, *Rwanda: Death, Despair and Defiance* (rev. edn). London: African Rights, 1995. Immense and harrowing depiction of the Rwandan holocaust; like nothing else in the literature.

Roméo Dallaire (with Brent Beardsley), *Shake Hands with the Devil: The Failure of Humanity in Rwanda*. New York: Carroll & Graf, 2004. Literate and passionate memoir by the Canadian leader of the UN assistance mission in Rwanda (1993–94).

Alison Des Forges, *Leave None to Tell the Story: Genocide in Rwanda*. New York: Human Rights Watch, 1999. Another indispensable human-rights report on the genocide.

Lee Ann Fujii, *Killing Neighbors: Webs of Violence in Rwanda*. Ithaca, NY: Cornell University Press, 2009. Insightful account of the local dynamics of the killing, and how community and personal bonds sometimes muted it.

Jean Hatzfeld, *Machete Season: The Killers in Rwanda Speak*, trans. Linda Coverdale. New York: Farrar, Straus & Giroux, 2005. Chilling testimony from imprisoned *génocidaires*. See also *Life Laid Bare: The Survivors in Rwanda Speak*.

Stephen Kinzer, *A Thousand Hills: Rwanda's Rebirth and the Man Who Dreamed It*. New York: John Wiley and Sons, 2008. As the subtitle suggests, a generally admiring portrait of Paul Kagame and his post-genocide rule in Rwanda.

René Lemarchand, *The Dynamics of Violence in Central Africa*. Philadelphia, PA: University of Pennsylvania Press, 2009. Places the Rwandan genocide in regional context, with superbly enlightening commentary on Burundi and Congo as well (see Box 9a).

Mahmood Mamdani, *When Victims Become Killers: Colonialism, Nativism, and the Genocide in Rwanda*. Princeton, NJ: Princeton University Press, 2001. How political identity was constructed for Hutus and Tutsis.

Linda Melvern, *Conspiracy to Murder: The Rwanda Genocide and the International Community*. London: Verso, 2004. Follow-up to the author's hard-hitting critique, *A People Betrayed: The Role of the West in Rwanda's Genocide* (2nd edn).

Gérard Prunier, *The Rwanda Crisis: History of a Genocide*. New York: Columbia University Press, 1997. A standard source on the origins of the genocide.

Carol Rittner, John K. Roth and Wendy Whitworth, eds, *Genocide in Rwanda: Complicity of the Churches?* St. Paul, MN: Paragon House, 2004. Insights into the churches' role.

Scott Straus, *The Order of Genocide: Race, Power, and War in Rwanda*. Ithaca, NY: Cornell University Press, 2006. Based on interviews with over two hundred jailed perpetrators; one of the most discussed recent works of genocide studies.

Allan Thompson, ed., *The Media and the Rwanda Genocide*. London: Pluto, 2007. The most extensive airing of debates over the media's role in the Rwandan holocaust.

Peter Uvin, *Aiding Violence: The Development Enterprise in Rwanda*. West Hartford, CT: Kumarian Press, 1998. Influential analysis of the genocide as an outgrowth of structural violence and foreign development assistance.

NOTES

1   John Quigley, *The Genocide Convention: An International Law Analysis* (London: Ashgate, 2006), p. 33.

2   Gérard Prunier, *The Rwanda Crisis: History of a Genocide* (New York: Columbia University Press, 1997), p. 261.

3   Christian P. Scherrer, *Genocide and Crisis: Conflict Roots, Mass Violence, and Regional War* (Westport, CT: Praeger, 2002), p. 109.

4   Colonel Luc Marchal, UNAMIR commander in Kigali; quoted in *Chronicle of a Genocide Foretold: Part 2, "We Were Cowards"* (Ottawa: National Film Board of Canada [hereafter, NFB], 1997).

5   International Panel of Eminent Personalities (IPEP) report, quoted in Kenneth J. Campbell, *Genocide and the Global Village* (New York: Palgrave, 2001), p. 78. The scenes at the psychiatric hospital, and the Belgian soldier's comment, are available in the NFB documentary *Chronicle of a Genocide Foretold: Part 2*.

6 Quoted in Maxim Kniazkov, "US 'Ran from Rwanda Responsibility,'" Agence France-Presse dispatch, August 22, 2001.

7 Linda Melvern, *A People Betrayed: The Role of the West in Rwanda's Genocide* (London: Zed Books, 2000), p. 174. See also Roméo Dallaire, *Shake Hands with the Devil: The Failure of Humanity in Rwanda* (New York: Carroll & Graf, 2004). The International Committee of the Red Cross (ICRC) also refused to abandon the field, performing extraordinarily dangerous and heroic work throughout the genocide (see Melvern, *A People Betrayed*, p. 215).

8 John Heidenrich, *How to Prevent Genocide: A Guide for Policymakers, Scholars, and the Concerned Citizen* (Westport, CT: Praeger, 2001), p. 199.

9 Linda Melvern, *Conspiracy to Murder: The Rwanda Genocide* (London: Verso, 2004), p. 240.

10 Quoted in NFB, *Chronicle of a Genocide Foretold*. Samantha Power wrote: "It is shocking to note that during the entire three months of the genocide, [President] Clinton never assembled his top policy advisers to discuss the killings. . . . Rwanda was never thought to warrant its own top-level meeting." Power, *"A Problem from Hell": America and the Age of Genocide* (New York: Basic Books, 2002), p. 366.

11 Quoted in Power, *"A Problem from Hell,"* p. 382.

12 Dallaire, *Shake Hands with the Devil*, p. 5. French Colonel Henri Poncet, arriving in Rwanda on April 8 with a well-armed force (Opération Amaryllis), "insisted to me that he was only here to evacuate expatriates and 'white people'" (p. 282).

13 Annan speaking at Memorial Conference on Rwanda Genocide, New York; United Nations Press Release, SG/SM/9223, AFR/870, HQ/631, March 26, 2004, http://www.un.org/News/Press/docs/2004/sgsm9223.doc.htm.

14 Mahmood Mamdani, *When Victims Become Killers: Colonialism, Nativism, and the Genocide in Rwanda* (Princeton, NJ: Princeton University Press, 2001), pp. 51, 70.

15 Prunier, *The Rwanda Crisis*, p. 39.

16 Ibid., p. 3.

17 Mamdani, *When Victims Become Killers*, p. 66.

18 Prunier notes that "by the end of the Belgian presence in Rwanda in 1959, forty-three [prefectural] chiefs out of forty-five were Tutsi as well as 549 sub-chiefs out of 559." *The Rwanda Crisis*, p. 27.

19 The myth still occasionally surfaces, as when Andrew Bell-Fialkoff refers to "the Hamitic Tutsi." Bell-Fialkoff, *Ethnic Cleansing* (New York: St. Martin's Griffin, 1999), p. 182.

20 René Lemarchand puts this very well: "The Hamitic idea, which presumed the innate cultural superiority of the Tutsi and claimed that Ethiopia was their original homeland, was pressed into service to legitimize Tutsi overrule under the Belgian colonizers. The inversion of this mythical discourse, emphasizing the foreignness, cunning, and perversity of Tutsi 'feudal exploiters,' played an equally decisive role in legitimizing Hutu ascendancy in the last years of colonial rule. It also lent ideological justification to the génocidaires." Lemarchand, *The Dynamics of Violence in Central Africa* (Philadelphia, PA: University of Pennsylvania Press, 2009), p. 92.

21 Christopher Taylor, *Sacrifice as Terror: The Rwandan Genocide of 1994* (Oxford: Berg, 1999), pp. 128–30.

22 See Mamdani, *When Victims Become Killers*, p. 88.

23 Melvern, *A People Betrayed*, p. 42. In March 2010, immediately following President Nicolas Sarkozy's visit to Rwanda (see note 33), France announced the detention of Agathe Habyarimana on an international warrant issued by the Rwandan government. It was not clear, as this book was going to press, whether or where Habyarimana would stand trial. See "Rwanda President's Widow Held in France over Genocide," *BBC Online*, March 2, 2010, http://news.bbc.co.uk/2/hi/europe/8545120.stm.

24 Scherrer, *Genocide and Crisis*, p. 105.

25 Many commentators have accused the RPF, under then-General, now-President Paul Kagame, of "recklessness" for launching this invasion. Bill Berkeley, for example, contends that "No rational person could have looked at the history of repeated mass

slaughters in Rwanda and Burundi since 1959 and doubted for a moment that at least one likely outcome of such an invasion would be massive violence against defenseless Tutsi civilians." Berkeley, "Road to a Genocide," in Nicolaus Mills and Kira Brunner, eds, *The New Killing Fields: Massacre and the Politics of Intervention* (New York: Basic Books, 2002), p. 114. See also Alan J. Kuperman, "Provoking Genocide: A Revised History of the Rwandan Patriotic Front," *Journal of Genocide Research*, 6: 1 (March 2004), pp. 61–84.

26 Alison Des Forges, *Leave None to Tell the Story: Genocide in Rwanda* (New York, Human Rights Watch, 1999), p. 122. According to Danielle de Lame, a Belgian anthropologist, "Already in 1989 [Rwandan] farmers described their situation as apocalyptic." Quoted in Jacques Sémelin, *Purify and Destroy: The Political Uses of Massacre and Genocide* (New York: Columbia University Press, 2007), p. 15.

27 Burundi, like Rwanda, has a large Hutu majority and a small but traditionally dominant Tutsi minority. In 1972, some 200,000 Hutus were slaughtered by the Tutsi-dominated army, in what has been termed an "eliticide": the primary targets were educated and/or wealthy Hutu males. The 1972 genocide was echoed by further outbreaks of mass killing of Hutu in 1988 (20,000 killed) and 1991 (a further 3,000 deaths). In October 1993 the Hutu president of the country was killed, leading to an outburst of genocidal violence against both Tutsis and Hutus that established a "basic pattern" for the events in Rwanda the following year (Scherrer, *Genocide and Crisis*, p. 3). Bill Berkeley estimates that "another hundred and fifty thousand have died in Burundi's continuing bloodshed" since 1993 (Berkeley, "Road to a Genocide," p. 110).

28 Catharine Newbury, "Ethnicity and the Politics of History in Rwanda," in David E. Lorey and William H. Beezley, eds, *Genocide, Collective Violence, and Popular Memory: The Politics of Remembrance in the Twentieth Century* (Wilmington, DL: Scholarly Resources, Inc., 2002), p. 76.

29 Melvern, *Conspiracy to Murder*, pp. 62–64.

30 Scherrer, *Genocide and Crisis*, p. 122.

31 Quoted in Melvern, *A People Betrayed*, p. 155.

32 This phrase is drawn from the title of ch. 8 of African Rights, *Rwanda: Death, Despair and Defiance* (rev. edn) (London: African Rights, 1995).

33 For more than a decade-and-a-half, controversy has swirled over the critical event of the downing of Habyarimana's presidential jet. It continues at a high pitch today. A great deal hinges on whether Hutu or Tutsi forces committed the act: if Hutus, for example, the evidence is stronger for a well-established extermination plan (as in Linda Melvern, *Conspiracy to Murder*); if Tutsis, there is greater support for a reactive and retributive framing, emphasizing Hutu fear and panic after the assassination of "their" president (e.g., Scott Straus, *The Order of Genocide*). At first, something of a consensus reigned that the plane was probably downed by the Hutu Power government, perhaps with the assistance of foreign agents or mercenaries, as part of a "coup d'état" against moderates and the opening salvo of a "final solution" to the Tutsi question. This theory then gave way gradually to arguments that the Tutsi-dominated RPF was in fact the party responsible. "Strong circumstantial evidence" for the involvement of the current Rwandan president, Paul Kagame, was outlined by a renegade from Kagame's regime, Lt. Abdul Joshua Ruzibiza, and by a French magistrate, Jean-Louis Bruguière, who investigated the plane crash and issued his findings in 2006. See Ruzibiza, *Rwanda: l'histoire secrète* (Paris: Éditions du Panama, 2005); an English translation of the Bruguière report, posted October 1, 2007, is available at http://cirqueminime.blogspot.com/2007/10/completed-bruguire-report-translated.html. It recommends that the International Criminal Tribunal for Rwanda (ICTR) charge Paul Kagame "for his presumed participation in the attack of 6 April 1994." René Lemarchand expresses general support for the findings in *The Dynamics of Violence in Central Africa* (pp. xii, 102). On the basis of these allegations, French officials in late 2008 extradited Rose Kabuye, President Kagame's chief of protocol, and charged her with "complicity in murder in relation to

terrorism" for her alleged involvement in the downing of Habyarimana's plane. (See "Rwandan Official Charged in France," AlJazeera.net, November 20, 2008.) Kabuye's trial process was ongoing at the time of writing. A new stage, and something of a return to the original consensus, may be indicated by a weighty investigation, the Mutsinzi report, unveiled in January 2010. It was sponsored by the Rwandan government, true, but was based on "more than five hundred interviews with former officers of the Hutu Power regime and other eyewitnesses," and cited the findings of foreign forensic experts that the Falcon jet was downed by missiles fired from a base under Rwandan government (hence Hutu) control. According to Philip Gourevitch, though the report is not conclusive, it "lays out [the] story in remarkably convincing detail," with witness accounts that "describe the events before, during, and after the assassination with convincing consistency." Gourevitch, "The Mutsinzi Report on the Rwandan Genocide," *The New Yorker*, January 8, 2010. See also Robert Marquand, "Rwanda Genocide: Will New Report Close the Book on Who Started It?," *The Christian Science Monitor*, January 12, 2010. Marquand notes that "with French Foreign Minister Bernard Kouchner in Rwanda . . . and with French president Nicolas Sarkozy traveling there this month – French leaders appear to be tacitly accepting the new findings" on the downing of the jet – and, it might be added, accepting the displacement of French influence symbolized by Rwanda's accession to membership in the anglophone Commonwealth of Nations. For an excellent summary of the findings and significance of this latest report, see Gerald Caplan, "Who Killed the President of Rwanda?," Pambazuka News, January 21, 2010, http://www.pambazuka.org/en/category/features/ 61625.

34 Dallaire, *Shake Hands with the Devil*, p. 328. He accords special praise to the stalwart contingent of Tunisian peacekeepers: "I can't say enough about the bravery of the Tunisians. They never shirked their duty and always displayed the highest standards of courage and discipline in the face of difficult and dangerous tasks" (p. 302). The same can be said of the heroic Red Cross staff throughout the genocide.

35 The deaths of the US troops in Somalia were recounted in the book and film *Black Hawk Down*.

36 Prunier, *The Rwanda Crisis*, p. 107. According to Chris McGreal, the pattern continued after April 6, 1994: "When the genocide started, Paris made no secret of where its loyalties lay. The French military flew in ammunition for government forces and, in the following weeks, a stream of Hutu officials travelled to Paris, including Jean-Bosco Barayagwiza, who was later convicted of genocide by the international tribunal, for meetings with President François Mitterrand and the French prime minister. Even as the mass graves filled across Rwanda, Paris engineered the delivery of millions of dollars' worth of weapons to the Hutu regime from Egypt and South Africa." McGreal, "France's Shame?," *The Guardian*, January 11, 2007, http://www.guardian.co. uk/world/2007/jan/ 11/rwanda.insideafrica. A book-length examination is Daniela Kroslak, *The French Betrayal of Rwanda* (Bloomington, IN: Indiana University Press, 2008).

37 Scherrer, *Genocide and Crisis*, p. 364.

38 Melvern, *Conspiracy to Murder*, p. 182.

39 Ibid., p. 168.

40 "The officers of UNAMIR believe to this day that had the European troops that came to rescue the expats stayed on in Rwanda, the killing could have been stopped there and then. . . . Together with the moderates in the Rwandan army and with the peacekeepers there would have been ample troops to restore calm. There were already 2,500 peace-keepers with UNAMIR, there were 500 Belgian para-commandos, part of the evacuation force, together with 450 French and 80 Italian soldiers from parachute regiments. In neighbouring Kenya there were 500 Belgian para-commandos, also a part of the evacuation operation. In Burundi there were 250 US Rangers, elite troops, who had come to evacuate the US nationals. There were 800 more French troops on standby." Ibid., p. 188.

41 Cited by Adam LeBor, who adds: "There are few, if any, more succinct summaries of the Clinton administration's responses to the genocidal crises of the early and mid-1990s." LeBor, *"Complicity with Evil": The United Nations in the Age of Modern Genocide* (New Haven, CT: Yale University Press, 2006), p. 178.

42 US Department of State, Daily Press Briefing, Friday, June 10, 1994. Full official transcript at http://dosfan.lib.uic.edu/ERC/briefing/daily_briefings/1994/9406/940610db.html. These are the comments referenced on p. 56, note 55, in partial justification of a slight shift in my preferred definition of genocide.

43 Dallaire, *Shake Hands with the Devil*, p. 325.

44 According to Christian Scherrer, "the map showing the places where the largest massacres occurred was almost identical with that of the religious centers in the various dioceses and parishes of Rwanda." Scherrer, *Genocide and Crisis*, p. 113.

45 African Rights, *Rwanda: Not So Innocent: When Women Become Killers* (London: African Rights, 1995), p. 26, emphasis added.

46 The death-tolls usually cited for these cases are 36,000 (Odessa) and 33,000 (Kiev); according to Eugen Kogon, the highest number of killings in a single day at Auschwitz-Birkenau was 34,000, and other estimates are lower. Kogon, *The Theory and Practice of Hell* (New York: The Berkley Publishing Company, 1980), p. 241.

47 African Rights, *Death, Despair and Defiance*, p. 922. As one *génocidaire* recalled: "The white priests took off at the first skirmishes. The black priests joined the killers or the killed. God kept silent, and the churches stank from abandoned bodies." Quoted in Jean Hatzfeld (trans. Linda Coverdale), *Machete Season: The Killers in Rwanda Speak* (New York: Farrar, Straus & Giroux, 2005), p. 142. On the churches' role more generally, see Timothy Longman, *Christianity and Genocide in Rwanda* (Cambridge: Cambridge University Press, 2010); Carol Rittner, John K. Roth and Wendy Whitworth, eds, *Genocide in Rwanda: Complicity of the Churches?* (St. Paul, MN: Paragon House, 2005).

48 Dona Tella Lorch, "Children's Drawings Tell Horror of Rwanda in Colors of Crayons," *The New York Times*, September 16, 1994.

49 African Rights, *Rwanda: Death, Despair and Defiance*, pp. 590–95.

50 Melvern, *Conspiracy to Murder*, p. 224.

51 African Rights, *Rwanda: Death, Despair and Defiance*, p. 665.

52 Ibid., p. 708.

53 Darryl Li, "Echoes of Violence," in Mills and Brunner, eds, *The New Killing Fields*, p. 125.

54 Mamdani, *When Victims Become Killers*, p. 225.

55 Adam Jones, "Gender and Genocide in Rwanda," in Jones, ed., *Gendercide and Genocide* (Nashville, TN: Vanderbilt University Press, 2004), p. 123.

56 African Rights, *Rwanda: Not So Innocent*, p. 88.

57 Prunier, *The Rwanda Crisis*, pp. 231–32.

58 See Des Forges, *Leave None to Tell the Story*, p. 734.

59 Linda Melvern wrote that "the French operation included everything UNAMIR needed. There were more than 2,500 elite soldiers from the French Foreign Legion, paratroopers, marines and special forces, all equipped with state-of-the-art weaponry, communications, one hundred armoured vehicles, heavy mortars, helicopters, and even jet aircraft. There was an armada of cargo aircraft." Melvern, *Conspiracy to Murder*, p. 243.

60 Prunier, *The Rwanda Crisis*, p. 267.

61 Michela Wrong, *In the Footsteps of Mr. Kurtz: Living on the Brink of Disaster in Mobutu's Congo* (New York: HarperCollins, 2001), p. 245.

62 See Marie Béatrice Umutesi, *Surviving the Slaughter: The Ordeal of a Rwandan Refugee in Zaire*, trans. Julia Emerson (Madison, WI: University of Wisconsin Press, 2004).

63 Scherrer, *Genocide and Crisis*, p. 198.

64 Melvern, *Conspiracy to Murder*, pp. 250–51.

65 Mamdani, *When Victims Become Killers*, p. 261.

66 Prunier, *The Rwanda Crisis*, p. 370.

67 Dallaire, *Shake Hands with the Devil*, pp. 175, 475–76.

68 Ibid., pp. 311, 358, 515.

69 See Sewell Chan and Dennis Hevesi, "Alison Des Forges, 66, Human Rights Advocate, Dies," *The New York Times*, February 13, 2009, http://www.nytimes.com/2009/02/14/nyregion/14desforges.html.

70 Gérard Prunier, *Africa's World War: Congo, the Rwandan Genocide, and the Making of a Continental Catastrophe* (New York: Oxford University Press, 2009), p. 349.

71 For a first-rate overview, see L.J. van den Herik, *The Contribution of the Rwanda Tribunal to the Development of International Law* (Leiden: Martinus Nijhoff Publishers, 2005).

72 On the so-called "media trials," see Dina Temple-Raston, *Justice on the Grass: Three Rwandan Journalists, Their Trial for War Crimes and a Nation's Quest for Redemption* (New York: The Free Press, 2005).

73 Amnesty International USA, "Rwanda Human Rights," 2009, http://www.amnestyusa.org/all-countries/rwanda/page.do?id=1011229.

BOX 9A CONGO AND DARFUR

In 2005, as the first edition of this book was being prepared for publication, genocide again stalked Africa. A brutal counter-insurgency war in Darfur – a western region of Sudan, Africa's largest country – had sparked international condemnation and application of the "genocide" label, but only limited international intervention. Probably over 100,000 people had already died. To the southwest, Congo was again threatening to descend into full-scale war, as Rwanda's army staged another invasion, supposedly to suppress remnants of Hutu forces that had murdered Tutsis in 1994 (Chapter 9). By 2008, while conflict in Darfur had significantly cooled, the complex and excruciatingly destructive conflict(s) in Congo had produced an estimated *5.4 million* "excess deaths," according to the International Rescue Committee (IRC).[1] "Malaria, diarrhoea, pneumonia and malnutrition, aggravated by conflict" were the leading causes of death;[2] roughly half the victims were children under the age of 5. This was human destruction on a scale not seen since the Second World War.

CONGO AND "AFRICA'S FIRST WORLD WAR"

Congo was the backdrop for one of the greatest but least-known genocides in modern history – the Belgian "rubber terror" (Chapter 2). After independence from Belgium in 1960, Congo fell under the sway of an army colonel, Mobutu Sese Seko. Mobutu proved to be corrupt and megalomaniacal, "a ruthless crook who fitted his palace with a nuclear shelter, hired [the] Concorde for shopping trips and so gutted the treasury that inflation between October 1990 and December 1995 totalled 6.3 billion per cent."[3]

The catalyst for Mobutu's downfall came from eastern Congo, thousands of kilometers from the capital, Kinshasa. In the final stages of the 1994 genocide in Rwanda, as Tutsi rebel forces closed in from the north and east, Hutu *génocidaires* staged a mass evacuation of populations under their control, across the Congolese border to the city of Goma (see Chapter 9). Ironically, it was *this* humanitarian crisis that galvanized the world, not the genocide against Tutsis. Ironically, too, the outside aid that flooded in was instrumental in permitting the *génocidaires* to reconstitute themselves, control the refugee population, and launch attacks against Tutsis in both Congo and Rwanda.

In the face of this threat, in 1997 Rwanda assisted the overthrow of the Mobutu regime by Laurent Désiré Kabila, viewed as a Rwandan proxy and partner in the struggle against Hutu killers. *En route* to Kinshasa, Kabila's force and the Rwandan army rampaged against Hutu populations in eastern Congo. By one estimate, some 200,000 people died in these little-known, RPF-engineered, and so far unprosecuted massacres.[4] It was, noted historian Gérard Prunier, "the first known instance of postcolonial imperial conquest in Africa by an African country."[5]

Once in power, however, Kabila fell under the sway of Hutu representatives in Kinshasa, supporting renewed cross-border attacks and killing operations in Rwanda.[6] Rwanda soon began plotting a coup against its former protégé. An attempted drive on Kinshasa by Rwandan forces and anti-Kabila Congolese was halted only by the military intervention of Angola and Zimbabwe. Together with Namibia and Chad, these formed the coalition that maintained Kabila in power until his 2001 assassination. (He was succeeded by his son Joseph, still in power as of early 2010.) Meanwhile, Rwanda, Uganda, and Burundi lined up with the anti-Kabila rebels who dominated the eastern half of the country. Congo had become "Africa's first world war." It was a continental struggle that "reached almost without interruption from the Red Sea to the Atlantic Ocean,"[7] and offered almost unlimited opportunities for looting of precious minerals, especially diamonds and, for a time, coltan (an ore used in cell phones and other devices).

This was also a prototypical "new war," of the kind examined in Chapter 12. Clashes between major concentrations of armed forces were rare. Many of the killers were paramilitaries, warlords, and freebooters, cut adrift from more traditional military forces. Of special note was the militia led by the Congolese Tutsi Laurent Nkundabagenzi (also known as Nkunda), operating from a power base among the Tutsi population of North Kivu. Nkunda's "record of violence in eastern Congo includes destroying entire villages, committing mass rapes, and causing hundreds of thousands of Congolese to flee their homes."[8] Other key actors were soldiers of the Congolese army, who felt abandoned by central authorities in Kinshasa: "Paid poorly, if at all, undisciplined and feeling abandoned, these fighters calculate they have more to gain from looting and shooting than maintaining the fiction of an integrated national army."[9] Internecine conflicts between these armed groups provoked refugee flows

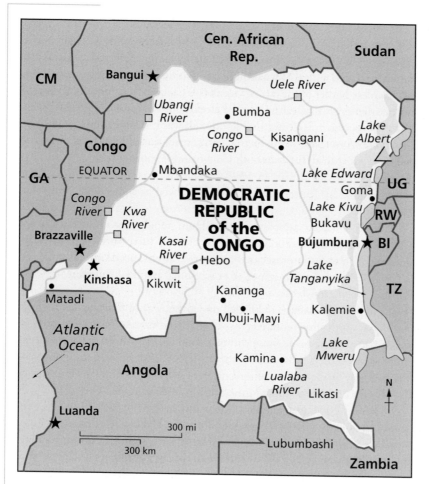

Map 9A.1   Congo

Source: Map provided by WorldAtlas.com.

numbering in the tens of thousands. Warlordism was rife amidst state collapse, with the Congolese government unable to "make [and] enforce laws, maintain order, deliver services, or ensure security."[10] Against this anarchic backdrop, as Prunier noted in his 2009 work *Africa's World War*, "civilians died partly because the soldiers killed them but, more often, because their living conditions (absence of health care, impossibility of steady cultivation, impossibility of trade, lack of shelter during the rainy season, constant displacement) caused their death."[11]

The rich mineral resources of Congo proved an irresistible lure for local militias and their foreign patrons. Competition for the spoils caused a falling-out between Rwanda and Uganda.[12] Both countries have experienced miraculous leaps in their export of key commodities – diamonds, gold, timber, and coltan – at levels that mysteriously far exceed domestic production.[13]

Starvation and disease caused most of the millions of deaths in the Congo wars, but tens or hundreds of thousands also died at the hands of rebel militias and the government. The forces of the FDLR (the Democratic Forces for the Liberation of Rwanda, born from the fleeing *génocidaires* of 1994) staged many attacks,[14] but it was the RCD rebels (the Congolese Rally for Democracy, supported by Rwanda and Uganda) that committed the most extensive atrocities against civilians. In 1999, UN Special Investigator Robert Garreton accused the rebels of running torture centers that amounted to "extermination" sites. Garreton declared: "The rebel forces must understand that they do not have any popular support and that they are seen as aggressors who have placed the people under a climate of terror."[15]

DARFUR

For half a century, Sudan was racked by a civil war that many observers have characterized as genocidal – between the Muslim Arab-dominated north (home to the capital, Khartoum) and the predominantly Christian and animist south. In recent decades, northern imposition of Arabic and *shariah*, or Islamic law, has fueled southern rebellion. The conflict exacted "a huge and terrible human toll," with possibly two million killed. Brookings Institution scholar Francis Deng characterized it in 2001 as "the worst humanitarian disaster in the world today."[16] A peace agreement was signed in 2005, but there were indications it might be unraveling in 2010, with a vote on South Sudanese independence scheduled for January 2011.

Curiously, it was a smaller-scale tragedy elsewhere in Sudan – in the remote region of Darfur, bordering Chad – that captured world attention in 2004. Darfur also provoked the most voluble debate over application of the "genocide" label since Rwanda in 1994.

For decades, sporadic conflict had flickered in Darfur between Arab pastoralists and African agriculturalists. The onset of recurring drought exacerbated tensions, pushing Arab northerners deeper into the African heartland. Feelings of marginalization, invasion, and exploitation provided a constituency for the rebellion that first erupted in June 2003, led by two rebel groups, the Sudan Liberation Army (SLA) and the Justice and Equality Movement (JEM).

Rebel attacks on Sudanese government offices, police, and military bases provoked an indiscriminately violent response from the military government in Khartoum, led by General Omar al-Bashir. Employing time-honored counterinsurgency strategies (precisely those that Khartoum had used for decades in the conflict with South Sudan), the government equipped an Arab militia, the *Janjaweed*, to mount attacks on African villages. (The name *Janjaweed* "translates roughly as 'evil men on horseback,' [and] was chosen to inspire fear.")[17] The assaults were carried out with the participation of Sudanese military forces, equipped with bombers and helicopters. The most violent of the militia leaders, Musa Hilal, wrote in August 2004 to a regional commander, "citing orders from President Bashir himself": "You are informed that directives have

Map 9A.2 Darfur and Sudan

Source: Reproduced with the permission of the Minister of Public Works and Government Services, UK.

been issued. . . to change the demography of Darfur and empty it of African tribes."[18]

The *Janjaweed* behaved much as Serb paramilitary units did in invading Bosnian Muslim or Albanian Kosovar villages (see Chapter 8). Adult male non-combatants were rounded up and murdered in gendercidal massacres.[19] African women were raped on a large scale, by assailants who called them "black slaves" and "rap[ed] them so that they [would] bear Arab children."[20] Civilian populations were dispossessed, starved, and put to flight:

> Government and Janjawiid forces destroyed everything that made life possible. Food that could be carried away was; the rest was burned. Animals that could be taken away were; the rest were killed. The simple straw buildings that served as clinics and schools were destroyed . . . and everything in them was stolen or torched. Pumps were smashed and wells polluted – often with corpses. Mosques were burned and Qurans desecrated.[21]

A US State Department report of September 2004 found that 61 percent of refugees interviewed had witnessed a member of their family killed (overwhelmingly a husband, son, or brother); 67 percent had seen others outside their family killed.[22] Up to 2,000 villages had been destroyed, damaged, and abandoned, leaving two million people uprooted and too terrified to return. With the collapse of agriculture, millions were dependent on outside food aid. As food supplies ran desperately short, "genocide by attrition" began to replace direct killing.

In the face of the systematic atrocities, a consensus emerged among many nongovernmental organizations, and some governments, that the campaign was genocidal.[23] According to the Aegis Trust in Britain, this conclusion was unavoidable. "Was the killing intentional? Yes. Was it systematically organised by the al-Bashir regime using government-armed Janjaweed militias, bombers and helicopter gunships? Yes. Were the victims chosen because of their ethnic and racial identity? Yes. This, in short, is genocide. The genocide continues."[24] Notably, in September 2004, US Secretary of State Colin Powell agreed. "We concluded – I concluded – that genocide has been committed in Darfur, and that the government of Sudan and the Janjaweed bear responsibility and that genocide may still be occurring."[25] However, as *The New York Times* pointed out, Powell's statement came "with the quick assurance that this didn't mean the United States was prepared to take any further action."[26]

"By the beginning of 2005, almost 2 million people had been driven to camps and towns inside Darfur and another 200,000 had sought refuge in Chad."[27] This, however, appears to have marked the peak of the devastation, as is considered further below. The death toll remains a subject of fierce dispute. Flint

Figure 9A.1 A young Darfuri man in a refugee camp in Chad, 2005.
Source: Courtesy Eric Markusen.

Figure 9A.2 A Darfuri woman in Oure Cassoni refugee camp, Chad, 2008.
Source: Courtesy Mia Farrow, www.miafarrow.org.

and de Waal estimated a total of 200,000 killed from all causes, the great majority in 2003-04. This was in keeping with UN estimates, at least through to April 2008, when John Holmes, the UN Under-Secretary General for Humanitarian Affairs, sparked controversy by claiming that up to 300,000 had died. The assertion was fiercely contested by the Khartoum authorities, but it also "reportedly surprised UN agencies and NGOs operating in Darfur."[28]

After the widespread accusations of genocide, an African Union peace-keeping force was deployed to Darfur. But it was just 6,700-strong in a territory as large as France, lacked a clear mandate to intervene to protect civilian lives, and was generally reduced to "watching the tragedy unfold."[29] Peace nego-tiations produced a tentative accord, the optimistically-dubbed Darfur Peace Agreement, between the government and the SLA, but it was rapidly flouted by both sides.[30] In August 2006, the UN Security Council declared its support for a "peacekeeping" force, but the Sudanese government bridled, and what emerged was instead a UN-AU hybrid, UNAMID (the UN-African Union Mission in Darfur). Originally intended to be 26,000 strong, it similarly encountered concerted resistance from the Sudanese authorities, who used every opportunity to impede and reduce its operations.[31] Nonetheless, by 2010 it had risen to 20,000 soldiers and police, and seemed to be settling in for a long-term presence.

In the first edition of this book, I suggested that as of 2005, some 10,000 people a month were dying in Darfur. This now appears inaccurate. According to the careful analysis by Julie Flint and Alex de Waal, violent deaths peaked in 2003–04. By 2006, thanks in large part to the heroic efforts of relief workers, "UN officials on the ground, in Darfur, estimated the correct figure at closer to two hundred deaths a month from violence, while mortality from hunger and disease remained comparable to pre-war levels and well below emergency thresholds."[32]

By then, though, the "Save Darfur" movement was beginning to peak, with comparisons being drawn to the Jewish Holocaust[33] and the genocide in Rwanda. For all its good intentions, Flint and de Waal accuse the movement of creating "a simplistic moral fable that portrayed the crisis as a battle between good and evil" – skating over, in large part, the role of rebel groups in fueling the violence.[34] (Three rebel leaders were indicted by the International Criminal Court in November 2008.)[35] "The conflict," wrote journalist Jennie Matthew late in 2008, "has mushroomed into a hugely complex web of violence fought between myriad groups and marred increasingly by banditry." The situation for remaining humanitarian workers, meanwhile, had "worsened considerably"; eleven aid workers were killed in 2008, and many others were assaulted or kidnapped for ransom.[36]

At the outset of 2010, a "fragile calm" had settled on Darfur. Rwandan Lt. Gen. Patrick Nyamvumba, commander of the UNAMID peacekeeping force, described the situation as "frozen" and "unpredictable."[37] Hundreds of thou-sands remained mired in refugee camps, unable to return to their homes. The ebbing of the worst violence was welcome, but with international indictments still outstanding, the evidence for Sudanese government-sponsored genocide and crimes against humanity in 2003–04 – and for a great deal of violence thereafter – remained strong. The fact that the genocide took the form of a counterinsurgency strategy, rather than a straightforward campaign of mass extermination on racial-ethnic grounds, does not preclude the "genocide" label. Rather, it places Darfur in the same category of other genocidal counterinsurgencies studied in this volume, from the Ottoman destruction of Christians (Chapter 4) to Guatemala (Box 3a) and East Timor (Box 7a).[38]

FURTHER STUDY

M.W. Daly, *Darfur's Sorrow: A History of Destruction and Genocide.* Cambridge: Cambridge University Press, 2007. Learned history, ranging from the mid-nineteenth century to (quite late in the volume) the genocide of recent years.

Julie Flint and Alex de Waal, *Darfur: A New History of a Long War.* London: Zed Books, 2008. Introduction to the Darfur conflict, by two authors with extensive experience in the region.

Amanda F. Grzyb, *The World and Darfur: International Responses to Crimes Against Humanity in Western Sudan.* Montreal: McGill-Queen's University Press, 2009. Compiles accounts and analyses by many of the leading scholars and activists of the Darfur genocide.

John Hagan and Wenona Rymond-Richmond, *Darfur and the Crime of Genocide.* Cambridge: Cambridge University Press, 2009. A criminological approach incorporating eyewitness testimonies.

Bryan Mealer, *All Things Must Fight to Live: Stories of War and Deliverance in Congo.* New York: Bloomsbury USA, 2008. Atmospheric account of Congo's collapse and conflict, by a former Associated Press correspondent.

Gérard Prunier, *Africa's World War: Congo, the Rwandan Genocide, and the Making of a Continental Catastrophe.* Oxford: Oxford University Press, 2009. Magisterial survey of the intricacies and atrocities of war and genocide in Congo. See also *Darfur: The Ambiguous Genocide.*

Christian P. Scherrer, *Genocide and Crisis in Central Africa: Conflict Roots, Mass Violence, and Regional War.* Westport, CT: Praeger Publishers, 2002. Another fine study of the politics of the African Great Lakes region.

Thomas Turner, *The Congo Wars: Conflict, Myth and Reality.* London: Zed Books, 2007. The best short introduction to the byzantine Congolese conflict.

Michela Wrong, *In the Footsteps of Mr. Kurtz: Living on the Brink of Disaster in Mobutu's Congo.* New York: Perennial, 2002. Journalistic account of life in Congo (then Zaire) under the Mobutu dictatorship.

NOTES

1 International Rescue Committee statistics cited in Amy Goodman, "DRC: The Invisible War," TruthDig.com, January 24, 2008, http://www.truthdig.com/report/item/20080123_the_invisible_war.

2 Joe Bavier, "Congo War-Driven Crisis Kills 45,000 a Month – Study," Reuters dispatch, January 22, 2007.

3 "Africa's Unmended Heart," *The Economist*, June 11, 2005. For an able and accessible overview, see Georges Nzongola-Ntalaja, *The Congo from Leopold to Kabila: A People's History* (London: Zed Books, 2003).

4 Kisangani Emizer, cited in Ola Olsson and Heather Congdon Fors, "Congo: The Prize of Predation," *Journal of Peace Research*, 41: 3 (2004), p. 325.

5 Gérard Prunier, *Africa's World War: Congo, the Rwandan Genocide, and the Making of a Continental Catastrophe* (New York: Oxford University Press, 2009), p. 333.

6 Christian P. Scherrer, *Genocide and Crisis in Central Africa: Conflict Roots, Mass Violence, and Regional War* (Westport, CT: Praeger, 2002), p. 267.

7 International Crisis Group (hereafter ICG), "How Kabila Lost His Way: The Performance of Laurent Désiré Kabila's Government," background paper, May 21, 1999. See also Jeremy M. Weinstein, "Africa's 'Scramble for Africa': Lessons of a Continental War," *World Policy Journal*, 17: 2 (Summer 2000), pp. 11–20; Thomas M. Callaghy, "Life and Death in the Congo: Understanding a Nation's Collapse," *Foreign Affairs*, 80: 5 (2001), pp. 143–49.

8 Howard W. French, "Kagame's Hidden War in the Congo," *The New York Review of Books*, September 24, 2009, http://www.nybooks.com/articles/23054. In January 2009, Rwanda suddenly turned on Nkunda and had him arrested. According to French, "the arrest took place just after the release of a UN report documenting Rwanda's close ties to the warlord, and concluding that he was being used to advance Rwanda's economic interests in Congo's eastern hinterlands. The report stated that Rwandan authorities had 'been complicit in the recruitment of soldiers, including children, have facilitated the supply of military equipment, and have sent officers and units from the Rwandan Defense Forces,' while giving Nkunda access to Rwandan bank accounts and allowing him to launch attacks on the Congolese army from Rwandan soil."

9 Rory Carroll, "Violence Threatens to Engulf Congo," *The Guardian*, November 26, 2004, http://www.guardian.co.uk/world/2004/nov/26/congo.rorycarroll. A 2008 report in the London *Times* suggested that little had changed: "It was the small hours of yesterday morning when they swept through Goma's neighbourhoods: Congolese government soldiers meant to protect the city's population, but who came instead as looters and killers. . . . Angry, drunk and in retreat, rogue gangs of soldiers who had given up the fight against the rebels stole what they could from homes and shops as panic gripped this tumbledown volcanic town on the banks of Lake Kivu. In one incident a Goma restaurant owner was shot dead, his bullet-riddled body left lying on the city centre's dusty, lava-blackened streets. At least eight other civilians were killed." Patrick Barth, "Drunk and in Retreat, Troops Unleash Wave of Death on Their Own People," *The Times*, October 31, 2008, http://www.timesonline.co.uk/tol/news/world/africa/article5051307.ece.

10 Weinstein, "Africa's 'Scramble for Africa.'"

11 Prunier, *Africa's World War*, p. 338.

12 See Lara Santoro, "False Dawn," *The New Republic*, July 3, 2000; French, "Kagame's Hidden War."

13 See Olsson and Fors, "Congo: The Prize of Predation." For an overview of the smuggling networks in Rwanda and Uganda, see Françoise Misser, "Looking for Scapegoats," *African Business*, 259 (November 2000).

14 See, e.g., Craig Timberg, "Rwanda's Tormentors Emerge from the Forest to Haunt Congo: Hutu Guerrillas Find New Victims," *The Washington Post*, February 10, 2005. Throughout the war, Rwanda exploited the 1994 genocide to justify invading its giant neighbor as and when it chose. "We know that there is an argument that the FDLR does not constitute a threat to the Rwandan government," stated Rwandan special envoy Richard Sezibera in December 2004. "Fine! But for us we start counting the dead from the 1 million plus in the 1994 genocide. In our view, even one death today caused by the FDLR is a continuation of the genocide." ICG, "Back to the Brink in Congo," *Africa Briefing*, December 17, 2004, p. 2.

15 ICG, "Africa's Seven-nation War," report, May 21, 1999, p. 18.

16 Francis M. Deng, "Sudan – Civil War and Genocide," in William L. Hewitt, *Defining the Horrific: Readings on Genocide and Holocaust in the Twentieth Century* (Upper Saddle River, NJ: Pearson, 2004), pp. 223–24.

17 Scott Straus, "Darfur and the Genocide Debate," *Foreign Affairs*, 84: 1 (2004), p. 126. According to Gérard Prunier, "Sociologically the *Janjaweed* seem to have been of six main origins: former bandits and highwaymen who had been 'in the trade' since the 1980s; demobilized soldiers from the regular army; young members of Arab tribes having a running land conflict with a neighbouring 'African' group . . . common criminals who were pardoned and released from gaol if they joined the militia; fanatical members of the Tajammu al-Arabi ['(Arab Union), a militantly racist and pan-Arabist organization which stressed the "Arab" character of the province']; and young unemployed 'Arab' men, quite similar to those who joined the rebels on the 'African' side." Gérard Prunier, *Darfur: The Ambiguous Genocide* (Ithaca, NY: Cornell University Press, 2005), pp. 45, 97–98.

18 Hilal quoted in Flint and de Waal, *Darfur*, p. 128.

19 For a compendium of reportage on gender-selective massacres and other atrocities, see Adam Jones/Gendercide Watch, "Gendercide in Darfur," http://www.gendercide.org/darfur01.htm.

20 Public International Law and Policy Group (PILPG), "Genocide in Darfur: A Legal Analysis," September 2004, http://www.africafiles.org/article.asp?ID=6727.

21 Ibid., p. 145.

22 State Department statistics cited in PILPG, "Genocide in Darfur."

23 "Organizations arguing that the massacres in Darfur fulfil the international legal definition of genocide include Physicians for Human Rights and the UK-based campaigning group Justice Africa. Human Rights Watch and the International Crisis Group have not employed the term 'genocide,' but both say Sudanese government forces and Janjawid militias are responsible for crimes against humanity, war crimes, and 'ethnic cleansing.' Amnesty International has called for the setting up of an international inquiry to examine charges of war crimes and 'allegations of genocide.'" John Ryle, "Disaster in Darfur," *The New York Review of Books*, 51: 13 (August 12, 2004), http://www.nybooks.com/articles/article-preview?article_id=17326. The UN International Commission of Inquiry on Darfur, reporting in 2005, argued that "the crucial element of genocidal intent appears to be missing, at least as far as the central government authorities are concerned," but stressed that "the crimes against humanity and war crimes that have been committed in Darfur may be *no less serious and heinous than genocide*" (quoted in Flint and de Waal, *Darfur*, p. 183, emphasis added) – a phrasing worth keeping in mind for the discussion of genocide versus crimes against humanity in Chapter 15 (pp. 538–41).

24 Aegis Trust report quoted in Anne Penketh, "Darfur: Never Again?," *The Independent*, January 26, 2005.

25 Terence Neilan, "Powell Says Sudan Abuses Qualify as Genocide," *The New York Times*, September 9, 2004.

26 Scott Anderson, "How Did Darfur Happen?," *The New York Times*, October 17, 2004.

27 Ibid.

28 Simon Tisdall, "Suffering Lost in a Numbers Game," *The Guardian*, April 29, 2008.

29 Prunier, *Darfur: The Ambiguous Genocide*, p. 145. See also Steve Bloomfield, "Darfur Peacekeepers Understaffed, Underequipped and Now Under Fire," *The Independent*, April 25, 2007, http://www.independent.co.uk/news/world/africa/darfur-peace keepers-understaffed-underequipped-and-now-under-fire-446062.html.

30 See Jonathan Steele, "It Was Meant to Bring Peace. Instead, British-brokered Deal Has Rekindled War," *The Guardian*, September 30, 2006, http://www.guardian. co.uk/world/2006/sep/30/sudan.jonathansteele.

31 Sudan was considerably aided in its obstinacy by its close economic and military relationship with China, which coveted and exploited the country's rich oil deposits to meet its spiraling domestic demand. Much of the pro-Darfur activism, particularly in the runup to the 2008 Beijing Olympics, focused on bringing pressure to bear on China to pressure, in turn, its Sudanese client – apparently with some limited success, at least in persuading China to appoint a special envoy to the territory, urge the Khartoum authorities to allow a limited UN peacekeeping presence in Darfur, and provide some 300 Chinese military engineers to the resulting UNAMID force to assist in reconstruction work. See, e.g., Jim Yardley, "China Defends Darfur Role," *The New York Times*, March 8, 2008; Edward Cody, "In China, a Display of Resolve on Darfur," *The Washington Post*, September 16, 2007; "China Appoints Envoy for Darfur," *BBC Online*, May 10, 2007; Howard LaFranchi, "Why Sudan Is Now Allowing UN Troops in Darfur," *The Christian Science Monitor*, April 18, 2007, http://www.csmonitor.com/2007/0418/p01s03-woaf.html; Helene Cooper, "Darfur Collides with Olympics, and China Yields," *The New York Times*, April 13, 2007, http://www.nytimes.com/2007/04/13/ washington/13diplo.html; Opheera McDoom, "China's Hu Tells Sudan It Must Solve Darfur Issue," Reuters dispatch, February 2, 2007, http://www.alertnet.org/ thenews/newsdesk/MCD261331.htm. However, China also wielded its veto power as a permanent member of the UN Security Council to ensure that UNAMID's mandate "would not have the power to disarm the warring factions or seize illegal weapons," and to head off any "threat of sanctions against Sudan's government." Denise Driscoll, "UN Darfur Force 'Will Be Too Weak,'" *The Sunday Telegraph*, August 5, 2007.

32 Flint and de Waal, *Darfur*, p. 190.

33 See, e.g., Nat Hentoff, "The Black Holocaust," *The Village Voice*, January 7, 2007, http://www.villagevoice.com/2007-01-02/news/the-black-holocaust/; Hentoff, "Holocaust in Plain Sight," *The Village Voice*, April 3, 2006, http://www. villagevoice.com/2006-03-28/news/holocaust-in-plain-sight/; "[George] Clooney Warns of 'Holocaust' in Sudan," ITV News, September 15, 2006.

34 Flint and de Waal, *Darfur*, p. 184. "Whereas the great majority of violent deaths in 2003–04 were due to attacks on civilians by the army and Janjawiid, from 2005 onwards most were caused by fighting among rebel groups and competition for pasture land among Arab militias – both of whom often fought with weapons supplied by the government, whose attacks continued" (p. 187). See also Edmund Sanders, "Death Rate Declines in Darfur," *The Los Angeles Times*, August 26, 2007.

On factional splits in the Darfurese rebel movements, see Steve Bloomfield, "War without End," *The Independent*, April 30, 2007, http://www.independent.co.uk/news/world/ africa/darfur-war-without-end-446777.html; Stephanie McCrummen, "Splintering of Rebel Groups Adds to Chaos in Darfur," *The Washington Post*, April 1, 2007; Edmund Sanders, "Rebels Pose a New Threat to Darfur's Displaced," *The Los Angeles Times*, March 13, 2007; Xan Rice, "Darfur's Rebel Forces Turn on Each Other," *The Guardian*, May 17, 2006, http://www.guardian.co.uk/world/2006/may/17/sudan.mainsection. In the genocide studies field, acknowledgment should be made of the work of Alan Kuperman, who, though not downplaying the atrocities of the Khartoum government in Khartoum, was and is skeptical of the one-sidedness of prevailing frameworks. See, e.g., Kuperman, "Strategic Victimhood in Sudan," *The New York Times*, May 31, 2006, http://www.nytimes.com/2006/05/31/opinion/31kuperman.html. Alex de Waal has written of "philanthropic imperialism" in the endeavor. See de Waal, "The Book Was Closed Too Soon on Peace in Darfur," *The Guardian*, September 29, 2006, http://www.guardian.co.uk/commentisfree/2006/sep/29/comment.sudan; see also Ben Wallace-Wells, "Darfuristan," *Rolling Stone*, December 24, 2009–January 7, 2010, http://www.rollingstone.com/politics/story/31343773/darfuristan.

35 Nora Boustany, "ICC Warrants Sought for 3 Sudanese Rebel Chiefs," *The Washington Post*, November 21, 2008.

36 Jennie Matthew, "Darfur Getting More Dangerous: UN Humanitarian Chief," Agence France-Presse dispatch on Yahoo! News, November 30, 2008.

37 Jeffrey Gettleman, "Fragile Calm Holds in Darfur after Years of Death," *The New York Times*, January 1, 2010, http://www.nytimes.com/2010/01/02/world/africa/02darfur.html.

38 Benjamin Valentino's emphasis on the insurgency/counterinsurgency dynamic in genocide and other collective killing is worth citing: Valentino, *Final Solutions: Mass Killing and Genocide in the 20th Century* (Ithaca, NY: Cornell University Press, 2004).

PART 3 SOCIAL SCIENCE PERSPECTIVES

CHAPTER 10

Psychological Perspectives

> Any broad historical examination of the phenomenon of genocide cannot fruitfully
> proceed without engagement with issues of collective human psychopathology.
>
> Mark Levene

Understanding genocide requires probing the minds of those who commit it, and those who seek to prevent or limit it. This is the province of psychology. Not surprisingly, many prominent scholars and analysts of genocide are psychologists and psychiatrists, including Israel Charny, Ervin Staub, Roy Baumeister, Robert Jay Lifton, and James Waller.

In approaching psychological contributions in this chapter, I will set aside one line of inquiry, focusing on the "authoritarian personality" and the mass psychology of fascism. Associated with central twentieth-century figures such as Theodor Adorno, Wilhelm Reich, and Erich Fromm, these investigations located fascism's psychological roots in childhood experiences of parental authoritarianism and repression. They also emphasized mechanisms of psychological projection, displacing onto others the violence derived from a lack of personal self-esteem (or, alternatively, hysterical narcissism), as well as various sexual neuroses. Projection strategies are considered further below, while some of the earlier Reichian attention to familial and social-psychological dynamics is paralleled in the closing discussion of genocidal perpetrators and rescuers.

NARCISSISM, GREED, FEAR, HUMILIATION

What motivates *génocidaires*? I see four psychological elements as essential: narcissism, greed, fear, and humiliation.

Narcissism

The Greek god Narcissus became so enraptured with his own reflection in a pool that he "fell in love with himself, and not being able to find consolation, he died of sorrow by the same pool."[1] The myth speaks to our propensity for hubristic self-love, a phenomenon first studied in a psychological and psychiatric context by Sigmund Freud (1856–1939). Freud described narcissism as a formative and necessary stage of ego development, but also sketched notes on a *narcissism of minor differences*. This refers, in Anton Blok's summary, to "the fact that the fiercest struggles often take place between individuals, groups and communities that differ very little – or between which the differences have greatly diminished."[2] Scholars of genocide are often struck by how groups that seem close linguistically, geographically, and/or religiously can succumb to bitter intercommunal conflict: Hutus and Tutsis, English and Irish,[3] Serbs and Croats, Catholics and Protestants. At a deeper level, Freud observed that "the communal feeling of groups requires, in order to complete it, hostility towards some

Figures 10.1 and 10.2   Malignant or pathological narcissism, generating a "cult of personality" buttressed by the intensive use of propaganda, is a regular feature of dictatorial and genocidal regimes. *Left:* Hubert Lanzinger's 1930s-era portrait of Adolf Hitler, *Der Bannerträger* (The Standard Bearer), shows the Führer as a heroic armored knight of old, reclaiming Germany's rightful place in the order of nations. *Source:* US Army Center of Military History, Washington, DC/US Holocaust Memorial Museum. *Right:* Kim Il Sung, absolute ruler of North Korea from 1948 to his death in 1994, is still depicted as a deity-like figure, as in this 2008 photo of a wall painting in the city of Wonsan. The photographer noted: "Paintings like this . . . are found in every city, town and village in the country. Major monuments aside, they are the only things that are illuminated at night[;] there are street lamps, but they are never switched on." Kim Il Sung's son, Kim Jong Il, ruled North Korea at the time of writing (March 2010; see Box 5.3 for more on the North Korean regime).

Source: Yeowatzup/Wikimedia Commons.

extraneous minority."[4] The psychological dynamic by which the "Self" and the "We" are defined against the "Other" is fundamental to genocide.[5]

Of equal significance is *malignant* or *pathological* narcissism, in which others exist only to fortify, magnify, and idolize the self.[6] Profound insecurity, anxiety, and unease often accompany this form of narcissism – a fear that without validation by others, the self will be undermined or annihilated.[7] But this seems to vanish at the extremes of malignant narcissism, where true *psychopathy* lies. This is a murderous egotism, incapable of empathy with others, that considers human destruction inconsequential if it increases personal power and glory.

Malignant narcissism and psychopathy are common among *génocidaires* in modern history. Consider Adolf Hitler, whose injured ego found transcendence in Holocaust. (How Hitler, the failed artist and rootless ex-soldier, must have reveled in the version of the Lord's Prayer devised by the League of German Girls: "Adolf Hitler, you are our great Leader. Thy name makes the enemy tremble. Thy Third Reich comes, thy will alone is law upon earth. . ."!)[8] Consider as well Joseph Stalin and Mao Zedong, "fanatics, poets, paranoiacs, peasants risen to rule empires whose history obsessed them, careless killers of millions"[9] – or Serbian ex-president Slobodan Milosevic, responsible for so much human devastation during the Balkan wars:

> US psychiatrists who have studied Milosevic closely describe him as having a "malignant narcissistic" personality. They see Milosevic as "strongly self-centered, vain, and full of self-love." He is also completely indifferent to almost anyone or anything else around him. A malignant narcissist such as Milosevic creates a core personality for himself and then shapes his own perception of the world to fit that personality. . . . Milosevic understands what is really going on, he knows that his own depictions of events that diverge from reality are lies, but at the same time he believes so strongly in his own lies that he sometimes gives the appearance of crossing the line into unreality.[10]

Collective pathological narcissism is also a factor in genocide. Shifting the analysis and diagnosis from the individual to the collective is a controversial move. But it seems appropriate when a majority or dominant minority of a nation's citizens hold that their country is innately superior, chosen by God or destiny, unique bearers of truth, or limitlessly capable. The philosopher Sam Vaknin has summarized the criteria for collective pathological narcissism:

> The group as a whole, *or members of the group* . . . feel grandiose and self-important. . . . [They are] obsessed with group fantasies of unlimited success, fame, fearsome power or omnipotence, unequalled brilliance, bodily beauty or performance, or ideal, everlasting, all-conquering ideals or political theories. . . . [They] are firmly convinced that the group is unique. . . . [They] require excessive admiration, adulation, attention and affirmation – or, failing that, wish to be feared and to be notorious. . . . [They] feel entitled. They expect unreasonable or special and favorable priority treatment. They demand automatic and full compliance with expectations. . . . They rarely accept responsibility for their actions . . . [They] are devoid of empathy. They are unable or unwilling to identify with

or acknowledge the feelings and needs of other groups. [They] are arrogant and sport haughty behaviors or attitudes coupled with rage when frustrated, contradicted, punished, limited, or confronted. . . . [All of] this often leads to anti-social behavior, cover-ups, and criminal activities on a mass scale.[11]

One of the countries of which I am a citizen, Great Britain, was probably the world leader in collective pathological narcissism during the nineteenth and early twentieth centuries. Generations of schoolchildren grew up imbibing their elders' conviction that Britain was God's gift to humankind, particularly to the darker races it was destined to rule. British culture and civilization were supreme, and British men and women were uniquely noble, brave, virtuous, and incorruptible. Traces of this mentality persist even in the post-colonial era, and can resurge with virulent passion in times of crisis, as I observed firsthand during a visit to Britain during the Falklands/ Malvinas War of 1982.[12]

In the past century, the societies that have most dramatically evinced a tendency towards collective pathological narcissism are three totalitarian states – Nazi Germany (1933–45), Stalinist Russia (1928–53), and Maoist China (1949–76) – and, since

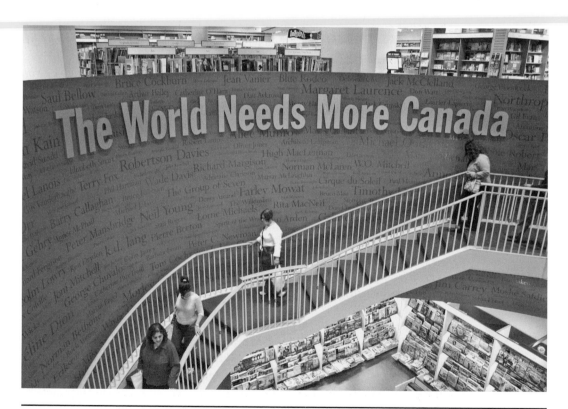

Figure 10.3   A popular Canadian slogan adorns a wall in a Toronto bookstore. Collective narcissism is the foundation of *nationalism*, which is widely recognized as a central ideological underpinning for modern genocide (see Chapter 16). It also fuels *patriotism*, generally – and dubiously – viewed as a benign and positive emotion. Nearly all states and peoples indulge in such narcissistic self-congratulation (see note 11, p. 415). At what point does it become dangerously pathological?

Source: Courtesy Gerry Chu/www.flickr.com/photos/gerrychu.

1945, a democratic one, the United States.[13] The presence of the US in this list, like its British predecessor, suggests that collective pathological narcissism is not tied to a particular political system or ideology. Psychologist Robert Jay Lifton has analyzed the contemporary US variant in his book *Superpower Syndrome*, pointing to

> a bizarre American collective mind-set that extends our very real military power into a fantasy of cosmic control, a mind-set all too readily tempted by an apocalyptic mission. The symptoms are of a piece, each consistent with the larger syndrome: unilateralism in all-important decisions, including war-making ones; the use of high technology to secure the ownership of death and history; a sense of entitlement concerning the right to identify and destroy all those considered to be terrorists or friends of terrorists, while spreading "freedom" and virtues seen as preeminently ours throughout the world; the right to decide who may possess weapons of mass destruction and who may not, and to take military action using nuclear weapons if necessary against any nation that has them or is thought to be manufacturing them; and underneath all of these symptoms, a righteous vision of ridding the world of evil and purifying it spiritually and politically.[14]

This mindset was fortified by the attacks of September 11, 2001, but it was not a product of them. Rather, distinctively American ideologies of unlimited space and power, combined with the country's unchallenged superpower status since the Second World War, generated a consensus (though very far from a universal view) that the US is destined to dominate the world and prevent any challenge to its hegemony. In past epochs, the mentality has spawned genocidal or proto-genocidal atrocities against Native Americans, Filipinos, Indochinese, and others. In more recent times, it has produced regular bouts of bellicosity and bullying internationally, with consequences that challenge conventional depictions of democratic state behavior, and are examined further in that context in Chapter 12.

Greed

"These people are like vultures swarming down, their eyes bleary, their tongues hanging out with greed, to feed upon the Jewish carcass." So wrote an appalled German businessman, observing the Nazi "Aryanization" of Jewish properties.[15] Yet few Germans shared his scruples. Most viewed the dispossession of the Jews of Germany as a once-in-a-lifetime opportunity, and made the most of it: "Looted Jewish property was a magnet which attracted millions brought up to believe in the myth of the Jewish wealth."[16] In the Nazi death camps, Jews were robbed not only of their few remaining possessions, but of their hair, which was sold for mattress stuffing – and (after death) of the gold fillings in their teeth, melted down for bullion.

In his 2005 work *Hitler's Beneficiaries*, German historian Götz Aly showed how critical was this massive apportioning of Jewish property (and goods and belongings seized from other subject populations) to the Nazis' hold on power and popular support. "The Holocaust," declared Aly, "will never be properly understood until it is seen as the most single-mindedly pursued campaign of murderous larceny in modern history." He pointed to "vast numbers of Germans [who] fell prey to the euphoria of a gold rush . . . as the state was transformed into a gigantic apparatus for plundering others" and distributing the bounty.[17] In the Nazi-occupied territories, too, "the insatiable greed for money or other spoils" was an important factor, along with "traditional hatred," in explaining the frequently enthusiastic support that Ukrainians and Poles displayed for the Nazi roundups and deportations of Jews.[18]

But the only unusual feature of the Nazi system was its extent. Greed is "an over-riding theme in human affairs,"[19] and a principal motive of genocidal perpetrators and bystanders alike. The opportunity to strip victims of their wealth and property – either by looting it outright, or purchasing it at desperation prices – and to occupy their emptied dwellings appears again and again in accounts of genocide. The Vendée genocide of the 1790s, inflicted by French revolutionaries on the people of a rebellious region (Chapter 1), "was also intended as an asset-stripping enterprise, the final recorded tally of confiscated goods [being] 46,000 farm animals, 153,000 hundred-weight of grain, 111,000 pounds of various metals, [and] a vast catalogue of other items, including fifty children's shirts."[20] As Armenians in 1915 were rounded up and massacred or driven away on death marches (Chapter 4), the US consul in Trebizond, Oscar Heizer, reported: "A crowd of Turkish women and children follow the police about like a lot of vultures and seize anything they can lay their hands on and when the more valuable things are carried out of the house by the police they rush in and take the balance. I see this performance every day with my own eyes."[21] At the height of Stalin's purges in the Soviet Union (Chapter 5), there was "frequent house-moving because every execution created a vacant apartment and dacha which were eagerly occupied by survivors and their aspirational Party housewives, ambitious for grander accommodation."[22] In Rwanda in 1994 (Chapter 9), would-be killers of Tutsis sometimes "didn't finish the job," a survivor recalled, "because they were in too much of a hurry to start looting. We could hear them getting into the cars, the vans, loading cases of Primus [beer], fighting over the furniture and everything else, rummaging under the beds for money."[23] "[We] had tasted comfort and overflowing plenty," one Hutu killer recalled. "Greed had corrupted us."[24]

Greed is more than a desire for material goods beyond those necessary for survival.[25] It is intimately connected to the existential hunger for power, domination, and prestige. "Man does not strive for power only in order to enrich himself economically," noted the sociologist Max Weber. "Power, including economic power, may be valued 'for its own sake.' Very frequently the striving for power is also conditioned by the social 'honor' it entails."[26] "Functionalist" analysts of the Jewish Holocaust emphasize the eagerness with which underlings sought to implement Hitler's grand plans, generating a dynamic that was to a considerable degree inde-pendent of direct orders.[27] Simon Sebag Montefiore noted that in Stalin's USSR, a "Terror entrepreneurialism" reigned, with a "succession of ambitious torturers who were only too willing to please and encourage Stalin by finding Enemies and killing them for him."[28] Often these individuals were designated next for execution; but there were always upwardly mobile men and women waiting to take their place.[29] The direct material rewards were considerable: "When an apartment was vacated by the arrest of its inhabitants, it was often taken over by the NKVD [secret police] officers, or divided up and occupied by other servitors of the Stalinist regime, such as office workers and chauffeurs, some of whom had no doubt been rewarded for giving information on the previous occupants."[30]

Even a brief moment in the sun may be enough to motivate *génocidaires*, as with the "street boys, rag-pickers, [and] car-washers" whom Gérard Prunier described as vengefully targeting Tutsis in Rwanda's genocide (see p. 358).[31] Greed reflects objective material circumstances, but also, like narcissism, the core strivings of ego. Greed is never satiated; but when it is fed, one feels validated, successful – even omnipotent. Perhaps the only force that can truly match it as a motivator for genocide is *fear*.

Fear

"No power so effectively robs the mind of all its powers of acting and reasoning as fear," wrote British statesman Edmund Burke.[32] To grasp the central role of fear and psychological anxiety in genocide, it is worth distinguishing between *mortal terror* and *existential dread*. Mortal terror is a largely "animal" response to a perceived threat to physical survival and integrity. Existential dread revolves around a sense of personal identity, destiny, and social place. It evokes, or threatens to evoke, feelings of shame, dishonor, and humiliation.

Mortal terror is "animal fear," perhaps in a double sense. In a form that is often hard to distinguish from simple reflex, it is common across species. We may have derived our first sense of it as humans from animals themselves – predatory ones. In her book *Blood Rites*, Barbara Ehrenreich linked phenomena as disparate as separation anxiety in infants, religious rituals including human sacrifice, and intercommunal warfare to the terrifying encounter of prehumans and primitive humans with predatory beasts. "Nothing gets our attention like the prospect of being ripped apart, sucked dry, and transformed into another creature's meal," she wrote.[33] The predator may have been the original "Other," transformed – as humans gained the upper hand over the animal kingdom – into the predatory out-group. The human "Other" in turn bounded and delineated the in-group (clan, tribe, ethnic group) where one found sustenance and support, including in collective self-defense.[34] Evolutionary psychologists – those who apply evolutionary biology to psychology – deploy such connections to argue that "human behavior is driven by a set of *universal reasoning circuits* that were *designed by natural selection* to solve *adaptive problems* faced by our *hunter-gatherer ancestors*."[35] But social psychologists – studying people in situations of group interaction – have also found that subjects "who believe others will attack them respond with more aggression than they direct against targets who do not elicit such a belief."[36]

Mortal terror attains a particular pitch of intensity in the human animal, owing to our apparently unique capacity to foresee our own extinction, beyond a context of proximate physical threat.[37] In the eyes of some scholars and philosophers, the resulting "death anxiety" is the worm in humanity's psychic apple. It is a key factor, obviously, in religious belief, which offers an escape from death to a paradisical afterlife. It is also (frequently via the religious route) central to acts of genocide. In those acts resides an element of psychological projection – a displacement of the perpetrator's own death anxiety onto a scapegoat[38] over whom one wields a

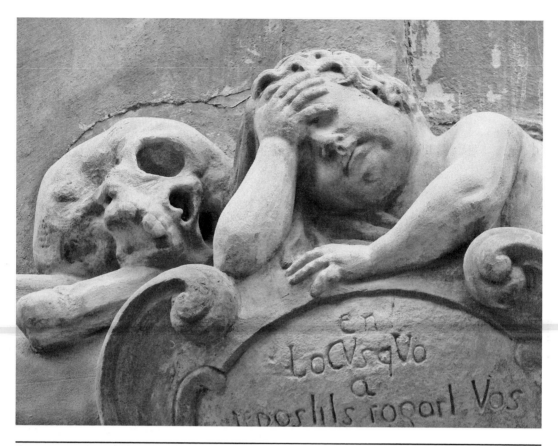

Figure 10.4 A baroque façade in Prague, Czech Republic, depicts the human apprehension of mortality and fear of inevitable death – the worm in our psychic apple. Genocidal leaders play on death anxiety to mobilize mass support for genocidal projects. They are themselves often spurred by a narcissistic desire to transcend death and quell their own anxieties through "immortal" acts of conquest, subjugation, and destruction. Yet the universal awareness of human fragility and vulnerability may also be a powerful force in generating empathy and solidarity across lines of social and cultural division.

Source: Author's photo, November 2009.

"death-defying," and death-inflicting, power. "Driven by nameless, overwhelming fears," wrote Israel Charny, "men turn to the primitive tools of self-protection, including the belief that they may spare themselves the terrible fate of death by sacrificing another instead of themselves."[39] As Ernest Becker likewise argued in what is still the most profound exploration of humans' death anxiety, *The Denial of Death*, "only scapegoats can relieve one of his own stark death fear: '*I* am threatened with death – let us kill plentifully.'" Becker pointed to the "transference" of the fear of death onto quasi-immortal leader/*Führer* figures: "the more they have, the more rubs off on us. We participate in their immortality, and so we create immortals," and buttress their pathologies and atrocities with our collective support. We are also led blindly to support "rational," technological solutions, and to fetishize scientific progress, even when it has destructive, indeed (in the nuclear age) species-threatening consequences.[40]

How has mortal terror influenced the course of genocides, both ancient and modern? Two of the central explanations offered for genocidal behaviour – *peer pressure* and *fear of contamination/pollution* – need to be considered. With regard to the former, both direct coercion and a more diffuse threat of alienation may be discerned. In numerous genocides, perpetrators who refuse to kill – or witnesses who protest the killing – are at mortal risk of sharing the fate of victims. In sentencing the Bosnian Serb soldier Drazen Erdemovic in 1998 for his participation in the mass slaughter of Bosnian Muslim men and boys at Srebrenica (Chapter 8), for example, the Trial Chamber of the International Criminal tribunal for the Former Yugoslavia found in partial mitigation of Erdemovic's crime that "the accused committed the offence in question under threat of death." "Your Honour, I had to do this," Erdemovic had told the tribunal. ". . . When I [at first] refused, they [commanding officers] told me: 'If you are sorry for them, stand up, line up with them and we will kill you too.'"[41] Erdemovic received just five years' imprisonment for his participation. Likewise, in Rwanda in 1994, many Hutus who "were outraged to see such vicious killing and burning" nonetheless refrained from interfering, according to Christine Nyiransabimana, a Tutsi survivor. "But it was quite dangerous to do more than murmur in protest, because the *interahamwe* [genocidal militia] killed – without fooling around – any Hutus having friendly dealings with their Tutsi neighbors."[42] Great Lakes specialist René Lemarchand agreed that "many Hutu were driven to kill their Tutsi neighbors because they knew they had no other option; refusal to comply meant that they themselves would be killed the next day."[43]

With regard to more diffuse forms of peer pressure, Jacques Sémelin has noted "the fear of being rejected by the group and, in a broader sense, of being ostracised by society" as critical to genocide perpetration.[44] When we consider the German "ordinary men" studied by Christopher Browning, leading perpetrators of the Nazi "Holocaust by Bullets" on the eastern front in 1941–42 (see Chapter 6), it is clear that the desire to remain part of the group (here, Police Battalion 101) was based on more than a sense of solidarity or belonging. In a context of extreme physical danger – in this case, the "barbarized" warfare evident from the first days of the Nazi–Soviet war (see p. 88) – group belonging offered the best, perhaps the only protection available. Shunning and anathematization by the group, even if it did not lead to direct execution or incarceration for refusing to participate in genocidal killing (and it did not), had tangible and possibly mortal implications. Submersion in the group, meanwhile, allowed perpetrators to diffuse the moral burden of their atrocities in actions undertaken by the collective – a standard feature of genocidal praxis, as Sémelin has also noted.[45]

The question of contamination/pollution and the quest for "purity," particularly in an age of science and pseudo-science, are similarly anchored in human perceptions of physical vulnerability and inevitable mortality. We are separated from the world and its multifaceted, often microbial threats by only a thin membrane of skin. The advent of modern biological science has produced a discourse of "viruses" and "cancers" and "bacilli" in the genocides of the past century or so. But the quest for purity through extermination of an impure Other, one who threatens the physical existence and solidaristic bonds of the perpetrator's own community, is lodged deep in the human psyche and human societies.

Mark Levene has argued that genocidal propaganda "fails to mask the underlying, essentially psychopathological nature of the anxiety" over purity and contamination. It produces one of the most prevalent features of genocidal discourse: "a theme of creeping contagion, corruption and contamination of both the individual and the social organism."[46] As usual, the Nazis' anti-semitic propaganda provides no shortage of examples, such as the propaganda poster described by Dawid Rubinowicz, a Polish Jewish diarist, in 1942: "A Jew is shown mincing meat and putting a rat into the mincer. Another is pouring water from a bucket into milk. In the third picture a Jew is shown stamping dough with his feet and worms are crawling over him and the dough."[47]

Daniel Chirot and Clark McCauley ascribed a central significance to this factor in their 2006 volume *Why Not Kill Them All?* "Fear of pollution," they wrote, "is at once the most intense, but also the psychologically most difficult cause to understand for those who do not share the sentiment that a particular group is so polluting that its very presence creates a mortal danger. . . . We cannot understand the horror of Europe's wars of religion, or of Stalin's destruction of millions, without understanding the fear of pollution." Passionate attachment to the in-group "means necessarily hate for the threatening out-group," with an abiding "fear of pollution . . . lead[ing] us to what would otherwise seem to be incomprehensible mass murder."[48]

The quest for purity also takes the form of the "cults of antiquity and agriculture" explored by historian Ben Kiernan in his 2007 study, *Blood and Soil.* "Even as they require technological dominance," Kiernan wrote, "genocide and extermination betray a preoccupation with restoring purity and order. In racial or geographical terms, this often demands eradication of foreign contamination and return to an imagined pure origin."[49] Two vivid examples are the Balkan wars and Rwandan genocide of the 1990s (see Chapters 8 and 9). Prominent among Serbs' historical memories were the genocidal atrocities inflicted upon them by the fascist Ustashe regime in Croatia during the Second World War. The revival of Ustashe-style symbolism and rhetoric by Franjo Tudjman's Croatian nationalist regime both evoked and marshaled deep anxieties, heightened when discrimination began against Serb professionals and officials within Croatia. In these varied ways "the Croats signaled the reasonableness of Serb fears," which was then "manipulated by Slobodan Milosevic, who needed the Croat issue to secure his power."[50]

The Rwandan holocaust of 1994 occurred in the aftermath of a massive (1993) blood-letting in neighboring Burundi, where between 50,000 and 100,000 civilians, overwhelmingly Hutus, were massacred by the Tutsi-dominated military following a failed coup. Some 350,000 Hutus fled to Rwanda, bringing firsthand accounts of atrocities; among these refugees were some of the most unrestrained genocidal killers of Tutsis in 1994.[51] The slaughter revived memories of an even greater killing of Hutus in 1972, when an "eliticidal" attempt was made to exterminate virtually all Hutus who had education or professional status (mainly adult males). Combined with the Tutsi-led rebel invasion of Rwanda in 1990, an "image of the Tutsi as the embodiment of a mortal danger . . . [was] hauntingly evident," according to René Lemarchand.[52] Scott Straus's study of perpetrators found "that most perpetrators participated in violence because they feared the consequences of not doing so. . . . What comes through [in interviews] . . . is a sense of acute insecurity, even panic, in the face of the president's death and the advancing Tutsi rebels."[53]

Even in the prototypical case of genocide against a completely defenseless and objectively non-threatening population – the Jewish Holocaust – mortal terror may have figured, though in heavily hystericized form. As Raul Hilberg notes, "the Germans drew a picture of an international Jewry ruling the world and plotting the destruction of Germany and German life."[54] "If we didn't defend ourselves, the Jews would exterminate us," Nazi propaganda chief Joseph Goebbels declared in March 1942. "It is a life-or-death struggle between the Aryan race and the Jewish microbe."[55] Linking Jews with bolshevism/communism created a fear-evoking dimension that was *not* purely hysterical, in the sense that Soviet Russia and Slavic civilization did pose logical threats to the German heartland.[56] (Ironically, the Jews were also depicted as *capitalist* plutocrats, plotting the subjugation, exploitation, and destruction of non-Jews everywhere. The only consistency in the portrait was thus the psychopathological hatred pervading it.)

Mortal terror contains a strong element of psychological *projection*. One justifies genocidal designs by imputing such designs to perceived opponents. The Tutsis/Croats/Jews/Bolsheviks must be killed because they harbor intentions to kill us, and will do so if they are not stopped/prevented/annihilated. Before they are killed, they are brutalized, debased, and dehumanized – turning them into something approaching "subhumans" or "animals" and, by a circular logic, justifying their extermination. A central aspect of this psychological dynamic is inflicting acts of mutilation, including on corpses. Sémelin has described this very well:

> Cruelty is truly a mental operation on the body of the other, intended to destroy his humanity. . . . And why stop once one has started? Why not continue dismembering the body, cutting off a woman's breasts, a man's penis, breaking their limbs? The vertigo of impunity hurls the executioner into a bottomless pit of cruelty. This spiral of bodily destruction can even continue after death. Although bereft of life, bodies can still resemble the living. And so they must be scalped, torn into pieces, crushed into unrecognisable objects; or, even worse, arranged in a variety of unimaginably grotesque positions, or carved up into pieces to turn them into waste material or even rubbish. In all these various acts of cutting and disemboweling it is the executioner who is protecting himself. Seen in this way, the perpetration of atrocities is the means by which perpetrators establish their own radical psychological distance from the victims, and convince themselves that these are in no way, and no longer, human beings.[57]

Projection also assists in displacing guilt and blame from genocidal perpetrators to their victims.[58] Wolfgang Sofsky noted that the Nazis designated Jews as the principal guards and hands-on oppressors of fellow Jews in the concentration camps, as well as those (the *Sonderkommandos*) who carried out much of the industrial processing of corpses in the death camps. It is "as though [the Nazi regime] wished to prove that the members of the subrace accepted any degradation and even killed one another: as though it wished to shift the burden of guilt onto the victims themselves."[59] In southwestern Rwanda, where thousands of Tutsis were reduced to hiding lice-ridden in swamps scoured by their would-be killers, a Tutsi survivor, Innocent Rwililiza, recalled: "I believe that seeing us like that, living like worthless wild things, made the

Hutus' work easier for them. Especially for those who were not consumed with a killing hatred." When caught, they were regularly exposed to torture, humiliation, and mutilative atrocity before being killed. "I feel . . . that they cut and mutilated to take humanity away from the Tutsis and kill them more easily that way," Rwililiza said.[60]

The possibility of physical/psychological displacement and dispossession is foundational to existential dread. "Desperation is a theme that runs through a great deal of ethnic violence," wrote Donald Horowitz. "A good many groups are convinced that they are or soon will be swamped, dominated, and dispossessed by their neighbors, perhaps even rendered extinct."[61] Since the physical annihilation of the individual is not impending, existential dread may appear subordinate to mortal terror. To view it as such would be a serious error. Group identity is so supreme a value that many individuals will sacrifice their lives to defend it. Likewise, people will often choose physical death over existential shame, dishonor, or loss of status and "respect" before one's peers.[62] Time-honored codes of warriorhood, masculine honor, and female virginity/sexual fidelity provide examples.

Finally, one should recognize that fear is pivotal to feelings of *humiliation*. As Chirot and McCauley wrote, this linkage is "why 'prestige' is so often important. Those who feel that their prestige has been diminished [i.e., that they have been humiliated] then feel they are vulnerable because they are seen as weak. This might embolden their enemies."[63] We turn to this phenomenon next.

Humiliation

> If I've learned one thing covering world affairs, it's this: The single most underappreciated force in international relations is humiliation.
>
> Thomas Friedman, *New York Times* columnist

What Friedman perceived in global affairs, psychologists and others have explored at the level of the individual. Humiliation is defined by Evelin Lindner as "the enforced lowering of a person or group, a process of subjugation that damages or strips away their pride, honor or dignity."[64] It is increasingly recognized as a primary motivating force in human behavior, particularly violent behavior. Lindner cited Suzanne Retzinger and Thomas Scheff's finding that "humiliated fury" plays a major role "in escalating conflict between individuals and nations."[65] Robert Jay Lifton wrote that "Humiliation involves feelings of shame and disgrace, as well as helplessness in the face of abuse at the hands of a stronger party. These are among the most painful and indelible of human emotions. He who has known extreme shame and humiliation may forever struggle to recover a sense of agency and self-respect."[66] Psychologist James Gilligan, who conducted research among hardened convicts in US prisons, went so far as to argue that "the basic psychological motive, or cause, of violent behavior is the wish to ward off or eliminate the feeling of shame and humiliation – a feeling that is painful and can even be intolerable and overwhelming – and replace it with its opposite, the feeling of pride."[67]

Humiliation thus figures prominently in the most extreme manifestations of human aggression: murder, war, genocide. Indeed, it is difficult to find a historical or contemporary case of genocide in which humiliation is not a key motivating force.[68] It suffices to consider the three best-known genocides of the twentieth century:

- In the case of the Ottoman destruction of minority Christians (Chapter 4), the Young Turk authorities in Constantinople were humiliated by military defeats in the Balkans and northern Africa (1909–13), and by the secession of imperial territories including Serbia, Bulgaria, and Albania. "Turks have awoken a national spirit, a national grudge," wrote the Turkish historian M. Cemil Bilsel. "They have infected people with a spirit that longs one day to settle accounts for the humiliation and oppression suffered by Turkdom."[69] In so doing, they were also humiliated by the presence of religious and ethnic minorities in their midst (overwhelmingly Christian) that played a prominent "middleman" role in the economy, and were supposedly assisting foreign plots against Turkey at a time of great vulnerability (the First World War). Moreover, it appears that Turkish authorities and commentators *today* would experience a sense of humiliation if they acknowledged and apologized for the Armenian and other genocides. Humiliation is thus a key underpinning of the government's campaign of genocide denial.[70]
- The Nazis rose to national prominence by exploiting national humiliation, which they translated into vengefulness and hatred against Germany's supposed tormentors. After four years of fighting in the First World War, the Germans were stunned by their army's collapse on the Western Front late in 1918. The defeated forces flooding back across the Rhine formed the core of the extreme right-wing groups that proliferated in the early 1920s – including one around Adolf Hitler, whose writings and statements blaze with anger at Germany's humiliation.[71] Outrage and humiliation greeted the imposition of the punitive Versailles Treaty in 1919, further fueling extremist and revanchist movements. Humiliation sought an outlet in scapegoating; the Nazis argued that it was the Jews who had delivered Germany a treacherous "stab in the back" to prostrate the country before the Western Allies, Bolshevism, and capitalism. As Germany moved from hyper-inflation in the 1920s to the Great Depression at decade's end, economic pressures and privation added to feelings of humiliation, especially among men whose self-image was intimately bound up with their "provider" status.[72]
- In Rwanda under Belgian colonialism, Tutsis were taught that they were descended from the "civilized" peoples of the Nile region, while Hutus were depicted as unrefined bumpkins. Tutsis were viewed (and came to view themselves) as tall, powerful, educated, attractive; Hutus as the humiliating antithesis. The 1959 revolution establishing Hutu political dominance was represented as a vanquishing of humiliation for the Hutu masses. Now Tutsis would be put "in their place." But when a Tutsi exile movement invaded from Rwanda in 1990, Hutu hegemony was threatened. The descent into economic crisis around the same time meant humiliating unemployment for hundreds of thousands of Hutus – again especially poignantly for adult men, who would be conscripted in huge numbers as agents of the genocide.

Humiliation also figures strongly in subaltern genocide, the "genocides by the oppressed" discussed in Chapter 1. There are, of course, both fantasies and realities of oppression. Nearly every *génocidaire* considers himself or herself oppressed by the target group: Turks by Christians, Germans by Jews, Hutus by Tutsis, Serbs by Kosovars, and so on. In many cases, these framings are the product of mythmaking and paranoia. In other instances, there may be a more objective character to the convictions. Hutus in Rwanda *had* experienced social subordination and humiliation at Tutsi hands. The Kosovar KLA extremists who waged a low-level campaign of persecution and – arguably – genocide against Serbs in Kosovo were motivated by years of Serb brutalization and oppression (Chapter 8). Islamist terrorism (see pp. 45–47) also carries a tinge of subaltern genocide: its exponents keenly feel the humiliation of centuries of conquest and domination by Western "Crusaders." "What America is tasting now is only a copy of what we have tasted," declaims Osama bin Laden. "Our Islamic nation has been tasting the same for more than 80 years, of humiliation and disgrace."[73] Commentators have often wondered how relatively privileged Arabs – even those directly exposed to and benefiting from the prosperity and cosmopolitanism of the West – can come to plan and perpetrate terrorist attacks that may include genocidal massacres. Humiliation is key to understanding this phenomenon; the educated and privileged may feel it even more powerfully than the masses.[74]

Finally, humiliation mingled with fear is central to an understanding of a commonly noted phenomenon in genocide: the use of dispossessed minorities and rootless refugees as perpetrators of mass atrocities. In considering imperialism and colonialism in Chapter 2, we cited Mark Levene's insight that the Scottish and Irish populations exposed to genocidal or proto-genocidal atrocities at English hands often supplied the vanguard of genocides against indigenous peoples in the Americas and Australia. "Brutalised by their previous experience, still looked down upon by their Anglo 'betters' as little more than savages themselves – the 'Scum of the Earth' and 'Refuse of Mankind,' not to say 'like the Goths and Vandals of old' – it was perhaps not that surprising that some of their number became serious native exterminators in their own right."[75] Other examples include the uprooted Balkan Muslims of the Ottoman Empire, who were readily turned against Christian populations during World War One; and the Burundian Hutus who fled Tutsi-sponsored terror in their homeland, took refuge in neighboring Rwanda, and are considered by some to have been especially eager tormentors of Tutsis during the 1994 genocide (see note 51).[76]

THE PSYCHOLOGY OF PERPETRATORS

> From our findings, we must conclude not only that such personalities are not unique or insane, but also that they could be duplicated in any country of the world today.
>
> Douglas Kelley, investigating psychiatrist at the
> Nuremberg Tribunal for Nazi war criminals

> Q. How do you shoot babies?
> A. I don't know. It's just one of those things.
>
> Paul Meadlo, US soldier who participated in the genocidal massacre
> of hundreds of Vietnamese civilians at My Lai (see pp. 75–76,
> Box 10.2 below), interviewed by Mike Wallace of CBS

In 1992, Christopher Browning published his groundbreaking book *Ordinary Men*, about a battalion of German police reservists and conscripts – mostly middle-aged men too old for active military service – who functioned as a killing squad on the eastern front in 1941–42. "The men of Reserve Police Battalion 101 were the unlikeliest of mass murderers. They did not represent special selection or even random selection. . . . They were simply ordinary people who went about completing the murderous tasks assigned them with considerable indifference."[77] As Daniel Goldhagen demonstrated in *Hitler's Willing Executioners*, these tasks included corraling and executing Jews and "saboteurs," including children and women, with rifle shots to the back of the head. Often the men emerged spattered with blood and brain matter. The sheer gruesomeness of their task led some to accept their commanding officer's offer to absent themselves from the slaughter without penalty. But surprisingly few bowed out: Browning estimates that 80 to 90 percent of the battalion eventually participated in close-up mass killings of Jews. Others felt queasy at the outset, but accustomed themselves to the killing, even coming to enjoy it. Some initially excused themselves, then returned. Most numbed themselves with intoxicants – a typical tactic of *génocidaires*, since alcohol and drugs "have the advantage of suppressing the individual's inhibitions and immersing him in an artificial state of well-being or even euphoria that helps him function in the blood and death-stained environment in which he is operating."[78]

How to explain this routinized participation in acts of unimaginable horror? Although criticized by Goldhagen for downplaying the role of Jew-hatred in the murders, Browning *did* acknowledge that the "deluge of racist and anti-Semitic propaganda" played a key role.[79] But he placed additional emphasis on "the mutually intensifying effects of war and racism"; obedience to authority; peer pressure and the "threat of isolation" from the group (with possibly mortal consequences in wartime); machismo; and feelings of obligation, duty, and honor.

Among the research that Browning cited to support his thesis was the twentieth century's most famous series of psychological studies, conducted by Stanley Milgram at Yale University beginning in the early 1960s, and known as "the Milgram experiments."[80] The basic design was elegantly simple, yet open to complex variations. A mild-mannered and agreeable middle-aged man, an accountant by profession, was trained to serve as the "learner" of the experiments (Figure 10.5). He was placed on one side of a wall, and a designated subject (the "teacher") was seated on the other, in front of a generator supposedly capable of administering shocks of increasing voltage to the learner. "The generator had thirty different switches running in fifteen-volt increments from 15 to 450 volts," wrote James Waller. "The higher levels of shock were labeled in big letters as 'Intense Shock,' 'Extreme Intensity Shock,' 'Danger: Severe Shock,' and, ominously, 'XXX.'" To give the subject a taste of the treatment supposedly to be meted out to the learner, he or she was administered a shock of 45 volts – "a level strong enough to be distinctly unpleasant." As the subject asked questions of the learner, incorrect answers were met with commands from a white-coated authority figure (the "experimenter") for the subject to administer "shocks" of ever-greater intensity to the learner. "At 300 volts, the learner vigorously pounded on the laboratory walls in protest. . . . The learner's pounding was repeated after 315 volts. Afterward, he was not heard from again," but the subject was instructed to disregard this, and to continue to turn the dial.[81]

Figure 10.5   The core of the Milgram experiments: an authority figure (the experimenter, top right) commands a subject to administer supposed shocks when a learner answers a question incorrectly. The subject is instructed to increase the voltage as the actor conveys first pain, then ominous silence. How far will an ordinary person turn the dial?

Source: Stanley Milgram, *Obedience to Authority* (New York: Random House, 1995).

The greatest shock of all was the experiment's results, which have echoed through the disciplines of psychology and sociology ever since. An absolute majority of subjects – twenty-six out of forty – "*obeyed the orders of the experimenter to the end, proceeding to punish the victim until they reached the most potent shock available on the generator.*"[82] Sometimes they did so stoically and dispassionately: the face of one subject is described as "hard, impassive . . . showing total indifference as he subdues the screaming learner and gives him shocks. He seems to derive no pleasure from the act itself, only quiet satisfaction at doing his job properly."[83] Most subjects, however, displayed tension, stress, concern, confusion, shame. When the experimental design was altered to make the learner dimly visible, some subjects sought to avoid the consequences of their actions by "avert[ing] their eyes from the person they were shocking, often turning their heads in an awkward and conspicuous manner."[84] But the experimenter assured them that he took full responsibility for the subject's actions. Moreover, the subject was told that he or she had "no other choice"; his or her continued participation was "essential." Despite clear misgivings, as noted above, the majority of subjects not only administered the "shocks" but stayed the course to the end.[85] A fair number projected their own stress and shame on to the learner, blaming him "for having volunteered for the experiment, and more viciously, for his stupidity and obstinacy." Interestingly, the obedience displayed by women "was virtually identical to the performance of men," though "the level of conflict experienced by the women was on the whole higher than that felt by our male [subjects]."[86]

Variations on the core experiment helped Milgram to zero in on some of the factors affecting obedience. Subjects placed in greater physical proximity to the learner, even touching him, were less likely to proceed than those more remotely positioned: "the changing set of spatial relations leads to a potentially shifting set of alliances over the several experimental conditions." Christopher Browning noted that "when not under the direct surveillance of the scientist, many of the subjects 'cheated' by giving lower shocks than prescribed."[87] When an ordinary-seeming person was substituted for the white-coated experimenter, "only a third as many [subjects] followed the common man as followed the experimenter." Furthermore, when other "subjects" were added and secretly instructed to rebel against the authority figure, "the effects of [such] peer rebellion [were] very impressive in undercutting the experimenter's authority." This led Milgram to conclude that "the mutual support provided by men for each other is the strongest bulwark we have against the excesses of authority." In a point relevant to our discussion of gender and genocide (Chapter 13), Milgram noted that selecting an adult male for the "learner" role probably affected the outcome. "As victims, [women] would most likely generate more disobedience, for cultural norms militate against hurting women even more strongly than hurting men. . . . Similarly, if a child were placed in the victim's role, disobedience would be much greater."[88]

Milgram summarized his results, which have been confirmed by dozens of subsequent studies:[89]

> What is surprising is how far ordinary individuals will go in complying with the experimenter's instructions. . . . It is the extreme willingness of adults to go to almost any lengths on the command of an authority that constitutes the chief finding of the study and the fact most urgently demanding explanation. . . . Ordinary people, simply doing their jobs, and without any particular hostility on their part, can become agents in a terrible destructive process. Moreover, even when the destructive effects of their work become patently clear, and they are asked to carry out actions incompatible with fundamental standards of morality, relatively few people have the resources needed to resist authority.[90]

Milgram emphasized that "every sign of tension" among the subjects was "evidence of the failure of authority to transform the [subject] to an unalloyed state of agency."[91] There was at least a latent capacity and desire to resist. In this context, it is worth examining the comportment of the minority of subjects who refused to "shock" the learner. One was a professor of Old Testament studies, who may have drawn on his religious convictions:

EXPERIMENTER: It's absolutely essential to the experiment that we continue.

SUBJECT: I understand that statement, but I don't understand why the experiment is placed above this person's life.

EXPERIMENTER: There is no permanent tissue damage.

SUBJECT: Well, that's your opinion. If he [the learner] doesn't want to continue, I'm taking orders from him.

EXPERIMENTER: You have no other choice, sir, you must go on.

SUBJECT: If this were Russia maybe, but not in America.[92]

Another subject, an industrial engineer, grew "incredulous and indignant" when ordered to continue administering the shocks:

EXPERIMENTER: You have no other choice.

MR. RENSALEER: I *do* have a choice. . . . Why don't I have a choice? I came here on my own free will. I thought I could help in a research project. But if I have to hurt somebody to do that, or if I was in his place, too, I wouldn't stay there. I can't continue. I'm very sorry. I think I've gone too far already, probably.[93]

To anticipate our discussion of the psychology of "rescuers," below, the resisters demonstrated a high degree of empathy for the learner – and of ego independence, symbolized by their refusal to submit blindly to an authority figure.[94] But they were, to repeat, a minority. Milgram voiced his expectation that outside of the laboratory environment – and especially in conditions of dictatorship or totalitarianism – they would be fewer still.

In his account of the experiments, Milgram moved beyond psychology to the sociology of modernity and bureaucratic complexity, which granted individuals a large measure of physical and psychological distance from the consequences of their actions. It is not surprising, therefore, to find the sociologist Zygmunt Bauman drawing on Milgram's work to support his contention that "the process of rationalization facilitates behaviour that is inhuman and cruel."[95] This theme is explored further in the discussion in Chapter 11 of sociological perspectives on genocide.

The Stanford prison experiments

Other insights into the psychology of genocide and group violence may be drawn from a second classic set of experiments, conducted by a Stanford University team under the social psychologist Philip Zimbardo in 1971. These were described in detail in Zimbardo's 2008 book, *The Lucifer Effect*.

"The rationale is this," Zimbardo told his team of researchers:

. . . Our research will attempt to differentiate between what people bring into a prison situation from what the situation brings out in the people who are there. By preselection, our subjects are generally representative of middle-class, educated youth. They are a homogeneous group of students who are quite similar to each other in many ways. By randomly assigning them to the two different roles, we begin with "guards" and "prisoners" who are comparable – indeed, are

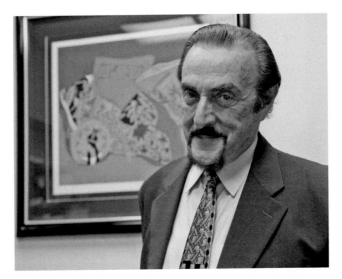

Figure 10.6 Dr. Philip Zimbardo, creator of the Stanford University prison experiments in 1971, went on to serve as an expert witness in the trials of US soldiers accused of abuses at the Abu Ghraib prison west of Baghdad, Iraq. In both instances, Zimbardo argued, the authoritarian environment of the prison (whether real or experimental) produced aberrant and abusive behavior by otherwise ordinary individuals. He is shown here on the Stanford campus in March 2007.

Source: Shams Shaikh.

interchangeable. The prisoners are not more violent, hostile, or rebellious than the guards, and the guards aren't more power-seeking authoritarians. At this moment "prisoner" and "guard" are one and alike. . . . In two weeks, will these youngsters still be so indistinguishable? Will their roles change their personalities? Will we see any transformations of their character?[96]

Zygmunt Bauman summarized the course and consequences of the experiment as follows:

In Zimbardo's experiment (planned for a fortnight, but stopped after one week for fear of irreparable damage to the body and mind of the subjects) volunteers had been divided at random into prisoners and prison guards. Both sides were given the symbolic trappings of their position. Prisoners, for example, wore tight caps which simulated shaven heads, and gowns which made them appear ridiculous. Their guards were put in uniforms and given dark glasses which hid their eyes from being looked into by the prisoners. No side was allowed to address the other by name; strict impersonality was the rule. There was [a] long list of petty regulations invariably humiliating for the prisoners and stripping them of human dignity. This was the starting point. What followed surpassed and left far behind the designers' ingenuity. The initiative of the guards (randomly selected males of college age, carefully screened against any sign of abnormality) knew no bounds. . . . The construed superiority of the guards rebounded in the submissiveness of the prisoners, which in its turn tempted the guards into further displays of their powers, which were then duly reflected in more self-humiliation on the part of the prisoners. . . . The guards forced the prisoners to chant filthy songs, to defecate in buckets which they did not allow them to empty, to clean toilets with bare hands; the more they did it, the more they acted as if they were convinced of the non-human nature of the prisoners, and the less they felt constrained in inventing and administering measures of an ever-more appalling degree of inhumanity.[97]

Bauman slightly overstates the case. In fact, the guards divided into three factions, with about one-third assuming "cruel, callous, sadistic, dominating, authoritarian, tyrannical, coercive, and aggressive roles." James Waller described a middle group as "tough but fair," while a final segment "emerged as 'good guards' and tried to help the prisoners when they could."[98] Christopher Browning pointed out that the behavior of Zimbardo's guards was strikingly similar to that of the "ordinary men" he studied for his eponymous book – from the "nucleus of increasingly enthusiastic killers who volunteered," through those who "performed . . . when assigned but who did not seek opportunities to kill," through "a small group (less than 20 percent) of refusers and evaders."[99] However, it must be remembered that Zimbardo's experiment was terminated after only a few days; it is impossible to say how many of the "tough but fair" group and the hold-outs would eventually have behaved sadistically, had it continued.

To the public, Zimbardo's results were as shocking as Milgram's. They depicted "the sudden transmogrification of likeable and decent American boys into near monsters of the kind allegedly to be found only in places like Auschwitz or Treblinka."[100] Contemporary readers are likely to think of the American men and women who abused inmates at Abu Ghraib prison near Baghdad, along with many other sites in occupied Iraq and at the US-run prison at Guantánamo Bay, Cuba. Indeed, in the wake of the Abu Ghraib revelations, many commentators cited the Zimbardo experiments as evidence that (in the words of criminologist David Wilson) "if you give a person power over someone who is powerless, someone who has been demonised or made to seem less human, then that absolute power corrupts absolutely."[101] Zimbardo himself offered expert counsel to the defense in one of the trials of Abu Ghraib perpetrators.

Viewing the lessons of the Stanford experiment from a quarter-century's perspective, Zimbardo wrote that it showed how

> within certain powerful social settings, human nature can be transformed in ways as dramatic as the chemical transformation in Robert Louis Stevenson's captivating fable of Dr. Jekyll and Mr. Hyde. . . . Good people can be induced, seduced, and initiated into behaving in evil ways. They can also be led to act in irrational, stupid, self-destructive, antisocial, and mindless ways when they are immersed in "total situations" that impact human nature in ways that challenge our sense of the stability and consistency of individual personality, of character, and of morality. . . . The [experiment] is a clarion call to abandon simplistic notions of the Good Self dominating Bad Situations. We are best able to avoid, prevent, challenge, and change such negative situational forces only by recognizing their potential power to "infect us," as it has others who were similarly situated.[102]

THE PSYCHOLOGY OF RESCUERS

> If you can do some good, why hesitate?
>
> John Rabe, German genocide rescuer during the
> "Rape of Nanjing" in 1937–38

Somehow, though, even in the darkest hour, a "Good Self" does seem able to trump Zimbardo's "Bad Situations" – or at least put in a regular enough appearance to be of real interest. The historical record is replete with accounts of brutal perpetrators, and bystanders whose "neutrality . . . helps the stronger party in an unequal struggle."[103] But it is also filled with testimonials to the brave individuals who interceded to save total strangers (as well as friends and acquaintances) from genocide.

The most famous of these figures are associated with the Jewish Holocaust, in part because that campaign of mass murder is better known and documented than all the others put together. Many readers will be familiar with the extraordinary collective opposition mounted by the people of Nazi-occupied Denmark, which, it should be conceded, had been "awarded a degree of autonomy that was unusual for a region under German occupation." In 1943, Nazi officials encountered "a local population unanimous in its resolve" to preserve Danish Jews from round-up and extermination. Virtually the entire Jewish population, several thousand strong, was successfully transferred by the operators of small boats to safety in neutral Sweden. According to Raul Hilberg, "help came from every quarter. The Danish police shielded the operators by warning them of danger, individuals helped to sell Jewish belongings, taxi drivers transported the Jews to the ports, house and apartment owners offered the victims shelter, Pastor Krohn [an advocate for the Jews] handed out blank baptismal certificates, druggists supplied free stimulants to keep people awake, and so on." It was, wrote Hilberg, "one of the most remarkable rescue operations in history."[104]

Among individual rescuers of Jews, at least before the release of Steven Spielberg's film *Schindler's List* – about the exploits of a German industrialist who saved hundreds of Jews from the gas chambers of Auschwitz-Birkenau – the most renowned was probably a Swedish representative in Budapest, Raoul Wallenberg (see p. 410):

> In 1944 the United States belatedly established the War Refugee Board (WRB) to aid and rescue the victims of Nazism. Fearing the imminent deportation of Hungarian Jewry, the WRB solicited the help of a number of neutral countries to protect this endangered community. Sweden embraced the American proposal and appointed Wallenberg as a special envoy to Hungary whose sole mission was to avert the deportation of Jews. Taking advantage of his diplomatic immunity and money contributed by private organizations like the American Jewish Joint Distribution Committee, Wallenberg issued bogus Swedish "protective passports," rented apartment buildings to serve as Jewish sanctuaries under Swedish protection, and personally whisked hundreds of Hungarian Jews off German transports on the pretext that they were wards of Sweden. Wallenberg's example inspired other neutral embassies and the International Red Cross office in Budapest to protect Jews too. According to some estimates, the rescue campaign launched by Wallenberg may have saved as many as 100,000 Jews.[105]

In the grimmest of ironies, Wallenberg the rescuer survived the Nazis, only to disappear into the custody of Soviet forces occupying Hungary. For reasons unknown, he appears to have spent years in detention before finally dying in the camps sometime in the 1950s.[106]

Equally striking is the story of Chiune Sugihara (Figure 10.9), the Japanese consul in Lithuania, who received a flood of Jews fleeing the Nazi-Soviet invasion of Poland in 1939. Sugihara

> willingly issued them transit visas by considerably stretching his own government's official rules, allowing the Polish Jews to cross Soviet territory en route to Japan and, from there, to anywhere they wished. Before the Japanese government reassigned him, Sugihara issued some 4,500 visas, many of them handwritten, and he did not stop issuing visas until literally the moment before his train carried him out. . . . His visas were also easy to counterfeit. Combined with those forgeries, Sugihara's efforts may well have saved some 10,000 Jews.[107]

"I cannot allow these people to die, people who had come to me for help with death staring them in the eyes" – so Sugihara recollected his feelings later. "Whatever punishment may be imposed upon me, I know I should follow my conscience."[108] Famous rescuers such as these took advantage of (and often risked) their professional positions to undertake their missions; but, of course, millions of people in the twentieth century alone utilized their occupational and bureaucratic positions to kill rather than save. What distinguishes individuals who choose to shelter and assist those at mortal risk of genocide, often at mortal risk to themselves?

In many cases, religious motivations played an important role. At its best and most humane, religion embodies universal values of compassion and mercy (see Chapter 16). Thus we find the Catholic cleric, Dompropst Bernard Lichtenberg of Berlin, rejecting the passivity and anti-semitism of the church hierarchy, and daring "to pray publicly for all Jews, baptized [as Christians] or not." When his efforts failed to save Jews from transportation to the death camps, he "*demanded that he be allowed to join [them] on their journey to the East.*" He was imprisoned, and picked up by the Gestapo upon his release; he died *en route* to Dachau.[109] Less demonstrative but no less religiously imbued were the actions of the "kind and gentle" Muslim notable recalled by a survivor of the Armenian genocide, who found refuge in his home:

> The bey followed Islamic law to the letter and was a devout believer. He prayed five times a day and fasted one month out of the year. I used to join him in these [observances]. He had also made a pilgrimage to Mecca and was thus called "Haji." He was a principled and just man. He felt genuine sorrow for the Armenian massacre and considered it a sin to bring any confiscated Armenian possessions into his home. He used to condemn the Turkish government, saying, "The Armenians are a hardy, intelligent, and industrious people. If there are any guilty among them, the government can arrest and punish them instead of slaughtering a helpless and innocent people."[110]

However, it is also the case that "more intense religiosity is frequently associated with greater prejudice" (Chapter 16);[111] and in any case, religious belief is by no means necessary to rescuers. Often it matters only that someone be "so overcome by the human tragedy of the genocide" that she or he feels impelled to intercede. During the Rwanda catastrophe of 1994, Paul Rusesabagina, Hutu proprietor of the Hotel

Mille Collines in Kigali, saved nearly 1,300 refugees – mostly Tutsi, as was his wife – from slaughter by Hutu militias, preserving them for the full two-and-a-half months of the genocide. Rusesabagina "rationed water from the swimming pool, had checkpoints removed, bribed killers with money and Scotch whisky and kept a secret telephone line open to the outside world." "I wanted to keep my people, the refugees, safe," he told a suddenly interested world. "That was my main objective and I tried to keep that up to the end . . . I rather take myself as someone who did his duties and responsibilities, someone who remained until the end when others changed completely their professions, and most of them became killers and others were killed."[112] (The 2004 film of Rusesabagina's exploits, *Hotel Rwanda*, brought international attention to this rescuer; see pp. 404–05, 410.)

BOX 10.1 "GOODNESS HAPPENED THERE": THE STORY OF LE CHAMBON

One of the most remarkable stories of Holocaust rescue centers on the village of Le Chambon-sur-Lignon in the isolated, mountainous region of Haute-Loire in southern France. In an overwhelmingly Catholic country, the villagers of Le Chambon were Protestant Huguenots, who elsewhere in France were mercilessly – Raphael Lemkin thought genocidally[113] – persecuted under the French *ancien régime*. While fighting raged beyond their region, the villagers of Le Chambon, wrote Philip Hallie, "fought no bloody battles with dragoons, but instead used the devices peculiar to mountain people: silence, cunning, and secrecy."[114] They concealed their faith, held services in the surrounding forests – and endured until the French Revolution declared religious freedom for all.

The heritage would stand the villagers of Le Chambon in good stead when, in the bitter winter of 1940–41, their village priest, Pastor André Trocmé, met with representatives of the American Friends Service Committee – the Quakers – in Marseilles. This religious organization had a reputation for indefatigable relief work in crisis situations – they were active in the "underground railroad" that transported escaped slaves from the US South to safety in Canada, and kept one-and-a-half million German children alive during the genocidal Allied blockade and famine after World War One. The Quakers told him they were looking for a French community that would give shelter and succor to refugees from fascism, especially the Jewish children of parents incarcerated by the Nazis' Vichy collaborators.[115] Was Le Chambon willing to assume this mortally dangerous role?

Trocmé promptly agreed – as his Quaker interlocutor put it simply, he was someone who "cared intensely for persons."[116] Shortly thereafter, the first of what would eventually number *thousands* of refugees – between 2,500 and 5,000 in all – arrived in the village. Pastor Trocmé and his wife, Magda (p. 409) arranged for their shelter with villagers. When Philip Hallie asked Magda, who was not herself religious, "why she found it necessary to let those refugees into her house, dragging after them all those dangers and problems," she responded as many genocide rescuers have: "Look. Look. Who else would have taken care of them if we didn't? They needed our help, and they needed it *then*. . . . I do not hunt around to find people to help. But I never close my door, never refuse to help somebody who comes to me and asks for something. This I think is my kind of religion. . . . When people come to my door, I feel responsible."

Moreover, Magda said, "I get pleasure from doing such things – yes, pleasure, the way some people get pleasure from the movies. It amuses me to help somebody, no matter what the cost." As for the Chambonnais villagers with whom the refugees were lodged for months or even years, Magda declared cheekily: "You know? Saving refugees was a *hobby* for the people of Le Chambon." [117] It was certainly an avocation, since as Hallie reports, "no Chambonnais ever turned away a refugee, and no Chambonnais ever denounced or betrayed a refugee." [118] Somehow their spirit tamed the Vichy and even the Nazi authorities dispatched to investigate reports that Le Chambon was "teeming with Jews." The Vichy official, according to Winton Higgins, "sat in his hotel room and wrote careful reports back to his superiors, assuring them that there were no Jews present at all," while the German official who replaced him when the Nazis occupied the remainder of France in 1942 "also found it prudent to pretend that Le Chambon's large and visible Jewish population didn't exist. . . . Throughout, the authorities realized there was little to be gained by trying to intimidate the fearless, stiff-necked Chambonnais, so they wisely desisted." [119]

The Nobel Prize-winning French writer, Albert Camus, lived for a year in Le Chambon in 1942, and wrote his masterpiece *The Plague* there. [120] The novel's central character, Doctor Rieux, "asserts the starkness and indivisibility of truth as the only basis for responsible action. The point," wrote Higgins, "encapsulates something essential to Le Chambon's response to its 'guests' and their predicament," as the villagers confronted their own pestilence – genocide. [121]

Some 75,000 French Jews were deported and murdered by the Nazis, but *every single refugee* sheltered by the Chambonnais, Jewish or otherwise, survived. After the liberation of France and the Nazi defeat, André Trocmé traveled the world, lecturing on non-violence. He died in 1971, and Magda in 1996, aged 94. [122] With Hallie's book, *Lest Innocent Blood Be Shed*, first published in 1979, the story of the Chambonnais became widely known. It is also the subject of a documentary film by one of the children born in Le Chambon, Pierre Sauvage, *Weapons of the Spirit* (1989).

On April 23, 2009 – Holocaust Remembrance Day – US president Barack Obama paid tribute to the villagers of Le Chambon-sur-Lignon:

> We also remember the number 5,000 – the number of Jews rescued by the villagers of Le Chambon, France – one life saved for each of its 5,000 residents.

Not a single Jew who came there was turned away, or turned in. But it was not until decades later that the villagers spoke of what they had done – and even then, only reluctantly. The author of a book on the rescue found that those he interviewed were baffled by his interest. "How could you call us 'good'?" they said. "We were doing what had to be done."

That is the question of the righteous – those who would do extraordinary good at extraordinary risk not for affirmation or acclaim or to advance their own interests, but because it is what must be done. They remind us that no one is born a savior or a murderer – these are choices we each have the power to make. They teach us that no one can make us into bystanders without our consent, and that we are never truly alone – that if we have the courage to heed that "still, small voice" within us, we can form a minyan[123] for righteousness that can span a village, even a nation.[124]

BOX 10.2 "KEEP YOUR PEOPLE IN PLACE. MY GUNS ARE ON YOU": HUGH THOMPSON, JR. AND THE MY LAI MASSACRE

The *Einsatzgruppen*-style massacre of hundreds of defenseless civilians at My Lai (see Chapter 2, pp. 75–76) produced no shortage of villains. But it also gave rise to a truly heroic act of genocide rescue.

Hugh Thompson, Jr. (see p. 410), was a 25-year-old helicopter pilot flying an observation craft on the morning of the slaughter. With him on the morning of March 16, 1968 were crew chief Glenn Andreotta and door gunner Lawrence Colburn, who was just 18 at the time.

Flying over My Lai hamlet, Thompson noted a number of corpses on the ground, including of some people he had previously seen lying injured. At a dike outside My Lai village, Thompson found a wounded young woman, and marked the spot with smoke, indicating that medical attention was urgently required. He took off again and hovered close to the ground, watching as a US infantry captain approached the wounded woman, "prodded her with his foot, and then killed her. Those in the helicopter could hardly believe what they were seeing."[125]

Hovering above the irrigation ditch depicted on p. 76, Thompson and his crew saw that it was filled with dead and wounded civilians. He landed again, exited the helicopter, and confronted a US sergeant. How could they help the civilians? he asked the sergeant. By putting them out of their misery, the sergeant responded. Another officer approached – Lt. William Calley, who would be the only killer convicted (and later pardoned) for the My Lai massacre. Calley told Thompson to mind his own business.

Lifting off again, Thompson witnessed the sergeant he had just conversed with shooting at the wounded in the ditch. That was the point at which he "snapped." Seeing a group of around ten Vietnamese fleeing toward a shelter, pursued by US soldiers, Thompson landed, interposing his helicopter between the troops and the panicked civilians. Turning to Colburn, he instructed him to train his machine gun on the US forces. If they fired at the villagers, Colburn should "Open up on 'em – blow 'em away." "They were the enemy then, I guess," he would recall years afterward.[126] "I could not live with myself unless I took some action to save the innocent."[127]

Exiting the helicopter, Thompson, armed only with a holstered handgun, demanded that the soldiers help him evacuate the civilians from their shelter. ". . . A lieutenant countered that they would be taken out with grenades. Refusing to back down, Thompson replied, 'I can do better than that. Keep your people in place. My guns are on you.' He then ordered two other helicopters to fly in for medical evacuation of the eleven wounded Vietnamese."[128]

Returning to the irrigation ditch, he found "a horrendous sight . . . Bodies were scattered along the edges of the ditch. There was blood, filth, and stench everywhere." "What do you call it when you march 100 or 200 people down in a ditch and line up on the side with machines [machine-guns] and start firing into it?" Thompson asked later. "Reminds me of another story that happened in World War Two, like the Nazis."[129] He pulled a small child, alive and miraculously unscratched, from the ditch. Weeping, he flew his craft back to Quang Ngai, the nearest city, and deposited the child at a hospital. Then, furious, he reported the massacre to his immediate superiors. This was the point at which instructions went out to the soldiers of Charlie Company to "stop the killing." The massacre ceased, and the massacre cover-up began. It would last for more than a year-and-a-half, until details of the slaughter broke in the US press, sparking a national scandal.

After the veil of silence was lifted, Thompson was awarded the Distinguished Flying Cross for supposedly having "greatly enhanced Vietnamese–American relations in the operational area." "Thompson later threw the decoration away,"[130] though in 1998 he accepted the Soldier's Medal for his heroism. His reporting of the massacre, and later his testimony to the investigative commission, drew the wrath of many in the United States who viewed him as a traitor to the military. "I'd received death threats over the phone. . . . It was scary. Dead animals on your porch, mutilated animals on your porch some mornings when you get up." But he felt he could not have behaved otherwise. "I saved the people because I wasn't taught to murder and kill. I can't answer for the people who took part in it," Thompson said. "I apologize for the ones that did. I just wished we could have helped more people that day."[131]

In 1998, on the massacre's thirtieth anniversary, he and Colburn revisited the scene of the massacre. In intensely moving encounters captured by a *60 Minutes* camera crew, they were reunited with two of the villagers they had rescued from the carnage. Hugh Thompson, Jr. died of cancer in January 2006, aged 62.

BOX 10.3   A HEROES' GALLERY

Figures 10.7–10.17   Some famous genocide rescuers and resisters. From top left: (1) Dominican friar **Bartolomé de las Casas**, "protector of the Indians" from Spanish depredations in the Americas (see Chapter 3). *Source*:   Wikimedia Commons. (2) Detail of Haitian banknote commemorating **Toussaint Louverture**, leader of the only successful slave rebellion in history, against one of the most genocidal slavery regimes ever devised. But did his subordinates and successors also commit genocidal atrocities against whites? See the discussion of "subaltern genocide" in Chapter 1. *Source*: Wikimedia Commons. (3) **Chiune Sugihara**, Japanese consul in Vilnius, Lithuania, who defied higher-ups to issue Japanese visas to thousands of Jews in 1941, enabling them to flee the advancing Nazis. *Source*: Wikimedia Commons. (4) The German businessman **John Rabe** (with glasses), alongside other organizers of the "International Safety Zone" in Nanjing, which saved thousands of Chinese from the depredations of the Japanese invaders in 1937–38 (see Chapter 2). *Source*: Forster Papers, Special Collections, Yale Divinity School Library. (5) **Pastor André and Magda Trocmé**, who led the village of Le Chambon-sur-Lignon in its resistance to Nazi and Vichy roundups of Jews, rescuing 5,000 refugees (see Box 10.1). *Source*: Chambon Foundation. (6) **Miep Gies** of Amsterdam, Holland, who sheltered the young Jewish diarist Anne Frank and her family until their arrest and deportation to the death camps. Madame Gies died in January 2010, aged 100. *Source*: Anne Frank House/Getty Images.

BOX 10.3 continued

Figures 10.7–10.17 continued   (7) **Sophie Scholl**, martyred member of the anti-Nazi White Rose movement at the University of Munich during World War Two. *Source*: Bayerischer Rundfunk/Learning from History. (8) **Oskar Schindler** (seated), the inspiration for Steven Spielberg's film *Schindler's List*, with Leopold Pfefferberg, one of the Jews he saved from the Nazis. *Source*: United States Holocaust Memorial Museum/Leopold Page Collection. (9) **Raoul Wallenberg**, who used his position at the Swedish embassy in Hungary to issue spurious documents to tens of thousands of Jews, preserving them from the Nazis' final round of anti-semitic slaughter (see p. 403). *Source*: St. Brendan School Network. (10) **Hugh Thompson, Jr.**, who landed his military helicopter between rampaging US troops and fleeing Vietnamese civilians at the hamlet of My Lai on March 16, 1968, and told his door gunner to fire on the US soldiers if the soldiers fired on the civilians (see Box 10.2). *Source*: US Army/Wikimedia Commons. (11) **Paul Rusesabagina**, inspiration for the film *Hotel Rwanda*. As manager of the Hotel Mille Collines in Kigali, Rusesabagina sheltered more than a thousand refugees throughout the genocide of April–July 1994, losing none to rampaging Hutu soldiers and militias. *Source*: AP Photo.

With the guidance of Samuel and Pearl Oliner, let us dig a little deeper into the psychology of rescuers. In 1988, the Oliners published a volume on "Rescuers of Jews in Nazi Europe," based on hundreds of interviews with those identified as such by the staff of the Yad Vashem museum. *The Altruistic Personality* has since become a classic, not only of Jewish Holocaust literature but of the social sciences.

What did the Oliners and their researchers discover about the motivations of those who aided, sheltered, and protected defenseless Jews, when most around them were turning their backs or actively assisting with the slaughter? Consider some of the testimonies of these otherwise ordinary individuals:

> I had contact all the time with people who were against Hitler. They told me the most horrible things – transports, gas chambers, drownings, gassing in trains – I knew that a huge injustice was taking place. I felt tense, I couldn't sleep.

> I could smell the smoke from Majdanek [death camp] . . .

> He had nobody else to help him. [The Jews] could not survive on their rations.

> . . . When [the Germans] started taking the Jewish people, that really lit my fire. They took them like sheep, throwing them into trains. I couldn't stand it anymore. . . . They took innocent people and I wanted to help.

> Somebody had to do it.

> . . . Unless we helped, they would be killed. I could not stand that thought. I never would have forgiven myself.

> Can you see it? Two young girls come, one sixteen or seventeen, and they tell you a story that their parents were killed and they were pulled in and raped. What are you supposed to tell them – "Sorry, we are full already?"

> . . . I was so ashamed of what other so-called Christians did that I felt I wanted to do the contrary.

> If you can save somebody's life, that's your duty.

> We helped people who were in need. Who they were was absolutely immaterial to us. It wasn't that we were especially fond of Jewish people. We felt we wanted to help everybody who was in trouble.[132]

The personal values and psychological orientations cited again and again by the Oliners revolve around these core themes: *altruism* (from the Latin: literally, "otherism"), *universalism, care* ("the obligation to help the needy"), *compassion* (literally, "together feeling"), *empathy, equity/egalitarianism, justice* (defined as "the right of innocent people to be free from persecution"), *respect, fairness, personal honor,* and *patriotism* (understood as "encompass[ing] national acceptance of pluralistic and diverse groups in relationships of equality rather than mere tolerance").[133] It is clear from the Oliners' account that these orientations have an abiding basis in rescuers' family upbringings. Rescuers were significantly more likely than non-rescuers to describe their parents as *benevolent, loving, kind, tolerant, compassionate, non-abusive,* prone to *explain* rather than punish, *extensive* rather than restrictive in their orientation toward others.[134] They were more likely to possess an "ego orientation" that emphasized these traits, along with *strength, autonomy,* and *independence* – "a certain non-conformity, a moral stubbornness, in refusing to adhere to the norms imposed upon them," as Donald Bloxham put it.[135] The Oliners wrote:

> Already attuned to conferring meaning on events through their particular moral sensibilities, [rescuers] depended on familiar patterns to discern the significance of the unprecedented events at hand. To a large extent, then, helping Jews was less a decision made at a critical juncture than a choice prefigured by an established character and way of life. As Iris Murdoch observes, the moral life is not something that is switched on at a particular crisis but is rather something that goes on continually in the small piecemeal habits of living. Hence, "at crucial moments of choice most of the business of choosing is already over." Many rescuers themselves reflected this view, saying that they "had no choice" and that their behavior deserved no special attention, for it was simply an "ordinary" thing to do.[136]

Even with these strong familial buttresses, the psychology of the rescuer did not necessarily arise "out of the blue" or manifest itself in a purely disinterested way. Geographical proximity, particularly in urban settings, facilitated matters. Nationalist sentiment was not absent: French rescuers were more likely to help Jews who were French citizens than stateless refugees. Frequently, rescuers had had previous positive relationships with Jews: as childhood friends, co-workers, neighbors. Sometimes Christian rescuers perceived Jews as a "chosen people," intimately related through the shared religious tradition. "Several rescuers acknowledged that they became dependent on the Jews they helped," for household chores, assistance with repairs and maintenance, and so on.[137] In some cases, rescuers had little idea what they were getting themselves into; small and low-risk acts of kindness would lead inexorably to acts of long-term and high-risk helping. Sometimes the rescued promised the rescuer a material reward after the war was over. More attractive and traditionally "innocent" Jews (particularly children) were especially likely to receive aid. Sometimes sexually intimate relationships developed, as they frequently do in situations of stress and shared danger.

At times, rescuers felt disappointed or disillusioned by the response of the rescued when the danger was over. This serves as a reminder that rescuer psychology is not to be romanticized. I do believe, however, that it is to be *idealized*, in the profoundest sense of the word. These people, who usually considered themselves utterly ordinary, point us to the human motivations that may one day bring an end to genocide in our world. Let us hope they are indeed ordinary – or at least more common than is generally realized. Because "if humankind is dependent on only a few autonomously principled people, then the future is bleak indeed."[138]

FURTHER STUDY

Roy F. Baumeister, *Evil: Inside Human Violence and Cruelty*. New York: W.H. Freeman, 1999. An engaging inquiry.

Philip Hallie, *Lest Innocent Blood Be Shed: The Story of the Village of Le Chambon and*

How Goodness Happened There. New York: HarperPerennial, 1994. Preachy, but the most detailed account we have of the villagers of Le Chambon-sur-Lignon (see Box 10.1).

Thomas Kenneally, *Schindler's List*. New York: Touchstone, 1993. Fact-based novel about the rescuer of Jews; basis for the film.

Neil J. Kressel, *Mass Hate: The Global Rise of Genocide and Terror*. New York: Plenum Press, 1996. Focuses on the psychology of genocidal perpetrators; usefully read alongside Waller (see below).

Robert J. Lifton, *The Nazi Doctors: Medical Killing and the Psychology of Genocide*. New York: Basic Books, 1986. Analyzes the complex psychology of medical workers/murderers at Auschwitz.

Stanley Milgram, *Obedience to Authority: An Experimental View*. New York: HarperPerennial, 1995. "The Milgram Experiments": a classic of social-scientific investigation.

Leonard S. Newman and Ralph Erber, eds, *Understanding Genocide: The Social Psychology of the Holocaust*. Oxford: Oxford University Press, 2002. Essays on perpetrators and bystanders in the Jewish and other genocides.

Samuel P. Oliner and Pearl M. Oliner, *The Altruistic Personality: Rescuers of Jews in Nazi Europe*. New York: The Free Press, 1988. Intensely moving large-sample study. See also Samuel P. Oliner, *Do Unto Others: Extraordinary Acts of Ordinary People*.

Irene Gut Opdyke with Jennifer Armstrong, *In My Hands: Memories of a Holocaust Rescuer*. New York: Anchor Books, 2001. Brief, potent memoir.

John Rabe, *The Good Man of Nanking: The Diaries of John Rabe*, trans. John E. Woods. New York: Alfred A. Knopf, 1998. Searing diary of the "Rape of Nanjing" by Japanese forces in 1937–38, and the "International Safety Zone" established by Rabe and others to save Chinese civilian lives.

Paul Rusesabagina, *An Ordinary Man: An Autobiography*. London: Penguin, 2006. Memoir of the rescuer who inspired the film *Hotel Rwanda*.

Ervin Staub, *The Roots of Evil: The Origins of Genocide and Other Group Violence*. Cambridge: Cambridge University Press, 1989. Early study of the psychology of genocide.

Nechama Tec, *When Light Pierced the Darkness: Christian Rescue of Jews in Occupied Europe*. Oxford: Oxford University Press, 1984. Rescuer behavior in Poland.

Samuel Vaknin, *Malignant Self-love: Narcissism Revisited* (5th rev. edn). Skopje: Narcissus Publications, 2003. Lengthy work by a leading authority on narcissism.

James Waller, *Becoming Evil: How Ordinary People Commit Genocide and Mass Killing*, 2nd edn. Oxford: Oxford University Press, 2007. The best social-psychological account of genocide, literate and engaging throughout.

Emmy E. Werner, *A Conspiracy of Decency: The Rescue of the Danish Jews*. Boulder, CO: Westview Press, 2002. The story of the remarkable rescue carried out during the Second World War.

Philip Zimbardo, *The Lucifer Effect: Understanding How Good People Turn Evil*. New York: Random House, 2007. Career-summarizing work by the designer of the Stanford prison experiments.

NOTES

1 Greek Mythology Link, "Narcissus," http://homepage.mac.com/cparada/GML/Narcissus.html.

2 Anton Blok, "The Narcissism of Minor Differences," ch. 7 in Blok, *Honour and Violence* (Cambridge: Polity Press, 2001), p. 115. Michael Ignatieff's exploration was influential in bringing Freud's concept to bear on ethnic conflict and genocide: "The Narcissism of Minor Difference," ch. 2 in Ignatieff, *The Warrior's Honour: Ethnic War and the Modern Conscience* (London: Penguin, 1998), pp. 27–65.

3 As Mark Levene noted, "it is striking . . . the degree to which the slanderous invocations made against American and later, antipodean 'first peoples' simply replicated Anglo venom directed at what were nearly always referred to as the 'wild' Irish." Levene, *Genocide in the Age of the Nation State, Vol. 2: The Rise of the West and the Coming of Genocide* (London: I.B. Tauris, 2005), p. 48. The real-world consequences were also comparable, in that "considered overall, an Irish population collapse from 1.5 or possibly over 2 million inhabitants at the onset of the Irish wars in 1641, to no more than 850,000 eleven years later represents an absolutely devastating demographic catastrophe" (p. 54).

4 Freud quoted in Blok, *Honour and Violence*, p. 117.

5 As Jacques Sémelin summarized the narcissism of minor differences: "Since [human beings] exaggerate their importance, this emotional investment becomes a cause of hostility among men. It is basically a narcissistic inclination: attention is shifted toward the other only to distinguish oneself and reinforce one's own self-esteem." Sémelin, *Purify and Destroy: The Political Uses of Massacre and Genocide* (New York: Columbia University Press, 2007), p. 28.

6 See Samuel Vaknin, *Malignant Self-love: Narcissism Revisited* (Skopje: Narcissus Publications, 2003).

7 "A narcissist openly reveals his megalomania, but craves admiration, praise, and flattery. He has little sense of humor, he cannot form significant relationships, and blows to his self-esteem can elicit violent anger. He has a paranoid distrust of others. He can appear self-confident and secure, but deep down feels shame, insecurity, and inferiority. . . . He may, at one moment, appear a charming, benign benefactor, and the next moment turn into a raging, aggressive attacker. . . . He has a distorted conscience. Depression is common." Neil J. Kressel, *Mass Hate: The Global Rise of Genocide and Terror* (New York: Plenum Press, 1996), p. 133.

8 Quoted in Barbara Ehrenreich, *Blood Rites: Origins and History of the Passions of War* (New York: Metropolitan Books, 1997), p. 210.

9 Simon Sebag Montefiore, *Stalin: The Court of the Red Tsar* (London: Phoenix, 2004), p. 617. In Maoist China, the cult of personality was all-pervasive, surpassing even the Stalinist exemplar. Gao Xingjian, later a Nobel laureate, described the ritual: "At six o'clock in the morning, the bugle call got people up, and they had twenty minutes to brush their teeth and have a wash. They then stood before the portrait of the Great Leader on the wall to seek 'morning instructions,' sang songs from Mao's *Sayings* and, holding high the little red book [of Mao's collected aphorisms], shouted out 'long live' three times before going to the dining room to drink gruel. Assembly followed, and Mao's *Selected Works* were recited for half an hour before people shouldered their hoes and pickaxes to work on the land." Quoted in Roderick MacFarquhar and Michael Schoenhals, *Mao's Last Revolution* (Cambridge, MA: The Belknap Press of Harvard University Press, 2006), p. 263. All of this must have been wonderful for Mao's ego; so too the endless stream of young female consorts handpicked for him (and by him) from the military and theater troupes. Chang and Halliday are merciless on this point (in *Mao: The Unknown Story*; see Chapter 5, Further Study) – justifiably, given that the debauchery occurred in what was otherwise one of the most austere and sexually puritan regimes in the world.

10 Louis Sell, *Slobodan Milosevic and the Destruction of Yugoslavia* (Durham, NC: Duke University Press, 2002), p. 173.

11 Vaknin, "Collective Narcissism," http://samvak.tripod.com/14.html; emphasis added, to stress that the "collective" character of such narcissism need not require unanimity or even a majority among the afflicted group. Precisely when ordinary grandiosity becomes pathological narcissism is difficult to discern. To some degree inherent in modern nationalism, as Mark Levene has noted, is *sacro egoismo*: "'the egotistic pursuit of the interest of one's own group, even if it involves the disregard and abuse of another,' the former, moreover, always being deemed 'sacred' and hence morally self-sufficient." Levene, *Genocide in the Age of the Nation State, Vol. 2*, p. 185, quoting George Mosse. An American correspondent, Kathleen Morrow, wrote: "An assumption of superiority is part of *every* national character. . . . If you listen long enough to any citizen of any nation, you will detect a trace of narcissistic unreality . . . part of the cultural mythology that holds the group together. (The French think they invented 'culture,' the Italians are sure they are the only people who really know how to 'enjoy life,' etc.) I tend to assume this almost universal tendency to national grandiosity is innocent enough – as long as the nation or group does not accumulate enough power to begin to try to impose its internal mythology on the rest of the world. . . . I suppose I'm arguing that US collective pathological narcissism is not a cultural or psychological problem as much as a systemic one. By systemic, I mean the global system, which at this point exhibits a number of power vacuums into which a too-powerful US can narcissistically rush." Morrow, personal communication, May 5, 2005.

12 For a pointed analysis of the collective narcissism of my other country of citizenship, see Clifford Krauss, "Was Canada Just Too Good to be True?," *The New York Times*, May 25, 2005.

13 Cambodia under the Khmer Rouge (see Chapter 7) is another candidate, but I consider Khmer Rouge fanaticism to have been too shallowly rooted in society as a whole to merit inclusion.

14 Robert Jay Lifton, *Superpower Syndrome: America's Apocalyptic Confrontation with the World* (New York: Thunder's Mouth Press/Nation Books, 2003), p. 190.

15 Quoted in Saul Friedländer, *Nazi Germany and the Jews, Volume 1: The Years of Persecution, 1933–1939* (New York: HarperCollins, 1997), p. 259.

16 Alexander Donat, *The Holocaust Kingdom* (Washington, DC: Holocaust Library, 1999), p. 197.

17 Götz Aly, *Hitler's Beneficiaries: Plunder, Racial War, and the Nazi Welfare State* (New York: Holt Paperbacks, 2005), pp. 285, 324. See also Martin Dean, *Robbing the Jews: The Confiscation of Jewish Property in the Holocaust, 1933–1945* (Cambridge: Cambridge University Press, 2008).

18 Saul Friedländer, *The Years of Extermination: Nazi Germany and the Jews, 1939–1945* (New York: HarperCollins, 2007), p. 535.

19 Patricia Marchak, *Reigns of Terror* (Montréal, PQ: McGill-Queen's University Press, 2003), p. 21.

20 Levene, *Genocide in the Age of the Nation State, Vol. 2*, p. 105.

21 Heizer quoted in Levon Marashlian, "Finishing the Genocide: Cleansing Turkey of Armenian Survivors, 1920–1923," in Richard G. Hovannisian, ed., *Remembrance and Denial: The Case of the Armenian Genocide* (Detroit, MI: Wayne State University Press, 1999), p. 115. (Heizer's statement dates from July 1915.) The US consul in Mamouret-ul-Aziz, Leslie A. Davis, similarly reported that "The scenes of that week [of deportation] were heartrending. The [Armenian] people were preparing to leave their homes and to abandon their houses, their lands, their property of all kinds. They were selling their possessions for whatever they could get. The streets were full of Turkish women, as well as men, who were seeking bargains on this occasion, buying organs, sewing machines, furniture, rugs, and other articles of value for almost nothing. . . . The scene reminded me of vultures swooping down on their prey. It was a veritable

Turkish holiday and all the Turks went out in their gala attire to feast and to make merry over the misfortunes of others." Davis quoted in Marchak, *Reigns of Terror*, p. 166.

22 Montefiore, *Stalin: The Court of the Red Tsar*, p. 265.

23 Marie-Louise Kagoyire, quoted in Jean Hatzfeld, *Life Laid Bare: The Survivors in Rwanda Speak* (New York: Other Press, 2006), p. 126.

24 Quoted in Jean Hatzfeld (trans. Linda Coverdale), *Machete Season: The Killers in Rwanda Speak* (New York: Farrar, Straus & Giroux, 2005), p. 87.

25 Levene defines greed as "the drive not only to take more than one needs, but to ingest much more than one could easily or safely manage" (*Genocide in the Age of the Nation State, Vol. 2*, p. 241).

26 H.H. Gerth and C. Wright Mills, eds, *From Max Weber: Essays in Sociology* (New York: Oxford University Press, 1954), p. 180.

27 Michael Burleigh, *Ethics and Extermination: Reflections on Nazi Genocide* (Cambridge: Cambridge University Press, 1997), p. 164.

28 Montefiore, *Stalin*, p. 626.

29 "Everybody could hope for speedy advancement because every day somebody was plucked from their midst and had to be replaced. Of course, everybody was also a candidate for prison and death, but during the day they did not think about it, giving full rein to their fears only at night." Nadezhda Mandelstam, *Hope Against Hope* (New York: Modern Library, 1999), p. 282.

30 Orlando Figes, *The Whisperers: Private Life in Stalin's Russia* (New York: Metropolitan Books, 2007), p. 265. In like fashion, during its campaigns against Chechen nationalists in the 1990s and 2000s, "Russian troops exploited the destruction of towns across the region and accompanying sweep operations with the undisguised objective of individual profit. . . . Their actions ranged from small-scale demands for cash and jewelry to the wholesale transportation of furniture and electronic equipment in open trucks. . . . The extortion of money for the return of detained civilians to combatants – dead or alive – was routine. . . . Direct evidence of the siphoning of oil and its transportation to surrounding republics by both the Chechen separatists and the Russian high command is difficult to obtain, but speculation is convincing." Emma Gilligan, *Terror in Chechnya: Russia and the Tragedy of Civilians in War* (Princeton, NJ: Princeton University Press, 2010), p. 7.

31 Gérard Prunier, *The Rwanda Crisis: History of a Genocide* (New York: Columbia University Press, 1997), pp. 231–32.

32 Burke quoted in Linda Green, "Fear as a Way of Life," in Alexander Laban Hinton, ed., *Genocide: An Anthropological Reader* (Malden, MA: Blackwell), p. 307.

33 Ehrenreich, *Blood Rites*, p. 76.

34 On the psychology of "in-group–out-group differentiation," see Ervin Staub, *The Roots of Evil: The Origins of Genocide and Other Group Violence* (Cambridge: Cambridge University Press, 1989), pp. 58–62.

35 James Waller, *Becoming Evil: How Ordinary People Commit Genocide and Mass Killing*, 2nd edn (Oxford: Oxford University Press, 2007), p. 149. Emphasis in original.

36 Donald L. Horowitz, *The Deadly Ethnic Riot* (Berkeley, CA: University of California Press, 2001), p. 151.

37 See J.S. Piven, *Death and Delusion: A Freudian Analysis of Mortal Terror* (Greenwich, CT: IAP Publishers, 2004).

38 In the Hebrew religious tradition, the scapegoat was "a live goat over whose head Aaron confessed all the sins of the children of Israel on the Day of Atonement. The goat, symbolically bearing their sins, was then sent into the wilderness." (Answers. com)

39 Charny quoted in Leo Kuper, *The Prevention of Genocide* (New Haven, CT: Yale University Press, 1985), p. 196. See also the discussion of psychological research on "mortality salience" and "terror management" in Kate Douglas, "Death Defying," *New Scientist*, August 28, 2004.

40 Ernest Becker, *The Denial of Death* (New York: The Free Press, 1973), pp. 148–49, 284. Jacques Sémelin's argument in *Purify and Destroy* is similar: "Beyond fear and hatred, [there] thus appears a fantasy of all-powerfulness in which this 'us' is victorious: it is regenerated by destroying 'them.' The death of an evil 'them' makes possible the omnipotence of 'us.' Such a psychological posture may seem 'primitive' or archaic – which, in fact, it is. We are still here in the realm of the *imaginaire*, but unlike that of death, it is one of omnipotence and glory. The two are inextricably linked. The two of them can be terribly effective because they affect the very foundations of the human psyche as explained, for example, by psychoanalysis." Sémelin, *Purify and Destroy: The Political Uses of Massacre and Genocide* (New York: Columbia University Press, 2007), p. 17.

41 "Prosecutor v. Drazen Erdemovic, Sentencing Judgement," March 5, 1998. From the Documentation Site of the Netherlands Institute of Human Rights, http://sim.law.uu.nl.

42 Nyiransabimana, quoted in Hatzfeld, *Life Laid Bare*, p. 140.

43 Réne Lemarchand, "Disconnecting the Threads: Rwanda and the Holocaust Reconsidered," *Journal of Genocide Research*, 4: 4 (2002), p. 513. A similar dynamic was evident in the Nazi SS, where (by contrast with the Order Police) not only was disobedience generally punished by execution, but a loss of employment in the camps could mean transfer to the mortal danger of the eastern front. Hence, according to Christopher Fettweis, "cowardice played an important role" in motivating SS members. "These men and women were well aware that to request a transfer might mean a trip to the Russian front, from which few people returned. The Jew-killing duties, while perhaps unpleasant, were relatively safe and provided a solid chance to survive the war. The Russian front must have provided quite an effective incentive to perform for those assigned to guard the trains, or to man the towers, or to work in the rear in the *Einsatzgruppen*." Fettweis, "War as Catalyst: Moving World War II to the Center of Holocaust Scholarship," *Journal of Genocide Research*, 5: 2 (2003), p. 229.

44 Sémelin, *Purify and Destroy*, p. 262.

45 "One thing is immediately obvious [in genocidal situations]: the killers are in a *group*. . . . Killings are thus carried out by battalions, gangs, crowds. Each group has a different story, and operates under different circumstances. But one thing is certain: It is the group that acts as the collective operator of mass murder. It is the group that gives rise to individuals transformed into killers." Ibid., pp. 240–41. Sémelin also points out (p. 273) that the forcible submersion of *victims* is frequently adopted as a strategy "to de-individualize them. Quantity depersonalizes and consequently desensitizes."

46 Mark Levene, *Genocide in the Age of the Nation State, Vol. 2*, p. 140.

47 Rubinowicz quoted in Friedländer, *The Years of Extermination*, p. 385.

48 Daniel Chirot and Clark McCauley, *Why Not Kill Them All? The Logic and Prevention of Mass Political Murder* (Princeton, NJ: Princeton University Press, 2006), pp. 36, 86.

49 Ben Kiernan, *Blood and Soil: A World History of Genocide and Extermination from Sparta to Darfur* (New Haven, CT: Yale University Press, 2007), p. 27.

50 Horowitz, *The Deadly Ethnic Riot*, p. 548.

51 The fact that these highly frustrated and alienated individuals were also outsiders made them additionally useful in jump-starting genocidal killing at the local level. An unidentified survivor of the Rwandan genocide, interviewed by Lee Ann Fujii, described killing sprees in Ngali, south of Kigali, in which "the Burundians would set an example for the Rwandan Interahamwe [genocidal militia] to kill and show them how to kill someone because the people from here in Ngali were scared and ashamed of killing their neighbors, their friends." Fujii, *Killing Neighbors: Webs of Violence in Rwanda* (Ithaca, NY: Cornell University Press, 2009), p. 86. This is just one example of "the transformation of refugee-generating conflict into conflict-generating refugees," in René Lemarchand's mordant phrasing (Lemarchand, *The Dynamics of Violence in Central Africa* [Philadelphia, PA: University of Pennsylvania Press, 2009], p. 20.) Lemarchand

also notes that following the Burundian genocide of 1972, "It is not a matter of coincidence that the few Hutu elites who survived the Burundi carnage were the first to articulate a stridently anti-Tutsi ideology . . . " (p. 58).

52 Lemarchand, "Disconnecting the Threads," p. 507.

53 Scott Straus, *The Order of Genocide: Race, Power, and War in Rwanda* (Ithaca, NY: Cornell University Press, 2006), pp. 139, 157.

54 Raul Hilberg, *The Destruction of the European Jews* (3rd edn), Vol. 3 (New Haven, CT: Yale University Press, 2003), p. 1093. Mark Levene also points disparagingly to the fantastic "notion that worldwide Jewry, despite its dispersal, minority status and history of persecution, was actually spearheading an international, even cosmic conspiracy to emasculate and ultimately wipe out not only the German people but all western civilization." Levene, "Why Is the Twentieth Century the Century of Genocide?," *Journal of World History*, 11: 2 (2000), p. 323.

55 Goebbels, quoted in Friedländer, *The Years of Extermination*, p. 335.

56 Such propaganda had a duly fear-evoking effect on German fighting forces, who came to view their mission of occupation and genocide as a fundamentally defensive one, especially with regard to the Slavic enemy. One soldier wrote in August 1941: "Precisely now one recognizes perfectly what would have happened to our wives and children had these Russian hordes . . . succeeded in penetrating into our Fatherland. I have had the opportunity here to . . . observe these uncultivated, multi-raced men. Thank God they have been thwarted from plundering and pillaging our homeland." Cited in Omer Bartov, *Hitler's Army: Soldiers, Nazis, and War in the Third Reich* (New York: Oxford University Press, 1992), p. 156.

57 Sémelin, *Purify and Destroy*, p. 297.

58 A Hutu killer in the Rwandan genocide also recalled: "The perpetrators felt more comfortable insulting and hitting crawlers in rags rather than properly upright people. Because they seemed less like us in that position." Quoted in Hatzfeld, *Machete Season*, p. 132.

59 Wolfgang Sofsky, *The Order of Terror: The Concentration Camp* (Princeton, NJ: Princeton University Press, 1999), p. 267.

60 Rwililiza quoted in Hatzfeld, *Life Laid Bare*, pp. 102, 113.

61 Horowitz, *The Deadly Ethnic Riot*, p. 393.

62 According to Terrence Des Pres, immersion in filth and excreta has much the same character, violating psychological taboos so deeply held that they are almost instinctive. "The shock of physical defilement causes spiritual concussion, and, simply to judge from the reports of those who have suffered it, subjection to filth seems often to cause greater anguish than hunger or fear of death. 'This aspect of our camp life,' says one survivor [of the Nazi camps, Reska Weiss], 'was the most dreadful and the most horrible ordeal to which we were subjected.' Another survivor [Leon Szalet] describes the plight of men forced to lie in their own excreta: they 'moaned and wept with discomfort and disgust. Their moral wretchedness was crushing.'" Des Pres, *The Survivor: An Anatomy of Life in the Death Camps* (Oxford: Oxford University Press, 1976), p. 66.

63 Chirot and McCauley, *Why Not Kill Them All?*, p. 28.

64 Evelin Lindner, "Gendercide and Humiliation in Honour and Human-rights Societies," in Adam Jones, ed., *Gendercide and Genocide* (Nashville, TN: Vanderbilt University Press, 2004), p. 40. Daniel Chirot and Clark McCauley define humiliation as "the emotion experienced when a public loss of status is imposed by another. This imposition is usually perceived as unfair and undeserved." Chirot and McCauley, *Why Not Kill Them All?*, p. 79; see their broader discussion of "Shame and Humiliation," pp. 77–80.

65 Retzinger and Scheff cited in Lindner, "Gendercide and Humiliation," p. 45.

66 Lifton, *Superpower Syndrome*, p. 103.

67 James Gilligan, "Shame, Guilt, and Violence," *Social Research*, 70: 4 (Winter 2003), p. 1154.

68 Donald Horowitz likewise wrote of "deadly ethnic riots" that "the reversal of invidious comparisons, the retrieval of imperiled respect, and the redistribution of honor are among the central purposive ideas embedded in the dramaturgy." Horowitz, *The Deadly Ethnic Riot*, p. 431.

69 Belsil quoted in Taner Akçam, *A Shameful Act: The Armenian Genocide and the Question of Turkish Responsibility* (New York: Metropolitan Books, 2006), p. 116.

70 Taner Akçam is strong on this: "Turkish nationalism arose as a reaction to the experience of constant humiliations. Turkish national sentiment constantly suffered from the effects of an inferiority complex. . . . Critical . . . was the fact that the Turks not only were continuously humiliated and loathed, but they were conscious of this humiliation. . . . A nation that was humiliated in this way in the past and is also conscious of that experience, will try to prove its own greatness and importance." Akçam, "The Genocide of the Armenians and the Silence of the Turks," in Levon Chorbajian and George Shirinian, eds, *Studies in Comparative Genocide* (London: Macmillan, 1999), p. 129. See also Akçam, *From Empire to Republic: Turkish Nationalism and the Armenian Genocide* (London: Zed Books, 2004), Chapters 2 and 3.

71 "Nazi doctors told me of indelible scenes, which they either witnessed as young children or were told about by their fathers, of German soldiers returning home defeated after World War I. These beaten men, many of them wounded, engendered feelings of pathos, loss, and embarrassment, all amidst national misery and threatened revolution. Such scenes, associated with strong feelings of humiliation, were seized upon by the Nazis to the point where one could say that Hitler rose to power on the promise of avenging them." Lifton, *Superpower Syndrome*, p. 111.

72 I explored the link between "Humiliation and Masculine Crisis in Iraq," focusing on the invasion of 2003 and subsequent occupation and uprising, in an article by this title in *Al-Raida* (Beirut: Institute for Women's Studies in the Arab World), Vol. 21, July 2004, available at http://www.iiav.nl/ezines/email/AlRaida/2004/No104-105.pdf.

73 Quoted in Gilligan, "Shame, Guilt and Violence," p. 1162. Jessica Stern's interviews with Palestinian suicide bombers provide further evidence of humiliation as a motivating force. See Stern, *Terror in the Name of God: Why Religious Militants Kill* (New York: Ecco Press, 2003).

74 This is also evident, with generally more positive outcomes, in the history of movements for national autonomy or independence. Clearly, the educated and otherwise privileged are disproportionately represented among the leaderships of such movements.

75 Levene, *Genocide in the Age of the Nation State, Vol. 2*, p. 60.

76 Scott Straus, however, rejected "the claim that Burundian refugees instigated the killing in Rwanda," contending that the population of Butare in southern Rwanda, where Burundian refugees were concentrated, arrived late and mostly unwillingly to the genocide. Straus, *The Order of Genocide*, p. 61.

77 Waller, *Becoming Evil*, pp. 72–73.

78 Sémelin, *Purify and Destroy*, p. 267.

79 Christopher Browning, *Ordinary Men: Reserve Police Battalion 101 and the Final Solution in Poland* (New York: Perennial, 1993), p. 184.

80 See Thomas Blass, *The Man Who Shocked the World: The Life and Legacy of Stanley Milgram* (New York: Basic Books, 2004).

81 Waller, *Becoming Evil*, p. 108.

82 Stanley Milgram, *Obedience to Authority: An Experimental View* (New York: HarperPerennial, 1995), p. 33; emphasis added.

83 Ibid., p. 40.

84 Ibid., p. 34. "Subjects seemed able to resist the experimenter far better when they did not have to confront [the 'victim'] face to face" (p. 62).

85 One might expect a degree of trauma to have resulted to the subjects from learning their capacity to do harm, but according to Milgram, this was not the case. Nearly all subjects expressed gratitude for the insights that the experiments had provided them. The

comment of one subject in a follow-up interview was: "I think people should think more deeply about themselves and their relation to their world and to other people." Ibid., p. 196.

86 Ibid., pp. 63, 161.

87 Browning, *Ordinary Men*, p. 172.

88 Milgram, *Obedience to Authority*, pp. 40, 62–63, 97, 118, 121.

89 See Waller, *Becoming Evil*, pp. 109–11. For recent evaluations of Milgram's work, see Thomas Blass, "Perpetrator Behavior as Destructive Obedience: An Evaluation of Stanley Milgram's Perspective, the Most Influential Social-psychological Approach to the Holocaust," ch. 4 in Leonard S. Newman and Ralph Erber, eds, *Understanding Genocide: The Social Psychology of the Holocaust* (Oxford: Oxford University Press, 2002), pp. 91–109; and Philip Zimbardo, *The Lucifer Effect: Understanding How Good People Turn Evil* (New York: Random House, 2007), p. 275, citing "a recent comparative analysis . . . of the rates of obedience in eight studies conducted in the United States and nine replications in European, African, and Asian countries." This found "comparably high levels of compliance by research volunteers in these different studies and nations. The majority obedience effect of a mean 61 percent found in the US replications was matched by the 66 percent obedience rate found across all the other national samples. The range of obedience went from a low of 31 percent to a high of 91 percent in the US studies, and from a low of 28 percent (Australia) to a high of 88 percent (South Africa) in the cross-national applications."

90 Milgram, *Obedience to Authority*, pp. 5–6.

91 Ibid., p. 155.

92 Ibid., p. 48.

93 Ibid., p. 51.

94 However, as Roy Baumeister notes, while "empathy may prevent cruelty in some cases . . . it can also serve it. The true sadist is not lacking in empathy – on the contrary, empathy helps the sadist to derive maximum pleasure and inflict the greatest pain." Roy F. Baumeister, *Evil: Inside Human Violence and Cruelty* (New York: W.H. Freeman, 1999), p. 247. For more on the psychology of torture and sadism, see Elaine Scarry, *The Body in Pain: The Making and Unmaking of the World* (New York: Oxford University Press, 1985), esp. ch. 1; and John Conroy, *Unspeakable Acts, Ordinary People: The Dynamics of Torture* (New York: Alfred A. Knopf, 2000).

95 Zygmunt Bauman, *Modernity and the Holocaust* (Ithaca, NY: Cornell University Press, 2000), p. 155.

96 Zimbardo, *The Lucifer Effect*, p. 33.

97 Bauman, *Modernity and the Holocaust*, pp. 166–67.

98 Waller, *Becoming Evil*, p. 238.

99 Browning, *Ordinary Men*, p. 168.

100 Bauman, *Modernity and the Holocaust*, p. 167.

101 Ryan Dilley, "Is It in Anyone to Abuse a Captive?," *BBC News Online*, May 5, 2004, http://news.bbc.co.uk/1/hi/magazine/3683115.stm.

102 Zimbardo, *The Lucifer Effect*, pp. 210–11.

103 Hilberg, *The Destruction of the European Jews*, Vol. 1, p. 318.

104 Hilberg, *The Destruction of the European Jews*, Vol. 2, pp. 589, 597–98.

105 Samuel P. Oliner and Pearl M. Oliner, *The Altruistic Personality: Rescuers of Jews in Nazi Europe* (New York: The Free Press, 1988), p. 20. Wallenberg's story has overshadowed those who facilitated his acts of rescue, such as the Swedish diplomat Per Anger. According to historian Henry Huttenbach, it was Anger who first "hit on the idea of issuing Jews temporary Swedish passports and identity cards. . . . Anger's undivided cooperation allowed Wallenberg to succeed. . . . It is safe to say that Wallenberg's mission to save Hungarian Jews from deportation would not have got off the ground had Wallenberg not had the total support from the Swedish Embassy, that is, from Per Anger." Henry R. Huttenbach, "In Memoriam: Per Anger, 1914–2002," *Journal of*

Genocide Research, 5: 2 (2003), p. 191. Saul Friedländer notes also the role of "the Swiss diplomats, Carl Lutz, and the delegate of the ICRC, Friedrich Born; the Italian Giorgio Perlasca, impersonated a 'Spanish chargé d'affaires'; [and] the Portuguese, Carlos Branquinho . . . ." Friedländer, *The Years of Extermination*, p. 642.

106 A concise and readable account of Wallenberg's efforts to save Hungarian Jews and his subsequent fate is John Bierman, *Righteous Gentile: The Story of Raoul Wallenberg, Missing Hero of the Holocaust* (rev. edn) (London: Penguin, 1995).

107 John G. Heidenrich, *How to Prevent Genocide: A Guide for Policymakers, Scholars, and the Concerned Citizen* (Westport, CT: Praeger, 2001), p. 122.

108 Sugihara, quoted in Samuel P. Oliner, *Do Unto Others: Extraordinary Acts of Ordinary People* (Boulder, CO: Westview Press, 2003), p. 50.

109 Hannah Arendt, *Eichmann in Jerusalem: A Report on the Banality of Evil* (New York: The Viking Press, 1965), p. 130; emphasis added.

110 Survivor testimony quoted in Donald E. Miller and Lorna Touryan Miller, *Survivors: An Oral History of the Armenian Genocide* (Berkeley, CA: University of California Press, 1999), p. 13.

111 Oliner and Oliner, *The Altruistic Personality*, p. 155. The Oliners consider religious belief "at best . . . only weakly related to rescue" of Jews during the Second World War (p. 156).

112 Mike Collett-White, "'Rwanda's Schindler' Saved 1,268 Lives," *The Scotsman*, December 30, 2004. Rusesabagina's alienation from the post-genocide regime in Rwanda is revealing: see Arthur Asiimwe, "'Hotel Rwanda' Hero in Bitter Controversy," Reuters dispatch, April 18, 2007.

113 Lemkin included the Huguenots in his unpublished world history of genocide. See http://www.americanjewisharchives.org/aja/FindingAids/Lemkin.htm.

114 Philip Hallie, *Lest Innocent Blood Be Shed: The Story of the Village of Le Chambon and How Goodness Happened There* (New York: HarperPerennial, 1994), p. 167.

115 After the fall of France in June 1940, the Germans occupied the northern and coastal regions of the country, leaving the remainder in the hands of a collaborationist government based in the spa town of Vichy. The Vichy authorities were strongly anti-semitic, and by summer 1942 had incarcerated some 20,000 French Jews in concentration camps. They often proved as virulent as the Nazis in their eagerness to incarcerate and eliminate Jews, regularly rounding them up on their own initiative.

116 Quoted in Hallie, *Lest Innocent Blood Be Shed*, p. 133.

117 Ibid., pp. 127, 152–53, 155, 195.

118 Ibid., p. 196.

119 Winton Higgins, "The Moral Capital of the World," in Adam Jones, ed., *Evoking Genocide: Scholars and Activists Describe the Works That Shaped Their Lives* (Toronto, ON: The Key Publishing House Inc., 2009), p. 154.

120 Albert Camus, *The Plague* (New York: Vintage, 1991).

121 Ibid., p. 155.

122 See Robert McG. Thomas Jr., "Magda Trocme, 94, Is Dead; Sheltered Victims of Nazis," *The New York Times*, October 19, 1996.

123 Minyan: "The minimum number of ten adult Jews or, among the Orthodox, Jewish men required for a communal religious service" (Answers.com).

124 "Remarks by the President at the Holocaust Days of Remembrance Ceremony," April 23, 2009, official White House transcript, http://www.whitehouse.gov/the_press_office/Remarks-by-the-President-at-the-Holocaust-Days-of-Remembrance-Ceremony.

125 Michael Bilton and Kevin Sim, *Four Hours in My Lai* (New York: Penguin, 1992), p. 136.

126 Ibid., pp. 138–39, 204.

127 Thompson quoted in Oliner, *Do Unto Others*, p. 118.

128 Zimbardo, *The Lucifer Effect*, pp. 474–75.

129 Rebecca Leung, "An American Hero: Vietnam Veteran Speaks Out About My Lai,"

CBSNews.com, 9 May 2004. http://www.cbsnews.com/stories/2004/05/06/60minutes/main615997.shtml.

130 Bilton and Sim, *Four Hours in My Lai*, p. 205. For excerpts from a televised interview with Thompson on *BBC Hardtalk*, see http://www.youtube.com/watch?v=hkFa2l SNAGc.

131 Leung, "An American Hero."

132 Oliner and Oliner, *The Altruistic Personality*, pp. 119, 134, 138, 143, 168–69, 197, 216–18.

133 Ibid., pp. 159, 209. I am struck as well by this almost surreal vignette from the Warsaw Ghetto, recorded by the diarist Emmanuel Ringelblum: "There is a policeman who is renowned as a model German. Nicknamed 'the gentleman,' he is the soul of honesty. He permits wagons through the gates of the Wall, refusing to take a bribe. He also permits Jewish children to pass to the Other Side by the dozen to buy food . . . Examples of his wondrous decency and honesty are recounted daily. He plays all sorts of games with the smuggler children. He lines them up, commands them to sing, and marches them through the gates." Jacob Sloan, ed. and trans., *Notes from the Warsaw Ghetto: The Journal of Emmanuel Ringelblum* (New York: Schocken, 1974), p. 265.

134 See also Barbara Coloroso's exploration of genocide's links to bullying – the "conscious, willful, deliberate activity intended to harm, to induce fear through the threat of further aggression, and to create terror in the target." Coloroso, *Extraordinary Evil: A Brief History of Genocide* (New York: Viking, 2007), pp. 51–80 (quoted passage from p. 55).

135 Donald Bloxham, *Genocide, The World Wars, and the Unweaving of Europe* (London: Vallentine Mitchell, 2008), p. 238.

136 Oliner and Oliner, *The Altruistic Personality*, p. 222. Such values and character traits may also be manifested collectively, as with the "conspiracy of decency" among Danes to preserve the country's Jewish population.

137 Ibid., p. 86.

138 Ibid., p. 257.

CHAPTER 11

The Sociology and Anthropology of Genocide

INTRODUCTION

The disciplines of sociology and anthropology are distinguished by the types of societies they study. Anthropologists have carried out work on the non-industrialized "Third World" or Global South, while sociologists have focused on social patterns and processes within the industrialized "First World" or Global North.[1] Anthropology also possesses a distinctive methodology: fieldwork. Nonetheless, the disciplines are linked by a common concern with societal and cultural processes, and it is appropriate to consider them together.

Sociology and anthropology also shared a reluctance, until fairly recently, to engage with genocide and state terror. "Many sociologists," stated Irving Louis Horowitz in the late 1980s, "exhibit a studied embarrassment about these issues, a feeling that intellectual issues posed in such a manner are melodramatic and unfit for scientific discourse."[2] Nancy Scheper-Hughes similarly described "the traditional role of the anthropologist as neutral, dispassionate, cool and rational, [an] objective observer of the human condition"; anthropologists traditionally maintained a "proud, even haughty distance from political engagement."[3]

Fortunately, Horowitz's evaluation is now obsolete, thanks to a host of sociologists who have contributed seminally to genocide studies. They include Kurt Jonassohn, Helen Fein, Zygmunt Bauman, Michael Mann, and Daniel Feierstein. Anthropological studies came later, but recent years have seen the first anthologies on anthropology and genocide, as well as groundbreaking works by Alexander Laban Hinton, Victoria Sanford, and Christopher Taylor, among others.[4]

In examining sociological perspectives, this chapter focuses on three key themes: (1) the sociology of modernity, which has attracted considerable interest from genocide scholars in the wake of Zygmunt Bauman's *Modernity and the Holocaust*; (2) the sociology of "ethnicity" and ethnic conflict; and (3) the role of "middleman" or "market-dominant" minorities. It then addresses anthropological framings of genocide, focusing also on the work of forensic anthropologists.

SOCIOLOGICAL PERSPECTIVES

The sociology of modernity

Is genocide a modern phenomenon?[5] At first glance, the question seems banal. We saw in Chapter 1 that the destruction of peoples on the basis of group identity extends back to early history, and probably to prehistory. Yet we also know that in recent centuries, and especially during the past hundred years, the prevalence of genocide has taken a quantitative leap. The central issue is: Has that leap also been *qualitative*? Is there something about modernity that has become *definitional* to genocide?

In one of the most discussed works on the Jewish Holocaust, *Modernity and the Holocaust*, sociologist Zygmunt Bauman delivered a resounding "yes" to this question. "Modern civilization was not the Holocaust's *sufficient* condition; it was, however, most certainly its *necessary* condition. Without it, the Holocaust would be unthinkable."[6] Bauman's argument revolved around four core features of modernity: nationalism; "scientific" racism; technological complexity; and bureaucratic rationalization. Modern nationalism divided the world "fully and exhaustively . . . into national domains," leaving "no space . . . for internationalism" and designating "each scrap of the no-man's-land . . . [as] a standing invitation to aggression." In such a world, European Jews – with their international and cosmopolitan identity – could be construed as alien. They "defied the very truth on which all nations, old and new alike, rested their claims; the ascribed character of nationhood, heredity and naturalness of national entities. . . . *The world tightly packed with nations and nation-states abhorred the non-national void. Jews were in such a void: they were such a void.*"[7]

This existential unease towards the Jew was combined with scientific racism, which Bauman depicted as a modern phenomenon,[8] overlaying traditional intercommunal antipathies with a veneer of scientific and medical rationality. This brought with it an impetus to total extermination of the racial Other: "The only adequate solution to problems posited by the racist world-view is a total and uncompromising isolation of the pathogenic and infectious race – the source of disease and contamination – through its complete spatial separation or physical destruction."[9]

How could such a totalizing project be implemented? For Bauman, the advent of modern technology and bureaucratic rationality was essential. The mass death that the Nazis developed and inflicted relied on products of the Industrial Revolution. Railway transport, gas chambers, Zyklon B cyanide crystals administered by men in gas masks – all were essentially modern inventions and had to be managed by a bureaucracy of death. The great German theorist of modern bureaucracy, Max Weber, emphasized "its peculiar, 'impersonal' character," which "mean[s] that the mechanism

. . . is easily made to work for anybody who knows how to gain control over it." Weber also argued that "the bureaucratization of all [social] domination very strongly furthers the development of 'rational matter-of-factness' and the personality type of the professional expert," distinguished by his or her cool amorality and devotion to efficiency. Moreover, bureaucracy cultivates secrecy: "the concept of the 'official secret' is the specific invention of the bureaucracy."[10]

The processing of millions of "subhumans" for anonymous death was unthinkable in the absence of such a culture, according to Bauman:

> By its nature, this is a daunting task, unthinkable unless in conjunction with the availability of huge resources, means of their mobilization and planned distribution, skills of splitting the overall task into a great number of partial and specialized functions and skills to co-ordinate their performance. In short, the task is inconceivable without modern bureaucracy.[11]

Moreover, this "splitting [of] the overall task" into isolated and fragmented units of time, space, and work created a vital psychological distance between the victims and those participating in their annihilation. No individual – except, by reputation, the distant and semi-mythical *Führer* figure – exercised overall authority or bore overall responsibility. One did not commit mass murder *per se*. Rather, one operated a railroad switch, or dropped a few cyanide crystals into a shaft: "a cool, objective operation . . . mechanically mediated . . . a deed performed at a distance, one whose effects the perpetrator did not see," in Wolfgang Sofsky's words.[12] Much the same set of values, procedures, and behaviors characterized the nuclear mentality, with its potential for rationally administered omnicide (Chapter 2).[13]

More recently, historian Mark Levene, in his magisterial work *Genocide in the Age of the Nation State*, has argued that "the problem of genocide lies in the very nature of modernity."[14] This, together with the subtitle of his second volume (*The Rise of the West and the Coming of Genocide*), suggests that genocide is *essentially* modern

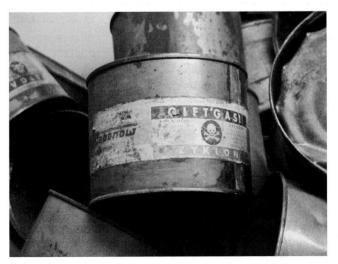

Figure 11.1 Are the technologies, ideologies, and state capacities of modernity inextricably linked to genocide? Some argue that the connection is so intimate that we should find another word for the mass killings of pre-modern ages. Even those who take a longer view, like this author, acknowledge distinctive features of genocide in the modern age. Pictured: a canister of Zyklon B, the chemical pesticide which the Nazis developed to murder Jews and others in the gas chambers.

Source: Michael Hanke/Wikimedia Commons.

and inextricably linked to the West's imperial expansion from the fifteenth century on (see Chapters 2 and 3): "the crystallization of the phenomenon we call 'genocide' – as opposed to other categories of mass murder – could only be really achieved in the context of an emerging, global, interlocking system of nation-states which finally came to its *fullest* fruition in the twentieth century."[15] While this was "accompanied by no overarching political agenda for the annihilation of foreign peoples," for Levene, it established "a broader cultural discourse in which such annihilation was considered perfectly acceptable." The bureaucratic features which Bauman emphasized resurfaced in Levene's contention that "we normatively name people as members of given tribes, nations, races, religions" because of "modernity's facility for reducing and simplifying complex phenomena – humans included – 'into a more manageable and schematized form,'" while failing or refusing "to imagine human beings as potentially possessing multi-layered identities and loyalties."[16]

Two main criticisms of this modernity-of-genocide thesis may be advanced. First, the supposed dividing line between historical and modern genocide seems more stylistic than substantive. It is simply not the case that "the Holocaust left behind and put to shame all its alleged pre-modern equivalents, exposing them as primitive, wasteful and ineffective by comparison," as Bauman contended.[17] Rather, the clear conviction of the founder of genocide studies, Raphael Lemkin, was that "genocide is not an exceptional phenomenon, but . . . occurs in intergroup relations with a certain regularity like homicide takes place between individuals."[18] Lemkin's own historical analysis of genocide encompassed millennia. The UN Genocide Convention that resulted from Lemkin's lobbying efforts likewise recognized in its preamble "that *at all periods of history* genocide has inflicted great losses on humanity" (emphasis added). Levene, for his part, is far too good a historian to ignore the continuities, so he hedges his bets at points – referring to "our phenomenon, *at least in its modern and contemporary manifestations*"; "genocide – *or at least a modern variant of it*"; "any *broad historical examination* of the phenomenon . . . "[19]

To explore the distinctively "modern" features of modern and contemporary genocides is a worthwhile inquiry, and both Bauman and Levene have made foundational contributions to the field. But precisely the same line of inquiry could be launched into the human institution most intimately allied with genocide – war. While we could note all manner of modern expansions and deadly innovations, we would not, I think, suggest that war thereby is *essentially* a modern creation.[20] So, too, with genocide. As Alex Alvarez argued, "What modernity has done is reshape genocide into a more efficient and rational endeavor capable of killing on an industrial scale. The modern age has not created genocide; rather it has altered its nature, application, and efficiency."[21]

Another criticism of the modernity-of-genocide thesis may be summarized in one word: Rwanda (see Chapter 9). There, around one million people were hunted, corraled, and exterminated in *twelve weeks* – a rate of killing exceeding by a wide margin that of the "modern" Nazi holocaust. Yet the genocide was not only more modern in chronological terms; it was carried out by men and women armed with little more than guns and traditional agricultural implements.[22] It involved no appreciable role for scientific or technical experts. And *the killing was conducted up close, often face-to-face, publicly*, with no resort to the physical and psychological distancing strategies and official secrecy supposedly necessary for "modern" mass slaughter.[23] One can argue that the Rwandan holocaust depended on a complex administrative apparatus; a racist ideology tinged with pseudo-science; and the industrial mass production of machetes, hoes, firearms, and grenades. But are these inherently "modern"? Bureaucracy is ancient, as various Chinese dynasties remind us.[24] One suspects that the ideology of hate developed by Hutu Power would have been just as functional without its vaguely modernist overtones.[25] With regard to Rwanda's technology of death, the basic implements of guns, machetes, and explosives all pre-date the Industrial Revolution.

ETHNICITY AND ETHNIC CONFLICT

> Loe, this is the payment you shall get, if you be one of them they terme, without.
> Thomas Merton, 1637

Few concepts are as amorphous and yet important as ethnicity. On one hand, ethnic identifications seem so fluid and mutable as to lack almost any "objective" character. On the other hand, ethnicity is arguably the dominant ideological impetus to conflict and genocide worldwide.

Three historical phenomena account for the prominence of ethnicity in today's "global society." The first is nationalism, touched on in Chapter 2. As medieval Europe moved away from a quilt of overlapping sovereignties and towards the formation of modern states, it first fell under the sway of strong, centralizing monarchs. With the onset of the democratic age via the American and French Revolutions, sovereignty was held increasingly to reside in "the people." But *which* people? How defined? The popular thrust gave rise in the nineteenth century to modern ethnic nationalism, as Western rulers and their populations sought an ideology to unify the new realms. The result was what Benedict Anderson called "imagined communities": geographically disparate but mutually identified agglomerations defining themselves as "French," "German," "British," "Italian," and so on.[26] The core idea was that the "imagined community" required a particular political form, the "nation-state," to achieve true realization.

On what basis were these communities imagined? It is worth pausing briefly to consider the bases or foundations of ethnicity, as they have been listed by a prominent scholar of the subject. Anthony Smith cited six foundations of ethnic identity: "1. a collective proper name, 2. a myth of common ancestry, 3. shared historical memories, 4. one or more differentiating elements of common culture, 5. an association with a specific 'homeland,' 6. a sense of solidarity for significant sectors of the population."[27]

While a refined concept of ethnicity is often considered to be a Western invention, this is open to challenge. Han Chinese, for example, had a well-developed ethnic sensibility well before the West's rise to dominance.[28] So too, clearly, did the peoples of the ancient Middle East, whose ethnic rivalries and extermination strategies were quite well-advanced, if the relevant religious texts are granted credence. (Even if the genocides mentioned in Chapter 1 were fantasies, the fact that people felt drawn to fantasize them speaks to ethnoreligious distinctions and divisions as sharp as any in modern times.) Indeed, it could be argued that ethnicity is at least latent in all societies, independent of Western penetration and influence. Other social units – notably extended family, clan, and tribe – evince many of the same solidaristic bonds as ethnicity; they may be considered proto-ethnic groupings. Like ethnic groups, moreover, these identifications are meaningless without an Other to define against oneself. There are no in-groups without out-groups, with what anthropologist Fredrik Barth has called "boundary maintenance mechanisms" serving to demarcate the two.[29]

When a dominant ethnic collectivity is established as the basis of a "nation-state," a quandary arises in dealing with the out-groups – "ethnic minorities" – that also find themselves within the boundaries of that state. Such minorities exist everywhere; even supposedly unified or organic nation-states (Japan is the most commonly cited example) have them. This often carries explosive consequences for intercommunal violence, including genocide, as we have had numerous opportunities to witness in these pages.

The second historical factor is the spread of Western imperialism and colonialism around the world (Chapter 2), which shaped the present-day configuration of nationalisms in important ways. Most obviously, it spurred the idea of ethnic nationalism (though some nationalisms, and a wide range of ethnic *identifications*, clearly existed independently of it). Despite the best efforts of colonizers to preserve those they subjugated from such dangerous influences, ethnic-nationalist ideologies were gradually absorbed and integrated into the anti-colonial movements that arose from the mid-nineteenth through mid-twentieth centuries. In addition, following the time-honored strategy of divide and rule, aimed at *preventing* nationalism, the colonialists typically gathered a host of clans, tribes, and long-established "national" entities into a single territorial and administrative unit. A glance at the ethnic composition of countries such as Nigeria, Congo, and Indonesia suffices to remind one of the enormous diversity of peoples that comprised the deliberately *un*imaginable "communities" of colonialism.

The nationalist leaders who sprang to prominence in the colonized world in the 1920s and 1930s were thus confronted with the crushing challenge of either forging a genuine sense of national community among diverse peoples, or negotiating a peaceful and viable fragmentation of the colonial unit. For the most part, they chose to maintain the colonial boundaries. In some cases, this produced viable multiethnic states (see Chapter 16), but in many instances it did not. Sometimes the managed breakup of multiethnic entities led to massive violence (India, Palestine); in states where the leadership chose to preserve an artificial unity, time-bombs were set for the future (Nigeria, Indonesia, Yugoslavia). The ethnic violence associated with the collapse of the Soviet empire in 1991 is a recent example of this trend.

A final historical conjuncture, often overlooked, is *globalization*. Although globalizing trends can be traced back many centuries, they have reached a new stage of complex interconnectedness at the turn of the millennium. One advantage of ethnic identifications is that they offer a strong sense of psychological rootedness amidst change and upheaval. Given the rapid transformations associated with globalization, where is a stable sense of "we," and therefore of "me," to be found? The anthropologist Clifford Geertz has argued that during the disorienting process of modernization . . . unintegrated citizens, looking for an anchor in a sea of changes, will grab hold of an increasingly anachronistic ethnic identity, which bursts onto the scene and then recedes as the process of structural differentiation moves toward a reintegrated society.[30]

One can question, though, whether such ethnic resurgence is a transitory phenomenon. As globalization is accompanied by intense nationalist sentiment in many parts of the world, the "transition" seems to be taking rather longer than expected. Part of the misunderstanding may lie in a tendency to believe that ethnic identifications are not primordial but fictional – created and manipulated by self-interested elites to mobilize their followers. (This line of argument has been bolstered by recent "postmodern" orientations in the humanities and social sciences.)

There *is* an important sense in which ethnic identifications are "imagined" or "mythical."[31] As I will show below, they are also subject to endless manipulations by elite figures and violence specialists. Ethnic identifications are protean in the sense that all of the six "bases" that Anthony Smith identifies for ethnicity can be altered, though not always at will or completely. One can change one's territorial base and recast one's primary ethnic identification, as generations of immigrants to the ethnic "melting-pot" of the United States have done (while often maintaining a secondary attachment to the previous identification). Ancestral myths can be revised, reinterpreted, or abandoned. Historical memory, language, culinary taste, forms of artistic expression – all are highly mutable.

Over time, however, ethnic identifications often achieve intergenerational stability. They assume a practical force in individual and group psychology, societal structure, and political behavior that is impossible to ignore, least of all by those seeking to understand and confront genocide and other mass violence.[32] In *Becoming Evil*, James Waller presented evidence from psychology, sociology, and anthropology to show that these identifications originate deep in human social behavior: "Knowing who is kin, knowing who is in our social group, has a deep importance to species like ours." Moreover, "We have an evolved capacity to see our group as superior to all others and even to be reluctant to recognize members of other groups as deserving of equal respect." Members of a cannibal tribe in Irian Jaya, Indonesia, convey this pointedly: they define themselves as "the human beings," and all others as "the edible ones."[33]

Ethnic conflict and violence "specialists"

Some defining work on the sociology of mass violence pointed to the role of individual and organizational actors in provoking and channeling violent outbreaks. Donald L. Horowitz, for example, stressed the importance of

organizations, often tied to ethnically based political parties, [that] reflect and reinforce interethnic hostility through propaganda, ritual, and force. They run the gamut from civilian to proto-military organizations, operating under varying degrees of secrecy and with varying degrees of coherence and military training. Their raison d'être is the alleged danger from the ethnic enemy.[34]

For his part, Paul R. Brass emphasized the role of violence "specialists" operating within "institutionalized . . . systems" of violence generation:

> The kinds of violence that are committed in ethnic, communal, and racial "riots" are, I believe, undertaken mostly by "specialists," who are ready to be called out on such occasions, who profit from it, and whose activities profit others who may or may not be actually paying for the violence carried out. In fact, in many countries at different times in their histories, there have been regions or cities and towns which have developed what I call "institutionalized riot systems," in which known actors specialize in the conversion of incidents between members of different communities into ethnic riots. The activities of these specialists are usually required for a riot to spread from the initial incident of provocation.[35]

The significance of this category of actors to the fomenting and implementing of genocide should be recognized.[36] Note some of the "specialists" that Brass identifies: "criminal elements and members of youth gangs," "local militant group leaders," "politicians, businessmen, religious leaders," "college and university professors," "pamphleteers and journalists . . . deliberately spreading rumors and scurrilous propaganda," "hooligans" (ranging from Nazi thugs to modern soccer hoodlums), "communal political elites."[37] Add to this list the violence specialists cited by Charles Tilly in his study of *The Politics of Collective Violence*: "Pirates, privateers, paramilitaries, bandits, mercenaries, mafiosi, militias, posses, guerrilla forces, vigilante groups, company police, and bodyguards."[38] Beyond the essential (and universally acknowledged) role of state officials and security force commanders, what we have here is a veritable who's-who of the leading *agents provocateurs* of genocide, its foot-soldiers, and its ideological defenders.

"MIDDLEMAN MINORITIES"

> The Greeks and Armenian merchants have been the leeches in this part of the world sucking the life blood out of the country for centuries.
>
> Admiral Mark L. Bristol, US High Commissioner to Turkey, 1922

Perhaps no collectivities are as vulnerable to hatred and large-scale killing as those "characterized as possessing an excess of enterprise, ambition, energy, arrogance, and achievement by those who believe themselves lacking such traits."[39] Such minorities are not necessarily immigrants or descendants of immigrants, but often they are, and this foreignness is a key factor in their targeting. Worldwide, reflecting both centuries-old patterns and more recent globalizing trends, populations have arrived or been introduced from outside the established society. Lacking access to land, as well as the network of social relations that dominant groups can utilize, such groups normally settle in the cities or towns – often in neighborhoods or zones that quickly acquire a minority tinge. Even when they are brought in by a colonial power as indentured laborers (as with the Indians whom the British imported to Uganda, South Africa,

Fiji, and elsewhere), there is a strong tendency for such groups to establish themselves in commercial trades.

Occupying an inherently vulnerable minority position, these sectors historically have been attractive to colonial powers as local allies and intermediaries. Such alliances allowed colonizers to "divide and rule," with the aid of a minority that was (1) less anchored to the territory and dominant culture in question, and therefore less prone to push for autonomy or national independence; and (2) heavily dependent on colonial favor, and therefore more likely to be loyal to the colonizers. Colonial favor often translated into greater educational opportunities and positions in lower and middle sectors of the bureaucracy. However, even in the absence of such colonial backing, and in the face of strong opposition from the dominant society, such groups almost universally emphasize education as a means of moving beyond their marginal position and attaining prosperity. They typically display strong bonds of ethnic, cultural, and material solidarity among their members, and they may have the advantage of access to capital and trading relationships through remaining ties with their (or their ancestors') countries of origin.

A frequent result is that these minorities establish a high degree of prominence, sometimes even outright dominance, in key sectors of the national economy. Well-known examples include Jews, whom Amy Chua refers to as "the quintessential market-dominant minority,"[40] and the Chinese of Southeast Asia. East Indians achieved a similar position in many East African economies, while Lebanese traders came to dominate the vital diamond trade in West Africa. The Dutch, British, and Portuguese-descended Whites of southern Africa may also be cited, along with the White "pigmentocrats" who enjoy elite status in heavily indigenous countries of Latin America. The potential for conflict, including for the violent or genocidal targeting of middleman minorities,[41] is apparent, though far from inevitable.[42] Through their common and preferential ties to colonial authorities, these minorities were easily depicted as agents of the alien dominator, opponents of national liberation and self-determination, and cancers in the body politic. Even today, their frequently extensive international ties and "cosmopolitan" outlook may grate on the majority's nationalist sentiments. Moreover, their previous relationship with a colonial power has often translated into a quest for alliances with authoritarian regimes in the post-colonial era. Elite Chinese businessmen in the Philippines and Indonesia, for example, were among the most enthusiastic and visible backers of the Marcos and Suharto dictatorships. When authoritarian rule collapsed, the mass hostility, resentment, and humiliation could be vented under democratic guise – a pattern that Chua has described well:

> In countries with a market-dominant minority and a poor "indigenous" majority, the forces of democratization and marketization directly collide. As markets enrich the market-dominant minority, democratization increases the political voice and power of the frustrated majority. The competition for votes fosters the emergence of demagogues who scapegoat the resented minority, demanding an end to humiliation, and insisting that the nation's wealth be reclaimed by its "true owners." Thus as America toasted the spread of global elections through the 1990s, vengeful ethnic slogans proliferated: "Zimbabwe for Zimbabweans," "Indonesia

for Indonesians," "Uzbekistan for Uzbeks," "Kenya for Kenyans," "Ethiopia for Ethiopians," "Yids [Jews] out of Russia," "Hutu Power," "Serbia for Serbs," and so on. . . . As popular hatred of the rich "outsiders" mounts, the result is an ethnically charged political pressure cooker in which some form of backlash is almost unavoidable.

Among the strategies of backlash, the "most ferocious kind . . . is ethnic cleansing and other forms of majority-supported ethnic violence," up to and including genocide.[43] Rwanda in 1994 is the best example of democratization helping to spawn genocide against a relatively prosperous minority. However, if we remove the democratic element from the equation, we can also add to the list the two other "canonical" genocides of the twentieth century. The relative wealth, industriousness, and educational attainment of the Armenian minority, even under conditions of discrimination and repression in the Ottoman lands, made them an easy target for the fanatical nationalism of the Young Turks (Chapter 4). Similar hatred or at least distaste towards Jews in Germany and other European countries contributed to popular support for the Holocaust against them (Chapter 6). Note that all three of these genocides featured massive looting and plundering along with mass murder (see the discussion of genocide and greed in Chapter 10). Genocide offers an unprecedented opportunity to "redress" an economic imbalance by seizing the wealth and property of the victims, and to inflict on them the kind of humiliation that the majority population may have experienced.

ANTHROPOLOGICAL PERSPECTIVES

A confession: I have long been envious of anthropologists. Political scientists like myself are commanded to maintain a detached, "objective" view of their subject. Our research stratagems are usually confined to the library and the office, with only occasional forays into the outside world. Anthropologists, by contrast, are allowed and encouraged to get their hands dirty. The defining method of anthropology – fieldwork – commands them to wade into the thick of their subject matter, and get to know the people they study. They may "emerge from the field exhausted," but they carry with them "a material of extraordinary richness and depth."[44] Reading anthropological case studies, one sees and hears the subjects, smells the air, tastes the food.

Anthropology "calls for an understanding of different societies as they appear *from the inside*,"[45] where anthropologists are seen as inevitable and integral participants in the cross-cultural encounter. They are expected to describe the impact of the experience on their own subjectivity. Assisting with the forensic excavation of mass graves in Guatemala, Victoria Sanford reported: "I'm not vomiting, I haven't fainted, what a beautiful valley, everything is greener than green, those are real bones, my god 200 people were massacred here, their relatives are watching."[46] It would be hard to describe such an experience as enjoyable. But it is certainly *revelatory*, both to author and reader, in a way that more detached analyses rarely are.

Consider the approach adopted in another recent and impressive work on the anthropology of genocidal conflict: Ivana Macek's *Sarajevo Under Siege: Anthropology in Wartime* (2009). In April 1992, Bosnian Serb forces closed a ring around the cosmopolitan city of Sarajevo, beginning a siege that lasted for nearly four years (see pp. 320–22). Macek – a Croat scholar from Zagreb whose anthropological research had previously focused on Africa – found herself drawn not to "aggressive Croatian nationalism," but to the besieged multiethnic population of Sarajevo, which was "being hit hardest by a nationalistic war." She decided "to let individuals' lived experiences of violence stand at the center of research and from that point to trace the effects of war on society and culture." In so doing, she consciously took "a poet's approach to fieldwork, as well as to writing." In contrast to the emotional disengagement and bloodless prose of most social-science writing, Macek proclaimed the anthropologist's right to adopt "a disciplined subjectivity [which] becomes not a flaw or obstacle but a crucial element for creating meaningful knowledge."

For six months over the period of the siege, during several visits, Macek shared the struggle and toil of Sarajevans, "employ[ing] all of my faculties . . . in order to manage from day to day, as well as record what they and I were undergoing." She emerged with a unique perspective: both insider/participant and rigorous scholarly observer. She documented the "deep sense of shame and humiliation" that always lurked, as people desperately clawed the means of subsistence from their austere and dangerous environment. But she also documented the strategies of coping and resistance: from the "fantastically inventive solutions to wartime shortages"; to the "magical thinking and small private magic routines" which people adopted as a "'childish' solution to an objectively unbearable situation"; to the gallows humor that citizens indulged in ("What is the difference between Sarajevo and Auschwitz? There is no gas in Sarajevo"). Perhaps surprisingly, and inspiringly, an outpouring of creative talent occurred as a reaction to life under siege, resulting in "an amazingly active artistic life": as one Sarajevan told her, "arts became the fount of the lifeforce. It gave back life to people, gave birth anew to optimism and strength, and gave meaning in a time when it looked as if life had lost all meaning." But Macek also witnessed expressions of "the emotional numbness and irrationality that followed an excess of pain": "People I saw who simply stood in open places during the shelling as if nothing was going on . . . "

Perhaps most poignantly, Macek captured the slow erosion of the cosmopolitan and interethnic identity that the overarching designation of "Sarajevan" had long sponsored and permitted. Increasingly, Sarajevans grew

> divided along ethnonational lines into Muslims, Serbs, and Croats. Ethnoreligious identities became politicized and grew more salient in everyday life. . . . Family members, friends, colleagues, and neighbors were judged by new, wartime standards, as people almost invariably tried to understand whether or not others' actions were influenced by their national identity. . . . Sarajevans started to "remember" the ethnoreligious traditions that most of them had lost during the secularization of society following the Second World War.[47]

The result of Macek's investigations was a portrait of a community under siege, with acts of genocide and urbicide underway (and resisted), with identities and memories summoned and reshaped. It provided further evidence that, in historian Anton Weiss-Wendt's assessment, it is anthropologists who "have made probably the most valuable contribution to genocide studies in . . . recent years."[48] However, this emergence of an anthropological critique in genocide studies required, and derived from, a broader shift in the discipline's focus: "a theoretical and ethnographic move away from studying small, relatively stable communities toward looking at those under siege, in flux, and victimized by state violence or insurgency movements."[49] The declaration issued in *Anthropology Today* in 1993, "Anthropologists Against Ethnic Violence," stated that "we must not shirk the responsibility of disputing the claims of demagogues and warning of the dangers of ethnic violence."[50]

The declaration, and the broader paradigm shift it represented, also reflected a conviction that anthropology had been deeply compromised, in the past, by its alliances with European imperialism and Nazism.[51] Most nineteenth-century anthropologists took for granted European dominance over subject peoples. Their schema of classification tended to revolve around hierarchies of humanity: they sifted and categorized the peoples of the world in a way that bolstered the European claim to supremacy. Modern "scientific" racism was one result. Even the most liberal anthropologists of the pre-First World War period, such as Franz Boas, viewed the disappearance of many primitive civilizations as preordained; "salvage ethnography" was developed in an attempt to describe as much of these civilizations as possible before nature took its supposedly inevitable course.[52]

Perhaps neither before nor since have anthropologists played such a prominent role in state policy as during the Nazi era (Chapter 6). Gretchen Schafft noted that "German and, to a lesser extent, Austrian anthropologists were involved in the Holocaust as perpetrators, from its beginning to its conclusion . . . Never had their discipline been so well respected and received. Never had practitioners been so busy . . . while the price for not cooperating was 'internal exile,' joblessness, or incarceration."[53] Prominent anthropologists such as Eugen Fischer, Adolf Würth, and Sophie Ehrhardt flocked to lend a scientific gloss to the Nazis' preposterous racial theories about Jews, Roma, and Slavs; many of these "scholars" continued their work into the postwar period.[54]

However, contradictorily and simultaneously, anthropology was emerging as the most pluralistic and *least* ethnocentric of the social sciences. Under the influence of the discipline's leading figures – Franz Boas, the revolutionary ethnographer Bronislaw Malinowski, the Englishman A.R. Radcliffe-Brown, and the American Margaret Mead – a methodology was developed that encouraged nonjudgmental involvement in the lives and cultures of one's subjects. Hierarchies of "development" were undermined by anthropologists' nuanced study of "primitive" societies that proved to be extraordinarily complex and sophisticated. And the supposedly scientific basis for racial hierarchy was powerfully challenged by work such as that of Boas, who "researched the change in head shape across only one American generation," thereby "demonstrat[ing] to the world how race, language, and culture are causally unlinked."[55] Anthropologists played a notable and little-known role in drafting the Universal Declaration of Human Rights, cautioning the UN Commission devoted to the task against "ethnocentrism, the assumption of the superiority of one's own cultural values."[56] With the great wave of decolonization after the Second World War, it was anthropologists above all who went "into the field" to grapple with, and in a sense validate, diverse "Third World" societies.

Anthropology's guiding ideal of cultural relativism requires that the practitioner "suspend one's judgement and preconceptions as much as possible, in order to better understand another's worldview." In studying genocidal processes, the relativist approach emphasizes "local understandings and cultural dynamics that both structure and motivate genocide," and examines them in their broader cultural context. Rather than "simply dismissing *génocidaires* as 'irrational' and 'savage,'" the approach "demands that we understand them and their perspective regardless of what we think of perpetrators."[57]

Arguably, though, cultural relativism has its limits. At some point, if one is to confront atrocities, one must adopt a universalist stand (i.e., that atrocities are always criminal, and cannot be excused by culture). Nancy Scheper-Hughes, among others, has criticized cultural relativism as "moral relativism" that is "no longer appropriate to the world in which we live." If anthropology "is to be worth anything at all, it must be ethically grounded."[58] Alexander Hinton likewise suggests that relativism "played a key role in inhibiting anthropologists from studying genocide," together with other forms of "political violence in complex state societies."[59]

Partly because of relativist influences, and partly because of its preference for "studying small, relatively stable communities,"[60] anthropology's engagement with genocide came relatively late. Only recently has a "school" begun to coalesce, developing a rich body of literature, particularly on terror and genocide in Latin America, Africa, and Southeast Asia. Deploying fieldwork-based ethnography (literally, "writing about ethnic groups"), these researchers have amassed and analyzed a wealth of individual testimonies about the atrocities. In Victoria Sanford's estimation, this "is among the greatest contributions anthropology can make to understanding social problems – the presentation of testimonies, life histories, and ethnographies of violence."[61] Together with the reports of human rights organizations and truth commissions (see Chapter 15), these provide important evidence, for present and future generations, of the nature and scale of atrocity.

Anthropologists go further still, to analyze how atrocity is ritualized within cultures, and how when collectively "performed," it serves to bolster communal identity and solidarity. A wide range of commentators have noted, for example, the atmosphere of festive cruelty that regularly pervades genocidal frenzies. Where the killing and celebrations of it are not tightly circumscribed, limited to a core genocidal cadre, they often assume a carnival-like flavor. In a North American context, one can recall the party atmosphere that prevailed among the all-white spectators at the lynching of two black men in Indiana (p. 485), or the Colorado militia perpetrators of the Sand Creek Massacre of Cheyenne (p. 115), who "put their accomplishments on public display, a deliriously received victory parade through Denver providing the opportunity for them to bedeck their horses, uniforms and other accoutrements with the various bodily parts – mostly female genitalia – that they had garnered as trophies."[62] In both cases, the performance and ritual celebration of genocidal acts helped to fortify white tribal solidarities, constructed against a threatening tide of "savage" Indians or "depraved" black males. Where these subaltern identifications are not fantastical but actual, one sees not only a similar ritual quality to acts of vengeance against (real) oppressors, whether localized or generalized, but the incorporation of *fantasies* of vengeance into cultural rituals and performances located along a continuum of subaltern genocide. My own exploration of this theme in *Genocides by the Oppressed* was strongly influenced by anthropological inquiries into ritual performances of retributive victory and atrocity.[63]

Questions of genocide and memory, explored further in Chapter 14, are also informed and interpreted by anthropological researchers: how coping strategies are adopted in the aftermath of mass atrocity;[64] how atrocities may become literally "part of the landscape" for communities, attached to familiar objects, irrupting to the forefront of consciousness at unexpected moments:

> [The] living memory of terror can reinvoke the physical and psychological pain of past acts of violence in unexpected moments. A tree, for example, is not just a tree. A river, not just a river. At a given moment, a tree is a reminder of the baby whose head was smashed against a tree by a soldier. The tree, and the memory of the baby it invokes, in turn reinvoke a chain of memories of terror, including witnessing the murder of a husband or brother who was tied to another tree and beaten to death – perhaps on the same day or perhaps years later.[65]

Culturally specific practices of terror are especially well suited to anthropological investigation. In his study of the Rwandan genocide, *Sacrifice as Terror*, Christopher Taylor showed how cultural dynamics, rituals, and symbolism may help to explain the particular course that the holocaust took. His analysis demonstrated – in Alexander Hinton's summary – that anthropological methods "explain why the violence was perpetrated in certain ways – for example, the severing of Achilles tendons, genital mutilation, breast oblation, the construction of roadblocks that served as execution sites, bodies being stuffed into latrines." The violence "was deeply symbolic," representing cultural beliefs about expulsion and excretion, obstruction and flow.[66] For example, Taylor pointed out the symbolism of the Nyabarongo River as a route by which murdered Tutsis were to be "removed from Rwanda and retransported to their presumed land of origin," thereby purifying the nation of its internal "'foreign' minority." Figure 9.1 on p. 354 shows the grim results. In Taylor's interpretation,

> Rwanda's rivers became part of the genocide by acting as the body politic's organs of elimination, in a sense "excreting" its hated internal other. It is not much of a leap to infer that Tutsi were thought of as excrement by their persecutors. Other evidence of this is apparent in the fact that many Tutsi were stuffed into latrines after their deaths.[67]

An intimate familiarity with day-to-day cultural praxis allows anthropologists to draw connections between "exceptional" outbursts of atrocity, such as genocide, and more quotidian forms and structures of violence. The leading theorist in this regard is Nancy Scheper-Hughes, whose classic study of a Brazilian village, *Death without Weeping*, explored the desensitization of women-as-mothers to the deaths of their infant children amidst pervasive scarcity.[68] This extended even to complicity in their offspring's deaths through the deliberate withholding of food and care, with the resulting mortality viewed as divinely ordained. Subsequently, Scheper-Hughes outlined a *genocidal continuum*, composed of a multitude of "small wars and invisible genocides" conducted in the normative social spaces of public schools, clinics, emergency rooms, hospital wards, nursing homes, court rooms, prisons, detention centers, and public morgues. The continuum refers to the human capacity to reduce others to nonpersons, to monsters, or to things that give structure, meaning, and rationale to everyday practices of violence. It is essential that we recognize in our species (and in ourselves) *a genocidal capacity* and that we exercise a defensive hypervigilance, a hypersensitivity to the less dramatic, *permitted*, everyday acts of violence that make participation (under other conditions) in genocidal acts possible, perhaps more easy than we would like to know. I would include all expressions of social exclusion, dehumanization, depersonalization, pseudo-speciation, and reification that normalize atrocious behavior and violence toward others.[69]

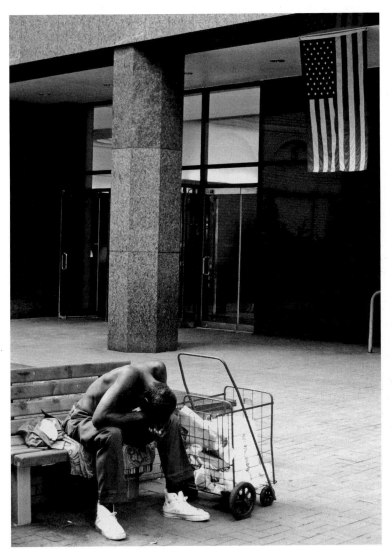

Figure 11.2 Nancy Scheper-Hughes's concept of the "genocidal continuum" focuses attention on "everyday acts of violence that make participation . . . in genocidal acts possible," especially strategies of social marginalization, anathematization, and exclusion. A homeless African American man sits on a bench in New York City, 2005.

Source: Colin Gregory Palmer/Wikimedia Commons.

She noted, for instance, that Brazilian "street children" experience attacks by police "that are genocidal in their social and political sentiments." The children "are often described as 'dirty vermin' so that unofficial policies of 'street cleaning,' 'trash removal,' 'fly swatting,' and 'pest removal' are invoked in garnering broad-based public support for their extermination." Through such practices and rhetoric, genocide becomes "socially incremental," something that is "experienced by perpetrators, collaborators, bystanders – and even by victims themselves – as expected, routine, even justified."[70] There seems a clear connection between such everyday rhetoric and the propaganda discourse of full-scale genocide, in which Native American children were referred to as "nits [who] make lice," Jews as "vermin," and Rwandan Tutsis as "cockroaches."

In closing this brief account of anthropological framings and insights, it is worth considering the role of *forensic anthropologists*. Bridging the natural and social sciences, they "have worked with health professionals, lawyers, photographers, and nongovernmental organizations to analyze physical remains and gather evidence with which to prosecute perpetrators."[71] Their core activities consist of the "search for, recovery, and preservation of physical evidence at the outdoor scene" of crimes and mass atrocities. They document how evidence relates to its "depositional environment," and use the data collected to reconstruct the events surrounding the deaths of the exhumed victims.[72]

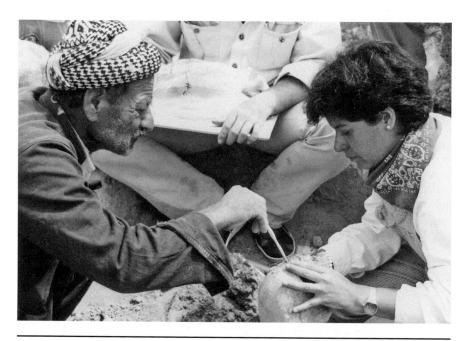

Figure 11.3   Isabel Reveco, a Chilean forensic anthropologist, examines the skull of a Kurdish victim of Saddam Hussein's Anfal Campaign against Iraqi Kurds (see p. 178). She is "helped by the father of two young men who were executed at Koreme," one of the major Anfal genocide sites. Saddam Hussein was tried and condemned to death for genocide against the Kurds, among other crimes; he was hanged on December 30, 2006. The evidence amassed and sifted by forensic anthropologists has been vital to sustaining charges of genocide and crimes against humanity in this and other prosecutions.

Source: Mercedes Doretti/Equipo Argentino de Antropología Forense (EAAF).

In recent years, forensic anthropologists have become the most visible face of anthropology in genocide investigation and adjudication. Among the pioneers of the field is Clyde Snow, a US specialist who in the 1990s oversaw the exhumations at the Balkan massacre sites of Vukovar and Srebrenica. These excavations form the basis of an inevitably gruesome but illuminating book of photographs and text, *The Graves* (see Further Study). As Snow described his task:

> When [societies] choose to pursue justice, we forensic anthropologists can put the tools of a rapidly developing science at the disposal of the survivors. We can determine a murder victim's age, sex and race from the size and shape of certain bones. We can extract DNA from some skeletons and match it with samples from the victims' relatives. Marks on the bones can reveal signs of old diseases and injuries reflected in the victims' medical histories, as well as more sinister evidence: bullet holes, cut marks from knives, or fracture patterns produced by blunt instruments. Taken together, such clues can tell us who victims were and how they died – clues crucial to bringing the killers to justice.[73]

Snow's earliest digs were conducted in Argentina during the 1980s, where he helped to train the Argentine Forensic Anthropology Team (Equipo Argentino de Antropología Forense, EAAF) that exhumed victims of the "Dirty War" (see Figure 11.3). "Ample forensic evidence" underpinned the report of the Argentine truth commission, *Nunca Más* (Never Again), and the prosecutions of former *junta* leaders.[74] The team went on to conduct exhumations in El Salvador, at the site of the military massacre of some 700 civilians at El Mozote.[75] With assistance from the American Association for the Advancement of Science (AAAS), Snow subsequently trained members of the Guatemalan Forensic Anthropology Team.[76] The team's investigations were equally vital to the truth commission report that labeled the military regime's campaign against Mayan Indians in the Guatemalan highlands as genocidal (see Box 3a), and assigned responsibility for more than 90 percent of the atrocities of the "civil war" to the government and the paramilitary forces it mobilized.[77]

Snow has conducted excavations at atrocity sites as geographically disparate as Ethiopia, Iraq, and the Philippines. His comment on the nature of his investigations summarizes the work of the conscientious anthropologists – and many others – who have informed our understanding of individual genocides: "You do the work in the daytime and cry at night."[78]

FURTHER STUDY

Zygmunt Bauman, *Modernity and the Holocaust*. Ithaca, NY: Cornell University Press, 2000. Influential sociological interpretation of the Jewish Holocaust.

Pierre L. van den Berghe, ed., *State Violence and Ethnicity*. Niwot, CO: University Press of Colorado, 1990. One of the best sociological works on genocide and state terror.

Paul R. Brass, ed., *Riots and Pogroms*. New York: New York University Press, 1996. Vigorous edited volume on the dynamics of ethnic violence.

Amy Chua, *World on Fire: How Exporting Free Market Democracy Breeds Ethnic Hatred and Global Instability*. New York: Anchor, 2004. Provocative overview of "market-dominant minorities."

Daniel Feierstein, *El genocidio como práctica social: Entre el nazismo y la experiencia argentina* [Genocide as a Social Practice: Between Nazism and the Argentine Experience]. Buenos Aires: Fondo de Cultura Económica, 2007. Sophisticated comparison of the sociology of Nazism with Argentina's culture of terror under military rule.

Helen Fein, *Genocide: A Sociological Perspective*. London: Sage, 1993. Short, influential treatise.

H.H. Gerth and C. Wright Mills, eds, *From Max Weber: Essays in Sociology*. New York: Oxford University Press, 1954. Writings of the great German theorist of authority, modernity, and bureaucracy.

Alexander Laban Hinton, ed., *Annihilating Difference: The Anthropology of Genocide*. Berkeley, CA: University of California Press, 2002. A groundbreaking anthology; see also *Genocide: An Anthropological Reader*; *Genocide: Truth, Memory, and Representation* (ed. with Kevin Lewis O'Neill).

Donald L. Horowitz, *The Deadly Ethnic Riot*. Berkeley, CA: University of California Press, 2001. Massive, eye-opening treatise on ethnic violence.

Irving Louis Horowitz, *Taking Lives: Genocide and State Power* (4th edn). New Brunswick, NJ: Transaction Publishers, 1997. Rambling sociological account.

Victoria Sanford, *Buried Secrets: Truth and Human Rights in Guatemala*. New York: Palgrave Macmillan, 2003. Sanford worked alongside the Guatemalan forensic anthropology team.

Gretchen E. Schafft, *From Racism to Genocide: Anthropology in the Third Reich*. Urbana, IL: University of Illinois Press, 2004. Explores anthropologists' complicity in Nazi social engineering.

James C. Scott, *Seeing Like A State: How Certain Schemes to Improve the Human Condition Have Failed*. New Haven, CT: Yale University Press, 1998. Fascinating study of "high-modernist" social planning, relevant to studies of state terror and totalitarian systems.

Jeffrey A. Sluka, ed., *Death Squad: The Anthropology of State Terror*. Philadelphia, PA: University of Pennsylvania Press, 2000. Another important anthology.

Anthony D. Smith, *National Identity*. London: Penguin, 1991. Fine primer on the ethnic and cultural roots of nationalism.

Wolfgang Sofsky, *The Order of Terror: The Concentration Camp*, trans. William Templer. Princeton, NJ: Princeton University Press, 1999. Essential book on the camps.

Eric Stover and Gilles Peress, *The Graves: Srebrenica and Vukovar*. Zurich: Scalo Publishers, 1998. Images and text of forensic excavations in Bosnia and Croatia.

Christopher C. Taylor, *Sacrifice as Terror: The Rwandan Genocide of 1994*. Oxford: Berg, 1999. Anthropological insights into the Rwandan holocaust.

Sarah E. Wagner, *To Know Where He Lies: DNA Technology and the Search for Srebrenica's Missing*. Berkeley, CA: University of California Press, 2008. Moving anthropological study of the exhumation of victims of the 1995 Srebrenica massacre, and continuing attempts to identify the dead.

NOTES

1 See Thomas Hylland Eriksen, *Small Places, Large Issues: An Introduction to Social and Cultural Anthropology* (London: Pluto Press, 2001), p. 29.

2 Horowitz quoted in Helen Fein, *Genocide: A Sociological Perspective* (London: Sage, 1993), p. 6.

3 Nancy Scheper-Hughes, "The Primacy of the Ethical: Propositions for a Militant Anthropology," *Current Anthropology*, 36: 3 (1995), pp. 410, 414.

4 See Alexander Laban Hinton, ed., *Annihilating Difference: The Anthropology of Genocide* (Berkeley, CA: University of California Press, 2002); Alexander Laban Hinton, ed., *Genocide: An Anthropological Reader* (London: Blackwell, 2002); Nancy Scheper-Hughes and Philippe Bourgois, eds, *Violence in War and Peace: An Anthology* (London: Blackwell, 2004); Jeffrey A. Sluka, ed., *Death Squad: The Anthropology of State Terror* (Philadelphia, PA: University of Pennsylvania Press, 1999).

5 "Modernity," as Hinton notes, "is notoriously difficult to define," but "can perhaps best be described as a set of interrelated processes, some of which began to develop as early as the fifteenth century, characterizing the emergence of 'modern society.' Politically, modernity involves the rise of secular forms of government, symbolized by the French Revolution and culminating in the modern nation-state. Economically, modernity refers to capitalist expansion and its derivatives – monetarized exchange, the accumulation of capital, extensive private property, the search for new markets, commodification, and industrialization. Socially, modernity entails the replacement of 'traditional' loyalties (to lord, master, priest, king, patriarch, kin, and local community) with 'modern' ones (to secular authority, leader, 'humanity,' class, gender, race, and ethnicity). Culturally, modernity encompasses the movement from a predominantly religious to an emphatically secular and materialist worldview characterized by new ways of thinking about and understanding human behavior." Hinton, "The Dark Side of Modernity: Toward an Anthropology of Genocide," in Hinton, ed., *Annihilating Difference*, pp. 7–8. For an ambitious anthology, see Stuart Hall *et al.*, eds, *Modernity: An Introduction to Modern Societies* (Malden, MA: Blackwell, 1996).

6 Zygmunt Bauman, *Modernity and the Holocaust* (Ithaca, NY: Cornell University Press, 2000), p. 13.

7 Ibid., pp. 53, 55; emphasis in original.

8 "As a conception of the world, and even more importantly as an effective instrument of political practice, racism is unthinkable without the advancement of modern science, modern technology and modern forms of state power. As such, racism is strictly a modern product. Modernity made racism possible." Ibid., p. 61.

9 Ibid., p. 76.

10 Max Weber, "Bureaucracy," in H.H. Gerth and C. Wright Mills, eds, *From Max Weber: Essays in Sociology* (New York: Oxford University Press, 1954), pp. 229, 233, 240. Lester R. Kurtz notes that bureaucracy evinces a tendency "to promote formal rather than substantive rationality, that is, the kind of thinking that emphasizes efficiency rather than moral or contextual considerations." Quoted in Robert Jay Lifton and Eric Markusen, *The Genocidal Mentality: Nazi Holocaust and Nuclear Threat* (New York: Basic Books, 1990), p. 180.

11 Bauman, *Modernity and the Holocaust*, p. 76.

12 Wolfgang Sofsky, *The Order of Terror: The Concentration Camp* (Princeton, NJ: Princeton University Press, 1999), p. 264. "Modern terror has no need of big criminals. For its purposes, the small-time tormentor suffices: the conscientious bookkeeper, the mediocre official, the zealous doctor, the young, slightly anxious female factory worker" (p. 278).

13 The classic study is Markusen and Kopf, *The Genocidal Mentality*.

14 Mark Levene, *Genocide in the Age of the Nation State, Vol. 1: The Meaning of Genocide* (London: I.B. Tauris, 2005), p. 10.

15 Ibid., p. 144. See also the emphatic formulation that "the specificity of genocide cannot be divorced from the very modern *framework* within which it occurs" (p. 155).

16 Levene, *Genocide in the Age of the Nation State, Vol. 1*, pp. 12–13, quoting Alexander Hinton.

17 Bauman, *Modernity and the Holocaust*, p. 89.

18 Lemkin, letter of July 22, 1948, quoted in John Docker, "Are Settler-Colonies Inherently Genocidal?," in A. Dirk Moses, ed., *Empire, Colony, Genocide: Conquest, Occupation, and Subaltern Resistance in World History* (New York: Berghahn Books, 2008), p. 87.

19 Levene, *Genocide in the Age of the Nation State, Vol. 1*, pp. 20, 130, 145. Emphases added.

20 Likewise with racism: though Levene correctly points to a modern scientific or pseudo-scientific discourse, he also acknowledges that "differentiating people on the basis of gradations of skin colour, and other physical attributes, as a tool whereby a dominant group legitimizes its social control over other groups is very old in history. It is certainly not exclusive to Europeans. One only has to look at the caste system in India to note its longevity and invidiousness." Levene, *Genocide in the Age of the Nation State, Vol. 2*, p. 189.

21 Alex Alvarez, *Governments, Citizens, and Genocide: A Comparative and Interdisciplinary Approach* (Bloomington, IN: Indiana University Press, 2001), p. 2.

22 Michael Mann similarly notes that in the Nazi genocide against the Jews, "foreign collaborators, Romanian and Croatian fascists, used primitive techniques to almost as devastating effect" as high-tech gas chambers. Mann, *The Dark Side of Democracy: Explaining Ethnic Cleansing* (Cambridge: Cambridge University Press, 2005), p. 241.

23 "As for the supposedly desensitizing effects of bureaucratic distancing, the brutal face-to-face murder of the Tutsis by tens of thousands of ordinary Hutus, many of them poor farmers, utterly disproves that thesis." Marie Fleming, "Genocide and the Body Politic in the Time of Modernity," in Robert Gellately and Ben Kiernan, eds, *The Specter of Genocide: Mass Murder in Historical Perspective* (Cambridge: Cambridge University Press, 2003), p. 103.

24 Levene likewise acknowledges "the military-bureaucratic power and organizing outreach of *pre-modern* states" (his emphasis). Levene, *Genocide in the Age of the Nation State, Vol. 1*, p. 148.

25 For a contrary view, defining the core features of the Rwandan holocaust as "manifestations of the modern world," see Robert Melson, "Modern Genocide in Rwanda: Ideology, Revolution, War, and Mass Murder in an African State," ch. 15 in Gellately and Kiernan, eds, *The Specter of Genocide*.

26 Benedict Anderson, *Imagined Communities: Reflections on the Origins and Spread of Nationalism* (London: Verso, 1991).

27 Anthony D. Smith, *National Identity* (London: Penguin, 1991), p. 21.

28 I am grateful to Benjamin Madley for this insight.

29 Barth cited in Andrew Bell-Fialkoff, *Ethnic Cleansing* (New York: St. Martin's Griffin, 1999), p. 73. As Alexander Hinton notes, "It is one of the most vexing problems of our time that imagined sociopolitical identities are so often forged out of hatred toward contrasting others." Hinton, *Why Did They Kill? Cambodia in the Shadow of Genocide* (Berkeley, CA: University of California Press, 2005), p. 220. For a famous reading of the phenomenon, examining the constitutive impact of the "Orient" upon the "West," see Edward Said, *Orientalism* (New York: Vintage Books, 1979).

30 Geertz quoted in Ray Taras and Rajat Ganguly, *Understanding Ethnic Conflict: The International Dimension* (New York: Longman, 1998), p. 14.

31 See John R. Bowen, "The Myth of Global Ethnic Conflict," ch. 15 in Hinton, ed., *Genocide: An Anthropological Reader*, pp. 334–43.

32 Nancy Scheper-Hughes wrote sardonically: "'Race,' 'ethnicity,' 'tribe,' 'culture,' and 'identity' were dutifully deconstructed and de-essentialized in Anthropology 101, where they were taught as historically invented and fictive concepts. Meanwhile . . . South African Xhosas and Zulus (manipulated by a government-orchestrated 'third force') daily slaughtered each other in and around worker hostels in the name of 'tribe,' 'ethnicity,' and 'culture.'" Scheper-Hughes, "The Primacy of the Ethical", p. 415.

33 James Waller, *Becoming Evil: How Ordinary People Commit Genocide and Mass Killing* (Oxford: Oxford University Press, 2002), pp. 153–54. He also points out (pp. 241–42) that in social–psychological experiments, "complete strangers arbitrarily assigned to groups, having no interaction or conflict with one another, and not competing against another group behaved as if those who shared their meaningless label were their dearest friends or closest relatives," and would rapidly come into conflict with those defined differently, but equally meaninglessly.

34 Donald L. Horowitz, *The Deadly Ethnic Riot* (Berkeley, CA: University of California Press, 2001), p. 243.

35 Paul R. Brass, "Introduction," in Brass, ed., *Riots and Pogroms* (Washington Square, NY: New York University Press, 1996), p. 12.

36 Horowitz makes explicit the link between ethnic rioting and genocide: "The deadly ethnic riot embodies physical destruction combined with degradation and the implicit threat of genocide. . . . The random, brutal killing of targets based merely on their ascriptive identity has . . . a proto-genocidal quality about it; it is an augury of extermination." Horowitz, *The Deadly Ethnic Riot*, pp. 432, 459.

37 Brass, "Introduction," pp. 12–13.

38 According to Charles Tilly, these actors "operate in a middle ground between (on one side) the full authorization of a national army and (on the other) the private employment of violence by parents, lovers, or feuding clans." Tilly, *The Politics of Collective Violence* (Cambridge: Cambridge University Press, 2003), p. 19.

39 Horowitz, *The Deadly Ethnic Riot*, p. 187. See also Walter P. Zenner, "Middleman Minorities and Genocide," in Isidor Wallimann and Michael N. Dobkowski, eds, *Genocide and the Modern Age: Etiology and Case Studies of Mass Death* (Westport, CT: Syracuse University Press, 2000), pp. 253–81. Groundbreaking genocide scholar Leo Kuper refers to these as "hostage groups"; that is, "hostages to the fortunes of the dominant group." Kuper, "The Genocidal State: An Overview," in Pierre L. van den Berghe, ed., *State Violence and Ethnicity* (Niwot, CO: University Press of Colorado, 1990), p. 44. See also the discussion in Kuper's *The Prevention of Genocide* (New Haven, CT: Yale University Press, 1985), p. 201.

40 Amy Chua, *World on Fire: How Exporting Free Market Democracy Breeds Ethnic Hatred and Global Instability* (New York: Anchor, 2004), p. 79.

41 Genocidal massacres may also be cited, such as the centuries of pogroms against European Jews, Indian uprisings against Whites in Upper Peru and Yucatán (Chapter 1), and the Hindu slaughter of Sikhs in India in 1984. Short of genocide or genocidal massacre, the strategy most commonly adopted against market-dominant minorities is mass expulsion. Idi Amin's banishing of Indians from Uganda in 1972 is an example; another is the "Boat People" expelled from Vietnam following the nationalist victory of 1975, aimed at "the elimination of ethnic Chinese and bourgeois Vietnamese from Vietnamese society." Richard L. Rubinstein, *The Age of Triage: Fear and Hope in an Overcrowded World* (Boston, MA: Beacon Press, 1983), p. 176. This was also, of course, the dominant Nazi policy towards German Jews between 1933 and 1938 (Chapter 6).

42 Horowitz, for example, argues that "in comparative perspective," the targeting of "unusually prosperous or advantaged ethnic groups . . . is only a minor factor in target selection [for deadly ethnic rioting], operative under certain, specific conditions of riot leadership. Quite often, prosperous minorities are not targeted even during the most brutal riots." Horowitz, *The Deadly Ethnic Riot*, p. 5.

43 Chua, *World on Fire*, pp. 124–25.

44 Eriksen, *Small Places, Large Issues*, p. 27.

45 Ibid., p. 7.

46 Victoria Sanford, *Buried Secrets: Truth and Human Rights in Guatemala* (New York: Palgrave Macmillan, 2003), p. 31.

47 Ivana Macek, *Sarajevo Under Siege: Anthropology in Wartime* (Philadelphia, PA: University of Pennsylvania Press, 2009). The quotes in these passages are drawn from pp. x, 4, 8, 11, 12, 31, 48–49, 53, 54–55, 62, 123, 161.

48 Anton Weiss-Wendt, "Problems in Comparative Genocide Scholarship," in Dan Stone, ed., *The Historiography of Genocide* (London: Palgrave Macmillan, 2008), pp. 42–70.

49 Alexander Laban Hinton, "The Dark Side of Modernity: Toward an Anthropology of Genocide," in Hinton, ed., *Annihilating Difference*, p. 2.

50 Declaration quoted in Macek, *Life Under Siege*, p. 28.

51 "The work of anthropology, in its earliest instances of practice, composed a necessary first step that gave substance and justification to theories of 'natural' hierarchy that would eventually be employed to rationalize racism, colonialism, slavery, ethnic purifications and, ultimately, genocide projects." Wendy C. Hamblet, "The Crisis of Meanings: Could the Cure be the Cause of Genocide?," *Journal of Genocide Research*, 5: 2 (2003), p. 243.

52 See also the discussion of Patrick Brantlinger's *Dark Vanishings* in Chapter 3.

53 Gretchen E. Schafft, "Scientific Racism in Service of the Reich: German Anthropologists in the Nazi Era," in Hinton, ed., *Annihilating Difference*, pp. 117, 131. See also Schafft's full-length book, *From Racism to Genocide: Anthropology in the Third Reich* (Urbana, IL: University of Illinois Press, 2004).

54 See Sybil Milton, "Holocaust: The Gypsies," ch. 6 in Samuel Totten *et al.*, eds, *Century of Genocide: Eyewitness Accounts and Critical Views* (New York: Garland Publishing, 1997). According to the Web Hyperdictionary, "physical anthropology" is "the scientific study of the physical characteristics, variability, and evolution of the human organism." See http://searchbox.hyperdictionary.com/dictionary/physical+anthropology.

55 Paul A. Erickson and Liam D. Murphy, *A History of Anthropological Theory* (Toronto, ON: Broadview Press, 2003), p. 76.

56 Geoffrey Robertson, *Crimes Against Humanity: The Struggle for Global Justice* (New York: The New Press, 2000), pp. 31–32. An anthropologist, W.G. Sumner, first used the term "ethnocentrism" in 1906, defining it as "the technical name for [a] view of things in which one's own group is the center of everything, and all others are scaled and rated with reference to it. . . . Each group nourishes its own pride and vanity, boasts itself superior, exalts its own divinities, and looks with contempt on outsiders." Quoted in Waller, *Becoming Evil*, p. 154.

57 Alexander Hinton, personal communication, July 24, 2005.

58 Scheper-Hughes, "The Primacy of the Ethical," p. 410.

59 Hinton, "The Dark Side of Modernity," in Hinton, ed., *Annihilating Difference*, p. 2.

60 Ibid.

61 Sanford, *Buried Secrets*, p. 210. In anthropological parlance, individual testimonies constitute the "emic" level of analysis, academic interpretations the "etic" level. See Eriksen, *Small Places, Large Issues*, p. 36.

62 Mark Levene, *Genocide in the Age of the Nation State, Vol. 2: The Rise of the West and the Coming of Genocide* (London: I.B. Tauris, 2005), p. 94.

63 Adam Jones, "'When the Rabbit's Got the Gun': Subaltern Genocide and the Genocidal Continuum," in Nicholas A. Robins and Adam Jones, eds, *Genocides by the Oppressed: Subaltern Genocide in Theory and Practice* (Bloomington, IN: Indiana University Press, 2009), pp. 185–207; see especially pp. 187–88.

64 See, e.g., Antonius Robben, "How Traumatized Societies Remember: The Aftermath of Argentina's Dirty War," *Cultural Critique*, 59 (Winter 2005), pp. 120–64.

65 Sanford, *Buried Secrets*, p. 143.

66 Hinton, "The Dark Side of Modernity," p. 19. Hinton argues that symbolism "mediate[s] all our understandings of the world, including a world of genocide" (personal communication, July 24, 2005). Jacques Sémelin also points to "the ways in which bodies are taken over, twisted, cut into pieces" as constituting "wholly cultural acts, through which the perpetrator expresses something of his own identity." Sémelin, *Purify and Destroy: The Political Uses of Massacre and Genocide* (New York: Columbia University Press, 2007), p. 301.

67 Christopher C. Taylor, *Sacrifice as Terror: The Rwandan Genocide of 1994* (Oxford: Berg, 1998), p. 130. The phenomenon has its counterpart in other genocides; as early as 1940,

the English novelist and essayist H.G. Wells pointed to "the victims smothered in latrines" in Nazi concentration camps, exemplifying "the cloacal side of Hitlerism." Quoted in Robertson, *Crimes Against Humanity*, p. 23. For another fascinating study of violent ritual and symbolism, see Antonius Robben, "State Terror in the Netherworld: Disappearance and Reburial in Argentina," in Robben, ed., *Death, Mourning, and Burial: A Cross-Cultural Reader* (London: Blackwell, 2005), which explored the symbolic violation of "disappearance" in a culture that ascribes great significance to the physical corpse and rituals of burial.

68 Nancy Scheper-Hughes, *Death without Weeping: The Violence of Everyday Life in Brazil* (Berkeley, CA: University of California Press, 1993).

69 Nancy Scheper-Hughes, "Coming to Our Senses: Anthropology and Genocide," in Hinton, ed., *Annihilating Difference*, p. 369. See also Scheper-Hughes, "The Genocidal Continuum: Peace-time Crimes," ch. 2 in Jeannette Marie Mageo, ed., *Power and the Self* (Cambridge: Cambridge University Press, 2002), pp. 29–47.

70 Scheper-Hughes, "Coming to Our Senses," pp. 372–73.

71 Hinton, "The Dark Side of Modernity," p. 33.

72 D.C. Dirkmaat and J.M. Adovasio, "The Role of Archaeology in the Recovery and Interpretation of Human Remains from an Outdoor Forensic Setting," in William D. Haglund and Marcella H. Sorg, eds, *Forensic Taphonomy: The Postmortem Fate of Human Remains* (New York: CRC Press, 1997), p. 58.

73 Clyde Snow, "Murder Most Foul," *The Sciences* (May/June 1995), p. 16.

74 Ibid., p. 20.

75 See Leigh Binford, *The El Mozote Massacre: Anthropology and Human Rights* (Tucson, AZ: University of Arizona Press, 1996); Mark Danner, *The Massacre at El Mozote: A Parable of the Cold War* (New York: Vintage, 1994).

76 "Originally a five-member group, the Guatemalan Forensic Anthropology Foundation now employs more than 60 people and has carried out more than 200 exhumations." Victoria Sanford, personal communication, June 15, 2005.

77 The activities of the Guatemalan forensic team are movingly described by Victoria Sanford in her book *Buried Secrets*, centering on exhumations in the Mayan village of Acul.

78 See the "Clyde Snow Information Page" at http://www.ajweberman.com/cs.htm.

CHAPTER 12

Political Science and International Relations

The core concern of political science is power: how it is distributed and used within states and societies. International relations (IR) examines its use and distribution among the state units that compose the international system. Historically, IR's overriding concern is with peace and war, though in recent decades the discipline has grappled increasingly with the growth of international "regimes": norms, rules, and patterns of conduct that influence state behavior in given issue areas.

The relevance to genocide studies of all these lines of inquiry is considerable. We have already drawn upon the contributions of political scientists and IR theorists, notably in Chapter 2 on "State and Empire; War and Revolution." The present chapter explores four further contributions of PoliSci and IR frameworks: empirical studies of genocide; the changing nature of war; the putative link between democracy and peace; and the role of ethical norms and moral entrepreneurs in constructing "prohibition regimes" worldwide, including the regime against genocide.

EMPIRICAL INVESTIGATIONS

The most influential empirical investigators of state-directed mass killing are the US political scientists R.J. Rummel, Barbara Harff, and Ted Gurr, the latter two often working in tandem. Their studies have clarified the scope and character of genocidal, "politicidal," and "democidal" murder in modern times. As with nearly all genocide scholars, their work is preventionist in orientation (see Chapter 6). They seek to determine the explanatory variables that can assist in identifying the genocide-prone societies of the present, and in isolating positive and constructive features that may inoculate societies against genocide and other crimes against humanity.

Rummel's book *Death by Government* (1997) coined the term "democide" to describe "government mass murder" – including but not limited to genocide as defined in the UN Convention. Examining the death-toll from twentieth-century democide, Rummel was the first to place it almost beyond the bounds of imaginability. According to his study, somewhere in the range of *170 million* "men, women, and children have been shot, beaten, tortured, knifed, burned, starved, frozen, crushed, or worked to death; buried alive, drowned, hung, bombed, or killed in any other of the myriad ways governments have inflicted death on unarmed, helpless citizens and foreigners."[1] If combat casualties in war are added to the picture, "Power has killed over 203 million people in [the twentieth] century."[2]

Rummel identifies the "most lethal regimes," in terms of numbers of people exterminated, as the Soviet Union under Lenin and Stalin (Chapter 5), communist China (Chapter 5), Germany under the Nazis (Chapter 6 and Box 6a), and Nationalist China (touched on briefly in Chapter 2). If the "megamurder" index is recalculated based upon a regime's time in power (i.e., as deaths per year), then Cambodia under the Khmer Rouge (Chapter 7), Turkey under Kemal Atatürk, and the Nazi puppet state in Croatia (1941–45) top the list.

Rummel discerned an underlying "Power Principle" in this human catastrophe, namely that "Power kills; absolute Power kills absolutely":

> The more power a government has, the more it can act arbitrarily according to the whims and desires of the elite, and the more it will make war on others and murder its foreign and domestic subjects. The more constrained the power of governments, the more power is diffused, checked, and balanced, the less it will aggress on others and commit democide.[3]

Accordingly, for Rummel, liberal democracies are the good guys. Only in situations of all-out international war, or when their democratic procedures are subverted by conniving elites, do they engage in democide on a significant scale. This argument ties in with the "democratic peace" thesis, and I will return to Rummel's work in addressing that thesis below. His significance, for the present, lies in his systematic attempt to tabulate the gory toll of twentieth-century mass killing, and to tie this to the exercise of political power (or "Power") worldwide.

Barbara Harff and Ted Gurr have approached genocide and "politicide" – mass killing on the basis of imputed political affiliation[4] – through the study of ethnic conflicts. In 1988, the authors compiled data for genocides and politicides between 1945 and 1980, and published a groundbreaking analysis that sought to isolate where, and under what conditions, these phenomena are most likely to occur. Harff summarized their findings as follows:

> Revolutionary one-party states are the likeliest offenders. Genocides occur with alarming frequency during or shortly after the revolutionary takeovers. Especially dangerous are situations in which long-standing ethnic rivalries erupt and radicalized groups armed with a revolutionary ideology gain the upper hand.

Communist ideologues tend to be most aggressive in their dealings with potential or past opposition groups. Interestingly enough, the length of democratic experience is inversely related to the occurrence of geno/politicides.[5]

The following year (1989), Gurr, working with James Scaritt, produced a valuable compendium of "minorities at risk," "distinguish[ing] ethnocultural minorities on the basis of present and past political discrimination, economic discrimination, their concentration regionally, numbers, and the minorities' political demands."[6] In recent years, Harff has conducted research at the US Naval Academy "in response to President Clinton's policy initiative on genocide early warning and prevention," utilizing statistical data of the State Failure Task Force.[7] Her important article for the *American Political Science Review* maintained a distinction between genocides and politicides that some find problematic;[8] but her findings have both buttressed and extended her earlier work with Gurr. "Empirically, all but one of the 37 genocides and politicides that began between 1955 and 1998 occurred during or immediately after political upheavals . . . 24 coincided with ethnic wars, 14 coincided with revolutionary wars, and 14 followed the occurrence of adverse regime changes."[9] She concluded that "the greater the magnitude of previous internal wars and regime crises, summed over the preceding 15 years, the more likely that a new state failure will lead to geno-/politicide." Among the key explanatory variables located by her study are:

- *Presence or absence of genocidal precedents:* "The risks of new [genocidal/politicidal] episodes were more than three times greater when state failures occurred in countries that had prior geno-/politicides."
- *Presence or absence of an exclusionary ideology:* "Countries in which the ruling elite adhered to an exclusionary ideology were two and a half times as likely to have state failures leading to geno-/politicide as those with no such ideology."
- *Extent of ethnic "capture" of the state:* "The risks of geno-/politicide were two and a half times more likely in countries where the political elite was based mainly or entirely on an ethnic minority."
- *Extent and depth of democratic institutions:* "Once in place, democratic institutions – even partial ones – reduce the likelihood of armed conflict and all but eliminate the risk that it will lead to geno-/politicide."
- *Degree of international "openness":* "The greater their interdependence with the global economy, the less likely that [national] elites will target minorities and political opponents for destruction."

Harff's research also turned up surprises. Ethnic and religious cleavages, in themselves, were strongly relevant only when combined with an ethnic minority's capture of the state apparatus. Poverty, which many commentators view as a virtual recipe for social conflict including genocide, could indeed "predispose societies to intense conflict," but these conflicts assumed genocidal or politicidal proportions only in tandem with features of the political system (a minority ethnicity in charge, the promulgation of an exclusionary ideology, and the like).

Harff concluded by arguing that "the risk assessments generated . . . signal possible genocides." Updating the risk assessments in 2009, she and Gurr cited progress as well as regress – and enduring danger-spots:

> The highest risk countries are the usual suspects: Sudan and Burma followed by Somalia, where no authority at present has the capacity to carry out mass killings. The future risks are nonetheless high, especially if an Islamist regime establishes control. Risks also remain high in Zimbabwe and Rwanda, and are greater than we previously estimated in Iran, Saudi Arabia, and China. They are lower in Afghanistan, Burundi, Uganda, and Sri Lanka. Some countries have dropped from previous lists because their revised risk scores, like those of Israel (included here as an example) have dropped near or below zero: among them are Bhutan, Bosnia, Côte d'Ivoire, Lebanon, and Nepal.[10]

In keeping with preventionist discourse, Harff urged policymakers to employ her and others' findings to make "timely and plausible assessments" and develop "anticipatory responses [that] should save more lives at less cost than belated responses after killings have begun."[11] The variables that she and Gurr have isolated are worth keeping in mind for the evaluation of genocide prevention and intervention strategies that concludes this volume.

THE CHANGING FACE OF WAR

> *Kalash au bilash; kalash begib al kash.*
> (You're trash without a Kalashnikov [automatic rifle]; get some cash with a Kalashnikov.)
> Popular saying in Darfur, Sudan (see Box 9a)

Methods of warfare have varied greatly over centuries and across human societies. Representatives of all of the disciplines explored in this section have provided a rich body of conflict case studies, and important exercises in comparative theory building.[12]

War in "primitive" societies ranges from the brutal and destructive (as with the Yanomami of Brazil and various New Guinean societies) to the largely demonstrative and symbolic (as among many native nations of North America).[13] The great empire builders of Central Asia laid waste to entire civilizations, but in Europe in the early modern period, war came to be waged by and against professional armies, with exemptions granted to civilians – in theory, and often in practice. Yet the two most destructive wars in history were centered precisely in civilized, modern Europe, where clashes of ideologies and national ambitions targeted principally the civilian population.

With the advent of the nuclear age, the potential destructive power of "total wars" grew limitless. The superpowers stepped back from the brink, confining their clashes to wars at the peripheries of their respective spheres of influence. One IR scholar even wondered whether an "end to major war" was nigh.[14] That speculation may have been valid – and may still be valid – in the case of international wars pitting centralized states against one another. Yet a tectonic shift in the nature of war occurred during this period. Most wars were now *civil* wars, pitting armed groups (usually guerrillas) against other armed groups (usually state agents and paramilitaries) within the borders of a single country. Often, too, these conflicts demonstrated a strong ethnic element, although this tended to be downplayed in commentary and scholarship, which focused on the government–guerrilla dyad. Examples are the wars in Burma, Ethiopia, Kashmir (divided between India and Pakistan), and Guatemala; many others could be cited.

Some scholars of international relations declared that the end of the Cold War marked a break in the trajectory of modern war. In fact, the civil wars and "limited" imperial wars of the Cold War era arguably laid the foundations for war as it is waged around the world today. Conflicts in Central America (Guatemala, Nicaragua, El Salvador) and Africa (Angola and Mozambique) were incredibly destructive – the Southern African conflicts alone killed well over a million people combined, and made refugees of millions more. Restraints on the targeting of civilians were either lax or non-existent. Terror strategies were widely employed, and by diverse actors: armies, paramilitary forces, freebooters, and mercenaries, with wide scope granted to criminal and profiteering elements. In Africa, the weapon of choice was the AK-47 automatic rifle – one of the rare Soviet products preferred over the capitalist competition.

The Cold War's demise magnified these trends, and added new ones. It is a truism that the withdrawal of the superpowers from extensive military engagement in the Third World "lifted the lid" from simmering or dormant ethnic conflicts in many countries. Ethnically fueled wars have increased worldwide – although it may be debated whether this primarily reflects older tensions and conflicts, or "more immediate and remediable causes: political manipulation, belief traps and Hobbesian fear."[15]

Many states that had been propped up by one of the superpowers (or had played off the US and Soviet Union against each other) collapsed in the face of popular resistance. This produced the great wave of democratization in East Asia, Latin America, and Eastern Europe at the end of the 1980s and into the 1990s, but it also led to "failed states," in which no central authority exerted effective control. Power and the means of violence devolved to decentralized networks of paramilitaries, warlords, freebooting soldiers or former soldiers, and brigands.

In such cases, these groups were often at odds or at war with one another – and usually with the civilian population as well. To shore up their power base, warlords and freebooters sought "rents" from the civilian population – in the form of mafia-style "protection money" or simple robbery – and from the sale of natural resources, so that wars in Congo, Liberia, Sierra Leone, and Colombia, among many others, were sustained by the windfall profits to be made from diamonds,[16] gold,[17] timber, oil, and drugs. These spoils were marketed internationally; the world had truly entered an age of *globalized* warfare, in which consumer decisions in the First World had a direct impact on the course and outcome of Third World conflicts.[18]

Gérard Prunier, who has witnessed the emergence and evolution of many such conflicts over four decades of academic work in Africa, described these "new wars" in 2009:

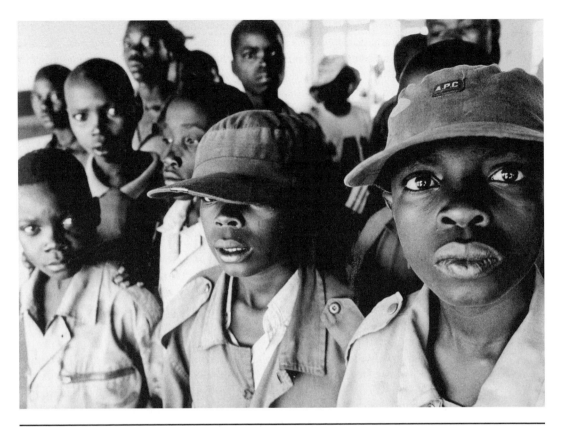

Figure 12.1   The new face of war: demobilized child soldiers in the Democratic Republic of the Congo, 2002.

Source: Courtesy Dimitri Falk.

Here economic predation, trafficking of all kinds, and looting both at the individual and at the collective level become essential features of the conflict because they are essential means of financing it. This has massive consequences [for] the way the war is fought. Because civilians are the ones from whom the military can take its means of survival, armed violence is more often directed at civilians (including, at times, those of one's own camp) than at the enemy army. Direct armed confrontation is often avoided, and straightforward military victory is only one of the various options in the field. It is actually this nonstate, decentralized form of violence that makes the conflicts so murderous and so hard to stop. Looting and its attendant calamities (arson, rape, torture) become routine operations for the "combatants," who are soon more akin to vampires than to soldiers.[19]

As Prunier's account suggested, the implications of these trends for genocides of the present and future are likewise "massive":

- The fact that most "new wars" are civil wars means that norms of state sovereignty are less powerful inhibitors than with international wars. The latter may be muted

451

or suppressed by collective security strategies deployed in recent decades. In any case, international wars are viewed as "threats to the system," and nearly always provoke an international outcry. No such effective "prohibition regime" exists in the case of civil conflicts (though one might be nascent). Contrast, for example, the response to Saddam Hussein's invasion of Kuwait with his much more severe depredations against Iraqi Kurds (mentioned in Box 4a).

- New wars feature a profusion of actors and agents, often making it difficult to determine who is doing what to whom. The most destructive war of recent times, in Congo (Box 9a), has killed up to six million people. But with a mosaic of local and outside forces, apportioning responsibility for genocide and other atrocities – and bringing effective pressure to bear on perpetrators – are tasks even more daunting than usual.

- To lend moral and political legitimacy to activities usually fueled by greed and power lust, new-war actors often play up ethnic and particularist identities. Campaigns of persecution against national and ethnic groups, including genocide, become a standard *modus operandi*. The wars of the 1990s in West and Central Africa and former Yugoslavia (Chapter 8) are prominent examples.

- The globalized arms trade and caches left over from Cold War struggles have flooded the territories in which new wars occur with cheap, light weaponry. In many countries, an AK-47 may be purchased for a few dollars. The loss of superpower sponsorship, and political–material competition among the various actors, spawn ever greater demands on the civilian population. Civilians may be mass-murdered if held to be in allegiance with one of the opposing groups, or insufficiently cooperative with extraction and taxation measures, or simply in the way.

- The ambiguous, uncertain, and shifting control over territories and populations that characterizes these wars vastly increases the complexity of conflict suppression and humanitarian intervention. IR scholars speak of "complex humanitarian emergencies" in which war, genocide, social breakdown, starvation, refugee flows, and internally displaced populations all combine to produce a downward spiral of suffering and destruction. Aid agencies, journalists, and human rights monitors are all at greater risk, and may be correspondingly more reluctant to enter the field or remain there. Without their expert witnessing and evaluations, events on the ground are further obscured, and considerable interventionist potential is squandered.

- If sufficient sources of "rent" can be extracted from the land and its population, these wars can become self-perpetuating and self-sustaining. The longer they drag on, the likelier is massive mortality from hunger and disease – and the likelier that the only viable source of income and self-respect (for young men but also, increasingly, for young women) is to join a warring faction.

It is difficult to say whether the new wars are more likely to produce genocide, but at the very least, they contain a strong genocidal *potential*. And, all too frequently, a genocidal dynamic is central to the unfolding conflict.

DEMOCRACY, WAR, AND GENOCIDE/DEMOCIDE

> Societies are known by their victims.
>
> Richard Drinnon

Are democracies less likely to wage war and genocide against each other than are non-democracies? Are they less likely *in general* to wage war and genocide?

These issues have provoked arguably the most vigorous single debate in the international relations literature over the past three decades – the so-called "democratic peace debate." They have also given rise to one of the few proclaimed "laws," perhaps the *only* one, in this branch of the social sciences. Democracies, it is claimed, do not fight each other, or do so only rarely. Why might this be so? As IR scholar Errol Henderson summarizes:

> Theoretical explanations for the democratic peace emphasize either structural/ institutional factors or cultural/normative factors in preventing war between democracies. The former posits that institutional constraints on the decision-making choices of democratic leaders make it difficult for them to use force in their foreign policies and act as a brake on conflict with other democracies. The latter assumes that democracies are less disposed to fight each other due to the impact of their shared norms that proscribe the use of violence between them.[20]

A "harder" version of the democratic peace hypothesis, advanced by R.J. Rummel, argues that democracies are far less likely than authoritarian states to commit democide, whether against their own populations or against others. Rummel conceded that democracies sometimes perpetrate democide, but "almost all of this . . . is foreign democide during war, and consists mainly of those enemy civilians killed in indiscriminate urban bombing." Acknowledging other examples, he claimed that they are the exceptions that prove the rule: "In each case the killing was carried out in a highly undemocratic fashion: in secret, behind a conscious cover of lies and deceit, and by agencies and power holders that had the wartime authority to operate autonomously. All were shielded by tight censorship of the press and control of journalists." In order for democratic states to become democidal, therefore, what makes them democratic has to be suspended, at least temporarily.[21]

There is much that is intuitively appealing about Rummel's formulations, and those of other proponents of the democratic peace hypothesis. First, it seems evident that genocides inflicted by democracies *against their own populations* are rare. One can think of exceptions – Sri Lanka is sometimes cited – but they do not come readily to mind. By contrast, this book is replete with examples of authoritarian, dictatorial, tyrannical, and totalitarian governments slaughtering their own populations (the USSR under Lenin and Stalin; China before and after the communist revolution; Cambodia under the Khmer Rouge; and so on). At a glance, too, the "law" that democracies do not fight each other seems empirically robust.

Things become more complicated, however, when we consider the history of colonizing liberal democracies; the nature of some of the indigenous societies they attacked; the secretive and anti-democratic character of violence by *both* democratic and authoritarian states; and the latter-day comportment of democracies, including the global superpower and non-Western democracies.

As we saw in Chapter 3, the strategy adopted towards indigenous peoples by Western colonial powers – in most cases, the most democratic states of their age – was frequently genocidal. Other, less democratic states were less likely to aggress internationally than the liberal democracies of the time (which were also the most technologically advanced countries, hence best equipped to impose violence on others).[22]

The character of the indigenous societies that the colonialists confronted, moreover, was often no less democratic than the colonial states themselves – sometimes more so. As sociologist Michael Mann has noted:

> The "democratic peace" school have excluded groups like the [North American] Indian nations from their calculations on the somewhat dubious grounds that they did not have permanent differentiated states of the "modern" type. Though this is convenient for the self-congratulatory tone of much of their writings . . . it is illegitimate even by their own definitions. For Indian nations did develop permanent constitutional states through the mid-nineteenth century – for example, the Cherokee in 1827, the Choctaw, Chickasaw and Creeks in the period 1856–1867.[23]

Thus, when genocidal campaigns were waged against these nations, "liberal democracies were actually committing genocide against other democracies, repeatedly." In fact, Mann suggested, "If we counted up separately the cases where 'the people' of the United States, Canada and Australia committed mass murder on the individual Indian and aboriginal nations, we could probably tip Rummel's statistical scales over to the conclusion that democratic regimes were more likely to commit genocide than were authoritarian states."[24] In *Genocide in the Age of the Nation State*, historian Mark Levene similarly argued that "in the time of intense nation-state formation, specifically in the late eighteenth and early nineteenth centuries . . . arguably the two most notable repeat-perpetrators of genocide were Britain and the United States."[25]

This phenomenon pervades the contemporary age as well. In examining *international* involvement in mass violence and atrocity, there is little doubt that the most consistently and aggressively violent country over the past fifty or sixty years is also the world's leading liberal democracy. Whatever the brutality of the Soviets in Hungary (1956) or in Afghanistan (see Chapter 2), no power approaches the United States when it comes to instigation of, and complicity in, conflicts and atrocities worldwide. The majority of this violence, moreover, was not conducted through formal participation in formally declared wars, but organized "covertly."[26] As we saw, Rummel generalized about this theme, claiming that democratic democide represents a stark departure from democratic norms. But then, wonders Errol Henderson, should these agents of mass violence really be classed as democracies?[27]

Mann, for his part, pointed out that the enabling variables which Rummel cited for "democratic democide" – secrecy, censorship, lying, deceit – are also those which have typically enabled mass killing by *non*-democratic states. Authoritarian genocides similarly tend to be inflicted in wartime, with attempts at secrecy. "Hitler committed almost all his murders during the war, and he did not dare make them public – indeed, nor did Stalin."[28]

Henderson, revisiting the data-set on democratic peace compiled by John Oneal and Bruce Russett (1997), pointed to sharp differences among Western liberal democracies, on one hand, and those he classified as "Hindu" democracies (India and Sri Lanka) and "Other" democracies (notably Israel), on the other. By retabulating Oneal and Russett's numbers, Henderson found that "Western democracies were significantly less likely to initiate interstate wars," but Hindu and other democracies "were significantly *more* likely to initiate them."[29]

On balance, and crucially including "extrastate" wars (wars against non-state entities, usually in a colonial and imperial context), "democratic states [are] in fact significantly *more likely* to become involved in – and to initiate – interstate wars and militarized international disputes," according to Henderson.[30] With regard to extrastate wars, "Western states – including the Western democracies – are more likely" to initiate and involve themselves in such conflicts. He concluded, provocatively and counter-intuitively, that "for all of its positive value as an egalitarian form of government, one of the key threats to peace for individual states is the presence of a democratic regime."[31]

What can we take away from these diverse arguments? First, even the skeptical Henderson acknowledged the "positive value" of democracy "as an egalitarian form of government." As Rummel argued, consolidated democratic regimes are much less likely to wage war and genocide against their own populations than are tyrannical states.

On the other hand, liberal democracy is no guarantee against domestic killing, as millions of indigenous peoples discovered. Nor, in a world where the greatest perpetrator of international violence is the liberal-democratic superpower, can democracy be seen as a cure-all.[32]

NORMS AND PROHIBITION REGIMES

International relations scholars have studied the role of norms and regimes in global affairs, notably (for our purposes) *humanitarian norms* and *prohibition regimes*. Regimes were defined by Stephen Krasner as "principles, norms, rules, and decision-making procedures around which actor expectations converge in a given issue-area." Norms are "specific prescriptions or proscriptions for action," while principles are "standards of behavior defined in terms of rights and obligations."[33]

Ethan Nadelmann defined prohibition regimes as sets of "norms . . . which prohibit, both in international law and in the domestic criminal law of states, the involvement of state and nonstate actors in particular activities." Such regimes emerge

> like municipal criminal laws . . . for a variety of reasons: to protect the interests of the state and other powerful members of society; to deter, suppress, and punish undesirable activities; to provide for order, security, and justice among members of a community; and to give force and symbolic representation to the moral values, beliefs, and prejudices of those who make the law.[34]

The key player in transforming norms into international regimes, especially prohibition regimes, is the *norm entrepreneur*, "an individual or organization that sets out to change the behaviour of others,"[35] and the *principled-issue networks* that norm entrepreneurs create. The history of the prohibition regime against genocide, weak and underdeveloped as it currently is, provides an excellent example of such entrepreneurship. Raphael Lemkin's decades-long campaign to develop a norm against genocide eventually generated a principled-issue network of scholars, government representatives, legal specialists, and human-rights activists; this network has grown exponentially, and exerted a real though limited influence on global politics.

Lemkin's campaign was described in general terms in Chapter 1. Here, I want to examine the nuts and bolts of his anti-genocide strategy, to demonstrate how successful norm entrepreneurship proceeds. (This discussion again draws heavily on Samantha Power's depiction of Lemkin's mission in *"A Problem from Hell."*)[36]

First, Lemkin perceived a void in existing international law. While legislation and even military intervention were countenanced in cases of interstate violence, states had free rein to inflict violence on their own populations. To generate a norm and prohibition regime against such actions, a powerful existing norm, and a defining regime of world affairs, had to be eroded. This was the norm of state sovereignty, and the international regime (the Westphalian state system) that it underpinned. As long as states forswore intervention in the "internal" affairs of other states, a principal cause of human suffering could not be confronted.

To define a new norm and sell it to the world, Lemkin invented a word that addressed the "crime without a name," as Winston Churchill had described Nazi atrocities in Eastern Europe. Lemkin struggled to find "a word that could not be used in other contexts (as 'barbarity' and 'vandalism' could) . . . one that would bring with it 'a color of freshness and novelty' while describing something 'as shortly and as poignantly as possible.'"[37] The term he finally settled on – genocide – proved to be one of the core *catalyzing ideas* of the twentieth century. With unprecedented speed, it led to the drafting of an international Convention against genocide, the foundation of a prohibition regime that today exhibits growing strength and complexity.

With his evocative term in hand, Lemkin physically planted himself at the heart of postwar international legislation and regime formation. In the surprisingly informal surroundings of United Nations headquarters, then housed in an abandoned war plant on Long Island, Lemkin obsessively lobbied delegates to the new organization, spending "endless hours haunting the drafty halls."[38] Few delegates escaped his (usually unwanted) attentions. From his one-room Manhattan apartment, Lemkin fired off literally thousands of letters to government officials and politicians, religious and cultural figures, newspapers and their editors and assistant editors and reporters. In addition, "friends, friends of friends, and acquaintances of acquaintances" were drafted to the cause, providing background information and fresh contacts.

Throughout his campaign, Lemkin engaged in *norm grafting*. The task of the norm entrepreneur is eased if s/he can point to previous, congruent norms that have achieved wide acceptance. If A, why not B? (If slavery is wrong, why not forced labor? If voting rights are extended to all adult males, why not to women?) Such grafting presumes a desire for moral and rhetorical consistency on the part of policymakers

Figure 12.2 "Our Countrymen in Chains": illustration for an 1837 poem by the Quaker activist John Greenleaf Whittier. Slavery was once even more deeply embedded in human society than genocide is today – indeed, while few people defend genocide as such, most people saw slavery as the natural order of affairs through to the nineteenth century. What changed minds, and finally pushed slavery to the margins of international society, were the slave uprisings in Haiti and elsewhere (see pp. 48–49) and the abolitionist movement launched in the West in solidarity with the enslaved. So if slavery can be abolished, why not genocide? This iconic image of the abolitionist movement displays tropes that have been common in "norm entrepreneurship" through to the present: the appeal to common humanity and empathy; a sentimental and religious dimension; and (unfortunately) the paternalistic portrayal of the victim as supplicant, dependent on the charity and good will of the privileged viewer.

Source: US Library of Congress Prints and Photographs Division/Wikimedia Commons. The image of the kneeling and prayerful slave was first deployed in England in the 1780s as the official seal of the Society for the Abolition of Slavery.

and publics.[39] Thus, Lemkin pointed to the huge gap in the evolving prohibition regime against war crimes and crimes against humanity. "If piracy was an international crime, he could not understand why genocide was not." In a similar vein, Lemkin wrote in *The New York Times*: "It seems *inconsistent* with our concepts of civilization that selling a drug to an individual is a matter of worldly concern [i.e., the basis for an international prohibition regime], while gassing millions of human beings might be a problem of internal concern."[40]

Norm entrepreneurs frequently exploit historical moments that provide a favorable environment for norm adoption and regime creation. These moments usually follow major upheavals that weaken preconceptions and undermine established frameworks. Lemkin's fortunate conjuncture was the "multilateral moment" (Power's phrase) immediately following the Second World War. In a few years, many of the international organizations, legal instruments, and regimes of today were first developed (often grafted onto previous institutions and regimes, as the UN grew out of the League of Nations). The revelation of the full horror of Nazi rule, especially the reports and images from the death camps, undermined the legitimacy of state sovereignty as a shield against intervention and prosecution on humanitarian grounds.

Lemkin's greatest achievement was the UN Genocide Convention. "Just four years after Lemkin had introduced 'genocide' to the world, the General Assembly had unanimously passed a law banning it." Lemkin now turned his efforts (which by this point were undermining his health) to lobbying for ratification of the treaty, and the transformation of his norm into an effective prohibition regime. Using classic tactics of the norm entrepreneur, Lemkin crafted his messages and appeals carefully, individually, and with an eye for utilitarian impact. "He sent letters out in English, French, Spanish, Hebrew, Italian, and German. Long before computers or photocopiers" – two of the most powerful tools of the contemporary norm entrepreneur – "he handcrafted each letter to suit the appropriate individual, organization, or country. . . . He wrote to the leaders of the most influential political parties, the heads of the private women's or civic groups, and the editors of prominent newspapers." He also "attempted to mobilize American grassroots groups" and "enlisted a panoply of American civic organizations, churches, and synagogues."[41] With few material resources of his own, he "borrowed stationery from supportive community organizations, applied for grants to pay for postage, and sent thousands of letters to absolutely anybody whose moral heartstrings he felt he might tug or on whose connections he might prey to get the ear of a US senator."[42]

According to Power, Lemkin "varied his pitch," tailoring his message carefully and sometimes cynically to the object of his appeal. "If a country had experienced genocide in the past, he reminded its citizens of the human costs of allowing it. But if a country had *committed* genocide in the past, as Turkey had done [against minority Christians], Lemkin was willing to keep the country's atrocities out of the discussion, so as not to scare off a possible signatory" to the convention.[43] For similar reasons, Lemkin avoided pushing for the inclusion of political groups in the UN definition of genocide. This, he feared, would provoke resistance among states fearful of having their political persecutions labeled as genocide. (In any case, Lemkin had never cared much about political groups. He did not consider them to be bearers of human culture in the same – archaic? – way that he viewed ethnonational groups.)

With his reluctance to include political groups, Lemkin contributed to some of the conceptual and legal confusion that has since surrounded the UN Convention.[44] On balance, though, it is hard to disagree with his own self-estimation (in pitching his story to publishers): that his life "shows how a private individual almost single handedly can succeed in imposing a moral law on the world and how he can stir world conscience to this end."[45]

IR theorists of norms and regimes describe a *tipping point* followed by a *norm cascade* in the diffusion of norms, analogous to the paradigm shifts in scientific knowledge studied by Thomas Kuhn.[46] One norm displaces another, decisively and definitively. At this point, norms become strongly entrenched in international regimes, including effective prohibition regimes.

With respect to the norm against genocide and crimes against humanity, we can observe that it has partially, not decisively, displaced the norm of state sovereignty. It appeared possible, in the immediate postwar period, that a tipping from sovereignty to cosmopolitanism and international governance could occur, but this idealistic vision faded rapidly with the onset of the Cold War, and does not seem a great deal closer today. Thus, while the drive to suppress and prevent genocide has indeed spawned a norm and a prohibition regime, it is applied only weakly and inconsistently – compared, say, with norms against state-sponsored slavery, nuclear proliferation, assassination of foreign leaders, or piracy and hijacking.[47] The anti-genocide movement is best classed with a range of other norms and regimes that have made significant strides, but have yet to entrench themselves in international affairs: those against capital punishment, trafficking (in human beings, drugs, and ivory), and theft of intellectual property, to name a few.

Nadelmann has developed a five-stage model for the evolution of prohibition regimes. At first, "most societies regard the targeted activity as entirely legitimate"; indeed, "states are often the principal protagonists." Then, the activity is redefined as morally problematic or evil, "generally by international legal scholars, religious groups, and other moral entrepreneurs." Next, "regime proponents begin to agitate actively for the suppression and criminalization of the activity." If this stage is successful, "the activity becomes the subject of criminal laws and police actions throughout much of the world." In the fifth and final stage, "the incidence of the proscribed activity is greatly reduced, persisting only on a small scale and in obscure locations."[48] Using this model, we can position the anti-genocide regime – and the other comparatively weak regimes mentioned above – between Nadelmann's third stage, with "regime proponents . . . agitat[ing] actively for the suppression and criminalization of the activity," and stage four, in which the regime is "the subject of criminal laws and police actions throughout much of the world."

Most weaker prohibition regimes suffer from a number of debilities. They may be relatively recent (many were at Nadelmann's first stage of evolution just a few decades ago). Their core concepts or "catalyzing ideas" may be prone to ambiguities of definition and application. Enforcement mechanisms are underdeveloped, and often corrupt – suggesting a lack of political will, and attesting to the failure of activist mobilization to spur political actors to meaningful effort. All of these factors are evident in the case of the anti-genocide regime.

Prohibition regimes are also hampered where strong counter-incentives exist. It remains in the interest of vast numbers of ordinary people (or smaller numbers of powerful people) to undermine the regime and weaken its application. Just as the lure of illegal drugs for both consumers and vendors outweighs the ability of states to suppress these substances, so genocide holds an enduring appeal as a problem-solving strategy for states and other actors.[49]

According to Nadelmann, however, prohibition regimes are *more* likely to succeed when the targeted activity has a strong transnational dimension; when unilateral and bilateral means of enforcement are inadequate; when a norm "reflects not just self-interest but a broadly acknowledged moral obligation"; and when the activity is vulnerable "to global suppression efforts by states."[50] IR theorists Margaret Keck and Kathryn Sikkink point out additionally that prohibition regimes are boosted when "the causal chain [is] short," when "causes can be assigned to the deliberate 'intentional' actions of identifiable individuals," and when a universalistic "concern with bodily harm" underlies the prohibition effort.[51] In all these respects, the anti-genocide regime holds considerable potential. This may bode well for its future strengthening.

▌ FURTHER STUDY

Susan Burgerman, *Moral Victories: How Activists Provoke Multilateral Action.* Ithaca, NY: Cornell University Press, 2001. Concise study with a Latin American focus.

Errol A. Henderson, *Democracy and War: The End of an Illusion?* Boulder, CO: Lynne Rienner, 2002. Myth-shattering analysis of democracies' involvement in international conflict.

Adam Hochschild, *Bury the Chains: Prophets and Rebels in the Fight to Free an Empire's Slaves.* Boston, MA: Houghton Mifflin, 2005. Study of the abolitionist movement, with many lessons for anti-genocide "norm entrepreneurs" today.

Kalevi J. Holsti, *The State, War, and the State of War.* Cambridge: Cambridge University Press, 1996. Arguably the best introduction to global transformations in warfare.

Adam Jones, ed., *Genocide, War Crimes and the West: History and Complicity.* London: Zed Books, 2004. "The most comprehensive treatment of Western responsibility for mass atrocity yet published" (Richard Falk); naturally I agree.

Mary Kaldor, *New and Old Wars: Organized Violence in a Global Era.* Stanford, CA: Stanford University Press, 2001. Like Holsti (above), a core text of the new security studies.

Margaret E. Keck and Kathryn Sikkink, *Activists Beyond Borders: Advocacy Networks in International Politics.* Ithaca, NY, and London: Cornell University Press, 1998. The role of transnational nongovernmental networks in norm entrepreneurship and regime formation.

Stephen D. Krasner, ed., *International Regimes.* Ithaca, NY: Cornell University Press, 1983. Groundbreaking study.

R.J. Rummel, *Death by Government.* New Brunswick, NJ: Transaction Publishers, 1994. Comprehensive survey of government-directed mass killing, marred by some dubious cheerleading for Western democracies.

Ward Thomas, *The Ethics of Destruction: Norms and Force in International Relations.* Ithaca, NY: Cornell University Press, 2001. Elegantly written study of normative constraints on war-making.

NOTES

1 R.J. Rummel, *Death by Government* (New Brunswick, NJ: Transaction Publishers, 1994). He considers this a fairly conservative estimate: "The dead could conceivably be nearly 360 million people." Rummel maintains an extensive website on democide at http://www.hawaii.edu/powerkills/.

2 Ibid., p. 13. "If all these dead were laid out head to toe, assuming each to be an average of 5 feet tall, they would reach from Honolulu, Hawaii, across the vast Pacific and then the huge continental United States to Washington DC on the East Coast, *and then back again almost twenty times*" (emphasis in original).

3 Ibid., pp. 1–2.

4 It is interesting to note that in her earlier writing (1987), Harff subsumed politicide under genocide: "My definition of genocide differs from the official definition . . . insofar as it broadens the scope of the victims and perpetrators. Thus, political opponents are included in my definition, though they lack the formal legal protection of the Convention on Genocide." Harff, "The Etiology of Genocide," in Michael N. Dobkowski and Isidor Wallimann, eds, *The Age of Genocide: Etiology and Case Studies of Mass Death* (Westport, CT: Greenwood Press, 1987), p. 44.

5 Harff quoted in Helen Fein, *Genocide: A Sociological Perspective* (London: Sage, 1993), p. 40.

6 Fein, *Genocide*, p. 96. See Ted R. Gurr and James R. Scaritt, "Minorities at Risk: A Global Survey," *Human Rights Quarterly*, 11: 3 (1989), pp. 375–405; more recently, Ted Robert Gurr, *Peoples versus States: Minorities at Risk in the New Century* (Washington, DC: US Institute of Peace Press, 2000).

7 Barbara Harff and Ted Gurr, "Assessing Country Risks of Genocide and Politicide in 2009," http://www.gpanet.org/webfm_send/76.

8 Barbara Harff, "No Lessons Learned from the Holocaust? Assessing Risks of Genocide and Political Mass Murder since 1955," *American Political Science Review*, 97: 1 (2003).

9 Ibid.

10 Harff and Gurr, "Assessing Country Risks of Genocide and Politicide in 2009."

11 Harff, "No Lessons Learned from the Holocaust?," p. 72.

12 For an extensive interdisciplinary sampling, see my "Bibliography of War" at http://adamjones.freeservers.com/bibliography_of_war.htm.

13 According to David Kertzer, "In many parts of the world, warfare itself is highly ritualized, with a special permanent site for the hostilities, special bodily adornment, special songs and verbal insults, and rules about the actual conduct of combat. In many of these cases, as soon as an individual is seriously wounded, hostilities cease and a round of post-battle ritual begins." Kertzer, quoted in Charles Tilly, *The Politics of Collective Violence* (Cambridge: Cambridge University Press, 2003), p. 86.

14 See John E. Mueller, *Retreat from Doomsday: The Obsolescence of Major War* (New York: Basic Books, 1989).

15 Jonathan Glover, *Humanity: A Moral History of the Twentieth Century* (New Haven, CT: Yale University Press, 1999), p. 141. For example, one of the most conflict-ridden countries in the world over the past three decades has been Somalia, yet this is "perhaps Africa's most homogeneous country from an ethnic point of view." Tilly, *The Politics of Collective Violence*, p. 72.

16 See Greg Campbell, *Blood Diamonds: Tracing the Deadly Path of the World's Most Precious Stones* (Boulder, CO: Westview Press, 2002).

17 See, e.g., Human Rights Watch, *The Curse of Gold*, June 2005, http://www.hrw.org/reports/2005/drc0505/.

18 This too has a precedent in the "limited" wars of the 1980s, when Nicaraguan *contra* rebels and the *mujahadeen* Islamists in Afghanistan trafficked drugs to finance weapons purchases, with the tacit approval and sometimes active complicity of the US government. See Peter Dale Scott and Jonathan Marshall, *Cocaine Politics: Drugs, Armies, and the CIA in Central America* (Berkeley, CA: University of California Press, 1991). For an overview of contemporary trends in historical context, see Peter Dale Scott, *Drugs, Oil, and War: The United States in Afghanistan, Colombia, and Indochina* (Lanham, MD: Rowman & Littlefield, 2003).

19 Gérard Prunier, *Africa's World War: Congo, the Rwandan Genocide, and the Making of a Continental Catastrophe* (New York: Oxford University Press, 2009), p. 337.

20 Errol A. Henderson, *Democracy and War: The End of an Illusion?* (Boulder, CO: Lynne Rienner, 2002), p. 4. See also Tarak Barkawi and Mark Laffey, *Democracy, Liberalism, and War: Rethinking the Democratic Peace Debate* (Boulder, CO: Lynne Rienner, 2001).

21 Rummel, *Death by Government*, pp. 14, 17. Among the other cases of "democratic democide" that Rummel cited in passing (pp. 14–16) were: "the large-scale massacres of Filipinos during the bloody US colonization of the Philippines at the beginning of [the twentieth] century, deaths in British concentration camps in South Africa during the Boar [*sic*] War, civilian deaths due to starvation during the British blockade of Germany in and after World War I, the rape and murder of helpless Chinese in and around Peking in 1900 [while crushing the Boxer Rebellion], the atrocities committed by Americans in Vietnam, the murder of helpless Algerians during the Algerian War by the French, and the unnatural deaths of German prisoners of war in French and US POW camps after World War II." However, as Mark Levene noted, Rummel displayed "an almost wilful myopia about mass murders committed directly or indirectly by liberal democratic regimes," especially more recent ones committed by his own country, the United States

(Levene, *Genocide in the Age of the Nation State, Vol. 1: The Meaning of Genocide* [London: I.B. Tauris, 2005], p. 54.) For example, while acknowledging that US forces did commit "democide" in Vietnam (Chapter 2), he suggested with a straight face that "the US democide in Vietnam seems to have killed at least 4,000 Vietnamese civilians, POWs, or enemy seeking to surrender, maybe as many as 10,000 Vietnamese" – this in a war that killed two to three million people, certainly including at least a million civilians, and kills them to this day through unexploded ordnance and environmental poisoning (Rummel, *Death by Government*, p. 277). In 2005, Rummel revised upward *more than fifty-fold* his estimate of all "colonial democide" in "colonized Africa and Asia [from] 1900 to independence," from an initial toll of 870,000 (a small fraction of the casualties in the Belgian Congo alone) to include *an additional 50 million victims*. Perhaps we may expect something similar, or even more expansive, in the case of US democide in Vietnam. Rummel, "Reevaluating Colonial Democide," Freedomspeace.blogspot.com, December 7, 2005.

22 I do not mean to suggest that *only* democracies aggressed in this fashion – the counter-examples of Tsarist Russia and Imperial Japan may be cited – but rather that democracy seems to have provided no check to such aggression.

23 Michael Mann, "The Dark Side of Democracy: The Modern Tradition of Ethnic and Political Cleansing," *New Left Review*, 235 (May–June 1999), pp. 18–46.

24 Mann, "The Dark Side of Democracy," p. 26. On the same page, Mann argues that "deliberate genocidal bursts were more common among British than Spanish or Portuguese settlers. In both cases, we find that the stronger the democracy among the perpetrators, the greater the genocide."

25 Levene, *Genocide in the Age of the Nation State, Vol. 1*, p. 162.

26 I have prepared a table of "Key Instances of US Involvement in Mass Violence against Civilians since 1953" to buttress this claim: see http://www.genocidetext.net/us_violence.pdf. In the four years since the first edition of this book was published, no-one has publicly challenged this claim and its supporting data, to my knowledge. See also the bibliography of much of the "dissident" literature on US state violence supplied in Adam Jones, "Introduction: History and Complicity," in Jones, ed., *Genocide, War Crimes and the West: History and Complicity* (London: Zed Books, 2004), pp. 26–30.

27 See Henderson, *Democracy and War*, p. 82. One should also note the overwhelming US dominance in foreign sales of the armaments that fuel wars and genocides worldwide. In 2009, the US accounted for an astonishing 68.4 percent of such sales. See Thom Shanker, "Despite Slump, US Role as Top Arms Supplier Grows," *The New York Times*, September 6, 2009.

28 Mann, "The Dark Side of Democracy," p. 20.

29 Henderson, *Democracy and War*, p. 66; emphasis added.

30 Ibid., p. 17.

31 Ibid.

32 It is also worth recalling the destruction inflicted by global capitalism under a liberal-democratic aegis, as noted in Chapter 1's discussion of structural violence.

33 Stephen Krasner, "Structural Causes and Regime Consequences: Regimes as Intervening Variables," *International Organization*, 36: 2 (1982), pp. 185–205.

34 Ethan Nadelmann, "Global Prohibition Regimes: The Evolution of Norms in International Society," *International Organization*, 44: 4 (1990), pp. 479–526.

35 Ann Florini, "The Evolution of International Norms," *International Studies Quarterly*, 40 (1996), p. 375.

36 Samantha Power, *"A Problem from Hell": America and the Age of Genocide* (New York: Basic Books, 2002). Power does not adopt the norm-entrepreneur framing, however; and I do not, of course, ascribe to Raphael Lemkin the vocabulary of norms, regimes, and so on.

37 Ibid., p. 42.

38 Ibid., p. 51.

39 The concept is similar to Keck and Sikkink's formulation of "moral leverage" as exercised by activist networks: "Material leverage comes from linking the issue of concern to money, trade, or prestige, as more powerful institutions or governments are pushed

to apply pressure. Moral leverage pushes actors to change their practices by holding their behavior up to international scrutiny, or by holding governments or institutions accountable to previous commitments and principles they have endorsed." Margaret E. Keck and Kathryn Sikkink, *Activists Beyond Borders: Advocacy Networks in International Politics* (Ithaca, NY: Cornell University Press, 1998), p. 201.

40 Power, and Lemkin quoted in Power, *"A Problem from Hell,"* p. 48; emphasis added. In similar fashion, activists seeking to memorialize certain genocides may also draw upon genocidal precedents. Thus, "proliferating Armenian discourses on [the genocide of] 1915 were coloured by connections with the Jewish Holocaust. This was entirely natural, given the proximity of the 'final solution,' the growing public awareness of it in the 1960s in the aftermath of the trial of Adolf Eichmann, and the fact that the Nazi campaigns of genocide had given decisive impetus to the establishment of the genocide convention." Donald Bloxham, *The Great Game of Genocide: Imperialism, Nationalism, and the Destruction of the Ottoman Armenians* (Oxford: Oxford University Press, 2005), p. 217.

41 Power, *"A Problem from Hell,"* p. 72.

42 Ibid., p. 71.

43 Ibid., pp. 63–64. John Cooper described similar strategies in his study of *Raphael Lemkin and the Genocide Convention* (London: Palgrave Macmillan, 2008): "Lemkin carefully avoided upsetting the Arab supporters of the genocide convention by . . . not singling out the fate of the Jews during the Second World War" (p. 147), and skated over Turkish crimes against the Armenians when wooing the Turkish government. He was also a grand flatterer. To the Mexican Ambassador to the UN, Padilla Nervo, Lemkin wrote: "Certainly, the great humanitarian tradition of your country, and the great prestige of its leaders throughout Latin America, in the United Nations, and in the world at large, qualifies Mexico as a natural champion and leader for the genocide convention" (p. 178). To the Haitian Foreign Minister, Dr. Vilfort Beauvoer, Lemkin eloquently declared: "Your ancestors, Excellency, were brought as slaves to this hemisphere. They were tortured and beaten; now you are a free people. . . . Your government should be in the forefront of this action" (p. 179). Meanwhile, in correspondence with a representative of the same French nation that had once enslaved the Haitians, Lemkin argued that "Quick ratification by France would start a strong ratification movement in the entire world because every country looks to France for guidance in matters of international law and new ideals" (p. 181).

44 Nor did Lemkin draw the line at behavior that many found boorish, if it would advance his cause. Power describes his "mix of flattery and moral prodding . . . [which] sometimes slipped into bluntly bullying his contacts and demanding that they acquire a conscience." *"A Problem from Hell,"* p. 71.

45 Lemkin quoted in ibid., p. 77.

46 The term "norm cascade" was coined by Martha Finnemore and Kathryn Sikkink in "International Norm Dynamics and Political Change," *International Organization*, 52: 4 (Autumn 1998), pp. 901–2. See also Thomas S. Kuhn, *The Structure of Scientific Revolutions* (Chicago, IL: University of Chicago Press, 1996).

47 "Piracy may be regarded as the very first 'crime against humanity,' its peculiarly barbaric quality derived from the taking of lives which were especially vulnerable while outside the protective realm of any nation." Geoffrey A. Robertson, *Crimes against Humanity: The Struggle for Global Justice* (New York: The New Press, 2000), p. 208. Accordingly, the international regime against piracy might be regarded as the first in history, with the possible exception of that against assassinating state leaders and diplomatic representatives.

48 Nadelmann, "Global Prohibition Regimes," pp. 484–86.

49 See Catherine Barnes, "The Functional Utility of Genocide: Towards a Framework for Understanding the Connection between Genocide and Regime Consolidation, Expansion and Maintenance," *Journal of Genocide Research*, 7: 3 (September 2005), pp. 309–30.

50 Nadelmann, "Global Prohibition Norms," p. 491.

51 Keck and Sikkink, *Activists Beyond Borders*, pp. 27, 53, 195.

CHAPTER 13

Gendering Genocide

> It is recommended that the definition [of genocide] should be extended to include a sexual group such as women, men, or homosexuals.
>
> Benjamin Whitaker, *Revised and Updated Report on the Question of the Prevention and Punishment of Genocide* (the UN Whitaker Report), 1985

The gender dimension of genocide and other crimes against humanity has only recently attracted sustained attention. Leading the way were feminist scholars, who paid particular attention to rape and sexual assault against women, and pressed for such crimes to be considered genocidal. Other scholars and commentators have concentrated on the gender-selective killing of infant girls through female infanticide, or the denial of adequate nutrition and health care resources to females at all stages of life.

The term "gender" is one of the most contested in the social sciences. Not long ago, it was assumed that gender could be clearly distinguished from biological/physiological sex. Gender meant the way that societies and cultures ascribed particular "feminine" and "masculine" roles, expectations, and values to (biological) males versus females. This vocabulary still has its strong proponents.[1] In the past couple of decades, however, the distinction between biological/physiological sex and cultural gender has begun to break down. Increasingly, scholars and activists argue that sex and gender overlap and are mutually constitutive. Such is the view of international relations scholar Joshua Goldstein, who views a strict gender–sex distinction as "construct[ing] a false dichotomy between biology and culture." Goldstein accordingly "use[s] 'gender' to cover masculine and feminine roles and bodies alike, in all their aspects, including the (biological and cultural) structures, dynamics, roles and scripts associated with each gender group."[2] His definition also guides discussion in this chapter. It allows us to explore the gendering of genocide both in its destructive impact on male and female bodies, and with regard to the cultural practices that shape embodied experience.

Gender is not synonymous with women/femininity, despite its close association with feminist-influenced scholarship and policy-making. Some feminists have contended that gender *means* the oppression of women by men,[3] resulting in a certain tone-deafness to the ways in which men and masculinities are often targeted, including in genocide. This chapter adopts a more inclusive view of gender. Indeed, it begins with one of the least-studied aspects of contemporary genocide: the gendercidal (gender-selective) killing of males.

GENDERCIDE VS. ROOT-AND-BRANCH GENOCIDE

> I saw the militias running in all directions, chasing men and boys to kill them.
> Eyewitness in East Timor (Box 7a), September 1999

The gendercidal targeting of a community's adult males, usually accompanied by slavery and/or concubinage for out-group women, has deep roots. In Homer's *Odyssey* (9:39–61), the hero Odysseus describes his raid on Ismaros: "I pillaged the town and killed the men. The women and treasure . . . I divided as fairly as I could among all hands."[4] The Greek historian Thucydides (fifth century BCE) recorded a dialog between Athenian representatives and delegates from Melos, resisting Athenian control. In the military show-down that resulted, wrote Thucydides, "the Melians surrendered unconditionally to the Athenians"; the latter then "put to death all the men of military age whom they took, and sold the women and children as slaves."[5]

It is impossible to know how common this pattern of gender-selective slaughter of males was, compared with the root-and-branch extermination of every member of the opposing group – women, children, and the elderly along with adult men. The term "root-and-branch" is also implicitly gendered: the root is the female that gives birth to the branch, the child. Thus, root-and-branch genocides are those that expand *beyond* adult males to remaining sectors of the targeted population.[6] When they do, the "branches" – children – are targeted in part because they may grow (a) to fight and take revenge, or (b) to give birth to new generations of resisters. The "roots" – women in their child-bearing years – may be slaughtered for their potential as bearers of the same new generations. ("Why were women and children considered enemies?" Scott Straus asked a convicted *génocidaire* in Ruhengeri, Rwanda. "The children and women would reproduce," he was told. "And if they reproduced?" "They would kill us again as they killed before, as is said in history."[7])

In the modern era, gendercides against "battle-age" males have been more frequent than campaigns of root-and-branch annihilation. There is a brutal logic in this. Genocide usually occurs in the context of military conflict, or precipitates it. Males are everywhere those primarily designated to "serve" in the military. A deranged form of military thinking dictates that all men of battle age, whether combatant or non-combatant, are legitimate targets.[8]

Figure 13.1 The gendercidal massacre of a community's males, often in acts of gender-selective "reprisal," is a standard feature of genocides throughout history. A frieze at the memorial museum in Lidice, Czech Republic, depicts the 1942 massacre by Nazi soldiers of 190 village males, in revenge for the assassination of Reinhard Heydrich (a key figure in planning the Holocaust of European Jews) in nearby Prague. Such mass execution scenes were repeated during the Armenian genocide (Chapter 4); by the Japanese at Nanjing in 1937–38 (Chapter 2); in Dhaka, Bangladesh in 1971 (Box 7a); and at Srebrenica in Bosnia-Herzegovina in 1995 (Chapter 8), to cite just a few examples. The children and women of Lidice were transported to concentration camps and death camps, where most were eventually killed. The gendercidal massacre of able-bodied males implies no long-term preservation of women, children, and the disabled. Instead, as in the Nazi case, it often serves as a precursor to "root-and-branch" genocide against entire populations.

Source: Author's photo, November 2009.

Figure 13.2 The face of gendercide against "battle-age" civilian men: the exhumed corpse of a victim of the Srebrenica massacre (see Chapter 8, pp. 325–27), blindfolded, hands tied behind his back, and executed by Bosnian Serb forces along with approximately 8,000 other Bosnian Muslim men and boys in July 1995.

Source: Courtesy International Criminal Tribunal for the Former Yugoslavia (ICTY).

In general, then, men are cast as "provocative targets," in Donald Horowitz's phrase:

> Experimental data indicate that provocative targets are more likely victims of aggression than are nonprovocative targets and that aggression may be regarded as less legitimate when the victim is weak or fails to retaliate. Men are attacked in riots and singled out for atrocities much more than women are, just as males are attacked more frequently than females are in experiments, and the skewing in both seems positively related to the strength of the target.[9]

As this suggests, there is also a logic to the physical preservation of women. They are deemed to pose no military threat, or a lesser one. They may have value as slaves and/or concubines. In addition, male-dominant society is overwhelmingly *patrilineal*, with descent traced through the father. The woman may be viewed as a "blank slate," able to adopt, or at least provide a conduit for, the ethnicity of a male impregnator; women may even be held to contribute nothing to the genetic mix *per se*. (This was a prominent theme as recently as the Rwandan genocide of 1994.)[10]

Reflecting such gendered assumptions and social structures, many cultures – perhaps most pervasively those of the Western world between the medieval era and the twentieth century – evolved norms of war that dictated protection for "civilians." This term also carried gendered connotations, so that even today the phrase "women and children" seems synonymous with "civilians."[11] Of course, once women and children have been removed from the equation, only adult men remain, implicitly consigning this group to *non*-civilian status and rendering it "fair game" – though degrees of protection may be extended on the basis of (old) age or demonstrable non-combatant status (e.g., handicapped or injured men).

A key question with regard to gender and mass killing is, therefore: Will genocidal forces view the slaughter of "battle-age" males as a sufficient expression of the genocidal impulse? Or will they also target children, women, and the elderly? The resolution to the question usually unfolds sequentially: *once* the younger adult male population group has been targeted, will remaining population groups *then* be slaughtered? Obviously, removing the group most closely associated with military activity, and hence military resistance, makes targeting other group members easier, logistically speaking. It may be much *harder*, however, to motivate genocidal killers to do their work, given norms against targeting these "helpless" populations.

The twentieth and twenty-first centuries have witnessed both core types of genocide, as we have seen throughout this volume. Typical of gendercidal strategies was the war in Bosnia-Herzegovina, with its crowning mass slaughter at Srebrenica (Chapter 8). To the Bosnian case we can add literally dozens of others in which gender selectivity channeled, and significantly limited, the *strictly murderous* dimension of the genocide (which is the critical one, by my preferred definition). They include Bangladesh in 1971; Cambodia between 1975 and 1979; Kashmir/Punjab and Sri Lanka in the 1980s and 1990s; the genocidal massacres of Sikhs in New Delhi in 1984; Saddam Hussein's Anfal Campaign against Iraqi Kurds in 1988; Kosovo and East Timor in 1999; Chechnya in the 1990s and 2000s; and Iraq after 2003.[12]

In New Delhi, for example, where more than five thousand Sikhs died in days of genocidal massacres, the gendered targeting of males was carried to almost surreal extremes:

> The nature of the attacks confirms that there was a deliberate plan to kill as many Sikh men as possible, hence nothing was left to chance. That also explains why in almost all cases, after hitting or stabbing, the victims were doused with kerosene or petrol and burnt, so as to leave no possibility of their surviving. Between October 31 and November 4, more than 2,500 men were murdered in different parts of Delhi, according to several careful unofficial estimates. There have been very few cases of women being killed except when they got trapped in houses which were set on fire. Almost all of the women interviewed described how men and young boys were special targets. They were dragged out of the houses, attacked with stones and rods, and set on fire. . . . When women tried to protect the men of their families, they were given a few blows and forcibly separated from the men. Even when they clung to the men, trying to save them, they were hardly ever attacked the way men were. I have not yet heard of a case of a woman being assaulted and then burnt to death by the mob.[13]

Delhi and, with it, Bangladesh, appear in Donald Horowitz's compendium of "deadly ethnic riots," which are closely linked to genocide (see also Chapters 11 and 12). Horowitz is emphatic about the gender dimension of such slaughters, and his comments may be used without qualification to describe genocide as well:

> While the violence proceeds, there is a strong, although not exclusive, concentration on male victims of a particular ethnic identity. The elderly are often left aside, and sometimes, though less frequently, so are children. Rapes certainly occur in ethnic riots, sometimes a great many rapes, but the killing and mutilation of men is much more common than is the murder or rape of women. Women are sometimes pushed aside or forced to watch the torture and death of their husbands and brothers. . . . Sometimes women are even treated courteously by their husbands' killers.[14]

It is important to point out that targeting "only" adult men is sufficient, under international law, to constitute genocide. This was confirmed in April 2004, when appeal judges of the International Criminal Tribunal for the Former Yugoslavia (ICTY) overturned a 2001 verdict against Bosnian Serb General Radislav Krstic, who had been found guilty "not of genocide but of aiding and abetting genocide" during the Srebrenica massacre. The appeals chamber determined that "by seeking to eliminate a part of the Bosnian Muslims" – those living in Srebrenica, and specifically by exterminating "the male Muslim" component of that group – genocide had indeed occurred under Krstic's supervision.[15] The original judgment outlined the legal justification as follows:

> The Bosnian Serb forces could not have failed to know, by the time they decided to kill all the men, that this selective destruction of the group would have a lasting

impact upon the entire group. Their death precluded any effective attempt by the Bosnian Muslims to recapture the territory. Furthermore, the Bosnian Serb forces had to be aware of the catastrophic impact that the disappearance of two or three generations of men would have on the survival of a traditionally patriarchal society . . . The Bosnian Serb forces knew, by the time they decided to kill all of the military aged men, that the combination of those killings with the forcible transfer of the women, children and elderly would inevitably result in the physical disappearance of the Bosnian Muslim population at Srebrenica.[16]

In its way, the verdict was as significant as that rendered earlier by the International Criminal Tribunal for Rwanda (ICTR) against Jean-Paul Akayesu. This established that the systematic rape of women could be considered genocidal when part of a broader campaign of group destruction (see the discussion of genocidal rape, below).

A very common result of gendercides against men is a glaring demographic disparity in the proportion of surviving women versus men. This is exemplified by cases such as Iraq, Cambodia, highlands Guatemala, and Rwanda – although one must be careful in evaluating the extent to which data truly reflect disproportionate male mortality, or alternatively an undercounting of males who may be in exile (as refugees or fighters), or in hiding to escape persecution and evade conscription.[17]

In the "root-and-branch" holocausts that the general public tends to view as the paradigm of genocide, a sequential progression is apparent along the lines described earlier. It is striking that all three of the "classic" genocides of the twentieth century – by the Turks against the Armenians; the Nazis against the Jews; and Hutus against Tutsis – followed roughly this pattern. The time separating the different stages was sometimes brief (in the Nazi case, only a few weeks), and the Rwandan case cannot be incorporated without serious qualification. Readers are invited to peruse the chapter-length treatments of these genocides through a "gendered" lens, to see how the progression from gendercidal to root-and-branch strategies occurred.

As noted in the Jewish Holocaust chapter, the shift from targeting "battle-age" non-combatant males, usually viewed as legitimate targets, to targeting children, women, and the elderly, may result in substantial emotional stress to killers. "While unarmed men seem fair game," wrote Leo Kuper, "the killing of women and children arouses general revulsion"[18] – though not in all situations, and not necessarily for long. Hence the escalation of Nazi killing of Jews, moving from adult males to other population groups;[19] hence, too, the development of distancing technologies such as gas vans and gas chambers, to reduce the trauma for murderers of women and children. One can also note the degeneration of more centralized control over genocidal killing in Rwanda. This appears to have been linked, in part, to concerns of ordinary Hutus that the murder spree was moving beyond acceptable targets.[20]

WOMEN AS TARGETS

The focus so far on the mass-murder component of genocide may have the unde-sirable effect of implying that women are exempted from the worst genocidal violence. Nothing could be further from the truth. First, root-and-branch genocides throughout history have killed tens or hundreds of millions of females. Many structural cases of genocide – such as mass famine, economic embargo, and so on – have an equal or greater impact on women and girls than on men and boys.

Second, the micro-managed gender strategies employed, for example, at Srebrenica, are fairly rare, especially in the contemporary era of "degenerate war" (see Chapters 2, 12). It is more common, as it was even in the Balkan genocides, for women to be exposed to direct abuses and atrocities. While these may be on average less deadly, they are no less "gendered." They range from verbal assault and humiliation, to physical attack and individual rape, to multiple and gang rape (often under conditions of protracted sexual servitude), to rape-murder on a large scale.

In December 1937, one of the most savage instances of genocidal rape inaugurated the so-called Rape of Nanjing. When Japanese forces seized the Chinese capital, up to a *quarter of a million* Chinese men were corraled and massacred, often after torture. Tens of thousands of women were also killed – usually after extended and excruciating gang rape. Kenzo Okamoto, a Japanese soldier, recalled: "We were hungry for women! Officers issued a rough rule: if you mess with a woman, kill her afterwards."[21] Another soldier stated: "Perhaps when we were raping [a female victim], we looked at her as a woman, but when we killed her, we just thought of her as something like a pig."[22] A Chinese eyewitness, Li Ke-hen, described "so many bodies on the street, victims of group rape and murder. They were all stripped naked, their breasts cut off, leaving a terrible dark brown hole; some of them were bayoneted in the abdomen, with their intestines spilling out alongside them; some had a roll of paper or a piece of wood stuffed in their vaginas." Almost no female was safe. Girls as young as eight, along with elderly women, were raped and killed. Even those not murdered immediately were liable to be "turned loose in such a manhandled condition that they died a day or two later."[23]

The Japanese rape of women in the Asian-occupied territories featured in the indictment at the postwar Tokyo Tribunal – though the systematic conscription and sexual exploitation of Korean, Indonesian, and other women (the so-called "comfort women" – see Chapter 14, p. 506) was not addressed. This may be because the victorious powers had overseen somewhat similar systems of female exploitation in their own spheres. Likewise, the mass rapes accompanying the Soviet conquest of eastern Germany in 1944–45 were not mentioned at the Nuremberg war crimes trials of 1945–46: the Soviets would never have permitted it.

Feminist author Susan Brownmiller's book *Against Our Will* (1975) marked the first systematic exploration of rape. It publicized the large-scale sexual violence against Bengali women during the Bangladesh genocide of 1971 (Box 8a), and the social rejection that raped women confronted in the aftermath. It was the Balkan wars of the 1990s, though, that exposed the issue of mass rape of women to international visibility (see the account of 16-year-old "E.," cited in Chapter 8). The term "genocidal rape" began to be widely employed to convey the centrality of sexual assault to the wider campaign of group destruction. Although rejected by some who argued that rape and genocide were distinct crimes, the concept gained further credibility with the events in Rwanda in 1994. As the UN Special Rapporteur on Rwanda, René Degni-Ségui, pointed out, "rape was the rule and its absence the exception" during this genocide.[24] While estimates of women raped in the Balkan genocides ranged between 20,000 and 50,000, in Rwanda they were *ten times* higher – between 250,000 and 500,000. Moreover, as at Nanjing, rape was standardly accompanied by "extreme brutality" above and beyond the specifically sexual assault. "Rape accompanied by mutilation [was] reported to include: the pouring of boiling water onto the genital parts and into the vagina . . . the cutting off of breast(s) and the mutilation of other parts of the female body."[25] And rape was very often followed by death – sometimes (and still) many years later, owing to the high proportion of Hutu rapists infected with the HIV virus. General Roméo Dallaire, recollecting the Rwandan holocaust years after he had failed meaningfully to impede it, found himself haunted above all by "the death masks of raped and sexually mutilated girls from women." But "even in the whitened skeletons" of the memorial sites, "you could see the evidence" of the masculine pathologies inscribed on their defenseless bodies:

> The legs bent and apart. A broken bottle, a rough branch, even a knife between them. Where the bodies were fresh, we saw what must have been semen pooled on and near the dead women and girls. There was always a lot of blood. Some male corpses had their genitals cut off, but many women and young girls had their breasts chopped off and their genitals crudely cut apart. They died in a position

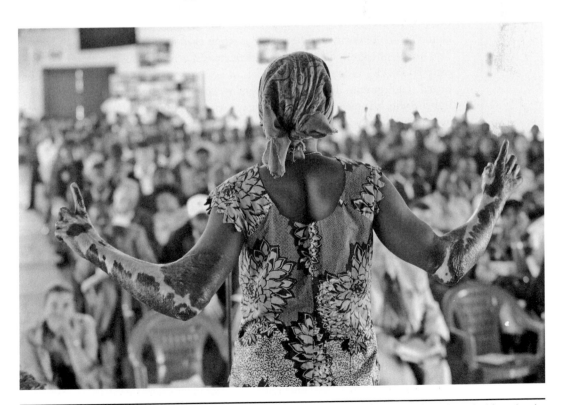

Figure 13.3   The increasing recognition in international law that rape can constitute a strategy of genocide resulted from decades of women's mobilizations against rape and sexual violence. Here, a rape survivor and burn victim tells her story at a UNICEF-sponsored gathering in Gisenyi, Rwanda, September 2008.

Source: Julien Harneis/Flickr.

of total vulnerability, flat on their backs, with their legs bent and knees wide apart. It was the expressions on their dead faces that assaulted me the most, a frieze of shock, pain and humiliation.[26]

In part as a result of the scale and savagery of the Rwandan rapes, and reflecting years of feminist-inspired mobilization around the issue, in September 1998 the ICTR convicted Jean-Paul Akayesu for acts of genocide including sexual violence. As Human Rights Watch noted, this marked "the first conviction for genocide by an international court; the first time an international court has punished sexual violence in a civil war; and *the first time that rape was found to be an act of genocide [intended] to destroy a group.*"[27]

Astonishingly, the record of mass rape in the Rwandan genocide was matched and even surpassed in the years following the holocaust – in neighboring Congo, where sexual violence has raged through to the present day. "Tens of thousands of women, possibly hundreds of thousands, have been raped in the past few years," wrote Jeffrey Gettleman of *The New York Times* in 2008.[28] Those responsible include virtually all the military and paramilitary forces operating in the east of the country – and even some of the "Blue Helmets" of MONUC, the UN peacekeeping force dispatched to restore order and protect civilians. John Holmes, coordinator of emergency relief for the UN, stated in 2007 that rape in Congo had become "almost a cultural phenomenon . . . The intensity and frequency is worse than anywhere else in the world."[29] "It's like a contagion," reported the advocate and actor Ashley Judd after a visit to eastern Congo. "When one man does it, it activates other men, and then the more brutal it becomes – looking for pregnant women to rape, and children. It's so unbelievably heinous that it's hard for us to wrap our minds around." As in Rwanda, apart from the psychological trauma and humiliation of rape, severe and often life-threatening physical injuries were the norm:

> The vagina will tear when being forced to accommodate either a rapist's anatomy or objects that are introduced: wood, rock, sticks, guns, bayonets. There will be perforation of the vaginal walls, perforation and ripping of the cervix, potentially, based on the extent of the penetration into the uterus. The wall between the rectum and vagina is ripped apart. The urethra, which goes to the bladder, is damaged. There is incontinence. The urine is constantly seeping out, because the muscles and mechanisms that hold the bladder intact are ruined; there is faecal incontinency, which of course can introduce faecal matter into the gut, which results in horrific infections. Does that paint the picture?[30]

GENDERCIDAL INSTITUTIONS

An appreciation of female vulnerability to genocide is greatly increased if we expand our framing beyond politico–military genocides, to the realm of "gendercidal institutions." I refer here to patterned behavior, embedded in human societies, that exacts a death-toll sufficiently large in scale and systematic in character to be considered gendercidal.

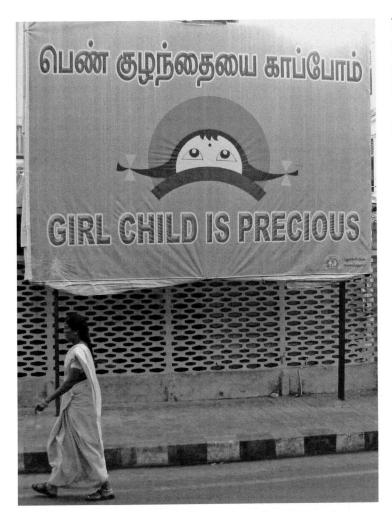

Figure 13.4   Female infanticide and female foeticide (sex-selective abortion) are among the most destructive "gendercidal institutions" against females, especially in India and China, the world's most populous countries. A sign outside the maternity hospital in Pondicherry, India, encourages a progressive approach to gender equality.

Source: Author's photo, June 2008.

For females, probably the most destructive such institution throughout history is female infanticide and neonaticide. The selective killing of newborn and infant girls reflects a culturally ingrained preference for male children. A nineteenth-century missionary in China, for example, "interviewed 40 women over age 50 who reported having borne 183 sons and 175 daughters, of whom 126 sons but only 53 daughters survived to age 10; by their account, the women had destroyed 78 of their daughters."[31] The Communist Revolution of 1949 made great strides in reducing discrimination against women and infant girls, but such millennia-old traditions are extremely difficult to root out. Today, numerous reports speak of large demographic disparities between males and females in parts of rural China, leading to widespread trafficking in women and adolescent girls as Chinese men seek to import wives from outside their regions.

The country where female infanticide and neonaticide are most widespread at present is India. For example, a study of Tamil Nadu state by the Community Service Guild of Madras found that "female infanticide is rampant" among Hindu families:

"Of the 1,250 families covered by the study, 740 had only one girl child and 249 agreed directly that they had done away with the unwanted girl child. More than 213 of the families had more than one male child whereas half the respondents had only one daughter."[32] Among wealthier families in both India and China, however, infanticide is being replaced by sex-selective abortion, following *in utero* screening procedures that have spread even to isolated rural areas.

Among other gendercidal institutions targeting females are gendered deficiencies in nutrition and health care (reflecting the prioritizing of male family members for these resources); "honor" killings of women and girls, particularly in the Middle East, South Asia, and the Caucasus; and dowry killings and *sati* in India, the former referring to murders of young women whose families cannot provide sufficient dowry payments to the family of their designated spouse, while the latter institution consigns women to die on the funeral pyres of their husbands.

Gendercidal institutions have also targeted males throughout history, and exacted a vast death-toll. Military conscription is a striking example. Less widely appreciated is *corvée* (forced) labor, which is both intimately related to and analytically distinct from military conscription. *Corvée* has overwhelmingly targeted adult men throughout history, killing in all likelihood hundreds of millions. There are grounds, in fact, for considering *corvée* the most destructive of all human institutions, even outstripping war. Ironically, forced labor remains legal today under the relevant international convention – but only when its targets are able-bodied adult males between the ages of 18 and 45.[33]

GENOCIDE AND VIOLENCE AGAINST HOMOSEXUALS

The phenomenon of discrimination and violence against homosexuals – especially gay men – is still pervasive. It is linked to the collective policing of gender, in which those who opt out of heterosexuality are seen as "asocial" threats. In the Nazi case (Box 6a), gay males were viewed as violating eugenic tenets. While the mentally handicapped were "useless eaters," gays were condemned as superfluous for their "failure" to help replenish the *Volk*.

In this book's first edition, I wrote that "perhaps only in the Nazi case has violence against homosexual men attained a scale and systematic character that might be considered genocidal." That judgment may still hold, but it has been challenged by the murderous campaign against homosexuals launched in post-2003 Iraq. In 2005, the leading Shia cleric, Grand Ayatollah Ali al-Sistani, issued a *fatwa* (religious injunction) calling for gay men and lesbians to be killed "in the worst, most severe way" (he lifted the decree against gay men the following year, but the *fatwa* against lesbians remained in place).[34] What had been one of the Arab world's livelier and more open gay scenes was replaced by a campaign of religious-fundamentalist terror that had killed an estimated four hundred people for alleged homosexual acts by 2007.[35] In that year, the United Nations Assistance Mission in Iraq (UNAMI) reported that "Islamic groups and militias have been known to be particularly hostile towards homosexuals, frequently and openly engaging in violent campaigns against them. There have been a number of assassinations of homosexuals." At "religious courts

. . . presided over by young, inexperienced clerics," homosexuals were given summary trials and sentences ranging "from 40 lashes to the death penalty."[36] In 2009, the UK *Observer* profiled a would-be judge and executioner, a young man who passed his days "cruising" Web sites to uncover hidden gays. The Net, he said, "is the easiest way to find those people who are destroying Islam and who want to dirty the reputation we took centuries to build up." "Animals deserve more pity than the dirty people who practise such sexual depraved acts," declared another member of the group. "We make sure they know why they are being held and give them the chance to ask God's forgiveness before they are killed."[37]

Those gays that had not fled the terror lived in fear, as related to *The New York Times* by "Mohammed [and] his friends":

> They described an underground existence, eked out behind drawn curtains in a dingy safe house in southwestern Baghdad. Five people share the apartment – four gay men and one woman, who says she is bisexual. They have moved six times in the last three years, just ahead, they say, of neighborhood raids by Shiite and Sunni death squads. Even seemingly benign neighborhood gossip can scare them enough to move. "We seem suspicious because we look like a cell of terrorists," said Mohammed, nervously fingering the lapel of his shirt. "But we can't tell people what we really are. A cell, yes, but of gays."[38]

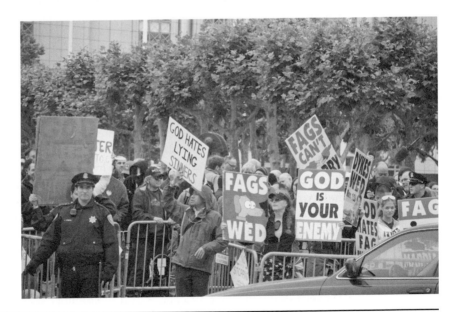

Figure 13.5   Protestors holding "God Hates Fag" and other signs demonstrate in San Francisco in June 2008. Homosexual men and women have been targeted for persecution and murder since the earliest days of many major societies and religious traditions. Today, in countries ranging from Colombia to Iraq to Uganda, their gender dissidence may incur the death penalty, whether imposed by state decree (as recently proposed in Uganda), religious *fatwa* (as in Iraq), or death-squads and vigilantes (as in Colombia and several other Latin American countries). (San Francisco is of course one of the global centers of gay and lesbian culture. The poster of this image, JP Puerta, noted, "It's amazing how in this country people with extremely different views can mix together in protests and mobs without anybody getting killed or seriously injured.")[39]

Source: JP Puerta/Wikimedia Commons.

Meanwhile, in Uganda as of early 2010, a bill was before parliament to formally enshrine the death penalty for homosexual relations in the country's legal code.[40] The measure was emblematic of a broader African trend toward anathematizing and criminalizing gays – again spurred by religious fundamentalism, this time predominantly of a Christian stripe.[41] In Latin American countries still reeling from the death-squad violence of the 1970s through the 1990s, gay males – especially male prostitutes, the transgendered, and drag queens – remain at extraordinary risk of vigilante-style killings in some Latin American societies. In Colombia between 1986 and 1990, "328 gay men were murdered in the city of Medellín alone."[42]

Globally, Amnesty International reports sampled by Stefanie Rixecker demonstrate that a wide range of violence is "directed at queer individuals based upon their actual or perceived sexual preference":

> The types of abuses range from complaints of ill treatment while in police custody to rape, sexual abuse, sexual realignment surgery, extrajudicial executions and disappearances, and state-sanctioned execution. The murder of gays and lesbians due to their sexuality, or to associated behaviors and illnesses (e.g. HIV and AIDS), not only means that the individuals are targeted, but also – due to the relatively small numbers of gays and lesbians – becomes tantamount to genocide and now, more specifically, gendercide.

"Although a full complement of the gay community is not murdered in such acts," Rixecker wrote, "the relatively small statistical populations of gays and lesbians overall means that the annual toll of queer identities can be regarded as a genocidal act."[43]

GENOCIDAL MEN, GENOCIDAL WOMEN

A cursory examination of classical and contemporary genocides shows that the overwhelming majority of genocidal planners, killers, and rapists are men, just as men predominate as architects and wagers of war. There is also the lesser, but still striking, disproportion of men among murderers worldwide (especially mass and serial murderers). One wonders, in fact, whether for many people, a *sufficient* explanation of genocide (and war, and murder) would not be simply: "Boys will be boys." Likewise, when we focus on disproportionate male *victimization*, at least for genocide's most lethal strategies, patterns of intra-male competition and conquest seem significant. They are evident not only in most human societies, as anthropologists have shown, but among the higher primates that are humanity's closest relatives.

Explanations for these tendencies and uniformities have spawned enduring, interdisciplinary, and so far inconclusive debates. Some of the most intriguing, but also ambiguous, data come from sociobiological investigations. In their book *Demonic Males*, Richard Wrangham and Dale Peterson drew direct comparisons between chimpanzee societies – in which prevail patterns of male bonding and hegemony-seeking, raiding, sexual assault, infanticide, and violent bloodlust – and human beings, a species that shares some 99 percent of its genome with chimpanzees. Some of the questions they asked about male chimps translate directly to human genocide, especially those pertaining to apparently "irrational" forms of violence: "Why kill the enemy, rather than simply drive him away? Why rape? Why torture and mutilate?"[44]

In *The Dark Side of Man* (which includes a chapter on "Genocide"), another researcher, Michael P. Ghiglieri, described a frankly stomach-churning act of massed killing of an isolated male chimp, comparable in central respects to a scene from the Rwandan genocide or a frenzied ethnic pogrom. He likened the results to the aftermath of a Nazi death-squad operation:

> In Gombe and Mahale [districts of Tanzania], after all the adult males in each vanquished community had been killed and all the adolescent males had sickened and died, seemingly from depression, the young females shifted their allegiance and home ranges and mated with the victorious males. The victors instantly expanded their territories to include part (Gombe) or most (Mahale) of the territories of the dead males. Both defeated communities ceased to exist, having been wiped out by genocidal warfare. Tanzanian chimps, like Hitler's storm troopers, had fought for lebensraum [living space].[45]

There are at least powerful common patterns, then, between these two closely-related species. Behavior such as bonding among in-group males to destroy out-group males; kidnapping and rape of females; frenzied/"sadistic" violence; and infanticide, all seem to some degree genetically coded, evolving over time amidst resource scarcity (which provokes "colonial"-style foraging along frontiers), and intramale competition for female mates, especially multiple mates.

How does this shape an understanding of nature versus nurture, physiology versus environment, in understanding gendered roles, identities, and performances? Ghiglieri made a case for hardwired male behavior, sardonically noting that "none of these apes learned these violent behaviors by watching TV or by being victims of socioeconomic handicaps – poor schools, broken homes, bad fathers, illegal drugs, easy weapons, or any other sociological condition." Only strict and lifelong discipline, he contended, would ever rein in males' basically "ethnocentric and xenophobic" disposition, their innate urge "to fight and kill other men genetically more distant from them in genocidal wars aimed at seizing or usurping what those other men possess, including the reproductive potential of their women."[46]

However, Wrangham and Peterson – along with Joshua Goldstein in his essential contribution *War and Gender* – considered the nature-versus-nurture argument a dead end. In their view, *both* physiology and environment are influential. In the ape world, another species also shares 99 percent of its genetic code with humans: the bonobo. But the bonobo is "the gentle ape"; there are "no reports of males forcing copulations, battering adult females, or killing infants," and they seem overall an amazingly benevolent bunch. Part of the explanation may lie in their more varied and plentiful food supply, contrasted with the foraging chimpanzee populations. This limits male intergroup and intragroup violence, as does the fact that bonobo females do not have manifestly fertile "periods," encouraging less territorial expansion for reproductive purposes, less competition (and rape) to access females during fertile periods, and a more relaxed and playful attitude toward sexuality (including homosexuality).

In addition, and in part for these reasons, female bonobos appear to act as a potent restraining force against male aggression and violence. If males "throw their weight around and become overly aggressive, they are liable to be suppressed by females . . . [who] form alliances that effectively protect them against male aggression."[47] This led the authors to stress (as did Ghiglieri) that females play a vital role in *validating* male violence by mating with the violent male – even in the context of a coercive "patriarchal bargain." "Women's evolved strategic responses to male demonism have included countermeasures and defiance, but they have also included collaboration. That is to say, while men have evolved to be demonic males, it seems likely that women have evolved to prefer demonic males . . . as mates."[48] The ubiquitous phenomenon of females "cheerleading" for male violence, addressed below, thus has its counterpart in the primate world. For Wrangham and Peterson, therefore, the resolution to the dilemma lay in humans' intelligence and capacity for empathy, which together could allow the human race to transcend its inbred and acculturated – and everywhere male-dominated – tendency to violence. This was not so far from elements of Ghiglieri's own "antidote to men's violence in America."[49]

In human societies, male hegemony is enshrined as the institution of *patriarchy* – "rule by the fathers," that is, rule by men as heads of family units and by older and more powerful men within communities, rather than rule by men as an undifferentiated gender class. However, by contrast with the chimpanzee "alpha male" who must constantly defend his status against challengers – or lose it – we see in human societies a displacement of the hegemonic struggle onto subordinate males. It is the patriarchs who choose to wage war and genocide against out-groups; but to this end, they must mobilize younger, subordinate males to inflict the actual violence. They are assisted by women as mothers and nurturers, who help to educate, train, and prepare younger generations of males for service as soldiers, cannon-fodder, and *génocidaires*. If they survive and succeed, they too are eligible to join patriarchal ranks, with all its consequences – including the privilege of mating with the most desirable females.

It is notable that while in some cultures, men flock to perform their assigned role as subordinate agents of violence, in most others they must be dragged unwillingly into these duties. The long, little-studied history of masculine resistance to military conscription, and the brutality of the "basic training" to which conscripts are exposed, suggest that male violence is not automatically activated – even, in many cases, that a more peaceable disposition must be broken down and reconstructed for warlike or genocidal purposes.

It is likewise the case among humans that, while those who commit murder, rape, and other violent crimes are overwhelmingly male, the majority of men in most cultures do *not* engage in such heinous acts. Nonetheless, the majority of men do partake, consciously or unconsciously, in the benefits of patriarchy, notably the subordinate and submissive role to which it consigns most females. And we must not pass over the human male's near-monopoly of the most violent crimes – like murder, rape, and genocide – quite so lightly. Psychologically complex humans have developed the psychologically complex ideology of *misogyny* – fear and hatred of females – as a key buttress of patriarchy. When combined with the active desire *for* females, as mates and cheerleaders, the mix is toxic indeed. No male is more dangerous than the frustrated and alienated male; and though he may ordinarily seek validation and a sense of superiority through the targeting of out-group males, he is also prone to seek it through existential violence against females. Allan D. Cooper has argued that "when men suffer from [an] acute masculine identity crisis, that is when they experience relative deprivation of masculinity, they often seek to end the crisis by destroying the desired object beyond their reach: a woman."[50] Thus the serial murderer or rapist of women is generally a dysfunctional and humiliated male. Thus too, perhaps, some of the wanton and mutilative savagery that attends male violence – both against females, as we have just seen, and against other males – occurs in societies at "peace," and in times of war and genocide as well.

In the specific context of genocide, Cooper has contended that most outbreaks of mass killing can be linked to an "emasculating moment," in which males, especially leaders, feel humiliated by a challenge to their masculinity, and react viciously – both to buttress the gendered status quo, and to reclaim an existential sense of masculine prowess.[51] Elisa von Joeden-Forgey has carried this analysis a step further, with her study of ideologies of "genocidal masculinity." She sees such ideologies as aimed *not* at preserving patriarchy, but at destroying it. Genocide relies upon subordinate and marginalized males who rebel against a patriarchal order which has frozen them out, denying them (among other things) access to females as the site of biological reproduction. In reacting to this sense of marginalization and humiliation, genocidal masculinity "rejects the old patriarchy and embraces an expression of power based on killing rather than life-giving." The result is a "ritualized cruelty" which often takes the form of what von Joeden-Forgey calls "life-force atrocities": "violence that targets the life force of a group by destroying both the physical symbols of the life force as well as the group's most basic institutions of reproduction, especially the family unit." She depicts these atrocities as falling into two broad categories:

The first are inversion rituals that seek to reverse proper hierarchies and rela-tionships within families, and thereby to destroy the sacred bonds that give our lives purpose and meaning. Such acts include forcing family members to watch the rape, torture and murder of their loved ones, and forcing them to participate in the perpetration of such crimes. Common versions of such atrocities includes fathers being forced to rape their children, mothers being forced to kill their children, children being forced to kill their parents, children being pulled scream-ing from their parents' arms to be killed, and parents being forced to watch as their children are slowly tortured and murdered. The second category of genocidal atrocity is the ritual mutilation and desecration of symbols of group reproduction, including male and female reproductive organs, women's breasts as the sites of lactation, pregnant women as the loci of generative powers, and infants and small children as the sacred symbols of the group's future. The evisceration of pregnant women and the use of infants for target practice are common examples. What ties these two categories of life force atrocity together is that in each, perpetrators betray a pronounced obsession with the destruction of the life-force of a group – not just the group's biological ability to bring children into the world, but also the structures of tenderness, love, protectiveness and loyalty that sustain family, and community, life.[52]

What, then, of women? Is their significance to the study of genocide primarily that of victims, as objects on which males write their genocidal "scripts"? Far from it. In fact, as Daniel Jonah Goldhagen has argued, "when we look to the populations in whose name eliminationist politics are perpetrated, women are no less supportive than men, and are no less desirous of the broader political and social transformations undergirding such politics than the men are."[53] Under patriarchy, women are generally reduced to supporting roles; but they perform them with enthusiasm. As "cheerleaders" for genocide, they offer moral and material support to male perpetrators; assist in ostracizing males who seek to evade involvement in the slaughter;[54] and provide political support, sometimes exceeding that of men, for genocidal leaders.[55]

Whatever the genetic and sociobiological inheritance, when women, along with men, are *mobilized, forced, encouraged, allowed* to participate in genocide and other atrocious violence, they generally display no more reluctance than (often reluctant) males. Readers' minds might leap to the revelations from Abu Ghraib prison near Baghdad, where female guards were prominent as agents of abuse. The scholar of

Figure 13.6 German women and adolescent girls were some of the Nazis' most ardent supporters – the party may have garnered more female than male votes in some elections, and Hitler received thousands of love letters and marriage proposals throughout his reign. Females are usually relegated to the roles of supporters and cheerleaders, as with these adolescent girls at a Nazi parade in Berlin in 1938. What happens when they are provided with positive and negative incentives to participate in the dirty work of genocide?

Source: Corbis.

genocide, moreover, encounters the direct involvement of women at many points in history: torturing and executing prisoners-of-war (as was standard in Native American civilizations); joining men in attacking and pillaging refugee convoys (as Kurdish women did in the Armenian genocide); and actively involving themselves in "euthanasia" killings and concentration-camp atrocities under the Nazis (female camp guards "murdered as easily [as men]; their sadism was no less," notes James Waller).[56]

Most dramatically, and apparently at levels unprecedented in history, women actively participated in perpetrating the Rwandan holocaust of 1994. "I had seen war before, but I had never seen a woman carrying a baby on her back kill another woman with a baby on her back," said a stunned officer with the United Nations Assistance Mission for Rwanda (UNAMIR).[57] Hutu women ululated their men into genocidal action, and were prominent after massacres in "finishing off" those still clinging to life: "Some were dead, some alive," one Hutu girl remembered. "We beat the ones who were not dead. The other women killed one each."[58] They gleefully looted the corpses afterward, "fighting over the fabric and the trousers," in the recollection of one Hutu perpetrator.[59] Nor were women limited to these subordinate roles: they assumed leadership positions at national, regional, and local levels. The most notorious (and high-level) case is Pauline Nyiramasuhuko, indicted by the International Criminal Tribunal for Rwanda (ICTR) for "personally direct[ing] squads of Hutu men to torture and butcher Tutsi men, and to rape and mutilate Tutsi women."[60] ("Before you kill the women, you need to rape them," Nyiramasuhuko reportedly urged the *interahamwe* militiamen whom she supervised.)[61] Rwanda, indeed, can serve as something of a test for the proposition that human females are more reluctant participants in violence and genocide than are males.

In light of the evidence from Rwanda and elsewhere, James Waller argued, "the challenge . . . is to transcend our gender expectations that women are basically innocent by nature, so that their acts of cruelty are viewed as deviant and abnormal, and instead approach their perpetration of extraordinary evil the same way we have that of men – as ordinary people influenced by cultural, psychological, and social constructions."[62]

In examining these constructions, can we discern specifically "feminine" roles, psyches, and personae among female perpetrators of genocide, and cheerleaders for it? The attempt is somewhat speculative, for the simple reason that the male perpetrator has overwhelmingly been the focus of inquiries into gender and violence, while female perpetrators have tended to be exoticized and sensationalized. However, several observations can be ventured.

First, we saw at the outset of this section that in male-dominant society, there may be a biological and cultural logic to female support for male violence, including its genocidal manifestations. Moreover, women under patriarchy are designated as the guardians of "home and hearth," especially children – meaning that they may feel especially keenly any threat to that domestic order, of the kind that designated "enemies" allegedly pose. A personal sense of vulnerability to violence – to sexual assault in particular – seems to have underpinned female support for genocidal actors and institutions, as with the US white women who willingly participated (as denouncers, spectators, and symbolic icons of female purity) in the lynchings of African-American men (see Box 13.1).

In asserting themselves as agents *beyond* the roles reserved for them under patriarchy, women may lay claim to a specific "female masculinity," according to Judith Halberstam[63] – appropriating and performing the kind of identities (as strong, potent, cruel) that are normally mapped onto males. Though no "matriarchal" society probably ever existed, some cultures have permitted women substantial public roles as social and economic actors, and these may facilitate greater and more direct female involvement in violence as well. Such cultures sometimes supply iconic images of the violent female, arguably validating and encouraging female expressions of violence – as the place of the bloodthirsty goddess Kali in Hindu culture has been linked to the prominent role women have played in the Hindu extremist movement.[64] Finally, to the extent that women are targeted in genocide, intrafemale rivalries may produce a kind of "gendered jubilation" at the destruction and humiliation of female rivals. This was powerfully evident in Rwanda, for example, where Hutu women had long been depicted as less attractive and desirable than their Tutsi counterparts. Many Hutu women accordingly took pleasure in Tutsi women's "comeuppance," and proved more than willing to assist in inflicting it.[65]

BOX 13.1 "STRANGE FRUIT" AND THE GENDERED POLITICS OF LYNCHING

Figure 13.7   Lynching victims Thomas Shipp and Abram Smith in Marion, Indiana, 1930.
Source: Bettman/Corbis.

The photograph opposite is one of the most infamous ever taken. It captures the festive atmosphere outside the midwestern US town of Marion, Indiana, on August 7, 1930. As police looked on, two young African-American men, Thomas Shipp and Abram Smith, were dragged from their jail cells, where they were being held on trumped-up allegations of rape and robbery. Shipp and Smith were beaten and tortured, then – like thousands of other African-American men, and some African-American women – murdered by lynching. In a typical "life-force atrocity" against out-group males (see p. 479), Smith, hanging at right, was castrated (hence the clothing arranged around his midsection – a photographer was there, after all, and one wouldn't want to offend popular sensibilities). The revelry continued, and the photographer snapped away: many such images of lynchings, and some even more gruesome, actually circulated as postcards in the US while lynching was at its height.

Soon after the events, a Brooklyn schoolteacher of a leftist bent, Abel Meeropol, saw the photograph. Meeropol dabbled as a poet and songwriter, and under the less foreign-sounding pseudonym of Lewis Johnson, he penned a song that indelibly depicted the lynched young men as *"strange fruit hanging on the poplar trees."* The explicit imagery of racial slaughter still has the power to shock:

. . . Pastoral scene of the gallant South,
The bulging eyes and the twisted mouth,
Scent of magnolia sweet and fresh,
And the sudden smell of burning flesh!
Here is a fruit for the crows to pluck,
For the rain to gather, for the wind to suck,
For the sun to rot, for a tree to drop,
Here is a strange and bitter crop.

Figure 13.8 Billie Holiday, the American jazz singer, recorded "Strange Fruit" in 1939. But she was hesitant about performing it live: some fans, clueless about the lyric's provenance, would ask her to "sing that sexy song about the people swinging." For more, see David Margolick and Hilton Als, *Strange Fruit: The Biography of a Song* (New York: Ecco, 2001). For an MP3 of Holiday's performance of the song, link to http://www.genocidetext.net/strange_fruit_billie.mp3; for a devastating live performance, see http://www.youtube.com/watch?v=h4ZyuULy9zs.

Source: Northern California Public Broadcasting, Inc. (NCPB).

First performed in New York clubs by the African-American singer Billie Holiday, "Strange Fruit" was recorded in 1939, and went on to entrench itself as one of the most iconic and influential songs of the century (in 2003, the British music magazine *Q* placed it at number 6 on its list of "100 Songs That Changed the World"). In 1997, the Richmond, Virginia-based hip-hop artist, Danja Mowf, reworked the song in a contemporary idiom. In a remarkable and deeply discomfiting move, Mowf took the listener inside the thoughts and tortured form of the lynching victim (incorporating details from another lynching, in 1930, of James Irwin in Ocilla, Georgia). In so doing, he drove home not only the gendered stigmatization that regularly produced murder, but the aspect that appalls so many viewers of the Marion, Indiana photograph: the festive unity that pervades the crowd, and the eclectic mix of white spectators represented.

> . . . This white girl identified me as a rapist
> Had me wishin' I was Harry Houdini, the great escapist . . .
> She said I kidnapped her, trapped her, slapped her
> Then after I tapped her, I fled through the pasture
> Nah, not me, 'cuz I knew I'd get acquitted
> But seemed every white face in town knew I did it
> Or done it, shit, about a hundred approachin' white figures
> Bearin' triggers, screaming, "Kill that nigger!" . . .
> Them cops ain't even yell "Freeze!," they just gave the mob the keys
> They beat me like I stole somethin', pistol-whipped me like a stickup
> Tied my hands behind my back, tied my feet to the bumper
> Of a pickup truck, now I'm gettin' shucked like corn
> Bein' drug through the town, face down
> To the gravel, my clothes and skin unravel
> They took me to a tree, hung me naked by my wrists
> When I beg and I plead I can't take it like this
> They shoved a pole in my mouth
> 'Cause you see, down South
> Lynchin' was a show, everybody came out.
> See, the mothers brought they daughters to come and check the slaughters,
> And fathers brought they sons, to see how it was done,
> They brung everyone, from the old to the young
> Cause it really was nuttin' to see a nigga get hung . . .
> My screams and tears brought more celebration and cheers
> Than twelve o'clock on New Year's
> A girl couldn't see, someone raised her higher
> So she could watch them breakin' out my teeth with the wire plier
> My one desire was to meet my Messiah, but they wouldn't let me die-ah
> Sayin', "Nigger, we gon' fry ya in the fire"
> I prayed that death was movin' near; that's when
> They castrated me and kept my nuts as souvenirs

Gasoline cleaned my wounds like liquor
Saw the match flicker, begged 'em do it quicker
Ahh yes, the smell of burning flesh
A hundred angry bullets penetrate my chest
Sweet death long awaited, I hang as a monument
A warning simply stated for a people that they hated . . .

> (Lyrics reprinted courtesy Danja Mowf, from his album *Word of Mowf* [1997]. Also by the artist's kind permission, the MP3 is available on this book's website at http://www.genocidetext.net/strange_fruit_danja.mp3.)

"Lynchin' was a show, everybody came out . . . " I have long been struck by a detail of the 1937 photo (Figure 13.9), anchored at left by a young white couple shyly holding hands, who look like they're headed to the prom afterward. We see here one of the starkest images ever captured of "ordinary" participants in genocidal atrocity, and something of the "banality of evil" that Hannah Arendt discerned in the Nazi Jew-killer, Adolf Eichmann. Evident as well, despite the fairly stable restriction of African-American lynching to male victims,[66] is how white complicity in this genocidal or proto-genocidal attack easily transcended age and gender, even in a context of quite traditional (mid-western 1930s) social relations. Those who seized, tormented, and lynched African-American men were overwhelmingly white

Figure 13.9   Detail of Figure 13.7.

males. But white women, too, "participated directly in [the] torture, execution, and mutilation" of the victims, according to Crystal N. Feimster's 2009 study *Southern Horrors*.[67] Moreover, white women were regularly deployed, and deployed themselves, as *justifications* for lynching (i.e., to inflict vengeance for acts of sexual assault and "dishonor" allegedly committed against them by demonized black males, and to protect them against the supposedly pervasive threat of future attack). Women were also essential to the dynamic of vigilantism and summary "justice." Rebecca Felton, an early Southern feminist and the first female member of the US Congress, declared in 1897 that "if it takes lynching to protect women's dearest possession from drunken, ravening human beasts, then I say lynch a thousand a week."[68] At the grassroots, women frequently issued the allegations and provided the testimony that led to black men like Shipp and Smith being seized, tortured, and murdered. And as we see in the photo, they were eager spectators of the ritual slaughter – even the grandmotherly figure gazing absently into the distance. Bonds of racial-ethnic solidarity, and fear of an "insurgent" racial minority, drew white men and women, girls and boys together to orchestrate and celebrate these grotesque spectacles of mutilation and race-murder.

Lynching was designed to terrorize African Americans, especially the restive and potentially rebellious black male, into political quiescence and economic servitude, after the US Civil War (1861–65) and the formal abolition of slavery in the former Confederacy. A heady, but tragically foreclosed, period of black emancipation and empowerment ("Reconstruction") saw African Americans flood into education, politics, agriculture and industry. But it spawned a vicious, arguably genocidal backlash among white ranks.[69] The racist "night riders" of the Ku Klux Klan were the most notorious result, responsible for many lynchings. The KKK's exploits were glorified in one of the masterworks of American film, D.W. Griffith's *Birth of a Nation* (1916), which for all its cinematic verve now seems pitched at about the same moral level as Leni Riefenstahl's paean to Adolf Hitler and Nazism, *Triumph of the Will* (1935).

Disciplined by the ever-present threat of vigilante violence, it was expected that blacks would return to the condition of subjugation and "social death"[70] that was their lot under slavery. Ruthless labor exploitation was an essential aspect, in the form of a system of quasi-slavery built around the prison system of the southern US. Every black man was liable to arrest on concocted and highly gendered charges of "delinquency," "vagrancy," or "miscegenation" (the last "an offense almost solely prosecuted against black men who engaged in sex with white women").[71] They were cast into work in mines, in quarries, and on plantations. Now even the minimal sense of reciprocal obligation present in southern slave society was replaced by a blatant hyperexploitation. More generally, and even in the northern states, urban blacks were squeezed into marginal and often squalid ghettoes. Rural blacks in the south were coerced into sharecropping arrangements (providing labor to a landowner in exchange for a plot of land to work for subsistence) that reimposed the economic dependency and illiteracy of the slavery period. And they probably experienced more chronic malnutrition than previously, since US slaves were generally fed a calorically adequate (if starchy and monotonous) diet.

We saw in Chapter 1 that lynching and other acts of physical and structural violence against African Americans were foundational to probably the first anti-genocide petition ever launched, submitted to the United Nations in 1951 (pp. 41–42). This was also at the vanguard of the civil rights movement that transformed, against violent resistance, the face of race relations in the US South.[72] Despite these accomplishments, however, the legacy of lynching, and the structures of political and economic marginalization that it helped to entrench, shape social formations to the present. As Douglas Blackmon wrote in his Pulitzer Prize-winning book, *Slavery by Another Name*: "There was no acknowledgment of the effects of cycle upon cycle of malevolent defeat, of the injury of seeing one generation rise above the cusp of poverty only to be indignantly crushed, of the impact of repeating tsunamis of violence and obliterated opportunities on each new generation of an ever-changing population outnumbered in persons and resources."[73]

The consequences of this reverberating violence, both directly and indirectly, are particularly stark in the case of younger black males. They disproportionately experience forms and levels of violence (intragroup or at the hands of security forces) – along with harassment, incarceration, and political disenfranchisement[74] – that are matched only by Native Americans. In 2004, gender scholar Augusta Del Zotto pointed to the phenomenon of "black male gendercide" in the United States, including practices of "quasi-morticide" ("self-destruction through deliberately dangerous action"), and patterns of "black-on-black violence . . . coinciding with drastic cutbacks in educational, vocational, and recreational" opportunities for youth. "Unlike many instances of gendercide," Del Zotto concluded, ". . . the practice of gendercide against African American males follows a long historical continuum and is contingent upon an unspoken de facto war involving race and class. Central to this sociopolitical condition is the systematic dismantling of kinship and cultural ties over time, making the African American male vulnerable to various forms of gendercidal targeting."[75]

A NOTE ON GENDERED PROPAGANDA

A useful application of a gender perspective in genocide studies is to genocidal propaganda, so central in mobilizing populations to support and commit atrocities. This issue may be approached from various angles.

If men, overwhelmingly, must be mobilized to do the "dirty work" of genocidal killing, how are their gender sensibilities exploited? Perhaps the most common strategy is to accuse males who evince qualms about participation of being cowards – failed bearers of masculinity. A Rwandan official visiting a commune that was deemed "negligent" in its genocidal duties demanded to know "if there were no more men there, meaning men who could deal with 'security' problems."[76] Men who "shirked" their duties were denounced in terms little less venomous than those employed against Tutsis: "What are those sons of dogs fleeing from?"[77]

Men's designated role as "protectors" of women and children fuels potent propaganda strategies. Nazi troops dispatched to the firestorm of the eastern front were exposed to speeches from their commanders, demanding to know "what would have happened had these Asiatic Mongol hordes succeeded to pour into . . . Germany, laying the country waste, plundering, murdering, raping?"[78] By implication, the German troops were justified in laying waste, plundering, murdering, and raping, as they did to an extent unseen since the days of the "Mongol hordes."

Women, as noted, are generally cast in supporting roles in genocidal campaigns. Propaganda directed at them emphasizes their role as guardians of home and children. This has the added advantage of bolstering the self-image of males as protectors of (passive, defenseless) "women and children."

A further important aspect of genocidal propaganda is the demonization of out-group men as a prelude to gender-selective round-ups and mass killing. The classic case is the construction of the "Eternal Jew" in Nazi propaganda, which paved the way for the Holocaust of 1941–45. This propaganda entrenched an image of the "wretched, disgusting, horrifying, flat-footed, hook-nosed dirty Jew"[79] – virtually always a *male* Jew. As Joan Ringelheim notes: "Legitimation for targeting Jewish men was plentiful in Nazi anti-Semitic and racist propaganda and, more to the point, in Nazi policy. The decision to kill every Jew did not seem to demand special justification to kill Jewish men. They were already identified as dangerous," thanks to years of grotesque imagery such as that depicted in Figure 13.10. "This was not so for Jewish

Figure 13.10   Poster for the Nazi propaganda exhibition *Der Ewige Jude* (The Eternal Jew), 1937. The sinister-looking male Jew is shown as addicted to lucre (the coins in his outstretched hand), oppressive (the whip in the other), and allied with international communism (Germany with the hammer-and-sickle crooked under his arm). Depictions of the Jewish male as dangerous and malevolent were central to their selective targeting at early stages of Nazi campaigns of persecution and, ultimately, genocide. More generally, such demonized depictions of out-group males are central to both genocidal propaganda and gendercidal massacre.

Source: Hoover Institution Archives Poster Collection.

Figure 13.11 "General Dallaire and his army have fallen into the trap of fatal women." Tutsi women, with badges/tattoos of support for the FPR (Rwandan rebel forces), are depicted seducing UN force commander Gen. Roméo Dallaire in this cartoon from the Hutu Power propaganda paper *Kangura* (February 1994). Genocidal propaganda against women often emphasizes their imputed sexual powers; in the Rwandan case, this paved the way for massive sexual violence against Tutsi women during the 1994 genocide.

Source: From Christopher Taylor, *Sacrifice as Terror: The Rwandan Genocide of 1994* (Oxford: Berg, 1994).

Figures 13.12 and 13.13 Men and women are assigned distinct, usually complementary, and highly constrained roles in war and genocide. In these Nazi propaganda images, the paramilitary SS male is depicted with a steely, implacable gaze, his phallic bayonet thrusting into the frame. The "Mother and Child" in the accompanying image symbolize what paramilitary masculinity was constructed as guarding and protecting: home and hearth, presided over by the fecund, nurturing figure of the German female.

Source: German Propaganda Archive/Robert D. Brooks.

women and children."[80] They were also depicted as sexually rapacious and invasive. Peter Fritzsche notes that "it was usually Jewish men who were imagined to prey on German women: the gender of the Jewish peril was male, while Aryan vulnerability was female."[81] It comes as little surprise, then, that adult male Jews were the first to be rounded up and executed *en masse* on the eastern front, as a means of acclimatizing the killers to subsequent root-and-branch genocide.

In a similar vein, consider the language typically directed at population groups to mark them out for persecution or genocide: terms such as "monster," "beast/bestial," "devil/demon," "bandit," "criminal," "rapist," "terrorist," "swindler," "vagabond," "subhuman," "vermin," "exploiter". . . . Now, though the task may be unpleasant, assign a human face to these caricatures. Is it a male or a female face that automatically leaps to mind?[82]

When women are targeted in genocidal and proto-genocidal propaganda, this tends to occur (1) on a smaller scale, (2) with a lesser variety of imagery, and (3) with a heavy concentration on the female's imputed sexual power (including her reproductive capacity) (see Figure 13.13). Hence the regular use of terms such as "seducer," "prostitute," "whore," "baby factory." This emphasis on sexual power and capacity no doubt fuels the rampant sexual violence against women and girls, including extreme humiliation and "life-force atrocities," that is a regular feature of genocidal campaigns. Women, and men, may also be targeted for their supposed links to the supernatural ("witch" and, relatedly, "baby-killer").

The implicit gendering of much genocidal propaganda seems fundamental to marshaling support for gendercide and all-out genocide. As such, it would seem to have implications for strategies of genocide prevention. I return to this subject in the concluding chapter.

FURTHER STUDY

African Rights, *Rwanda: Not So Innocent: When Women Become Killers*. London: African Rights, 1995. Taboo-shattering account of women's participation in the 1994 genocide.

R. Charli Carpenter, *"Innocent Women and Children": Gender, Norms, and the Protection of Civilians*. London: Ashgate, 2006. Innovative study of gender and humanitarian intervention, focusing on the vulnerabilities of civilian males.

Gendercide Watch, www.gendercide.org. Website featuring two dozen detailed case studies of gendercide.

Michael P. Ghiglieri, *The Dark Side of Man: Tracing the Origins of Male Violence*. Cambridge, MA: Perseus Books, 2000. Argues that men are biologically programmed to wage war and commit genocide.

Joshua S. Goldstein, *War and Gender: How Gender Shapes the War System and Vice Versa*. Cambridge: Cambridge University Press, 2001. Captivating interdisciplinary overview.

Jessica Hubbard, *Understanding Rape as Genocide: A Feminist Analysis of Sexual Violence and Genocide*. Saarbrücken: VDM Verlag Dr. Müller, 2008. More of a graduate paper than a book, but a reasonable primer.

Human Rights Watch, *Shattered Lives: Sexual Violence During the Rwanda Genocide and Its Aftermath*. New York: Human Rights Watch, 1996. Examines the targeting of women for rape in the Rwandan holocaust; available on the Web at http://hrw.org/reports/1996/Rwanda.htm.

Adam Jones, ed., *Gendercide and Genocide*. Nashville, TN: Vanderbilt University Press, 2004. The most wide-ranging book on gender-selective killing. See also *Gender Inclusive: Essays on Violence, Men, and Feminist International Relations*.

Claudia Koonz, *Mothers in the Fatherland: Women, the Family and Nazi Politics*. New York: Basic Books, 1987. Inquiry into the diverse roles of German women under Nazism.

Nicholas D. Kristof and Sheryl WuDunn, *Half the Sky: Turning Oppression into Opportunity for Women Worldwide*. New York: Knopf, 2009. Vignettes of women's inspiring advances and continued subjugation.

Rohit Lentin, ed., *Gender and Catastrophe*. London: Zed Books, 1997. Essays on the gendering of genocide, slavery, poverty, and famine, with an emphasis on women.

Lois Ann Lorentzen and Jennifer Turpin, eds, *The Women and War Reader*. New York: New York University Press, 1998. Anthology of writings on women's victimization and agency in wartime.

Caroline O.N. Moser and Fiona C. Clark, eds, *Victims, Perpetrators or Actors? Gender, Armed Conflict and Political Violence*. London: Zed Books, 2001. Groundbreaking edited collection.

Elenor Richter-Lyonette, ed., *In the Aftermath of Rape: Women's Rights, War Crimes, and Genocide*. Givrins: Coordination of Women's Advocacy, 1997. Examines genocidal rape, with emphasis on the Balkans and Rwandan cases.

Alexandra Stiglmayer, ed., *Mass Rape: The War against Women in Bosnia-Herzegovina*. Lincoln, NB: University of Nebraska Press, 1995. The standard source on sexual violence against women in the Balkan wars.

Klaus Theweleit, *Male Fantasies, Volume 1: Women, Floods, Bodies, History*, trans. Stephen Conway. Minneapolis, MN: University of Minnesota Press, 1987. Profound psychoanalytical study of fascist and paramilitary masculinities.

Samuel Totten, ed., *Plight and Fate of Women During and Following Genocide*. New Brunswick, NJ: Transaction Publishers, 2009. Part of a series of "critical bibliographic reviews" of genocide; a very useful resource.

Mary Anne Warren, *Gendercide: The Implications of Sex Selection*. Totowa, NJ: Rowman & Allanheld, 1985. Coined the term "gendercide," with a focus on reproductive technologies.

NOTES

1 See, e.g., R. Charli Carpenter, "Beyond 'Gendercide': Operationalizing Gender in Comparative Genocide Studies," in Adam Jones, ed., *Gendercide and Genocide* (Nashville, TN: Vanderbilt University Press, 2004), pp. 230–56, esp. pp. 232–38.

2 Joshua Goldstein, *War and Gender* (Cambridge: Cambridge University Press, 2001), p. 2.

3 For instance, Mary E. Hawkesworth wrote: "In principle, a gendered practice could privilege men or women. But the history of male dominance has resulted in systematic male power advantages across diverse social domains. Feminist usage of the adjective

'gendered' reflects this male power advantage. *Hence a gendered practice is synonymous with androcentric* [male-centered] *practice* in common feminist terminology." Hawkesworth, "Democratization: Reflections on Gendered Dislocations in the Public Sphere," in R.M. Kelly *et al.*, eds, *Gender, Globalization, and Democratization* (Lanham, MD: Rowman & Littlefield, 2001), p. 235, n. 2; emphasis added.

4 Excerpts in Kurt A. Raaflaub, handout for Brown University Classics course (CL56), "War and Society in the Ancient World."

5 Thucydides, *The Peloponnesian War*, quoted in Frank Chalk and Kurt Jonassohn, *The History and Sociology of Genocide: Analyses and Case Studies* (New Haven, CT: Yale University Press, 1990), p. 73.

6 See Adam Jones, "Why Gendercide? Why Root-and-Branch? A Comparison of the Vendée Uprising of 1793–94 and the Bosnian War of the 1990s," *Journal of Genocide Research*, 8: 1 (2006), pp. 9–25.

7 Scott Straus, *The Order of Genocide: Race, Power, and War in Rwanda* (Ithaca, NY: Cornell University Press, 2006), p. 164.

8 A disturbing strand of just-war theory even justifies gender-selective extermination of males. The Enlightenment philosopher Vitoria stated: "Everyone able to bear arms should be considered dangerous . . . they may therefore be killed unless the opposite is clearly true." Michael Walzer wrote: "a soldier who, once he is engaged, simply fires at every male villager between the age of 15 and 50 . . . is probably justified in doing so." Vitoria quoted in R. Charli Carpenter, "'Women and Children First': Gender, Norms, and Humanitarian Evacuation in the Balkans 1991–95," *International Organization*, 57: 4 (Fall 2003), p. 672; Walzer quoted in Carpenter, "Beyond 'Gendercide,'" p. 252, n. 13.

9 Donald L. Horowitz, *The Deadly Ethnic Riot* (Berkeley, CA: University of California Press, 2001), p. 148. Horowitz added that "In experiments, males are also more selective in their choice of targets; females distribute shocks more equally among targets. Perhaps selective targeting itself is a sex-skewed phenomenon"; that is, males are more likely to aggress against males selectively and disproportionately than are women (p. 148).

10 See Adam Jones, "Gender and Genocide in Rwanda," in Jones, ed., *Gendercide and Genocide*, p. 111.

11 See R. Charli Carpenter, "'Women, Children and Other Vulnerable Groups': Gender, Strategic Frames and the Protection of Civilians as a Transnational Issue," *International Studies Quarterly*, 49 (2005), pp. 295–334.

12 Most of these cases receive extended treatment on the Gendercide Watch site, http://www.gendercide.org. A question commonly asked is whether in such cases, men are being targeted "as a group" or "as such," rather than (for example) as combatants or potential combatants. The question is a valid one, in part because as noted in the discussion of "Multiple and Overlapping Identities" in Chapter 1 (pp. 34–36), *gender always combines with other variables* to produce genocidal outcomes. The most obvious are *ethnicity/ nationality/ race/religion/perceived political affiliation* (that is, there is no targeting of males as a global gender group, but rather of males belonging to one of these designated groups); *age* (with "battle-age" males more liable to be targeted than very young or very old ones); *community prominence* (the disproportionate representation of men among elites means that when "eliticides" occur, as in Burundi in 1972, the victims are overwhelmingly male); and *perceived military capacity* (given the prevailing cultural and practical identification of males with combatants). Often implicit in the question, however, is the notion that women and girls *are* victimized "as such" – primarily because they are female. In my view, this is untenable. When women are the victims of politico–military genocide, it is similarly on the basis of their ethnicity, perceived political affiliation, and so on (or because of their family relationship with men of these designated groups). The Nazis who killed Jewish women *en masse* did not kill German women – in fact, their slaughter of the Jews was often justified by the supposed need to protect German women. Even in the cases where a misogynistic worldview seems predominant, other variables are crucial. Female infanticide does not target females as a group, but rather those of a particular age, and usually of a particular (poorer) social class. The European witch-hunts of the

medieval and early modern era, which resulted in a death-toll about 75 percent female, likewise did not designate all women as targets, but women perceived as a threat for their supposed liaisons with dark powers. *Age* and *marital status* were other important variables, with the majority of women designated as "witches" being older and more likely to be widows. Clearly, however, the gender variable is decisive in all these cases – as it is in the case of gendercidal killings of men. Finally, does the gendered hatred of women – misogyny – that factors in all these cases have a counterpart for male victims (misandry)? I contend that it does, and that it is evident, for example, in gendered propaganda. For further discussion, see Adam Jones, "Problems of Gendercide," in Jones, ed., *Gendercide and Genocide*, pp. 257–71.

13 Madhu Kishwar, "Delhi: Gangster Rule," in Patwant Singh and Harji Malik, eds, *Punjab: The Fatal Miscalculation* (New Delhi: Patwant Singh, 1985), pp. 171–78.

14 Horowitz, *The Deadly Ethnic Riot*, pp. 73, 123, n. 261.

15 Ian Traynor, "Hague Rules Srebrenica was Genocide," *Guardian*, April 20, 2004, http://www.guardian.co.uk/world/2004/apr/20/warcrimes. See also the comments by Daniel Goldhagen concerning the Nazis' early gendercidal massacres of Jewish males on the Eastern front: "Even if . . . the initial order was to kill 'only' teenage and adult Jewish males – the order was still genocidal and clearly was understood by the perpetrators as such. . . . The killing of the adult males of a community is nothing less than the destruction of that community." Daniel J. Goldhagen, *Hitler's Willing Executioners: Ordinary Germans and the Holocaust* (New York: Vintage, 1997), p. 153.

16 Judgment of August 2, 2001, cited in John Quigley, *The Genocide Convention: An International Law Analysis* (London: Ashgate, 2006), p. 197.

17 See, e.g., the discussion of the Rwandan case in Jones, "Gender and Genocide in Rwanda," pp. 123–25; and of the Cambodian case in May Ebihara and Judy Ledgerwood, "Aftermaths of Genocide: Cambodian Villagers," in Alexander Laban Hinton, ed., *Annihilating Difference: The Anthropology of Genocide* (Berkeley, CA: University of California Press, 2002), pp. 275–80.

18 Leo Kuper, *Genocide: Its Political Use in the Twentieth Century* (London: Penguin, 1981), p. 46. Richard Rhodes also noted that "Men prepared to kill victims who are manifestly unthreatening – the elderly, unarmed women, small children, infants – behave differently from men prepared to kill victims such as men of military age who can be construed to be at least potentially dangerous." Rhodes, *Masters of Death: The SS-Einsatzgruppen and the Invention of the Holocaust* (New York: Alfred A. Knopf, 2002), p. 69. According to Rhodes (p. 167), the Nazis even "established mental hospitals and rest areas" to care for SS men "'who [had] broken down while executing women and children.'" "I must admit openly that the gassings had a calming effect on me," confessed Rudolf Höss, the former commander of the Auschwitz death camp. ". . . I was always horrified of death by firing squads, especially when I thought of the huge numbers of women and children who would have to be killed. . . . Now I was at ease. We were all saved from these bloodbaths." Quoted in Mark Levene, *Genocide in the Age of the Nation State, Vol. 1: The Meaning of Genocide* (London: I.B. Tauris, 2005), p. 102.

19 See the analysis of this escalation in Goldhagen, *Hitler's Willing Executioners*, pp. 149–51.

20 On this phenomenon, see Jones, ed., *Gendercide and Genocide*, pp. 24–25, 117–18.

21 James Yin and Shi Young, *The Rape of Nanking: An Undeniable History in Photographs* (Chicago, IL: Triumph, 1996), p. 188.

22 Iris Chang, *The Rape of Nanking: The Forgotten Holocaust of World War Two* (London: Penguin, 1998), pp. 49–50.

23 Historian David Bergamini, quoted in Yin and Young, *The Rape of Nanking*, p. 195.

24 Quoted in Elenor Richter-Lyonette, "Women after the Genocide in Rwanda," in Richter-Lyonette, ed., *In the Aftermath of Rape: Women's Rights, War Crimes, and Genocide* (Givrins: Coordination of Women's Advocacy, 1997), p. 107.

25 Ibid., p. 107.

26 Roméo Dallaire, *Shake Hands with the Devil: The Failure of Humanity in Rwanda* (New York: Caroll & Graf Publishers, 2003), p. 430.

27 "Human Rights Watch Applauds Rwanda Rape Verdict," Human Rights Watch press release, September 2, 1998, http://www.hrw.org/en/news/1998/09/02/human-rights-watch-applauds-rwanda-rape-verdict; emphasis added. See also Teaching Human Rights Online, "Rape and Genocide in Rwanda: The ICTR's Akayesu Verdict," http://homepages. uc.edu/thro/rwanda/RwandaRapeCase2. htm.

28 Jeffrey Gettleman, "Rape Victims' Words Help Jolt Congo into Change," *The New York Times*, October 17, 2008, http://www.nytimes.com/2008/10/18/world/africa/18congo. html.

29 Stephanie McCrummen, "Prevalence of Rape in E. Congo Described as Worst in World," *The Washington Post*, September 9, 2007. See also "Rape a Weapon of War, Activists in Congo Say," CNN.com, October 17, 2009, http://www.cnn.com/2009/WORLD/africa/10/16/amanpour.congo.rape.documentary/index.html.

30 Judd quoted in Christopher Dickey, "Ashley Judd's Heart Of Darkness," *Newsweek*, October 30, 2008, http://www.newsweek.com/id/166488. See also Anna Husarska, "The Hidden Wounds of Congo's Wars," Slate.com, January 4, 2008, http://www.slate.com/id/2181274. On efforts to help survivors, see Stephanie Hanes, "Life after Rape in Congo," *The Christian Science Monitor*, April 25, 2007, http://www.csmonitor.com/2007/0425/p13s02-woaf.html.

31 Ansley J. Coale and Judith Banister, "Five Decades of Missing Females in China," *Demography*, 31: 3 (August 1994), p. 472.

32 Malavika Karlekar, "The Girl Child in India: Does She Have Any Rights?," *Canadian Woman Studies*, March 1995.

33 For detailed case studies of gendercidal institutions against females and males, see the Gendercide Watch website.

34 Cara Buckley, "Gays Living in Shadows of New Iraq," *The New York Times*, December 18, 2007, http://www.nytimes.com/2007/12/18/world/middleeast/18baghdad.html.

35 Buckley, "Gays Living in Shadows."

36 Doug Ireland, "UN Human Rights Report Confirms Iraqi Gay Killings," ZNet.org, January 27, 2007. See also Rasha Moumneh, "Iraq's New Surge: Gay Killings," *Foreign Policy*, September 9, 2009, http://www.foreignpolicy.com/articles/2009/09/09/iraqs_new_surge_gay_killings.

37 Afif Sarhan and Jason Burke, "How Islamist Gangs Use Internet to Track, Torture and Kill Iraqi Gays," *The Observer*, September 13, 2009, http://www.guardian.co.uk/world/2009/sep/13/iraq-gays-murdered-militias.

38 Buckley, "Gays Living in Shadows."

39 Puerta quoted at http://commons.wikimedia.org/wiki/File:2008_Anti-gay_protestors_in_San_Francisco.jpg; I have corrected a couple of typos. Puerta's comment is worth bearing in mind for the discussions of free speech/genocide denial (Chapter 14) and US cosmopolitanism (Chapter 16, pp. 592–93).

40 See Jeffrey Gettleman, "After Americans Visit, Uganda Weighs Death for Gays," *The New York Times*, January 3, 2010, http://www.nytimes.com/2010/01/04/world/africa/04uganda.html (the accompanying photo by Marc Hofer of anti-gay demonstrators in Kampala is also striking).

41 Fran Blandy, "Homosexual Africans Face Prison, Intolerance and the Death Penalty," *The Telegraph*, January 11, 2010, noting that "38 out of 53 [African] countries have criminalised consensual gay sex."

42 Amnesty International UK report, *Breaking the Silence*, cited in Stefanie Rixecker, "Genetic Engineering and Queer Biotechnology: The Eugenics of the Twenty-first Century?," in Jones, ed., *Gendercide and Genocide*, p. 188.

43 Rixecker, "Genetic Engineering and Queer Biotechnology," p. 188.

44 Richard Wrangham and Dale Peterson, *Demonic Males: Apes and the Origins of Human Violence* (New York: Mariner, 1996), p. 23.

45 Michael P. Ghiglieri, *The Dark Side of Man: Tracing the Origins of Male Violence* (Cambridge, MA: Perseus Books, 2000), p. 173.

46 Wrangham and Peterson, *Demonic Males*, p. 214.

47 Ibid., pp. 208, 227.

48 Ibid., p. 239.

49 Ghiglieri called "for the vast majority of US citizens to make the individual decision to cooperate as a group . . . to teach children, all children, from day one, self-control, self-discipline, and self-responsibility in a world where we ourselves show that offensive violence is wrong. . . . Boys becoming young men must already have been socialized with these deep human values (in a palatable form, more or less as Boy Scouts of America wishes to do) *by their parents*. Second, we must decide to cooperate to make felonious violence – rape, murder, offensive war, genocide, and terrorism – not only 'not pay' for the perpetrator but also reap pain. In short, to stop violence, we must decide that our justice is *lex talionis* justice" – at which point Ghiglieri's prescriptions cease to persuade me (*The Dark Side of Man*, p. 256). See also the discussion in John Docker, "Chimpanzees, Humans, Agricultural Society," ch. 2 in Docker, *The Origins of Violence: Religion, History and Genocide* (London: Pluto Press, 2008), pp. 13–38. After surveying some of the same terrain explored by Wrangham/Peterson, Ghiglieri, and Joshua Goldstein, Docker expressed support for a "sophisticated anti-determinism . . . which allows a powerful space for plasticity of brain and mind, the capacity not to be predetermined, the talent to be transformative, to be able to change and reverse and invert, to be unpredictable. In these terms, while there may be shared characteristics between chimpanzees and early humans, these may act in human history as potentialities, as possibilities, rather than as inevitable or binding; and they may not be carried through at all" (p. 28).

50 Allan D. Cooper, *The Geography of Genocide* (Lanham, MD: University Press of America, 2009), p. 42.

51 Ibid.; see ch. 6, "The End of Masculinity," and the lengthy appendix (Appendix 2) exploring "The Emasculating Moment of Historic Genocides."

52 Elisa von Joeden-Forgey, "Genocidal Masculinity," in Adam Jones, ed., *New Directions in Genocide Research* (London: Routledge, forthcoming 2011).

53 Daniel Jonah Goldhagen, *Worse Than War: Genocide, Eliminationism, and the Ongoing Assault on Humanity* (New York: Basic Books, 2009), p. 215. See also Alan Hall, "Behind Every Nazi Mass Murderer Was a Woman: New Book Claims Women under Hitler Were Just as Ruthless as Men," *The Daily Mail*, February 3, 2009, profiling the research of German historian Kathrin Kompisch, not yet published in English.

54 "In Britain and America during [World War One], women organized a large-scale campaign to hand out white feathers to able-bodied men found on the streets, to shame the men for failing to serve in combat. . . . The white feather campaign was briefly resurrected in World War II, and the British government had to issue badges for men exempt on medical grounds." Goldstein, *War and Gender*, p. 272. "Many feminists, such as England's Isabella Pankurst, set the struggle for suffrage aside for an equally militant jingoism, and contented themselves with organizing women to support the war effort. 'The war is so horribly exciting but I cannot live on it,' one British suffragette wrote. 'It is like being drunk all day.'" Barbara Ehrenreich, *Blood Rites: Origins and History of the Passions of War* (New York: Metropolitan Books, 1997), p. 13.

55 It seems that at least as many women as men, perhaps more, supported Hitler and the Nazi regime; Tim Mason wrote that "a variety of different sources convey the impression that in the later 1930s the Third Reich enjoyed a large measure of active and passive support among women, *a larger measure than it gained from among men*" (quoted in Robert Gellately, *Backing Hitler: Consent and Coercion in Nazi Germany* [Oxford: Oxford University Press, 2001], p. 16, emphasis added). Gellately explained this as follows: "Conservative, Catholic, and even liberal women by and large shared the point of view advocated by the Nazis, as to a 'naturally' determined sexual division of labour, and that it was important to reconstruct a 'community of the people' in which they would be involved primarily as wives and mothers, and 'not be forced to compete with men for scarce jobs and political influence'" (p. 10, citing Ute Frevert, *Women in German History*). Owing to gender-separated voting booths, we also know that more women than men

voted in favor of perpetuating Augusto Pinochet's dictatorial rule in Chile in a 1989 plebiscite; "51% of women and 58% of men voted 'no'" to the dictator. (See the fine documentary, *In Women's Hands*, PBS/Annenberg Project, *Americas* series, 1993; statistic available at http://people.rit.edu/cakgss/inwomenshands.html.) In both cases, one wonders whether the fact that it was predominantly men who were targeted for harassment, detention, incarceration, torture, and murder by the regimes in question (the Jewish Holocaust apart) may have prompted a greater proportion of men to express opposition to those regimes when it was safe to do so. Finally, the recent prominence of women in the proto-genocidal Hindu-extremist movement in India has received increasing scholarly attention (see note 64).

56 James Waller, *Becoming Evil: How Ordinary People Commit Genocide and Mass Killing*, 2nd edn (Oxford: Oxford University Press, 2007), p. 267.

57 Quoted in Alison Des Forges, *Leave None to Tell the Story: Genocide in Rwanda* (New York: Human Rights Watch, 1999), p. 261. For numerous examples, see the ground-breaking African Rights report, *Rwanda: Not So Innocent: When Women Become Killers* (London: African Rights, 1995). For more on Nyiramasuhuko, see Carrie Sperling, "Mother of Atrocities: Pauline Nyiramasuhuko's Role in the Rwandan Genocide," *Fordham Urban Law Journal*, January 1, 2006. Her trial, underway when the first edition of this book appeared in 2006, was still ongoing as the second neared completion in 2009! – the longest of all the trials supervised by the ICTR (International Criminal Tribunal for Rwanda).

58 Quoted in *Crimes against Humanity*, film produced by the Imperial War Museum, London, December 2002 (from the official transcript).

59 Léopord Twagirayezu, quoted in Goldhagen, *Worse Than War*, p. 102.

60 Kimberlee Acquaro and Peter Landesman, "Out of Madness, A Matriarchy," *Mother Jones*, January/February 2003. Available at http://motherjones.com/politics/2003/01/out-madness-matriarchy. The article is a good overview of women's position in Rwanda after the genocide, including the "unplanned – if not inadvertent – movement of female empowerment driven by national necessity."

61 For a lengthy profile of Nyiramasuhuko, see Peter Landesman, "A Woman's Work," *The New York Times Magazine*, September 15, 2002, http://www.nytimes.com/2002/09/15/magazine/a-woman-s-work.html

62 Waller, *Becoming Evil*, pp. 268–69.

63 Judith Halberstam, *Female Masculinity* (Durham, NC: Duke University Press, 1998); cited in von Joeden-Forgey, "Genocidal Masculinity."

64 On Hindu women's militancy, see Parita Mukta, "Gender, Community, Nation: The Myth of Innocence," in Susie Jacobs *et al.*, eds, *States of Conflict: Gender, Violence and Resistance* (London: Zed Books, 2000), pp. 163–78; Atreyee Sen, "Reflecting on Resistance: Hindu Women 'Soldiers' and the Birth of Female Militancy," *Indian Journal of Gender Studies*, 13: 1 (2006), pp. 1–35.

65 See Adam Jones, "Gender and Genocide in Rwanda," in Jones, *Gender Inclusive: Essays on Violence, Men, and Feminist International Relations* (London: Routledge, 2009), p. 123.

66 See the list of over 150 "Recorded Cases of Black Female Lynching Victims" between 1886 and 1957, compiled by Maria Delongoria for her doctoral dissertation, "'Stranger Fruit': The Lynching of Black Women: The Cases of Rosa Richardson and Marie Scott." Available at http://edt.missouri.edu/Fall2006/Dissertation/DeLongoriaM-120506-D6091/research.pdf (Appendix A, p. 160).

67 Crystal N. Feimster, *Southern Horrors: Women and the Politics of Rape and Lynching* (Cambridge, MA: Harvard University Press, 2009), p. 147. Feimster noted: "Thousands of white women . . . participated in southern lynchings as a display of racial and gender solidarity; to exercise violent power over African Americans, and to express their desire to move freely without threat of violence. In this sense, mob violence served as a perverse demonstration of the New Woman's desire for authority and autonomy. . . . Southern white women . . . were most visible at lynchings of black men accused of sexually threatening or assaulting white women and girls. More than any other alleged crime the

accusation of rape or attempted rape brought white women and men together at southern lynchings [*n.b.* and in the Marion, Indiana case]. Not only an expression of racial solidarity, support for and participation in mob violence also brought white women together across class lines on the issue of sexual violence and protection" (pp. 145, 149).

68 "Rebecca Latimer Felton," Women in Congress, http://womenincongress.house.gov/member-profiles/profile.html?intID=74. See also David Brion Davis, *Inhuman Bondage: The Rise and Fall of Slavery in the New World* (New York: Oxford University Press, 2006), p. 29.

69 See Eric Foner, *Forever Free: The Story of Emancipation and Reconstruction* (New York: Vintage, 2005); Stephen Budiansky, *The Bloody Shirt: Terror after the Civil War* (New York: Plume, 2009).

70 The reference is to Orlando Patterson's magisterial work, *Slavery and Social Death: A Comparative Study* (Cambridge, MA: Harvard University Press, 1982), though Patterson cites Michel Izard as originator of the term. The "social death" concept has been deployed in the genocide studies literature, notably by Claudia Card in her article "Genocide and Social Death," *Hypatia*, 18: 1 (2003), pp. 63–79. "Social death, central to the evil of genocide (whether the genocide is homicidal or primarily cultural), distinguishes genocide from other mass murders. Loss of social vitality is loss of identity and thereby of meaning for one's existence. Seeing social death at the center of genocide takes our focus off body counts and loss of individual talents, directing us instead to mourn losses of relationships that create community and give meaning to the development of talents" (from the article's abstract). The usage thus ties in with discussions of cultural genocide (Chapter 1) – and also with discussions of gender and genocide. The raped woman in a traditional society, for instance, is exposed to much the same kind of shame, stigmatization, and anathematization as the slave. In a genocidal and post-genocidal situation, the intent is often (and the consequences more often still) to undermine the "relationships that create community" and erode the cohesion of the targeted ethnic or national group.

71 Douglas A. Blackmon, *Slavery by Another Name: The Re-Enslavement of Black Americans from the Civil War to World War II* (New York: Anchor Books, 2009); see also www.slaverybyanothername.com. The institution of widespread "post-slavery" slave labor, channeled through the prison system, was almost unknown until the publication of this Pulitzer Prize-winning book by a *Wall Street Journal* editor. Blackmon describes "hundreds of forced labor camps . . . scattered throughout the [post-Civil War] South – operated by state and county governments, large corporations, small-time entrepreneurs, and provincial farmers. These bulging slave centers became a primary weapon of suppression of black aspirations" (p. 7). Conditions in the camps and plantations filled with "black men, and a small number of women" (p. 54) often differed little from those at Mauthausen or Auschwitz III-Monowitz under the Nazis. Thousands, probably tens of thousands, were directly killed by the mistreatment, or had their lives drastically cut short. Not untypical of the system in the 1870s was the death toll recorded in Alabama, where "in the first two years that [the state's penal system] leased its prisoners [to plantation and mine owners], nearly 20 percent of them died. In the following year, mortality rose to 35 percent. In the fourth, nearly 45 percent were killed" (p. 57). At the Coalburg slave camp, "of 648 forced laborers at the mine in 1888 and 1889, 34 percent did not survive. At the Pratt Mines, 18 percent died. All but a handful were black" (p. 98). Noting the pattern of restitution claims against German corporations who profited from slave labor under the Nazis (see Chapters 6, 14), Blackmon asked: "What would be revealed if American corporations were examined through the same sharp lens of historical confrontation as the one . . . being trained on German corporations that relied on Jewish slave labor during World War II and the Swiss banks that robbed victims of the Holocaust of their fortunes?" (p. 3).

72 See Taylor Branch, *Parting the Waters: America in the King Years, 1954–63* (New York: Touchstone, 1988).

73 Blackmon, *Slavery by Another Name*, p. 6.

74 The razor-thin margin by which George W. Bush won election in 2000, for example, was decisively swung by the absent male (notably minority male) voter in Florida. Traditionally he was not only a he, but a Democrat; but he was stripped from the electoral rolls by laws that disenfranchise Florida convicts. See Marc Mauer, "Disenfranchisement of Felons: The Modern-Day Voting Rights Challenge," *Civil Rights Journal*, 6 (Winter 2002), pp. 40–43, available at http://www.sentencingproject.org/doc/publications/mauer-crj.pdf; also Michelle Alexander, *The New Jim Crow: Mass Incarceration in the Age of Colorblindness* (New York: The New Press, 2010), and Alexander's article "The New Jim Crow" in *The Nation*, March 9, 2010, http://www.thenation.com/doc/20100322/alexander.

75 Augusta C. Del Zotto, "Gendercide in a Historical-Structural Context: The Case of Black Male Gendercide in the United States," in Jones, ed., *Gendercide and Genocide*, pp. 158, 166. For arguments along similar or parallel lines, see Orlando Patterson, *Rituals of Blood: Consequences of Slavery in Two American Centuries* (Washington, DC: Civitas/Counterpoint, 1998); and João H. Costa Vargas, *Never Meant to Survive: Genocide and Utopias in Black Diaspora Communities* (Lanham, MD: Rowman & Littlefield, 2008), esp. ch. 1, "Genocide in the African Diaspora: United States, Brazil, and the Imperatives of Holistic Analysis and Political Method." There is also a countervailing phenomenon of subaltern hate-crimes with a quasi- or proto-genocidal dimension, for example, in much rape and gang-rape in US jails. See Adam Jones, "'When the Rabbit's Got the Gun': Subaltern Genocide and the Genocidal Continuum," in Nicholas A. Robins and Adam Jones, eds., *Genocides by the Oppressed: Subaltern Genocides in Theory and Practice* (Bloomington, IN: Indiana University Press, 2009), pp. 194–95 (and *passim*).

76 Quoted in Des Forges, *Leave None to Tell the Story*, p. 459.

77 Quoted in African Rights, *Rwanda: Death, Despair and Defiance* (rev. edn) (London: African Rights, 1995), p. 82.

78 Commander of the Wehrmacht's II Corps to his troops, late December 1941; quoted in Omer Bartov, *Hitler's Army: Soldiers, Nazis, and War in the Third Reich* (New York: Oxford University Press, 1992), p. 132.

79 Saul Friedländer, *Nazi Germany and the Jews, Volume 1: The Years of Persecution, 1933–1939* (New York: HarperCollins, 1997), p. 124.

80 Joan Ringelheim, "Genocide and Gender: A Split Memory," in Ronit Lentin, ed., *Gender and Catastrophe* (London: Zed Books, 1997), p. 19. See also the heavily-gendered depiction of the Jew in Adolf Hitler's *Mein Kampf* (Boston, MA: Houghton Mifflin, 1943), pp. 300–27.

81 Peter Fritzsche, *Life and Death in the Third Reich* (Cambridge, MA: The Belknap Press of Harvard University Press, 2008), p. 129. Jeffrey Herf's portrait of the "Jewish enemy" was gendered throughout, both in presenting exclusively male Jews in the propaganda images reproduced as color plates, and in numerous passing references throughout the text (Herf, *The Jewish Enemy: Nazi Propaganda during World War II and the Holocaust* [Cambridge, MA: The Belknap Press of Harvard University Press, 2006]; see, e.g., pp. 32, 33, 128, 143, 222). However, Herf did not explore gender as an overarching theme or variable.

82 See Adam Jones, "Genocide and Humanitarian Intervention: Incorporating the Gender Variable," *Journal of Humanitarian Assistance*, February 2002, http://www.jha.ac/articles/a080.htm.

PART 4 THE FUTURE OF GENOCIDE

CHAPTER 14

Memory, Forgetting, and Denial

> Memory is life. It is always carried by groups of living people, and therefore it is in permanent evolution. It is subject to the dialectics of remembering and forgetting, unaware of its successive deformations, open to all kinds of use and manipulation . . . Memory always belongs to our time and forms a lived bond with the eternal present.
>
> Pierre Nora

"You speak about history," Soviet dictator Joseph Stalin told a gathering of his subordinates. "But one must sometimes correct history."[1] Never was that task pursued more surreally than under Stalin. Old photographs were doctored to eliminate Stalin's former Bolshevik colleagues, now labeled "saboteurs" and "enemies of the people" (see Chapter 5). The history of the Communist Party was rewritten to accord Stalin a central and heroic role. Inconvenient evidence was expunged, such as Lenin's warning shortly before his death that Stalin should be distrusted and marginalized. When the Nazi–Soviet pact was signed in August 1939, the erstwhile epitome of evil – the fascist German regime – became a friend and business partner. Less than two years later, Germany had launched the most destructive invasion of all time against the Soviet Union. Overnight, Soviet public opinion and official history had to shift again to accommodate total war against the former friend (and, prior to that, mortal enemy).

As satirized by George Orwell in *Nineteen Eighty-Four*, Stalinism and other totalitarianisms have become classic cases of the manipulation of history and memory. Usually, however, things are not as clear-cut as dictatorial imposition. Rather, memory and history reflect an ongoing contestation and evolution, within both societies and individual hearts and minds. Elizabeth Jelin has written of "'legitimacy' struggles over memory – who has what rights to determine what should be remembered and how":

> Such moments of contestation over commemorations and memorials are markers which provide clues to the processes of remembrance at the subjective and the symbolic levels, where the memories of different social actors are enacted and become "the present," making it easier to analyze the construction of collective, social and public memories.

At these points, Jelin adds, "memories are multiple and at times in conflict."[2] In large part, this reflects one's positioning in the historical drama. Is one an older person, with direct memories of the events? Is one younger, seeking to uncover the secrets of one's elders, or alternatively to "let the past take care of the past" and move on? Is one a former collaborator with the repressive regime, anxious to justify the collaboration or mitigate one's guilt through confession and public repentance? Is one a victim of the regime who feels that personal suffering constitutes "the basic determinant of legitimacy and the claim to truth"?[3] Or does such suffering mean that one is unable to adopt an "objective" approach to the events?

Figure 14.1   Genocide memorials have proliferated around the world in recent decades, as a way of conscientizing new generations to the horrors – and lessons – of the past. Visitors' expressions reflect their reaction at a September 2009 ceremony for a new monument commemorating victims of the Babi Yar massacre. The Nazis rounded up and shot 33,700 Jews at Babi Yar, outside Kiev in Ukraine, over a period of 48 hours (September 29–October 1, 1941) – the largest such massacre of the Holocaust.

Source: AP Photo/Efrem Lukatsky.

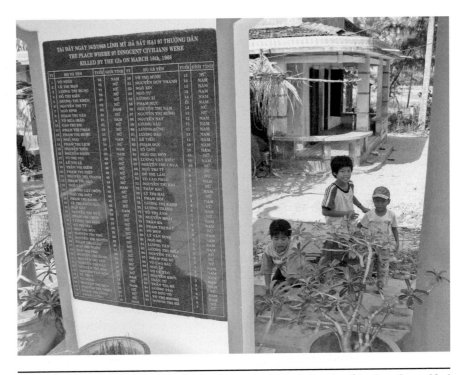

Figure 14.2   Vietnamese children gather beside a memorial in the hamlet of Co Luy, Quang Ngai Province, listing 97 victims of the My Lai massacre by US soldiers in March 1968 (see Chapter 2, pp. 75–76).

Source: Author's photo, July 2009.

The answers to these questions tell us something about how individual identities are constructed through selective memory (as all memory is). Cumulatively, they also say a great deal about how a society remembers, and *why* it remembers: that is, with what collective or public purpose.[4] To understand this more deeply, let us consider four cases in which genocide and crimes against humanity, or forceful allegations thereof, have spawned far-reaching debate, self-analysis, and denial.

CONTESTED MEMORIES: FOUR CASES

I. Germany

Germany's reckoning with its Nazi past may be divided into three principal stages. The first, extending from the war's end to about the mid-1960s, was one of willful amnesia, as Germans sought to put the war behind them. It has been argued that this act of forgetting (see further below) was significant in allowing West Germans to build a prosperous and democratic state, while in Soviet-controlled East Germany, Nazi sins could be displaced onto "fascism" and the communist entity depicted in a heroic light. In West Germany, to the extent that victims were memorialized and commemorated, they were overwhelmingly *German* victims – such as the hundreds of thousands of German POWs who remained in Soviet camps, in many cases into the 1950s. The West German government under Konrad Adenauer did initiate substantial reparations payments to Jews in the form of tens of billions of deutschmarks in financial transfers to Israel. This evoked some public opposition, but most Germans appear to have welcomed it as a means of bolstering their alliance with the West – rather than as an *entrée* to memorialization of Jewish suffering and German guilt.

The upheavals of the 1960s radically destabilized this historical narrative. Survivors and scholars of the genocide against the Jews explored the Holocaust systematically for the first time. German scholars asserted historical continuities between the Nazi and post-Nazi periods, including the role of large capitalist enterprises that had managed the transition smoothly from fascism to democracy. Many younger Germans made pilgrimages to Israel to atone for the sins of their forebears. The *Schuldfrage* (guilt issue) took center stage, symbolized by Chancellor Willi Brandt's famous kneeling apology for Nazi crimes (the so-called *Kniefall*) on a July 1970 visit to Poland.[5] In academia, the ferment spilled over into the *Historikerstreit* (historians' debate) of the 1970s and 1980s, "a scholarly controversy over the place and significance of National Socialism and the Holocaust in the narrative of modern German history."[6] An older generation concerned with maintaining, for example, a distinction between Nazi and German Army practices was confronted by mostly younger scholars who challenged the assumptions and evasions of their seniors (see also Chapter 6).

This second stage saw the German and Nazi past rendered more complex and problematic to ordinary Germans. Society was prone to "irruptions of memory" of the kind described by Alexander Wilde: "public events that break in upon [the] national consciousness, unbidden and often suddenly, to evoke associations with symbols, figures, causes, ways of life which to an unusual degree are associated with a political past that is still present in the lived experience of a major part of the population."[7]

One such irruption belonged to the realm of popular culture: the January 1979 broadcast of the US television mini-series *Holocaust*, starring Meryl Streep and James Woods, which despite its soap-opera stylings offered Germans perhaps their first sustained depiction of Jewish persecution under Nazism. Quite unexpectedly, it was *Holocaust* that first rent the public fabric in a decisive way, as Heinz Hoehne noted in *Der Spiegel*:

> An American television series, made in a trivial style, produced more for commercial than for moral reasons, more for entertainment than for enlightenment, accomplished what hundreds of books, plays, films, and television programs, thousands of documents, and all the concentration camp trials have failed to do in the more than three decades since the end of the war: to inform Germans about crimes against Jews committed in their name, so that millions were emotionally touched and moved.[8]

Another irruption was prompted by the visit of US President Ronald Reagan to the Bitburg military cemetery, where German soldiers, including SS officers, were interred. The German soldiers were "victims of Nazism also," Reagan proclaimed. "They were victims, just as surely as the victims in the concentration camps."[9] His comments sparked a furor among US military veterans, as well as among Jewish intellectuals and activists. In Germany, they provoked intense public discussion over whether Jewish and German victimization should be mentioned in the same breath.

A third, somewhat amorphous stage began in the 1990s, in the wake of the *Historikerstreit*, and carried over into the new millennium. It centered on the public debate over three controversial books. Daniel Jonah Goldhagen's *Hitler's Willing Executioners* accused "ordinary Germans" of perpetrating many of the genocidal atrocities of the Second World War. The book attracted a huge audience in Germany, especially among the younger generation. Günter Grass's *Im Krebsgang* (*Crabwalk*), meanwhile, described events at the end of the war, when the *Wilhelm Gustloff* cruise liner was torpedoed by a Soviet submarine, killing thousands of German civilian refugees. Lastly, Jörg Friedrich's *Brandstätten* (*Fire Sites*) provided grisly photographic evidence of the effects of Allied fire-bombing of German cities. (See Box 6a for more on Grass's and Friedrich's books.) Friedrich ably described the public's response to his book in terms that captured the emotional stress of suppressing memories, and the catharsis of expressing them:

> The bombing left an entire generation traumatised. But it was never discussed. There are Germans whose first recollections are of being hidden by their mothers. They remember cellars and burning human remains. It is only now that they are coming to terms with what happened . . . [But] Germans in their seventies and eighties have not forgotten. Their memories are still vivid. People stand up in my public lectures and describe what befell their families. They have tears in their eyes and they can't breathe.[10]

Also significant was the late 1990s controversy over a traveling exhibition of photographs, organized by the Hamburg Institute for Social Research, that provided vivid and chilling evidence of German Army participation in atrocities against Jews, Soviet prisoners-of-war, and others. The longstanding distinction between Nazi "evil" and army "honor" was decisively and probably durably undermined.[11]

Can a new, usable collective memory or public history be constructed out of these diverse strands and fragments? Robert Moeller, a leading scholar of the subject, appeared to believe so. He favored narratives that "move beyond a language in which the categories of victim and perpetrator were mutually exclusive," seeking instead "to capture the complexities of individual lives and 'mass fates' by exploring how during the Third Reich it was possible both to suffer and to cause suffering in others."[12] Yet any such project is, it is fair to say, in its early stages.

II. Japan

Japan's struggles over memory mirror in key respects those in Germany, the other major Axis power defeated in the Second World War. Postwar German governments, however, offered both effusive apologies and tens of billions of dollars in restitution payments, while German scholars often took a lead in exposing German crimes. By contrast, Japanese authorities have only grudgingly conceded that their overseas empire was founded on slave labor, and with rare exceptions have resisted formal apologies. Japanese scholars and activists, too, have often sought to paper over the country's criminal record, while glorifying the actions of the Japanese military.

In the 1980s and 1990s, Asians enslaved either in the Japanese homeland or the wartime empire – Koreans and Chinese above all – launched a concerted campaign to win restitution from the Japanese government. They were joined by former Allied prisoners of war, some 300 of whom petitioned in 2008 for recognition of the unpaid labor they had been forced to perform for the Aso Mining Company in 1945. The claim was particularly volatile, given that Aso was the family firm of the then-prime minister, Taro Aso. Aso was additionally notorious for "his combative reputation as a historical revisionist," centered on what *The New York Times* denounced as "nostalgic fantasies about Japan's ugly past." Apart from the relatively small number of POWs, some 10,000 Koreans had also "worked under severe conditions in the company's mines between 1939 and 1945; many died and most were never properly paid." Nonetheless, the Aso Group's official corporate history "omitted all mention" of the forced laborer, and bluntly refused to provide details about both the POWs and Koreans enslaved there.[13]

The cases of slave labor that received the greatest attention were those of the so-called "comfort women": tens of thousands of women tricked and coerced into serving as sex slaves to Japanese soldiers throughout the "Greater Asian Co-Prosperity Sphere." Following the Japanese invasion of Manchuria in 1931, the Japanese army began to construct a network of hundreds of "comfort stations" across the occupied territories, "dup[ing] or forc[ing] Korean, Taiwanese, Chinese, Indonesian, Filipino, Japanese and Dutch women to work in them." Estimates of the number dragooned and exploited in this fashion range between 140,000 and 200,000.[14] Those who survived (about one in six did not) faced continued shame and suffering upon their return home, and like so many atrocity survivors kept their experiences quiet for decades. Only in the 1980s did they begin to seek compensation for their suffering from the Japanese government.

In 1993, in a rare and groundbreaking move, the Japanese government officially recognized the system of sexual slavery, and established a small private fund for compensation.[15] Disbursements ended in 2007, however, and in that same year, Japanese prime minister Shinzo Abe sparked an international outcry by effectively rescinding Japan's recognition of the sexual slavery. The women, he claimed, had willingly served as prostitutes, in order to earn money for their families. "There is no evidence to prove there was coercion, nothing to support it," Abe declared. "So, in respect to [the 1993] declaration, you have to keep in mind that things have changed greatly."[16] Japanese courts rejected claims for restitution, though the struggle continued at the time of writing (March 2010).[17]

The refusal to offer recognition and compensation to wartime victims attested to a wider memory struggle in Japan, played out in the fields of political and religious ritual, education, and popular culture. For decades, it had been customary for Japanese political leaders to visit the Yasukuni shrine in Tokyo (see Figure 14.3), to pay tribute to the nearly two-and-a-half million soldiers, officers, and government functionaries who are not only memorialized there, but designated as deities in the pantheon of the Shinto religion. Over time, the shrine became a brazen monument to Japanese militarism, with an attached museum full of weaponry and housing a statue honoring Japanese *kamikaze* (suicide pilots) – with no mention of the atrocities inflicted by Japanese forces throughout the "Greater Asian Co-Prosperity Sphere." Right-wing extremists, proclaiming they are defending Japanese "honor," have made the shrine a point of pilgrimage, sparking counter-demonstrations by communists and other anti-imperialists.[18]

The contemporary controversy arose after 1959, when the names of more than a thousand war criminals convicted and executed for atrocities committed during World War Two were added to Yasukuni's rolls. In 1978, fourteen "Class A" war criminals were similarly honored, including wartime prime minister Hideki Tojo, executed by the International Military Tribunal for the Far East in 1948. For a Japanese prime minister to visit Yasukuni and pay homage to those memorialized there "could be likened to [a German] Chancellor . . . paying his respects at monuments to Himmler and Goebbels, or even Hitler himself," wrote Christopher Reed.[19] But it became a tradition to do so, thereby setting an official seal on what, since the war, has been a privately-owned memorial. In 2001, Prime Minister Junichiro Koizumi prayed at the shrine, repeating the ritual five times more before leaving office

Figure 14.3 The Yasukuni shrine in Tokyo – a homage to Japanese war dead that has become a key site in the struggle over memories of Japan's World War Two-era atrocities.

Source: David Monniaux/Wikimedia Commons.

in 2006.[20] His successor, however – Shinzo Abe, already under fire for his comments about slave laborers – avoided those same ceremonies, while expressing remorse for the "tremendous damage and suffering" Japan had inflicted on neighboring nations.[21]

No Japanese leader has visited Yasukuni since, but the controversy endures. In 2008, a documentary film on the shrine commemorations[22] became the object of vigorous criticism from the nationalist right. The protests prompted a number of cinemas to pull the film from their screens – which only sent crowds flocking to other showings, to find out what all the fuss was about. It was only one of the arguments over what constituted "acceptable" forms of cultural expression and public criticism about Japan's imperial record. Perhaps the most notable furor erupted over another documentary film – this one a brazenly revisionist account of the "Rape of Nanjing" (see Chapter 2, pp. 72–73) directed by Satoru Mizushima, a prominent TV mogul. After allegedly conducting "exhaustive research" on the subject, Mizushima emerged with the conclusion that not a single Chinese had been massacred by Japanese troops: "The evidence for a massacre is faked. It is Chinese Communist propaganda . . . If we remain silent, anti-Japanese propaganda will spread across the world. What is important is to correct the historical record and send the right message."[23] *The Truth of Nanjing*, released in 2008, prompted angry protests from the Chinese government, but it catered to a substantial constituency of Japanese convinced that the country's honor was being besmirched by its enemies. That this constituency encompassed senior figures in the Japanese establishment was demonstrated by a "true modern history" essay contest held in 2008. The winning entry was authored by none other than General Toshio Tamogami, air force chief of staff. Tamogami considered it "certainly a false accusation to say that our country was an aggressor nation" in the war. Rather, "many Asian countries take a positive view" of Japan's wartime policies, which, he alleged, had actually promoted positive race relations: "If Japan had not fought the Great East Asia War at that time, it might have taken another 100 or 200 years before we could have experienced the world of racial equality that we have today."[24] This, though, was too much for a government increasingly sensitive to international criticisms of its war record and the failure to acknowledge atrocious conduct. Tamogami was fired from his post within a day of the prize announcement.

III. Russia

Few if any countries in history have witnessed so dramatic a political, economic, and demographic collapse as the Soviet Union. The end of communism, formalized in 1991, saw the "socialist republics" of Ukraine, Belarus, Kazakhstan, the Baltic states, and other parts of the realms seize independence from Moscow's rule. Millions of ethnic Russians were left "stranded" in the newly independent states. Almost overnight, the USSR was transformed from a global superpower to a crumbling post-Soviet polity. The imposition of brutal neoliberal measures spawned a cataclysmic collapse in living and health standards, as well as an unprecedented demographic decline particularly affecting Russian males, whose life expectancy fell *by* a decade

Figure 14.4 The "Solovetsky Stone" in the Troitskaya gardens in St. Petersburg, Russia (there is another in Moscow). Designed by E.I. Ikhnalev and Y.A. Rybakov, it was sponsored by the Memorial Society (see Map 5.1) and incorporates a granite boulder from the Solovetsky Islands, where one of the most feared slave-labor camps of the Soviet Gulag was located. The stone purportedly was mined 50 meters from the main prisoner execution site. The inscription includes dedications to "victims of communist terror" and "freedom fighters," along with a line from the poem "Requiem" by Anna Akhmatova: "I'd like to name you all by name, but . . ."

Source: Mark A. Wilson/Wikimedia Commons.

in a decade. (See p. 62, note 137 for Stephen Cohen's estimate that the collapse and attendant economic measures shortened the lives of perhaps *one hundred million* people.)

Though the material devastation was extensive, equally significant was a pervasive psychological dislocation and humiliation, as Russia seemed to be returning to its historical role as a poor and backward source of raw materials for prosperous Western states. Even attempts to return the wayward territory of Chechnya to the fold proved incompetent, despite the application of massive, arguably genocidal violence (see Box 5a).

The first post-Soviet governments, steered by the bumbling Boris Yeltsin (1931–2007), gave way in December 1999 to a regime headed by Vladimir Putin, a former agent of the Soviet secret police (KGB). (Putin turned over the presidency to his protégé Dimitri Medvedev in May 2008, but is widely seen as still pulling the strings, and seemed in early 2010 to be angling for a return to the presidency in 2012.) Apart from prosecuting the Chechnya war with renewed, eventually "successful" ferocity, Putin recognized that Russians yearned for a return to stability and a sense of national pride. That required waging a concerted struggle over memory, in three key areas: (1) the imperial past of Russia/the USSR; (2) the "Great Patriotic War" (1941–45); and (3) the legacy of Joseph Stalin, the Soviet dictator who killed millions (Chapter 5), but also led the "union" to superpower status and victory over Nazi invaders.

In Chapter 2 (Figure 2.9, p. 82), we saw how the memory of the titanic sacrifices of World War Two had been used to regenerate a sense of national pride in Russia's far-flung, still ethnically diverse population.[25] To the same end, in 2007 Putin's government bluntly pressured neighboring Estonia to re-erect a statue of a Red Army soldier that authorities in Tallinn had removed as a vestige of Estonia's imperial subjugation by the USSR. For most Estonians, in the words of the country's president Toomas Hendrik Ilves, "this soldier stands for deportations and murders, the destruction of our country, not liberation. It is a monument to mass murder." But for Putin's government, and for the approximately one-third of the Estonian population that is ethnically Russian, the statue's dislocation was a "blasphemous" repudiation of Russian heroism. Russia threatened to break diplomatic relations; the ethnic Russian minority in Estonia staged three days of violent riots; and in short order, Estonia capitulated, returning the statue to its plinth.[26]

Russia's concern to validate its imperial past vis-à-vis constituent units of the Russian Federation was evident in its trampling of Chechen lives – and historical memories – in the devastating assaults of the post-Soviet period.[27] It was also attested by the 2007 decision to counter mobilizations by Circassian organizations, denouncing as "genocide" their conquest by Russian Cossacks in the nineteenth century, with a celebration of the supposedly "voluntary accession of Circassia to Russia." Murat Berzegov, head of the Circassian Congress in Adygeia, depicted the celebrations as evidence that "the [Russian] authorities have reverted to the myths of Soviet times." He called instead for "recognition of the Circassian genocide as a historical truth, and rehabilitation for a nation that has suffered so much on its own lands."[28]

No aspect of late-Soviet and post-Soviet struggles over memory has been so fraught as the question of how to address the Stalinist period in mainstream and official readings of history. After the "destalinization" campaign launched by Nikita Khrushchev in 1956, Stalin occupied an uneasy place in the Soviet firmament. His crimes were recognized as substantial "excesses," but not so severe as to challenge the legitimacy of the system *tout court*. Stalin's role as wartime leader and economic modernizer was generally praised in official texts and declarations.

Under Mikhail Gorbachev, whose liberalization measures in the 1980s eventually prompted the collapse of the Soviet empire and the USSR itself, this relatively rosy portrait was subjected to withering challenge. It was under Gorbachev that the non-governmental organization Memorial formed to document and denounce Stalinist crimes. Post-Soviet leaders permitted its continued operation, along with other efforts to memorialize Stalin's victims, such as the "Solovetsky Stones" in St. Petersburg and Moscow (see Figure 14.4).[29] Both Putin and his formal successor, Medvedev, have paid public tribute to Stalin's victims. In laying a wreath at a memorial site in Moscow in 2007, Putin declared that "hundreds of thousands, millions of people were killed and sent to camps, shot and tortured." Such atrocities, he stated, "happen when ostensibly attractive but empty ideas are put above fundamental values, values of human life, of rights and freedom."[30]

But a starkly different trend has also been evident. In December 2008, Russian authorities raided the offices of Memorial, confiscating computer drives and disks containing the St. Petersburg branch's archive: "databases of victims of repression in Leningrad, and memoirs, letters, recordings and transcripts of interviews, photographs, and other documents about the history of the Gulag and the Soviet Terror from 1917 to the 1960s."[31] In the same year, a new history textbook – published by the same company, Prosveshenije, that held a textbook monopoly in Soviet days – declared that Stalin's murderous terror during the 1930s occurred because the dictator "did not know who would deal the next blow, and for that reason he attacked every known group and movement, as well as those who were not his allies or of his mindset." It was important, the text declared, "to show that Stalin acted in a concrete historical situation" and behaved "entirely rationally – as the guardian of a system, as a consistent supporter of reshaping the country into an industrialised state." "We are not defending Stalin," claimed Alexander Danilov, editor of the new textbook. "We are just exploring his personality, explaining his motives and showing what he really achieved."[32]

Mass media followed suit. A 2007 television miniseries, *Stalin Live*, depicted "an elderly Stalin, in the last weeks of his life, recalling episodes in his younger days, most presenting him in a favorable light." Though reviled by many critical Russians, the series was popular with Stalin's supporters, who remain numerous (see Figure 5.4, p. 204). A 2005 opinion survey, carried out by the All-Russian Public Opinion Research Center on the sixtieth anniversary of the Soviet victory over the Nazis, "showed a nation roughly divided between the pro- and anti-Stalin camps, with those sympathetic to the dictator holding a modest edge. . . . 20% of respondents described his role as 'very positive,' and 30% called it 'somewhat positive.' Only 12% described it as 'very negative.'"[33] Another opinion poll, in which some *fifty million* Russians allegedly voted by telephone, chose Stalin as the third-greatest Russian of all time, behind medieval hero Alexander Nevsky and Petr Stolypin, the architect of tsarist reforms.[34]

Stalin's enduring popularity among broad sectors of the Russian population attested to the nostalgia many feel for a time when the country was ruled by a "firm hand," modernized at a dramatic pace (and a mass-murderous cost), and finally achieved victory in the most gargantuan military conflict ever waged. It also reflected dissatisfaction with the post-Soviet trajectory of social breakdown and spiraling economic inequality; political corruption; and ideological individualism and consumerism. The new authoritarians in Russian politics – Vladimir Putin above all – seemed prepared to nurture at least an ambivalent stance toward the Stalinist dictatorship, and to glorify significant aspects of Soviet life under the tyrant.

IV. Argentina

In 1976, against a backdrop of mounting social and economic chaos, a military regime under General Jorge Rafael Videla took power in Argentina. A state of siege

Figure 14.5   The Naval Mechanics School (ESMA) in the Buenos Aires suburb of Palermo, Argentina, where hundreds of victims of the country's military dictatorship from 1976 to 1983 were interned, tortured, and murdered. Today, as the banner hanging between the pillars proclaims, it has been designated as a "Memory Space" (*Espacio para la Memoria*). But for whose memory? Years later, the issue is still in dispute.

Source: Author's photo, January 2005.

was declared. For the next seven years, Videla and his fellow generals presided over the most brutal of South America's modern military dictatorships. Between 10,000 and 30,000 people – suspected of involvement with leftist guerrillas, or vaguer subversions – were "disappeared" by the authorities. Generally, they were tortured to death or executed; in many cases their bodies were dumped out of airplanes and into the Atlantic Ocean.[35] Pregnant detainees were often allowed to give birth before being killed; the infants were then turned over to be adopted by military families.[36]

In 1982, following Argentina's defeat by Great Britain in the war over the Falkland Islands,[37] military rule began to crumble. In 1983, the state of siege was lifted, and free elections held. Raúl Alfonsín of the Radical Civic Union (UCR) was sworn in as president in December. That month also saw the creation of the National Commission on Disappeared People (CONADEP), which investigated the fate of those who vanished under the military regime. Its report was released in 1984 under the title *Nunca Más* (Never Again) – echoing the call of those who memorialize the Jewish Holocaust. The report "catalogued 8,960 unresolved 'disappearances,' but warned that the true figure might be higher. It also listed 340 clandestine abduction centers in Argentina, which it said were in use at the height of the repression."[38] In Argentina, the events are regularly referred to as "genocide," although the designation would be disputed by some genocide scholars.[39]

The most notorious of the state detention facilities was the Naval Mechanics School (Escuela de Mecánica, ESMA) in the Palermo suburb of Buenos Aires (Figure 14.5). Over time, the movement to memorialize the disappeared and compensate survivors began to push for the creation of a museum on the forty-two-acre property. In 2004, the government of Nestor Kirchner bowed to the pressure. It expropriated the site and declared it would house a "Museum of Memory," to educate current and future generations about the period of state terror.

But which memories, and whose, should be reflected? Was this form of memorialization even appropriate, with the atrocities still fresh in the national consciousness? An account by journalist Larry Rohter in *The New York Times* described "sharp differences" over these issues among human-rights activists.[40] The Mothers of the Plaza de Mayo had gathered throughout the military dictatorship in the central square of Buenos Aires, demanding information and the return of their disappeared loved ones. Some members of the group argued that "museums mark the end of a story, and we haven't reached that point in Argentina yet," in the words of one leader, Hebe de Bonafini. "It's much too soon to be setting up a museum, because the historical events in question are too recent." Other organizations, however, strongly supported the project. One, called *Memoria Abierta* (Open Memory), compiled an archive of over 4,000 photographs and a range of oral histories for deposit in the museum. According to Patricia Valdez, director of Memoria Abierta: "We do not want this museum for ourselves, but for Argentine society. It has to be a place that transcends the fluctuations of Argentine politics and lets the facts speak for themselves."

Even among those who generally supported the initiative, the appropriate range and limits of this "memory space" (*espacio para la memoria*) aroused controversy. In announcing the museum's creation on March 24, 2004, the anniversary of the 1976 *coup d'état*, President Kirchner "seemed to be suggesting that the focus will be on the military dictatorship that dominated the country from 1976 to 1983." Kirchner was leader of the Peronist Party, whose activists had been targeted during the so-called "Dirty War." But Peronism, too, stood accused of atrocities during the 1970s. They included the formation of paramilitary organizations and death squads blamed for some 300 murders, as well as bombings and kidnappings. Limiting the museum's coverage to the 1976–83 period "would only distort historical realities," argued the Peronists' conservative opponents. Mabel Gutiérrez of the Group of Relatives of the Disappeared and Detained rejected the criticisms. "We are going to try to be as impartial as possible in telling the story, but if those on the other side don't like it, let them make their own museum. They have the money of the reactionaries of the right."[41]

The struggle took place against a backdrop of on-again, off-again attempts to prosecute Argentina's military leaders and their henchmen for crimes committed under the dictatorship. After a series of "demonstration coups" by disgruntled military officers following the return to democracy, President Alfonsín declared a *punto final* (full stop) to the prosecutions in 1985. Those already jailed were pardoned by his Peronist successor, Carlos Menem, who declared he was acting in the interests of national unity and reconciliation.[42] But as in neighboring Chile, as the country stabilized, as a new generation of once-repressed youths took power,[43] and as electorates responded favorably to justice-seeking measures, initiatives were relaunched. The

Argentine Supreme Court in 2005 lifted the immunity granted to officials of the former regime, and at the time of writing (March 2010), a lengthy legal process was drawing to a close in which some 60 convictions had been won for human rights abuses, with no fewer than 627 "former military officers, policemen and officials" charged and scheduled to stand trial in 2010 and after – more than any other Latin American country. The focus of the high-profile series of trials as this edition went to press was the top leadership of the ESMA complex, including Alfredo Astíz, the "Blond Angel" accused of committing crimes against humanity there. Said Gastón Chillier, director of a leading Argentine human rights organization: "I think and I hope this is the beginning of the end of a long process that began in 1983 with the return of democracy."[44]

Under fire by prosecutors, the military reacted vengefully. Key witnesses to the dictatorships' crimes were "disappeared" or killed.[45] When they finally evacuated the ESMA site in 2007, reported the UK *Telegraph*, "soldiers nailed a shooting-target to the front door of one of the buildings and then systematically wrecked the place . . . Signs of this destruction are everywhere still: ripped floors, flooded basements and destroyed bathrooms, with only the sound of water dripping from broken pipes coming from inside. This havoc has dashed hopes that the entire ESMA complex, apart from the two buildings that have just opened, will be accessible to the public in the near future."

Disagreements among the groups struggling to define collective memory continued to "mak[e] matters worse," with "little agreement on how to develop the rest of the complex. Some insist that certain buildings should be brought down; others want to preserve the place as it stands." According to Nenina Bouliet of the Memory Institute, "Besides divisions on what to include, we're swamped with proposals from Argentinian artists . . . Unfortunately, we lack museum experts in Argentina with experience on how to transmit the horrors that took place here."[46] Though this author was granted a tour of the ESMA complex in 2007, along with other delegates to a genocide conference in Buenos Aires, the public opening of the "Museum of Memory" has yet to materialize.

THE POLITICS OF FORGETTING

In 2002, Patrick Desbois, a French Catholic priest, arrived in the Ukrainian town of Rawa-Ruska, where the Nazis had transported his grandfather as a forced laborer after invading Ukraine in 1941. His grandfather had told Desbois stories of terrible things that occurred in the town during the early period of the Nazi occupation. Reports stated that Jews had been murdered there *en masse*. But when he sought further information, he encountered "a black hole. There was nothing in the books."[47] Nor, on his 2002 visit, could (or did) the town's mayor enlighten him.

Returning to Rawa-Ruska the following year, Desbois enlisted instead the deputy mayor, who proved much more forthcoming. Yaroslav Nadiak helped him to solicit eyewitness accounts from ageing townspeople. They were present on the dreadful day in 1941 when about 1,500 Jews were gathered and slaughtered by the Nazi *Einsatzgruppen*; they gathered silently at the site in the forest where the

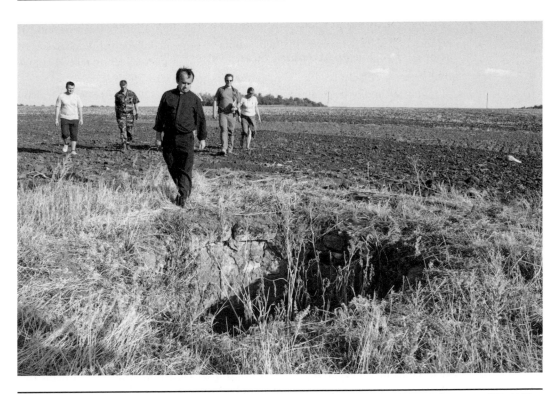

Figure 14.6   Father Patrick Desbois walks the edge of a well in Bogdanovka, Ukraine, where Jewish victims of Nazi killing squads (*Einsatzgruppen*) were thrown, living or dead, during 1941–42. Desbois devotes his life to documenting the Nazis' Jewish victims, reclaiming for a contemporary age the "Holocaust by Bullets" in which 1.5 million Jews were murdered.

Source: AP Photo/Efrem Lukatsky, July 2007.

Jews were buried underfoot. "I realized that the memory of the genocide existed," said Desbois, "and that it was the humble people, country farmers, who carried it."[48]

The Jews of Rawa-Ruska were victims of the campaign of mass murder now known, thanks to Desbois, as "The Holocaust by Bullets." At the time, the Holocaust of the Jews was overwhelmingly linked in the public mind with the death camps and gas chambers of Auschwitz-Birkenau, Treblinka, and elsewhere. Yet, as we saw in Chapter 6, one-and-a-half to two million Jews were instead slaughtered by up-close gunfire, mostly before the camps began their deadly work. As Desbois wrapped up the first of his interviews with eyewitnesses, the deputy mayor told him: "Patrick, this is what I could do for one village; I can do the same thing for a hundred villages." "Alright!" responded Desbois. "Let's do it!"[49]

The result was an odyssey that has brought Father Desbois, and the atrocities he has so painstakingly cataloged, to global attention. Traipsing through the Ukrainian and Belarussian countryside, Desbois has located hundreds of mass graves of Jews and other victims of the Nazis (see the project's website at www.memorialdelashoah.org). His team has collected and cataloged ballistic evidence at about 750 murder sites as of 2009, some with multiple mass graves; Desbois estimates there may be as many as 1,800 overall. Most significantly, he has solicited, and recorded, the testimony of hundreds of local witnesses, many of whom were speaking about the massacres of 1941–44 for the first time. "It's like they have been waiting for years to talk," Desbois told *Time*. "They always ask: 'Why have you come so late?'"[50]

Their testimony is encouraged by Desbois's status as a priest. According to Paul Shapiro, director of the Center for Advanced Holocaust Studies at the United States Holocaust Memorial Museum: "When a priest comes, people open up. He brings to the subject a kind of legitimacy, a sense that it's OK to talk about the past. There's absolution through confession."[51] Desbois is also careful to adopt a non-judgmental attitude toward them: "I do not ask who is guilty and who is not guilty. I deal just with victims."[52] He must also conceal his emotional response to the witnesses' narratives: "I cannot react to the horrors that pour out. If I react, the stories will stop."[53]

Early in his investigations in Rawa-Ruska, Desbois was struck by the handsome, foreign-funded cemetery for the German war dead in the area. German foundations had supported the meticulous collection, identification, and reburial of every soldier's bones that could be located, and their loving commemoration. "While the mass graves of the thousands of Jews who were shot are untraceable," Desbois wrote in his 2008 book, *The Holocaust by Bullets*, "every German killed during the war has been reburied and identified by name . . . Thus, under the ground, everything is still in order according to the hierarchy of the [Third] Reich." For Desbois, such one-sided memorializing was grotesque. "We cannot give a posthumous victory to Nazism. We cannot leave the Jews buried like animals. *We cannot accept this state of affairs and allow our [European] continent to be built on the obliterated memory of the victims of the Reich*."[54] He more than anyone has rescued the "Holocaust by Bullets" from relative historical obscurity, the Babi Yar massacre aside (see Figure 14.1). In so doing, he has resurrected in contemporary memory hundreds of thousands of previously forgotten victims of the Nazis.

Such forgetting is memory's intimate partner and *alter ego*. Together with preventing future genocides, and closely related, the struggle against forgetting is probably *the* central task of genocide scholars and activists worldwide. On a societal level, "memoricide" – Mirko Grmek's term – obliterates the recollection of atrocities' victims (see p. 28). Nations glorify their past, conspicuously "forgetting" its unsavory aspects. Attention to the "Holocaust by Bullets," in which the "ordinary men" of Christopher Browning's famous book played so prominent a role,[55] upsets a somewhat comforting view of the Holocaust as a genocide perpetrated by a small coterie of Nazi leaders, bureaucrats, and death-camp technicians. *These* mass murders were inflicted by large numbers of mass murderers, prompting the kind of questions about German society and its pervasive anti-semitism that Daniel Goldhagen raised in his controversial 1996 work, *Hitler's Willing Executioners*.[56]

On an individual level, perpetrators seek to consign their atrocities to memory's dustbin. Forgetting may represent a final stage of revision, reinterpretation, and denial, canceling any dissonance with one's preferred self-image. A common strategy is to displace others' victimization onto oneself. Atrocities that one perpetrated, supported, or ignored are crowded out by memories of personal and collective victimization, whether experienced or imagined.

However, victims too may seek to forget: whether because it is painful to remember; because remembering prevents them from "getting on with their lives"; or because they are convinced no one will listen to their stories. Such was the case with many survivors of the Armenian and Jewish holocausts, who spent decades after the events seeking to consign them to the past and build new lives. Today, genocide survivors are often encouraged to tell their stories, on the assumption that doing so will bring them relief. But whatever the benefits of their doing so for a public audience, the emotional and psychological implications for the survivors are more uncertain. Relating their experiences may bring to the surface trauma that survivors had long worked to suppress.

Moreover, while many people welcome survivors' accounts for the unique perspective they supply on atrocious events, some – perhaps only a vocal fringe; perhaps the majority – will accuse them of falsification or exaggeration. Such testimonies upset the delicate project of forgetting within perpetrators' societies. And they destabilize a central strategy in such forgetting: *denial*. Assertions of genocide denial have surged in recent years, as ever more historical events have come to be labeled as "genocide." I explore the phenomenon of genocidal denial next, together with the vexing issue of how to counter it.

GENOCIDE DENIAL: MOTIVES AND STRATEGIES

Denial is the final stage of genocide, and an indispensable one from the viewpoint of the *génocidaires*. "The perpetrators of genocide dig up the mass graves, burn the bodies, try to cover up the evidence and intimidate the witnesses. They deny that they committed any crimes, and often blame what happened on the victims."[57] As Richard Hovannisian has written:

> Following the physical destruction of a people and their material culture, memory is all that is left and is targeted as the last victim. Complete annihilation of people requires the banishment of recollection and the suffocation of remembrance. Falsification, deception, and half-truths reduce what was to what may have been or perhaps what was not at all.[58]

The phenomenon of genocide denial is overwhelmingly associated with the Jewish Holocaust. Since this resurged in the public consciousness in the early 1960s, a diverse and interlinked network of Holocaust deniers has arisen. In Europe, a centuries-old tradition of anti-semitism (see Chapter 6) underlies their activities, which overlap with neo-Nazi violence against Jews and their property. In North America, the neo-Nazi element is also strong. In both "wings" of the denialist movement, however, academic figures – such as Arthur Butz in the US, Robert Faurisson in France, and David Irving in Great Britain (jailed for three years for Holocaust denial in Austria in 2006)[59]– have also sought to lend the enterprise a veneer of respectability.

We will consider specific denial strategies below, but before we do, it is important to stress that the Jewish Holocaust is not officially denied by any state or national elite (though denial is common intellectual currency in the Arab and Muslim worlds).[60] Thus, in the West at least, deniers of the Jewish catastrophe remain relatively marginal figures, with little access to the mainstream.

However, the broader phenomenon of genocide denial is far more deeply entrenched, often representing a societal consensus rather than a fringe position. Individual and collective narcissism (Chapter 10) plays a pivotal role. In many contexts, a denialist stance heads off "cognitive dissonance" between one's preferred view of self and country, and the uglier reality. There is also generally an element of material self-interest. Denial can pay well, since it fortifies the status quo and serves powerful and prosperous constituencies, both political and corporate. Positive rewards are combined with sanctions. Failure to deny (that is, a determination to acknowledge) may result in loss of employment; decreased social standing and career prospects; dismissal as a "kook" or a "radical"; and so on.

Among the most common discourses of genocide denial are the following:

"*Hardly anybody died.*" Reports of atrocities and mass killings are depicted as exaggerated and self-serving. (The fact that some reports *are* distorted and self-interested lends credibility to this strategy.) Photographic and video evidence is dismissed as fake or staged. Gaps in physical evidence are exploited, particularly an absence of corpses. Where are the bodies of the Jews killed by the Nazis? (Incinerated, conveniently for the deniers.)[61] Where are the bodies of the thousands of Kosovars supposedly killed by Serbs in 1999? (Buried on military and police bases, or dumped in rivers and down mineshafts, as it transpired.) When the genocides lie far in the past, obfuscation is easier. Genocides of indigenous peoples are especially subject to this form of denial. In many cases, the groups in question suffered near-total extermination, leaving few descendants and advocates to press the case for truth.

"*It was self-defense.*" "The onset of [genocidal] killing," wrote Jacques Sémelin, "almost always seems to involve this astounding sleight of hand that assimilates the destruction of civilians with a perfectly legitimate act of war. From that moment on, massacre becomes an act of self-defense."[62] Murdered civilians – especially adult males (Chapter 13) – are depicted as "rebels," "brigands," "partisans," "terrorists." The state and its allies are justified in eliminating them, though unfortunate "excesses" may occur. Deniers of the Armenian genocide, for example, play up the presence of armed elements and resistance among the Armenian population – even clearly defensive resistance. Likewise, deniers of Nazi genocide against Jews turn cartwheels to demonstrate "that *Weltjudentum* (world Jewry) had declared war on Germany in 1933, and the Nazis, as the ruling party of the nation, had simply reacted to the threat."[63] Jews were variously depicted as predatory capitalists, decadent cosmopolitans, and leaders of global communism. The organizers of the third canonical genocide of the twentieth century, in Rwanda, alleged that the assault on Tutsis was a legitimate response to armed invasion by Tutsi rebels based in Uganda, and the supposed machinations of a Tutsi "fifth column" in Rwanda itself.

Genocide may also be depicted as an act of *pre-emptive* self-defense, based on atrocities, actual or alleged, inflicted on the perpetrator group in the past – sometimes the very distant past. Sémelin, for example, has explained Serbs' "insensitivit[y] to the suffering they caused" in the Balkan genocide of the 1990s in terms of their inability to perceive any but "their own woes, as a martyred people who had themselves been victims of 'genocide' during the Second World War." Former Serb president Biljana

Plavsic, then on trial at the International Criminal Tribunal for the Former Yugoslavia (ICTY; see Chapter 15), acknowledged that the "obsession with no longer being victims transformed us into bullies" – and in some cases *génocidaires*.[64]

A substrategy of this discourse is the claim that "*the violence was mutual.*" Where genocides occur in a context of civil or international war, they can be depicted as part of generalized warfare, perhaps featuring atrocities on all sides. This strategy is standard among the deniers of genocides by Turks, Japanese, Serbs, Hutus, and West Pakistanis – to name just a few. In Australia, Keith Windschuttle used killings of whites by Aboriginals to denounce "The Myths of Frontier Massacres in Australian History."[65] (See also "*We* are the real victims," below.) Sometimes the deniers seem oblivious to the content of their claims, reflecting deeply embedded stereotypes and genuine ignorance, rather than malicious intent – as with the CNN reporter who blithely referred to the world standing by and "watch[ing] Hutus and Tutsis kill each other" during the Rwandan genocide of 1994.[66]

"*The deaths weren't intentional.*" The difficulties of demonstrating and documenting genocidal intent are exploited to deny that genocide occurred. The utility of this strategy is enhanced where a longer causal chain underpins mass mortality. Thus, when diverse factors combine to cause death, or when supposedly "natural" elements such as disease and famine account for many or most deaths, a denialist discourse is especially appealing. It buttresses most denials of indigenous genocides, for example (see Chapter 3). Deniers of the Armenian and Jewish holocausts also contend that most deaths occurred from privations and afflictions that were inevitable, if regrettable, in a wartime context – in any case, not genocidal.

"*There was no central direction.*" Frequently, states and their agents establish deniability by running off-duty death squads, or employing freelance forces such as paramilitaries (as in Bosnia-Herzegovina and Darfur), criminal elements (e.g., the *chétés* in the Armenian genocide), and members of the targeted groups themselves (Jewish *kapos* in the Nazi death camps; Mayan peasants conscripted for genocide against Mayan populations of the Guatemalan highlands). State attempts to eliminate evidence may mean that documentation of central direction, as of genocidal intent, is scarce. Many deniers of the Jewish Holocaust emphasize the lack of a clear order from Hitler or his top associates to exterminate European Jews. Armenian genocide denial similarly centers on the supposed freelance status of those who carried out whatever atrocities are admitted to have occurred.

"*There weren't that many people to begin with.*" Where demographic data provide support for claims of genocide, denialists will gravitate towards the lowest available figures for the targeted population, or invent new ones. The effect is to cast doubt on mortality statistics by downplaying the victims' demographic weight at the outbreak of genocide. This strategy is especially common in denials of genocide against indigenous peoples, as well as the Ottoman genocide of Christian minorities.

"*It wasn't/isn't 'genocide,' because . . .*" Here, the ambiguities of the UN Genocide Convention are exploited, and combined with the denial strategies already cited. Atrocious events do not qualify as "genocide" . . . because the victims were not members of one of the Convention's specified groups; because their deaths were unintended; because they were legitimate targets; because "only" specific sectors of the target group (e.g., "battle-age" men) were killed; because "war is hell"; and so on.

"*We would never do that.*" Collective pathological narcissism (see Chapter 10) occludes recognition, or even conscious consideration, of genocidal culpability. When the state and its citizens consider themselves pure, peaceful, democratic, and law-abiding, responsibility for atrocity may be literally unthinkable. In Turkey, notes Taner Akçam, anyone "dar[ing] to speak about the Armenian Genocide . . . is aggressively attacked as a traitor, singled out for public condemnation and may even be put in prison."[67] In Australia, "the very mention of an Australian genocide is . . . appalling and galling and must be put aside," according to Colin Tatz. "A curious national belief is that simply being Australian, whether by birth or naturalisation, is sufficient inoculation against deviation from moral and righteous behaviour."[68] Comedian Rob Corddry parodied this mindset in the context of US abuses and atrocities at Abu Ghraib prison near Baghdad. "There's no question what took place in that prison was horrible," Corddry said on *The Daily Show*. "But the Arab world has to realize that the US shouldn't be judged on the actions of a . . . well, we shouldn't be judged on actions. It's our principles that matter, our inspiring, abstract notions. Remember: just because torturing prisoners is something we did, doesn't mean it's something we *would* do."[69]

"*We are the real victims.*" For deniers, the best defense is often a strong offense. With its "Day of Fallen Diplomats," Turkey uses Armenian terrorist attacks against Turkish diplomatic staff to pre-empt attention to the Turkish genocide against Armenians. In the case of Germany and the Nazi Holocaust, there is a point at which a victim mentality concentrating on German suffering leads to the horrors that Germans inflicted, on Jews and others, being downgraded or denied. In the Balkans, a discourse of genocide was first deployed by Serb intellectuals promoting a nationalist–xenophobic project; the only "genocide" admitted was that against Serbs, whether by Croatians in the Second World War (which indeed occurred), or in Kosovo at the hands of the Albanian majority (which was a paranoid fantasy). Notably, this stress on victimhood provided powerful fuel for unleashing the genocides in the first place; the discussion of humiliation in Chapter 10 is worth recalling.

DENIAL AND FREE SPEECH

What are the acceptable limits of denialist discourse in a free society? Should *all* denial be suppressed? Should it be permitted in the interest of preserving vigorous debate in a liberal public sphere?

In recent years, many countries in the West have grappled with these questions. Varied approaches have been adopted, ranging from monitoring denialist discourse, to punitive measures including fines, imprisonment, and deportation. At the permissive end of the spectrum lies the United States. There, notorious deniers of the Jewish Holocaust, as well as neo-Nazi and Ku Klux Klan-style organizations, operate mostly unimpeded, albeit sometimes surveilled and infiltrated by government agents. A much harder line has been enforced in France and Canada. In France, Holocaust denier Robert Faurisson was stripped of his university teaching position and hauled before a court for denying that the Nazi gas chambers had existed. Eventually, in July 1981, the Paris Court of Appeals assessed "personal damages" against Faurisson, based

Figure 14.7 Denial of the Jewish Holocaust has been pushed to the fringes in Western societies. In some regions, however – notably the Arab and Muslim worlds[70] – it remains a standard feature of public and media discourse. The world's most notorious genocide denier is Iranian president Mahmoud Ahmadinejad, shown here speaking at Columbia University, New York City, in September 2007.

Source: Wikimedia Commons.

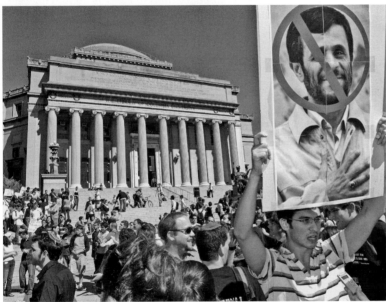

Figure 14.8 Demonstrators protest Ahmadinejad's presence at Columbia. Ahmadinejad hosted a conference of Holocaust deniers and skeptics (and bizarrely, a few ultra-orthodox Jews) in Tehran in December 2006, and has repeatedly called the Holocaust a "myth" in speeches and interviews.

Source: David Shankbone/ Wikimedia Commons.

Figure 14.9 Those who call for the legal suppression of Holocaust and genocide denial link it to outbreaks of racism and xenophobia, as with this anti-semitic graffito on a Milan, Italy street. But who decides which genocides are to receive official recognition, and which expressions of genocide denial are to be censured and punished?

Source: Giovanni Dall'Orto/Wikimedia Commons.

on the likelihood "that his words would arouse in his very large audience feelings of contempt, of hatred and of violence towards the Jews in France."[71] In Canada, Alberta teacher Jim Keegstra "for twelve years . . . indoctrinated his students with Jewish conspiracy explanations of history . . . biased statements principally about Jews, but also about Catholics, Blacks, and others."[72] In 1982, Keegstra was dismissed from his job and, in 1984, charged with promoting racial hatred. In 1985, he was convicted, and sentenced to five months in jail and a $5,000 fine. The decision was overturned by the Alberta Court of Appeal, citing Canada's Charter of Rights and Freedoms, but Canada's Supreme Court delivered a seminal 1990 decision in Keegstra's case, ruling that hate speech was *not* constitutionally protected.[73]

Undoubtedly the most famous trial involving a genocide denier is the libel case brought in 2000 by David Irving, an amateur historian of some repute who nonetheless cast doubt and aspersions on the genocide of the Jews. Deborah Lipstadt accused Irving of genocide denial in her book *Denying the Holocaust*, referring to him as a "discredited" scholar and "one of the most dangerous spokespersons for Holocaust denial."[74] She also pointed to his links with neo-fascist figures and movements. Irving exploited Britain's loose libel laws to file a suit for defamation. The resulting trial became a *cause célèbre*, with prominent historians taking the stand to outline Irving's evasions and obfuscations of the historical evidence, as well as the character of his personal associations. The final, 350-page judgment by Judge Charles Gray cited Irving for nineteen specific misrepresentations, and contended that they were deliberate distortions to advance a denialist agenda. Irving's suit was dismissed, leaving him with a £2 million bill for legal costs – though he was subject to no legal sanction *per se*.

The spectrum of policies toward deniers, from permissive to prosecutory, is mirrored by the debate among genocide scholars and anti-genocide advocates. Those who call for punitive measures against deniers stress the link between denial and genocide, including future genocides, as well as the personal suffering that denial inflicts on a genocide's survivors and their descendants. This argument was made eloquently by Roger Smith, Eric Markusen, and Robert Jay Lifton, who held that

> denial of genocide [is] an egregious offense that warrants being regarded as a form of contribution to genocidal violence. Denial contributes to genocide in at least two ways. First of all, genocide does not end with its last human victim; denial continues the process, but if denial points to the past and the present, it also has implications for the future. By absolving the perpetrators of past genocides from responsibility for their actions and by obscuring the reality of genocide as a widely practiced form of state policy in the modern world, denial may increase the risk of future outbreaks of genocidal killing.

They especially condemned the actions of some professional scholars in bolstering various denial projects:

> Where scholars deny genocide, in the face of decisive evidence that it has occurred, they contribute to a false consciousness that can have the most dire reverberations. Their message, in effect, is: murderers did not really murder; victims were not

really killed; mass murder requires no confrontation, no reflection, but should be ignored, glossed over. In this way scholars lend their considerable authority to the acceptance of this ultimate human crime. More than that, they encourage – indeed invite – a repetition of that crime from virtually any source in the immediate or distant future. By closing their minds to truth such scholars contribute to the deadly psychohistorical dynamic in which unopposed genocide begets new genocides.[75]

The opposing view does not dispute the corruption of scholarship that genocide denial represents. However, it rejects the authority of the state to punish "speech crimes"; it stresses the arbitrariness that governs *which* genocide denial is prohibited; and it calls for proactive engagement and public denunciation in place of censorship and prosecution. A leading exponent of such views is the linguistics scholar and political commentator Noam Chomsky, whose most bitter controversy revolves around a defense of the right of Robert Faurisson to air his denialist views. In an essay titled "Some Elementary Comments on the Rights of Freedom of Expression," published (without his prior knowledge) as a foreword to Faurisson's *Mémoire en défense*, Chomsky depicted calls to ban Faurisson from teaching, even to physically attack him, as in keeping with authoritarian traditions:

> Such attitudes are not uncommon. They are typical, for example, of American Communists and no doubt their counterparts elsewhere. Among people who have learned something from the 18th century (say, Voltaire) it is a truism, hardly deserving discussion, that the defense of the right of free expression is not restricted to ideas one approves of, and that it is precisely in the case of ideas found most offensive that these rights must be most vigorously defended. Advocacy of the right to express ideas that are generally approved is, quite obviously, a matter of no significance . . . Even if Faurisson were to be a rabid anti-Semite and fanatic pro-Nazi . . . this would have no bearing whatsoever on the legitimacy of the defense of his civil rights. On the contrary, it would make it all the more imperative to defend them.[76]

Each of these perspectives brings important ideas to the table. To expand on Smith *et al.*'s reasoning: in most societies, some speech is subject to legal sanction – libelous, threatening, and obscene speech, for instance. It can reasonably be asked whether genocide denial does not do greater harm to society, and pose a greater threat, than personal libel or dirty words. Does not genocide denial libel an entire people? And is the threat it poses not extreme, given that denial may sow the seeds of future genocides?

The case is a powerful one, and yet I find myself generally in agreement with Chomsky. Free speech *only* has meaning at the margins. Banning marginal discourses undermines liberal freedoms. Moreover, only a handful of deniers – principally those assailing the Jewish and Armenian genocides – have attracted controversy for their views. The president (François Mitterrand) of the same French state that prosecuted Robert Faurisson not only actively supported Rwanda's *génocidaires* – before, during, and after the 1994 catastrophe – but when asked later about the genocide, responded:

"The genocide or the genocides? I don't know what one should say!" As Gérard Prunier noted, "This public accolade for the so-called 'theory of the double genocide' [i.e. by Tutsis against France's Hutu allies, as well as by Hutus against Tutsis] was an absolute shame."[77] It advanced a key thesis of genocide deniers: that the violence was mutual or defensive in nature. But Mitterrand's words were widely ignored; he was certainly in no danger of being arraigned before a tribunal. *Sed quis custodiet ipsos custodes?* – Who will guard the guards themselves?

One wonders, as well, whether the names and views of people such as Irving, Faurisson, and Keegstra would be remotely as prominent, if prosecutions and other measures had not been mounted against them.[78] (Indeed, it makes me queasy to print them here.) Deborah Lipstadt, for one, thinks not. The scholar who defended her work against David Irving's charge of libel told the BBC in 2006: "I am uncomfortable with imprisoning people for speech . . . I don't find these laws efficacious. I think they turn Holocaust denial into forbidden fruit, and make it more attractive to people who want to toy with the system or challenge the system."[79] In my view, denialist individuals, and the initiatives they sponsor, are best confronted with a combination of monitoring, marginalization, and effective public refutation. Such refutation can be accomplished by visible and vocal denunciation, informed by conscientious reportage and scholarship, as well as by proactive campaigns in schools and media.

While genocide denial in the public sphere may be destructive, for genocide scholars and students its consequences may actually be productive. Professional deniers have spurred scholarship in areas that otherwise might not have attracted it.[80] Moreover, not all "denial" is malevolent. Whether a genocide framework should be applied in a given case is often a matter of lively *and legitimate* debate. In recent decades, the character and content of mass killing campaigns in Bosnia and Kosovo, Darfur, Biafra (Nigeria), East Timor, Guatemala, and Vietnam have been intensively analyzed and hotly disputed. I believe this is to be encouraged, even if I find some of the viewpoints disturbing and disheartening. Keeping denial of *all* genocides out of the realm of crime and punishment may be the price we pay for this vigorous exchange.[81]

FURTHER STUDY

Ian Buruma, *The Wages of Guilt: Memories of War in Germany and Japan*. London: Atlantic Books, 2009. Originally published in 1994, Buruma's book explores how World War Two's main aggressors came to terms with their past – or failed to.

Stanley Cohen, *States of Denial: Knowing about Atrocities and Suffering*. Cambridge: Polity Press, 2001. Insights into denial, and efforts to counter it, on both personal and societal levels.

Father Patrick Desbois, *The Holocaust by Bullets: A Priest's Journey to Uncover the Truth behind the Murder of 1.5 Million Jews*. London: Palgrave Macmillan, 2008. Describes the efforts of the French priest, profiled in this chapter, to document atrocities against Jews on the eastern front.

Richard J. Evans, *Lying About Hitler: History, Holocaust, and the David Irving Trial*. New York: Basic Books, 2001. Brisk account of Irving's defamation suit, by a historian who served as a defense witness.

John R. Gillis, ed., *Commemorations: The Politics of National Identity*. Princeton, NJ: Princeton University Press, 1994. How collective memory shapes national identity.

Jeffrey Herf, *Divided Memory: The Nazi Past in the Two Germanys*. Cambridge, MA: Harvard University Press, 1997. Intricate rendering of Germany's "search for a usable past."

Herbert Hirsch, ed., *Genocide and the Politics of Memory: Studying Death to Preserve Life*. Chapel Hill, NC: University of North Carolina Press, 1995. Early and wide-ranging collection.

Richard G. Hovannisian, ed., *Remembrance and Denial: The Case of the Armenian Genocide*. Detroit, MI: Wayne State University Press, 1999. Armenian genocide denial and its place in collective memory.

Adam Jones, ed., *Evoking Genocide: Scholars and Activists Describe the Works That Shaped Their Lives*. Toronto, ON: The Key Publishing House Inc., 2009. Explores, in sixty mini-essays, how genocide was memorialized and interpreted in cultural works, and how those works in turn influenced genocide educators and anti-genocide advocates.

Deborah E. Lipstadt, *Denying the Holocaust: The Growing Assault on Truth and Memory*. New York: Plume, 1994. Survey of denial's exponents that prompted David Irving's failed legal action against Lipstadt.

David E. Lorey and William H. Beezley, eds, *Genocide, Collective Violence, and Popular Memory: The Politics of Remembrance in the Twentieth Century*. Wilmington, DE: Scholarly Resources, 2002. Still the best primer on genocide and memory.

Peter Novick, *The Holocaust in American Life*. Boston, MA: Mariner Books, 2000. Fascinating exploration of how the Jewish Holocaust was remembered and deployed by American Jews and others.

George Orwell, *Nineteen Eighty-Four*. London: Penguin, 1983. Dark satire of the manipulation of history and memory under totalitarianism.

Michael Shermer and Alex Grobman, *Denying History: Who Says the Holocaust Never Happened and Why Do They Say It?* (rev. edn). Berkeley, CA: University of California Press, 2000. Carefully documented rebuttal of Holocaust deniers.

Jay Winter, *Sites of Memory, Sites of Mourning: The Great War in European Cultural History*. Cambridge: Canto, 1998. History, memory, and memorialization in post-First World War Europe.

John C. Zimmerman, *Holocaust Denial: Demographics, Testimonies and Ideologies*. Lanham, MD: University Press of America, 2000. Like Shermer (above), a systematic and effective counter to denialist claims.

NOTES

1 Simon Sebag Montefiore, *Stalin: The Court of the Red Tsar* (London: Phoenix, 2004), p. 142.

2 Elizabeth Jelin, "The Minefields of Memory," *NACLA Report on the Americas*, 32: 2 (September/October 1998), p. 25. Martha Minow wrote: "Memorials can name those who were killed; they can depict those who resisted and those who rescued. They can accord honor and confer heroic status; they can express shame, remorse, warning, shock. Devoting public space to memories of atrocities means devoting time and energy to decisions about what kinds of memories, images, and messages to embrace, critique, and resist . . . Vividly capturing and recasting memory, fights over monuments in the streets and in debates usefully disturb congealed memories and mark important junctions between the past and a newly invented present," Minow, *Between Vengeance and Forgiveness: Facing History after Genocide and Mass Violence* (Boston, MA: Beacon Press, 1998), pp. 138, 140.

3 Jelin, "The Minefields of Memory," pp. 26, 28.

4 For some nuanced and cautionary comments on public memory, see Jay Winter, "The Generation of Memory: Reflections on the 'Memory Boom' in Contemporary Historical Studies," *GHI Bulletin*, 27, http://www.ghi-dc.org/publications/ghipubs/bu/027/b27 winterframe.html.

5 For text and a vivid photograph, see "Encyclopedia: Warschauer Kniefall," Nation Master. com, http://www.nationmaster.com/encyclopedia/Warschauer-Kniefall. "The event made Brandt widely unpopular in Germany, especially among conservatives and liberals but also many social democrats, and he was heavily criticized by the press for being unpatriotic . . . Eventually, [however,] even many Germans came to see it as a courageous and honorable decision."

6 Robert G. Moeller, "War Stories: The Search for a Usable Past in the Federal Republic of Germany," in David E. Lorey and William H. Beezley, eds, *Genocide, Collective Violence, and Popular Memory: The Politics of Remembrance in the Twentieth Century* (Wilmington, DE: Scholarly Resources, 2002), pp. 206, 211.

7 Alexander Wilde, "Irruptions of Memory: Expressive Politics in Chile's Transition to Democracy," in Lorey and Beezley, eds, *Genocide, Collective Violence, and Popular Memory*, p. 4.

8 Hoehne quoted in Ian Buruma, *The Wages of Guilt: Memories of War in Germany and Japan* (London: Atlantic Books, 2009), p. 88.

9 Quoted in Moeller, "War Stories," p. 210. On Bitburg, see also Jeffrey Herf, *Divided Memory: The Nazi Past in the Two Germanys* (Cambridge, MA: Harvard University Press, 1997), pp. 350–54.

10 Friedrich quoted in J.M. Coetzee, "Victims" (review of Günter Grass, *Crabwalk*), *New York Review of Books*, June 12, 2003.

11 See the companion volume for the exhibition: Hamburg Institute for Social Research, *The German Army and Genocide: Crimes Against War Prisoners, Jews, and Other Civilians in the East, 1939–1944* (New York: New Press, 1999). An excellent documentary on the controversy surrounding the Wehrmacht exhibition is *The Unknown Soldier*, dir. Michael Verhoeven (First Run Features, 2008).

12 Moeller, "War Stories," p. 216. See also Nicholas Kulish, "Facing German Suffering, and Not Looking Away," *The New York Times*, February 26, 2009, http://www.nytimes. com/2009/02/27/world/europe/27poland.html.

13 William Underwood, "WWII Forced Labor Issue Dogs Aso, Japanese Firms," *The Japan Times*, October 28, 2008, http://search.japantimes.co.jp/cgi-bin/fl20081028zg.html. By contrast, as Christopher Reed notes, "Germany has chosen a path of reconciliation by proactively settling wartime forced labor accounts. The 'Remembrance, Responsibility and the Future' Foundation was established in 2000, with funding of some $6 billion provided by the German federal government and more than 6,500 industrial enterprises.

As reparations payments drew to a close in late 2005, about 1.6 million forced labor victims or their heirs had received individual apologies and symbolic compensation of up to $10,000. Similarly, the Austrian Reconciliation Fund recently finished paying out nearly $350 million to 132,000 workers forced to toil for the Nazi war machine in that country, or their families" (Reed, "Family Skeletons: Japan's Foreign Minister and Forced Labor by Koreans and Allied POWs," n.d., *The Asia-Pacific Journal: Japan Focus*, http://www.japanfocus.org/-Christopher-Reed/1627).

14 The "comfort women" experienced treatment that "was almost universally barbaric. They were forced to have sex with as many as 50 men a day, some were tied to beds with their legs open, and many were beaten by drunken soldiers." Velisarios Kattoulas, "No Comfort for the Women," *Far Eastern Economic Review*, March 15, 2001. According to George Hicks, "The comfort system consisted of the legalised military rape of subject women on a scale – and over a period of time – previously unknown in history." George Hicks, *The Comfort Women: Japan's Brutal Regime of Enforced Prostitution in the Second World War* (New York: W.W. Norton, 1994), pp. 16–17.

15 David McNeill, "Korea's 'Comfort Women': The Slaves' Revolt," *The Independent*, April 24, 2008; Norimitsu Onishi, "Japan's 'Atonement' to Former Sex Slaves Stirs Anger," *The New York Times*, April 25, 2007.

16 Norimitsu Onishi, "Abe Rejects Japan's Files on War Sex," *The New York Times*, March 2, 2007, http://www.nytimes.com/2007/03/02/world/asia/02japan.html.

17 See Jun Hongo, "Sex Slave Victims Press for Apology," *The Japan Times*, November 26, 2008, http://search.japantimes.co.jp/cgi-bin/nn20081126a5.html.

18 For an overview of the controversy surrounding the Yasukuni shrine, see John Breen, ed., *Yasukuni, the War Dead and the Struggle for Japan's Past* (New York: Columbia University Press, 2008); and Buruma, *The Wages of Guilt*, pp. 219–28.

19 Christopher Reed, "When the Victors Memorialize Their Massacres: Koizumi and the Rape of Nanking," *Counterpunch*, October 19, 2005, http://www.counterpunch.com/reed10192005.html.

20 Chisaki Watanabe, "Suit Over Japan War Shrine Visits Rejected," Associated Press dispatch in *The Guardian*, September 29, 2005.

21 Miwa Suzuki, "Japan's Leader Shuns Controversial War Shrine," *The Sydney Morning Herald*, August 16, 2007.

22 A.O. Scott, "Entwined at a Japanese Shrine, the Nobility and Horrific Brutality of War," *The New York Times* (review of *Yasukuni*, dir. Li Ying), August 12, 2009.

23 Mizushima quoted in David McNeill, "Propaganda War is Declared in Cinemas over Nanking Massacre," *The Independent*, December 5, 2007, http://news.independent.co.uk/world/asia/article3223694.ece; and Justin McCurry, "China Angered by Nanjing Massacre Film," *The Guardian*, January 25, 2007, http://www.guardian.co.uk/film/2007/jan/25/china.world.

24 Tamogami quoted in Blaine Harden, "WWII Apologists Persist Despite Japanese Policy," *The Washington Post*, November 3, 2008.

25 In May 2009, representatives in the Russian Duma actually went so far as to "propose a law that would criminalize the denial of the Soviet victory in World War II," in the words of Sergei Shoigu, the co-chairman of Putin's United Russia party. Another United Russia MP, Valery Ryazansky, stated: "Those who attempt to interpret the outcome of World War II, to turn everything upside down, to represent those who liberated countries from the Nazi invaders as subjugators" would face punishment. See John Wendle, "Russia Moves to Ban Criticism of WWII Victory," *Time*, May 8, 2009, http://www.time.com/time/world/article/0,8599,1896927,00.html.

26 See Jenny Booth, "Russia Threatens Estonia over Removal of Red Army Statue," *The Times*, April 27, 2007, http://www.timesonline.co.uk/tol/news/world/europe/article1714401.ece; and "Russian MPs Visit Estonia as Soviet War Statue is Re-erected," Associated Press dispatch in *The Guardian*, May 1, 2007, http://www.guardian.co.uk/world/2007/may/01/russia.international.

27 As Anne Applebaum has written, "If the Russian people and the Russian elite remem-
    bered – viscerally, emotionally remembered – what Stalin did to the Chechens, they could
    not have invaded Chechnya in the 1990s, not once and not twice. To do so was the moral
    equivalent of post-war Germany invading western Poland. Very few Russians saw it that
    way – which is itself evidence of how little they know about their own history."
    (Applebaum, "The Gulag: Lest We Forget," *Hoover Digest*, 2005: 1, http://www.hoover.
    org/publications/digest/3001971.html).

28 Marina Marshenkulova and Azamat Bram, "Outrage at 'Fake' Circassian Anniversary,"
    Institute for War and Peace Reporting, October 5, 2007. "By way of compromise, the
    local authorities offered to use the word 'union' more frequently than 'voluntary acces-
    sion.'"

29 For another example, see "Memorial Raised to Victims of Stalin," Agence France-Presse
    dispatch in *The Times*, August 9, 2007, http://www.timesonline.co.uk/tol/news/world/
    europe/article2224591.ece: "A three-storey cross has been erected on a site where
    thousands of victims of Stalin's purges were executed 70 years ago. About 500 people
    gathered in the southern [Moscow] suburb of Butovo for a religious service after the
    12.5m (41ft) wooden cross was raised by hand and then fixed in place with rocks. More
    than 20,000 were killed at the site during Stalin's campaign against "enemies of the
    people" . . . The cross was carved from cedar and pine from Solovetsky Monastery in
    Siberia, one of Stalin's most notorious prison camps." Another "Solovetsky Stone," this
    one in St. Petersburg, is depicted in Figure 14.4, p. 509.

30 "Putin Honors Stalin Victims 70 Years after Terror," Reuters dispatch, October
    30, 2007, http://www.reuters.com/article/idUSL3072723020071030. For his part,
    Medvedev stated in October 2009 that "even now we can hear voices saying that these
    numerous deaths were justified by some supreme goals of the state. Nothing can be valued
    above human life, and there is no excuse for repressions . . . It is . . . important to prevent
    the justification, under the pretext of putting historical records straight, of those who
    killed their own people." Ellen Barry, "Don't Gloss Over Stalin's Crimes, Medvedev
    Says," *The New York Times*, October 30, 2009, http://www.nytimes.com/2009/10/31/
    world/europe/31russia.html.

31 Orlando Figes, "The Raid on Memorial," *New York Review of Books*, 56: 1 (January 15,
    2009), http://www.nybooks.com/articles/22248.

32 Will Stewart, "Stalin's Mass Murders Were 'Entirely Rational' Says New Russian
    Textbook Praising Tyrant," *Daily Mail*, September 3, 2008.

33 David Holley, "TV Series on Stalin Divides Russian Audience," *The Los Angeles Times*,
    March 30, 2007.

34 "Stalin Voted Third-Best Russian," *BBC Online*, December 28, 2008, http://news.bbc.
    co.uk/2/hi/europe/7802485.stm.

35 See Nick Allen, "Airline Pilot Arrested over Argentine 'Death Flights,'" *The Telegraph*,
    September 24, 2009.

36 An essential source is Antonius C.G.M. Robben's *Political Violence and Trauma in
    Argentina* (Philadelphia, PA: University of Pennsylvania Press, 2005). Two English-
    language overviews are Martin Edwin Andersen, *Dossier Secreto: Argentina's Desaparecidos
    and the Myth of the "Dirty War"* (Boulder, CO: Westview Press, 1993), and Paul H.
    Lewis, *Guerrillas and Generals: The "Dirty War" in Argentina* (Westport, CT: Praeger
    Publishers, 2002). A concise summary from a genocide studies perspective is "The
    Disappearances: Mass Killing in Argentina," ch. 14 in Ervin Staub, *The Roots of Evil: The
    Origins of Genocide and Other Group Violence* (Cambridge: Cambridge University Press,
    1989), pp. 210–31. The kidnapping of infants was the subject of an Oscar-winning
    Argentine film, *The Official Story* (1985).

37 The Falkland Islands are known as Islas Malvinas to Argentines.

38 Amnesty International, "Argentina: The Military Juntas and Human Rights," in William
    L. Hewitt, ed., *Defining the Horrific: Readings on Genocide and Holocaust in the Twentieth
    Century* (Upper Saddle River, NJ: Pearson, 2004), p. 247.

39 In November 2003, together with a small group of other foreign scholars, I attended what

was probably the first international conference on genocide in South America, held at the University of Buenos Aires. At a guess, 75 or 80 percent of the presentations dealt with the "genocide in Argentina" under military rule. Without exception, all the presenters took it as a given that the events in question had constituted genocide. This would be much more controversial among genocide scholars in the West, given the limited number of victims, and the fact that the violence was targeted against alleged members of a political group. In conversation with some of the Argentine scholars, though, it became clear to me that not only did they consider the term valid, but they regarded its application as *vital to memorializing the events and validating victims' suffering.*

40 Larry Rohter, "Debate Rises in Argentina on Museum of Abuses," *The New York Times*, April 19, 2004. Unless otherwise specified, all quotes in this discussion of the Museum of Memory are drawn from Rohter's article.

41 Quoted in ibid.

42 However, *junta* leader General Videla was jailed in June 1997 for the kidnapping of children, which was held to lie beyond the boundaries of the *punto final.*

43 As noted in Chapter 15, Chile's outgoing president at the time of writing, Michele Bachelet, was a political prisoner under General Augusto Pinochet's military regime (1973–90).

44 Juan Forero, "Argentina Puts Officials on Trial over the Abuses of the 'Dirty War,'" *The Washington Post*, December 28, 2009.

45 "Police Probe Death of Witness in Argentina Human Rights Trial," CNN.com, October 20, 2009, http://www.cnn.com/2009/WORLD/americas/10/20/argentina.witness/ index.html; Tom Hennigan, "'Dirty War' Torture Witness Goes Missing," *The Times*, September 28, 2006, http://www.timesonline.co.uk/tol/news/world/us_and_americas/ article652322.ece.

46 Alfonso Daniels, "Argentina's Dirty War: The Museum of Horrors," *The Telegraph*, May 17, 2008, http://www.telegraph.co.uk/culture/3673470/Argentinas-dirty-war-the- museum-of-horrors.html.

47 Desbois quoted in Vivienne Walt, "Genocide's Ghosts," *Time*, January 16, 2008, http:// www.time.com/time/magazine/article/0,9171,1703919-1,00.html.

48 Desbois quoted in Isabel de Bertodano, "Two Faiths Together," *The Tablet*, February 7, 2009, http://www.thetablet.co.uk/article/12644.

49 Father Patrick Desbois, *The Holocaust by Bullets: A Priest's Journey to Uncover the Truth behind the Murder of 1.5 Million Jews* (London: Palgrave Macmillan, 2008), p. 37. See also Desbois's project's website at http://holocaustbybullets.wordpress.com, and an excellent CBC documentary on Desbois's work at http://www.youtube.com/watch?v= H5DSH2EqZ54.

50 Desbois quoted in Walt, "Genocide's Ghosts."

51 Desbois quoted in Elaine Sciolino, "A Priest Methodically Reveals Ukrainian Jews' Fate," *The New York Times*, October 6, 2007, http://www.nytimes.com/2007/10/06/world/ europe/06priest.html.

52 Desbois quoted in Walt, "Genocide's Ghosts."

53 Desbois quoted in Sciolino, "A Priest."

54 Desbois, *The Holocaust by Bullets*, p. 34. Emphasis added.

55 Christopher Browning, *Ordinary Men: Reserve Police Battalion 101 and the Final Solution in Poland* (New York: HarperPerennial, 1993).

56 Daniel Jonah Goldhagen, *Hitler's Willing Executioners: Ordinary Germans and the Holocaust* (New York: Vintage, 1997). Whatever the flaws of Goldhagen's central thesis (see Chapter 6 for further discussion), both he and Christopher Browning deserve great credit for helping, with their careful archival research, to resurrect the "Holocaust by Bullets" for contemporary memory.

57 Gregory H. Stanton, "Eight Stages of Genocide," http://www.genocidewatch.org/about genocide/8stagesofgenocide.html.

58 Richard G. Hovannisian, "Denial of the Armenian Genocide in Comparison with Holocaust Denial," in Hovannisian, ed., *Remembrance and Denial: The Case of the Armenian Genocide* (Detroit, MI: Wayne State University Press, 1999), p. 202.

59 See Ian Traynor, "Irving Jailed for Denying Holocaust," *The Guardian*, February 21, 2006, http://www.guardian.co.uk/world/2006/feb/21/thefarright.highereducation.

60 For a summary, with many examples, see Anti-Defamation League, "Holocaust Denial in the Middle East: The Latest Anti-Israel Propaganda Theme," http://www.adl.org/holocaust/denial_ME/Holocaust_Denial_Mid_East_prt.pdf. For a consideration of the broad trends in the Arab world, see Meir Litvak and Esther Webman, *From Empathy to Denial: Arab Responses to the Holocaust* (London: Hurst and Company, 2009).

61 Thus, in the context of the "Holocaust by Bullets" just discussed, German Reichsführer Heinrich Himmler issued an order in July 1942 that "all mass graves [on the eastern front, mostly filled with Jewish victims] were to be opened and the corpses burned. In addition the ashes were to be disposed of in such a way that it would be impossible at some future time to calculate the number of corpses burned." A similar procedure was followed at the Auschwitz II-Birkenau death camp in Poland: "Elevators carried the corpses to the ground floor [of the gas chamber/crematorium complex], where several ovens reduced them to ashes. After the grinding of bones in special mills, the ashes were used as fertilizer in the nearby fields, dumped in local forests, or tossed into the river, nearby." Both passages from Saul Friedländer, *The Years of Extermination: Nazi Germany and the Jews* (New York: HarperCollins, 2007), pp. 404, 503.

62 Jacques Sémelin, *Purify and Destroy: The Political Uses of Massacre and Genocide* (New York: Columbia University Press, 2007), p. 248.

63 Michael Shermer and Alex Grobman, *Denying History: Who Says the Holocaust Never Happened and Why Do They Say It?* (Berkeley, CA: University of California Press, 2002), p. 40.

64 Ibid., p. 213. The point of *reductio ad absurdum* was reached with the Kosovo conflict of 1998–99, during which Serb acts of genocide against Kosovar Albanians were justified by the Albanian "occupation" of historic Serb lands. Serb extremists traced the alleged trend back no fewer than six centuries, to the Battle of Kosovo Polje in 1389, and used it to justify the first public accusations of "genocide" occurring in a contemporary Balkans context – that is, by Kosovar Albanians against Serbs! (See Chapter 8.) For Sémelin, such tropes serve as a reminder that "the word [genocide] is used as much as a symbolic shield to claim victim status for one's people, as a sword raised against one's deadly enemy" (p. 313).

65 For a summary and debunking, see Ben Kiernan, "Cover-up and Denial of Genocide: Australia, the USA, East Timor, and the Aborigines," *Critical Asian Studies*, 34: 2 (2002), pp. 180–82.

66 CNN International broadcast, December 31, 2004.

67 Taner Akçam, *From Empire to Republic: Turkish Nationalism and the Armenian Genocide* (London: Zed Books, 2004), p. 209.

68 Colin Tatz, *With Intent to Destroy: Reflecting on Genocide* (London: Verso, 2003), p. 137.

69 Corddry quoted in Alan Shapiro, "American Treatment of Iraqi and Afghan Prisoners: An Introduction," TeachableMoment.org, http://www.teachablemoment.org/high/prisoners.html.

70 See John Bunzl, "Islam's Holocaust Denial Trap," Haaretz.com, February 10, 2006, available at http://www.lebanonwire.com/0602MN/06021003HZ.asp.

71 Paris court judgment cited in Shermer and Grobman, *Denying History*, pp. 10–11. In 2007, the European Union adopted hate-crime legislation that "urges EU nations to impose prison sentences of up to three years for individuals convicted of denying genocide, such as the mass killing of Jews during World War II or the massacres in Rwanda in 1994.The rules would require countries to prosecute offenders in connection with killings that have been recognized as genocides by the International Criminal Court in The Hague." Molly Moore, "EU Ministers Agree on Rules against Hate Crimes, Racism," *The Washington Post*, April 20, 2007.

72 David Bercuson and Douglas Wertheimer, quoted in Luke McNamara, "Criminalising Racial Hatred: Learning from the Canadian Experience," *Australian Journal of Human*

Rights, 1: 1 (1994). Available online at http://www.austlii.edu.au/au/other/ahric/ajhr/ V1N1/ajhr1113.html.

73 See McNamara, "Criminalising Racial Hatred." The case of Ernst Zündel, a German-born denier of the Jewish Holocaust, has also generated controversy. Zündel became "a political hot potato to immigration officials in Canada and the United States." Moving from Canada to the US when the Canadian government denied his application for citizenship, Zündel was then deported back to Canada, and then on to Germany, where in 2007 he was convicted on "14 counts of inciting racial hatred and for denying that the Nazis killed six million Jews during World War II." See "Jail for German Holocaust Denier," *BBC Online*, February 15, 2007, http://news.bbc.co.uk/2/hi/europe/6364951. stm.

74 Richard J. Evans, *Lying About Hitler: History, Holocaust, and the David Irving Trial* (New York: Basic Books, 2001), p. 6. Evans was one of the historians who testified at the trial; his book provides an excellent overview of the proceedings.

75 Roger W. Smith, Eric Markusen, and Robert Jay Lifton, "Professional Ethics and the Denial of the Armenian Genocide," in Hovannisian, ed., *Remembrance and Denial*, pp. 287, 289.

76 Noam Chomsky, "Some Elementary Comments on the Rights of Freedom of Expression," http://www.chomsky.info/articles/19801011.htm. Much controversy attached to Chomsky's comment in this essay that "As far as I can determine, he [Faurisson] is a relatively apolitical liberal of some sort."

77 Gérard Prunier, *The Rwanda Crisis: History of a Genocide* (New York: Columbia University Press, 1997), p. 339.

78 After the David Irving decision, historian Andrew Roberts claimed the judgment against Irving was at best a partial victory, since "the free publicity that this trial has generated for him and his views has been worth far more than could ever have been bought for the amount of the costs." Quoted in Evans, *Lying About Hitler*, p. 235.

79 Lipstadt quoted in "'Irving? Let the Guy Go Home,'" BBC Online, January 4, 2006, http://news.bbc.co.uk/1/hi/uk/4578534.stm. See also Michael Shermer, "Free Speech, Even If It Hurts," *The Los Angeles Times*, February 26, 2006; Ben MacIntyre, "We Can't Deny the Deniers," *The Times*, January 20, 2006, http://www.timesonline.co.uk/tol/ comment/columnists/ben_macintyre/article715852.ece.

80 According to Colin Tatz, "for all the company they keep, and for all their outpourings, these deniers assist rather than hinder genocide and Holocaust research," in part by "prompt[ing] studies by men and women of eminence . . . who would otherwise not have written on genocide." Tatz, *With Intent to Destroy*, pp. 139–40.

81 For a discussion of responsible versus malicious denial of a genocide framework in the Cambodian case, see Ben Kiernan, "Bringing the Khmer Rouge to Justice," *Human Rights Review*, 1: 3 (April–June 2000), pp. 92–108. In fact, Jörg Menzel's article, "Justice Delayed or Too Late for Justice? The Khmer Rouge Tribunal and the Cambodian 'Genocide,' 1975–79," *Journal of Genocide Research*, 9: 2, pp. 215–33, strongly questions the "genocide" appellation for the Cambodian case, as the quote marks in the title suggest. "It is . . . far from clear if the criteria of genocide, as established under current international criminal law, are met by the crimes of the potential candidates of the ECCC . . . The genocide question may therefore be relevant more on a dogmatic and a psychological level" (ibid., pp. 222–23). I would consider Menzel's critique a "responsible" one in Kiernan's terms; yet it is notable that his skeptical and quite dismissive framing appeared in the leading journal in the field of comparative genocide studies.

CHAPTER 15

Justice, Truth, and Redress

What can justice mean when genocide is the issue?

Terrence Des Pres

The legal strictures against genocide constitute *jus cogens*: they are among the laws "accepted and recognized by the international community of States as a whole from which no derogation is permitted." Jus cogens is associated with the principle of *universal jurisdiction* (*quasi delicta juris gentium*), which "applies to a limited number of crimes for which any State, even absent a personal or territorial link with the offence, is entitled to try the offender."[1]

There is theory, however, and there is practice. After the UN Convention came into force in 1951, genocide was all but ignored in international law. In the international arena, the word was commonly deployed for propaganda purposes. For example, the resurgence of interest in the Jewish Holocaust, and the roughly contemporary rise of Israel to major-power status, made "genocide" an attractive verbal weapon for Palestinians and their Arab allies. National-level trials occasionally employed prosecuted the crime, as with Israel's prosecution of Adolf Eichmann in 1961 and Ethiopia's proceedings against members of the Dergue regime (see below). Yet overall, a conspiracy of silence prevailed in diplomatic quarters and at the United Nations. Diplomatic norms militated against such grave accusations, while states' bloody hands meant that there was always a danger that allegations could rebound on the accuser, through the defense of *tu quoque* – "a plea that the adversary committed similar atrocities."[2]

Despite this passivity, the twentieth century *did* produce revolutionary new forms of international justice. Formal mechanisms ranged from the humanitarian law of the

Hague Conventions (1899, 1907) and Geneva Conventions (culminating in 1949); to war crimes tribunals at Nuremberg and for Yugoslavia, Rwanda, and Sierra Leone; and most recently to an International Criminal Court (ICC) with universal jurisdiction though, alas, not yet universal membership. These were accompanied by less formal institutions, such as the "truth commissions" mounted under both national and international aegis, and investigative bodies that may blow the whistle on genocide, whether past, present, or incipient. Such efforts also feature substantial public involvement, especially by religious and human rights NGOs, academics, and legal professionals – a phenomenon that can be traced back to the international campaigns against slavery and the Congo "rubber terror" in the nineteenth and early twentieth centuries.

This penultimate chapter explores the interrelation of justice, truth-seeking, and redress as they have evolved both nationally and internationally.

LEIPZIG, CONSTANTINOPLE, NUREMBERG, TOKYO

The move towards tribunals for war crimes and "crimes against humanity" reflected the growing institutionalization and codification of humanitarian instruments during the latter half of the nineteenth century. This was evident in the formative efforts of Henri Dunand and his International Committee of the Red Cross, founded in 1864. The Red Cross was a pioneering institution in addressing suffering that offends the human conscience. Leaders were also becoming aware of "crimes against humanity" (Box 15.1), albeit selectively. Consider British politician William Gladstone's 1870 fulmination against Ottoman atrocities in the Balkans:

> Certain it is that a new law of nations is gradually taking hold of the mind, and coming to sway the practice, of the world; a law which recognises independence, which frowns upon aggression, which favours the pacific, not the bloody settlement of disputes, which aims at permanent and not temporary adjustments; above all, which recognises, as a *tribunal* of paramount authority, the general *judgment of civilised mankind*.[3]

Much the same speech could have been given for the drafting of the Rome Statute of the International Criminal Court (1998), suggesting that Gladstone was overly optimistic in his assessment. But his generation did witness substantial advances in human freedom. The abolition of slavery in the United States (1861) and Brazil (1888) were high-water marks. They were accompanied by campaigns against the Congo "rubber terror," pogroms against Russian Jews, and early Ottoman massacres of Armenians (1894–96), presaging the genocide of Christian minorities during World War One.

At century's end, Russian Tsar Nicholas convened an international conference on war prevention at The Hague in Holland. This led to two seminal conventions, in 1899 and 1907, that placed limits on "legitimate" methods of warfare, including bans on civilian bombardments and the use of poison gas. All sides abrogated the agreements only a few years later, during the First World War (1914–18). But the new framings shaped the postwar world – including the 1927 Protocol against chemical and biological warfare, which remains in force.

As part of the punitive peace imposed on Germany at Versailles, a few desultory trials of alleged war criminals took place before German courts at Leipzig. They ended in fiasco, with the Allies divided, and German opposition to the initiative effectively unchallenged. A similar dynamic prevailed in the trials that Allied occupiers imposed on Turkey, described in Chapter 4.

More high-profile and successful were the international tribunals at Nuremberg and Tokyo following the Second World War.[4] Trials were by no means foreordained as a strategy for handling German and Japanese war criminals. Intense debates on this topic occurred among members of the Allied coalition during 1943–45. Both Winston Churchill and Joseph Stalin pushed for summary executions of those in the Nazi leadership strata.[5] Franklin Roosevelt considered the wholesale demilitarization, deindustrialization, and dismemberment of Germany (the so-called "Morgenthau Plan"). This was in keeping with public opinion in the Allied countries: few people viewed tribunals as the optimal way of dealing with enemy war crimes.

However, a legal process was finally settled upon in both the German and Japanese cases. This was, indisputably, a major advance in international jurisprudence. Nuremberg featured "the first official mention of genocide in an international legal setting," as all the German defendants were accused of "conduct[ing] deliberate and systematic genocide, viz., the extermination of racial and national groups, against the civilian populations of certain occupied territories."[6] Raphael Lemkin's tireless lobbying had paid dividends, though, as noted in Chapter 1, "genocide" formed no part of the Nuremberg verdicts. (Nor could it have, since it was not at the time a crime under international law.)[7]

Both tribunals were flawed. Leaders were tried only for crimes committed in wartime. Nazi actions against the Jews prior to September 1, 1939, for example, were absent from the Nuremberg indictments. Nazi crimes against Jews, Roma, and other groups were downplayed, while charges of waging aggressive war were emphasized. Japanese atrocities against Chinese and other Asian civilians were similarly under-stressed, by contrast with allegations of the murderous abuse of Allied prisoners-of-war.

The long-established principle of *nullum crimen sine lege* – no crime without an accompanying law – was implemented in "an extremely loose and controversial" way at Nuremberg. Leaders were tried for crimes that had not formally existed when they were committed.[8] In addition, prosecutors at both the Nuremberg and Tokyo tribunals avoided charging Germans and Japanese with atrocities that the Allies had also inflicted. Thus, while indiscriminate bombardment of civilians was long established as a core war crime, it could not be prosecuted without providing the accused with a ready-made *tu quoque* defense. Even so, an Indian judge at Tokyo, Rahadbinod Pal, dissented from the majority verdict, labeling the trial a sham for its inattention to the Allies' own crimes.[9] In one case – that of unrestricted submarine warfare – the charges manifestly *did* overlap with Allied practice. Here, German Admiral Karl Dönitz's *tu quoque* defense was successful, leading to his acquittal, though Dönitz was convicted on "counts . . . [of] crimes against peace and war crimes – and sentenced to 10 years in prison."[10]

Figure 15.1 Judgment at Nuremberg, 1946: accused Nazi war criminals in the dock after the Second World War.

Source: United States Holocaust Memorial Museum.

For the Tokyo trials, the Allies did not prosecute Emperor Hirohito, the man who "had personally approved all his country's barbaric military ventures" before and during the Second World War. They allowed him to remain on the Japanese throne, albeit de-deified.[11] Nor was Hirohito the only accused war criminal allowed to evade justice. The US was particularly interested in military technology, including biological weapons. Thus, Japanese scientists associated with the Unit 731 biological experiments – which led, among other things, to the release of live plague bacilli over Chinese cities – were granted immunity from prosecution, in return for sharing their research and expertise with the Americans. In Europe, police and security forces were deemed vital to both sides in the emerging Cold War struggle, regardless of the role they had played in fascist persecutions. Soviet occupiers, for instance, incorporated Nazi-era personnel wholesale into the new Stasi security force of East Germany.

The tribunals were victor's justice, but they were also groundbreaking. Nuremberg established "two central precedents: that of individual criminal responsibility, and that of the universal jurisdiction over crimes against humanity."[12] Out of twenty-four indictments, two were dropped and three defendants acquitted; another seven were imprisoned and not executed. (In the Tokyo proceedings, seven defendants were sentenced to death, sixteen to life in prison, and two others to lighter terms.) There is also no discounting the bonanza that the tribunals represented for historical scholarship and the documentation that underpins it. Alan Bullock called Nuremberg, with its bounty of Nazi documents on public display, "an absolutely unqualified wonder . . . the greatest coup in history for historians."[13]

THE INTERNATIONAL CRIMINAL TRIBUNALS: YUGOSLAVIA AND RWANDA

It is one of history's ironies that the International Criminal Tribunal for the Former Yugoslavia (ICTY) was created to deflect accusations of Western complacency in the face of genocide.[14] In spring 1992, with war raging in Bosnia, voices were raised for the establishment of a UN-sponsored tribunal to try the perpetrators of atrocities. In May 1993, the Security Council created the ICTY at The Hague (hence, "the Hague tribunal"). For some time following, this was as far as the West was willing to go. The Balkan wars continued for another three years, with the worst single atrocity occurring near their end (the Srebrenica massacre of July 1995). The tribunal's creation did not prevent a new eruption of conflict in Kosovo in 1998–99.

Following the Dayton peace agreement of 1996, the ICTY process gradually gathered steam. The unwillingness of occupying forces to seize indicted individuals, for fear of destabilizing the transition process, gave way to a more assertive attitude. The pace of arrests and prosecutions picked up substantially. With growing cooperation from Croatian authorities, more than half of the ICTY's indicted figures were in custody by 2001. In that year, the process climaxed with the extraordinary transfer of former Yugoslav President Slobodan Milosevic to the tribunal. "For the first time in human history, a head of state was brought to international legal accountability for crimes committed as a result of his rule."[15] Though Milosevic died before a conviction could be rendered, by 2009 his partner in crime, Bosnian Serb president Radovan Karadzic, was gazing dolefully from the dock (Figure 8.7, p. 333).[16] In December of that year, the UN Security Council extended the ICTY's mandate, originally scheduled to expire in 2010, through to 2012.

The ICTY won praise for impartiality. Its first conviction was issued against a Croatian (albeit one who served with Serb forces). The indictments of Croatian General Ante Gotovina and Kosovo Prime Minister Ranush Haradinaj helped to balance the emphasis on Serb crimes against Bosnian Muslims, Croats, and Kosovar Albanians. However, the ICTY was criticized for ruling out war crimes prosecutions of NATO leaders of the Kosovo war, accused of attacks on civilian targets and other breaches of international law.[17]

With the Hague tribunal in place, the UN could hardly avoid establishing a tribunal for the Rwanda genocide of 1994. The International Criminal Tribunal for Rwanda (ICTR) was housed at Arusha, Tanzania, where the abortive 1993 peace agreements had been signed (Chapter 9). The ICTR's gears ground painfully slowly, however. Understaffed and underfunded, it was prone to allegations that it focused exclusively on Hutu killers of Tutsis, with no consideration of Tutsi reprisal killings of Hutus.[18] Its operations also appeared distorted by the more extensive genocide trials in Rwanda. These imposed the death penalty, while ICTR proceedings did not, leading to the paradox that *génocidaires* could escape execution at the ICTR, while their underlings could be (and were) sentenced to death by Rwandan judges.[19] In Gérard Prunier's scathing 2009 assessment, the Rwanda tribunal

combined three different evils: it was an embodiment of the worst aspects of UN bureaucratic inefficiency; a muted, closed arena for jousting over all the unacknowledged political contradictions of the genocide; and a swamp of nepotistic and corrupt practices. . . . The result was that, whereas it had taken the Nuremberg Tribunal one year (from November 1945 to November 1946) to judge twenty-four Nazis and hang ten, the ICTR had managed to carry out only twenty procedures in ten years at a cost of around $700 million.[20]

Originally set to conclude in 2009, the ICTR trials were extended by Security Council fiat until December 2010, to allow processes then underway to conclude. The balance-sheet of the ICTR operations seems, overall, less impressive than the ICTY's. Leaving aside the efficacy of their justice measures, however, the two ad-hoc tribunals have contributed more to legal interpretations and applications of the Genocide Convention than all authorities in the preceding forty-five years. Some examples follow.

Jurisdictional issues

For decades, applications of international humanitarian law were impeded by the difficulty of determining which legal instruments could be imposed on sovereign states, and when – in peacetime, or solely in war? In civil wars, or only international ones? These matters are now largely resolved. In its "exhaustive analysis of customary and conventional international humanitarian law," the Hague tribunal concluded by decisively "severing . . . the category of crimes against humanity [including genocide] from any requirement of a connection to international wars, *or indeed to any state of conflict*."[21] In the estimation of legal scholar Christopher Rudolph, this ICTY precedent "opened the door to international adjudication of internal conflicts."[22] It was seized upon by the Arusha tribunal in extending relevant international law to a "civil conflict" (the Rwanda genocide). The precedent has become a touchstone for advocates of universal jurisdiction in cases of genocide and other crimes against humanity.

The concept of a victim group

Many have criticized the UN Genocide Convention's exclusion of political and other potential victim groups. Moreover, the four core groups that the Convention *does* recognize – "national, ethnical, racial, and religious" – are notoriously difficult to define and distinguish "as such." Confronted with genocide in Rwanda, where populations sharing most of the usual ethnic markers – language, religion, a common history – descended into savage intercommunal killing, the ICTR chose to define an ethnic group as "one whose members share a common language and culture; or, a group which distinguishes itself as such (self identification); or, *a group identified as such by others, including perpetrators of the crimes (identification by others)*."[23] Identities may now be *imputed* to a collectivity, as well as avowed by one.

Gender and genocide

According to Steven Ratner and Jason Abrams, the ICTY's "indictments and jurisprudence have highlighted the role of sexual violence in the Balkan conflict and more clearly defined the status of such offenses in international criminal law."[24] For instance, in the Celibici case, the ICTY ruled that rape could constitute torture. The ICTR went further still. With the Akayesu decision of 1998, the Arusha tribunal, "in one of its significant innovations, defined rape as a form of genocide, in that it constitutes serious bodily or mental harm in accordance with article II(b) of the [UN] Convention."[25] Rape was also depicted as a form of "preventing births within the group," both physically and through inflicting psychological trauma on women.[26] From both perspectives, female rape victims are now viewed as victims in their own right, rather than as a medium through which dishonor and dislocation are visited upon a family or community. This new sensitivity, "a significant advance in international jurisprudence,"[27] reflects decades of successful feminist mobilization around the issue of rape, including groundbreaking analyses of rape in war and genocide.[28]

Neither the ICTY nor the ICTR has accompanied these advances with systematic attention to rape and sexual violence against males, especially in detention centers and prison camps. The ICTY tribunal reacted with unease to forays on the subject, while the ICTR has ignored it altogether.[29] However, the tribunals *did* make one essential contribution to legal understandings of gendercidal atrocities against men. In 2001, Bosnian Serb General Radislav Krstic became the first person to be convicted by the ICTY of aiding and abetting genocide. Krstic's lawyers had argued that because "only" adult males were killed at Srebrenica, the strategy was not genocidal against the community as a whole. In its 2004 verdict on Krstic's appeal, the court rejected these arguments, contending that selective killing of males constituted destruction of the Bosnian-Muslim population "in part," and this was sufficient to characterize the slaughter as genocide.[30]

BOX 15.1 "GENOCIDE" VS. "CRIMES AGAINST HUMANITY"

The concept of "crimes against humanity" predates that of genocide. It was first used in an international context in 1915. As the Ottoman genocide against Christian minorities raged (see Chapter 4), the Allies of the Triple Entente – Russia, France, and Great Britain – gathered to issue a statement of protest and concern. The proposed Russian wording condemned "crimes . . . against Christianity and civilization," but the other Allies felt this could bring yet more persecution upon the ravaged Christian populations of Anatolia. Accordingly, an agreement was struck to change the text to denounce instead crimes "against humanity and civilization."

Thus was born one of the most potent concepts of human rights and, eventually, international law. The Nuremberg tribunal of 1945–46 employed the language of crimes against humanity, along with "crimes against peace" and "war crimes," to prosecute Nazi war criminals for acts that included "murder, extermination, enslavement, deportation, and other inhumane acts committed against any civilian population, before or during the war. . ." The Rome Statute of the International Criminal Court, adopted in 1998, added the crimes of torture, "rape, sexual slavery, enforced prostitution, forced pregnancy, enforced sterilization, or any other form of sexual violence of comparable gravity"; "persecution against any identifiable group or collectivity on political, racial, national, ethnic, cultural, religious, gender . . . or other grounds"; "forced disappearance of persons"; and "the crime of apartheid." It also emphasized that the "other inhumane acts" referenced at Nuremberg consisted of those "of a similar character [to those cited] intentionally causing great suffering, or serious injury to body or to mental or physical health."[31]

For genocide scholars and students, the areas of conceptual crossover and divergence with the UN Genocide Convention are worth noting. Crimes against humanity are characterized by two main requisites: they must be "widespread or systematic," and they must be committed in the course of an attack "directed against any civilian population" (Rome Statute). Neither of these requirements is found in the Genocide Convention, though in practical application and prosecution, genocide has generally been viewed as targeting civilians (or at least non-combatants). The "widespread" scale and "systematic" character of atrocities likewise supply important evidence that a campaign of genocide is underway.

Importantly, the "murder" and "extermination" provisions of crimes against humanity legislation do *not* require that the civilian victims be members of a particular national, ethnic, racial, or religious collectivity, as the Genocide Convention does. Moreover, the Rome Statute's prohibition against "persecution" of "identifiable group[s]" references a wider range of collectivities than does the Convention, including "political," "cultural," and "gender" groups.

There is an intriguing overlap between the "extermination" provisions of crimes against humanity legislation and Article 2(c) of the Genocide Convention, which bans "deliberately inflicting on the group conditions of life calculated to bring about its physical destruction in whole or in part." The Rome Statute defines "extermination" in similar, at times identical, language: it is "the intentional infliction of conditions of life, inter alia [among other things] the deprivation of access to food and medicine, calculated to bring about the destruction of part of the population." Like Article 2(c), therefore, "extermination" emphasizes *indirect* destruction through denial of the means of subsistence, especially "food and medicine." Faminogenic crimes (see pp. 68–69), as well as certain strategies of blockade and ghettoization, can either be considered genocidal under international law (when directed against members of one of the groups designated in the Convention), or exterminatory under crimes against humanity provisions (so long as they are "widespread or systematic" and target a civilian population).

In international-legal practice, crimes against humanity after Nuremberg faded into the background – as indeed did the Genocide Convention after it entered into law in 1951. When mass killing and other crimes erupted in the Balkans, Rwanda, and elsewhere in the 1990s, it was allegations of genocide which captured the imagination of publics, political leaders, and legal specialists – in part because the interethnic dimension of the killing was so pronounced. However, prosecutors at the Yugoslavia and Rwanda tribunals – and those that have followed – quickly ran up against limitations and ambiguities in the Genocide Convention, most notably its requirement that *intent to destroy a particular group* be demonstrated. Not only does crimes against humanity legislation incorporate a much wider range of crimes (notably including torture, forcible deportation, and sexual assault), but a prosecutor need only demonstrate that acts were intentionally inflicted against civilians, rather than a designated group.[32] If she or he *can* so demonstrate, then the punishment imposed on the perpetrator – usually life imprisonment or incarceration for decades – will likely be similar to that imposed for genocide.[33]

The result has been a subtle but noticeable shift in international tribunals away from genocide and toward crimes against humanity as the preferred legal framework. This was prominently displayed in the International Criminal Court's indictment of Sudanese president Omar al-Bashir in 2008 (as well as a former Sudanese interior minister and *Janjaweed* militia leader) for crimes allegedly committed in the Darfur region of western Sudan (see Box 9a). Prosecutors requested an indictment for genocide, along with war crimes and crimes against humanity. But the ICC's pre-trial chamber at first demurred: "the material provided by the Prosecution in support of its application for a warrant of arrest failed to provide reasonable grounds to believe that the Government of Sudan acted with specific intent to destroy, in whole or in part, the Fur, Masalit and Zaghawa groups" of Darfur.[34] (As this book headed to press in early 2010, however, the prosecution's appeal had been allowed, and a way was potentially open for genocide to be added to the charge sheet.) The former Liberian leader and warlord, Charles Taylor, was similarly on trial by the UN-sponsored Special Court for Sierra Leone in 2010 for war crimes and crimes against humanity – but not genocide (see further below).

The trend might be expected to grow in coming years. In some ways, this strikes me as an important validation of a concept which has generally been sidelined by the recent emphasis on genocide. "Crimes against humanity" is, on its own terms, a revolutionary notion. It suggests that the atrocities in question target not only the proximate victim, but the entire human collective and its core values. It is thus an elegant and rather moving encapsulation of the tendency toward universalism and cosmopolitanism, from which ideas of "human rights" derive.

The growing prominence of crimes against humanity in legal and public discourse also points to something I have long sensed: that the most significant deployment of "genocide" may *not* be as a legal-prosecutorial device, but as an intellectual concept and – recognizing the term's unequalled rhetorical power – an advocacy tool to arouse public concern, shame perpetrators, and press for intervention.[35] This may also free the term from its unnecessarily restrictive framing in the UN Genocide Convention, with its limited target groups and high evidentiary requirement of genocidal intent.

Readers interested in the concept of crimes against humanity are invited to consult my recent book, *Crimes Against Humanity: A Beginner's Guide* (Oneworld, 2008, www.crimesagainsthumanity.ca), which aims to provide the first systematic treatment of the subject for a general audience.

NATIONAL TRIALS

Prosecution of genocide and other crimes at a national rather than international level carries certain advantages. Mechanisms for indictment, prosecution, and adjudication usually exist, at least in name: this is a definitional feature of the modern state. Moreover, in countries where genocide and crimes against humanity have been committed, the matter is deeply personal:

> Where trials take place in the country where the offenses occurred, the entire process becomes more deeply connected with the society, providing it with the potential to create a strong psychological and deterrent effect on the population. This factor, combined with the greater access to evidence, witnesses, victims, and perpetrators, gives such tribunals a significant potential advantage over international tribunals.[36]

Unfortunately, perpetration of genocide on a national territory often correlates with underdeveloped and compromised legal institutions. Thus, the capacity for administering justice may be sorely lacking. In Ethiopia, for instance, President Meles Zenawi's government charged more than five thousand representatives of the brutal Dergue dictatorship with offenses that included crimes against humanity and genocide; but these "highly ambitious" prosecutions suffered from a "judicial system [that was] weak and lacking any tradition of independence."[37] Rwanda's formal postgenocide trials, as distinct from the *gacaca* experiment (see below), aroused strong international criticism for their selective and sometimes shambolic character.

National trials can also arouse national sentiment, to the detriment of the proceedings. This derailed the tribunals at Leipzig and Constantinople after the First World War. Even contemporary, advanced legal systems may be unduly swayed by such sentiment. Israel, for example, mishandled the trial of John Demjanjuk, a US citizen extradited on charges of having served as a brutal guard ("Ivan the Terrible") at the Treblinka death camp. According to Geoffrey Robertson, some Israelis "wanted so badly to convict Demjanjuk that three experienced judges ignored exculpatory evidence and presided over an outrageously unfair show trial," sentencing the prisoner to death. Only when incontrovertible proof of mistaken identity was submitted at the appeal stage was Demjanjuk "grudgingly" cleared – for the time being.[38]

In addition to Ethiopia's proceedings against the Dergue and Israel's against Demjanjuk, some major national trials for war crimes and crimes against humanity include:

- Proceedings against thousands of accused war criminals in Germany after World War Two, following on the Nuremberg tribunal but conducted by German courts. Result: minimal "denazification," with most former Nazi functionaries left unprosecuted.
- Israel's abduction and trial of leading Nazi bureaucrat Adolf Eichmann (1960–61). Result: Eichmann's conviction and execution (1962).[39]
- Argentina's prosecution and incarceration, in the mid-1980s, of leaders of the former military *junta*. Result: five leaders convicted and jailed, but pardoned several years later; renewed prosecutions in the 2000s as immunity is lifted (see Chapter 14).
- Trials of accused *génocidaires* in Rwanda. Result: some trials and executions, general chaos, and the introduction of less formal *gacaca* proceedings (see below).
- The trials in post-2003 Iraq of Saddam Hussein and several of his henchmen for genocide against Shias and Kurds (Box 4a). Result: Saddam and his cousin, Ali Hassan al-Majid ("Chemical Ali"), convicted and hanged; others convicted and awaiting execution at the time of writing.

Domestic legislation on genocide is sometimes intriguing for its application of the Genocide Convention. Incorporation of the Convention into national law can be restrictive, based on "reservations" that are often self-serving.[40] But domestic framings can also be expansive and inclusive, perhaps charting a course for developments at the international level. This is especially notable in the case of designated victim groups for genocide. Bangladesh – with memories of the 1971 genocide still fresh (Box 8a) – added political groups to the Convention definition, as did Costa Rica in 1992 and Panama in 1993. Peru includes social groups, while Finland adds "a comparable group of people" to the Convention's core list of collectivities.[41] Another distinctive example is Cambodia, where, in light of the Khmer Rouge's strategies, genocide was defined in a Decree Law of July 1979 as including "planned massacres of groups of innocent people; expulsion of inhabitants of cities and villages in order to concentrate them and force them to do hard labour in conditions leading to their physical and mental destruction; wiping out religion; [and] destroying political, cultural and social structures and family and social relations."[42]

THE "MIXED TRIBUNALS": CAMBODIA AND SIERRA LEONE

The tribunals agreed for Cambodia and the West African nation of Sierra Leone provide an innovative "mixed" model that combines national and international representation. The trend-setter is Cambodia, where the model emerged after hard bargaining between the United Nations and the Cambodian government. The UN – supported in this by human rights NGOs in Cambodia and abroad – declared the country's post-genocide legal system incapable of administering justice. Not only was the system ramshackle and underfunded, the argument ran, but it was vulnerable to intervention and control by the authoritarian Hun Sen government. Government representatives, by contrast, stressed the importance of homegrown justice. After tortuous twists and turns a compromise was reached, and a UN–Cambodia Agreement was signed in June 2003. According to Tom Fawthrop and Helen Jarvis, the mixed tribunal was "a carefully crafted structure designed to provide sufficient checks and balances. International jurists, lawyers and judges will occupy key roles as the co-prosecutor, co-investigating judge and two out of five trial court judges, and must be a party to conviction or exoneration of any accused."[43] The first trial, of Kaing Guek Eav (alias "Duch"), was described in Chapter 7 (see p. 304); it concluded in November 2009, with no verdict rendered at the time of writing. The trials of four more Khmer Rouge leaders were in the works – senior figures only, so as not to risk destabilizing the process of recovery and reconciliation underway in Cambodian society. As Jörg Menzel summarized it, "the Cambodian approach to transitional justice is minimalist in nature: a symbolic criminal trial against a few main perpetrators. This is not much, but probably better than nothing."[44]

Although it took the Cambodian framework as its guide, the Special Court for Sierra Leone was first off the ground. It, too, includes both national and foreign justices, adjudicating under both domestic and international laws. But in a unique twist, two cities on different continents hosted the proceedings. Trials of the leaders of three different militia formations (the RUF, CDF, and AFRC) took place in Freetown, the Sierra Leonean capital. But a chamber of the International Criminal Court at The Hague was employed as the venue for Charles Taylor's trial – a special case, owing to Taylor's role as former president of Liberia (he was charged with orchestrating atrocities in Sierra Leone), and his status as a highly divisive figure in this traumatized region of West Africa. The possibility that a public trial would destroy nascent processes of reconciliation and reintegration of former combatants prompted the United Nations to approve the move. Taylor's trial at The Hague began in June 2007, and continued as this edition went to press. Three former leaders of the AFRC (Armed Forces Revolutionary Council) had already been convicted for war crimes and crimes against humanity (none of those before the court is charged with genocide); their convictions were upheld on appeal, while the convictions of three RUF figures were being appealed at the time of writing. Unquestionably the court's most notable legal contributions, thus far, were the conviction of AFRC figures for forcibly conscripting children, and the 2009 conviction of three RUF leaders for inflicting forced marriage on women. In each case, this was the first time such a verdict had been rendered under international law.[45]

ANOTHER KIND OF JUSTICE: RWANDA'S *GACACA* EXPERIMENT

Following the seizure of power in Rwanda by Paul Kagame's RPF rebels, well over 100,000 detainees were jailed for years without trial, in squalid and overcrowded conditions. Their incarceration was usually based on genuine suspicion of involvement in the genocide; some accusations, though, were surely concocted to settle personal scores or seize property. Clearly, the country's shattered legal system could not hope to clear the backlog of cases.

The solution eventually settled upon was *gacaca* (ga-CHA-cha). The word means "on the grass," a reference to the open-air proceedings chaired by "260,000 lay judges – old and young, men and women, Hutu and Tutsi," elected by popular vote in October 2001.[46] *Gacaca* tribunals, which began to function in 2005, were established at four levels, from cell through sector and district to province. The lowest-level tribunal handled Category 4 offenses, those against property only. Sector tribunals assessed crimes involving injury, while district-level trials handled cases of killing, but not – at the outset – the organization and direction of killing (Category 1 crimes). Until 2008, these latter crimes fell outside the *gacaca* framework, but in that year the tribunals' mandate was extended to include *local*-level planners and organizers of genocidal crimes. Provincial tribunals served as courts of final appeal for all *gacaca* cases.[47]

At the trials, victim and perpetrator were brought face to face, with witnesses speaking for each, and with each allowed an opportunity to address the tribunal. The "array of participants . . . include[d] all those affected by the crimes and also those who will be affected by the suspect's return to the community."[48] Judges, nine in number, were volunteers, usually community notables.

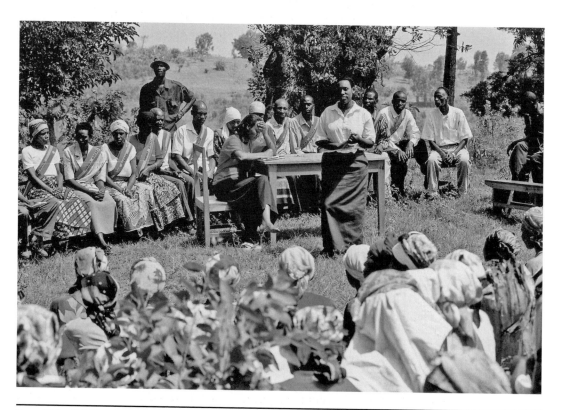

Figure 15.2 "It's Vestine's turn to talk about what happened to her family before the gacaca, the village court."

Source: Mark Vuori/World's Children's Prize/www.worldschildrensprize.org. In 2006, the AOCM, organization of Rwanda's genocide orphans, was awarded the prize by millions of children voting around the world.

The ensuing procedure "clearly contains elements that are distinctly retributive in nature," such as the emphasis on individual guilt and the imposition of punishments, as legal scholar Nicholas A. Jones acknowledged. However, *gacaca* also featured important elements of *restorative* justice:

> An offender who willingly accepts responsibility, takes ownership of his or her actions, and demonstrates his or her contriteness and willingness to tell the truth about the events that occurred, may receive a reduced sentence and an earlier return to the community through the application of the community service aspect of the plea. The [*gacaca*] legislation provides the accused with an avenue through which they may attempt to make amends for the harm they have caused. Additionally, this may present offenders with an opportunity to increase their likelihood for re-integration into the community, because other members of the community witness those attempts at restitution.[49]

In the evaluation offered by one of Jones's interviewees,

> I think that the Gacaca can bring people together because once you bring people together to dialogue, to discuss the issues that affect them directly, to discuss about whether they took part – one accused of murdering another, the other saying "you did this," "I didn't do this," "I did this, I'm sorry, can you forgive me?" That's a very important dialogue, and finally, starting from the hard facts is difficult, but finally you reach a consensus, whatever the case. Once people come together, you will definitely come up with a changed attitude. Previously people didn't want to even look at one another, but now they can hope to, they can hope to sit down and they can discuss issues.[50]

Critics of *gacaca* pointed to the political selectivity of the process – Tutsi killers of Hutus during and after the genocide against Tutsis were not called to account – as well as to the lack of Western-style judicial safeguards, such as defense lawyers and a presumption of innocence, and the "low standards of evidence" that left "ample room for manipulation and corruption."[51] There was also the perpetual problem of post-genocide justice: individuals' exploitation of inadequate legal infrastructure, and the prevailing confusion, fear, and paranoia, to saddle innocent people with genocide-related charges, thereby displacing them as political, professional, or even romantic rivals.

Moreover, an abstract concept like "reintegration" is fraught with complexity. What does it mean when thousands of killers and their accomplices are reintroduced to communities that include their victims and relatives of their victims? This process, which is not unique to Rwanda (see further below), will doubtless be closely tracked and studied in coming years.[52]

At this point, near the end of the *gacaca* experiment (they were scheduled to conclude in 2010),[53] one can say it seems a reasonably inspired indigenous response to a vast challenge – administering justice in a post-genocidal society with daunting resource constraints. The raw numbers were certainly impressive: by mid-2009, some 1.5 *million* cases had been heard.[54]

THE PINOCHET CASE

General Augusto Pinochet was first among equals in the military *junta* that overthrew the elected regime of Salvador Allende in Chile on September 11, 1973.[55] The coup was followed by a campaign against the Left, in which several thousand Chileans died. Many more were scarred physically and psychologically by torture, and tens of thousands forced into exile. Activists who fled one Southern Cone* country for refuge in another were hunted down and murdered in death-squad operations coordinated jointly by the region's dictators, Pinochet included.

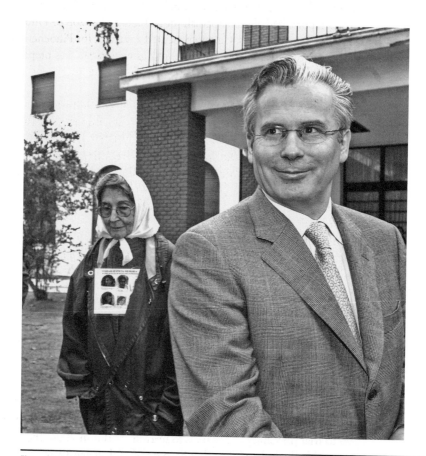

Figure 15.3 Spanish judge Baltasar Garzón is shown in August 2005 at the Naval Mechanics School in Buenos Aires, Argentina (ESMA; see Figure 14.5 and related discussion), together with a member of the Mothers of the Plaza de Mayo (the "Mothers of the Disappeared"). Garzón, whose extradition request to Great Britain sparked the Augusto Pinochet case, has sought to use "universal jurisdiction" provisions to extend Spain's role in prosecutions for genocide and crimes against humanity committed outside its territory. However, his campaign hit a roadblock in 2009, with the declared opposition of the Spanish government to allowing the country's legal system to serve as a "World Court."[56]

Source: Presidency of the Nation of Argentina/Wikimedia Commons.

---

* The "Southern Cone" of South America consists of Argentina, Chile, Paraguay, and Uruguay.

In 1974, Pinochet appointed himself president. Repression, torture, and death-squad activity continued, albeit on a reduced scale. In 1989, confident that his free-market reforms and social conservatism would sway a majority of Chileans, Pinochet submitted to a plebiscite. A majority – though not a large one – rejected him. Pinochet duly left office in 1990, and a centrist government took power.

Pinochet lived on, wealthy and comfortable except for persistent back problems. In search of relief, he consulted physicians in London, where the former Conservative Prime Minister, Margaret Thatcher, was his regular visitor; she had staunchly backed Pinochet during her years in power. For its part, the Blair government dispatched Foreign Office staff to attend to the aging dictator's needs and concerns.

Press reports had alerted Spanish judge Baltasar Garzón to Pinochet's presence in Britain. In October 1998, Garzón procured a warrant for Pinochet's extradition. The former dictator, aware that legal proceedings were afoot, was preparing to flee when police detained him. He would remain under house arrest while the British considered Garzón's extradition request.

On March 24, 1999, the same day that NATO bombs began falling on Kosovo (Chapter 8), a panel of the House of Lords – the supreme British tribunal – voted 6-1 that norms of diplomatic immunity did not extend to Pinochet in his current situation.[57] British domestic opinion was divided over the detention and extradition request, however, with Lady Thatcher leading a chorus of protest. In the end, *Realpolitik* (loosely, "reality politics") won out. In March 2000, a year-and-a-half after Pinochet's arrest, UK Home Secretary Jack Straw released him by government fiat on "compassionate" grounds.[58]

This seemed an abortive conclusion. Nonetheless, the Pinochet case was recognized as a watershed in international humanitarian law. For the first time since the legally ambiguous Eichmann case,[59] a former leadership figure, accused of committing grave abuses in one state (but not war crimes *per se*), was detained in another state for possible extradition to a third. Considerations of sovereign immunity were no longer determinant. As one of the British Law Lords wrote: "The trend was clear. War crimes had been replaced by crimes against humanity. The way in which a state treated its own citizens within its own borders had become a matter of legitimate concern to the international community."[60]

In a neat example of a political "feedback loop," international legal proceedings against Pinochet influenced the Chilean domestic agenda.[61] In closing his 2000 account of the Pinochet case, Geoffrey Robertson opined that Pinochet was "as likely to go to trial [in Chile] . . . as he is to heaven."[62] But in 2004, the Chilean Supreme Court suddenly declared Pinochet fit to stand trial, at age 89, for murders committed under his aegis. Shortly after the renewed legal process was announced, Pinochet entered hospital with a supposed "stroke." The Supreme Court was unimpressed. In the first days of January 2005, it reiterated that the process should go ahead, and placed the former dictator under house arrest.[63] In September 2005, Pinochet was formally stripped of his immunity from prosecution. Impunity for Pinochet's colleagues and underlings had also evaporated, with "more than 300 retired officers, including 21 generals . . . in jail or facing charges."[64]

Where would it all end? For Pinochet, only death in December 2006 brought relief. But in the wake of his prosecution (and Yugoslavia's surrender of Slobodan

Milosevic to The Hague shortly thereafter), a certain vulnerability now attended dictators and their henchmen worldwide.[65] Former Peruvian president Alberto Fujimori was repatriated from Chile, put on trial, and convicted in April 2009 of kidnapping and murder for death-squad massacres and "disappearances" of leftist opponents. He was "sentenced to 25 years in what was described as a landmark ruling for human rights cases in Latin America."[66] And fewer of those ensconced in power felt secure after the Yugoslavia tribunal (ICTY) indicted Slobodan Milosevic for crimes in Kosovo in 1999 (and secured his extradition), or when the International Criminal Court followed by indicting Sudanese president Omar al-Bashir for crimes against humanity in Darfur in March 2009.

Even for those who did not face courts or formal indictments, travel arrangements were disrupted. Cuban President Fidel Castro allegedly "cancelled at least two trips out of Cuba, apparently fearing he could be arrested on US criminal charges." The former chief of Ethiopia's Dergue regime, Mengistu Haile Mariam, "faced an arrest threat in South Africa while receiving medical treatment there, causing him to return to safer exile in Zimbabwe."[67] Alleged architects of Israeli atrocities against Palestinians cancelled trips to the United Kingdom for fear of detention and arrest under universal jurisdiction provisions.[68] Not even the policy elite of the world's leading democracy was safe from such challenges. In March 2009, none other than Baltasar Garzón, "the crusading investigative judge who ordered the arrest of the former Chilean dictator Augusto Pinochet," moved to open an investigation of "six former high-level Bush administration officials" accused of "violat[ing] international law by providing the legal framework to justify the torture of prisoners at Guantánamo Bay, Cuba . . ." Those named included former attorney general Alberto R. Gonzales, and various legal specialists who had bent the law to permit the torture of prisoners in US custody.[69] This, however, was a step too far for Spain's attorney general. He promptly moved to squelch the investigation, cautioning that US courts were the appropriate venue for such charges, and Spain's should not become "a plaything" for political agendas.[70] The veto was widely seen to mark a cresting of the universal-jurisdiction movement that Spain, and Garzón, had done so much to spearhead. But as with legal-humanitarian interventions more generally, the slackening could well be only temporary.

THE INTERNATIONAL CRIMINAL COURT (ICC)

> Implicit within the logic of the term "crime against humanity" is the need for an international court.
>
> David Hirsh

The concept of a permanent international tribunal for war crimes and crimes against humanity is a venerable one. According to legal scholar William Schabas, Gustav Moynier of the Red Cross outlined an early plan in the 1870s.[71] But for most of the twentieth century, the one court with a claim to global jurisdiction – the International Court of Justice (ICJ) at The Hague, also known as the World Court – was limited mostly to territorial claims and resource disputes. When Nicaragua launched proceedings against the US in the 1980s for acts of material sabotage and support for *contra* rebels, the US at first argued that the ICJ lacked jurisdiction. When the ICJ begged to differ, the US withdrew from the proceedings and refused to abide by any judgment against it. The ICJ ruled in Nicaragua's favor, but was impotent to enforce its decision. "A court with teeth" in the humanitarian and human rights arena existed only in the Western European regional context: the European Court of Justice's decisions are binding on all European Union members. However, the mounting impetus for a global prohibition regime against genocide, war crimes, and crimes against humanity led, in 1994, to the UN drafting a statute for a legal body along the lines of the Yugoslavia tribunal, but with global jurisdiction. A final version was agreed in Rome, with the "Rome Statute" passed on July 17, 1998. In April 2002, sixty-six countries – six more than required – voted to adopt the Statute, and it entered formally into force. By early 2010, 108 "state parties" had ratified it in their national legislatures. Eighteen judges, including seven women, were appointed, and Luis Moreno Ocampo was selected as the first independent prosecutor. Notably, Moreno Ocampo first came to prominence through his prosecution of former *junta* leaders in Argentina.

The court was envisaged as an adjunct to legal proceedings at the national level. Only when national mechanisms prove incapable of handling a case can the ICC come into play. Individuals from states who are not signatories to the Rome Statute may still be tried, though only if referred to the Court by a signatory state. In general, ICC proceedings are to be activated only by a request from a member state, though some loopholes do exist. The independent prosecutor can initiate investigations on his or her own (*proprio motu*), while the UN Security Council may command the prosecutor to apply the court's jurisdiction even if s/he is reluctant to do so. A Pre-Trial Chamber will then issue warrants for the arrest of indicted individuals (it is individuals, not states or other entities, that are the focus of the ICC's operations).

The Court's mandate extends to genocide, war crimes, crimes of "aggression," and crimes against humanity. The definition of "genocide" adopted by the ICC is identical to that of the UN Convention. Worth noting also is the emphasis on "crimes against humanity" in the Rome Statute. As we saw above (Box 15.1), this category of crimes overlaps with the Genocide Convention in some measure, and is likely – for practical and conceptual reasons – to figure more prominently than genocide in future legal prosecutions.

Despite the broad international consensus behind the ICC, many governments, including the US, have shied from it. The Clinton government signed the Rome Statute in the knowledge that it was unlikely to be ratified by Congress.[72] The issue of universal jurisdiction, along with the semi-independent role of the prosecutor, were key sticking points. In May 2002, the Bush administration renounced the treaty, and declared that it would not tolerate the detention or trial of any US national by the ICC. Later the same year, Bush signed into law the "American Servicemembers Protection Act," authorizing the US president "to use all means . . . necessary to bring about the release of covered US persons and covered allied persons held captive by or on behalf of the [ICC]."[73] Wags referred to this as the "Invade the Hague Act," conjuring images of US troops descending on Dutch detention centers to free Americans accused of abuses and atrocities. The tone was certainly eased by Barack

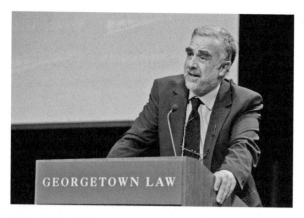

Figure 15.4   Luis Moreno Ocampo, former scourge of Argentine war criminals, appointed in 2003 as the first prosecutor of the International Criminal Court (ICC). Ocampo is shown speaking at Georgetown University in Washington, DC, in April 2008.

Source: Ralph Alswang/Center for American Progress.

Figure 15.5   The ICC building in The Hague, Netherlands.

Source: Hanhil/Nederlandstalige Wikipedia.

Obama's succession in 2009, but the new civility did not extend to the US actually becoming a state party to the court.

The ICC is "the body that may ultimately play the greatest role in interpreting the prohibition against genocide."[74] To this point, though, "its power as part of the atrocities [prohibition] regime remains contested and indefinite."[75] Its broad mandate and intended permanence bode well, as does its popularity in most countries of the world. On the other hand, concessions made to placate US and other concerns (including an opt-out clause lasting seven years) provoked concern that the ICC might become just another toothless legal body.

Since the first edition of this book was published, the Court has launched investigations into Congo, Darfur, the Central African Republic, and Northern Uganda, issued a dozen indictments (four of the accused were in custody), and tried its first case – against a Congolese militia chief, Thomas Lubanga, accused of conscripting child soldiers.[76] Whether and when the ICC's purview would extend beyond these important but politically "safe" African cases remained uncertain as this edition was prepared.[77]

INTERNATIONAL CITIZENS' TRIBUNALS

Often called "international people's tribunals," these bodies substitute accusations and public shaming for due process and enforcement. The formation of a citizens' tribunal implies that regular means of justice are inadequate – corrupt or compromised. "The people" – certain interested people – seize the initiative and stage a quasi-trial. This may publicize atrocities, raise public consciousness, or shatter taboos, for example about Western state involvement. (It is usually Western democracies that are both hosts and subjects of the proceedings.) Tribunals can place vital evidence on the public record, and point to gaps between legislation and its application, highlighting the immunity often extended to sovereign states and their representatives.

Citizens' tribunals received a rare comparative analysis in a book by political scientists Arthur and Judith Klinghoffer.[78] The authors pointed out that, in many ways, the most remarkable and successful citizens' tribunal was the first. In February 1933, the month after Adolf Hitler came to power, the Reichstag Parliament building in Berlin was burned down. Three foreign and one German communist, along with the Dutchman Marinus van der Lubbe, were charged with the crime. The Nazis seized on the fire to declare a state of emergency, suspend the Weimar Constitution, and begin their mass round-ups of communist suspects (Box 6a). Fearing that the German courts were too cowed to try the matter fairly, various public intellectuals, along with prominent socialists and communists, convened "The Commission of Inquiry into the Origins of the Reichstag Fire" in London in September 1933. Held a week before official proceedings were due to get underway in Germany, the tribunal pulled the rug out from under the Nazis' planned show-trial. Placed in the hot seat by international media attention, a court in Leipzig convicted only van der Lubbe (he was subsequently executed). The four communists were acquitted. "The first international citizens' tribunal had taken on Nazi Germany, and had won," wrote Arthur Klinghoffer. "Intellectuals had confronted a totalitarian state, and had successfully used public opinion as a weapon to further their cause."[79]

Four years later, supporters of exiled Russian communist Leon Trotsky organized a citizens' tribunal at his new (and final) home in Coyoacán, a Mexico City suburb. The intent of the Dewey Commission, chaired by the eponymous philosopher, was to denounce Soviet show-trials and accusations against Trotsky. The tribunal achieved some success in countering Stalinist propaganda, although its geographic remove from centers of Western public opinion limited its impact.

Much more visible was the International War Crimes Tribunal to judge US actions in the Vietnam War in 1967, known as the Russell Tribunal. Delegates voted unanimously that US actions did constitute genocide against the Vietnamese and other Indochinese peoples (for more on the US war in Vietnam, and these findings, see Chapter 2). According to Ann Curthoys and John Docker, "the Tribunal made a significant and eventually influential contribution to debates over the morality and conduct of the war in Vietnam."[80] However, "this decision on genocide had little impact on the American public and was generally viewed by the press as verbal excess."[81]

Since the 1970s, tribunals have publicized the restitution claims of indigenous peoples; the Japanese "comfort women" issue; Western wars and sanctions against Iraq;[82] and the social damage associated with neoliberal economic measures imposed by the First World on the Third. As these examples suggest, "In essence, tribunals have become a weapon of the radical left in its battle with 'global capitalism.'"[83]

It has been argued that "these tribunals do make some contribution to the pathetically limited possibilities of action for the punishment of genocide."[84] However, many observers consider them to be kangaroo courts: their "investigations sometimes seem perfunctory, and the verdict seems preordained," in Leo Kuper's words.[85] Richard Falk referred to the Russell Tribunal as "a juridical farce."[86] Law Professor Peter Burns likewise argued that "the desired conclusion[s]" of such tribunals are "inextricably woven into the accusations and process itself." He considered them "a form of overt morality play, relying upon polemic and theatre to achieve results that may be desirable ethically, but may or may not be desirable legally."[87]

TRUTH AND RECONCILIATION

Like *gacaca* in Rwanda, truth and reconciliation commissions are driven by a vision of restorative justice that "seeks repair of social connections and peace rather than retribution against the offenders." As such, these commissions have become the preferred option for societies (or at least their decision-makers) who wish to avoid arduous and possibly destabilizing trials. For victims, such commissions provide a forum, perhaps the first they have had, for speaking of the horrors inflicted upon them or upon those whom they loved. Ideally, the result is *catharsis* – in this context, the mastering of one's pain through its articulation. "By confronting the past, the traumatized individuals can learn to distinguish past, present, and future. When the work of knowing and telling the story has come to an end, the trauma then belongs to the past; the survivor can face the work of building a future."[88] Validation may also lie in having one's testimony heard, corroborated, and integrated into a commission's published findings. A degree of moral order is restored to the world when one's suffering is taken seriously, and its perpetrators viewed with obloquy. (Truth-telling may also have a darker side, however, considered below.)

Key questions for truth commissions include the following. *How long will the commission operate for?* The general trend is from a few months to a couple of years. *Who will fund it?* Significant resources may be available domestically, as in South Africa. In other cases foreign funding is crucial, and in a pair of instances the UN has played a formative role (El Salvador) or a prominent one (Guatemala). *Who will staff the commission?* The emphasis has been on prominent public figures from the country in question, widely seen as fair-minded and compassionate. *Will the commission examine alleged abuses by all sides in a given conflict, or one side only?* The strong tendency has been towards examining all sides' conduct, since this greatly bolsters the credibility of the commission's procedures and final report. *Will the commission have the power to dispense justice and grant amnesty?* Justice, no; and only South Africa's commission could grant amnesty to those who confessed before it.

In conducting its operations, *how will the commission elicit testimony?* Sessions may be held in public or behind closed doors. Anonymous testimony might be permitted, especially in the case of sexual crimes. *What standard of evidence will be required to draw publishable conclusions?* According to Hayner, the trend is towards "the 'balance of probabilities' standard for basic conclusions of fact. This . . . suggests that there is more evidence to support than to deny a conclusion, or that something is more likely to be true than not based on the evidence before the commission."[89] *Will the commission's report include prescriptions and recommendations?* In general, yes. Special attention is often paid to reforming the state security forces. Commissions may also provide critical documentation for subsequent criminal trials. *Will the commission name names?* More rarely.[90] There is a delicate balance to be struck between holding individuals accountable while risking (1) overturning the applecart of a delicate political transition, or (2) provoking threats and acts of violence against witnesses and commission staff. The UN-sponsored commission in El Salvador *did* name names, despite intense opposition from the Salvadoran government and military. The Guatemalan commission, by contrast, chose not to, though it left no doubt that state agents had committed the overwhelming majority of the atrocities (see Box 3a).

Will truth commissions consider the roles of foreign actors? Generally not, though when such investigations *are* conducted, they may be revelatory. The 1992 report of the Chad truth commission, for example, produced a hard-hitting assessment of US aid to the goons of the Habré regime. The US also came under close scrutiny by the Guatemalan Commission for Historical Clarification. The commission obtained extensive documentation of the US role in overthrowing a democratic government in Guatemala (1954), then installing and sustaining the military dictators who eventually turned to full-scale genocide against Mayan Indians and domestic dissenters.

However, "most truth commissions have not investigated this international role at any depth; few have addressed the issue at all in their final report."[91] This reflects material and evidentiary constraints, as well as the complexity of some international involvements. (One balks at assessing the international dimension of the Congo conflict, for example, if a truth commission is ever struck with this mandate.) Sometimes the reluctance may derive from practical considerations. Many truth commissions, as noted, rely on international financial support – frequently from the United States.

Truth commissions resemble citizens' tribunals in compensating for a lack of "teeth" in their deliberations by creating ripples in the public sphere. In the commissions' case, this can produce a kind of quasi-legal sanction against offenders. Some of those named by commissions may avoid foreign travel, fearing arrest. At a more informal level, Hayner has vividly described the treatment accorded to leaders and high-profile agents of the former *junta* in Argentina. Many were never formally tried; some were jailed but released under an amnesty. Nevertheless, the revelation of their deeds, primarily through the Argentine truth commission and its *Nunca Más* report, carried lasting consequences for these individuals. "Whenever they venture into the streets or public places, [Generals] Videla, Massera, Camps, and several others have experienced spontaneous though nonviolent acts of repudiation: waiters refuse to serve them, other patrons leave the place or sit far away from them, some actually defy their bodyguards and confront them with the opinion that most Argentines have of them."[92]

A question remains: Is the truth always desirable? In personal terms, truth-telling about atrocity is often deeply traumatizing for the teller. Yael Fischman and Jaime Ross describe the "recurring themes" of torture survivors in therapy:

fear of destroying others, such as relatives and therapists, by relating the trauma; fear of loss of control over feelings of rage, violence, and anxiety; shame and rage over the vulnerability and helplessness evoked by torture; rage and grief at the sudden and arbitrary disruption of individual, social, and political projects, and at the violation of rights; guilt and shame over surviving and being unable to save others; guilt over bringing distress on self and family and over not protecting them . . . fear and rage at the unpredictability of and lack of control over events; grief over the loss of significant others, through both death and exile; and loss of aspects of the self, such as trust and innocence.[93]

Outside a formal therapeutic environment, though, almost no mechanism to elicit truth-telling – be it a truth commission, a human rights investigator, or a journalist – provides meaningful follow-up to traumatized survivors. Truth-divulging may also be "dangerous and destabilizing" on a national level, according to Hayner, "disrupt[ing] fragile relationships in local communities recently returned to peace."[94] She cited Mozambique, where "people across the political spectrum, including victims, academics, government officials and others . . . said, 'No, we do not want to reenter into this morass of conflict, hatred, and pain. We want to focus on the future. . . . We prefer silence over confrontation, over renewed pain. While we cannot forget, we would like to pretend that we can.'"[95]

These attitudes were not ostrich-like. Rather, they signaled a process of peace and reconciliation that had come about "remarkably quickly" in Mozambique, many observers describing it "with a sense of wonder." From the day a peace agreement was signed ending one of Africa's most brutal twentieth-century wars, "the former warring enemies have lived in peace virtually without incident." Rituals of purification and reconciliation were performed at the village level, beyond the reach of state initiatives.[96] "We were all thinking about how to increase peace and reconciliation," said one Mozambican official, "but when we came to the grassroots, they were reconciling already. Our ideas were only confusing and stirring up trouble."[97] In 2009, Malangatana Ngwenya, a renowned Mozambican poet and artist who lost many members of his family in the war, told the UK *Guardian*: "If we had had a truth commission, it would just have caused tension. I don't want to know who killed my family. It would be stupid to know. And even if by chance I learned who took my brother's life, I wouldn't waste time on starting to hate."[98]

A similar reconciliation process prevailed in East Timor following the final expulsion of Indonesian forces from the territory in 1999 (Box 7a). While the Indonesian architects of genocide in East Timor enjoyed immunity in their homeland, the quarter-century-long occupation also drew many Timorese onto the Indonesian side as collaborators. For those accused of "nonserious crimes," the post-independence Timorese authorities sponsored a community reconciliation program (PRK) described by anthropologist Elizabeth F. Drexler:

Individuals wishing to be reconciled with particular communities (deponents) submitted statements of nonserious crimes. These statements were reviewed by the deputy general prosecutor for serious crimes to establish that the deponent applying for reconciliation was not sought on other charges of more serious crimes. In the community hearings deponents testified to their actions, often emphasizing their lack of power or control in an overall system of intimidation and forced participation in the campaign of terror orchestrated by infamous militia leaders who remained just over the border in Indonesia. Community members in attendance had the opportunity to question what happened, often producing responses that attributed culpability to other militia members who remain in West Timor. . . . Most communities agreed to accept the deponent and promised to no longer ostracize him or her after the symbolic act of reconciliation was fulfilled (e.g., cleaning the church). Thus in community reconciliation hearings, testimony had immediate effects, and the community was bound to act as if the narrative given were true.

While "some victims . . . criticized the process because they felt pressured to accept statements from the perpetrator that were not as complete or remorseful as they had hoped," the program has nonetheless "been celebrated as a major innovation," according to Drexler.[99]

THE CHALLENGE OF REDRESS

- *Israel/Germany, December 2009.* The Israeli press reports that Israel will formally press Germany for half a billion to a billion euros in further compensation for Jews used as slave labor during World War Two. German Finance Minister Yuval Steinitz was scheduled to "present German government with the demand on behalf of 30,000 Israeli survivors of forced labor in wartime ghettos, during a joint session scheduled to take place in early 2010 in Berlin." The initiative to renegotiate the 1950s agreement between Germany and Israel, under which successive German governments paid tens of billions of dollars in reparations to the Israeli state on behalf of the Jewish people, followed a successful campaign against banks and other business enterprises, in Switzerland and elsewhere, for claims derived from Jewish capital deposits and hyperexploited labor. But it also followed the September 2009 rejection by Germany's highest court of a claim to return "land seized by the Nazis from its Jewish owner in 1933. . . . The Nazis later sold the homes to their occupants, who are now the owners."[100]
- *Providence, Rhode Island, USA, May 2009.* A commission created by the Steering Committee on Slavery and Justice at Brown University, a member of the US's privileged Ivy League, announces it will erect a memorial to educate the community "about how slavery was intertwined with the University's early benefactors." Rhode Island "was the heart of the American slave trade," with "more than 110,000 enslaved Africans" transiting the city en route to New World plantations. "Brown University, for its part, was financed in part with donations from John and Moses Brown, who were the most prominent Providence slave traders, as well as other Rhode Island slave traders and southern plantation owners. Slaves also helped to construct the first building on the campus, now known as University Hall." In the 2000s, Brown University took a lead in engaging with its slaving heritage. Responding to earlier recommendations by the Steering Committee, it "created a $10-million target for an endowment for Providence Public Schools," among other measures designed to improve educational opportunities for slavery's

descendants. In the wake of the university's decision to replace "Columbus Day" celebrations with a "Fall Weekend" – since Columbus was an early slaver – calls were even heard to rename the university itself.[101]

- *United Kingdom/Australia, September 2009.* The skull and jawbone of two aboriginal individuals, held by the Royal College of Surgeons in London and National Museums Scotland, arrive home in Tasmania to an indigenous ritual "to welcome the remains and their spirits back to their country" after an exile approaching two centuries. One set of remains was acquired by a Christian missionary around 1830. "National Museums Scotland believes it acquired its skull about 1823, but has no further information other than that it came from Tasmania. 'That usually means the remains were grave-robbed,' the Tasmanian Aboriginal Centre's Sara Maynard said. 'In such cases the grave robber rarely provided detailed documentation.'" The Royal College of Surgeons had earlier unearthed five other jawbones of aborigines in its collection, and returned them in 2002. "Since 1996, more than 1000 indigenous remains have been brought back to Australia," but "more than 1000 are still held in museums worldwide." The Tasmanian Aboriginal Centre calls for legislation to ensure "that all Aboriginal remains in British institutions are returned to Australia."[102]

These three vignettes bear upon the central issue of *redress* for past atrocities. The *Concise Oxford Dictionary* defines redress as to "set right, remedy, make up for, get rid of, rectify . . . [a] distress, wrong, damage, grievance, [or] abuse." Political scientist Colin Tatz, summarizing the arguments of Mari Matsuda, cited "five prerequisites for a meritorious claim for redress: a 'human injustice' must have been committed; it must be well-documented; the victims must be identifiable as a distinct group; the current members of the group must continue to suffer harm; and such harm must be causally connected to the past injustice."[103]

Forms of redress are numerous, and sometimes amorphous. Penalties imposed by official tribunals, such as the ICTR and ICTY, certainly qualify, as do the decisions of less formal processes (such as *gacaca* in Rwanda). The healing that ideally accompanies truth commissions and formal acts of reconciliation may also constitute redress. Compensation is a regular feature: it can take the form of monetary payments (as in the Israeli–German case), territorial agreements, restitution of property or cultural objects (like aboriginal remains), profits from exploitation of natural resources, and affirmative action policies in public and private sector employment (such as in South Africa after 1994).

A critical role may be played by formal *apologies*. Martha Minow emphasized "the communal nature of the process of apologizing," which "requires communication between a wrongdoer and a victim. . . . The methods for offering and accepting an apology both reflect and help to constitute a moral community."[104] Memorable apologies include:

- German Chancellor Willi Brandt's *Kniefall* (kneeling apology) at a Polish war memorial in 1970.
- Queen Elizabeth's 1995 *mea culpa* to New Zealand Maoris for British violation of the Waitingi Treaty of 1840: "The Crown expresses its profound regret

and apologizes unreservedly for the loss of lives because of hostilities arising from this invasion and at the devastation of property and social life which resulted."[105]

- The annual "Sorry Day," instituted by white Australians after the publication of *Bringing Them Home*, the report of the Aboriginal and Torres Strait Islander Commission (Chapter 3).[106]
- President Bill Clinton's 1998 half-apology at Kigali airport for Western inaction during the genocide in Rwanda.[107]
- The 2004 statement by Heidemarie Wieczorek-Zeul, Germany's development aid minister, to Namibian Hereros for "atrocities . . . [that] would have been termed genocide" (see Chapter 3).
- Australian prime minister Kevin Rudd's February 2008 apology, "without qualification" and as his government's first act of parliament, for the forcible transfer of Australian aboriginals to white-run institutions that sought to extirpate the native culture from their hearts and minds. Rudd apologized "to the mothers, the fathers, the brothers, the sisters, the families and the communities whose lives were ripped apart by the actions of successive governments under successive parliaments" (see Chapter 3).[108]
- The apologies by the US Congress and Senate – which still awaited a harmonized wording and final approval after the Senate vote of June 2009 – to African Americans for the institution of slavery, and the "Jim Crow" apartheid measures that followed its formal repeal. The Senate wording, which passed unanimously, "acknowledges the fundamental injustice, cruelty, brutality, and inhumanity of slavery and Jim Crow laws" and "apologizes to African-Americans on behalf of the people of the United States." However, the Senate tacked on a disclaimer that "Nothing in this resolution authorizes or supports any claim [for compensation/restitution] against the United States."[109]

Perhaps the most unusual of the recent welter of apologies was Denmark's to Ireland. On an August 2007 visit to Ireland, Danish culture minister Brian Mikkelson expressed remorse for brutal Viking raids in Ireland, "pillaging monasteries and massacring inhabitants" – some 1,200 years ago! ". . . We are not proud of the damages to the people of Ireland that followed in the footsteps of the Vikings," Mikkelson told his hosts. "But the warmth and friendliness with which you greet us today . . . show us that, luckily, it has all been forgiven."[110]

One can question whether genuine issues of reparation and restitution arise in the Viking case. With regard to more recent atrocities, however, there remains a danger that apology may serve as a cheap substitute for meaningful redress. Does it not "merely whitewash the injustice?" wondered Elazar Barkan.[111] In the wake of Kevin Rudd's historic apology to the "Stolen Generations," Tony Barta also inquired whether the terms of the *mea culpa* in fact served to "bur[y] a history of genocide."[112]

However, apologies may also serve as the *entrée* to significant material compensation and institutional transformation. A US congressional apology to Japanese Americans for their internment during the Second World War came as part of a Civil Liberties Act, under which the US government paid out 80,000 claims worth $1.6 billion, in addition to opening a Japanese American National Museum in Los

Angeles. Queen Elizabeth's declaration to the Maoris was accompanied by a substantial land settlement and the granting of extensive fishing rights. Profits from these sources "within a few years . . . became a significant source of Maori income."[113] In Canada, a Royal Commission on Aboriginal Peoples acknowledged in 1996 that "great wrongs have been done" to Native Indians. This half-apology was followed by the allotting of hundreds of millions of dollars "to community-based healing initiatives for victims" of the residential school system (see Chapter 3); the designation of Indians as "first nations" (as in the US); and the creation in April 1999 of a new territory, Nunavut, for northern Inuit peoples, with a concomitant share of profits from the land's abundant natural resources (see p. 593).[114]

By contrast, a failure or refusal to apologize usually signifies intransigence toward material and institutional forms of redress. Notable *non*-apologies of recent times include Turkey's for the genocides of Christian minorities during World War One; Central European countries' for the mass expulsion of ethnic Germans at the end of the Second World War and after; and Israel's for the "ethnic cleansing of Palestine" in 1947–48.[115] Nonetheless, the apologetic trend prevails, suggesting a strengthening of the humanitarian regime first forged in the mid-nineteenth century.

FURTHER STUDY

Hannah Arendt, *Eichmann in Jerusalem: A Report on the Banality of Evil*. New York: The Viking Press, 1965. Arendt's controversial account of the trial in Israel of Adolf Eichmann, the ultimate bureaucratic killer.

Elazar Barkan, *The Guilt of Nations: Restitution and Negotiating Historical Injustices*. New York: W.W. Norton, 2001. Wide-ranging overview of contemporary forms of redress.

Roy Gutman and David Rieff, *Crimes of War: What the Public Should Know*. New York: W.W. Norton, 1999. Richly (sometimes disturbingly) illustrated encyclopedia.

Priscilla B. Hayner, *Unspeakable Truths: Confronting State Terror and Atrocity*. New York: Routledge, 2001. Energetic insider account of truth commissions.

L.J. van den Herik, *The Contribution of the Rwanda Tribunal to the Development of International Law*. Leiden: Martinus Nijhoff, 2005. Overview of the ICTR's shaping of the law of genocide and crimes against humanity.

David Hirsh, *Law against Genocide: Cosmopolitan Trials*. London: Glasshouse Press, 2003. Focuses on four recent trials related to genocide and crimes against humanity.

Michael J. Kelly, *Nowhere to Hide: Defeat of the Sovereign Immunity Defense for Crimes of Genocide and the Trials of Slobodan Milosevic and Saddam Hussein*. New York: Peter Lang, 2005. How the immunity previously granted to leaders of sovereign states eroded in the twentieth and twenty-first centuries.

Antjie Krog, *Country of My Skull: Guilt, Sorrow, and the Limits of Forgiveness in the New South Africa*. New York: Three Rivers Press, 2000. Searing study of the truth and reconciliation process after apartheid.

Martha Minow, *Between Vengeance and Forgiveness: Facing History after Genocide and Mass Violence*. Boston, MA: Beacon Press, 1998. A good introduction to issues of truth and redress.

Nunca Más: The Report of the Argentine National Commission on the Disappeared. New York: Farrar Straus Giroux, 1986; Spanish version online at http://www.nuncamas.org/index.htm; English version at http://web.archive.org/web/2003 1004074316/nuncamas.org/english/library/nevagain/nevagain_001.htm. The groundbreaking investigation of crimes committed by the Argentine military *junta* (1976–83).

Steven R. Ratner and Jason S. Abrams, *Accountability for Human Rights Atrocities in International Law: Beyond the Nuremberg Legacy* (2nd edn). Oxford: Oxford University Press, 2001. Best read alongside Schabas (see below), with a useful Cambodia case study.

W. Michael Reisman and Chris T. Antoniou, eds, *The Laws of War: A Comprehensive Collection of Primary Documents on International Laws Governing Armed Conflict*. New York: Vintage, 1994. Core texts with commentary.

Antonius C.G.M. Robben, *Political Violence and Trauma in Argentina*. Philadelphia, PA: University of Pennsylvania Press, 2005. Examination of the military dictatorship in Argentina (1976–83) and its impact on society.

Geoffrey Robertson, *Crimes against Humanity: The Struggle for Global Justice* (3rd edn). New York: The New Press, 2007. Thin on genocide, but elegantly written and bracingly opinionated.

William A. Schabas, *Genocide in International Law: The Crime of Crimes* (2nd edn). Cambridge: Cambridge University Press, 2009. Comprehensive and massively detailed; an indispensable reference work.

Sarah B. Sewall and Carl Kaysen, eds, *The United States and the International Criminal Court: National Security and International Law*. Lanham, MD: Rowman & Littlefield, 2000. Essays analyzing the ICC initiative in historical context.

Adam M. Smith, *After Genocide: Bringing the Devil to Justice*. Amherst, NY: Prometheus Books, 2009. Wide-ranging portrait of the accomplishments and travails of the international search for justice.

Eric Stover and Harvey M. Weinstein, eds, *My Neighbor, My Enemy: Justice and Community in the Aftermath of Mass Atrocity*. Cambridge: Cambridge University Press, 2004. Now-classic collection of essays with a grassroots emphasis and expertise, focusing on the Bosnian and Rwandan cases.

NOTES

1   William A. Schabas, *Genocide in International Law: The Crime of Crimes* (Cambridge: Cambridge University Press, 2000), p. 354. Some examples of crimes that command universal jurisdiction are "hijacking and other threats to air travel, piracy, attacks upon diplomats, [threats to] nuclear safety, terrorism, *apartheid* and torture."

2   Ibid., p. 341.

3   Gladstone quoted in Gary Jonathan Bass, *Stay the Hand of Vengeance: The Politics of War Crimes Tribunals* (Princeton, NJ: Princeton University Press, 2000), p. 33; emphasis added.

4   The official names of the tribunals were the International Military Tribunal (Nuremberg, created in August 1945) and the International Military Tribunal for the Far East (Tokyo, created in January 1946). For more on the tribunals, see Joseph E. Persico, *Nuremberg: Infamy on Trial* (London: Penguin, 1995), and Arnold C. Brackman, *The Other Nuremberg: The Untold Story of the Tokyo War Crimes Trials* (New York: William Morrow, 1987).

5   See Richard Overy, "Making Justice at Nuremberg, 1945–1946," http://www.bbc.co.uk/history/worldwars/wwtwo/war_crimes_trials_01.shtml.

6   Samantha Power, *"A Problem from Hell": America and the Age of Genocide* (New York: Basic Books, 2002), p. 50 (quoting the Nuremberg indictments). Although their trials received far less public attention than did those of the top Nazi leaders, Nuremberg also tried members of the *Einsatzgruppen* killing squads who rampaged through Polish and Soviet territories in 1941–42. These defendants "had been *directly* involved in the supervision and implementation of mass murder, war crimes, and genocide. Of the twenty-four accused, twenty-two were convicted. Among those, two commanders, ten leaders, and two officers were sentenced to death by hanging. One commander and one leader were sentenced to life imprisonment. The remaining six defendants were given lesser sentences." James Waller, *Becoming Evil: How Ordinary People Commit Genocide and Mass Killing*, 2nd edn (Oxford: Oxford University Press, 2007), p. 96.

7   "Genocide was mentioned at Nuremberg, but was not included in the charges against the defendants and was not an operative legal concept." Arthur Jay Klinghoffer and Judith Klinghoffer, *International Citizens' Tribunals: Mobilizing Public Opinion to Advance Human Rights* (New York: Palgrave, 2002), p. 195 (n. 5).

8   Steven R. Ratner and Jason S. Abrams, *Accountability for Human Rights Atrocities in International Law: Beyond the Nuremberg Legacy* (2nd edn) (Oxford: Oxford University Press, 2001), p. 22. Martha Minow points out that "no prior law made it clear that individuals could be charged with the crime of waging aggressive war; the same held true for crimes against humanity, including murder, extermination, enslavement, and persecution on the basis of views or identities." Minow, *Between Vengeance and Forgiveness: Facing History after Genocide and Mass Violence* (Boston, MA: Beacon Press, 1998), p. 33.

9   Geoffrey Robertson, *Crimes against Humanity: The Struggle for Global Justice* (New York: The New Press, 2000), p. 224.

10 David Hirsh, *Law against Genocide: Cosmopolitan Trials* (London: Glasshouse Press, 2003), p. 42.

11 Robertson, *Crimes against Humanity*, p. 222.

12 Hirsh, *Law against Genocide*, p. xvi.

13 Bullock quoted in Richard J. Goldstone and Gary Jonathan Bass, "Lessons from the International Criminal Tribunals," in Sarah B. Sewall and Carl Kaysen, eds, *The United States and the International Criminal Court: National Security and International Law* (Lanham, MD: Rowman & Littlefield, 2000), p. 54.

14 Bass wrote that the ICTY "was an act of tokenism by the world community, which was largely unwilling to intervene in ex-Yugoslavia but did not mind creating an institution that would give the *appearance* of moral concern." Bass, *Stay the Hand of Vengeance*, p. 214.

15 Louis Sell, *Slobodan Milosevic and the Destruction of Yugoslavia* (Durham, NC: Duke University Press, 2002), p. 361.

16 By the end of 2009, the ICTY had passed 92 judgments (listed at http://www.icty.org/sid/10095), far more than the ICTR. Fifteen cases were in process; only two accused were still at large, including Ratko Mladic, supervisor of the Srebrenica slaughter in 1995.

17 For a nuanced examination, see David Bruce MacDonald, "The Fire in 1999? The United States, NATO and the Bombing of Yugoslavia," ch. 16 in Adam Jones, ed., *Genocide, War Crimes and the West: History and Complicity* (London: Zed Books, 2004), pp. 276–98.

18 Rory Carroll, "Genocide Tribunal 'Ignoring Tutsi Crimes,'" *The Guardian*, January 13, 2005. "A former prosecutor, Carla del Ponte, promised to charge members of the RPF [the Tutsi-led Rwandan Patriotic Front] but before doing so she was removed from her post by a unanimous vote in the UN security council in August 2003. Her successor, Hassan Bubacar Jallow, showed no such zeal."

19 See Minow, *Between Vengeance and Forgiveness*, p. 41. As of April 2004, the ICTR had completed nine cases (including appeal stages) with twelve cases being tried or pending appeal. Ten defendants were "sentenced to life imprisonment, three were acquitted, while the rest received different jail terms ranging from 10 to 35 years. Out of the 12 cases pending appeal, two of them have been acquitted at the trial stage." Twenty-three defendants were in custody awaiting trial. Fondation Hirondelle, "ICTR/Genocide/ Commemoration – Basic Facts on the ICTR," http://www.hirondelle.org/hirondelle. nsf/0/d5df8df93c71b8aac1256e69004c22ce?OpenDocument.

20 Gérard Prunier, *Africa's World War: Congo, the Rwandan Genocide, and the Making of a Continental Catastrophe* (New York: Oxford University Press, 2009), p. 309.

21 Robertson, *Crimes against Humanity*, p. 296; emphasis added.

22 Christopher Rudolph, "Constructing an Atrocities Regime: The Politics of War Crimes Tribunals," *International Organization*, 55: 3 (2001), p. 667.

23 Yusuf Aksar, "The 'Victimized Group' Concept in the Genocide Convention and the Development of International Humanitarian Law through the Practice of Ad Hoc Tribunals," *Journal of Genocide Research*, 5: 2 (2003), p. 217; emphasis added.

24 Ratner and Abrams, *Accountability for Human Rights Atrocities*, p. 201.

25 Schabas, *Genocide in International Law*, p. 384.

26 Ibid., p. 174.

27 Nicholas A. Jones, *The Courts of Genocide: Politics and the Rule of Law in Rwanda and Arusha* (London: Routledge, 2010), p. 143.

28 See, e.g., Susan Brownmiller, *Against Our Will: Men, Women, and Rape* (New York: Bantam, 1975); Alexandra Stiglmayer, ed., *Mass Rape: The War against Women in Bosnia-Herzegovina* (Lincoln, NB: University of Nebraska Press, 1994).

29 On the rape of males in conflict and genocide, see Sandesh Sivakumaran, "Sexual Violence Against Men in Armed Conflict," *The European Journal of International Law*, 18: 2 (2007), pp. 253–76; and Augusta Del Zotto and Adam Jones, "Male-on-male Sexual Violence in Wartime: Human Rights' Last Taboo?," paper presented to the Annual Convention of the International Studies Association (ISA), New Orleans, LA, March 2002, available at http://adamjones.freeservers.com/malerape.htm. For a recent mainstream-media report on the subject, see Jeffrey Gettleman, "Symbol of Unhealed Congo: Male Rape Victims," *The New York Times*, August 4, 2009, http://www. nytimes.com/2009/08/05/world/africa/05congo.html. A truly groundbreaking docu- mentary film on gender-based violence (GBV) against males is "Gender Against Men," produced in 2009 by the Refugee Law Project of Faculty of Law, Makerere University, Kampala, Uganda. It focuses on atrocities against men (including gendercidal killing and rape) in Congo and Uganda. The full 45-minute film can be downloaded from http://www.forcedmigration.org/video/gender-against-men/media.

30 Judge Meron stated: "By seeking to eliminate a part of the Bosnian Muslims, the Bosnian Serb forces committed genocide. They targeted for extinction the 40,000 Bosnian Muslims living in Srebrenica, a group which was emblematic of the Bosnian Muslims in general. They stripped all the male Muslim prisoners, military and civilian, elderly and young, of their personal belongings and identification, and deliberately and methodically killed them solely on the basis of their identity." Ian Traynor, "Hague Rules Srebrenica Was Genocide," *The Guardian*, April 20, 2004, http://www.guardian. co. uk/print/ 0,3858,4905287-103645,00.html.

31 For the full text of the Rome Statute, see http://untreaty.un.org/cod/icc/statute/romefra. htm.

32 See Robert Marquand, "Why Genocide is Difficult to Prosecute," *The Christian Science Monitor*, April 30, 2007, http://www.csmonitor.com/2007/0430/p01s04-wogi.html.

33 L.J. van den Herik has written of the Rwanda tribunal (ICTR) that "an examination of the legal description of crimes against humanity . . . reveals that this crime has been formulated to serve as a kind of safety net in case genocide could not be proved." Van den Herik, *The Contribution of the Rwanda Tribunal to the Development of International Law* (Leiden: Martinus Nijhoff Publishers, 2005), pp. 254–55.

34 Zachary Manfredi, "Implications of the Absence of Genocide Charges for Bashir," *ICC Observers*, March 5, 2009, http://iccobservers.wordpress.com/2009/03/05/icc-observers-commentary-implications-of-the-abscence-of-genocide-charges-for-bashir.

35 As Daniel Jonah Goldhagen argues, "We should use 'genocide' . . . regularly and liberally for mass murders," since "more than any other term, [it] conveys the magnitude of the horror of what perpetrators do to their victims." Goldhagen, *Worse Than War: Genocide, Eliminationism, and the Ongoing Assault on Humanity* (New York: Basic Books, 2009), p. 525.

36 Ratner and Abrams, *Accountability for Human Rights Atrocities*, p. 182.

37 Ibid., p. 175.

38 Robertson, *Crimes against Humanity*, p. 240. As of 2010, however, Demjanjuk was again on trial, having been extradited from the US to Germany to face charges of serving as a prison guard at Sobibor (not Treblinka). See Madeline Chambers, "Nazi Guard Demjanjuk Wheeled into Munich Trial," Reuters dispatch, November 30, 2009.

39 "Eichmann managed to escape [Germany] and flee to Argentina. Eventually abducted by Israeli intelligence agents in Argentina in May 1960, he was brought to Israel to stand trial. He was charged with fifteen counts of crimes against the Jewish people and against humanity, and of war crimes. Eichmann's trial opened on April 11, 1961, and ended on August 14 of the same year. He was found guilty and sentenced to death (Israel allows the death penalty only for crimes of genocide). An appeal of his death sentence was rejected in May 1962. Eichmann was hanged in the Ramla prison on the night of May 31, 1962. His body was cremated and his ashes spread over the sea, outside the territorial waters of Israel." Waller, *Becoming Evil*, p. 99.

40 For a complete list, see Prevent Genocide International, "Declarations and Reservations to the Convention on the Prevention and Punishment of the Crime of Genocide," http://www.preventgenocide.org/law/convention/reservations/.

41 Schabas, *Genocide in International Law*, p. 351 (n. 28).

42 Cited in Tom Fawthrop and Helen Jarvis, *Getting Away with Genocide? Elusive Justice and the Khmer Rouge Tribunal* (London: Pluto Press, 2004), p. 223.

43 Ibid., p. 240.

44 Jörg Menzel, "Justice Delayed or Too Late for Justice? The Khmer Rouge Tribunal and the Cambodian 'Genocide' 1975–79," *Journal of Genocide Research*, 9: 2 (2007), p. 224.

45 See "'Forced Marriage' Conviction a First," IRIN dispatch, February 26, 2009, http://www.irinnews.org/Report.aspx?ReportId=83160. See also the Special Court's website at http://www.sc-sl.org.

46 Lyn S. Graybill, "Ten Years After, Rwanda Tries Reconciliation," *Current History*, May 2004, p. 204.

47 George Packer, "Justice on a Hill," in Nicolaus Mills and Kira Brunner, eds, *The New Killing Fields: Massacre and the Politics of Intervention* (New York: Basic Books, 2002), pp. 133–34.

48 Alana Erin Tiemessen, "After Arusha: Gacaca Justice in Post-Genocide Rwanda," *African Studies Quarterly*, 8: 1 (2004), http://www.africa.ufl.edu/asq/v8/v8i1a4.htm.

49 Jones, *The Courts of Genocide*, p. 69.

50 C. Kayitana quoted in ibid., p. 51.

51 Packer, "Justice on a Hill," p. 135.

52 Anne Aghion's 2009 documentary film, *My Neighbor My Killer* (www.gacacafilms.com), powerfully documents the reintegration process, and provides a useful overview of the *gacaca* process as a whole.

53 "Gacaca Courts Wind Up Proceedings," Hirondelle News Agency dispatch, December 17, 2009, http://www.hirondellenews.com/content/view/13079/309.

54 "Rwanda: Jury Still Out on Effectiveness of 'Gacaca' Courts," IRIN dispatch on *Refworld*, June 23, 2009, http://www.unhcr.org/refworld/publisher,IRIN,,RWA,4a433 cf217,0.html.

55 Allende died in the coup, apparently by his own hand as military forces invaded the Moneda presidential palace.

56 See Helene Zuber, "Spain's 'World Court' May Be Restricted," *Spiegel Online*, June 2, 2009, http://www.spiegel.de/international/world/0,1518,628112,00.html.

57 A technical consideration dictated, however, that Pinochet could be extradited only for crimes committed after Britain's incorporation of extraterritorial torture as a crime under domestic law. Thus, only offenses from the final two years of Pinochet's rule – not the most repressive – could be extraditable.

58 A good investigation of the events, with many key documents, is Diana Woodhouse, *The Pinochet Case: A Legal and Constitutional Analysis* (Oxford: Hart Publishing, 2000).

59 "Ambiguous," because Eichmann's arrest by Israeli agents was technically a violation of Argentine sovereignty (and was protested as such); furthermore, Eichmann was dispatched clandestinely to Israel to stand trial, rather than being formally extradited.

60 Lord Millet quoted in Robertson, *Crimes against Humanity*, p. 395.

61 Ernesto Verdeja also refers to the Pinochet detention as "an example of how international events can redefine domestic political contours," and this was well before the Chilean Supreme Court's declaration that Pinochet was fit to stand trial. Verdeja, "Institutional Responses to Genocide and Mass Atrocity," in Jones, ed., *Genocide, War Crimes and the West*, p. 339.

62 Robertson, *Crimes against Humanity*, p. 400.

63 They were, of course, sometimes put on trial for other things, such as corruption (as with Arnoldo Alemán of Nicaragua and Carlos Andrés Pérez of Venezuela).

64 "Writing the Next Chapter in a Latin American Success Story," *The Economist*, April 2, 2005. In August 2007, the Chilean Supreme Court confirmed a life sentence for Hugo Salas Wenzel, convicted of murdering twelve of Pinochet's opponents; he was "the first such senior military officer to receive a life term for human rights violations." Daniel Schweimler, "Chile Ex-General Jailed for Life," *BBC Online*, August 29, 2007, http://news.bbc.co.uk/2/hi/americas/6967974.stm. Later in the same year, fifteen figures in Pinochet's regime were given sentences ranging from five to eighteen years in jail "for the revenge killings of three dissidents," following a failed assassination attempt on Pinochet in 1986. "Ex-Pinochet Agents Sentenced in Revenge Killings," Associated Press dispatch on CNN.com, December 28, 2007. In April 2008, five senior naval officers were indicted for atrocities committed in the immediate wake of the 1973 military coup: see "Retired Navy Officers Indicted in Chile for Killing, Torture of Priest," Associated Press dispatch in *The Los Angeles Times*, April 19, 2008. It is worth noting, and probably not coincidental, that Michelle Bachelet, Chile's president from 2005 to 2009, was herself a political prisoner under Pinochet.

65 See Marc Weller, "On the Hazards of Foreign Travel for Dictators and Other International Criminals," *International Affairs*, 75: 3 (1999), pp. 599–617.

66 Rory Carroll, "Former Peruvian President Alberto Fujimori Sentenced to 25 Years," *The Guardian*, April 7, 2009, http://www.guardian.co.uk/world/2009/apr/07/alberto-fujimori-peru.

67 John G. Heidenrich, *How to Prevent Genocide: A Guide for Policymakers, Scholars, and the Concerned Citizen* (Westport, CT: Praeger, 2001), p. 67.

68 "In 2005, a retired Israeli general, Doron Almog, returned to Israel after landing in London because he was tipped off that police planned to arrest him. The warrant for Almog – who allegedly oversaw the bombing of a Gaza building in which 14 people were killed – was later cancelled. Other Israeli leaders, including former military chief Moshe Yaalon and ex-Shin Bet security chief Avi Dichter, have cancelled trips to Britain in recent years for the same reason." Ian Black, "Tzipi Livni Arrest Warrant Prompts Israeli Government Travel 'Ban,'" *The Guardian*, December 15, 2009, http://www.guardian.co.uk/world/2009/dec/15/tzipi-livni-arrest-warrant-israeli.

69 Marlise Simons, "Spanish Court Weighs Inquiry on Torture for 6 Bush-Era Officials," *The New York Times*, March 28, 2009, http://www.nytimes.com/2009/03/29/world/europe/29spain.html.

70 Valerie Nichols, "Spain Rejects 'Bush Six' Torture Trial," Atlantic Council, April 16, 2009, http://www.acus.org/new_atlanticist/spain-rejects-bush-six-torture-trial.

71 Schabas, *Genocide in International Law*, pp. 368–69.

72 For a summary of the US position on the Genocide Convention, see Samantha Power, "The United States and Genocide Law: A History of Ambivalence," ch. 10 in Sewall and Kaysen, eds, *The United States and the International Criminal Court*, pp. 165–75.

73 For the complete text of the bill, see http://www.state.gov/t/pm/rls/othr/misc/23425.htm.

74 Alexander K.A. Greenawalt, "Rethinking Genocidal Intent: The Case for a Knowledge-based Interpretation," *Columbia Law Review*, 99 (1999), p. 2269.

75 Rudolph, "Constructing an Atrocities Regime," p. 678.

76 Catherine Philp, "Thomas Lubanga Becomes First to Stand Trial for War Crimes at the ICC," *The Times*, January 26, 2009, http://www.timesonline.co.uk/tol/news/world/africa/article5586688.ece.

77 For an up-close portrait of the court's early operations, see Thomas Darnstädt, Helen Zuber and Jan Puhl, "The International Criminal Court's Dream of Global Justice," *Spiegel Online*, January 14, 2009, http://www.spiegel.de/international/world/0,1518,druck-601258,00.html.

78 Klinghoffer and Klinghoffer, *International Citizens' Tribunals*.

79 Arthur Jay Klinghoffer, "International Citizens' Tribunals on Human Rights," in Jones, ed., *Genocide, War Crimes and the West*, pp. 350–51.

80 Ann Curthoys and John Docker, "Defining Genocide," in Dan Stone, ed., *The Historiography of Genocide* (London: Palgrave Macmillan, 2008), p. 24.

81 Klinghoffer and Klinghoffer, *International Citizens' Tribunals*, p. 156.

82 See, e.g., the "Criminal Complaint" filed by former US Attorney General to the International Court [People's Tribunal] on Crimes Against Humanity Committed by UN Security Council on Iraq held in Spain in November 1996: Jones, ed., *Genocide, War Crimes and the West*, pp. 270–73; and, most recently, "Declaration of the Jury of Conscience – World Tribunal on Iraq," Istanbul, June 23–27, 2005, http://www.wagingpeace.org/articles/2005/06/27_jury-of-conscience-declaration.htm.

83 Klinghoffer and Klinghoffer, *International Citizens' Tribunals*, p. 10.

84 Leo Kuper, *The Prevention of Genocide* (New Haven, CT: Yale University Press, 1985), p. 193.

85 Ibid.

86 Falk quoted in Klinghoffer and Klinghoffer, *International Citizens' Tribunals*, p. 134.

87 Professor Peter Burns of the University of British Columbia, personal communication, May 12, 2005.

88 Minow, *Between Vengeance and Forgiveness*, pp. 60, 67.

89 Priscilla B. Hayner, *Unspeakable Truths: Confronting State Terror and Atrocity* (New York: Routledge, 2001), p. 232.

90 "While most commissions have had the power to name perpetrators, however, only a few have done so: El Salvador, Chad, the second commission of the African National Congress, and the South African Truth and Reconciliation Commission." Hayner, *Unspeakable Truths*, pp. 107–8.

91 Ibid., p. 75.

92 Ibid., p. 111.

93 Fischman and Ross, article on "Group Treatment of Exiled Survivors of Torture," in the *American Journal of Orthopsychiatry*; quoted in Victoria Sanford, *Buried Secrets: Truth and Human Rights in Guatemala* (New York: Palgrave Macmillan, 2003), p. 241.

94 Hayner, *Unspeakable Truths*, p. 185.

95 Ibid.

96 See also Carolyn Nordstrom, "Terror Warfare and the Medicine of Peace," in Catherine Besteman, ed., *Violence: A Reader* (New York: Palgrave Macmillan, 2002), pp. 273–96.

97 Hayner, *Unspeakable Truths*, pp. 190–91. For a similar report from Uganda, see Marc Lacey, "Atrocity Victims in Uganda Choose to Forgive," *The New York Times*, April 18, 2005. "Remarkably, a number of those who have been hacked by the rebels [of the Lord's Resistance Army], who have seen their children carried off by them or who have endured years of suffering in their midst say traditional justice must be the linchpin in ending the war. Their main rationale: the line between victim and killer is too blurred."

98 Ngwenya quoted in Jonathan Steele, "A Healing in Mozambique," *The Guardian*, November 20, 2009, http://www.guardian.co.uk/commentisfree/2009/nov/20/mozambique-civil-war-peace.

99 Elizabeth F. Drexler, "Addressing the Legacies of Mass Violence and Genocide in Indonesia and East Timor," in Alexander Laban Hinton and Kevin Lewis O'Neill, eds, *Genocide: Truth, Memory, and Representation* (Durham, NC: Duke University Press, 2009), p. 229.

100 "Israel to Seek Another 1b Euros Holocaust in [*sic*] Reparations from Germany," Haaretz.com, December 20, 2009, http://www.haaretz.com/hasen/spages/1136383.html.

101 "Brown University to Erect Slave Trade Memorial," The Living Consequences (blog), March 18, 2009; "Slavery and Justice Commission Recommends a Memorial to Acknowledge Slave Trade Ties," Brown University press release, March 16, 2009, http://news.brown.edu/pressreleases/2009/03/memorial; Joshua Rhett Miller, "Brown University Should Consider Name Change Due to Slave Ties, Critics Say," FOXNews.com, April 17, 2009, http://www.foxnews.com/story/0,2933,516982,00.html.

102 "Britain to Return Aboriginal Bones," *The Sydney Morning Herald*, September 13, 2009; Paul Carter, "Aboriginal Remains Repatriated," *The Sydney Morning Herald*, September 21, 2009.

103 Colin Tatz, *With Intent to Destroy: Reflecting on Genocide* (London: Verso, 2003), p. 105.

104 Minow, *Between Vengeance and Forgiveness*, p. 114.

105 Queen Elizabeth quoted in Elazar Barkan, *The Guilt of Nations: Restitution and Negotiating Historical Injustices* (New York: W.W. Norton, 2001), p. 264.

106 "A 'Sorry Day' in Australia," *BBC Online*, May 26, 1998, http://news.bbc.co.uk/1/hi/world/asia-pacific/100476.stm.

107 Clinton's semi-apology ran as follows: "It may seem strange to you here, especially the many of you who lost members of your family, but all over the world there were people like me sitting in offices, day after day after day, who did not fully appreciate the depth and the speed with which you were being engulfed by this unimaginable terror. The international community, together with nations in Africa, must bear its share of responsibility for this tragedy as well. We did not act quickly enough after the killing began. We should not have allowed the refugee camps to become safe haven for the killers. We did not immediately call these crimes by their rightful name: genocide. We cannot change the past. But we can and must do everything in our power to help you build a future without fear and full of hope." Cited in *PBS Online News Hour*, http://www.pbs.org/newshour/ bb/africa/jan-june98/rwanda_3-25a.html.

108 "Text of Australian Prime Minister Kevin Rudd's Apology to Aborigines," *The Hindu*, February 13, 2008, http://www.thehindu.com/nic/auspmapology.htm. For those inclined to dismiss such apologies as "only words," Hall Greenland captures something of the impact of Rudd's parliamentary declaration: "There were tears in Kevin Rudd's eyes as the parliament, the crowded gallery and huge crowd outside rose to give him a standing ovation. And there was not a dry eye among the thousands that assembled at the open-air broadcast in Eveleigh Street in the Sydney suburb of Redfern – Australia's little Harlem. All over Sydney the Aboriginal flag flew from town halls, schools and even Sydney University two blocks from Eveleigh Street. . . . For many kids this day will be like the day of the moon landing, or the day Martin Luther King was assassinated, or

Che [Guevara] murdered, or JFK shot, was for previous generations; they will remember where they were if only because lots of schools watched the apology. It means these rising generations will inherit an Australia which has, if not a clean sheet, at least an honest one." Greenland, "Australia's Finest Hour," Counterpunch.org, February 13, 2008, http://www.counterpunch.org/greenland02132008.html.

109 See Krissah Thompson, "Senate Backs Apology for Slavery," *The Washington Post*, June 19, 2009; text of the Senate resolution available at http://www.opencongress.org/bill/111-sc26/text.

110 Owen Bowcott, "Danes Say Sorry for Viking Raids on Ireland," *The Guardian*, August 16, 2007, http://www.guardian.co.uk/world/2007/aug/16/ireland.

111 Barkan, *The Guilt of Nations*, p. 323.

112 Tony Barta, "Sorry, and Not Sorry, in Australia: How the Apology to the Stolen Generations Buried a History of Genocide," *Journal of Genocide Research*, 10: 2 (2008), pp. 201–14.

113 Barkan, *The Guilt of Nations*, pp. 30, 273.

114 Tatz, *With Intent to Destroy*, p. 167.

115 On Israel-Palestine, see Ilan Pappé, *The Ethnic Cleansing of Palestine* (Oxford: Oneworld, 2006). With regard to the ethnic German expulsions, a small step was taken by the Czech government in August 2005, apologizing to expellees who were "active opponents of Nazism." See "Czechs Apologize for Mistreating German Anti-Nazis in WWII," Reuters dispatch in Haaretz.com, August 30, 2005. However, see also the European Court of Human Rights decision of October 2008 "reject[ing] a land claim by ethnic Germans who lost homes in Poland during World War II," on the grounds that "modern Poland bears no responsibility for the expulsion of ethnic Germans by the Soviets . . . because it had no governmental control of the land," and therefore was not obliged "to enact laws providing for rehabilitation, restitution of confiscated property or compensation for property lost by the individual applicants." "Court Throws out Restitution Claim by Ethnic Germans," Deutsche Welle dispatch, October 10, 2008.

CHAPTER 16

Strategies of Intervention and Prevention

The slogan "Never Again," said human rights scholar Thomas Cushman, "embodies in crystalline form the preventative discourse" that pervades comparative genocide studies:

> through empirical and scientific observation of operationally defined cases of genocide, one can isolate the variables and causal mechanisms at work and predict future genocides. Armed with such predictions, one can take specific practical steps to intervene and stop genocides from occurring. The key to success is the development of political mechanisms or structures, which will heed the scientific understanding and possess the political will, which means basically the ability and the physical force necessary to intervene to stop genocide.[1]

Cushman viewed such optimism skeptically. He rejected the notion that all genocides can be prevented or suppressed. But he recognized that *some* can be, and he argued for strategies sensitive to historical context and the practical limitations on key actors. With such cautions in mind, this chapter tries to avoid easy answers and pat solutions. But it recognizes, and indeed typifies, the concern of the vast majority of genocide scholars and advocates, not only with regard to past genocides, but in confronting present genocidal outbreaks and preventing them in future.

Why should genocide be prevented? For most people who have read this far, the answer may be self-evident: to preserve people and groups at risk of destruction. But what if moral considerations are excluded, and rational self-interest is emphasized? This would at least have the advantage of appealing to a broader range of potential allies.

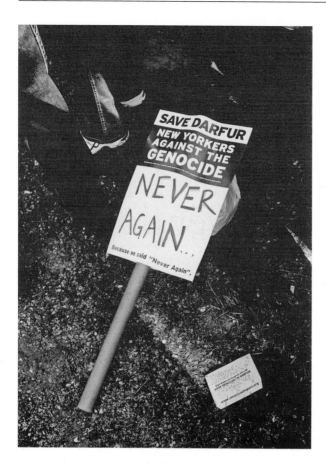

Figure 16.1 Never again . . . but how? Sign at a "Save Darfur" rally in New York City, April 2006.

Source: Kate Mereand/Wikimedia Commons.

In his thoughtful book *How to Prevent Genocide*, John Heidenrich addressed this question head-on. He pointed out that genocides typically generate refugee flows that can overwhelm neighboring countries and destabilize whole regions. Today, up to 27 million people may also be "internally displaced" worldwide as a result of genocide. "Such global multitudes of homeless and often stateless people have repeatedly drained the resources of the world's emergency aid services." He added that "every major genocidal crisis also shakes the international order. No one in 1994 expected that, within two years, mass killings in tiny Rwanda would plunge the enormity of Zaire/Congo into a civil war drawing in countries from almost half of Africa – but that is what happened."[2]

It is thus in the interest of humanity – both morally and practically – to oppose the crime against humanity that is genocide. What are the most reliable warning signs and facilitating conditions of this phenomenon? What ideas have been proposed for genocide intervention and prevention? What might we add to the mix? And what is the role of central actors, from the international community and its constituent organizations, to nongovernmental organizations (NGOs), civil society, and concerned – or potentially genocidal – individuals?

WARNING SIGNS

> Genocide . . . rarely comes out of the blue anymore [*sic*] than it picks on a group of people for no reason whatsoever.
>
> Mark Levene

What are the most reliable indicators that a genocide is impending? Although there is no "general 'essence' of genocide . . . across time and space," some traits and enabling conditions may serve as red flags.[3] In outlining them, I touch on possible intervention strategies, but postpone a more substantial engagement with this theme for later in the chapter.

- *A history of genocide and intercommunal conflict.* As political scientist Barbara Harff reminded us, "perpetrators of genocide often are repeat offenders, because elites and security forces may become habituated to mass killing as a strategic response to challenges to state security."[4] Genocide is frequently dependent on pre-existing patterns of state behavior and state–society relations. Psychologist Ervin Staub pointed to "ideologies of antagonism" among communal groups, "the outcome of a long history of hostility and mutual violence."[5]

- *Severe economic crisis.* Few factors seem so influential in genocidal violence as economic upheaval and catastrophe. When the material base of people's lives is thrown into question, they are prone to seek scapegoats among minorities (or majorities); to heed an extremist political message; and to be lured by opportunities to loot, pillage, and supervene. Economic crisis may undermine the legitimacy and administrative capacity of state authorities, who may lash out genocidally as a means of maintaining power. Such crises also encourage rebellious, revolutionary, and secessionist movements. These movements may fuel the ruling authorities' paranoia, and sometimes contain a genocidal seed and impetus of their own.

- *Mobilization along lines of communal cleavage.* It is natural for people of a particular religion, language, or history – the usual markers of "ethnic" identity – to associate with others who share those traits. Social and political mobilization along such lines is not inherently bad and violence-provoking. Indeed, if successfully managed, it may *forestall* outbreaks of violence. No one anticipates a genocidal outbreak in Belgium or Switzerland, for example – two countries whose political systems are largely structured along communal or "consociational" lines.[6]

  Nonetheless, a healthy and nongenocidal society will, in place of or in addition to such mobilizations, include a range of "cross-cutting" forums, movements, and socialization mechanisms that encourage people to move beyond limited identifications toward a more cosmopolitan vision. Such relations can help offset us-and-them thinking, as Ervin Staub wrote: "To evolve an appreciation of alikeness and a feeling of connectedness, members of subgroups of society must live together, work together, play together; their children must go to school together. Members of different nations must also work and play together . . . To reduce prejudice requires positive contact."[7]

National and, in particular, federal governments have a central responsibility to ensure that communal identities are successfully managed, and that constituencies are fairly represented in the halls of political and economic power. In an interview, political scientist Kal Holsti argued that "the most important [variable] is inclusiveness":

> There must be a deliberate policy by governments not to exclude specific groups from participating in the political system. If you look at Rwanda, Burundi, or Liberia and other places, the one thing they have in common is that one group – whether a minority or a majority – systematically excludes other groups from political participation, from government largesse, and from government programs. In some cases excluded groups were thrown out of the country; in other cases they were killed in genocides or politicides; in yet other cases they were simply denied the vote or in other ways discriminated against. In the countries that have succeeded, there is an attempt to be politically inclusive . . . There is no single formula, but the common characteristic . . . is an inclusive political system and political parties that transcend ethnic and language groups and that focus instead on policy differences.[8]

- *Hate propaganda.* A standard feature of genocidal mobilization is hate propaganda, including in mass media, public political speech, websites, graffiti, and more diffuse discourse strategies, such as rumor and gossip. The proliferation of media organs and other institutions devoted to hate speech is usually identifiable, though an increase in frequency and/or intensity of annihilationist rhetoric may be harder to measure. To the extent that it can be gauged, it may identify future *génocidaires* – and their targets. Hate speech underpins "exclusionary ideologies . . . that define target groups as expendable."[9] And if there is one message I would seek to impart above all others in the study and prevention of genocide, it is: *Let the perpetrators or would-be perpetrators tell you, by their words and deeds, who their targets are. Then confront them accordingly.*

  How does one confront hate propaganda? Pluralistic societies encounter some of the same vexing questions as in the case of genocide denial (Chapter 14), notably: is it legitimate to suppress dissident speech? Whereas denialism can be confronted with logical and empirical refutation, and includes a grey area of legitimate discussion and debate, hate propaganda directly incites violence. But repressing it may only spur the hatred that underlies it, and give publicity to the propagandists. Constructive countermeasures – support for pluralistic media projects and political initiatives; effective use of education systems – are generally preferable. However, while this argument may be comfortably advanced in democratic living rooms, it has different implications in societies where history and current indicators warn of genocide. Suppressing ethnic hate propaganda in Rwanda, for instance, may run counter to cherished liberal principles, but I, for one, would not object to it.
- *Unjust discriminatory legislation and related measures.* Some discriminatory ("affirmative action") legislation may actually help to suppress a potential genocide (see, e.g., the discussion of the *Bumiputra* policy in Malaysia, pp. 583–84).

In general, though, discrimination embodied in law (and in deliberately unequal systems of "justice") serves to marginalize and isolate designated groups – perhaps as a prelude to their extermination.

Another kind of discriminatory legislation deserves attention: that aimed at restricting possession of firearms. My liberal sympathies incline me towards effective gun control as a measure of a civilized society. However, the argument advanced by Jay Simkin *et al.*, members of the odd-sounding group Jews for the Preservation of Firearm Ownership (www.jpfo.org), rings true. They contend that most instances of mass killing have been preceded by systematic campaigns to seize arms from intended targets.[10] A reasonable middle ground might lie in allowing restricted firearm ownership in plural societies, while recognizing that campaigns to suppress private gun ownership in illiberal and repressive societies *may* aim to deny a minority the means to resist genocide.

- *Severe and systematic state repression.* Repression and state terror are especially trenchant indicators that a genocidal campaign may be brewing. Regardless of whether genocide ensues, such abuses must be denounced and suppressed. The imposition of emergency measures; restrictions on civil liberties; the banning or harassing of opposition parties and organizations; arbitrary detentions and large-scale round-ups of civilians; the advent or increased use of torture as state policy; substantial flows of refugees and internally displaced persons (IDPs) – all these should arouse deep concern, and may well presage a genocidal outbreak.

These acts are predominantly inflicted in authoritarian and developing societies, but citizens of democratic countries should acknowledge that they are not immune to creeping societal repression. They should be alert to violations of democracy and human rights at home and abroad, exploiting liberal democracy's broad freedoms in doing so.

The groups most likely to be targeted for repression include ethnic, racial, and religious minorities; "middleman" groups, especially those occupying an envied place in the economy (see Chapter 11); political dissidents and accused "enemies of the people," especially those involved in nationalist and secessionist movements or class rebellions; and finally, groups labeled as "outcasts," "asocials," and "rootless and shiftless," or depicted as outside the "universe of obligation," as sociologist Helen Fein theorized it (Chapter 1).

My own contribution to early-warning mechanisms revolves around the vulnerability of adult males, notably men of "battle age" (roughly 15–55). As I argued in Chapter 13, there are grounds for claiming that this group, usually described as the most impervious to violence, is in fact *most* vulnerable to genocide and the repression that routinely precedes it – if by "most vulnerable" we mean most *liable* to be targeted for mass killing and other atrocities.[11] The United Nations and other international organizations, governmental and nongovernmental, require a paradigm shift in their thinking on gender, violence, and humanitarian intervention – one that allows specific (certainly not exclusive) attention to be paid to adult men and male adolescents. How, for example, might greater sensitivity to the vulnerability of "battle-age" males at Srebrenica have assisted in heading off the gendercidal massacres of July 1995?[12]

▌ HUMANITARIAN INTERVENTION

> Throughout history, it has been the inaction of those who could have acted; the indifference of those who should have known better; the silence of the voice of justice when it mattered most; that has made it possible for evil to triumph.
>
> Haile Selassie, former Ethiopian emperor

The 1990s inaugurated a new age of humanitarian intervention. With the end of the Cold War, the way lay open for hard-nosed *realpolitik* to be set aside in favor of efforts to help suffering and persecuted peoples. The United Nations would finally come into its own as the arbiter and peace-builder that Franklin Roosevelt originally envisaged. Regional actors would step up to address nearby trouble spots.

At the same time, the collapse of the Soviet empire and of superpower rivalries had allegedly "lifted the lid off" a host of simmering conflicts, mostly ethno-national in nature. One prominent observer warned of a "coming anarchy" of state collapse and untrammeled violence.[13] In many parts of the world – Africa, former Soviet Central Asia, the Caucasus, the Balkans – anarchy did indeed arrive.

During this period, "humanitarian intervention" came to be associated with a military response to atrocities, separating warring factions, supervising negotiations, and brokering political settlements. The four key cases of, and debates over, humanitarian intervention in the 1990s – Iraqi Kurdistan (1991); Bosnia-Herzegovina (1992–95); and Kosovo and East Timor (both 1999) – all featured such interventions. However, might such military interventions instead represent *failures*, in the same way that successful fire-fighting may attest to inadequate fire prevention? In this discussion, I first address *non*-military intervention strategies. Military solutions should be a last resort, although mounted resolutely and with all dispatch when necessary.

The authors of a Canadian-sponsored report, *The Responsibility to Protect*, propose a useful range of non-military strategies. These "may come in the form of development assistance and other efforts to help address the root cause of potential conflict; or efforts to provide support for local initiatives to advance good governance, human rights, or the rule of law; or good offices missions, mediation efforts and other efforts to promote dialogue or reconciliation."[14] Lending political support – whether good offices, formal mediation, or simply rhetorical support – to governments that act respectfully towards their citizens is one of the most constructive interventionist measures.

Conversely, *withholding* aid may be a potent intervention strategy. It is essential that military and "security" aid not be provided to forces of repression. However, recent history suggests that such forces are often favored aid recipients. France, for instance, armed and trained the Rwandan *génocidaires* even when their murderous intentions were plain, and continued to support them after they had slaughtered up to a million of their fellow citizens. As noted in Chapter 12, the United States is without equal in the post World-War Two period in supporting forces of atrocity and genocide beyond its borders.

With regard to economic intervention, it is worth abiding by medicine's Hippocratic oath: First, do no harm. Interventionist economic policies such as "austerity" measures and "structural adjustment" programs may increase social stress in a way that contributes directly or indirectly to genocide. Rwanda and, arguably, Yugoslavia in the 1980s and 1990s provide examples. Cheerleading for wholesale economic "globalization" should thus be rejected. As international legal theorist Richard Falk has written, "Economic globalisation . . . weakens the overall capacity and will of governments to address human wrongs either within their own society or elsewhere. . . . It seems appropriate to link economic globalisation with a high threshold of tolerance for human wrongs, at least for now."[15] Moreover, if structural and institutional violence can themselves constitute genocide, then structural adjustment measures and the like may be not only a *cause* of genocide, but a *form* of it.

Sanctions

Economic and political sanctions lie at an intermediate point between "soft" intervention strategies and military intervention. As *The Responsibility to Protect* summarized such measures, they may include "arms embargoes," "ending military cooperation and training programmes," "financial sanctions," "restrictions on income-generating activities such as oil, diamonds . . . logging and drugs," "restrictions on access to petroleum products," "aviation bans," "restrictions on diplomatic representation," "restrictions on travel," and "suspension of membership or expulsion from international or regional bodies."[16] To this list might be added judicial sanctions, such as indictments for war crimes and genocide.

The difficulty with sanctions lies in targeting them to impede a repressive or genocidal leadership, without inflicting general human suffering. In two twentieth-century cases, human destruction caused by malevolent and/or misdirected sanctions could be considered genocidal. The economic blockade imposed on Germany during *and after* the First World War killed up to three-quarters of a million people.[17] The sanctions imposed on the Iraqi population in peacetime provide a second case (see Chapter 1).

Partly as a result of the Iraqi catastrophe, "blanket economic sanctions in particular have been increasingly discredited in recent years," because they impose "greatly disproportionate . . . hardships" on civilians.[18] Appropriately targeted measures, however, may repress would-be *génocidaires*. These actions can include freezing of bank accounts; travel bans; and (more controversially) sporting, cultural, and academic boycotts.

The United Nations

The UN has an abysmal record in confronting and forestalling genocide. According to Leo Kuper and others, this reflects the organization's founding on Westphalian norms of state sovereignty (Chapter 12), and the desire of most member states to avoid shining a spotlight on their own atrocities, past or present.

There is and always has been another side to the UN, however, typified by its extraordinarily effective specialized agencies (UNICEF, the World Food Program, the

High Commissioner for Refugees [UNHCR], and many others), as well as by the UN's contribution to peacekeeping and peacebuilding around the world. Since the late 1980s, the UN has increasingly stressed peace*building*, described by UN Secretary-General Kofi Annan as

> the creation or strengthening of national institutions, monitoring elections, promoting human rights, providing for reintegration and rehabilitation programmes, as well as creating conditions for resumed development. Peacebuilding does not replace ongoing humanitarian and development activities in countries emerging from crises. Rather, it aims to build on, add to, or reorient such activities in ways that are designed to reduce the risk of a resumption of conflict and contribute to creating conditions most conducive to reconciliation, reconstruction and recovery.[19]

These measures are vital to making "Never Again" a reality. Peacebuilding has been implemented most visibly in three Central American countries (El Salvador, Nicaragua, and Guatemala) after their civil wars. In coordination with nongovernmental organizations, both indigenous and foreign, the UN oversaw the demobilization and reintegration of fighting forces; constructed new societal

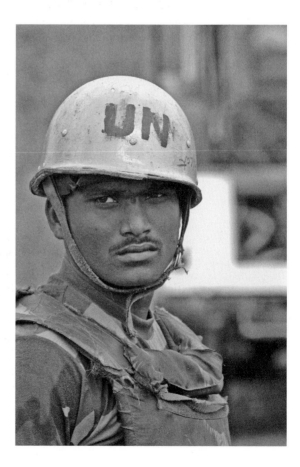

Figure 16.2 An Indian soldier of the United Nations Mission in the Democratic Republic of the Congo (MONUC) on a military escort mission in February 2007. For all their flaws, the United Nations and its dedicated peacekeeping corps remain perhaps the most effective agents of humanitarian intervention and post-conflict reconstruction.

Source: Julien Harneis/Flickr.

institutions virtually from scratch; organized and supervised elections; monitored violations of human rights; and assisted in the work of truth-and-reconciliation commissions, among other duties. On balance, this must be counted as a major UN success, providing a wealth of knowledge and practice for future genocide prevention and conflict resolution.

Overall, evidence supports the assertion of *The Responsibility to Protect* that the UN "is unquestionably the principal institution for building, consolidating and using the authority of the international community."[20] As John Heidenrich noted, "by signing the UN Charter, every member has obligated itself to adhere to the most basic norms of civilized conduct, which means that only through outright hypocrisy can a government commit a crime as grievous as genocide." Moreover, "only the United Nations has the Security Council, the only international body with the global legal right to compel countries to adhere to international humanitarian treaties and customs, by force if necessary."[21]

WHEN IS MILITARY INTERVENTION JUSTIFIED?

Kenneth Roth, executive director of Human Rights Watch, set a useful standard for military intervention. "Given the death, destruction, and disorder that are often inherent in war and its aftermath," he wrote, "humanitarian intervention" – by which he means *military* intervention – "should be reserved as an option only in situations of ongoing or imminent mass slaughter. Only the direst cases of large-scale slaughter can justify war's deliberate taking of life." Thus, Roth argued,

> Military action must be the last reasonable option. Second, the intervention must be primarily guided by a humanitarian purpose. Third, it should be conducted to maximize respect for international human rights law. Fourth, it must be reasonably likely to do more good than harm. Finally, it should ideally, *though not necessarily*, be endorsed by the UN Security Council or another body with significant multilateral authority.[22]

In the wake of the Kosovo intervention, carried out without UN Security Council authorization, a Swedish-sponsored Independent International Commission was formed under the stewardship of South African Judge Richard Goldstone (who spent two years as head of the ICTY tribunal at The Hague, and would also issue the devastating report on Israel's 2009 attack on the Gaza Strip – see p. 253). A commission member, political scientist Mary Kaldor, summarized the commission's conclusion: "that the Kosovo intervention was illegal, because there was no Security Council resolution, *but legitimate* because it resolved a humanitarian crisis and had widespread support within the international community and civil society." The "illegal but legitimate" verdict was an elegant one, but attested to "very dangerous" gaps and imprecisions in international law and interventionist policies.[23]

BOX 16.1 THE GENOCIDE PREVENTION TASK FORCE AND THE WILL TO INTERVENE (W2I) PROJECT

In the United States and Canada, in 2008 and 2009 respectively, two major commissions on genocide and crimes against humanity submitted their reports.

The Genocide Prevention Task Force was established in November 2007 "by a consortium of non-governmental agencies – the US Holocaust Memorial Museum, the American Academy of Diplomacy, and the US Institute of Peace – under the joint chairmanship of Madeleine Albright and William Cohen," respectively secretaries of state and defense under Bill Clinton.[24]

The Task Force stressed at the outset of its report, *Preventing Genocide: A Blueprint for US Policymakers*, that "preventing genocide is an achievable goal. Genocide is not the inevitable result of 'ancient hatreds' or irrational leaders. It requires planning and is carried out systematically. There are ways to recognize its signs and symptoms, and viable options to prevent it at every turn if we are committed and prepared. Preventing genocide is a goal that can be achieved with the right organizational structures, strategies, and partnerships – in short, with the right blueprint."[25] That blueprint centered on five major intervention strategies:

1. *Early Warning: Assessing Risks and Triggering Action.* "Acute warning of potential genocide or mass atrocities must be made an 'automatic trigger' of policy review."
2. *Early Prevention: Engaging before the Crisis.* "With international partners, we must engage leaders, develop institutions, and strengthen civil society within high-risk countries. Doing so will reduce capacities and motivations for mass violence while increasing social and institutional safeguards."
3. *Preventive Diplomacy: Halting and Reversing Escalation.* "Even when signs of preparation for genocide are apparent, there are opportunities to alter leaders' decisions, interrupt their plans, and halt and reverse escalation toward mass atrocities." The Task Force recommended creation of an Atrocities Prevention Committee "to improve our crisis response system and better equip us to mount coherent and timely strategies for preventive diplomacy."
4. *Employing Military Options.* "US leaders must consider how to leverage all instruments of national power to prevent and halt genocide and mass atrocities, including military assets . . . The United States should redouble its support for international partners such as the United Nations and the African Union to build their capacities to deploy effective military responses to mass atrocities."
5. *International Action: Strengthening Norms and Institutions.* "America has an interest in promoting strong global norms against genocide so that sovereignty cannot be used as a shield. We must also make international and regional institutions more effective vehicles for preventing mass atrocities."[26]

In Scott Straus's summary, "the report takes a comprehensive strategic approach that . . . emphasizes US leadership (which is appropriate for a policy statement aimed at influencing US policy) but still recognizes the importance of international processes and actors."[27] Some criticized, though, the record of the co-chairs. Madeleine Albright's credibility with regard to the prevention of and intervention in genocide was questioned in light of the Clinton administration's failure to intervene in Rwanda in 1994, and Albright's infamous comment about the half-million Iraqi children killed by the UN sanctions regime (see pp. 44–45). Cohen was Defense Secretary at the time of the 1999 Kosovo campaign, so how one evaluates that intervention (see Chapter 8) will influence an evaluation of his own credibility.

In Canada, the report of the **Mobilizing the Will to Intervene (W2I) initiative** was modeled on, and sought to concretize, the Responsibility to Protect (R2P) framework established by the International Commission on Intervention and State Sovereignty (ICISS) several years earlier (see above, p. 572). The W2I consultation and interview process was directed by Roméo Dallaire, commander of UN forces in Rwanda (Chapter 9) and subsequently a Canadian senator, together with Frank Chalk of the Montreal Institute for Genocide and Human Rights Studies (MIGS). The authors declared:

> First, we must recognize that the United Nations and other international insti-
> tutions are made up of national governments whose primary concern is the
> retention of political support from their domestic constituencies. Consequently,
> the key to mobilizing international support is to first garner domestic support
> . . . A vocal and broad-based constituency must emerge with the ability to
> advocate the case for governmental action in a persuasive manner.

"Mobilizing political will" to intervene in mass atrocities relied upon four key elements:

> leadership from the executive and legislative branches of government; inter-
> departmental coordination within the government; well developed civilian and
> military capacity; and knowledge sharing and pressure by civil society groups
> and the news media to raise awareness among decision makers and the public.

Communication was essential: not only between public and political spheres, and through the media, but in the need for streamlined communication *within* government bureaucracies. The Will to Intervene initiative, like the Genocide Prevention Task Force, emphasized this latter point. It proposed a Coordinating Office for the Prevention of Mass Atrocities to "create standard operating procedures for disseminating intelligence concerning the risks of mass atrocities throughout the whole of government."

The report urged humanitarian and nongovernmental organizations to "move beyond well-meaning but simplistic calls for the government to 'do something' to prevent mass atrocities, and provide precise proposals for action founded on results-based analysis." These should then be presented to policymakers, through well-maintained channels: "It is imperative that advocates build and sustain long-term relationships with key civil servants, politicians, and members of the executive, so that they may strategically reach all levels of government with their proposals for action."

The Will to Intervene authors lamented that the momentum for humanitarian intervention had notably flagged in the wake of September 11, 2001, and the long, draining invasions and occupations of Iraq and Afghanistan. These, they contended, "have depleted much of Canada and the United States' defense, diplomatic, and development resources, vastly diminishing the political will to engage in human-itarian intervention."[28] The humanitarian justifications offered for the Iraq War, meanwhile, delegitimized appeals for humanitarian intervention, especially as the dimensions of that disaster became clear (Box 4a).

Many commentators, however, have criticized military interventions as currently framed, because they tend to grant *carte blanche* to powerful states (themselves at no risk of military intervention) to dictate to the world's weaker states. In the view of law professor Stephen Holmes, this may extend to mounting invasions on supposedly "humanitarian" grounds. For all the lofty rhetoric that accompanies them, Holmes argued, military interventions are usually selective, self-interested, and counterpro-ductive.[29] A leftwing cottage industry bloomed after the 1999 Kosovo intervention, depicting it as malign US/NATO imperialism rather than an altruistic venture.[30] The broader point – that "humanitarian" intervention often masks imperial motives – is cogent. Calls for intervention may legitimately be analyzed for possible ulterior motives, but the existence of such motives should not necessarily rule out intervention altogether. I personally supported military intervention in both Kosovo and East Timor in 1999.

It is worth considering the place of ***regional actors*** in the intervention equation. Such actors have played *the* key role in virtually all successful interventions against genocide over the past three-and-a-half decades (success being measured by a halt to the killing). In 1971, India, the regional hegemon of South Asia, intervened to stop the genocide against Bengalis in East Pakistan (see Box 8a). In 1979, Tanzania over-threw the Idi Amin government in Uganda, ending his depredations (though installing a new regime under Milton Obote that proved little better). Also in 1979, Vietnam invaded Cambodia and pushed the Khmer Rouge regime to the margins. NATO's 1999 intervention in Kosovo brought an end to Serb genocide in the province, and allowed 800,000 ethnic Albanian refugees to return. Later that year, Australia played the leading role in ending Indonesia's genocidal occupation of East Timor; at the dawn of the new millennium, Nigeria headed the interventions in Sierra Leone and Liberia staged by ECOWAS (the Economic Community of West African States).

In none of these interventions, with the possible exception of Australia in East Timor and the NATO countries in Kosovo, did moral and humanitarian considerations act as primary catalysts – *from the perspective of the intervening state.*[31] Ulterior motives were always present (see Box 16.2). Yet in a world of states that is still run according to classical notions of sovereignty and *realpolitik*, one arguably takes what one can get. Ulterior motives may even be welcome for the added spur they provide to necessary state intervention. And the Timor case (see Box 16.2) shows us, like no other recent instance of successful intervention, how powerfully morally-infused activism can influence the equation.

BOX 16.2 "IF YOU LEAVE US HERE, WE WILL DIE": INTERVENTION IN EAST TIMOR, 1999

In Box 7a, we explored one of the most dramatic of recent humanitarian interventions, in Indonesian-occupied East Timor in September 1999. Violence erupted after referendum results showed a clear majority of Timorese in favor of independence from their powerful neighbor. An unusually rapid, direct, and successful intervention quelled it, however, and set East Timor on course to the independent statehood it had been denied after decolonization from Portugal in 1975. Geoffrey Robinson has supplied a riveting eyewitness account of the 1999 events.[32]

Robinson was a political affairs officer with the unarmed UN team, known as UNAMET, that supervised the referendum and witnessed its aftermath. "In a few short months," he reported, "the vast majority of international UNAMET staff had become so deeply committed to the [referendum] process that they were prepared to work exceptionally long hours and, quite literally, to place their lives on the line to ensure its success." Many were worried, however, by the decision to leave security in the hands of the Indonesian occupiers. Their worst fears were confirmed when it became known that a large majority of Timorese had voted for independence.

The resulting crackdown and killing spree by Indonesian-sponsored militias prompted those at UN headquarters to order a staff pullout from the Dili compound. But some 1500 terrified refugees had gathered there, and according to instructions issued on September 8, they would be left behind. The announcement provoked "outrage" and "a storm of protest within the compound," wrote Robinson. It "brought to a head fundamental questions about the United Nations' priorities and its responsibilities to the people of East Timor." To many observers, "it seemed that the United Nations was drawing an invidious distinction among its employees, based solely on their race or national origin."

The objections were communicated to New York. In the end, eighty-one UN staffers and others were allowed to remain in the compound, while most foreign and local staff were evacuated on September 10. Remaining staffers and journalists, accompanied by all refugees who wished to leave, departed safely for Darwin on September 14.

Memorable and, one hopes, trendsetting though the rebellion was, it was just one of the factors that encouraged the US superpower and its Australian ally to sponsor an armed intervention in East Timor under UN auspices within days of the outbreak of post-referendum violence (though too late to save hundreds or thousands of Timorese murdered by militias). This overrode the traditional commands of *realpolitik*, which would have dictated support for Indonesia rather than Timorese independence – as had indeed prevailed in the international community over the preceding quarter-century. According to Robinson, the "unusual conjuncture of events and conditions" encouraging intervention included "dramatic media coverage, the existence of a longstanding network of NGO and church organizations, and the surprisingly effective diplomacy of the UN Security Council and the secretary-general himself. More than anything else, though, it shows that the actions of a relatively small number of people, some but not all of them powerful, profoundly influenced the course of events" not only through the rebellion at the UN compound, but "by keeping the spotlight of media attention on East Timor, and by making a compelling moral case for intervention."

After perhaps wavering before the rebellion of September 8, Annan, recalling the fiascoes in Rwanda and Bosnia (Srebrenica) during his tenure as UN peacekeeping chief, mounted "an extraordinary campaign of personal diplomacy, urging world leaders to contribute to an international force and exert pressure on Indonesia to accept it." He also announced "emphatically" that "the United Nations is [not] abandoning the people of East Timor in their hour of greatest need."

Annan felt obliged to issue the declaration, in part, by the "thousands of messages I have received from all over the world." This attested to the power of the global protests mounted by civil society and nongovernmental organizations, especially in Australia, the UK, North America, and Portugal. A dedicated core of activists had utilized every communications strategy open to the "norm entrepreneur" over the previous quarter-century,[33] to publicize Indonesian atrocities and promote Timorese self-determination. Now they activated their networks to bring thousands of demonstrators into the streets of major cities.

Efforts to marshal a humanitarian response were further assisted by a favorable historical moment. A referendum might never have taken place in East Timor had a new Indonesian president, B.J. Habibie, not replaced the dictator Suharto and shifted policy on the Timor issue. When the consequences of the vote became plain, proponents of intervention could cite the recent confrontation with Serbia over Kosovo, in which NATO intervention was justified by all manner of humanitarian rhetoric which could now be deployed to justify aiding East Timor (Chapter 8). More generally, the 1999 events took place during an unusually propitious post-Cold War phase of international politics, bookended by the US and Allied interventions in Iraq (the first in 1990, establishing a Kurdish protected area on humanitarian grounds; the second in 2003, cloaking adventurism in humanitarian guise, to the detriment of the cause). Such "moments" cannot be predicted in advance, but they can be exploited when they arise, and promoted through patient and dedicated advocacy.

The advantages of intervention by regional actors are several. Geographical contiguity minimizes logistical difficulties, although this may be offset by resource constraints (apart from the Australian case, all the interventions cited above were carried out by poor developing nations). With contiguity often comes a degree of ethnocultural kinship, making it less likely that interventions will be seen as foreign or imperial in nature. Regional powers may also have a vested interest in guarding against the spill-over of genocide, something that more distant actors might not share.

At the same time, however, vested interests operate, and may undermine the intervention. The conflict in Congo – Africa's "first world war" (Box 9a) – fed the expansionist and pillaging ambitions of a host of African nations. Logistical difficulties are likely to prevail where regional actors are underdeveloped, with limited resources. In such cases, material assistance from the developed world is critical. Political scientist Alan Kuperman has argued that "only the US military has a large, long-haul cargo air fleet," without which "rapid reaction to most parts of the world is impossible."[34] Journalist Michael Hirsh goes so far as to argue that the "most important future role for the UN" might be that of "a legitimizer for local forces" to intervene, with assistance and logistical backing from the developed countries, primarily the US who supply most of the UN's budget.[35]

A standing "peace army"?

In a contribution to his edited *Encyclopedia of Genocide*, Israel Charny proposed the creation of an International Peace Army as a "standing machinery . . . for responding to eruptions of genocide, at any time or place in the world." Such a force

> would move automatically into action any time that authenticated reports are received of the mass killing of any group of unarmed civilians, such as the ethnic cleansing of a village or a region. The basic mandate of the *International Peace Army* would be to take action in the same way that we are accustomed today in democratic countries to call on the police at the first evidence of murder or even possible murderous assault.[36]

The Peace Army would be pluralistic in composition (with "nationals from a very wide range of countries"). Charny divided the Peace Army into three units: one military, another medical and humanitarian, and a third designed "for the Rebuilding of Safe and Tolerant Communities." In a nod to the growing scope and complexity of UN peacekeeping and peacebuilding operations from the late 1980s onward, this last component would bring "skilled administrators and technicians for reestablishing the basic structure of community life." It would also aim to "mobilize indigenous leaders of the peoples involved in the conflict – religious leaders, political leaders, popular folk heroes including media celebrities, sports stars, beloved popular singers, leaders in education, and so on of the indigenous culture – who will agree to speak to the building of a new era of tolerance and reconciliation."[37]

A Peace Army might seem utopian, but contemporary developments may make it less so. For one thing, Charny's imagined force would be an "affiliated police arm" of the United Nations.[38] In the new millennium, the UN took steps to establish a standing army that, with the input of humanitarian organizations, could fulfill many of the functions Charny envisaged. The plan called for twelve nations – Canada and Denmark have already signed on – to contribute to a 6,000-strong force on standby for a call from the Secretary-General and the Security Council. A different, possibly complementary, Dutch proposal called for a "fire brigade" of 2,500 to 5,000 soldiers as "a permanent, rapidly deployable brigade" to intervene in genocidal outbreaks. Five thousand troops is roughly the force that Major-General Roméo Dallaire pleaded for in 1994 when the Rwandan genocide was underway. "If I had had such a force available to me while I was the UNAMIR Force Commander sometime in mid-April, we could have saved the lives of hundreds of thousands of people," Dallaire asserted.[39]

The European Union, which after the UN may represent the world's leading force for democracy, peace, and humanitarianism (see below, pp. 591–92), has discussed an "EU Rapid Reaction Force" (ERRF), capable of deploying up to 60,000 soldiers within sixty days and maintaining them in the field for up to one year. The EU also floated the idea of "battle groups" consisting of elite battalions of 1,500 soldiers, able to deploy within fifteen days and stay in the field for a month. Not to be left out, the African Union also sought to develop an African Standby Force consisting of "regionally-based standby brigades, numbering between 3,500 and 5,000 troops," deployable within two weeks.[40] All these initiatives were guided by a perception that the hidebound, bureaucratic process of deploying peacemaking and peacekeeping operations gives *génocidaires* and war criminals too great a head start. For the UN and the Europeans alike, there was the added attraction of developing a military force that does not rely on the US for funding and logistics. Unfortunately, at the time of writing (March 2010), none of these forces had seen the light of day.

Finally, there is the possibility of an "international legion of volunteers," as Heidenrich discussed. Such corps have played an important role in some conflicts, from the Spanish Civil War to the French Foreign Legion's varied postings. Some proposals even envisage the use of mercenaries in this role, arguing that the unsavory reputation attached to such forces is outdated.[41]

BOX 16.3 SUCCESS STORIES?

Any study of genocide must reckon not just with genocidal outbreaks, of the kind examined throughout this book, but with cases where genocide has *not* occurred – despite significant ethnoreligious divisions and, often, histories of intercommunal conflict. What can we learn about genocide prevention and intervention from apparent examples of coexistence and successful conflict management? And how must their successes be qualified?

Malaysia

Figure 16.3 Mahathir bin Mohamed, prime minister of Malaysia from 1981 to 2003. He combined a sometimes authoritarian style of rule with affirmative-action measures for indigenous Malays, and modernizing measures to expand the economic pie for all citizens. He thereby continued Malaysia's generally successful policies to mute ethnic conflict between Malays and ethnic Chinese. Mahathir also established himself as a leading voice of the developing world against untrammeled neoliberalism. He is shown speaking to the World Economic Forum in Davos, Switzerland, in January 2003.

Source: Sebastian Derungs/Flickr.

Malaysia (formerly Malaya) achieved independence from Great Britain in 1959, by which point its communal makeup reflected the demographic transformations wrought by colonialism. In addition to a sizable Indian population, originating with the indentured laborers whom the British brought to work the highland tea plantations, roughly a quarter of the population is ethnic Chinese. As elsewhere in Southeast Asia, the Chinese moved into business and industry, particularly after the departure of British capital. Their growing economic power, and allegations of subversive links to communist China, generated the same hostility from native Malays that has occasionally led to rioting in neighboring Indonesia.

Malaysia, too, saw its outbreak of anti-Chinese rioting in 1969, with several hundred killed. The Malay-dominated government, however, responded intelligently, if in a somewhat authoritarian fashion. It launched an affirmative-action campaign – the *Bumiputra* ("sons of the soil") policy – to boost the presence of Malays in higher education and the national economy, without alienating ethnic Chinese to the point that they abandoned the country. Just as significantly, they ensured that a rising tide would float all boats – that is, by generating economic prosperity, all communities would benefit. The modernization of the country proceeded apace. "From 1970 to 1995, the per capita Malay income grew by 830 percent while the per capita Chinese income grew by 635 percent," reducing – though not eliminating – the income gap between the two main groups. "Middle-class and entrepreneurial Malays share common interests in Malaysia with middle-class Chinese, and this lessens ethnic conflict," emphasizing the importance of such interests "cut[ting] across ethnic, religious, or regional lines." As a result, wrote Daniel Chirot and Clark McCauley, while "Malaysia has hardly been a model of perfect toleration," it has managed to combine "a relatively accommodating policy toward the more entre-preneurial minority, affirmative action for the poorer majority, and acceptance of multiculturalism."[42] Tensions and rivalries remain, and at the close of 2009, the small Christian minority vigorously protested discriminatory measures reflecting the Islamism of the ruling regime.[43] But though the protests threatened to spill over to rioting and communal violence, no such full-scale eruption had occurred in the four decades since 1969.

Source: Edmund Gomez, *The State of Malaysia: Ethnicity, Equity and Reform* (RoutledgeCurzon, 2004).

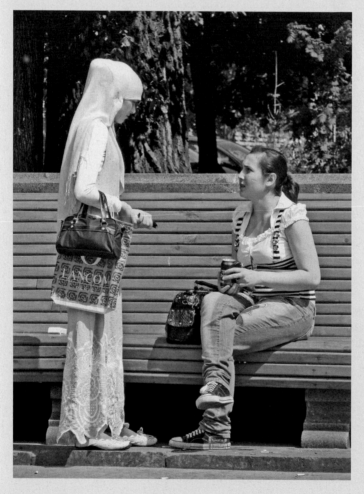

Figure 16.4 Young women in traditional and Western dress chat outside Kazan's main university. The city, capital of the Tatarstan Republic in Russia, offers a particularly encouraging example of Muslim–Christian and religious–secular coexistence.

Source: Author's photo, June 2008.

Kazan, Tatarstan Republic (Russia)

In how many other places on earth do Muslims and Christians live peacefully side by side, in similar demographic proportions? In a country like Lebanon, this eventually proved a recipe for communal conflict and civil war. One might expect something similar in Kazan. After all, the fierce rivalry and battles between ethnic Russians and the Bulgar- and Mongol-descended Tatars was a defining feature of Russia's emergence as a modern state. In 1552, Ivan the Terrible besieged and annexed the Tatar Khanate, and a flood of Russian colonists followed, continuing under successive tsarist regimes and during the period of Soviet communism (Chapter 5). Russians now account for fully 40 percent of the population, versus the Muslim Tatars' 50 percent.

Elsewhere in the Russian Federation and beyond, tensions between indigenous Muslim populations and Russians have spawned genocide (in the Caucasus) and secessionist aspirations (not only among Muslims in Chechnya [see Box 5a], but in Crimea and eastern Ukraine, with their large Russian populations). In Kazan, however, an almost surreal coexistence reigns. The minarets of the magnificent Kul-Sharif mosque, opened in 2005, rise adjacent to the steeples of the Russian Orthodox cathedral.

This is the result of enlightened political leadership, interfaith dialogue, and a careful apportioning of material resources among the different ethnoreligious communities. In the post-Soviet period, the Republic of Tatarstan was granted a large measure of political autonomy and control over exploitation of the republic's rich oil and gas resources; Moscow appears to view the republic as a model for its relations with Russian Muslims and the wider Muslim world. The Kul-Sharif mosque, for example, was built on the site of a mosque razed by the sixteenth-century Russian conquerors, as a subtle gesture of restitution.

Tatarstan's Council for Religious Affairs manages relations among the faiths – ensuring, for instance, that "when the state pays for a mosque to have a new roof structure, it ensures at the same time that a Russian-Orthodox church receives similar funding, for new chairs."[44] One result is that religious fundamentalism, usually fueled by feelings of persecution and humiliation, has found little foothold in Kazan. Among Muslims, women in Western dress mingle easily with more tradition-minded coreligionists (see Figure 16.4). Orthodox Christians and Muslims alike throng the city's beautiful boulevards, and flock to its lively cafés and pizzerias. "When people live directly next to one another they get a feeling for how to respect one another," said Renat Nakifovich Valiullin, head of the Council for Religious Affairs. A skeptic might note that the same was said of Sarajevo in Bosnia – a model of intercommunal harmony until Yugoslavia collapsed into war and genocide in the 1990s (Chapter 8). For now, though, Kazan's example shines brightly.

Source: Ray Nayler, "Kazan: Phoenix in the Snow," *Passport Magazine*, http://www.passport magazine.ru/article/1101/.

Figure 16.5 Nelson Mandela addresses the crowd at the concert to celebrate his 90th birthday in London, UK, June 27, 2008. Mandela's vision of racial reconciliation and a "rainbow nation" in South Africa brought about one of the seminal transitions of modern times, from a white-ruled apartheid system to a liberal democracy. (46664 was Mandela's ID number during his 27 years as a prisoner. Today, it is the name of his educational foundation to combat HIV/AIDS – see www.46664.com.)

Source: Paul Williams/Flickr.

South Africa

Few countries could have been considered less promising arenas for a peaceful transition from racial despotism to multiracial democracy than South Africa in the 1970s and 1980s. Since the first arrival of European whites in what would become the "Cape Colony" around Cape Town, the indigenous population was dispossessed of its land and reduced to a marginal existence. The system of apartheid imposed by the Dutch-descended Afrikaner population built on previous patterns and legislation of racial exclusion by imposing a system of *apartheid* ("apartness") when the National Party seized power in whites-only elections. Exploitation of the poorly paid, poorly housed African population was combined with all the petty racial humiliations – "Whites Only" signs, separate public facilities, and so on – familiar from (and inspired by) the US Deep South in the pre-civil rights era. The African National Congress, founded in 1912 to confront the Land Act (which banned black Africans from land ownership across South Africa's most fertile territories), was driven underground and into exile by the 1960s, and its leader, Nelson Mandela, jailed for life. He would eventually spend 27 years in prison, most of it on Robben Island off Cape Town.

Popular protest gathered force, with the Soweto Uprising of 1976 – ruthlessly repressed by the Afrikaner security forces – serving as something of a watershed.

The state sought to head off the threat of majority rule by turning black against black, with the internecine (perhaps genocidal) warfare between Xhosa, the largest ethnic group, and the Zulu population concentrated in Natal province. The violence was fueled and manipulated throughout by the Afrikaner regime, in keeping with the time-honored colonial strategy of divide-and-rule. As instability spiraled out of control, however, and with the waning of the Cold War reducing the resonance of appeals to "anticommunism," negotiations were finally opened with Mandela and other ANC leaders in jail or exile.

The result was the freeing of the ANC figures, the dismantling of the formal apartheid system, and finally the joyous free elections of April 27, 1994 (which unfortunately had the effect of crowding out the Rwandan genocide, then raging, from global headlines). Nelson Mandela was installed as the country's first black president. He became a pivotal voice of reconciliation, and the principal purveyor of a vision of South Africa as a "rainbow nation at peace with itself and the world," encompassing all races and ethnic groups.[45] Work began on a new constitution, finalized in 1996, which was perhaps the most liberal and progressive in the world. It guaranteed equal rights for all, and granted official status to no fewer than nine indigenous languages (Xhosa, Pedi, Ndebele, Swazi, Sotho, Zulu, Tsonga, Venda, and Tswana), together with English and Afrikaans. A Truth and Reconciliation Commission (TRC) angered some by granting amnesty to those on all sides of the country's political divides who confessed to engaging in political violence and terrorism during the apartheid era. Nonetheless, it has served as a model for similar processes in the wake of mass atrocities worldwide (see Chapter 15).

South Africa's progress has been uneven since. The economic gulf between whites and blacks, entrenched by apartheid, has barely begun to be addressed; unemployment for blacks approaches 50 percent. Relatedly, violence may be even more out of control than in the 1980s – though now it takes the form of rampant crime rather than state terror. HIV-AIDS is at epidemic levels, exacerbated by the criminally cavalier policies of Mandela's successor as president, Thabo Mbeki (who gave way to Jacob Zuma in May 2009). Tens of thousands of whites, feeling themselves frozen out by "affirmative action" measures targeting the black majority, have emigrated. Most stayed, however, and adjusted to their newly subordinate political role (being comparatively rich helped). Ethnic tensions between Xhosa and Zulu gradually became muted, and democracy has endured. The "long walk to freedom," to cite the title of Mandela's autobiography,[46] remains incomplete – if emancipation includes meaningful economic equity and personal security. But nearly two decades after official apartheid was consigned to the dustbin, there is much to commend and admire in South Africa's transformations.

Source: Allister Sparks, *Beyond the Miracle: Inside the New South Africa* (University of Chicago Press, 2009).

Rwanda

Most of the "success stories" in this section emphasize pluralism, consociationalism, and democracy as key factors in inoculating societies against outbreaks of genocide and crimes against humanity. The Malaysian example, however, points to a more authoritarian and *dirigiste* framing that can also be judged as "successful," in this respect at least. In both Malaysia and Rwanda, the model has been based on economic development that gives all communities at least some sense, though not necessarily an equal one, of growing prosperity. This can mute the sense of discrimination and marginalization that so often gives rise to social conflict.

In the Rwandan case, however (see Chapter 9), the government is more authoritarian, and a verdict of "success" correspondingly more controversial. Founded on the RPF guerrilla movement which seized power in Kigali in July 1994, it has been classed by many observers as an *ethnocracy* – a political order in which a particular ethnic group is hegemonic. The genocidal "Hutu Power" regime gave way to a Tutsi-dominated one under President Paul Kagame;[47] many would concur with René Lemarchand's evaluation of the government as "a thinly disguised Tutsi dictatorship."[48] But advancing any such argument in Rwanda is bound to land one in trouble – or worse – with the authorities. Officially, after 1994, there are no longer ethnicities in the country. Citizens are neither Hutu nor Tutsi, but Banyarwanda. Acknowledging continuing ethnic tensions and inequalities is viewed as a subversive echo of the genocidal past.

Figure 16.6   Rwandan president Paul Kagame, leader of the ruling Rwandese Patriotic Front (RPF), is shown in June 2009 attending the World Economic Forum on Africa in Cape Town, South Africa. Kagame, a Rwandan Tutsi exile from Uganda, has blended harsh authoritarianism with measures to promote economic growth, attract foreign investment and aid, and suppress ethnic mobilizations of the kind that produced the 1994 genocide (see Chapter 9).

Source: Eric Miller/Wikimedia Commons.

Kagame won 95 percent of the presidential vote in the first post-genocide elections in 2003, and the RPF was returned to power in 2008 in a vote which, again, no opposition party was allowed to contest. According to the UK *Economist* in 2008, Kagame "allows less political space and press freedom at home than Robert Mugabe does in Zimbabwe," while "anyone who poses the slightest political threat to the regime is dealt with ruthlessly."[49] Press freedom is heavily curtailed, with Rwanda ranking 147th out of 169 countries surveyed by Reporters Without Borders in 2007 (183rd out of 195 in a Freedom House survey released the following year).[50]

Even with such heavy-handed tactics, however, it is difficult to deny that post-1994 Rwanda has witnessed remarkable transformations. The ban on mobilizing around ethnic constituencies and platforms has helped to suppress civil violence (and ethnically-imbued hate speech). Internationally, the Kagame regime has positioned Rwanda as a poster child for foreign investment and overseas development assistance; over half a billion dollars in foreign aid flooded in during 2005 alone.[51] The RPF regime also set a seal on the country's removal from the French zone of influence, securing entry to the British Commonwealth instead, in late 2009. Economic growth has averaged an impressive 6 percent annually – albeit from a very low base, and with a half-acknowledged boost from the looting of eastern Congo's rich resources, following the extension of Rwandan power there in 1996 (see Box 9a). New industries (such as specialty coffees) have been promoted, and the government has worked hard to attract tourism, depicting the country as an oasis of peace and social order on the troubled African continent.[52] A reservoir of Western guilt for the genocide was an enormous boon, at least until the Kagame regime's depredations in eastern Congo squandered much goodwill. Meanwhile, the *gacaca* process within (see pp. 543–45) allowed hundreds of thousands of alleged Hutu accomplices to the genocide to be judged by local communities and reintegrate in society, following models of restorative justice rather than, in general, raw retribution.

A striking feature is that Rwanda today has the highest female political representation of any country in the world. The 2003 constitution guaranteed women 30 percent of seats in the national parliament, but in fact they have surged far beyond this point, as *The Washington Post*'s Stephanie McCrummen reported:

> Women hold a third of all cabinet positions, including foreign minister, education minister, Supreme Court chief and police commissioner general. And Rwanda's parliament [in September 2008] became the first in the world where women claim the majority – 56 percent, including the speaker's chair. One result is that Rwanda has banished archaic patriarchal laws that are still enforced in many African societies, such as those that prevent women from inheriting land. The legislature has passed bills aimed at ending domestic violence and child abuse, while a committee is now combing through the legal code to purge it of discriminatory laws.[53]

Is the Rwandan model a viable one for post-genocidal societies? Observers have found much to criticize, and to commend.

Source: Stephen Kinzer, *A Thousand Hills: Rwanda's Rebirth and the Man Who Dreamed It* (Wiley, 2008).

India

It may seem odd to cite India as a "success story" of coexistence and conflict management. After all, the country was born of genocide (the Partition violence of 1947–48, in which half a million to a million Indians perished).[54] Since then, India has experienced waves of secessionist and counterinsurgent violence in Punjab and Indian-occupied Kashmir; Maoist guerrilla violence against "class enemies," provoking an indiscriminate state backlash; Muslim–Christian clashes in the desperately poor states of the northeast; and regular rounds of Hindu–Muslim and Hindu-Sikh violence, at times spilling over into genocide – as with the Delhi massacre of Sikhs following Prime Minister Indira Gandhi's assassination in 1984, or the mass killings of Muslims in Gujarat in 2002. A powerful Hindu nationalist party, the Bharatiya Janata Party (BJP), has led coalition governments at both state and federal levels, and its thuggish ally, the Shiv Sena party, was known for threats and vigilantism against those it designated as ethnic or political enemies.[55]

Yet it is perhaps remarkable – given India's immense size, abiding poverty, and ethnoreligious divisions spilling over into international conflict (the seemingly perpetual crisis in relations with neighboring Pakistan) – that the state has held together at all, and coexistence has *generally* prevailed over violence. In part, this is thanks to the kind of enlightened leadership at the municipal level that we saw operating in Kazan, Russia (above).[56] More generally, observers stress the significance of India's democratic political system, with its cross-cutting political cleavages. Referring to the Hindu militants of Shiv Sena, for example, *The Economist* concedes that "India's democracy has spawned many [such] opportunist outfits . . . fermenters of ethnic, religious, or caste-based grievance. But it is also in part self-correcting. No communal interest is big enough to secure state-level or national power. To forge alliances extremists have to moderate."[57] The appeal of the Hindu-nationalist BJP, too, has waned since its peak in the late 1990s.

India's founding prime minister, Jawaharlal Nehru, famously described his country as "an ancient palimpsest on which layer upon layer of thought and reverie had been inscribed, and yet no succeeding layer had completely hidden or erased what had been written previously. . . . Though outwardly there was diversity and infinite variety among our people, everywhere there was that tremendous impress of oneness, which had held all of us together for ages."[58] Nehru's idealistic vision of a unified subcontinent was shattered by Partition, and is challenged on many fronts today. But his idea of India as a federal, multicultural, democratic society remains a powerful unifying force. And then there's cricket . . . ![59]

Source: Sunil Khilnani, *The Idea of India* (Farrar, Straus & Giroux, 1999).

Figure 16.7   Flags of the European Union (EU) fly outside European Commission headquarters in Brussels, Belgium.

Source: Xavier Häpe/Wikimedia Commons.

The European Union (EU)

For hundreds of years, the conflict dyad of Britain and France was one of the most war-prone in the world. The entrance of a unified Germany in 1871, and Germany's determination to win "a place in the sun" alongside the other imperial powers, directly contributed to the two world wars of the twentieth century. Yet today, these three countries are not only at peace, but members of a wider union encompassing most of Europe outside Russia. The EU project began in 1951 with the formation of the European Coal and Steel Community, in which erstwhile enemies France and (West) Germany took a leading role. In 1957, these two countries, together with Italy, Belgium, Luxembourg, and the Netherlands, formed the European Economic Community (EEC). It gradually expanded to include, first, Great Britain, and since the fall of communism in 1989, a number of the former Soviet satellite states in

Central Europe. The European Union (EU) formally came into being in 1993, and now comprises fully 27 member states.

Today, war between EU members is almost inconceivable. Moreover, member states must agree to respect the rights of ethnic, religious, and sexual minorities enshrined in the Convention for the Protection of Human Rights and Fundamental Freedoms (the European Convention on Human Rights), and to defer to the judgments of the European Court of Human Rights (ECtHR) – one of the few international legal institutions with real teeth, and generally considered the strongest rights-protection body in the world.[60] (Whether this has made Europeans in general more tolerant of ethnic and religious minorities is questionable, however, in light of the apparent rise in hate crimes and growing hostility to immigrants – particularly Muslims – reflected in large-sample opinion surveys.)[61]

The benefits of belonging to the EU can also act as a spur to reform and reconciliation in countries aspiring to membership. There is no doubt that Croatia's growing willingness to extradite accused war criminals to the Hague tribunal, and accept the return of Serbs expelled from the Krajina region during "Operation Storm" in 1995 (see Chapter 8), is closely linked to a desire to curry favor with the EU, which it applied to join in 2003. (Croatia remained a non-member at the time of writing, but it has been granted candidate status, and seemed on track to join in 2012.) Turkey's on-again, off-again ascent to EU membership is also linked to its repeal, after 2003, of bans on the Kurdish language in education, media, and public discourse.

Source: Jeremy Rifkin, *The European Dream: How Europe's Vision of the Future Is Quietly Eclipsing the American Dream* (Tarcher, 2005).

The United States and Canada

These two North American countries, which share the longest undefended border in the world, are themselves a model of *international* coexistence. Internally, as we have seen, both countries have wrestled with the consequences of European colonialism: the continuing marginalization of indigenous peoples and, in the US case, the legacy of slavery and discrimination against African Americans. Nonetheless, whether we consider the "melting pot" model in the US or the doctrine of "multiculturalism" which has come to dominate Canadian political discourse, both countries have significantly advanced values of pluralism and cosmopolitanism within their borders. The umbrella appellation "American" has proved a successful device for integrating new waves of immigrants to the US, with a decreasing emphasis on assimilating to the hegemonic (white-Protestant) culture. Even after the horrors of September 11, 2001, there was no significant violent backlash against US Muslims. Nor have present tensions over undocumented migrants, especially from Mexico, led (so far) to widespread vigilantism. The US still naturalizes more immigrants annually than any other country.

The election of the nation's first African American president, Barack Obama, was a watershed. In his "Speech on Race," delivered in March 2008, Obama outlined his "own American story" as follows:

> I am the son of a black man from Kenya and a white woman from Kansas. . . . I've gone to some of the best schools in America and lived in one of the world's poorest nations. I am married to a black American who carries within her the blood of slaves and slaveowners – an inheritance we pass on to our two precious daughters. I have brothers, sisters, nieces, nephews, uncles and cousins, of every race and every hue, scattered across three continents, and for as long as I live, I will never forget that in no other country on Earth is my story even possible.[62]

As for my own country, Canada, it has – despite a major hiccup in 1970[63] – wrestled peacefully with the challenge of nationalism and separatism in the predominantly French-speaking province of Quebec. In the wake of sweeping policies of accommodation, acceptance of the Parti Québecois's affirmative action measures for francophones following its provincial election victory in 1976, and two referendums on Quebec "sovereignty" which failed (the second only narrowly), the secessionist impetus in Quebec appears to have waned. Meanwhile, Canada's previous emphasis on encouraging immigration from "white" Europe has given way to a much greater openness to the wider world, so that cities like Toronto and Vancouver are today among the most multicultural on the planet. Reconciliation efforts with the country's marginalized aboriginal populations – including recognition of land rights and resource claims – have also proceeded, though natives' standards of living and health remain far below those of non-aboriginals.[64] In 1999, as noted in Chapter 15, the federal territory of Nunavut was carved out of the Northwest Territories, accompanied by a substantial devolution of political authority to the native Inuit population, and an agreement to share the proceeds from the territory's rich mineral resources. Canada also "finali[zed] a C$1.9 billion ($1.7 million) class-action settlement for 80,000 surviving former inmates" of the residential schools, "with extra payments for those who suffered physical and sexual abuse."[65] In a declaration before the Canadian parliament in June 2008, Conservative Prime Minister Stephen Harper rendered a formal apology for "a sad chapter in our history," and a truth and reconciliation process was underway at the time of writing (March 2010).[66]

Sources: John D. Buenker and Lorman A. Ratner, eds, *Multiculturalism in the United States: A Comparative Guide to Acculturation and Ethnicity*, rev. edn (Greenwood Press, 2005); Augie Fleras and Jean Leonard Elliott, *Engaging Diversity: Multiculturalism in Canada*, 2nd edn (Nelson Thomson Learning, 2002).

IDEOLOGIES AND INDIVIDUALS

Who am I and of what am I capable?

James Waller

Our analysis now shifts from the national and international–political sphere to the more intimate level of human beings' minds and hearts. What difference can individual witnessing make to genocide? How do ideologies, whether religious or secular, spur us to perpetrate – and prevent – genocide? And how can we confront and mitigate our own potential to inflict or support genocidal acts?

The role of the honest witness

Witnessing and transmitting are central to genocide prevention and intervention. The key is *honest, accurate* witnessing, combined with the capacity to communicate what one has witnessed. The "relentless keepers of the truth," as Russian intellectual Nadezhda Mandelstam called them, are genocide's most powerful opponents, and "the best proof that good, not evil, will prevail in the end."[67] Conversely, those who fail to witness honestly – who turn away, distort, and deny – are reliable allies of the *génocidaires*.

A fascinating contrast in honest versus dishonest witnessing is provided by the terror-famine in Ukraine (1932–33). At the height of the famine, with millions dying throughout the countryside, British socialists Sidney and Beatrice Webb traveled to the USSR. They kept well away from the starving rural areas, and subsequently wrote "a glowing account" of their visit (*Soviet Communism – A New Civilisation*, published in 1935). *The New York Times*'s Moscow correspondent, Walter Duranty, likewise avoided all mention of the famine and the state's genocidal manipulation of it. Duranty's reports influenced the Roosevelt administration's decision to recognize the Soviet government – in 1933, as famine, collectivization of the countryside, and the crushing of peasant resistance all reached their zenith.[68]

The witnessing of British journalist Malcolm Muggeridge was radically different. Arriving in the Soviet Union in 1933, Muggeridge adopted the simple expedient of buying a train ticket to journey through the heartland of Ukraine and the North Caucasus. *En route*, he witnessed some of the horrific scenes of famine described in Chapter 5. "*Whatever else I may do or think in the future, I must never pretend that I haven't seen this,*" Muggeridge wrote in his diary.[69] He returned to publish an account of "millions of starving peasants, their bodies often swollen from lack of food," struggling with "soldier members of the GPU [secret police] carrying out the instructions of the dictatorship of the proletariat." The Stalinist forces, Muggeridge wrote, "had gone over the country like a swarm of locusts and taken away everything edible . . . [and] had reduced some of the most fertile land in the world to a melancholy desert."[70] His example was echoed by the journalist Gareth Jones (see Figure 16.8).

Like Muggeridge, the diplomats, missionaries, and some German soldiers who witnessed the genocide of the Armenians during the First World War were central to catalyzing international protest, and some small measure of intervention in the

Friday, March 31, 1933. THE EVENING

FAMINE RULES RUSSIA

The 5-year Plan Has Killed the Bread Supply

By GARETH JONES

Mr. Jones is one of Mr. Lloyd George's private secretaries. He has just returned from an extensive tour on foot in Soviet Russia. He speaks Russian fluently—and here is the terrible story the peasants told him.

A FEW days ago I stood in a worker's cottage outside Moscow. A father and a son, the father a Russian skilled worker in a Moscow factory, and the son a member of the Young Communist League, stood glaring at one another.

The father, trembling with excitement, lost control of himself and shouted at his Communist son: "It's terrible now. We workers are starving. Look at Cheliabinsk, where I once worked. Disease there is carrying away numbers of us workers and the little food there is is uneatable. That is what you have done to our Mother Russia."

The son cried back: "But look at the giants of industry which we have built. Look at the new tractor works. Look at the Dnieprostroy. That construction has been worth suffering for."

"Construction indeed!" was the father's reply. "What's the use of construction when you have destroyed all that's best in Russia?"

What that worker said at least 96 per cent.

MR. GARETH JONES.

"The cattle have nearly all died. How can we feed the cattle when we have only fodder to eat ourselves?"

"And your horses?" was the question I asked in every village I visited. The horse is now a question of life and death, for without a horse how can one plough? And if one cannot plough, how can one sow for the next harvest? And if one cannot sow for the next harvest, then death is the only prospect in the future.

The reply spelled doom for most of the villages. The peasants said: "Most of our horses have died and we have so little fodder that the remaining ones are scraggy and ill."

If it is grave now and if millions are dying in the villages, as they are, for I did not visit a single village where many had not died, what will it be like in a month's time? The potatoes left are being counted one by one, but in so many homes the potatoes have long run out. The beet, once used as cattle fodder, why run out in many huts before the new food comes in June, July and August, and many have not even beet!

The situation is graver than in 1921, as all peasants stated emphatically. In that year

CHILD BEGGARS IN MOSCOW

there was famine in several great regions, but in most parts the peasants could live. It was a localised famine, which had many millions of victims, especially along the Volga. But to-day the famine is everywhere, in the formerly rich Ukraine, in West Russia, in Central Asia, in North Caucasus—everywhere.

What of the towns? Moscow as yet does not look so stricken, and no one staying in Moscow would have an inkling of whi

Figure 16.8   Whether accurate information about genocide is disseminated depends on whether mass media and other actors invest the necessary resources in documenting the events, and whether witnesses report honestly. While many pro-Soviet journalists and intellectuals ignored or covered up the mass famine sweeping the Soviet Union during the 1930s, a small handful of witnesses emerged with their integrity intact. Malcolm Muggeridge of *The Guardian* was one (see main text); another was Gareth Jones, a British diplomatic attaché who organized his own tour of the Soviet countryside at the height of the famine, and published dispatches like the one pictured, from the London *Evening Standard* (March 31, 1933).

Source: http://www.garethjones.org

Armenian plight. Their writings and photographs are essential to our current understanding of the genocide, and serve as a bulwark against those who deny it (see Chapters 4 and 14). By contrast, the withdrawal of nearly all media and most foreign observers from Rwanda in the early stages of the 1994 genocide meant that only the most fragmentary imagery and testimony of that holocaust reached the outside world. Even in an age of globalized mass communication, the Rwandan *génocidaires* inflicted their horrors with only rare outside witnesses, and no outside intervention.

Often, honest witnessing must be carried out at great risk of capture, torture, and death. At such times it inspires real awe. A dramatic example is Jan Karski, a Polish diplomat in his late twenties, who sought to convey the truth of the Jewish Holocaust to the outside world. Operating throughout Nazi-occupied Poland, Karski "disguised himself as a Jew, donning an armband with the Star of David, and smuggled himself through a tunnel into the Warsaw ghetto. Posing as a Ukrainian militiaman, he also infiltrated Belzec, a Nazi death camp near the border between Poland and Ukraine." One marvels at the danger and deception hinted at in this passage. At the end of 1942, Karski escaped to London. He immediately sought a meeting with representatives of the Jewish community. Passing on Karski's reports to the World Jewish Congress in New York, Ignacy Schwartzbart, a prominent London Jew, urged his audience to *"BELIEVE THE UNBELIEVABLE."*[71] Even leading Jews, however, found the information unfathomable: "I cannot believe you," US Supreme Court justice Felix Frankfurter told Karski in a private meeting. It was not that he was accusing Karski of lying, Frankfurter stressed; it was just that he did not possess the evidence that would allow him to absorb such a mind-boggling account. This serves as a painful reminder that no link need exist between honest witnessing and genocide prevention. A host of unpredictable factors – above all, public attention, political will, and private/elite sponsorship – must come into play if information is to translate into action.[72]

In the contemporary age, the witnessing of human rights organizations and activists is indispensable. Global NGOs such as Human Rights Watch, Amnesty International, the Red Cross, and Doctors Without Borders, as well as legions of national and regional projects, provide the most detailed and informed analyses of rights violations and human suffering. One activist describes their core approach as *"promoting change by reporting facts."*[73]

Other activist initiatives preserve past traumas, including genocide, in historical memory – another form of witnessing. One example is the Russian Memorial Society (see Map 5.1). "Memorial was founded by a group of young historians, some of whom had been collecting oral histories of [Gulag] camp survivors for many years," wrote Anne Applebaum. "Later, Memorial would also lead the battle to identify the corpses buried in mass graves outside Moscow and Leningrad, and to build monuments and memorials to the Stalinist era." By the end of the 1990s, Memorial had established itself as "the most important centre for the study of Soviet history, as well as for the defence of human rights, in the Russian federation." Its publications were "known to Soviet scholars around the world for their accuracy, their fidelity to facts, and their careful, judicious archives."[74]

Ideologies, religious and secular

> The imagination and the spiritual strength of Shakespeare's evildoers stopped short at a dozen corpses. Because they had no *ideology*.
>
> Alexander Solzhenitsyn, *The Gulag Archipelago*

The role of religious belief in genocide prevention and intervention may be examined from two perspectives. On one hand, religious believers throughout history have derived from their faith an abiding love and respect for humanity. In a practical sense, this has led them to cross lines of religion, ethnicity, and social class to help genocide's victims. In colonial Spanish America, Bartolomé de las Casas denounced atrocities against the Indians with a passion that still cuts through cant nearly five centuries later (though las Casas supported the importation of African slaves to reduce the burden on indigenous peoples). Catholics in Poland during the Second World War regularly sheltered Jews (see Chapter 10). One such rescuer, Irene Gut Opdyke, was a devout believer who wrote in her memoirs: "Courage is a whisper from above: when you listen with your heart, you will know what to do and how and when."[75] Post-genocide

Rwanda witnessed a surge of converts to Islam, since the country's Muslim minority, by contrast with its Catholic Church, saved Tutsi coreligionists, rather than assisting in their massacre. Surely, the humane and cosmopolitan vision guiding much religious belief and practice is to be acknowledged and admired.

The case of Rwanda's Catholic Church, however, reminds us that religious believers often act negligently or murderously in genocide.[76] "The very worst things that men have ever done," said British politician William Gladstone, "have been done when they were performing acts of violence in the name of religion."[77] In the opinion of the great sociologist Barrington Moore, Jr. – summarized by his student Charles Tilly – monotheistic religions, in particular, foster "gross intolerance, hence readiness to kill outsiders, because of their sharply drawn distinctions between the worthy and the unworthy, the pure and the impure."[78] But polytheism provides no barrier to fanaticism, as Muslim and Sikh survivors of Hindu nationalist violence can attest.

The distinguishing element here is not religious belief *per se*, but *extremism and exclusivism* passed through a religious filter. There are few more important tasks of genocide prevention than confronting religious extremists and fundamentalists, at home and abroad – not with persecution or bombs, which would only fuel their martyr complexes, but with a pluralistic, humanistic education system, and a cosmopolitan[79] counter-discourse (including by religious moderates).

Secular ideologies are also Janus-faced in relation to genocide. Democratic and pluralistic ideologies are primarily responsible for our concern over genocide and human rights violations. The very idea of "human rights" is a product of the secular Enlightenment in Europe, though it resonates with many religious and philosophical traditions. These ideologies have underpinned enormous positive changes in human civilization. State-sponsored slavery is no more.[80] The most blatant forms of colonialism have mostly been expunged from the earth. Major wars and genocides across a range of previously conflictive "dyads" are now unlikely or unthinkable (France and Germany is the most commonly cited pairing). Institutions whose gratuitous cruelty has something in common with the sadism of genocide – such as drawing-and-quartering or breaking on a wheel[81] – are also historical relics.

Secular-humanist ideologies have given rise to the idea of global civil society and "world citizenship," vital to transcending the differences of culture, class, and religion that can fuel genocides. A world citizen holds that:

> Everyone is an individual endowed with certain rights and subject to certain obligations; everyone is capable of voluntaristic action seeking rational solutions to social problems; everyone has the right and obligation to participate in the grand human project; everyone is, therefore, a citizen of the world polity. World citizenship is the institutional endowment of authority and agency on individuals. It infuses each individual with the authority to pursue particularistic interests, preferably in organizations, while also authorizing individuals to promote collective goods defined in largely standardized ways.[82]

But secular ideologies have also *underpinned* most genocides of the past two centuries. One thinks of the genocidal expansionists into an economically "unexploited" North America; the Young Turk modernizers of the Ottoman Empire, and their counterparts in Stalinist Russia; the Nazis with their fanatical racism and nationalism; and the Khmer Rouge communists in Cambodia. The genocidal consequences of much secular ideology were eloquently conveyed by a repentant Communist Party activist, speaking about the imposition of famine and collectivization in the Soviet countryside:

> With the rest of my generation I firmly believed that the ends justified the means. Our great goal was the universal triumph of Communism, and for the sake of that goal everything was permissible – to lie, to steal, to destroy hundreds of thousands and even millions of people, all those who were hindering our work or could hinder it, everyone who stood in the way. And to hesitate or doubt about all this was to give in to "intellectual squeamishness" and "stupid liberalism," the attribute of people who "could not see the forest for the trees" . . . I was convinced that I was accomplishing the great and necessary transformation of the countryside; that in the days to come the people who lived there would be better off for it; that their distress and suffering were a result of their own ignorance or the machinations of the class enemy; that those who sent me – and I myself – knew better than the peasants how they should live, what they should sow and when they should plow.[83]

A mirror image of such thinking in the capitalist West depicts those who stand in the way of "modernization" and "development" as backward and disposable, while the millions of casualties inflicted by colonial famines or contemporary "structural adjustment" policies are justified by the noble ends of market liberalism.

It is at this point that secular ideologies blend with religious ones, and begin to realize their true genocidal potential. A replacement is found for the supernatural goals of religion (salvation, paradise, oneness with the creator, and so on). Such bounties are now promised in one's own lifetime, or at least within a few generations. It is in this sense that the English historian A.J.P. Taylor refers to Marx and Engels's *Communist Manifesto* as a "religious book," guided by a figure (Marx) who was "essentially . . . a prophet, not a philosopher"; "if events did not fit in with his system," Taylor wrote, "so much the worse for events."[84]

All of this serves as a reminder that a critical individual dimension – in both senses of the word "critical" – exists in religious and secular ideologies alike. Each person must monitor, as objectively and skeptically as possible, the tendency to hatred and exclusivism that is present in us all. There is always a temptation to believe we are superior and in the right – whether we buttress this with religious belief, a secular stance, or a mixture of the two. Actually, we *might* be "superior" and in the right! I do believe some epistemologies (strategies of knowing), moral frameworks, and social options are superior to others, or I would not be writing this book. But we must guard against hubris. As the US indigenous activist Ruby Plenty Chiefs reminds us: "Great evil has been done on earth by people who think they have all the answers."[85]

Personal responsibility

How can you as an individual monitor your beliefs, and reduce (forgive me) your genocidal potential?[86]

- *Educate yourself broadly and deeply.* If your beliefs are congruent with reality and a viable moral framework, they should not collapse in the face of opposed views. Expose yourself to those viewpoints, by consulting a wide range of media – something that is now easier than ever. Learn from contrary-minded others. Surprisingly often, you will find that those who think differently become more familiar, even genuine friends. This may make you less likely to support their persecution and extermination.
- *Travel if you can.* This is also easier than ever, even outside the privileged West. My own most intensive learning has come from traveling as much of the world as time and money have allowed. Talk to people in those distant lands, like-minded and otherwise. The vast majority will be welcoming and receptive, and will open their hearts and lives to you. You are bound to discover strong bonds of community; and again, when you have immersed yourself in a place and interacted with its people, you are probably less likely to want to kill them some day, or support anyone with that agenda. Travel also serves as an antidote to the kind of narcissistic, triumphalist thinking about one's own nation and culture that is such a vital underpinning of genocidal enterprises (see Chapter 10).[87]

  If you *can't* travel, or won't, then at least read voraciously (history, current affairs, travel accounts, even guides); watch the History Channel and Discovery and National Geographic; surf the Net for relevant perspectives and insights. As always, balance your receptivity with critical thinking and a healthy dose of skepticism.
- *"Keep [y]our consciences soft and vulnerable."* "Only then," wrote Donald and Laura Miller, "will we rise up to challenge the suffering that surrounds us. Denial of evil is a defense mechanism that a just world simply cannot afford."[88] Be open to the distress and persecution of others. As the Argentine revolutionary Ché Guevara wrote in a 1966 letter to his children: "Above all, be capable always of feeling to your very depths any injustice committed against anyone in any part of the world."[89] Similar were the words of Holocaust survivor and Nobel Peace Prize-winner Elie Wiesel, accepting his award in 1986:

  > Sometimes we must interfere. When human lives are endangered, when human dignity is in jeopardy, national borders and sensitivities become irrelevant. Whenever men or women are persecuted because of their race, religion, or political views, that place must – at that moment – become the center of the universe.[90]

It is easy to allow crimes like genocide and other mass violence to slide into abstractions. Aid agencies speak of "compassion fatigue." Allen Feldman pointed to a "cultural anesthesia" born of "generalities of bodies – dead, wounded, starving, diseased, and homeless . . . pressed against the television screen as mass articles."[91] Soviet dictator Joseph Stalin famously commented, "One death is a tragedy; a million deaths is a statistic."[92]

The solution lies in empathy and learning. I recall sitting in a restaurant in Colombia in 1994, watching fragmentary images on TV of dozens of bodies floating down a river somewhere very far away. These are today among the indelible images of the Rwandan holocaust (see Figure 9.1). My thought at the time? "Oh jeez, more tribal violence in Africa." Only after plowing through a few thousand pages of testimony and reportage on the genocide, material that stunned and changed me, did I feel I had expiated the shame of that first ignorant reaction.

- *Question authority.* I do not say "Reject authority." Much authority is *authoritative* rather than *authoritarian*. It derives its legitimacy from suasion and moral appeal. On the other hand, the great majority of genocides are carried out under authoritarian rule of one kind or another, and formally democratic societies are far from immune to these temptations – especially in times of proclaimed emergency. Many if not most readers of this book will be called upon, at some point in their lives, to decide whether to support a call to large-scale collective violence. Is that call warranted, or is it a summons to atrocity? All authority rests on conformity, and conforming *may* be immoral, or inhuman. When this is the case, move beyond questioning to active opposition. ". . . Any form of domination, hierarchy, control has a burden of proof. It's not self-justifying. It has to demonstrate that it's legitimate, just as any use of force or coercion does. Therefore it deserves to be challenged. And if it's challenged, and it cannot justify itself, it should be dismantled."[93]

- *Support worthy causes.* You know a few already. Some of those devoted specifically to genocide prevention may be found on the webpage for this book (www. genocidetext.net). Consider supporting by *participating*, not just by contributing money. Participation brings you into contact and solidarity with other human beings. This is essential to building a global movement against genocide and other mass crimes.

  Proponents of worthy causes may sometimes use violence to achieve their goals – typically, to bring an end to violence (including structural violence) by an oppressor. These actions may not be pretty, but neither, unfortunately, are they obsolete. Violent resistance to the planners and perpetrators of genocide, *while it is underway*, is an incontestable right. Likewise, all people have the right to resist aggressive war waged against them, if their resistance does not descend into atrocity.

  Beyond this, I offer only tentative comments about whether to support a given movement that practices violence. In my life, I have strongly backed movements that used violence to defend civilian populations, for positive social revolution, and for national independence (the Sandinistas in Nicaragua; the FMLN guerrillas in El Salvador; South Africa's ANC; Fretilin in East Timor). I have also supported state-led military interventions that suppressed genocide – Vietnam in Cambodia, or NATO in Kosovo (though in the latter case, I criticized the military strategy, based on high-altitude bombing, as cowardly and ineffective).

  As Alan Kuperman has pointed out, however, violent resistance and military intervention may provide just the "provocation" that would-be *génocidaires* seek to justify implementation of their "final solution." Thus, violence should be employed, and such movements be supported, only *in extremis*: as a defensive response to manifestly intolerable treatment or (Kuperman) "grossly disproportionate" state attack or counterattack.[94] It is a cliché to say that non-violent means should be tried first, second, and third. It becomes less of a cliché when we appreciate the demonstrable power of non-violent resistance, which has toppled dictatorships around the world.[95]

CONCLUSION

This book has tried to provide an introduction to the concept and practice of genocide. We have considered both genocide's roots in antiquity and its manifestations in modern and contemporary periods. The intimate relationships between genocide, war, imperialism, and social revolution have been explored, together with diverse social science perspectives on the phenomenon. We have examined how legal institutions and mechanisms evolved to confront genocide; how genocides worked their way into collective memory; and the role that gender plays.

One might express optimism or pessimism about the chances of establishing an effective anti-genocide regime. But a mood changes nothing.

Anything in the human order that can be understood can be confronted. In the case of a blight as pernicious and enduring as genocide, we are morally obliged to do so. Actions taken today carry special significance, with so many human and planetary issues demanding attention. To stage an effective confrontation, we need to perceive the linkages between genocide and other pressing challenges. Hence, in part, my preference for a broad and inclusive genocide framework, rather than a conceptually restrictive or narrowly legalistic one. Meaningful "peace" cannot exist alongside massive inequalities in wealth, health, and education. And it will do us little good to suppress genocide and establish amity among peoples, if the earth itself finally rebels against the species that has caused it so much ecocidal damage.

The odds of overcoming these multifarious challenges are impossible to estimate, but I believe we have an obligation to face them squarely. I hope I have persuaded you, if you needed persuading, that the effort to suppress genocide deserves a prominent place on the human agenda. May I welcome you to the struggle?

FURTHER STUDY

Gary J. Bass, *Freedom's Battle: The Origins of Humanitarian Intervention.* New York: Alfred A. Knopf, 2008. The dawn of "humanitarian" interventions in the nineteenth and early twentieth centuries.

Daniel Chirot and Clark McCauley, *Why Not Kill Them All? The Logic and Prevention of Mass Political Murder.* Princeton, NJ: Princeton University Press, 2006. Particularly thoughtful on the institutional and political mechanisms necessary to confront genocide.

Timothy W. Crawford and Alan J. Kuperman, *Gambling on Humanitarian Intervention: Moral Hazard, Rebellion and Civil War*. Abingdon: Routledge, 2006. Cautionary tales of "moral hazard" in humanitarian interventions.

John G. Heidenrich, *How to Prevent Genocide: A Guide for Policymakers, Scholars, and the Concerned Citizen*. Westport, CT: Praeger, 2001. Emphasizes strategies of military intervention.

Leo Kuper, *The Prevention of Genocide*. New Haven, CT: Yale University Press, 1985. Kuper's second and final book on genocide focuses on UN performance and preventive strategies.

Adam Lebor, *"Complicity with Evil": The United Nations in the Age of Modern Genocide*. New Haven, CT: Yale University Press, 2006. Disturbing overview of the UN's failed interventions in the 1990s and 2000s.

Nicolaus Mills and Kira Brunner, eds, *The New Killing Fields: Massacre and the Politics of Intervention*. New York: Basic Books, 2002. Exceptional essays, with a journalistic tinge.

Mobilizing the Will to Intervene: Leadership and Action to Prevent Mass Atrocities. Report of The Will to Intervene Project (Montreal Institute for Genocide and Human Rights Studies, 2009). Available online at http://migs.concordia.ca/W2I/documents/ENG_MIGS_finalW2IAugust09.pdf. The Canadian counterpart to the US-based Genocide Prevention Task Force, with policy recommendations for both Canadian and US governments, publics, and media.

PreventGenocide.org. http://www.preventgenocide.org. Indispensable resources and prevention strategies.

Preventing Genocide: A Blueprint for US Policymakers. Report of the Genocide Prevention Task Force, Washington, DC: US Holocaust Memorial Museum *et al.*, 2008. Available online at http://www.ushmm.org/genocide/taskforce/pdf/report.pdf. The Albright–Cohen report, focusing on a US leadership role in prevention and intervention.

Neal Riemer, ed., *Protection Against Genocide: Mission Impossible?* Westport, CT: Praeger, 2000. Short, readable volume on genocide prevention.

Geoffrey Robinson, *"If You Leave Us Here, We Will Die": How Genocide Was Stopped in East Timor*. Princeton, NJ: Princeton University Press, 2009. How an effective intervention was marshaled, by one of the participants and rebels (see Box 16.2).

Peter N. Stearns, *Global Outrage: The Impact of World Opinion on Contemporary History*. Oxford: Oneworld, 2007. Engaging survey of the emergence of global public opinion on humanitarian issues.

Nicholas Wheeler, *Saving Strangers: Humanitarian Intervention in International Society*. Oxford: Oxford University Press, 2000. The classic study.

NOTES

1 Thomas Cushman, "Is Genocide Preventable? Some Theoretical Considerations," *Journal of Genocide Research*, 5: 4 (2003), pp. 528, 531.
2 John G. Heidenrich, *How to Prevent Genocide: A Guide for Policymakers, Scholars, and the Concerned Citizen* (Westport, CT: Praeger, 2001), p. 18.
3 Cushman, "Is Genocide Preventable?," p. 525.

4 Barbara Harff, "No Lessons Learned from the Holocaust? Assessing Risks of Genocide and Political Mass Murder since 1955," *American Political Science Review*, 97: 1 (February 2003), p. 62.

5 Ervin Staub, "The Psychology of Bystanders, Perpetrators, and Heroic Helpers," in Leonard S. Newman and Ralph Erber, eds, *Understanding Genocide: The Social Psychology of the Holocaust* (Oxford: Oxford University Press, 2002), p. 30.

6 For a discussion of consociationalism in the context of a genocide-afflicted region, see René Lemarchand, "Consociationalism and Power Sharing in Africa: Rwanda, Burundi, and the Democratic Republic of the Congo," *African Affairs*, 106 (2007), pp. 1–20.

7 Ervin Staub, *The Roots of Evil: The Origins of Genocide and Other Group Violence* (Cambridge: Cambridge University Press, 1989), p. 274.

8 Personal interview with Kal Holsti, Vancouver, BC, January 2001.

9 Ted Robert Gurr and Barbara Harff, *Ethnic Conflict in World Politics* (Boulder, CO: Westview Press, 1994), p. 80.

10 For an overview of the empirical evidence, see David Kopel, review of Jay Simkin *et al.*, *Lethal Laws* (Milwaukee: Jews for the Preservation of Firearm Ownership, 1994), in *New York Law School Journal of International and Comparative Law*, 15 (1995), pp. 355–98.

11 R. Charli Carpenter has deepened and problematized this framing of "vulnerability" in important respects, emphasizing physical capacity as well as liability to violent victimization. See Carpenter, "Women and Children First: Gender Norms and Humanitarian Evacuation in the Balkans, 1991–1995," *International Organization*, 57: 4 (Fall 2003), pp. 661–94. More generally, Carpenter's 2006 volume, *"Innocent Women and Children": Gender, Norms and the Protection of Civilians* (London: Ashgate, 2006) is an essential and eye-opening contribution.

12 See Adam Jones, "Genocide and Humanitarian Intervention: Incorporating the Gender Variable," in Jones, *Gender Inclusive: Essays on Violence, Men, and Feminist International Relations* (London: Routledge, 2009), pp. 255–82.

13 See Robert D. Kaplan, *The Coming Anarchy: Shattering the Dreams of the Post Cold War* (New York: Random House, 2000).

14 International Commission on Intervention and State Sovereignty (hereafter, ICISS), *The Responsibility to Protect* (Ottawa, ON: International Development Research Centre, 2001), p. 19.

15 Richard Falk, "The Challenge of Genocide and Genocidal Politics in an Era of Globalisation," in Tim Dunne and Nicholas J. Wheeler, eds, *Human Rights in Global Politics* (Cambridge: Cambridge University Press, 1999), p. 191.

16 ICISS, *The Responsibility to Protect*, pp. 30–31.

17 "After the Armistice [of November 1918], the blockade was extended to the Baltic ports and continued until the Allies were satisfied with German compliance with their demands. The journalist Walter Duranty visited Lübeck in 1919 and found people living on potatoes and black bread. They had no meat, butter, milk or eggs. A doctor told him that 90 per cent of the children were anaemic or below weight, and that more than half of them had rickets or tuberculosis. . . . The senior German delegate at Versailles, Graf Ulrich von Brockdorff-Rantzau, expressed some of the [German] resentment: 'The hundreds of thousands of noncombatants who have perished since November 11 because of the blockade were destroyed coolly and deliberately, after our opponents had won a certain and assured victory. Think of that, when you speak of guilt and atonement.'" Jonathan Glover, *Humanity: A Moral History of the Twentieth Century* (New Haven, CT: Yale University Press, 1999), pp. 65–66.

18 ICISS, *The Responsibility to Protect*, p. 29.

19 Annan quoted in ibid., p. 40.

20 Ibid., p. 48.

21 Heidenrich, *How to Prevent Genocide*, p. 61.

22 Kenneth Roth, "Setting the Standard: Justifying Humanitarian Intervention," *Harvard International Review* (Spring 2004), p. 59; emphasis added. For a similar (and earlier)

framing, see Nicholas Wheeler, *Saving Strangers: Humanitarian Intervention in International Society* (Oxford: Oxford University Press, 2000), pp. 33–34. Wheeler's book offered the best argument for a "solidarist" approach to intervention in what he calls "supreme humanitarian emergencies," defined as "extraordinary situations where civilians in another state are in imminent danger of losing their life or facing appalling hardship, and where indigenous forces cannot be relied upon to end these violations of human rights" (p. 50).

23 Mary Kaldor in "Humanitarian Intervention: A Forum," *The Nation*, July 14, 2003, p. 13. "The commission went on to argue that a gap between legality and legitimacy is very dangerous and needs to be removed by specifying conditions for humanitarian intervention." This was the challenge taken up, not entirely successfully in my view, by the ICISS.

24 "Editor's Introduction," Symposium on the Genocide Prevention Task Force Report, *Genocide Studies and Prevention*, 4: 2 (2009), p. 147.

25 *Preventing Genocide: A Blueprint for US Policymakers*, US Holocaust Memorial Museum *et al.*, 2008, p. xv.

26 Ibid., pp. xvii–xviii.

27 Scott Straus, "A Step Forward," Symposium on the Genocide Prevention Task Force Report, *Genocide Studies and Prevention*, 4: 2 (2009), p. 186.

28 *Mobilizing the Will to Intervene: Leadership and Action to Prevent Mass Atrocities*, report of The Will to Intervene Project (Montreal: Montreal Institute for Genocide and Human Rights Studies, 2009). Quoted passages from pp. 2, 32, 37, 52–53, 62; the full text of the report is available online at http://migs.concordia.ca/W2I/documents/ENG_MIGS_finalW2IAugust09.pdf.

29 Stephen Holmes, "Looking Away," *London Review of Books*, November 14, 2002.

30 See Michael Parenti, *To Kill a Nation: The Attack on Yugoslavia* (London: Verso, 2000); Noam Chomsky, *The New Military Humanism: Lessons from Kosovo* (Monroe, ME: Common Courage Press, 1999); Philip Hammond and Edward S. Herman, eds, *Degraded Capability: The Media and the Kosovo Crisis* (London: Pluto Press, 2000); and Diana Johnstone, *Fools' Crusade: Yugoslavia, NATO, and Western Delusions* (New York: Monthly Review Press, 2003).

31 India relished the opportunity to deal a blow to its erstwhile rival Pakistan by severing its eastern wing. It was also confronted by an unmanageable flood of refugees from the genocide, as was Tanzania in the Ugandan case. (The regime that replaced Amin in Uganda, that of Milton Obote, was also no less murderous than its predecessor.) Vietnam had deep political rivalries with the Khmer Rouge, close ties to the Vietnamese minority in Cambodia, and desires to establish itself as the regional hegemon. Member countries of NATO were profoundly concerned by the security implications of hundreds of thousands of Kosovar refugees destabilizing neighboring countries in a corner of Europe that had already spawned one world war. Only in the East Timor case, I have argued (Box 7a and Box 16.2), was moral suasion by morally motivated actors truly decisive in the equation: it persuaded Australia to lead the intervention, when considerations of *realpolitik* dictated otherwise. However, to the extent that it became politically untenable for the Australian government to act otherwise, we may also argue that practical considerations outweighed humanitarian ones.

32 Geoffrey Robinson, *"If You Leave Us Here, We Will Die": How Genocide Was Stopped in East Timor* (Princeton, NJ: Princeton University Press, 2010). The quoted passages are drawn from pp. 155, 175, 179, 186, 191, and 194.

33 For broader discussion, see Adam Jones, "Wired World: Communications Technology, Governance, and the Democratic Uprising," ch. 8 in Edward Comor, ed., *The Global Political Economy of Communication: Hegemony, Telecommunication and the Information Economy* (London: Macmillan, 1994), pp. 145–64; available at http://adamjones.freeservers.com/wired.htm.

34 Alan J. Kuperman, "Humanitarian Hazard: Revisiting Doctrines of Intervention," *Harvard International Review*, Spring 2004, p. 67.

35 Michael Hirsh, "Calling All Regio-Cops: Peacekeeping's Hybrid Future," *Foreign Affairs* (November–December 2000), p. 5.

36 Israel W. Charny, "An International Peace Army: A Proposal for the Long-range Future," in Charny, ed., *The Encyclopedia of Genocide* (Santa Barbara, CA: ABC-CLIO, 1999), p. 650.

37 Ibid., pp. 650–52.

38 Ibid., p. 650.

39 Dallaire quoted in Heidenrich, *How to Prevent Genocide*, pp. 200–1. Heidenrich's ch. 12, "The Evolution of an Idea," explores the various proposals for a UN standing force.

40 See Tim Pippard and Veronica Lie, "Enhancing the Rapid Reaction Capability of the United Nations: Exploring the Options," United Nations Association-UK, July 2004.

41 See, e.g., the analysis of a British government Green Paper on the subject in "Peacekeeping 'Role' for Mercenaries," *BBC Online*, February 13, 2002, http://news.bbc. co.uk/1/hi/uk_politics/1817495.stm.

42 Daniel Chirot and Clark McCauley, *Why Not Kill Them All? The Logic and Prevention of Mass Political Murder* (Princeton, NJ: Princeton University Press, 2006), pp. 166–67.

43 See "Christianity's Modern-Day Martyrs," *Spiegel Online*, February 28, 2010, http:// www.spiegel.de/international/world/0,1518,680349,00.html.

44 Verena Hütter, "German–Russian Exchange," Goethe-Institut, July 15, 2009, http:// www.goethe.de/uun/bdu/en4821332.htm.

45 Mandela's inaugural address as president, May 14, 1994, quoted in Samuel P. Oliner, *Do Unto Others: Extraordinary Acts of Ordinary People* (Boulder, CO: Westview Press, 2003), p. 154.

46 Nelson Mandela, *Long Walk to Freedom: The Autobiography of Nelson Mandela* (New York: Back Bay Books, 1995).

47 René Lemarchand, for example, claims that "a fundamental reality of the Kagame regime" is that "one ethnocracy has replaced another." Lemarchand, "A History of Genocide in Rwanda" (review article), *The Journal of African History*, 43: 2 (2002), pp. 307–11.

48 René Lemarchand, *The Dynamics of Violence in Central Africa* (Philadelphia, PA: University of Pennsylvania Press, 2009), p. x.

49 "A Flawed Hero," *The Economist*, August 21, 2008.

50 "Eritrea Ranked Last for First Time While G8 Members, Except Russia, Recover Lost Ground," Reporters Without Borders press release, October 16, 2007, http://www.rsf. org/Eritrea-ranked-last-for-first-time,24025.html; Howard W. French, "Kagame's Hidden War in the Congo," *The New York Review of Books*, September 24, 2009. http:// www.nybooks.com/articles/23054

51 $576 million, to be precise; see http://www.indexmundi.com/rwanda/economic_aid_ recipient.html.

52 For an example of the upbeat media coverage that has resulted, see Shashank Bengali, "Rwanda Economy Thriving as Country Moves Past Genocide," McClatchey Newspapers on Yahoo! News, March 1, 2008.

53 Stephanie McCrummen, "Women Run the Show in a Recovering Rwanda," *The Washington Post*, October 26, 2008, http://www.washingtonpost.com/wp-dyn/content/ article/2008/10/26/AR2008102602197.html.

54 For a survey of recent literature on the Indian Partition and its relevance for genocide studies, see my review article in *Journal of Genocide Research*, 10: 4 (2008), pp. 625–32.

55 See Gendercide Watch, "Kashmir/Punjab/The Delhi Massacre," http://www.gendercide. org/case_kashmir_punjab.html; on Gujarat, see Garda Ghista, *The Gujarat Genocide: A Case Study in Fundamentalist Cleansing* (Authorhouse, 2006).

56 Indian researcher Ashutosh Varshney "has found evidence to suggest that the single most critical variable in determining which cities in India have or have not experienced inter-communal violence between Muslims and Hindus is the strength of their civil society institutions. In cities where community leaders were in regular contact through integrated

civic organizations and could reassure each other at times of heightened political tension that they would keep their communities quiet, and when they could use their organizational authority to tell their own people to remain peaceful, there was little violence, even when other nearby places were erupting in deadly ethnic riots." Chirot and McCauley, *Why Not Kill Them All?*, p. 190; see Varshey, *Ethnic Conflict and Civic Life: Hindus and Muslims in India* (New Haven, CT: Yale University Press, 2002). See also Martha C. Nussbaum, *The Clash Within: Democracy, Religious Violence, and India's Future* (Cambridge, MA: The Belknap Press of Harvard University Press, 2007).

57 "A Bollywood Song and Dance," *The Economist*, February 20, 2010.

58 Nehru quoted in Shashi Tharoor, *Nehru: The Invention of India* (New York: Arcade Publishing, 2004), p. 225.

59 "In India, cricket is [a] 'religion.' The country comes to a stop when a cricket match is being played – the roads are deserted, parties and weddings are postponed, operations in hospitals are rescheduled, parliament goes in for early closing. North-south, east-west, rich-poor, men-women, rural-urban, Hindu-Muslim – a craze bordering on madness unites the nation when it comes to cricket." Vinod Mehta, "Letter: India's Cricketing 'Religion,'" *BBC Online*, October 14, 2004, http://news.bbc.co.uk/2/hi/programmes/3734038.stm.

60 The European Convention is also binding on the 47 countries that compose the Council of Europe, including 20 that are not (yet) members of the EU.

61 See the website of the EU-sponsored Fundamental Rights Agency, http://fra.europa.eu/fraWebsite/home/home_en.htm.

62 "Barack Obama's Speech on Race," *The New York Times*, March 18, 2008.

63 I refer to the "October Crisis" of 1970, when the government of Prime Minister Pierre Trudeau imposed the War Measures Act in response to bombings and kidnappings by the Quebec Liberation Front (FLQ). Some of my first memories of life in Canada are of soldiers and armoured vehicles stationed outside the parliament buildings in Ottawa.

64 See, e.g., Bill Curry, "Aboriginals in Canada Face 'Third World'-Level Risk of Tuberculosis," *The Globe and Mail*, March 10, 2010, http://www.theglobeandmail.com/news/national/aboriginals-in-canada-face-third-world-level-risk-of-tuberculosis/article1496790/.

65 Debora Mackenzie, "Canada Probes TB 'Genocide' in Church-Run Schools," *New Scientist*, May 5, 2007.

66 "PM Cites 'Sad Chapter' in Apology for Residential Schools," CBC News, June 11, 2008, http://www.cbc.ca/canada/story/2008/06/11/aboriginal-apology.html.

67 Nadezhda Mandelstam, *Hope Against Hope* (New York: Modern Library, 1999), p. 383.

68 Ian Hunter, "A Tale of Truth and Two Journalists," in William L. Hewitt, ed., *Defining the Horrific: Readings on Genocide and Holocaust in the Twentieth Century* (Upper Saddle River, NJ: Pearson Education, 2004), p. 134.

69 Muggeridge quoted in Hunter, "A Tale of Truth," p. 135; emphasis added.

70 Muggeridge quoted in Robert Conquest, *The Harvest of Sorrow: Collectivization and the Terror-Famine* (New York: Oxford University Press, 1986), p. 260.

71 Samantha Power, *"A Problem from Hell": America and the Age of Genocide* (New York: Basic Books, 2002), p. 32.

72 Staub, *The Roots of Evil*, p. 282.

73 Quoted in Margaret E. Keck and Kathryn Sikkink, *Activists Beyond Borders: Advocacy Networks in International Politics* (Ithaca, NY: Cornell University Press, 1998), p. 19; emphasis added. For an overview of the history and activities of Amnesty International, see Jonathan Power, *Like Water on Stone: The Story of Amnesty International* (London: Penguin, 2002).

74 Anne Applebaum, *Gulag: A History* (London: Penguin, 2003), p. 497. The contribution of artists, writers, and other shapers of cultural form also provides a potent form of witnessing, albeit usually at some remove from events. It would be hard to overstate the importance of films such as *Schindler's List* and *The Killing Fields* to increasing public consciousness of the Jewish and Cambodian genocides, respectively. "Norm entre-

preneurs" (Chapter 12) frequently use books – both non-fiction and fiction – to confront genocide and other crimes against humanity. Sometimes these can become true "culture carriers." Harriet Beecher Stowe's *Uncle Tom's Cabin* alerted millions of nineteenth-century readers to slavery's depredations; in contemporary times, Jonathan Schell's *The Fate of the Earth* strongly inspired the anti-nuclear movement. Finally, though they are always vulnerable to charges of grandstanding, celebrities have brought important visibility to genocide's victims or potential victims – as with Mia Farrow and Darfur, Richard Gere and Tibet, and Sting with the rainforest Indians of Brazil. I have explored the diversity of cultural offerings on genocide in my edited volume, *Evoking Genocide: Scholars and Activists Describe the Works That Shaped Their Lives* (Toronto, ON: The Key Publishing House, 2009).

75 Irene Gut Opdyke with Jennifer Armstrong, *In My Hands: Memories of a Holocaust Rescuer* (New York: Anchor Books, 2001).

76 The controversy over the Catholic and Protestant churches' actions during the Jewish Holocaust may be revisited in this context (see Chapter 6).

77 Quoted in Peter Balakian, *The Burning Tigris: The Armenian Genocide and America's Response* (New York: HarperCollins, 2003), p. 121.

78 Charles Tilly, *The Politics of Collective Violence* (Cambridge: Cambridge University Press, 2003), p. 8; see also Barrington Moore, *Moral Persecution in History* (Princeton, NJ: Princeton University Press, 2000).

79 The term "cosmopolitan" was first deployed in the modern era by Immanuel Kant in *Perpetual Peace* (1795). Mary Kaldor "use[s] the term . . . to refer both to a positive political vision, embracing tolerance, multiculturalism, civility and democracy, and to a more legalistic respect for certain overriding universal principles which should guide political communities at various levels, including the global level." Kaldor, *New and Old Wars: Organized Violence in a Global Era* (Stanford, CA: Stanford University Press, 2001), p. 116. See also the discussion of "the re-emergence of cosmopolitanism" in David Hirsh, *Law against Genocide: Cosmopolitan Trials* (London: Glasshouse Press, 2003), pp. 13–17; and S. Vertovec and R. Cohen, eds, *Conceiving Cosmopolitanism* (Oxford: Oxford University Press, 2002).

80 Ethan Nadelmann claims that "no other international prohibition regime so powerfully confirms the potential of humanitarian and similar moral concerns to shape global norms as does the regime against slavery and the slave trade." Nadelmann, "Global Prohibition Regimes: The Evolution of Norms in International Society," *International Organization*, 44: 4 (Fall 1990), available at http://www.criminology.fsu.edu/transcrime/articles/Global ProhibitionRegimes.htm.

81 For a grisly description of the kinds of public execution common in "civilized" Europe as recently as the eighteenth century, see the opening pages of Michel Foucault's *Discipline and Punish: The Birth of the Prison* (New York: Vintage, 1979) – but not before lunch.

82 John Boli and George M. Thomas, "INGOs and the Organization of World Culture," in Boli and Thomas, eds, *Constructing World Culture: International Nongovernmental Organizations since 1875* (Stanford, CA: Stanford University Press, 1999), pp. 39–40. See also Peter N. Stearns's study of the emergence (and limitations) of "world opinion" in *Global Outrage: The Impact of World Opinion on Contemporary History* (Oxford: Oneworld, 2007); Lynn Hunt, *Inventing Human Rights: A History* (New York: W.W. Norton & Co., 2007); Micheline R. Ishay, *The History of Human Rights: From Ancient Times to the Globalization Era* (Berkeley, CA: University of California Press, 2008); and Keck and Sikkink, *Activists beyond Borders*.

83 Testimony quoted in Conquest, *The Harvest of Sorrow*, p. 233. Nadezhda Mandelstam wrote of "this craving for an all-embracing idea which would explain everything in the world and bring about universal harmony at one go." Under Stalinism, "Life was deviating from the blueprints, but the blueprints had been declared sacrosanct and it was forbidden to compare them with what was actually coming into being." Mandelstam, *Hope Against Hope*, pp. 115, 163.

84 A.J.P. Taylor, "Introduction," in Karl Marx and Friedrich Engels, *The Communist Manifesto* (Harmondsworth: Penguin, 1970), pp. 27, 46. Hence also state socialism in practice (Stalin, Mao, the Kims of North Korea, and others; see Chapter 5). Christopher Hitchens notes that "Communist absolutists did not so much negate religion, in societies that they well understood were saturated with faith and superstition, as seek to *replace* it. The solemn elevation of infallible leaders who were a source of endless bounty and blessing; the permanent search for heretics and schismatics; the mummification of dead leaders as icons and relics; the lurid show trials that elicited incredible confessions by means of torture . . . none of this was very difficult to interpret in traditional terms." Hitchens, *God is Not Great: How Religion Poisons Everything* (Toronto, ON: McClelland & Stewart, 2007), p. 246. See also the discussion in Mark Levene, *Genocide in the Age of the Nation State, Vol. 2: The Rise of the West and the Coming of Genocide* (London: I.B. Tauris, 2005), pp. 200–06. John Gray has explored the ideological and programmatic connections among utopian projects which claim both religious and secular inspiration in *Black Mass: How Religion Led the World into Crisis* (Toronto, ON: Anchor Canada, 2007). The quasi-religious character of contemporary capitalist thinking about "development," "modernization," "freedom," and other lofty themes has been critiqued by Karl Polanyi, Noam Chomsky, Vandana Shiva, Amartya Sen, Naomi Klein, and many others. How a hubristic faith in such prescriptions produced disaster (and arguably genocide) in Vietnam is captured by David Halberstam in *The Best and the Brightest* (New York: Ballantine, 1993). The title has become a catch-phrase for the technocratic mindset and bright-eyed naïveté that produced hecatombs of dead and debilitated in the "developing" world.

85 Ruby Plenty Chiefs quoted in Martha Minow, *Between Vengeance and Forgiveness: Facing History after Genocide and Mass Violence* (Boston, MA: Beacon Press, 1998), p. 8.

86 Jacques Sémelin wrote: "The eternal question always crops up: how on earth is it possible? How can human beings suddenly become executioners of their fellow man [and woman]? Yet if our own country sank into an increasingly serious economic crisis, with dismal parades of millions of unemployed, if it was harassed by a rise in terrorist attacks, each one bloodier than the last, how long would we remain impervious to this way of thinking? We would have to find enemies, not only beyond our borders but also within them, and – who knows? – maybe even right where we live: in our town, village, street, our own building." Sémelin, *Purify and Destroy: The Political Uses of Massacre and Genocide* (New York: Columbia University Press, 2007), p. 9.

87 "Travel is fatal to prejudice, bigotry, and narrowmindedness, and many of our people need it sorely on these accounts. Broad, wholesome, charitable views of men and things cannot be acquired by vegetating in one little corner of the earth all one's lifetime." Mark Twain, *The Innocents Abroad* (1869). Thanks to Jennie Walker for this source. Unfortunately, Twain's views were not always in keeping with these lofty sentiments, especially with regard to US indigenous peoples (see p. 107).

88 Donald E. Miller and Lorna Touryan Miller, *Survivors: An Oral History of the Armenian Genocide* (Berkeley, CA: University of California Press, 1999), p. 5.

89 Guevara letter in the Museo Ernesto Che Guevara, Alta Gracia, Argentina; author's transcription and translation. Kurt Gerstein, a Nazi SS officer, witnessed the stripping, brutalization, and murder by gassing of a transport of Jews to the Belzec death camp in 1942. He subsequently made a greater effort than perhaps any other German "Aryan" to alert the world to the Nazi extermination campaign. In a March 1944 letter to his staunchly pro-Nazi father, Gerstein wrote: "However tight the limitations on a man may be and however much, in many things, he may follow the principle that discretion is the better part of valor, he must never lose his standards or his ideas. He must never exonerate himself before his conscience and before the higher order of things to which he is subject by saying: that is not my business, I can do nothing to change things. . . . He keeps silent but he thinks: that is my business. I am involved in this responsibility and guilt, having knowledge of what is happening and a corresponding measure of blame." Quoted in Saul Friedländer, *The Years of Extermination: Nazi Germany and the Jews, 1939–1945* (New York: HarperCollins, 2007), pp. 539–40. However, Gerstein continued to deliver Zyklon

B gas pellets to the death camps, thus remaining a "member of the extermination system," albeit "a morally tormented and 'treasonous'" one (Friedländer, p. 540).

90 Wiesel quoted in Samuel P. Oliner, *Do Unto Others: Extraordinary Acts of Ordinary People* (Boulder, CO: Westview Press, 2003), p. 159.

91 Feldman quoted in Liisa H. Malkki, "Speechless Emissaries: Refugees, Humanitarianism, and Dehistoricization," in Alexander Laban Hinton, ed., *Genocide: An Anthropological Reader* (Malden, MA: Blackwell, 2002), p. 353.

92 Stalin quoted in David Remnick, *Resurrection: The Struggle for a New Russia* (New York: Vintage, 1998), p. 288.

93 Noam Chomsky, BBC Hardtalk, November 3, 2009. "Authoritative" interpretations of history, enshrined for example in school textbooks, must also be critically examined and regularly challenged, lest they "reinstil the ideological seeds of tomorrow's conflicts," according to Jacques Sémelin. "Therefore the prevention of mass-scale violence must include work on the memories of the past memories that could just as well serve to stir up passions as to contain them in working for reconciliation." Sémelin, *Purify and Destroy*, p. 372. Taner Akçam wrote along similar lines that "all studies of large-scale atrocities teach us one core principle: To prevent the recurrence of such events, people must first consider their own responsibility, discuss it, debate it, and recognize it. In the absence of such honest consideration, there remains the high probability of such acts being repeated, since every group is inherently capable of violence; when the right conditions arise this potential may easily become reality, and on the slightest of pretexts. There are no exceptions. Each and every society needs to take a self-critical approach, one that should be firmly institutionalized as a community's moral tradition regardless of what others might have done to them." Akçam, *A Shameful Act: The Armenian Genocide and the Question of Turkish Responsibility* (New York: Metropolitan Books, 2006), p. 2. For a fascinating case-study of an attempt to write a collaborative, consultative, pluralistic regional history of the Balkans, and the quite inspiring results, see Nicole Itano, "To Avoid 'Us vs. Them' in Balkans, Rewrite History," *The Christian Science Monitor*, March 14, 2007, http://www.csmonitor.com/2007/0314/p01s02-woeu.html, describing an initiative in which "more than 60 scholars and teachers from around the Balkans have joined to create a new series of history books that tackle some of the most controversial periods in the region['s history]." In the Balkans, Itano wrote, "history is often served up as a nationalistic tale that highlights the wrongs perpetrated by others." The new history books, "which are being translated into 10 regional languages, present history from various perspectives and excerpt historical documents to challenge interpretations of key events like the Ottoman conquest of Constantinople." They will provide an alternative to "government-issued texts in which wars – and there have been many in the region over the centuries – are portrayed in 'us versus them' terms with ancient wrongs visited again and again." Such initiatives deserve imaginative extension and enthusiastic support.

94 Alan J. Kuperman, "Wishful Thinking Will Not Stop Genocide: Suggestions for a More Realistic Strategy," *Genocide Studies and Prevention*, 4: 2 (August 2009), pp. 191–99. Kuperman argued (p. 193) that "the international community should refuse to intervene in any way – diplomatic, economic, or military – to help sub-state rebels unless state retaliation is grossly disproportionate. This would discourage militants within vulnerable sub-state groups from launching provocative rebellions that recklessly endanger civilians in hopes of garnering foreign intervention. At the same time, by retaining the intervention option for cases of disproportionate retaliation, this reform also would discourage states from responding to rebellion by intentionally harming civilians. All sides in civil conflicts would thus have incentives for less violent action."

95 The lives and writings of twentieth-century figures such as Mahatma Gandhi, Martin Luther King, the Dalai Lama, and Aung San Suu Kyi provide important insights and inspiration, as does Jonathan Schell's study, *The Unconquerable World: Power, Nonviolence, and the Will of the People* (New York: Metropolitan Books, 2003). See also Peter Ackerman and Jack DuVall, *A Force More Powerful: A Century of Nonviolent Conflict* (New York: Palgrave, 2000).

INDEX

[*Note:* Scholars are referenced only where there is a significant engagement with their work, not each time that work is cited.]